CENSUS OF INDIA 1891

Census of India 1871-1951, 9 Sets In 384 Bindings (9788121258876) Rs. 700000

Census of India 1891, 28 Vols. In 49 Bindings (978-81-212-7129-5) Rs. 125000

1. General Report (9788121269834) Rs. 1450
2. General Tables For British Provinces And Feudatory States (9788121269810) Rs. 2710 (Vol. I)
3. General Tables For British Provinces And Feudatory States (9788121269797) Rs. 950 (Vol. II)
4. Assam - Report (9788121269773) Rs. 2390 (Vol. I, V.1)
5. Assam - Tables (9788121269759) Rs. 2210 (Vol. II, V.2)
6. Assam - Provincial Tables (9788121269735) Rs. 1310 (Vol. II, V.3)
7. The Lower Provinces of Bengal and their Feudatories - The Report (9788121269711) Rs. 1660 (Vol. III)
8. The Lower Provinces of Bengal and their feudatories - The Administrative Tables (9788121269698) Rs. 4200 (Vol. IV)
9. The Lower Provinces of Bengal and their feudatories - The Caste Tables (9788121269674) Rs. 2600 (Vol. V, Pt. 1)
10. Lower Provinces of Bengal - The Provincial Tables (9788121269650) Rs. 1980 (Vol. V, Pt. 2)
11. Berar or the Hyderabad Assigned Districts (9788121269636) Rs. 3360 (Vol. VI)
12. Bombay and Its Feudatories - Report (9788121269612) Rs. 4010 (Vol. VII, Pt. 1)
13. Bombay And Its Feudatories - Imperial Tables (9788121269599) Rs. 790 (Vol. VIII, Pt. 2)
14. Imperial Series - Burma Report (9788121269575) Rs. 2320 (Vol. IX-V.1)
15. Imperial Tables - Burma Report (9788121269551) Rs. 3360 (Vol. X-V.2)
16. Provincial Tables Burma Report (9788121269537) Rs. 3510 (Vol. X-V.3)
17. Provincial Tables Burma Report (9788121269513) Rs. 3630 (Vol. X-V.4)
18. The Central Provinces And Feudatories - The Report (9788121269490) Rs. 2290 (Vol. XI, Pt. 1)
19. The Central Provinces And Feudatories - Imperial tables and supplementary returns (9788121268936) Rs. 2010 (Vol. XII)
20. Madras The Report On The Census (9788121269476) Rs. 2870 (Vol. XIII)
21. Madras - Tables I to XVII-C, British Territory (9788121269452) Rs. 3490 (Vol. XIV)
22. Madras - Tables A TO E, British Territory. Tables for feudatory States and A Caste Index (9788121269438) Rs. 2820 (Vol. XV)
23. The North Western Provinces and Outh - Report and Provincial Tables (9788121268912) Rs. 3100 (Vol. XVI, Pt. 1)
24. The North - Western Provinces and Oudh- Imperial Tables (9788121269414) Rs. 2000 (Vol. XVII, Pt. 2)
25. The North - Western Provinces and Oudh- Imperial Caste Tables (9788121269391) Rs. 3020 (Vol. XVIII, Pt. 3)
26. Punjab and Its Feudatories - The Report on the Census (9788121269377) Rs. 2710 (Vol. XIX, Pt. 1)
27. Punjab and Its Feudatories - Imperial Tables and Supplementary Returns for the British Territory (9788121269353) Rs. 1370 (Vol. XX, Pt. 2)
28. Punjab and Its Feudatories - Imperial Tables and Supplementary Returns for the Native States, Together With A Caste Index (9788121269339) Rs. 4910 (Vol. XXI, Pt. 3)
29. Report on The Census of The Districts of Ajmere-Merwara (9788121269056) Rs. 720 (Vol. XXII)
30. His Highness The Nizam's Dominions - Report (9788121269315) Rs. 2240 (Vol. XXIII, Pt. 1)
31. His Highness The Nizam's Dominions - Report (9788121269292) Rs. 2410 (Vol. XXIII, Pt. 2)
32. His Highness The Nizam's Dominions - Imperial And Supplementry Tables and Caste Index (9788121269278) Rs. 3390 (Vol. XXIII, Pt. 3)
33. Baroda - Report (9788121269254) Rs. 3810 (Vol. XXIV, Pt. 1)
34. Baroda - Tables (9788121269230) Rs. 2620 (Vol. XXIV, Pt. 2)
35. Mysore - Report (9788121269216) Rs. 2590 (Vol. XXV, Pt. 1)
36. Mysore - Imperial Tables (9788121269193) Rs. 1600 (Vol. XXV, Pt. 2)
37. Mysore - Tables (9788121269179) Rs. 5320 (Vol. XXV, Pt. 3)
38. Mysore - Supplementary Tables (9788121269155) Rs. 3590 (Vol. XXV, Pt. 4)
39. Mysore- Supplement to the Mysore census report of 1891 being a list of villages in the Mysore province and : comparing the population as per Censuses of 1891, 1881 & 1871 (9788121279024) Rs. 5350 (Vol. XXV, Pt. 5)
40. Rajputana - The Report, Imperial Tables And Supplementary Returns (9788121269131) Rs. 2330 (Vol. XXVI, Pt. 1)
41. Rajputna - The Provincial Tables and Remarks (9788121269117) Rs. 550 (Vol. XXVI, Pt. 2)
42. Central India (9788121269094) Rs. 2000 (Vol. XXVII)
43. Kashmir State - The Report on the census and Imperial and supplementary Tables (9788121269070) Rs. 2290 (Vol. XXVIII)
44. The Census of Calcutta (9788121269032) Rs. 890
45. Report on the census of Cochin (9788121269018) Rs. 790 (Pt. 1)
46. Report on the census of Cochin - The Final Census Tables with Appendices (9788121268998) Rs. 910 (Pt. 2)
47. Report on the Census of Coorg (9788121268974) Rs. 730
48. Report on the census of Travancore -Report (9788121274029) Rs. 4220 (Vol. I)
49. Report on the census of Travancore -Appendix (9788121268950) Rs. 5300 (Vol. II)

Owing to the antiquity and rarity of this book, certain pages are regrettably absent, and readability is compromised due to the blurring of the original text. If you possess any insights regarding the availability of these missing sections, kindly inform us. Your assistance is crucial in ensuring the completion of this significant work for the benefit of future generations.

CENSUS OF INDIA, 1891

BOOK-14: VOL. IX

IMPERIAL SERIES

BURMA REPORT

PART-I

OPERATIONS AND RESULTS

H. L. Eales

GYAN

Published by

GYAN

Gyan Publishing House
5, Ansari Road
Daryaganj, New Delhi-110002
Phone: 011-47034999, 9811692060
E-mail: books@gyanbooks.com

Distribution Network
gyanbooks.com
India, USA, Canada, UK, Australia

ISBN: 978-81-212-7129-5 (Set) 28 Vols. In 49 Bindings
978-81-212-6957-5 (PB) Book-14, Vol. IX, Part-I

First Published, 1892

2nd Impression 2024

Printed at: Gyan Press, Delhi.

CENSUS OF INDIA 1891

GOVERNMENT OF INDIA.

CENSUS OF 1891.

IMPERIAL SERIES.

VOLUME IX.

BURMA REPORT.

VOLUME I.

OPERATIONS AND RESULTS,

WITH

TWO MAPS, FOUR DIAGRAMS AND FOUR APPENDICES.

BY

H. L. EALES, I.C.S., Provincial Superintendent of Census Operations.

RANGOON:

PRINTED BY THE SUPERINTENDENT, GOVERNMENT PRINTING, BURMA.

1892.

PREFACE.

A Census Report differs in some respects from the ordinary Blue Book. It appeals more directly to the general public, as the general public is after all the subject of it. Moreover, it has been the custom of Superintendents to write prefaces to the reports of other provinces in the hope, perhaps, that what they have written with so much toil may find some readers and not repose in undisturbed dignity on the shelves of Government almirahs. This is the excuse for the present preface. The Report on the Census of Burma consists of four volumes—the Report and its comparative statements and appendices, the Imperial Tables of Burma, and two volumes of District Tables. There are altogether 2,430 pages comprised in these volumes.

My task is over, and, now it is finished, it is but right I should here state the sense of obligation I feel to those who have offered me their help so willingly in the preparation of the report. If in any chapter of this report there is matter of interest to the general reader, it is to those who have ungrudgingly helped me that the credit is due. In Chapter III on Religion I gratefully acknowledge the help I have received from the Lord Bishop of Rangoon Dr. Strachan, from the Right Reverend Bishop Bigandet, the Rev. Dr. Marks, the Rev. Dr. Cushing, and Major Temple. In the chapter on Infirmities Dr. Pedley very kindly read my proofs and gave me valuable hints on the points referred to. Chapter VII, Education, was written after I had discussed the question with Mr. Pope, the Director of Public Instruction. I trust my critics will deal gently with Chapter VIII, which deals with the languages spoken in Burma. In it I have ventured to discuss the classification of the languages of Burma and their kindred tongues. But for the help I received from Dr. Cushing, Major Temple, Dr. Shaw, and Mr. Houghton of the Burma Commission, and from Mr. C. O. Blagden of the Straits Settlements Civil Service, I should have hesitated to publish this attempt at the reclassification of languages. In Chapter X I have again to acknowledge the help received from Dr. Cushing and Mr. Houghton. Mr. E. C. S. George and Mr. Merrifield have also furnished me with interesting monographs on the subjects of the races in the Bhamo and Mergui districts.

Several officers have very kindly helped to revise my proofs; chief amongst them are Mr. Smeaton and Dr. Shaw. Mr. Pereira, the Township Officer of Magwe, has also very kindly assisted me in the correction of the proofs of several chapters of this report. To Mr. Regan, the Superintendent of the Government Press, I am in no small measure indebted for hints as to the shape in which the report now appears and for the patient care that has been displayed in producing the four volumes. I have already, in my report, acknowledged how much of the success of the Census depended on the prompt working of the Government Press.

I cannot, however, close this preface without mentioning the loyal help I have received from my Census Establishment. In the work of organization I received the most willing assistance from Mr. Noyce, who, in the anxious days before the enumeration, worked early and late. Subsequently Mr. Stubbs was appointed the Manager of the Central Office. I cannot easily express the sense of obligation I am under to him for his untiring industry. At one time there were more than 400 clerks employed in the Census Office. The management of such an office requires tact and judgment. Mr. Stubbs proved himself well fitted for the task. He gave me entire satisfaction. Of the subordinate establishment, where so many worked well, it would seem invidious to pick out individuals, but amongst the Burmese Clerks, Maung Saw Maung and Maung Bo, and amongst the Bengali Clerks, Babu B. K. Chatterji, well deserve mention, not merely for the hard work they did, but for the excellent example they set to their subordinates. To the last named in particular my thanks are due. His industry and conscientious hard work are worthy of especial recognition.

MAGWE :
The 13th August 1892.

TABLE OF CONTENTS.

CHAPTER I.

General description of Burma.

	Para.	Page.
Increase of census area by the annexation of Upper Burma	1	1
The boundaries of the province	2	ib.
The Dependent States	3	ib.
Distribution of area over which the census was taken	4	3
Excluded tracts	5	ib.
Physical features	6	ib.
The coast line	7	4
The rivers of Burma	8	ib.
The Irrawaddy	9	ib.
The lakes of Burma	10	5
The geology of Burma	11	ib.
The products of the soil	12	6
Rainfall	13	ib.
Cause of variety in rainfall	14	8
Administrative divisions and the changes since 1881	15	ib.
The census administrative divisions	16	9
The recent census was the third taken in Lower and the first in Upper Burma ...	17	10
The attitude of the people	18	11
The preparation of the provisional total of population	19	12
The census returns	20	ib.
The distribution of the population by area	21	15
Comparison with the density of population in other countries	22	17
Distribution of the population by towns and villages	23	ib.
The disproportion in the growth of the population and the number of towns and villages in the last two intercensal periods discussed as a means of ascertaining the true growth of the population between 1872 and 1881	24	19
The urban population	25	21
The disproportion in the increase of villages and towns in the two intercensal periods discussed as a test of the accuracy of the returns of the rate of increase ...	26	ib.
The growth of the chief towns of Lower Burma	27	22
The areality of townships, villages, and occupied houses	28	23
The mean proximity	29	24
The return of occupied houses	30	25
The definition of a census house	31	ib.
The average number of residents in each occupied house	32	27
The average size of the village	33	29
Boat population	34	31

CHAPTER II.

Movement of the Population.

	Para.	Page.
The two points of view from which the census returns may be discussed	34a	35
The natural increment	34b	37
Annual returns of vital statistics	35	38
Increase due to excess of immigrants over emigrants	36	41
Movement of the population within the province	37	42
Growth of the population in the rural tracts	38	44
Stationary districts	39	46
Corrected rate of annual increase	40	ib.
Rangoon	41	47

CHAPTER III.

Religion.

	Para.	Page.
The religions of Burma	42	51
Strength of the various religions	43	52
Relative strength of the various chief races in the eight administrative divisions ...	44	55
Buddhism	45—56	58—68
Nat-worship or animistic religion	57	68
Shamanism	58, 59	69, 70
Mahomedanism	60	71
Hinduism	61	72
Christianity	62—68	73—77
Church of England	69	77
The Roman Catholics	70	79
Presbyterians	71	80
Baptists	72	ib.
Christianity no longer an exotic religion in Burma	73	81
Wesleyans and the Methodists	74	ib.
The Lutherans and Armenians	75	82
Sikhism	76	ib.
Jews	77	83
Parsis	78	ib.
Religions "Not returned"	79	ib.

CONTENTS.

CHAPTER IV.

Sex and Age.

	Para.	Page.
General review of the scope of the chapter	80	85
Distribution by sexes in Upper and Lower Burma compared with other countries ...	81	ib.
Birth-rate of males and females	82	86
Accuracy of the returns	83	88
Disparity of the sexes	84	ib.
Proportionate strength of the sexes at various ages	85	89
Comparative strength of the sexes in Burma distributed by religions and age periods ...	86	90
Buddhists	ib.	ib.
Nat-worshippers	ib.	91
Hindus and Musalmans	ib.	ib.
Christians	ib.	ib.
Proportion of females to 1,000 males at every age period	87	92
Comparison with the returns of 1872 impossible	88	95
Returns of sexes of Lower Burma in 1872, 1881 and 1891 contrasted	89	ib.
Returns of birth-place an explanation of the variance in the return of sexes... ...	90	96
The age returns	91	ib.
The general inaccuracy of all age returns	92	ib.
Explanation of Diagram B	93	97
Explanation of Diagram C	94	ib.
Consideration of the comparative statement of age periods on the various provinces of India	95	100
The causes of these anomalous returns of the age of children	96	ib.
Distribution by age periods of 10,000 of the population of each sex	97	101
Comparative table showing degree of accuracy in the return of children's ages in the various districts	98	105
Comparison of age periods in aggregates of 10 and 20 years	99	106
The age at which the population is evenly divided	100	108
Ages of the population by sexes in every year of their life per 10,000 of the total population excluding the population of Rangoon	101	ib.
Age returns in Rangoon	102	109
Proportionate strength of population within the reproductive age period	103	110
The mean age of the population	104	ib.

CHAPTER V.

Civil Condition.

	Para.	Page.
Marriage	105	111
Divorce	106	ib.
Comparison of the strength of the tendency to marriage in Burma and in other couutries	107	112
Why married people are proportionately less numerous in Burma than in India ...	108	113
Civil condition of the population by age	109	ib.
Polygamy comparatively rare in Burma	110	114
Polygamy in Burma	111	115
The mean age of married persons in Burma	112	116
The tendency to marriage among those professing the different religions returned ...	113	ib.
Distribution of population by civil condition in every 10,000 of each age-period by religion	114	117
Distribution of 10,000 of each sex and of each condition by age periods	115	118
The reproductive age period	116	119

CHAPTER VI.

Infirmities.

	Para.	Page.
The returns of the four chief infirmities, insanity, deaf-mutism, blindness and leprosy ...	117	121
The various forms of insanity	118	125
Comparative prevalence of insanity in Burma, India and Europe	119, 120	125, 126
Causes of insanity	121	126
Local distribution of insanes	122	127
Distribution of insanes by age periods	123	ib.
Infirmities distributed by caste and race	124	128
Insanes distributed by religions they profess	125	ib.
Distribution by sex	126	ib.
Tendency to insanity amongst males and females	127	ib.
Deaf-mutism	128	ib.
Local distribution of deaf-mutes	129	129
Cause of variance in the return of deaf-mutes	ib.	ib.
Absence of deaf-mutism in the earliest age period	130	ib.
Distribution of deaf-mutes by caste or race	131	ib.
Distribution of deaf-mutes by religion	ib.	130
The comparative prevalence of blindness	132	130
Cause of blindness	133	131
Smaller percentage of blindness amongst Indian immigrants	134	ib.
Females afflicted with blindness more than males	135	ib.
Comparative prevalence of blindness in the sexes distributed by races	136	132
Leprosy	137	ib.
Comparative prevalence of leprosy	138	ib.
Local distribution of leprosy	139	ib.
Venereal disease as a cause of leprosy	140	133
Distribution of those afflicted with leprosy by age periods	141	ib.

	Para.	Page.
Prevalence of leprosy amongst the indigenous races and religions	142	133
Infirmity returns of Burma contrasted with those of India, &c.	143	ib.

CHAPTER VII.

EDUCATION.

The scope of the census returns	144	135
Proposal to restrict return to literates and illiterates	145	ib.
Comparison of the state of education in Burma with that of other provinces and countries	146	136
Educational returns of 1881 in Lower Burma contrasted	147	ib.
Causes of position held by Burma	148	137
Education and religion	149	138
Education in Upper Burma and attitude of the pôngyis	150	ib.
State of education in the different districts of Burma	151	139
Education amongst males	152	141
Education amongst females	153	ib.
Education in relation to age	154	143
Education amongst men	155	144
Education amongst women	156	ib.
The future prospects of education in Burma	157	ib.

CHAPTER VIII.

LANGUAGES.

Substitution of parent-tongue for mother-tongue as the term used for denoting the language spoken	158	145
Classification of languages	159	146
Group A, Languages of Burma—(a) Burmese and its dialects	160	ib.
Returns of those speaking dialects of Burmese in Lower Burma in 1881 and 1891 ...	161	147
The Chin dialects	162	ib.
The Kuki dialects	163	148
The Chingpaw and Lishaw dialects	164	ib.
The Môn-Anniam dialects	165	ib.
Karen dialects	166	149
Taik Shan dialect	167	ib.
Selung or Selôn dialect	168	ib.
Group B, Languages of India	169	150
Group C, Languages of Asia beyond India and Burma	170	ib.
Group D, Languages of Europe and Africa	171	151
Classification prescribed by the Government of India	172	152
The Aryan, the Semitic and Turanian families	173	153
Discussion of the classifications already made	174	ib.
Terrien de la Couperie's classification	175	154
Max Müller's theory regarding the origin of speech	176	155
The evolution of articulate language out of ejaculation	177	156
The term polytonic proposed	178	ib.
Reason for adopting the term polytonic	179	ib.
The definition of the term Tone	180, 181	157, 158
The classification of the languages	182	158
Dr. Cushing's opinion	183	159
The languages of Burma classified	184	ib.
Burmese and its dialects	185	160
Arakanese	186	ib.
Tavoy	187	ib.
Yaws	188	161
Chaungtha	189	ib.
Kudo or Kadu and Danu dialects	190	ib.
The Yabein dialect	191	ib.
The Chin-Lushai group	192	ib.
Shandu or Shendu and Kyau or Chaw	193	163
The Kachin-Naga group	194	164
The Karen dialects	195	ib.
Môn or Talaing	196	166
The decay of the Môn and Talaing languages	197, 198	166, 167
The Môn-Annam kingdom	199	167
Shan or Tai dialect	200, 201	167—169
The Selung or Selôn language	202	169

CHAPTER IX.

BIRTH-PLACE.

The objects of the enquiry into birth-place	203, 204	171
Divisions of the enquiry	205	174
Comparative mobility of the population in India and Burma	206	ib.
Comparison with the returns of 1881	207	ib.
Persons born in Burma enumerated in India	208	175
The two classes of emigrants from Burma	209	ib.
Relative number of emigrants from the chief provinces of India	210	ib.
Comparison of the returns of birth-place, religion, and parent-tongue	211	ib.
Explanation of the disparity	212	176

	Para.	Page.
The immigration and emigration statistics collected in the ports of Burma	213	176
Summary of the returns of the past five years of immigrants and emigrants ...	214	177
Cause of the discrepancy in the returns	215	ib.
Movement of the population between Upper Burma, Lower Burma, and the Shan States	216	178
Causes of this movement of the population	217	ib.
Movement of the population from district to district	218	183
The cause of immigration from India	219	ib.
Comparative mobility of the population in the districts of Burma—Immigration ...	220	ib.
Comparison with the returns of districts in Indian provinces—Emigration ...	221	184
Mobile disposition of the Burmans	222	ib.

CHAPTER X.

Caste or Race.

	Para.	Page.
The return of caste for the first time in Burma	223	185
Parent-tongue and birth-place as a substitute for the return of race	224	186
Reasons for making the return of caste and race	225	ib.
Imperial and Provincial classifications	226	187
The Imperial classification unsuited to Burma	227	ib.
Classification of the races	228	188
Imperial classification	229	ib.
Relative strength of indigenous races, Hindu aud Mahomedan tribes	230	189
Relative strength of the nationalities enumerated in Lower Burma in 1872 and 1891 ...	231	193
The Burmese	232	ib.
The Burmese tribes	233—236	193—196
The Arakanese	237	196
Tavoyer	238	197
Kudo	239	198
Yaw	240	ib.
Yabeins	241	ib.
Chaungthas	242	199
Danus and Danaws	243	ib.
Chins	244	ib.
Taungthas or Kukis	245	200
Kachins	246	ib.
Shans	247	ib.
The Ahoms or Assamese	248	204
The Môns or Talaings	249	205
Karens	250	206
The Taungthus	251	207
Malays	252	208
Chinese	253	212
Panthès	254	ib.
Musalman tribes	255	ib.
Indian immigrants from Southern India	256	ib.
Hindu castes	257, 258	214, 215
The European nationalities	259	216
Eurasians	260	ib.

CHAPTER XI.

Occupations.

	Para.	Page.
Variety in the occupations returned and the method of compilation	261	217
The Imperial Tables XVII A and B	262—264	218
The classification adopted	265	ib.
Comparison of the two classifications	266—268	219
The arrangement of the classes	269—271	220, 221
The Abstracts A, B and C	272	234
Class A, Service of Government	273	252
The pastoral and agricultural class B	274	ib.
The classification of herdsmen	275	253
Order V, Agriculture	276	ib.
Comparison of the results of the two classifications of agriculturists	277	254
The four groups of Order V	278	255
Item 38, Land occupants cultivating	279	256
Item 41, Tenants and sharers	280	ib.
Group 11, Agricultural labourers	281	ib.
Group 12, Growers of special produce	282, 283	257, 258
The explanation of Abstract E	284	258
Growers of special products	285	259
Class C, Personal and household service	286	ib.
Class D, The preparation and supply of material substances	287	ib.
Group 17, The suppliers of animal food	288	260
Item 98, Toddy-drawers and sellers	289	ib.
Dealers in oil	290	261
Order IX, Builders and dealers in building materials	291	ib.
Groups 25 and 26, Boat-builders and makers of vehicles	292	ib.
Supplementary requirements	293	ib.
Press proprictors and printers	294	262

	Para.	Page.
Wood-carvers and lacquerers	295	262
Group 36, Tool-makers	296	ib.
Order XII, Makers of textile fabrics	297	263
Group 40, Workers in cotton	298	ib.
Weavers	299	ib.
Group 41, Workers in jute, coir, &c.	300	264
Group 42, Drapers and workers in articles of attire	301	ib.
Order XIII, Workers and dealers in precious metals and stones	302	ib.
Blacksmiths	303	ib.
Item 298, Potters	304	265
Order XV, Workers in wood, cane, and leaves	305	ib.
Item 304, Carpenters	306	266
Group 50, Bamboo-workers, &c.	307	ib.
Order XVII, Workers in leather, horns, and bones	308	267
Class E, Commerce, transport, and storage	309	ib.
General merchants, shopkeepers, and brokers	310	ib.
Carriers by land and water	311	ib.
Boat-owners and boatmen	312	268
Class F, Professions	313	ib.
Item 401, Priests, ministers, and missionaries	314	ib.
The Burmese religious orders	315	ib.
Group 65, Literary men	316	269
Group 66, The legal profession	317	ib.
Group 67, The medical profession	318	270
Class G, Indefinite and independent	319	ib.

CHAPTER XII.

Administration of the Census Operations.

	Para.	Page.
The Agra Conference	320	273
Appointment of the Provincial Superintendent of the Census Operations	321	ib.
Distribution of the area of the province	322	274
Distribution of the regular census area into synchronous and non-synchronous census tracts	323	ib.
The agency employed	324	275
The adjustment of the census administration to the lines of the revenue administration	325	275
The subdivisional and circle registers	326	276
The translation of the schedule and instructions	327	277
Amendment of Circle Registers **A** and **B**	328	278
House-numbering	329	ib.
The preliminary and final indents for schedule books and the printing	330	ib.
Stationery	331	279
Areas requiring special arrangements	332	280
Special arrangements for the enumeration of coolies	333	ib.
The enumeration of the population afloat	334	281
The *personnel*	335	ib.
Classes from which census officers were recruited	336	282
The enumeration	337	283
Census holidays	338	ib.
Preparation of the enumerator's abstract	339	284
The special arrangement adopted in Burma to secure an early return of the population	340	ib.
The preparation of the provisional totals	341	286
The compilation of the figures	342	287
Abstraction	343	ib.
The tabulation	344	289
Method devised for classifying and tabulating occupations and castes	345	290
The tabulation of castes and races	346	ib.
Employment of British soldiers in the census office	347	291
Compilation	348	ib.
Imperial tables	349	292
The cost of the report	350	ib.
Printing	351	293
Cost of the census year by year, 1890-91 to 1892-93	352	295
The accuracy of the returns	353	296
Services of officers	354	297

APPENDICES.

A.—The enumeration in the tracts excluded from census operations	i—xlv.
B.—Index of castes, tribes, and races found in Burma—Census 1891	xlvii—l.
C.—Circulars, instructions, and specimen forms	li—xcv.
D.—Extracts from the reports of Deputy Commissioners and Presidents of Municipalities	xcvii—cxlvi.

ADDITION TO ADDENDA AND CORRIGENDA OF VOLUME I, BURMA CENSUS REPORT.

Page 191, Statement C, column 17, line 10, *for* "67" *read* "467."

" Statement C, column 21, line 10, *for* "70,137" *read* "103," and in line 11, *for* "83" *read* "38,477."

ADDENDA AND CORRIGENDA.

Page 7, *for* "sub-mountane" *read* "submontane."

" 8, line 17 from top, *for* "sub-mountane" *read* "submontane."

" 11, " 24 " " "it" " "they."

" 22, " 4 from bottom, " "Maulmein" " "Ma-ubin."

" 45, in the table of variation in the area under cultivation, *for* "Shwegyin" *read* "Toungoo," and *for* "Toungoo" *read* "Shwegyin."

" 51, *for* "Shwe Yeo" *read* "Shway Yoe."

" 63, line 7 from bottom, the word "Atthakathâ or Commentaries" should be in brackets.

" 96, " 5 from top, *for* "4,015,461" *read* "4,015,451."

" 102, Pegu district, male, under age 1, *for* "191" *read* "192."

" 102, " female, " 2, " "348" " "349."

" 102, " male, " 4, " "249" " "247."

" 102, Kyauksè district, female, " 1, " "145" " "144."

" 146, line 10 from bottom, *for* "7,303·00" *read* "7,303·30."

" 187, " 13 from top, " "Group" " "Class."

" 262, " 27 " " "15" " "14."

Page 56. In the table showing the comparative strength of the various nationalities by religions the Burmanized Kachins are included in the number of Burmese Buddhists and Burmese Nat-worshippers, while the Taungthus are included under the Shans.

REPORT

ON THE

CENSUS OF BURMA.

Taken on the 26th February 1891.

CHAPTER I.

General description of Burma. The Rainfall, Administrative, and Census divisions. The Census returns. Attitude of the people, comparison of the returns of Burma with those of India. Distribution of population by area. Rate of progress. Comparisons of the returns of Lower Burma at the three enumerations of 1872, 1881, and 1891. Urban and Rural population. Return of boat population.

THE physical geography of Lower Burma has been already described in Sir William Hunter's *Imperial Gazetteer of India* and even still more fully in Colonel Spearman's *British Burma Gazetteer*. But the annexation of the kingdom of Upper Burma and the States dependent on it not only necessitates a short account of the physical features of the newly acquired territory, but as the annexation has removed the former artificial division of the valley of the Irrawaddy, the Upper and Lower provinces have now become so identified that any description of the former would be incomplete without the inclusion of the latter.

The boundaries of the province.

2. Although the northern and north-eastern boundaries of the province have not yet been finally demarcated, the province may be said to extend from the Pakchan river 9° 55″ north lat. in the south, to the Kachin hills which divide the Bhamo district from Yunnan in 27° 15″ circa., north lat., in the north, and from the Bay of Bengal on the west to the eastern boundary of the dependent Shan States. This eastern boundary is not yet demarcated. The extreme length from north to south is about 1,200 miles and at its broadest part, which is in latitude 21°N., it extends for about 480 miles from the boundary of Chittagong on the west to the eastern boundary of the tributary Trans-Salween States on the east. Lower Burma was formerly somewhat imaginatively described as resembling a bird flying from east to west, Arakan and Tenasserim forming the wings and Pegu the body. But the annexation of Upper Burma, by altering the shape, has destroyed this fanciful resemblance.

On the north the dependent State of Manipur and the Kachin hills and the Chinese province of Yunnan form the boundaries. The Siamese Shan States and Siam bound the province on the east and the Bay of Bengal on the south and west, and Chittagong on the north-west. The area of Upper Burma is estimated at 83,473 square miles. This area does not include the townships of Sinbaungwè, Taingda, and Minhla, which have been incorporated with the Thayetmyo district and which cover about 737 square miles. The area of Lower Burma before the annexation was returned at 87,220 square miles. Thus, the total area is about 87,957 square miles in Lower and 83,473 square miles in Upper Burma, or 171,430 square miles for the whole province. The area of the Northern and Southern Shan States is computed to be about 40,000 square miles.

The Dependent States.

3. Within these boundaries, but still treated as semi-dependent States, are the States of Thaungthut (Hsawnghsūp) and Zinglein Kanti (Singkaling Hkamti) in the Upper Chindwin

district, the State of Baw (Maw) in the Kyauksè district, the State of Kantigyi (Hkāmti Lōng) in the Bhamo district, while the States of Kale and Wuntho have recently been taken under the direct administration of British Officers. On the east we have the following States :—

(1) Momeik (Möng Mit) with its dependency Mohlaing (Möng Lang) under the supervision of the Commissioner, Northern Division.

(2) The Northern Shan States under the supervision of the Superintendent, Northern Shan States—

Taungbaing (Tawng Peng), North Theinni (Hsin Wi), South Theinni (Hsin Wi), Thibaw (Hsi Paw), with its dependencies Mainglôn (Möng Long), East and West.

Thônzè (Hsum Hsai) and Maingtôn (Möng Tung).

(3) The Southern Shan States under the supervision of the Superintendent and Political Officer, Southern Shan States—

Maingnaung (Möng Nawng), Kyithi Bansan (Kehsi Mansam), Monè (Möng Nai), with its dependency Kyaingtaung (Keng Tawng), Maingseik (Möngsit), Maingpan (Möng Pan), with its Trans-Salween dependencies Maingta (Mönghta), Mainghan (Möng Hang), Maingsut (Möng Kyawt), and Maingthat (Möng Hsat) ; Thatôn (Hsahtung), including Tabet (Tam Hpak) and Letmaing (Manglôn) ; Banyin (Wanyin) ; Naungmun (Nawng Wawn) ; Yatsauk (Lawk Sawk) ; Saga (Samka), with its dependency Pöngmu ; Sagwe (Sakoi) ; Nyaungywè (Yawng Hwe), with it dependencies Letthet (Lai Hsak), Inleywa (Anleywa), Kyauklat (Kyawkhtap), and Thigyit (Hsikip) ; Maingkaing (Möng Kung) ; Lègya (Lai Hka) ; Maingpun (Möng Pawn) ; Maingpyin (Möng Ping) ; Kyaingkan (Kenghkam) ; Maukmè (Mawkmai), with its Trans-Salween dependencies Mesakôn (Mehsakun) and Maingmaw (Möng Mau);

Hopôn (Hopong) including Helôn (Hai Long) ;
Nankôk (Nam Hkôk) ;
Mobyè (Möng Pai) ;
Maingshu (Möng Hsu) ;
Maingsin (Möng Sang) ;
Kyainglun (Keng Lôn) ;

(4) The Myelat under the supervision of the Superintendent and Political Officer, Southern Shan States—

Ywangan (Ye Ngan) ;
Pwehla (Pwela) ;
Bawzaing (Mawsôn) ;
Nankôn (Namsong) ;
Pinhmi (Pangmi) ;
Lwèmaw (Loimaw) ;
Nantôk (Namtôk) ;
Bawnin (Mawnang) ;
Kyaukkuleywa (Kyawkku Hsiwan) ;
Pindaya (Pangtala) ;
Kyôn (Kyong) ;
Thamakan (Hang Möng Hkan), including Magwe (Makwe), Lwean (Loi An), Taunghla (Tawngla), and Myinmati (Menghti) ;
Lwè-e (Loi Ai) ;
Nanke (Nam Hkai) ;
Lwèlôn (Loi Long).

The eastern boundary of these Shan States is still uncertain and the area covered by them can therefore only be estimated approximately.

Distribution of area over which the census taken.

4. Over the whole of Burma except in these dependent States and certain excluded tracts the census was taken and the census schedule duly filled in. In some of the remoter and wilder hill tracts the experience acquired in past census showed that the census could not be taken synchronously. Special instructions were therefore issued and the census schedule books were checked within a few days before and after the 26th February 1891. The area over which the census was not taken synchronously bears but a slight proportion to the whole area of the province. The point will be more fully dealt with in Chapter XII. It will be sufficient to note here that the area in Lower Burma over which the census was taken non-synchronously in 1881 was reduced from about 11,000 to about 4,000 square miles. This improvement is due to the firmer hold the administration had obtained over the hill tracts in the Tharrawaddy and Toungoo districts, to the efforts of the missionaries who have successfully laboured to improve and enlighten the wild Karen villagers, and in part also to the better arrangements made by the respective Deputy Commissioners, especially in the Salween Hill Tracts, where the whole area of the district was included within the synchronous census tract.

Excluded tracts.

5. In Bhamo, Upper Chindwin, and the Shan States special arrangements were made with the sanction of the Government of India. The Superintendent of the Northern Shan States, Mr. Daly, proposed an enumeration form in which the population of each village is entered and this form was accepted for the whole of excluded States. The arrangements made will be found in full detail in Chapter XII.

Physical features.

6. Now that the artificial political boundary of Upper and Lower Burma has been removed the province is divided solely by its physical features. The physical divisions of Burma are its mountain ranges, which run north and south and divide the country longitudinally. They are the Arakan Yoma, the Pegu Yoma, the Paunglaung range, and the Shan Hills. The two last ranges are generally considered to form but one series. The Arakan Yoma is a continuation of the mountain chain known as the Naga Hills which form the eastern boundary of Assam. Running almost due south they divide the Arakan division from the basin of the Irrawaddy. The Pegu Yoma rises in the high land of Meiktila, south of Mandalay, and, running parallel to the Arakan Yoma, divides the basin of the Irrawaddy from that of the Sittang. The Paunglaung range rises in the high lands of the Shan States and divides the basin of the Sittang from the Salween. This range, unlike the Pegu Yoma, has some hills of considerable height, one peak rising to about 8,000 feet. The range sinks down into the plain of Thatôn. Between the Paunglaung range and the last and easternmost range of the Shan Hills, flows the Salween which rises in the Chinese Shan States. This easternmost range of mountains divides the basin of the Salween from the Mekong, and further south it divides British territory from the neighbouring kingdom of Siam, and further south still ends in the Malay Peninsula.

Burma thus divided by its mountain chains falls into four great divisions: Arakan on the west, Tenasserim on the east, and between them the basins of the Irrawaddy and Sittang, which are divided from each other by the Pegu Yoma. In lieu of the former political frontier between Upper and Lower Burma the physical boundary between the upper and lower province coinciding as it did with the former political division between the Talaing and Burman kingdoms would naturally be drawn at the northern limit of the delta of the Irrawaddy. The delta of the Irrawaddy may be said to begin near the village of Yegin Mingyi, a few miles south of Myanaung. At about this spot the flood-waters of the Irrawaddy spread over and mingle with the water of the Myitmaka chaung and hence Mr. Theobald has fixed on this spot as the apex of the delta. The sides of the delta measure 179 miles on the west and 126 miles on the east, and the base, measured from Elephant Point to Cape Negrais, is 137 miles in length. The area thus comprised is, roughly speaking, about 12,000 square miles. With the exception of the laterite hills near Myaungmya and the Eocene sandstone range near Thamandewa in the same township, but a few miles further south, the whole of this area is a vast plain gradually sloping down to the sea shore. How gradual the fall is may be judged by the fact that the tide is said to be felt as far north as Yegin Mingyi. Hence the name "Yegin." It is estimated that at least 2,000 square miles or one-sixth of this area is below the level of the highest spring tides.

This delta, together with the lowlying land lying to the west of the estuary of the Sittang in the Pegu and Shwegyin districts, comprises what should, from a physical point of view, be considered as the lower province. The physical aspect of these districts is the same. Till lately they were covered with dense tree and bamboo jungle and with water-logged swamps, clothed with elephant grass. The extension of cultivation and the draining of these swamps have changed the aspect of the country within the memory of persons still living. The climate of the delta is cooler and more temperate than in Upper Burma, and this is shown somewhat strangely and yet very markedly in the difference between the complexion and physique of the dwellers of the delta and of the drier and hotter districts of the upper province. A traveller ascending the Irrawaddy will notice that the people of the southern province are fairer and stouter than those further north until he reaches Bhamo, where the infusion of foreign blood predominates and other types of the Tibeto-Burman family prevail. North of the apex of the delta and the boundary between the deltaic and inland tracts, which we may fix at Yegin Mingyi, the rainfall gradually lessens till we arrive at Minbu, where what was formerly called the rainless zone commences and extends as far as Katha. Northward of this point the rainfall increases, till at Bhamo the annual rainfall reaches an average of about 70·106 inches, which is almost the same as the average rainfall at Yegin Mingyi.

The coast line.

7. The coast line of the province extends for about 1,200 miles from the mouth of the Naaf to the estuary of the Pakchan and apart from the mouths of its chief rivers, which are the Kuladan, the Ngawun (or Bassein mouth of the Irrawaddy), the Hlaing (or Rangoon river), the Salween, and the Dawe (or Tavoy river), there are no harbours of any importance except at Kyaukpyu and Mergui, where the harbours are formed by the islands that lie off the coast.

The Arakan and Tenasserim coast during the south-west monsoon is exceedingly dangerous on account of numerous small islands that stud it, while the Gulf of Martaban, which forms the estuary of the Sittang, is also useless as a roadstead, exposed as it is to the full force of the south-west monsoon and rendered still more dangerous by the bore formed by the tide forcing its way up over the shoals which lie between its funnel-shaped banks.

The rivers of Burma.

8. From its position and the plentiful rainfall Burma, as might be expected, abounds in rivers. In Arakan there are three, the Naaf, the Kuladan, and the Lemyo or Lemro. In Tenasserim the chief rivers are the Sittang, the Belin, and the Salween, into which the Gyaing, Yônsalin, and Attaran, themselves considerable rivers, fall; and further south the Tavoy and the Tenasserim. None of these rivers are of great value as navigable streams as only small launches and country-boats can ascend them to any distance from their mouths.

The Irrawaddy.

9. But the chief glory of the country, as it is the most important factor in its past and present history, is the magnificent stream of the Irrawaddy. For 900 miles and more of its course it is navigable even when its stream is lowest by steam-ships of over 100 tons burden, and its chief tributary, the Chindwin, has been successfully navigated in a large launch as far as 300 miles from its junction with the Irrawaddy. At its mouth the Irrawaddy has formed a large delta which is almost unsurpassed by any in the world for area and the fertility of the soil.

Unlike the three other great rivers of the Indo-China peninsula, the Salween, the Mekong, and the Red river, the Irrawaddy is for most of its course unencumbered with rocks and rapids and is easily navigated at all seasons of the year. It thus forms the natural highway into Southern and Central China. To the Irrawaddy and to the abundant rainfall are due the productiveness of the country and its comparative immunity from serious famines.

The tributaries of the Irrawaddy are the Mogaung river which falls in north of Bhamo from the west, the Tapeng from the east, and the Shwele which also falls in from the east after Bhamo has been passed. For nearly 200 miles there is no tributary of importance till the Myitngè falls in at Ava. The Chindwin is the next affluent and further south during the rains the drainage of the eastern and western hills is brought down by the Yenangyaung, Pin, Yin, Sadôn, and Mongyaung streams. These latter are unnavigable for any distance at any time and quite inconsiderable, except in the rains. South of the old frontier the Kyini, Butle, and Nawin on the east, and the Mindôn, Made, Kyaukbu, and Patashin on the west, are the only remaining affluents. Of these, only the Mindôn is navigable by boats of any size throughout the year.

The lakes of Burma.

10. In Burma Proper there are no real lakes of any importance except the Inma lake in Prome, the Tu and Duya in Henzada, the Shagègyi and the Yegyi in Bassein. The Meiktila lake and the Aungpinle lake near Mandalay are artificial reservoirs. In the high lands of the Shan Hills are the Inle lakes near Nyaungywe and the Indawgyi lake near Mogaung. The other lakes are marshes formed after the fall of the waters of the rivers and which are wholly or partly dried up in the hot season.

The geology of Burma.

11. A detailed description of the geology of Burma would be out of place in a Census report. Soil, climate, and rainfall, the configuration and height of its mountain ranges, the number and size of its rivers, undoubtedly do directly influence the character and hence indirectly the religions and customs of the races inhabiting the province and the density of its population, but though a brief description of the soil is necessary, geological details would be out of place. The geology of Upper as well as of Lower Burma has been reported on by Messrs. Theobald, Mallet, Oldham, and Blandford, and a short *résumé* of their writings, which has been kindly revised by Dr. Noetling, is all that is necessary here. Of the mountain ranges already mentioned the westernmost or Arakan Yoma is in most part composed of beds of early tertiary age resting on cretaceous beds which rise to the surface in the western face of the range. Here and there are found hills of nummulitic limestone and occasionally outcrops of serpentine. The surface rocks are generally sandstone and shales. Coal has been found, but hitherto has not paid for its working. Lime is burnt in the Bassein and Thayetmyo districts. The next range is the Pegu Yoma, which is composed wholely of beds of later tertiary age, consisting chiefly of either sandstone or shale. The third range is the Paunglaung. It formed a portion of the margin of the vast oceanic bed in which the beds composing the Arakan and Pegu Yomas were deposited. So far as is known it consists of two distinct groups, the Gneissose formation and limestone, which has been supposed to be of lower carboniferous age, but which, according to recent investigations, more probably belongs to the lower Silurian formation. The fourth mountain range, which is divided from the Paunglaung by the Salween river, has not yet been explored. It probably belongs to the same formation as the Paunglaung and, so far as it is geologically considered, forms but one mountain system. The hills that skirt the Irrawaddy north of Mandalay are Silurian limestone locally changed into crystalline limestone, the matrix of rubies, metamorphic rocks composed of gneiss and hornblendic schist, and opposite Kyaukmyaung greenstone and basalt are found. On the west of the river the formation of the Sagaing hills is partly metamorphic and partly tertiary. The latter are composed of sandstones and shales of the Miocene period.

The delta of the Irrawaddy is said to be composed chiefly of "older" and not "river alluvium." This is explained by Mr. Theobald to be due to the fact that the delta of the Irrawaddy has been formed by elevation by subterraneous forces and not by the accumulation of fluviatile beds of recent origin. North of the delta the formation between the Arakan Yoma on the west and the Pegu Yoma on the east is of alluvial clays and sand resting on sandstone of the Miocene period. Further north, between the old frontier and Pagan, we find but little alluvial soil, and the hills which bound the river on both sides are chiefly composed of sandstone and shales containing fossil wood and bones. South-east of Pagan we find the extinct volcano of Poppadaung. This volcano is supposed by Mr. Blandford to have been in action during the Pliocene period. Coal has been found in the Thayetmyo, Upper Chindwin, Henzada, Hanthawaddy, Shwebo, Amherst, and Mergui districts, but hitherto all attempts to work it profitably have failed. Gold was, so Dr. Mason reports, found in most of the rivers of Burma, but in such small quantities as not to pay for the working. The tin mines in Mergui have, within the last two years, been again reported on by Mr. Hughes, of the Geological Survey, but though his report is on the whole favourable, hitherto only the Chinese have been able to make the working remunerative. The ruby mines of Burma, of which so much was expected, but from which as yet so little has been gained, are too well known to require further notice. In the Mogaung subdivision of the Bhamo district, not far from Maingkhwan, are the amber mines. The amber is much inferior in quality to the European amber. The jade mines are to the west of Lamaing. They have been worked profitably by the Chinese. Last, but not least, come the earth-oil wells. These wells are to be found on both sides of the Arakan Yoma. On the western side hitherto they have not been worked by Europeans to a profit. On the eastern side the oil-bearing strata is cut in two by the Irrawaddy. Borings have shown that oil is to be found on both the Minbu as well as the Yenangyaung (or Magwe) side of the river. These wells have been worked for many years past by the Burmans. It is yet too early to say whether the exploitation of these oil-fields by European capital will or will not be a financial success. The Yenangyaung field appears to be of limited extent.

But with the exception of the oil-fields, so far the efforts to win the mineral wealth of Burma have not as yet proved successful, nor is there at present any probability that a sudden development of mining industry is ever likely to divert the movement of the population or to make any great change in the returns of the occupations they at present pursue.

The products of the soil.

12. Apart from its mineral wealth, which has played but a small part in the history of the races inhabiting Burma, the province is remarkable for the fertility of its soil. In the delta of the Irrawaddy and in the alluvial plains of Arakan and Tenasserim the staple product is rice. In Mandalay, Sagaing, Kyauksè, Pyinmana, and Taungdwingyi, as well as in the plains of Shwebo and in the valley of the Chindwin, rice is largely cultivated. It is generally said that the Burman selects the cultivation of rice because it suits best his lazy nature and that he has only to scratch the ground in order that it may smile into plenty in his face. Any one who is acquainted with the cultivation of rice knows that this charge is untrue. Not only does the ploughing of the water-logged field impose very severe labour on the ploughman, but the rice plants are in most cases transplanted which is unnecessary in the case of other grains. The real reason why rice, and rice alone, is grown in the places before mentioned is because the localities are especially fitted for this species of cultivation. Of late years the efforts of the Agricultural Department have been devoted to inducing cultivators to grow tobacco, wheat, and sugar-cane, and with some success. Further north of the delta, in places where from various causes rice cannot be successfully cultivated, Indian-corn, peas, millet, and sessamum are grown in large quantities.

Rainfall.

13. The area of Burma is so vast and the physical conditions are so varied that to give the mean annual rainfall of Burma would be simply misleading. Mr. Theobald divided Lower Burma into three zones, the littoral, embracing Mergui, Kyaukpyu, and Akyab; the sub-littoral, including Moulmein, Amherst, Tavoy, and Sandoway; and the inland, embracing such places as Thayetmyo, Myanaung, and Prome. It is not easy to see what was the principle underlying this classification, as it is difficult to understand how the conditions of Moulmein, Tavoy, and Sandoway vary from those of Mergui and Akyab. The term sub-littoral is equally applicable to Rangoon as to Tavoy. This classification is on the face of it fanciful and dictated rather by a slight and perhaps accidental variance of the amount of the rainfall than by the physical conditions of the districts themselves. During the last few years observations have been made in Upper as well as in Lower Burma. The accompanying table will show the returns of the average annual rainfall for the past 10

years in Lower and of the past 5 years in Upper Burma classified in accordance with the arrangement hereafter recommended.

Division.	District.	Mean annual rainfall.	Remarks.
Arakan	Akyab	184·6	Littoral.
	Northern Arakan	127·49	Sub-mountane.
	Kyaukpyu	196·8	Littoral.
	Sandoway	209·7	
Pegu	Rangoon Town	94·4	Deltaic.
	Hanthawaddy		
	Pegu	116·66	
	Tharrawaddy	87·5	
	Prome	43·9	Central.
Irrawaddy	Thôngwa	86·7	Deltaic.
	Bassein	110·3	
	Henzada	84·9	
	Thayetmyo	36·9	Central.
Tenasserim	Amherst	182·2	Littoral.
	Tavoy	200·3	
	Mergui	183·7	
	Toungoo	83·6	Central.
	Shwegyin	137·5	Deltaic.
	Salween	100·31	Sub-mountane.
Northern	Mandalay	27·616	Central.
	Bhamo	70·106	Sub-mountane.
	Shwebo	30·289	Central.
	Katha	46·97	
	Ruby Mines	83·88	Sub-mountane.
Central	Ye-u	34·556	Central
	Sagaing	26·97	
	Lower Chindwin	28·347	
	Upper Chindwin	73·587	Sub-mountane.
Southern	Myingyan	23·90	Central.
	Pakôkku	23·18	
	Minbu	24·134	
	Magwe	34·956	
Eastern	Kyauksè	22·70	Central.
	Meiktila	29·968	
	Yamèthin	33·76	
	Pyinmana	50·666	

A comparison of these returns with the map of Burma would appear to suggest the distribution of the area of Burma somewhat after the following lines of classification :—

(1) *Littoral.*—The littoral area embraces the whole sea coast of Arakan and Tenasserim. The mean annual rainfall in the Arakan coast does not vary much from the annual rainfall in the Tenasserim sea coast districts. The physical conditions are precisely similar as we find in both a high range of hills running parallel with the coast line and at no great distance from it. Here the mean annual rainfall varies from 182·2 inches at Moulmein to 209·7 at Sandoway.

(2) *Deltaic.*—In this division are included the districts of Bassein, Henzada, Thôngwa, Hanthawaddy, Tharrawaddy, Pegu, and part of Toungoo and Shwegyin. Except in the eastern half of the Shwegyin district, where the rainfall is much heavier, the climatic conditions and physical features of all these districts are similar. There is no range of mountains to arrest the rain-charged clouds, and the result is that the rainfall is less heavy, though the actual duration of the rainy season is nearly as long as in the littoral area.

In these districts the mean annual rainfall varies from 84·9 in Henzada to 137·5 in the Shwegyin district. The rainfall at Shwegyin is exceptionally heavy because of the neighbouring hills of the Paunglaung range. The mean annual rainfall at Pyuntaza is about 14 inches less than the record of rainfall at Shwegyin.

(3) *Central.*—This tract includes the districts of Toungoo, Prome, and Thayetmyo in Lower, and Pyinmana, Yamèthin, Meiktila, Kyauksè, Magwe, Minbu, Myingyan, Pakôkku, Mandalay, Katha, Shwebo, Sagaing, Ye-u, and Lower Chindwin in Upper Burma, thus including the whole of the Eastern, Southern, and parts of the Northern and Central divisions. In this area the rainfall varies from an average annual fall of 83·6 in Toungoo, 50·66 in Pyinmana, and 43·9 in Prome, where the rainfall is generally sufficient for rice-cultivation, to an annual average fall of about 22·7 inches in Kyauksè, 23·18 in Pakôkku, which form what is commonly called the dry zone.

(4) *Sub-mountane.*—Under this head should be included the districts of Upper Chindwin, Bhamo, Ruby Mines, Northern Arakan, Salween, and part of Shwegyin and Toungoo. The rainfall here is considerably heavier than in the Central zone and varies from 70·106 at Bhamo to 127·49 in the Northern Arakan Hill Tracts.

Cause of variety in rainfall.

14. The variation in the rainfall is clearly due to the following causes :—

(1) The heavily charged rain-clouds brought up by the south-west monsoon are partly arrested by the peaks of the Arakan Yoma and the Tenasserim hills, which drain them of most of their contents, accordingly the rainfall is heaviest in the littoral zone. In the delta the rainfall is still heavy, though not so heavy as in the littoral tracts of Arakan and Tenasserim, where the hill-ranges act as condensers. The clouds that escape the Arakan hills in their passage to the north-west do not suffer so much as those that pass directly over them, and accordingly we find the rainfall heavier in Pyinmana in the east than in Minbu on the Irrawaddy to the west, though they are situated in about the same parallel of latitude.

In the same way Thayetmyo and Prome, which are more sheltered by the Arakan Yoma, have a much smaller fall than Toungoo enjoys, where the rain-clouds arrive after passing over the plains of the delta and the comparatively insignificant hills of the Pegu Yoma.

(2) The scanty rainfall of the Central zone is further aggravated by the want of forests, which is noticeable in all except the southern districts of this zone. For, unlike the rest of Burma, if we except the districts of Toungoo, Pyinmana, Prome, and part of Thayetmyo and Magwe, this Central tract contains no forests of importance such as undoubtedly help to increase the rainfall in the deltaic districts.

The importance of the rainfall is best gauged in relation to the question of the movement of the population, which is dealt with in the next chapter.

Administrative divisions and the changes since 1881.

15. The administrative divisions of the province do not, however, correspond with the physical boundaries, though in Lower Burma they adhere more closely to them than in the Upper Province. In Lower Burma in 1881 there were but three divisions : Arakan, comprising the districts of Akyab, Northern Arakan, Kyaukpyu, and Sandoway ; Tenasserim, which included Toungoo, Salween, Amherst, Moulmein, Tavoy, and Mergui ; and the great deltaic division of Pegu, which then included Rangoon, Hanthawaddy, Prome, Tharrawaddy, Henzada, Bassein, Thôngwa, and Thayetmyo. On the 1st June 1881 the Commissionership of Pegu was divided into two : Pegu, which kept Rangoon, Hanthawaddy, Tharrawaddy, and Prome ; and Irrawaddy, to which Bassein, Thôngwa, Henzada, and Thayetmyo were assigned.

A glance at the map will show that this division is, on geographical grounds, somewhat amorphous. Thayetmyo, which belongs to Irrawaddy, is cut off from the other part of the division by the Prome district. But mere geographical reasons were outweighed by administrative difficulties. The former administrative boundaries that obtained in 1881 were further obliterated by the division of the

Hanthawaddy district into two parts, a new district being formed out of the Pegu, Paunglin, and Syriam townships, and the Laya circle of the Shwegyin district. This district was called Pegu.

In 1885 the Kingdom of Ava was annexed and the territory so acquired was divided into four Commissionerships or Divisions; Northern, to which Mandalay, Myadaung, Bhamo, and Shwebo were assigned; Central, which first included Kyauksè and Ava, as well as Sagaing, Ye-u, and the Upper and Lower Chindwin districts; Southern, which included the Myingyan, Pagan, Minhla, and Taungdwingyi districts; and Eastern, to which were given Pyinmana, formerly known as Ningyan, Yamèthin, and Meiktila. As experience was gained and occasion for changes arose, this original division into districts and divisions has been altered from time to time. The Myadaung district has been deprived of the Malè township, which has been given to Shwebo, and of the Ruby Mines, which have been formed into a separate district, while its name Myadaung has been changed to Katha. The State of Wuntho, lying between Katha, Bhamo, and Upper Chindwin, has since been annexed owing to the sudden rising of the Sawbwa, and its area will be added to the Katha district. The Central division has been deprived of Kyauksè, which has been transferred to the Eastern division, and the small district of Ava has been made into a subdivision of the Sagaing district. The Eastern division has experienced no change except that, as before stated, Kyauksè has been given over to it, as since the railway line was opened between Toungoo and Mandalay Kyauksè was more easily accessible to the Eastern than the Central Commissionership. The Southern Commissionership has experienced the most change. In fact, the areas of the districts have all been redistributed. The townships of Taingda, Minhla, and Sinbaungwè, known to the Burmans since the annexation of Pegu in 1852 as Myedè Kyan or "what is left of Myedè," have been added to the Thayetmyo district in Lower Burma. The headquarters of the Minhla district were removed early in 1886 from Minhla to Minbu, which was formed into a district, and Taungdwingyi and Magwe were constituted into a separate district and called Magwe. The district of Pagan, which at first lay on both sides of the Irrawaddy, was broken up and Pagan subdivision was added to Myingyan, which at the same time gave up the area on the west of the Irrawaddy which formerly belonged to it, and the two subdivisions of Myingyan and Pagan which lay on the west bank of the Irrawaddy were formed into the Pakôkku district. The changes were made gradually, and as these changes in the administrative divisions in Upper Burma have assimilated the administrative more closely to the natural divisions, there has been a gain in symmetry as well as in administrative convenience. Looking at the map it will be seen that the Northern division includes the basin of the Irrawaddy above its junction with the Chindwin; the Central embraces the valley of the Chindwin; the Eastern takes in the uplands of Meiktila and the basin of the Sittang, while to the Southern falls the lower portion of Irrawaddy basin. If further alterations occur between the present and the next succeeding census, the line of change may be confidently expected to follow in the same direction. The distinction between Upper and Lower Burma will be completely lost by the inclusion of the Thayetmyo in the Southern division, and of Myingyan, Mandalay, or Toungoo in the Eastern. These divisions will then lose their, at present, significant names.

The census administrative divisions.

16. Since the administrative divisions are now probably fairly permanent, they have been adopted as convenient units in dealing with the census returns, especially as they will form a ready means of comparison in future years. The experience gained at the last preceding census had shown that there were considerable areas even in Lower Burma where the census schedule could not be checked in one night. Furthermore, there were parts of the province where, for a variety of reasons, the officer in charge reported that any regular census could not possibly be taken. The province, from a purely census point of view, therefore, fell into three divisions: First, the tract over which the information acquired for filling up the census schedule could not be collected; these tracts were therefore excluded from the regular operations of the census and were called "the excluded tracts." Under this term

were comprised parts of Bhamo and Katha in the Northern division, the States of Kanti, Taungthut, and Kale in the Upper Chindwin, Wuntho and the Shan States to the east of the Irrawaddy. The area thus treated is shaded blue in Census Map II. Secondly, the area over which the returns required by the standard census could be prepared, but where, owing to the sparsity of the population, the illiteracy of the village headmen, and the difficulty of communications the census schedule could not be synchronously checked on the night of the 26th February. These areas were called the "non-synchronous census tracts" and are shaded yellow on the map. Over all the rest of the province the census was taken synchronously. This area is left uncoloured.

On the occasion of the census of 1881 the province of Lower Burma was divided into synchronous and non-synchronous census areas and there were no excluded tracts, and though in the report of 1881 it is stated that the census of 1881 was practically synchronous throughout the province, it would appear that in Northern Arakan, Salween, and parts of Shwegyin, Toungoo, and Amherst, Mergui and Tharrawaddy districts the preparation of the returns was spread over the months of January and February.

The advance made in the last decade in the spread of education by the missionaries amongst the wild Karens of Toungoo, Shwegyin, and Tharrawaddy, as well as the stronger grip that the administration of the districts has gained over these remoter tracts, have naturally tended to decrease the area which could not be synchronously censused in 1881. Accordingly the Deputy Commissioner of Tharrawaddy, with the aid of the Forest Department, was able to arrange for the synchronous census of the whole of the tract comprising, so far as can be now ascertained, 1,000 square miles, or nearly half the area of the whole district which had been excluded from the synchronous census in 1881. In the same way the non-synchronous census areas both in Shwegyin and Toungoo were largely decreased. This subject is more fully discussed in Chapter XII, where the arrangements made by the Deputy Commissioners both in Upper and Lower Burma are described. The administration of the census operations is fully dealt with in Chapter XII of this report. It will be sufficient here to state that the census operations followed as closely as possible the lines of the revenue administration of the province. The unit of enumeration was the block. The size of a census block varied according to the local conditions, but in order to preserve, as far as possible, the identity of the lowest unit of administration, which is the village, orders were passed that one or more villages were not to be grouped into one block as it was found that by so doing in 1881 the returns of the villages grouped in this way could not be separated. A village therefore consisted of one or more blocks according to its size. Blocks for census purposes were grouped for the purpose of superintendence into census circles under circle supervisors, and the census circles were placed under the charge of Superintendents. There was no difficulty in rural tracts in treating townships as Charges, but owing to the fact that revenue circles in Lower Burma often contain 50 or 60 and sometimes even more villages, the revenue circle was often too large to correspond with the census circle, which ordinarily should not contain more than 10 or 15 blocks. On the other hand, in Upper Burma the revenue circles are sometimes very small, and in some districts, such as Kyaukse̱ and Myingyan, contain but one village. No hard-and-fast rule could therefore be successfully applied, and accordingly arrangements were made for each district in concert with the Deputy Commissioner.

17. On the night of 26th February the census was taken in Burma as in the rest of the Indian Empire. It was the third census taken in Lower Burma, but the first ever attempted in the Upper Province. In August 1872 the first census was taken in Lower Burma. This was followed after a lapse of eight and-a-half years by the census of 17th February 1881. We have therefore some means of judging the growth of the population and of testing the accuracy of our figures by comparing our returns for Lower Burma with those of previous enumerations. Unfortunately the Kings of Ava never attempted to make any numberings of the inhabitants of their kingdom. The records of the Hlutdaw or *Aula Regis* and of the district "kayaings," even if they were available, would be useless for purposes of comparison, as they

are confined to details of revenue and not of population. The operations in the Upper Province were, however, so well carried out by the District Officers that there is every reason to believe that the enumeration was on the whole made quite as accurately as in the earlier acquired province.

The attitude of the people.

18. Owing to the trouble and confusion consequent on the subversion of the Kingdom of Ava and the difficulty experienced in reducing the turbulent upcountry Burmans to order, some doubt was at first experienced as to whether a synchronous census could be successfully carried out. Even in Lower Burma, which had caught the infection of dacoity and anarchy, at one time the census promised to be a task of difficulty. But so thoroughly was the task of reducing the turbulent districts to order carried out in the three years immediately preceding the census, that even less opposition was experienced in Upper Burma on this occasion than in Lower Burma at the previous enumeration in 1881. The collection of statistics cannot but suggest to those enumerated the intention to collect revenue. In 1872 the wildest rumours were current, and even in 1881 the reports current among the villagers would have been ludicrous if they had not been inconvenient. That these rumours were believed in 1881 is proven by the fact that all the inhabitants of two villages on the Siam frontier emigrated *en bloc* into Siam. Nor can we wonder that ignorant Burman villagers or Karen foresters are troubled in mind when we read that in England no census was taken till 1801, and that the Bill which was introduced into the House of Commons in 1753 for the purpose of legalizing the taking of a census was received with such virulence of language and such absurd predictions of future disasters and epidemics as would seem now to be incredible were it not on record. One member of Parliament stated that he " did not believe that there was any set of men or indeed any individual of the human species so presumptuous and so abandoned as to make the proposal we have just heard. The new Bill will direct the imposition of new taxes, and indeed the abolition of a very few words will make it the most effectual engine of rapacity and oppression that was ever used against an injured people." Another Member gravely said that " the people looked on the proposal as ominous and feared lest some public misfortune or an epidemical distemper should follow the numbering." The Bill was eventually thrown out. In a newly conquered country there was ample reason for fearing lest the enumeration would be thwarted by the suspicious doubts of the enumerated; as a fact, however, these fears proved to be groundless. In not one district was any opposition offered, and even in Bhamo, where the people are not of Burmese blood and are extremely illiterate, no active opposition was offered. No more significant proof of the thoroughness of the pacification of Upper Burma could be asked for or obtained. In the reports of the District Officers the attitude of the people is the subject of favourable comment. In Lower Burma the dread of an increase of taxation as the result of the census was no longer a cause of disquietude. The householders even took pride in the census numbers given to their houses, and in more than one case the house number was elaborately carved and hung up with pardonable pride in front of the artist's house. In Upper Burma the original feeling regarding the census was no doubt tempered with alarm, but the influence of the District Officers and their own common sense showed the villagers that they had nothing to fear, and even in Upper Burma the census operations were regarded in a spirit of benevolent neutrality. In Lower Burma some of the better educated took an interest in the census. One pôngyi in Rangoon who imagined that he had escaped enumeration felt so aggrieved that he reported the omission and he was no doubt agreeably surprised to find that the President of the Municipality had not forgotten him.

The Burman is not prevented by motives of false shame from revealing the true facts regarding himself and his wife and family. Whereas in England the census enumerator might be thought to ask impertinent questions regarding the age of those whom he enumerates and in India the Mahomedan refuses to give his wife's name, a Burman, on the contrary, is willing to supplement the information asked for with details not usually required in census returns. The attitude of the people was a most satisfactory feature of the operations, and there need be no apprehension on this score regarding future enumerations.

There is every reason therefore for anticipating that the Shan States, which were necessarily excluded from the operation of the regular census, and where, on this occasion, a much more simple form of enumeration was adopted, will in 1901 fall within the scope of the regular synchronous census.

The census was taken synchronously on the night of the 26th February throughout the synchronous area, and in the non-synchronous tracts the census schedule books were corrected on the day preceding and on the two days following the census. The methods followed for overcoming the difficulty of enumerating travellers by land and water are detailed in Chapter XII.

The preparation of the provisional total of population.

19. The next important point was the early submission of the returns of the population.

On the occasion of the last census much delay was experienced owing to the fact that the enumerators were found to be unable to add up and submit the total number of the population of their blocks. This necessitated the books being collected and being forwarded to the Head Central office, where, after much further delay owing to the irregular submission of the schedule books, the returns were obtained. The necessity of obviating this waste of time and of utilizing the enumerator to the utmost of his ability was no slight task. Special arrangements were made in conjunction with the District Officers for the prompt compilation of the returns of occupied houses and of the population by sexes.

In Chapter XII the arrangements that were made will be fully dealt with. It will suffice to say here that notwithstanding the fact that in Lower Burma in the rural tracts communications are still imperfect, owing to lack of roads and railways and telegraphs, and that in the upper province the novelty of the work and the huge areas of some of the districts rendered the work of compiling this return within the time allowed by the Census Commissioner a matter of impossibility, yet on the whole these returns were compiled by the District Officers with, in most instances, praiseworthy accuracy and despatch. The operations in Upper Burma were further hampered and the success of the census in the Katha, Upper Chindwin, Ye-u, and Shwebo districts imperilled by the sudden rising of the Wuntho Sawbwa. This rising was in no way connected with or caused by the census; most fortunately the arrangement that had been made in concert with the Deputy Commissioner of Katha for compiling the returns of the preliminary enumeration prevented the failure of the work. The Provisional returns of the Upper Burma districts show more accurate results than those of the lower province. In Minbu, where the population amounted to 224,475 persons, spread over an area of 3,210 square miles, the final figures checked in the Central Office only show a difference of 203, although the Deputy Commissioner, Mr. Hartnoll, submitted his returns within the six days prescribed by the Census Commissioner. Equal promptitude and almost equal accuracy was shown in the submission of the returns of the Sandoway, Thayetmyo, Toungoo, Shwegyin, Bhamo, Akyab, Hanthawaddy, Tharrawaddy, Prome, Tavoy, Ye-u, Lower and Upper Chindwin, Pakôkku, Kyauksè, Katha, Pyinmana, Yamèthin, Magwe, and Ruby Mines districts. The result of the comparison of the final with the preliminary returns fully justified the experiment of having the return of population by sexes and of occupied houses compiled locally instead of submitting the schedule books to the abstraction offices for compilation and thereby delaying the early return of the total population. But for carelessness in one district, Bassein, the error would have been inappreciable.

The Census returns.

20. The total population of Upper and Lower Burma, inclusive of the State of Wuntho, but exclusive of the Shan States, is now ascertained to be 7,722,053; the population of the Shan States is returned as 375,961. This includes the population of the synchronous census tract of the Shan States, which was confined to the British Civil and Military stations. In this area the census schedules were duly filled up and checked on the night of the 26th February. The total population of this tract is shown separately in all the Imperial tables. It amounted to 2,992 souls. The total population of the whole province thus amounts to 8,098,014 persons. As this was the first census ever taken of the upper province no comparison can be drawn so far as Upper Burma is concerned; but the following statement will

show how rapidly the returns of the population of the lower province have increased since 1872, in which year the first census was taken :—

1872.	1881.	Increase.	Percentage.	1891.	Increase.	Percentage.
2,747,148	3,736,771	989,623	36·02	4,658,627	921,856	24·67

Rapid as was the growth of the population since 1881, it was not judged by statistics alone so rapid as in the eight and a-half years which elapsed between the census of 1872 and that of 1881. But a careful perusal of the report of the census of 1872 will show that a large number of persons admittedly escaped enumeration in that year. On the 15th July 1872 the orders were first issued to the Commissioners. From that date to the 15th August, on which the census was to have been taken, the time was so short that it is not surprising that even in Rangoon itself the census was not taken till the 16th August. The enumeration in Rangoon was so palpably wrong that the Deputy Commissioner allowed 2½ per cent. for persons who had escaped notice. What must have occurred in the remoter parts of the province can only be deduced from the fact that the work was apparently intrusted to the thugyis, who in some cases, it is stated, had barely time to "scramble" back to their circles after receiving orders to carry out the census. Moreover, it must be remembered that as the thugyi collects the "capitation-tax," an accurate census would betray the shortcomings of his own "capitation-tax rolls." It is recorded "that no attempt was made to obtain a record of the "Salôn population, while for most of the Karens in the Pegu Yomas and other "mountainous and wild parts of the country, as well as for Northern Arakan, the "thugyis' returns were accepted as an approximate statement of the numbers of "the people." The whole of the population of the Hill Tracts was omitted, and in the Amherst district the Deputy Commissioner in consternation reported that in one circle the population according to the census returns was actually 1,340 below even the thugyis' annual figures. One means of judging how the work in 1872 was done is to take the figures for a race, such as the Karens, whose numbers are rarely recruited by immigration, and to compare the returns of 1872 with those of 1881. Mr. Copleston, in paragraph 229 of his report, states regarding the increase in the Karens as follows :—

"Of all kinds of Karens there are 518,294. At the census of 1872 the numbers returned amounted to 331,255. The increase of 56 per cent. cannot in any considerable part be attributed to immigration, and it is therefore necessary, as has before been said, to suppose that many Karens were omitted from the enumeration of 1872."

On the other hand, the census of 1881 was taken with much greater care and accuracy. Instead of one bare month being allowed for preparation, the work of preparation was commenced as early as 21st May 1880, when instructions were issued to Commissioners. Accordingly, as might have been expected, the more carefully prepared census operations in 1881 prevented any large number of persons escaping enumeration, and, while it thus showed a most abnormal increase in the growth of population between August 1872 and February 1881, it effectually prevented the next census from showing any such extraordinary return. If we confine the comparison to the Town of Rangoon, where the short notice given in 1872 might naturally be expected to be less liable to create blunders and errors in enumeration, we find that in 1872 the population, excluding the 2½ per cent. addition which the Deputy Commissioner wished to add for faulty enumeration, was returned at 98,745 persons. In 1881 the population had risen to 134,176, an increase of 35·88 per cent. This rate of increase is lower than the general rate of increase in the province, which is returned at 36·02. If we add the 2½ per cent. which represented the number who are supposed to have escaped enumeration, in 1872, the increase between 1872 and 1881 is reduced to slightly under 33 per cent. In 1891 the population of Rangoon was returned at 180,324, which gives an increase of 34·3 per cent. in the decade. It is clear therefore that Rangoon has been growing at a steady rate since 1872, while, if the figures of 1872 are correct, the growth of the population outside Rangoon was abnormally fast, faster even than Rangoon for eight and a-half years, and then apparently fell to about two-thirds of its previous rate of progression.

But although the rate of increase has fallen from the abnormal return of 36·02 per cent. for the eight and a-half years ending in February 1881 to 24·67 for the 10 years ending in February 1891, yet this latter rate is far in excess of any of the returns of the other provinces of the Empire as the following table will show:—

Province.	Area in square miles.	Occupied houses.		Population.						Variation per cent. since last census.			Persons per square mile, 1891.
				Total.		*Male.*		*Female.*					
		1891.	1881.	1891.	1881.	1891.	1881.	1891.	1881.	Total.	Male.	Female.	
Madras	141,193	6,705,517	5,641,914	35,630,440	30,812,745	17,619,395	15,250,617	18,011,045	15,562,128	+ 15·63	+ 15·53	+ 15·73	252·35
Bombay and Sind ...	125,064	3,373,232	2,825,469	18,857,044	16,471,107	9,763,067	8,506,581	9,093,977	7,964,526	+ 14·48	+ 14·77	+ 14·18	150·77
Bengal	149,725	13,569,179	10,531,228	71,336,617	66,589,553	35,556,460	33,122,832	35,780,157	33,466,721	+ 7·12	+ 7·34	+ 6·91	476·45
North-Western Provinces and Oudh.	107,954·3	8,224,075	6,866,503	46,903,102	44,107,869	24,302,135	22,912,556	22,600,967	21,195,313	+ 6·34	+ 6·06	+ 6·63	434
Punjab	111,016	3,841,558	2,707,091	25,130,127	22,703,947	13,580,077	12,314,376	11,550,050	10,389,571	+ 10·7	+ 10·4	+ 11·2	226·3
Ajmere-Merwara ...	2,711	*	64,118	*	460,722	*	248,844	*	211,878	...	...	...	...
Central Provinces ...	115,936	2,567,764	2,712,259	12,944,805	11,548,511	6,486,315	5,827,122	6,458,490	5,721,389	+ 12·1	+ 11·3	+ 12·9	111·7
Berar	17,717·87	591,008	466,027	2,897,491	2,672,673	1,491,826	1,380,492	1,405,665	1,292,181	+ 8·41	+ 8·06	+ 8·78	163·53
Coorg	1,583	...	22,357	173,055	178,302	95,907	100,439	77,148	77,863	− 2·94	− 4·51	− 0·91	109·3
Assam	49,004	1,118,885	859,388	5,476,833	4,881,426	2,819,703	2,503,703	2,657,130	2,377,723	+ 10·87	+ 11·20	+ 10·51	111·76
Lower Burma ...	87,957	869,132	677,362	4,658,627	3,736,771	2,462,296	1,991,005	2,196,331	1,745,766	+ 24·67	+ 23·67	+ 25·80	52·96
Upper Burma ...	83,473	561,728	...	3,063,426	...	1,424,860	...	1,544,081	...	...	...	...	36·69
Total British Territory ...	993,333·90	*	33,373,716	*	204,163,626	*	104,158,567	*	100,005,059	...	...	...	...

* The figures are not yet available as the returns of Ajmere-Merwara have not been received.

It is evident therefore from this table that the growth of the lower province is still extraordinarily rapid. The annual rate of increase is 2·23 per cent., which corresponds to 24·67 per cent. for the decade. This means that if this rate of increase be maintained, the population of Lower Burma will be doubled in 31·428 years.

The growth of the population in the various towns and districts of the lower province is discussed *seriatim* in Chapter II of the report which deals with the movement of the population in detail.

The distribution of the population by area.

21. The area of the province, including the Upper Burma districts, but excluding the Shan States, of which the area is estimated at 40,000 square miles, is returned at 171,430 square miles; accordingly there are on an average 45·04 persons living on each square mile throughout the province. In Lower Burma in 1872 there were only 31·5 persons to the square mile, while in 1881 the returns showed that there were then 42·8 to the same area. In 1891 the density had risen to 52·96 persons to the square mile.

Map II shows the density of the population of the province and its distribution over the various townships of the different districts. For the purpose of classification the returns of density have been divided into six grades—0-10, 11-25, 26-50, 51-100, 101-150, 151 and over.

The subjoined table will give more fully the return of density for each district in Upper and Lower Burma, giving at the same time the population and area of each district and its relative position to the rest of the province.

Table.

Name of district.	Area.	Population.	Ratio of area to total area of province.	Serial order graded by area.	Ratio of population to total of province.	Serial order graded by population.	Density per square mile.	Serial order graded by density.
1	2	3	4	5	6	7	8	9
LOWER BURMA.								
ARAKAN DIVISION—								
Akyab	5,535	416,305	·0323	11	·0540	4	75·21	13
Northern Arakan ...	1,015	14,628	·0059	35	·0018	36	14·41	29
Kyaukpyu ...	4,309	163,832	·0251	17	·0212	21	38·02	22
Sandoway	3,667	77,134	·0214	19	·0100	31	21·03	26
Total ...	**14,526**	**671,899**	**·0847**	**6**	**·0870**	**6**	**46·25**	**4**
PEGU DIVISION—								
Rangoon Town ...	22	180,324	·0001	36	·0234	20	8,196·54	1
Hanthawaddy ...	1,948	267,039	·0114	31	·0346	12	137·08	5
Pegu	2,428	301,420	·0142	27	·0390	11	124·14	8
Tharrawaddy ...	2,014	347,454	·0117	29	·0450	9	172·51	4
Prome	2,887	360,252	·0168	25	·0466	7	124·78	7
Total ...	**9,299**	**1,456,489**	**·0542**	**8**	**·1886**	**2**	**156·62**	**1**
IRRAWADDY DIVISION—								
Thôngwa	5,413	446,076	·0316	14	·0578	2	82·41	11
Bassein	7,047	475,002	·0411	6	·0615	1	67·40	17
Henzada	1,948	380,927	·0114	31	·0493	5	195·54	2
Thayetmyo	3,134	250,161	·0183	22	·0324	13	79·82	12
Total ...	**17,542**	**1,552,166**	**·1024**	**5**	**·2010**	**1**	**88·48**	**2**
TENASSERIM DIVISION—								
Amherst	15,203	417,312	·0887	2	·0540	3	27·44	24
Tavoy	7,150	94,921	·0418	5	·0123	28	13·27	30
Mergui	7,810	73,748	·0455	4	·0096	32	9·44	33
Toungoo	6,354	162,132	·0371	7	·0210	22	25·51	25
Shwegyin	5,427	198,521	·0316	13	·0257	19	36·58	23
Salween	4,646	31,439	·0271	16	·0041	34	6·76	35
Total ...	**46,590**	**978,073**	**·2718**	**1**	**·1267**	**4**	**20·99**	**8**

Table—concluded.

Name of district.	Area.	Population.	Ratio of area to total area of province.	Serial order graded by area.	Ratio of population to total of province.	Serial order graded by population.	Density per square mile.	Serial order graded by density.
1	2	3	4	5	6	7	8	9
UPPER BURMA.								
NORTHERN DIVISION—								
Mandalay	2,100	374,060	·0122	28	·0484	6	178·12	3
Bhamo ... ... } Bhamo, excluded tracts }	9,800	92,660	·0572	3	·0120	29	9·45	32
Katha ... ... } Katha, Kawlin ... } Katha, Wuntho ... } Katha, excluded tracts... }	6,000	115,411	·0350	9	·0150	26	19·23	27
Ruby Mines ...	2,000	26,134	·0117	30	·0034	35	13·06	31
Shwebo	2,680	135,255	·0156	26	·0175	24	50·46	19
Total ...	**22,580**	**743,520**	**·1317**	**3**	**·0963**	**5**	**32·92**	**6**
CENTRAL DIVISION—								
Ye-u	5,000	92,549	·0292	15	·0119	30	18·51	28
Sagaing	1,836	248,207	·0107	33	·0321	14	135·18	9
Lower Chindwin ...	3,400	232,245	·0199	20	·0301	15	68·31	16
Upper Chindwin ...	19,000	75,785 }	·1108	1	·0127	27	5·14	36
Upper Chindwin, Uyu township.	...	22,008 }						
Total ...	**29,236**	**670,794**	**·1706**	**2**	**·0868**	**7**	**22·94**	**17**
SOUTHERN DIVISION—								
Myingyan	3,737	351,411	·0218	18	·0454	8	94·03	10
Pakôkku	6,160	303,753	·0359	8	·0394	10	49·31	20
Minbu	3,210	224,475	·0187	21	·0291	16	69·92	14
Magwe	5,500	219,190	·0321	12	·0284	17	39·85	21
Total ...	**18,607**	**1,098,829**	**·1085**	**4**	**·1423**	**3**	**59·05**	**3**
EASTERN DIVISION—								
Kyauksè	1,050	126,622	·0061	34	·0164	25	120·59	9
Meiktila	3,000	206,650	·0175	23	·0268	18	68·88	15
Yamèthin	3,000	160,662	·0175	23	·0208	23	53·55	18
Pyinmana	6,000	56,349	·0350	9	·0073	33	9·39	34
Total ...	**13,050**	**550,283**	**·0761**	**7**	**·0713**	**8**	**42·16**	**5**
Total Lower Burma ...	87,957	4,658,627	·5131	...	·6033	...	52·96	...
Total Upper Burma ...	83,473	3,063,426	·4869	...	·3967	...	36·69	...
Total ...	**171,430**	**7,722,053**	...	...	...	...	**45·04**	...
Shan States, synchronous tract }	40,000	{ 2,992	...	...	·79	...	...	...
Shan States, non-synchronous tract. }		{ 372,969	...	...	99·21	...	...	...
Total Shan States ...	**40,000**	**375,961**	...	...	...	...	...	...

As might have been expected, the returns show that there is a great difference between the most densely and the least densely populated districts of the province. It may be said that the density varies almost inversely with the size of the district. The Upper Chindwin, of which the area is returned at 19,000 square miles, itself a principality two and a-half times as large as Wales, has but 5·14 persons to each square mile. Henzada possesses the densest population, there being 195·54 persons to each square mile. In 1881 the returns showed 163 persons for the same area. Next to Henzada, Mandalay district shows the highest actual return of 178 to the square mile, but it must be remembered that the urban population of Mandalay city is included therein, without which the district rural tracts only show 91·6 persons to the square mile.

Tharrawaddy, with 172 inhabitants to the square mile, Hanthawaddy, with 137, and Sagaing, with 135 inhabitants to the square mile, come next in order after Mandalay.

Comparison with the density of population in other countries.

22. If we compare the returns of the density of the population of the province as a whole, or the various districts in the province with the returns of other countries, we find that notwithstanding its rapid growth of late years Burma still ranks low. The accompanying table shows the relation of population to area in some of the chief States of Europe and America, as well as in the other provinces of the Indian Empire :—

Name of Province or State.	Year of enumeration.	Area.	Population.	Density.
Upper Burma	1891	83,473	3,063,426	36·69
Lower Burma	1891	87,957	4,658,627	52·96
United Province	1891	171,430	7,722,053	45·04
England and Wales	1891	58,186	29,001,018	498
Scotland	1881	30,417	4,033,103	132
Ireland	1881	32,583	5,174,836	159
Islands	1881	295	141,260	479
United Kingdom	1881	121,481	35,026,108	288
France	1886	204,092	37,930,759	186
Italy	1880	114,410	28,459,628	249
Prussia	1885	136,075	28,318,470	208
Saxony	1885	5,856	3,182,003	543
Bavaria	1885	29,632	5,420,199	183
Baden	1885	5,891	1,601,255	272
Wurtemburg	1885	7,619	1,995,185	262
Hesse	1885	3,000	956,611	319
Alsace, Lorraine	1885	5,668	1,564,355	276
German Empire	...	...	...	...
Russia in Europe	1887	2,130,462	95,870,810	45
Servia	1890	19,050	2,096,043	110
Sweden	1880	170,979	4,565,668	27
Norway	1875	123,205	1,806,900	15
Denmark	1890	14,124	2,185,159	155
Holland	1889	12,648	4,548,596	360
Belgium	1889	11,373	6,093,798	536
Canada	1881	3,470,257	4,324,810	5*
Brazil	1872	3,209,878	9,930,478	3
Ceylon	1891	25,364	3,008,239	118
Indian Empire	...	†	†	...
Madras with Feudatories	1891	150,802	39,331,062	260·81
Bombay and Sind	1891	125,064	18,857,044	150·77
Bengal	1891	149,725	71,336,617	476·45
North-Western Provinces and Oudh	1891	107,954	46,903,102	434·47
Punjab	1891	111,016	25,130,127	226·3
Ajmere—Merwara	1891	2,711	†	...
Central Provinces	1891	115,936	12,944,805	111·7
Berar	1891	17,718	2,897,491	163·53
Coorg	1891	1,583	173,055	109·3
Assam	1891	49,004	5,476,833	111·76

* Omitting the territories. | † Final figures not yet available.

It will be seen that Upper and Lower Burma, even if we exclude the Shan States, form the largest province of the Indian Empire in the matter of size, but with the exception of Assam they contain the fewest inhabitants. It is, moreover, the least densely populated of any. The easiest way of appreciating the immense size of the province is by comparison with other countries. Burma by itself is as large as Great Britain and two islands as large as Ireland. In population it contains nearly twice as many inhabitants as Scotland did in 1881. The average size of a district in Burma, including the Rangoon district, the area of which is only 22 square miles, is 4,761·94 square miles, that is to say, larger than the three counties of Kent, Sussex, and Hampshire.

The largest district is Upper Chindwin, which is almost as big as Servia, but only contains as many inhabitants as the town of Huddersfield.

There are 15 districts above and 21 districts below the average size. The average population of a district is 214,501 persons, and there are 17 districts which contain more and 19 that contain less than this number.

Distribution of the population by towns and villages.

23. Imperial Table III gives the return of towns and villages in every district classified by population. The first difficulty encountered in preparing this table was to distinguish between the terms village and town. The Census

Commissioner, in his note L., dated the 19th July 1890, laid down the following broad rules for the guidance of Provincial Superintendents :—

(*a*) the population should not be less than 5,000, residing in houses more or less contiguous, not in scattered collection such as hamlets;

(*b*) the place, if not containing the above population, should be under the operation of some Municipal Chaukidari Act;

(*c*) the place, though containing the above population, should not be merely a large village, but should have some distinctly urban character, as that of a market town;

(*d*) where a town is made up of several distinct portions, each should be shown separately for the purpose of Final Tables IV and V as municipal limits, suburbs, and cantonment respectively.

According to the instructions the list of towns has been prepared and the return of these towns classified by population and religion will be found in detail in Imperial Tables IV and V. Imperial Table III is also interesting as it gives the number of the various classes of villages and towns classified by their population for the whole of Burma.

In preparing the list of the towns in Upper Burma I had no returns of any previous census to guide me. Moreover, I was aware that owing to the recent date of the annexation there might be places which were in reality towns, whose population was uncertain and which had not yet been placed under the operation of any Municipal Act. Knowing, however, that the trade and population of the province is expanding and is likely to continue to expand, rapidly, I construed the definition liberally and included such places as Yenangyaung, the centre of the oil industry, thinking that even if its population did not amount to 5,000, yet to all intents and purposes its inhabitants belong to the urban and not rural class, and their inclusion and separate return on this occasion would facilitate comparison on the occasion of the next census. There are then two cities, Rangoon and Mandalay, and 58 towns and 28,709 villages in Burma. The urban population amounts to 946,649, being 12·44 per cent. of the total population of the whole province.

Before examining the returns in Imperial Table III we must recollect that the returns of the excluded tracts in the Bhamo and Katha districts do not give the population or number of villages belonging to each of them. In the Kawlin township of the Katha district and in the Uyu township of the Upper Chindwin district the census schedule books were burnt and consequently they were treated as excluded tracts. As there were no towns in these tracts no difficulty occurs in calculating the distribution of the urban population, but it must be borne in mind that the return of villages and village population distributed amongst the villages only embraces 7,605,560 of the total population.

On examining Imperial Table III we find that of the 28,769 towns and villages in Burma 16,659 or 57·9 per cent. were villages containing less than 200 inhabitants, and these 16,659 villages contained 1,723,743 inhabitants or 22·6 per cent. of the total population, namely, 7,605,560. In Lower Burma there were 10,207 villages containing each less than 200 inhabitants, being 57·3 per cent. of the total number of towns and villages in Lower Burma and containing altogether 1,067,930 persons or 22·9 per cent. of the inhabitants of Lower Burma. In 1881, 9,963 or 62·8 per cent. of all the towns and villages contained less than 200 inhabitants each, but as the population of these various grades of villages is not given separately in the 1881 report, it is therefore not available for comparison. The number of villages containing from 200—499 inhabitants naturally shows a very considerable decrease, from 16,659 to 9,490, but though so much fewer in number, they contain 2,927,915 inhabitants or 38·4 per cent. of the total population. In Lower Burma there were 6,040 villages of this size containing 1,858,797 or 39·9 per cent. of the total population of the Lower Burma province. It will be seen that both in the whole province as well as in Lower Burma by far the greater part of the population live in villages containing less than 500 inhabitants. Of villages containing upwards of 500 and less than 1,000 inhabitants there are 2,141 in the united province and that they contain 1,383,563 inhabitants or 18·1 per cent. of the total population. Of these 1,282 containing 823,993 inhabitants belong to Lower Burma. Of villages containing 1,000 and less than 2,000 inhabitants there are only 374, which contain altogether 500,513 or 6·5 per cent. of the total population. Of these 374 villages 202 were in Lower Burma, whereas there were only 93 of this size in 1872 and 142 in 1881. Of towns and villages containing from 2,000 to 2,999 inhabitants there were 41 in all in Burma, containing 100,031 inhabitants or 1·3 per cent. of the total population. Of these 41 villages 21 were in the lower province as against 19 in 1881 and 16 in 1872. Of towns and villages whose inhabitants number 3,000 and more and less than 5,000 there were 21 with a total population of 76,565 or 1·006 per cent. of the total population. All of the remaining grades are classed as towns and their inhabitants are included in the return of urban population. In 1881 there were in Lower Burma 15,837 villages and 20 towns. The definition of what constituted a town was purely arbitrary, the term being confined to all places containing upwards of 5,000 inhabitants. Following this classification for the purpose of comparison it will be found that there were 17,763 villages and 25 towns in Lower Burma in 1891, being an increase of 12·1 per cent. in the number of the former and 25 per cent. in that of the latter.

The accompanying statement will show the number of villages and towns in Lower Burma graded according to the number of their inhabitants in 1872, 1881, and 1891.

Year.	With less than 200 inhabitants.	200—499.	500—999.	1,000—1,999.	2,000—2,999.	3,000—4,999.	5,000—9,999.	10,000—14,999.	15,000—19,999.	20,000—49,999.	50,000 and over.
1872	9,875	3,594	503	93	16	8	10	3	3	3	1
1881	9,963	4,886	819	142	19	8	10	2	4	2	2
Percentage of increase since 1872.	·8	35·9	62·8	52·6	12·5	...	...	50*	33·3	50*	100
1891	10,207	6,040	1,282	202	21	11	11	4	4	4	2
Percentage of increase since 1881.	2·4	23·6	56·5	42·8	10·5	37·4	10	100	...	100	...

* Decrease.

In comparing the figures of 1881 with those of 1872 Mr. Copleston remarked—

"It appears from these figures that the total increase in the number of villages is 1,748; those with less than 200 inhabitants are but slightly more numerous than in 1872. The villages have been growing more populous and the chief part of the increase in the numbers forming the different classes is among those possessing over 200 souls each. The falling off in the numbers of villages in Northern Arakan and Salween (Final Form XVIII) is probably apparent only and is due to a different method of classification. Many single tès containing several families, and many small hamlets which in 1872 were dignified with the title of villages, though at no great distance apart, have perhaps on this occasion been grouped together. In Bassein, while the area of the district has been reduced from 8,739 to 7,047 square miles, the number of villages has increased from 1,486 to 1,699. The larger villages may be expected to continue to increase in a higher ratio than the smaller ones as the population expands and as the Karens and other hill tribes gradually move down into the plains, gathering in larger communities than it is possible to form where the taungya or jhoom system of cultivation is in vogue."

The disproportion in the growth of the population and the number of towns and villages in the last 2 intercensal periods discussed as a means of ascertaining the true growth of the population between 1872 and 1881.

24. The return of 1891 throws fresh light on this matter. In the first place it will be noticed that notwithstanding an apparent increase in the population between 1872 and 1881 at the rate of 36·02 per cent., the total number of villages and towns in Lower Burma only showed an increase of 1,748 or 12·3 per cent., whereas though in the last decade the population has only increased at the rate of 24·67 per cent., yet the total number of villages and towns in Lower Burma has advanced to 17,788, an increase of 1,931 or 12·17 per cent.

From this comparison the inference might be drawn that whereas the villages and towns did not escape enumeration in 1872 many of their inhabitants did, and hence the disproportion between the increase of population and the increase in the number of towns and villages. This is, I believe, the true explanation. But it might be urged that the disproportion was caused by a flocking of the population to the towns and larger villages. This is disproved by the fact that the population of urban to the total population was 13 per cent. in 1872, and this had fallen to 11·4 per cent. in 1881. In 1891 the return is 12·44 per cent., but this increase over 1881 is due to the fact that not only have all towns over 5,000 inhabitants been included as towns, but several containing less than 5,000 inhabitants have been so returned. If we adhere to the arbitrary rules of 1881 and 1872 we find that the urban population of Lower Burma has risen from 425,775 to 540,672, an increase of 26·9 per cent. only, so that the proportions of urban to the total population which is now 11·6 per cent. remains practically unchanged. But it may be urged that the people, though they did not flock to the towns, went to the larger villages. The best way therefore will be to take each of the various grades separately. We find that the number of villages under 200 inhabitants increased between 1872 and 1881 at the rate of ·8 per cent., and between 1881 and 1891 at 2·4 per cent. The number of villages from 200 to 499 inhabitants increased between 1872 and 1881 at the rate of 35·9 per cent., and between 1881 and 1891 at the rate of 23·6 per cent. As these two classes of villages contained in 1891 62·8 of the total population of Lower Burma, and though the corresponding figures are not, as has already been stated, available for the census of 1872 or 1881, we may conclude that the distribution of the population by these grades of villages has not suffered any proportional change. The remaining towns and villages have been increased between 1872 and 1881 by 368 and in the decade between 1881 and 1891 by 533. The increase in the number of these larger villages and towns was no doubt caused not by the founding of new villages that have suddenly outgrown the first two classes (which for brevity we may shortly call classes **A** and **B**) since 1872, but more probably by recruitment from either **A** or **B** of villages that have outgrown the limit of 500 inhabitants. By leaving out these villages of over 500 inhabitants no appreciable difference will be caused in following deductions which may be drawn from the increase in the number of villages as compared with the increase in the population in the corresponding periods of time. If these towns and villages were included it will easily be seen that they would really strengthen rather than weaken the argument advanced, as in the second intercensal period classes **A** and **B** have lost by this increase in the number of their inhabitants 533 as against 368 villages, which is the total increase in the higher grades between 1872 and 1881. Taking then these two grades of villages **A** containing less than 200 and **B** containing from 200 to 499 inhabitants, we find that in 1872 and 1881 there is scarcely any increase in the number of **A**, but a very large increase in **B**. There was in fact an increase of 88 under **A** and 1,292 under **B** or 1,380 altogether. In the next decade we find that there is an increase of 244 villages of **A** size and 1,154 villages of **B** size. Thus it would seem that while the population was increasing at the rate of 36·02 per cent., the number of villages of the two smallest classes which we have taken as a gauge of the increase of the population show an increase at the rate of about 10 per cent., or, to be exact, 10·24 per cent., while in the next decade, when the total population only increased at the rate of 24·67, the number of villages of classes **A** and **B** increased at the rate of 9·5 per cent., notwithstanding the fact that 533 villages which were formerly in this grade have now to be included in the 500—999 grade.

No tendency then has so far been discovered amongst Burmans to congregate in large in preference to setting up in smaller villages. The increase in the net number of villages since 1881 disproves this. Why then is there not a proportionate increase in the number of villages between 1872 and 1881? If there had been a falling off since 1881 in the number of new villages as compared with the increase of the population, the war with Upper Burma and the consequent troublous times in Lower Burma would have been taken as a cause for the falling off. But just the contrary was the case; the population increased in proportion to the villages faster in the intercensal period between 1872 and 1881 than in the next decade between 1881 and 1891, when the rate of increase of the villages was more nearly approximate to the rate of growth of the population. The only deduction to be drawn from this is that either there was a disinclination to found new villages between 1872 and 1881, which disinclination has since disappeared, or, what is really the true explanation, villages whose existence could not be easily ignored were duly included in 1872, whereas a large number of their inhabitants were omitted. This will account for the small increase in the number of villages in Class **A** in 1881 and the disproportionate increase in Class **B** at the same enumeration. New villages were founded between 1872 and 1881, and a few more which had been omitted in 1872 were included in the returns of 1881; but we may take it that a great part of the 36·02 increase was not the real increase which is gauged by the number of new villages, but was gained by the more careful enumeration of the inhabitants of the old villages already in existence. This is, I venture to say, a conclusive argument that the rate of progress of the lower province since 1881 has as a fact kept pace with the real and not the nominal rate of progress of the previous intercensal period.

The urban population.

25. Adhering to the classification of towns adopted at the last census for the purpose of comparison, we find that in 1872 the urban population was returned as 357,648, or 13 per cent. of the total population in Lower Burma. In 1881, owing to better enumeration, whereby fewer villages and their inhabitants were omitted, although the total urban population had risen to 425,775, the proportion of the urban to the total population had fallen to 11 per cent. In 1891 the population of all towns containing upwards of 5,000 inhabitants amounted to 540,672, or 11·6 per cent. of the total population.

It stands to reason, even if we had not the express avowal of the reports of 1872, that enumeration of the wilder tracts in 1872 must have been faultier than that of the larger towns which were immediately under the ken of the District Officers and where the arrangements for taking the census were necessarily more easily made, better revised, and more carefully supervised.

The disproportion in the increase of villages and towns in the two intercensal periods discussed as a test of the accuracy of the returns of the rate of increase.

26. Accordingly, unless there were some great migration of the country population to the towns or the town population to the country, we should expect that the increase of the town and rural population would to some extent coincide, but we find that, while the urban population had increased by 19 per cent. between 1872 and 1881, the population of the rural tracts had increased at the rate of 38·6 per cent. Mr. Copleston's explanation of this, based as it was on the admittedly imperfect data of the returns of 1872, is not satisfactory. He says:

"The causes of this disproportion of increase are not far to seek. In February many persons who have their house in the town are away trading or are employed in agricultural pursuits elsewhere."

This is certainly not the case, for we rarely find the town trader taking up agricultural work in February at any rate. He goes on to say:

"Rangoon and Akyab during the busy season receive large numbers of coolies, who work in the rice-mills and the ports. But with these exceptions the number of immigrants in the towns as they are above defined is small."

Mr. Copleston omits to take into consideration the fact that nearly all the Indian and most of the Chinese immigrants who are not coolies are also nearly all settled permanently in the towns, and he appears to have under-rated the immense number of coolies who flock from Chittagong and Madras to work in our Burman rice-mills in the working season, during which the census of 1881, as well as that of 1891, was taken. Considering that the census of 1872 was taken in August after the returns of the rice-mill coolies to their homes, we should have expected that the census of 1881, taken in February at the height of the busy season, would have shown an increase and not a decrease in the proportion of the urban population to the rest of the inhabitants of the country. Here again the only explanation is that the urban population of Burma was, as might be expected, much more carefully enumerated in 1872, and that many inhabitants of the rural tracts escaped enumeration; thus the more accurate census of 1881 shows a disproportional growth in the rural population since 1872.

I have gone into this question of the faulty enumeration of 1872 from more points of view than one as I feel that this apparent falling off in our rate of progress is worthy of as full and thorough an explanation as can be offered. The matter is more fully discussed in Chapter II, which treats the census return from the dynamic and not the static point of view.

The growth of the chief towns of Lower Burma.

27. We have, as the returns show, in Lower Burma 25 towns containing upwards of 5,000 inhabitants instead of only 20 as in 1881. But not only has the number of towns increased, but the population of each and all of the 20 chief towns, except Pantanaw, shows a satisfactory increase. The subjoined table will show at a glance the progress made by the chief towns of Lower Burma since 1872.

The following table shows the population of the 20 towns whose population exceeded 5,000 in 1872 and 1881, and the increase at each enumeration :—

Name of town.	Population in 1872.	Population in 1881.	Percentage of increase.	Percentage of decrease.	Population in 1891.	Percentage of increase.	Percentage of decrease.
Rangoon	98,745	134,176	35·88	...	180,324	34·393	...
Moulmein	46,472	53,107	14·28	...	55,785	5·042	...
Akyab	19,230	33,989	76·75	...	37,938	11·618	...
Prome	31,157	28,813	...	7·52	30,022	4·196	...
Bassein	20,688	28,147	36·05	...	30,177	7·212	...
Toungoo	10,732	17,199	60·25	...	17,517	1·848	...
Henzada	15,307	16,724	9·25	...	19,555	16·927	...
Thayetmyo	15,142	16,097	6·31	...	17,101	6·237	...
Tavoy	14,469	13,372	...	7·58	15,099	12·915	...
Yandoon	9,680	12,673	30·92	...	20,235	59·67	...
Shwedaung	12,654	12,373	...	2·22	12,424	·41	...
Mergui	9,737	8,633	...	11·34	10,137	17·42	...
Kyangin	8,477	7,565	...	10·76	8,116	7·28	...
Shwegyin	7,871	7,519	...	4·47	8,754	16·42	...
Paungdè	5,630	6,727	19·48	...	10,233	52·11	...
Pantanaw	5,888	6,174	4·86	...	6,036	...	2·33
Pegu	4,416	5,891	33·40	...	10,762	82·68	...
Allanmyo	9,697	5,825	...	39·93	9,012	52·99	...
Myanaung	5,636	5,416	...	3·90	5,489	1·34	...
Lemyethna	5,331	5,355	·45	...	5,614	4·83	...

The table requires very little explanation. It is satisfactory to remark that the decay of the towns of Prome, Tavoy, Shwedaung, Mergui, Kyangin, and Shwegyin has been arrested. The increase of the following towns,—Pegu, Allanmyo, Yandoon, and Paungdè,—is so startling as to require some further explanation. In the case of Pegu the increase is due to the inclusion within municipal limits of the large village called Zaingganaing on the west bank of the Pegu river and also to the impetus given to the growth of the town by the opening of the Sittang Valley Railway and the selection of the town for the headquarters of the Pegu district, which was separated from the Hanthawaddy district in April 1883. Yandoon is the headquarters of the flourishing subdivision of that name in the Thôngwa district. It has shared in the expansion of the district consequent on the immense spread of cultivation that has taken place in the last 10 years. The increase in Allanmyo is probably due to the inclusion of Ywataung village in the returns and to better enumeration. On referring to the returns of 1872 we find that the population of Allanmyo was given as amounting to 9,697. The decrease of 39 per cent. was not explained. It was due no doubt to the fact that the Ywataung quarter was omitted from the returns. In Paungdè the only explanation of the abnormal increase there, as in Allanmyo, is that the enumeration was more carefully made and that the town has flourished on account of the opening of the Irrawaddy Valley State Railway during the last intercensal period, the full value of which may not have been felt in Paungdè till after 1881. The decrease in Pantanaw is very slight. The Deputy Commissioner of Moulmein reports that "the place is rapidly decaying, the river has silted both above and below the town, and the traders and brokers have deserted it for Wakèma, Yelegalè, and other places."

The areality of townships, villages, and occupied houses.

28. The most ordinary method of conveying an impression of the proportion of the number of the inhabitants to the area of the country inhabited by them is to give the average number living on each square mile. A map, No. II, has been prepared showing the density of the population township by township. Another and almost more forcible way of conveying the same impression is to give the areality of the townships, villages, and houses, that is, in other words, the average area assignable to each unit of these different classes. The following table is therefore the converse of the statement giving the average density of the population.

The accompanying statement will show at a glance the areality of the townships, villages, and occupied houses in the various districts throughout the province.

District.	Areality of townships in square miles.	Areality of villages in square miles.	Areality of occupied houses in acres.
1	2	3	4
LOWER BURMA.			
ARAKAN DIVISION—			
Akyab	691·87	3·19	42·75
Northern Arakan	10·15	3·67	169·56
Kyaukpyu	861·8	4·02	80·50
Sandoway	1,222·33	6·69	168·03
PEGU DIVISION—			
Rangoon Town	22	22	·49
Hanthawaddy	487	1·66	24·59
Pegu	485·6	3·46	31·15
Tharrawaddy	402·8	1·69	19·94
Prome	412·42	1·58	24·92
IRRAWADDY DIVISION—			
Thôngwa	676·625	3·79	45·42
Bassein	783	3·33	52·96
Henzada	324·66	1·84	17·42
Thayetmyo	447·71	3·33	40·89
TENASSERIM DIVISION—			
Amherst	1,266·91	12·42	135·06
Tavoy	1,787·5	23·36	239·51
Mergui	1,562	21·63	370·03
Toungoo	1,059	7·27	118·42
Shwegyin	1,085·4	7·02	89·42
Salween	464·6	23·23	439·92
UPPER BURMA.			
NORTHERN DIVISION—			
Mandalay	210	2·42	17·46
Bhamo	1,960	*	*
Katha	...	...	...
Ruby Mines	1,000	16·39	321·68
Shwebo	446·66	7·14	57·97
CENTRAL DIVISION—			
Ye-u	1,000	10·61	165·41
Sagaing	306	3·13	25·80
Lower Chindwin	566·66	3·82	52·33
Upper Chindwin	...	*	*
SOUTHERN DIVISION—			
Myingyan	467·12	4·29	42·46
Pakôkku	770	5·07	70·28
Minbu	401·25	3·75	48·30
Magwe	687·5	9·85	100·74
EASTERN DIVISION—			
Kyauksè	210	1·93	21·81
Meiktila	600	2·97	50·69
Yamèthin	1,000	3·57	65·13
Pyinmana	1,500	18·86	364·70
Mean areality, Lower Burma ...	862·32	4·94	64·76
Mean areality, Upper Burma ...	657	5·92	70·89
Mean areality, Burma ...	766·64	5·29	67·08

* No return of areality of villages and houses could be made for the Bhamo, Katha, and Upper Chindwin districts as the total number of villages in these districts is not known.

The mean proximity.

29. Another way of regarding the question of the density of the population is to show the mean average distance between towns and villages supposing they were placed at equal distances from each other. The accompanying statement is then the correlative of the areality statement.

Proximity Statement.

Name of district.	Mean proximity of towns in miles.	Mean proximity of villages in miles.	Mean proximity of persons in yards.
1	2	3	4
LOWER BURMA.			
ARAKAN DIVISION—			
Akyab	...	1·91985	218·0710
Northern Arakan	...	2·06069	498·2964
Kyaukpyu	...	2·15742	306·7222
Sandoway	...	2·78225	412·1024
Total Arakan Division ...	**64·6067**	**2·14805**	**277·7596**
PEGU DIVISION—			
Rangoon Town	...	...	20·8896
Hanthawaddy	...	1·38714	161·5305
Pegu	...	2·00129	169·7405
Tharrawaddy	21·556	1·40030	143·9873
Prome	33·3348	1·35460	169·2873
Total Pegu Division ...	**32·7682**	**1·48456**	**151·1164**
IRRAWADDY DIVISION—			
Thôngwa	39·5297	2·09728	208·3347
Bassein	45·1031	1·96333	230·3558
Henzada	23·7137	1·46016	135·2449
Thayetmyo	...	1·96314	211·6822
Total Irrawaddy Division ...	**38·0373**	**1·91456**	**201·5200**
TENASSERIM DIVISION—			
Amherst	76·4037	3·79164	360·9672
Tavoy	...	5·20281	519·0627
Mergui	...	5·00505	615·4579
Toungoo	...	2·99068	374·3995
Shwegyin	...	2·85278	319·2446
Salween	...	5·17916	727·0296
Total Tenasserim Division ...	**82·0042**	**3·79877**	**412·7692**
Total Lower Burma ...	**53·1152**	**2·40414**	**260·1684**
UPPER BURMA.			
NORTHERN DIVISION—			
Mandalay	...	1·67431	141·7053
Bhamo	...	*	615·0548
Katha	...	*	431·2204
Ruby Mines	...	4·36485	523·7918
Shwebo	...	2·87651	266·5238
Total Northern Division ...	**80·7359**	*	**329·5811**
CENTRAL DIVISION—			
Ye-u	...	3·51294	439·5881
Sagaing	26·614	1·90857	162·6584
Lower Chindwin	...	1·67019	228·8299
Upper Chindwin	...	*	833·6416
Total Central Division ...	...	*	**394·7732**
SOUTHERN DIVISION—			
Myingyan	...	2·22965	195·0308
Pakôkku	...	2·42255	269·3257
Minbu	30·4409	2·08823	226·1600
Magwe	45·607	3·35196	296·8486
Total Southern Division ...	**44·19546**	**2·48297**	**246·1078**
EASTERN DIVISION—			
Kyauksè	...	1·49703	172·2215
Meiktila	...	1·85565	227·8724
Yamèthin	...	2·03438	258·4348
Pyinmana	...	4·67499	617·1352
Total Eastern Division ...	**61·3776**	**2·36199**	**291·2455**
Total Upper Burma ...	**62·0923**	**2·96594**	**312·1852**
Total Burma ...	**56·9657**	**2·62586**	**285·0531**

* This return is not available for villages in Bhamo, Katha, and Upper Chindwin, and in the Northern and Central Divisions, as the total number of villages is not known.

In calculating the mean proximity equal distribution is of course assumed. The formula used is practically the same as the one used for the English, Bombay, and Punjab Censuses. The mean proximity of towns and villages was not shown at the last census, but the mean proximity of persons in Lower Burma was 289 yards, so that the increase of the population is represented by the fact that persons are now 29 yards closer to each other.

The return of occupied houses.

30. Intimately connected with the distribution of the population by towns and villages is the return of the occupied houses. In Imperial Table I is given the number of occupied houses both in towns and villages, district by district, throughout the province. It will be seen that on the occasion of the present census no attempt has been made to classify houses according to the structure or materials of which the house is composed. Such a return in Burma, where the majority even of the best houses are built of wood, would be valueless if not actually misleading. The last attempt to classify houses for the Imperial return was on the occasion of the Census of 1872. In 1881 no attempt was made to classify houses except in British Burma, but it was considered advisable to repeat the experiment here on the ground that the house often forms the basis of local taxation. At the same time all houses, whether occupied or not, were returned, but were shown separately. It is quite clear that the classification of houses belongs rather to revenue than to purely census operations. Such a return, to be of any value, would involve much greater detail than the very rough means of classification adopted. Accordingly the attempt of classifying houses was not renewed. Again, the return of unoccupied as well as of occupied houses would have been of no value in Burma, where since the majority of houses are built of flimsy materials, an unoccupied house soon falls into ruin, and after a short time ceases to exist if left unoccupied. Moreover, since the preliminary census is taken when the country-folk are mostly engaged in harvesting their crops, a large number of houses would be shown unoccupied because the owners were living in temporary huts or tès in their fields and near their threshing-floors; thus there would be shown a large return of houses in excess of the usual number. For these reasons at the Agra Conference it was decided to make no attempt to return the number of unoccupied houses.

The definition of a census house.

31. But while no attempt was made to include returns that were not actually required for statistical purposes, an endeavour was made to determine the definition of a census house. At the Conference of Census Superintendents held at Agra it was found impossible to make any hard-and-fast rules as to what was and what was not a census house as the customs and circumstances of the inhabitants of the various provinces were so dissimilar. In Burma, however, there is generally little difficulty in distinguishing between what is and what is not a census house. The two chief ideas that underlie what we call a household, namely, (1) commensality or the messing together of all the members of a family, and (2) the almost universal custom that each household should have a separate domicile in which the family lives apart from other households, are ideas which commend themselves alike to Briton and to Burman. Accordingly outside of our larger towns no difficulty was experienced. In the towns, however, we have a large Indian element and want of space perforce compels people to live close together in terrace or barrack houses. With the Census Commissioner's approval the following definition of a census house was issued: "For census purposes a house "may be taken to mean either a separate building or tenement completely sepa-"rated by partitions from the rest of the building, *e.g.*, a house in a terrace in "England. If the inhabitants of separate tenements in a barrack house do not "mess together, the separate tenements, if they have a separate opening on "to a public way, may with safety be numbered as separate census houses." On the occasion of his visit to Burma in October 1890 the Census Commissioner himself inspected the blocking and numbering of the houses in Mandalay, Rangoon, Pakôkku, Myingyan, Pagan, Minbu, Thayetmyo, and Prome, and expressed himself satisfied with the method of procedure adopted except in the case of Pakôkku, where an over-zealous enumerator had construed the instructions too liberally. On the occasion of the preceding census of 1881 an attempt was

made to subdivide the numerous and thickly-peopled lodging-houses into separate houses in Rangoon and Moulmein, but there was apparently no uniform rule throughout the province. The necessity for issuing such an order is best exemplified by the report of 1881, where we find that in Moulmein 1,414 persons were returned as living in two houses and 4,635 living in 18 houses in Rangoon. Accordingly, as might be expected, after deducting the houses returned in the three townships of Taingda, Minhla, and Sinbaungwe, amounting to 9,397 houses, the number of occupied houses in Lower Burma has been increased from 677,362 in 1881 to 869,132 in 1891, being an increase of 191,770 or 28 per cent. The result of this order is best understood when we compare the returns of occupied houses and of the total population. We find that while the number of occupied houses has been increased, as already stated, the population has only grown at the rate of 24·67 per cent. The excess in the growth of the number of houses may be traced to a careful compliance with the instructions of the Census Commissioner and not to any change in the previous habits of the people. There were altogether 1,430,860 occupied houses in Upper and Lower Burma, that is to say, there are on an average 5·39 persons living in each house, which is slightly less than the return 5·5 recorded at the last census.

The following statement shows the number of occupied houses to the square mile in each district in Upper and Lower Burma and the average number of persons living in each house separately for towns and vilages in each district :—

District.	Number of houses to each square mile.	Average density per house in towns.	Average density per house in villages.
LOWER BURMA.			
ARAKAN DIVISION—			
Akyab	14·96	6·06	4·94
Northern Arakan	3·77	...	3·81
Kyaukpyu	7·94	4·18	4·81
Sandoway	3·80	5·76	5·51
PEGU DIVISION—			
Rangoon Town	1,288·5	6·36	...
Hanthawaddy	26·02	...	5·26
Pegu	20·54	5·83	6·05
Tharrawaddy	32·08	5·68	5·36
Prome	25·67	5·14	4·81
IRRAWADDY DIVISION—			
Thôngwa	14·08	5·74	5·85
Bassein	12·08	5·64	5·57
Henzada	36·73	5·40	5·31
Thayetmyo	15·65	5·78	5·03
TENASSERIM DIVISION—			
Amherst	4·73	5·28	5·90
Tavoy	2·67	4·93	4·97
Mergui	1·72	5·36	5·47
Toungoo	5·40	5·04	4·68
Shwegyin	7·15	5·19	5·10
Salween	1·45	...	4·65
Total Lower Burma ...	**9·88**	**5·69**	**5·31**

District.	Number of houses to each square mile.	Average density per house in towns.	Average density per house in villages.
UPPER BURMA.			
NORTHERN DIVISION—			
Mandalay	36·64	4·929	4·79
Bhamo	1·04	6·78	5·11
Katha	...	7·54	...
Ruby Mines	1·98	...	6·56
Shwebo	11·03	6·08	4·48
CENTRAL DIVISION—			
Ye-u	3·86	4·65	4·78
Sagaing	24·80	5·04	5·49
Lower Chindwin	12·22	5·36	5·59
Upper Chindwin	...	...	...
SOUTHERN DIVISION—			
Myingyan	15·07	5·89	6·27
Pakôkku	9·10	5·007	5·45
Minbu	13·89	2·30	6·43
Magwe	6·35	5·91	6·30
EASTERN DIVISION—			
Kyauksè	29·33	4·35	4·09
Meiktila	12·62	5·11	5·45
Yamèthin	9·82	5·57	5·44
Pyinmana	1·75	5·92	5·20
Total Upper Burma ...	**6·72**	**4·62**	**5·39**
GRAND TOTAL BURMA ...	**8·34**	**5·22**	**5·34**

The average number of residents in each occupied house.

32. The average number of persons who were found to be living in each inhabited house is 5·69 per house in Lower Burma towns and 5·31 in the houses in rural tracts. The position is reversed in Upper Burma, and the total of Upper and Lower Burma shows that the houses in the rural tracts are more densely populated than the houses in the towns. The returns of Lower Burma are normal; the slight decrease in the density which is now returned as being 5·36 for the whole of the lower province is due, as already noticed, to the more careful enumeration of the houses and the breaking up of long lines of barrack houses into separate census houses. But the return of Upper Burma is, on the face of it, somewhat extraordinary and requires explanation. The figures given in the statement show that in the Ye-u, Sagaing, Lower Chindwin, Myingyan, Pakôkku, Minbu, Magwe, and Meiktila districts the density of the population per house in the rural tracts exceeds the density of the population per house in the towns. In the Katha and the Upper Chindwin districts the return of the density per house in the rural tracts could not be obtained because there were in both of these districts tracts in which the census schedule returns could not be prepared. In the Ruby Mines and Upper Chindwin districts there were no towns, so that there was no return of the urban population to serve for comparison. In Mandalay, Bhamo, Shwebo, Yamèthin, and Pyinmana the density of the population is greater in the urban

than in the rural tracts. Taking these last districts, we find the reason why the density per house should be greater is at once apparent. In the first three towns we have a strong military garrison lodged in barracks where we should naturally expect the density per house to be high. In Pyinmana and Yamèthin we had a large military police battalion and a considerable number of European and Indian residents. The fact that the natives of India herd together in crowded houses was pointed out in the last report as the cause fo r the greater average density per house of our town population in Lower Burma. If the figures given above are correct, it is clear that the general tendency is for a greater number of persons to live together in village than in town houses in Upper Burma. It might easily be understood, if such were the case, why there should be no difference in the returns, because our town spaces in Upper Burma are not yet crowded with houses. But the reason why the villages should show greater density than the towns is not at once apparent. Moreover, why should not the same occur in Lower Burma? Here we have the solution of the question. In Upper Burma the thathameda was assessed on the villages according to the return of houses therein. In Lower Burma the number of houses in a village is not considered in the apportionment of the capitation-tax or of the land-tax. The Upper Burma villager is naturally more reluctant to set up a separate establishment, and it is to the interest of the villagers to conceal the full number of the houses in the village. It is true that the District Officers generally found, in preparing the subdivisional registers, which show the name of every village and number of houses in each village in their districts, that a large number of fresh houses were found whose existence was unknown before. The explanation of this sudden increase given by the local Burman officials was that villagers who had gone to Lower Burma had returned to their north country homes. If we turn to the Revenue Administration Report of 1890-91 we find that there was an increase of 18 per cent. in the amount of the demand and of 15 per cent. in the collection of the thathameda in 1890-91 over those of the previous year. The Financial Commissioner says, "the general rise of the thathameda demand was due partly, it is said, to the return of people to their old villages, but mainly to the closer scrutiny of the assessable households." Leaving Minbu town out, as the returns here were so abnormal that a separate explanation has been furnished by the Deputy Commissioner, we find that in the ordinary Burman town and village, where the returns of the urban population are not swollen by the presence of an overwhelming number of foreigners, the density of the population per house is invariably greater in the rural tracts. That there is no mistake in the compilation of the returns is clear, because the error is one which could not have passed unnoticed, firstly, because the number of houses was prepared and checked twice before taking of the census, in the district circle, and subdivisional registers, and the return of occupied houses was again prepared in the district offices from the census schedules after the census, and, lastly, the return has again been carefully compiled in the Central Census Office. We may take it then that the number of houses as now compiled is a correct compilation of the returns of the village officials. If there be any error, it must be in the preparation of this return by the local enumerators, who are the local tax-gatherers, and who were thus forced to criticize their own returns. The result is that the assessment of the thathameda rose 18 per cent. But the most significant fact still is that the density is even yet higher in the villages, and the explanation is to be found in the Financial Commissioner's remarks. It stands to reason that the number of assessable houses could not so easily escape scrutiny in towns which are the headquarters of the District Officers as in remote villages. The inference then is that a large number of houses in villages were not included in the census returns. Moreover, as this is the first census ever taken in Upper Burma, the village folks could not help feeling sure that the information so collected was simply to serve as a basis for the enhancement of their household-tax, and accordingly, despite the closer scrutiny of the officials, many houses must have escaped notice, while there was no temptation, as in 1872 in Lower Burma, to leave out individuals. In Lower Burma not only do the villagers know that the number of houses in a village has no effect on the revenue, but two previous enumerations have passed without the imposition of new forms of taxation, and hence they are wiser and consequently less reluctant to make true returns.

The returns of Minbu are so abnormal that it was impossible to accept them without some further explanation. The Deputy Commissioner, however, states that there were two causes for these abnormal returns. The first one is that Minbu, which was a mere village in 1886, was raised suddenly to the rank of a garrison town and became the headquarters of the third brigade. Barracks were built for the troops and a large native followers' bazaar sprang up. The garrison has since been taken away and we have thus naturally a large number of ready-built houses in the bazaar at the disposal of the townsfolk. But the chief cause, and one which forms a ready explanation for the abnormal return, was the fact that the Shwesetdaw festival had just been held and that it had been largely attended by the townspeople of Minbu, Sinbyugyun, and Salin. This would not only reduce the density of the towns, but would increase that of the villages where the townspeople who attended the festival were enumerated.

The remarks of the Deputy Commissioner are worth quoting. He says,—

"So far as I know of Salin, Minbu, and Sinbyugyun, the average density (per house) is more than 2·3—being about five, I should say—but when I have been at Minbu and Salin during the festival the towns have looked to be nearly deserted."

A third cause is given for the high density of the rural tracts in this district, and that is, the habit of the Chins of living crowded together in their tès. Only one other district in Burma contains more Chins than were found in Minbu, where the number enumerated amounted to 16,099.

There is, however, a real reason for a denser population per house in Upper Burma than we should expect to find in the lower province. The troublous time of 1886-87 and 1887-88 not only caused the destruction of many villages which were burnt by the dacoits, but the villagers, for their own protection, preferred to live in large rather than in small villages, and the villages being generally fenced, the house-room naturally was cramped. Accordingly the return of the next comparative statement, which exhibits the average number of houses and inhabitants to each village, shows that notwithstanding the greater sparsity of the population as compared with the total area of Upper Burma, the villages contain on an average more houses and a larger number of inhabitants than in the lower province.

33. Comparing the returns of the number of houses with those of towns and villages with the rural population, district by district, we find we have the following interesting table :—

The average size of the village.

District.	Average number of houses to each village.	Average number of inhabitants to each village.
LOWER BURMA.		
ARAKAN DIVISION—		
Akyab	44·16	218·20
Northern Arakan	13·88	53
Kyaukpyu	30·53	147·05
Sandoway	24·73	136·38
PEGU DIVISION—		
Rangoon Town	...	...
Hanthawaddy	43·36	228·43
Pegu	68·62	415·22
Tharrawaddy	52·80	283·46
Prome	35·16	169·27
IRRAWADDY DIVISION—		
Thôngwa	49·21	288·34
Bassein	36·61	204·01
Henzada	60·91	323·74
Thayetmyo	47·42	238·60
TENASSERIM DIVISION—		
Amherst	48·38	285·62
Tavoy	52·61	261·71
Mergui	32·27	176·69
Toungoo	35·01	163·87
Shwegyin	46·96	239·74
Salween	33·79	157·19
Total Lower Burma	43·26	230·02

District.	Average number of houses to each village.	Average number of inhabitants to each village.
UPPER BURMA.		
NORTHERN DIVISION—		
Mandalay	44·69	214·15
Bhamo	25·69	131·27
Katha	...	...
Ruby Mines	32·61	214·21
Shwebo	74·98	336·59
CENTRAL DIVISION—		
Ye-u	39·70	190·15
Sagaing	70·35	386·65
Lower Chindwin	45·49	254·42
Upper Chindwin	...	...
SOUTHERN DIVISION—		
Myingyan	59·56	373·52
Pakôkku	42·33	230·86
Minbu	34·71	223·19
Magwe	57·89	364·99
EASTERN DIVISION—		
Kyauksè	53·87	220·74
Meiktila	37·51	204·73
Yamèthin	33·80	184·08
Pyinmana	26·33	136·98
Total Upper Burma ...	**43·94**	**237·06**
GRAND TOTAL BURMA ...	**43·52**	**232·71**

It will be seen that the figures for Upper and Lower Burma approximate to each other very closely. The greater density in Upper Burma is no doubt due to the fact that fear of dacoits has tended to keep the country-folk together in large villages for mutual protection. In comparing the returns of the present census for Lower Burma with those of 1881, we find two difficulties,—firstly, in the change in the definition of what constitutes a town; secondly, in the fact that the report of 1881 does not discriminate between town and village in calculating the average number of houses and population. In all towns and villages taken together in 1881 there were on an average 45·4 houses and 236 persons. In 1872 the figures were 38 and 194 respectively. Taking the villages apart it will be found that there were only 210 persons in villages alone against 236 in towns and villages taken together. As the return of occupied houses was not made separately for towns and villages, it is not now possible to discriminate how many houses there were to each village if the towns were excluded. If the classification of 1881 were adopted in our present returns for the purposes of comparison, we should find that there are 48·8 houses and 261 inhabitants on an average to each town or village, and that in all villages and places containing less than 5,000 inhabitants there are on an average in Lower Burma in 1891 231 inhabitants to each village or place containing less than 5,000 inhabitants against 210 in 1881 and 194 in 1872.

This means that the average density of population in the villages of Lower Burma increased at the rate of 10 per cent. between 1881 and 1891. In the returns of 1872 the mean population is calculated without excluding the urban population. It is impossible to ascertain now what the correct population for each village really was. It is impossible therefore to infer from the incomplete return of 1872 that any change has taken place in the conditions which determine the size of the villages in Lower Burma. The only inference we can draw is that the greater density is due to the growth of the population and not to any aversion to found new villages.

34. In Burma, with its numerous waterways, the boat population forms an important factor in the return. Special arrangements, which will be detailed at length in Chapter XII, were made to secure a careful enumeration. The Irrawaddy Flotilla Company, whose huge river steamers often carry people enough to populate two villages of the average size, were through the courtesy of their Manager enumerated apart from the rest of the province. It will be unnecessary to repeat here the details of the arrangements that were made; but care was taken to allot to each district the boat blocks that belonged to it and the totals of the population so enumerated are shown in the district returns. In some places where fishing or trading boats collected separate boat blocks were formed. In ports also where of necessity special arrangements were required the boat population is not included in either town or village blocks. Lastly, boats that were in transit were enumerated apart, but with these exceptions boats were included in village or town blocks and enumerated by the village or town enumerators and have by them been included in the population of the village. The accompanying statement will show the districts in which returns of boat population were made compared in the case of the Lower Burma districts with the returns of 1881. No corresponding figures for 1872 are available.

Boat population.

Comparative statement of boat population.

District.	1881.	1891.	Variation.
LOWER BURMA.			
ARAKAN DIVISION—			
Akyab	8,477	4,853	— 3,624
Northern Arakan	58	287	+ 229
Kyaukpyu	1,569	659	— 910
Sandoway	387	420	+ 33
Total Arakan Division ...	10,491	6,219	— 4,272
PEGU DIVISION—			
Rangoon Town	10,150	7,246	— 2,904
Hanthawaddy ... ... } Pegu ... ... }	10,112	{ 3,065 { 1,374	— 5,673
Tharrawaddy	1,099	600	— 499
Prome	2,490	1,125	— 1,365
Total Pegu Division ...	23,851	13,410	— 10,441
IRRAWADDY DIVISION—			
Thôngwa	14,805	16,506	+ 1,701
Bassein	11,552	7,690	— 3,862
Henzada	3,440	3,313	— 127
Thayetmyo	1,790	5,338	+ 3,548
Total Irrawaddy Division ...	31,587	32,847	+ 1,260
TENASSERIM DIVISION—			
Amherst including Moulmein Town ...	5,066	12,159	+ 7,093
Tavoy	490	473	— 17
Mergui	1,423	2,599	+ 1,176
Toungoo	709	1,216	+ 507
Shwegyin	1,312	885	— 427
Salween	386	297	— 89
Total Tenasserim Division ...	9,386	17,629	+ 8,243
Total Lower Burma ...	75,315	70,105	— 5,210

Comparative statement of boat population—concluded.

District.	1881.	1891.	Variation.
UPPER BURMA.			
NORTHERN DIVISION—			
Mandalay	...	1,784	...
Bhamo	...	2,813	...
Katha	...	637	...
Ruby Mines	...	150	...
Shwebo	...	287	...
Total Northern Division ...	...	5,671	...
CENTRAL DIVISION—			
Ye-u	...	...	...
Sagaing	...	413	...
Lower Chindwin	...	1,152	...
Upper Chindwin	...	2,712	...
Total Central Division ...	...	4,277	...
SOUTHERN DIVISION—			
Myingyan	...	1,325	...
Pakôkku	...	787	...
Minbu	...	523	...
Magwe	...	1,143	...
Total Southern Division ...	...	3,778	...
EASTERN DIVISION—			
Kyauksè	...	...	...
Meiktila	...	...	...
Yamèthin	...	...	...
Pyinmana	...	...	...
Total Eastern Division ...	...	...	...
Total Upper Burma ...	...	13,726	...
GRAND TOTAL BURMA ...	...	83,831	...

While the population of Lower Burma has grown so rapidly at first sight it seems strange that the boat population should not show a corresponding increase. There is on the contrary a decrease of 6·9 per cent., while we have large decreases in the following districts: Akyab, Kyaukpyu, Rangoon, Hanthawaddy, Pegu, Tharrawaddy, Prome, Bassein, and Shwegyin.

Before entering into an explanation of these variations the value of the figures recorded must be ascertained on the occasion of the census of 1891. Orders were issued that as far as possible all boats should be included in the village blocks, except in places where they were numerous; hence a large number of scattered boats belonging to villagers were enumerated by the Village enumerator and their inhabitants were enumerated in their houses ashore. Our boat population is not like the boat population of Canton, or of Bangkok, or of our English canals, and every Burman hle-thugyi or boat-owner has his house ashore. Careful preparations, moreover, had been made by the District Officers for the enumeration of boats on the move, and patrols were started and boats enumerated from the morning of 26th February. Every river and creek was parcelled out and boatmen soon found out that they would have to be stopped and enumerated. Any one who has gone through the process of stopping a big paddy-boat with the usual complement of oarsmen will know how tedious and slow the process of filling up all the entries must necessarily be; besides this, while one boat is being enumerated, the others would have to wait their turn. The Burman boatman, sooner than undergo this bother and worry, would prefer to accept "the inevitable" and gladly welcome the excuse for a day's idleness, and thus prefer to stay ashore and be enumerated in the village at which the boat halted. The system of patrolling and enumerating boats on the move was an unavoidable consequence of the census. As the patrolling was on this occasion begun earlier than on 17th February 1881 and before the census commenced ashore, many boats halted for the day till the census night was over. On the occasion of the last census the enumeration of the boat population did not commence till nightfall and was continued for the three following days. Thus boatmen did not have the chance of being enumerated on dry land. The enumeration of the boat population could not by any possibility be finished in one night. On this occasion the time of enumeration was more evenly divided and work on the boats began earlier. This had no doubt the effect of inducing the easy-going Burman to prefer in many instances to be enumerated ashore. This is the true explanation of the apparent decrease in the boat population in those districts which show a comparatively small decrease. But smallness of the increase in Thôngwa and the decrease in Hanthawaddy, Pegu, and Bassein is also in part due to the fact that the extension of the cultivable area brought about by the bunds on the Lower Irrawaddy and canals in the Hanthawaddy district, while they interfered with the fishing revenue, have compensated the fishermen themselves by inducing many of them to live ashore as cultivators. This change has tended to check the growth in our boat population. But the main cause of the decrease in the boat population of Pegu and Hanthawaddy, which is by far the most noticeable, is undoubtedly to be traced, as the Deputy Commissioner of Pegu points out, to the opening of the Pegu and Sittang Valley Railway, which has stopped the passenger traffic on the Pegu river, and to the extension of launch traffic in the smaller creeks of the Tuntè and Syriam townships. It is now no longer necessary for travellers by water in these districts to take more than one day over their journey within these districts. The decrease in Shwegyin district is also probably due to the opening of the railway. The decrease in Rangoon is due in great measure to the fact that, whereas in 1881 the number of sailing ships engaged in the rice trade was very large and these ships were accustomed to come to the port early for their charters, within this last intercensal period the carrying trade has passed almost wholly into the hands of the steam-ship companies, and the harbour is now no longer crowded with sailing ships awaiting their sailing orders. Steam-ships can rely on arriving punctually and are not forced to arrive early for fear of meeting contrary winds. This is the explanation which the Port Officer and Collector of Customs have submitted for this falling off in the boat population of Rangoon, and the enquiries that have been made confirm the truth of their explanation. But, while we have a total decrease of 5,210 in the aggregate and a deficit in 13 districts, in six districts we find an increase, and in one of them, Amherst, a very large one. This would appear to be all the more puzzling after the explanation given above. Taking the cases in their order, we find the increase in Northern Arakan proves that the explanation given for the decrease in other districts is true. For, strange to say, in Northern Arakan the enumeration was carried out on the same lines as in 1881. The census on both occasions was non-synchronous; hence there was no greater temptation for boatmen to stay and be enumerated ashore on this than on the previous occasion, whereas in other districts the apparent decrease was no doubt caused by the earlier commencement of the boat enumeration in 1891 than in 1881. In Northern Arakan then, as this cause was inoperative, we might expect an increase in the boat population. The increase in Toungoo is due to the greater care exercised in enumerating the raftsmen on the Sittang, while the increase in Mergui is entirely due to the more careful numbering of the Selungs or Salôns. Special arrangements were made by the Deputy Commissioner and

Mr. Hughes of the Geological Survey, who with his survey parties was on duty in the Mergui Archipelago, and who lent valuable assistance and secured a much more complete enumeration of this strange tribe of sea-gypsies. The increase in Thayetmyo is probably due to the inclusion of the three Upper Burma townships with their boat population, and also probably to the fact that the boats were more carefully enumerated at Allanmyo and Thayetmyo and could not now escape enumeration by crossing the frontier. But the most astonishing increase is in the case of the Amherst district, where the return has suddenly leapt from 5,066 to 12,159, an increase of 140 per cent. These figures seemed to be so astounding that I had them checked both in the returns of the present and last census. I have been unable to trace any error in our present returns, but I found some omissions in the return of 1881. It is useless, therefore, to attempt to explain the discrepancy, which perhaps may not exist in reality. There are no returns of 1872 to help as a guide in the matter. The return of occupations, Imperial Tables XVII-A and B, when compared with the returns of the census of 1881, afford no clue to these variations in the boat population. Indeed, it would appear that if the number of the boat population were correct, the number of fishermen and of those engaged in carrying by water were understated in 1881. Mr. Copleston states with regard to the return of 20,355 persons who were enumerated as being fishermen that "it cannot be said that these figures include all persons who are "engaged in fishing." It is more than probable that a large number of the 949,891 persons, or 48 per cent. of the total male population in 1881 who were shown under the indefinite and unproductive class, should have been returned as fishermen and boatmen. No criticism, therefore, of the returns of the boat population can be made by comparing the occupation tables of the present with those of the last report.

In England and Wales, where we have a large navy, a magnificent mercantile fleet, immense docks as well as a large fishing industry, and a network of canals on which there are barges inhabited by people who are born, bred, and die in them, the maritime population was returned in 1871 as being only 76,163 altogether, and of these 66,187 were enumerated in seagoing ships. In 1881 the number of seamen, boat and bargemen, and others engaged in water traffic enumerated in England and Wales amounted to 136,644, being 0·5 per cent. of the population. Of these only part were enumerated on board their vessels and boats as no record was on this occasion made of the number enumerated in seagoing ships and boats on inland waters. These figures were extracted from the returns of occupations. The number of the boat population recorded in Burma, though smaller than at the preceding enumeration, yet comprises 1·5 per cent. of the population of Lower Burma, and therefore is greatly in excess of the proportion borne to the total by the maritime population of the most maritime nation in the world.

CHAPTER II.

MOVEMENT OF THE POPULATION.

Consideration of the dynamics of the Census returns Comparative statement of district variations. General increase in all districts. The proportion of the increase due to natural increment and to excess of immigration over emigration. Vital statistics in Burma and Rangoon. Movement of the population within the province. Movement from Urban to Rural and from Rural to Urban tracts. The growth of our towns due chiefly to foreign immigration. Progressive and stationary districts. Rangoon Town.

The two points of view from which the Census returns may be discussed.

34*a*. In the previous chapter the census returns have been discussed with reference to the number and distribution of the population on the night of the 26th February, that is to say, from the purely statistical point of view. In this present chapter the returns are considered in order to ascertain the dynamic forces that have been exerted as exemplified by the growth and movement of the population in the intercensal period. We have in Chapter I discussed the rate of increase between 1872 and 1881 and compared it with the results of the past enumeration in order to ascertain the accuracy of the returns and their value as a standard of measure. The conclusion then drawn was that faulty enumeration in 1872, and more carefully prepared and more accurately collected returns in 1881, made it appear that the population of Burma was growing at an abnormally rapid rate, but an examination of the returns has shown that this rate of increase was consequently exaggerated and did not in all probability exceed the rate obtained in the last decade. We have now to discuss the rate of progress with a view to ascertain the forces that have produced this increase in the intercensal period just past and to estimate as far as possible their effect in the future.

Imperial Table II exhibits the population of Burma district by district and compares the returns of the Lower Burma districts with the returns obtained from them in 1881. As this is the first Census that has been taken in Upper Burma, we have not the same opportunity of gauging the forces at work there; the scope of the present chapter is consequently limited to an examination of the returns of the lower province.

Imperial Table IV is a similar return to Imperial Table II. It compares the returns of the population of the towns in Lower Burma with the figures recorded in 1881. It does in fact for the towns the duty performed by Table II for the districts of the province.

In addition to these Imperial Tables, the Provincial Tables which will be found in Volumes III and IV of the Census Report of Burma, give in detail, district by district, township by township, circle by circle, and village by village, the population distributed by sex, religion, education, and language. The returns of every district, town, and township in Lower Burma are there compared with the figures obtained in 1881.

Owing to the numerous changes in the area of the revenue circles, any comparison with the returns of the Census of 1881 would have been of small value, while any such attempt would have increased the size of the Provincial volumes, already sufficiently large. The consideration in detail of the returns of any administrative unit smaller than a district or town does not lie within the scope of the Imperial Report.

The subjoined comparative table of district variations exhibits the variation per cent. in the number of males and females and of occupied houses in the districts and divisions of the lower province since 1881. It also shows the growing density of the population.

Comparative Table of District Variations.

District.	Variation per cent in number of — *Male.* Increase.	*Male.* Decrease.	*Female.* Increase.	*Female.* Decrease.	*Total.* Increase.	*Total.* Decrease.	Variation in the specific population per square mile. Increase.	Decrease.	Variation per cent. in the number of occupied houses. Increase.	Decrease.
1	2	3	4	5	6	7	8	9	10	11
Lower Burma.										
Arakan Division.										
Akyab	18·435	...	18·717	...	15·735	...	10·22	...	21·73	...
Northern Arakan ...	1·781	...	...	·05	·889	...	0·13	...	13·91	...
Kyaukpyu ...	7·340	...	12·110	...	9·731	...	3·37	...	19·29	...
Sandoway ...	19·223	...	21·857	...	20·503	...	3·57	...	20·00	...
Total ...	**12·328**	...	**16·757**	...	**14·362**	...	**5·80**	...	**20·69**	...
Pegu Division.										
Rangoon Town ...	36·351	...	30·195	...	34·393	...	2,097·63	...	37·24	...
Hanthawaddy ...	21·194	...	30·297	...	25·210	...	27·60	...	} 39·46	...
Pegu	32·269	...	41·806	...	36·342	...	33·03	...	}	...
Tharrawaddy ...	22·229	...	27·770	...	24·913	...	34·40	...	29·62	...
Prome	9·859	...	13·668	...	11·760	...	13·13	...	18·04	...
Total ...	**22·920**	...	**26·626**	...	**24·590**	...	**29·71**	...	**30·30**	...
Irrawaddy Division.										
Thôngwa	59·166	...	54·644	...	57·034	...	29·93	...	54·38	...
Bassein	20·668	...	23·401	...	21·977	...	12·14	...	21·97	...
Henzada	19·944	...	19·572	...	19·759	...	32·26	...	28·91	...
Thayetmyo ...	43·714	...	51·591	...	47·535	...	9·08	...	43·89	...
Total ...	**33·463**	...	**33·908**	...	**33·678**	...	**19·39**	...	**35·06**	...
Tenasserim Division.										
Amherst	16·491	...	19·413	...	17·820	...	4·15	...	20·41	...
Tavoy	11·382	...	11·980	...	11·687	...	1·38	...	23·54	...
Mergui	32·299	...	28·337	...	30·391	...	2·20	...	32·96	...
Toungoo	21·920	...	30·269	...	25·832	...	5·23	...	23·93	...
Shwegyin	26·617	...	14·634	...	20·669	...	5·84	...	21·88	...
Salween	6·525	...	2·882	...	4·765	...	0·30	...	5·82	...
Total ...	**19·522**	...	**19·277**	...	**19·406**	...	**3·32**	...	**21·91**	...
Total Lower Burma ...	**23·677**	...	**25·809**	...	**24·669**	...	**10·12**	...	**28·31**	...

This table explains itself and will be noticed in detail hereafter. It will be sufficient to remark here that the greater proportional increase in the number of females may either be due to more careful enumeration or to the fact that immigrants from Upper Burma, India, and elsewhere are beginning to bring their women with them. The abnormal increase in Thayetmyo district has already been explained in Chapter I. There is but one decrease, and that a very slight one, in the Northern Arakan Hill Tracts. Here there is a slight falling off in the number of the women. This is due to the fact that the Hill Tracts are a wild rugged country which is inhabited by semi-civilized tribes who, when they become civilized, naturally emigrate to the plains. The variation in the number of houses has already been explained.

There are only two ways in which the population of the province as apart from the numbers returned could have increased (*a*) by natural increment, that is to say, by the excess of births over deaths, and (*b*) by excess of immigrants over emigrants. It is true that there may in our Census returns be a third cause present in cases where a hastily taken census, such as the enumeration of 1872, is followed by a much more careful one, and thus the apparent growth of the population is made to appear greater than it actually is, and the real rate of increase is exaggerated. Fortunately, however, the returns of 1881 were on the whole accurate, and though perhaps some of the outlying tribesmen may have successfully evaded enumeration, the main results were sufficiently trustworthy. Closely allied to the discussion of the rate of progress of the province as a whole are the questions of movement of the population from district to district within the province itself and from rural tracts into towns. The treatment of these topics, therefore, falls within the scope of the present chapter.

34*b*. The natural increment. The Malthusian axiom that population tends to outgrow the means of its support does not yet apply to Burma, as the richness of its soil and the superabundance of culturable land bid defiance to the doctrine of "diminishing returns." War, epidemic diseases, and famine are the three extraordinary factors which tend to diminish the ordinary rate of natural increment. In Lower Burma we have in the last decade had no open war, but the anarchy consequent on the downfall of the kingdom of Ava has no doubt to some extent reacted on the districts of the lower province. In the troubles that followed in Lower Burma but few persons lost their lives, and the slight falling off in the birth-rate, as shown in the vital statistical returns, is probably due, not to births being fewer, but to the negligence of the registrars and the want of supervision which might naturally be expected when the time of District Officers was occupied with more urgent work. It is in this matter impossible to speak with absolute certainty, but nearly all District Officers in Lower Burma will agree that the troublous times of 1886-87 probably affected the buoyous-natured Burman very slightly and left but slight impression on the birth-rate; marrying and giving in marriage went on much as usual. For on inspecting the returns of births and deaths registered in Burma, which will be found on the next page, it will be seen that the death-rate also suffered in these two years, and there can therefore be little doubt that the falling off in both cases is due to more than usual carelessness in registration. Moreover, the loss to the population, if any, in Lower Burma was probably more than counterbalanced by the immigration of Burmans from the still more disturbed districts of Upper Burma.

The next disturbing factor is epidemic disease. On reviewing the annual sanitary reports we find that the years 1881, 1882, 1883, 1886, 1887, 1889, and 1890 were fairly healthy. In 1884 the report states that the year was exceptionally unhealthy, but no disease was reported as epidemic. In 1885 and 1888 cholera is reported as having been epidemic, and the death-rates in both instances were comparatively high, yet in neither case did they exceed the birth-rate. No pestilence of such appalling virulence ravaged the country in the last ten years as to seriously interfere with the natural increment of the population.

Of the third and last disturbing factor, famine, in Lower Burma we are happily free. Failure of crops and deficient rainfall in Upper Burma only tend to swell the tide of immigration into the more favoured districts of the lower province.

We may therefore conclude that in Lower Burma we have had no extraordinary disturbing external influences to check the growth of our population. Again the "margin of comfort," that is to say, the excess of the average earning-power over the average cost of living, is certainly greater in Burma than in any other Indian province, and, taking into consideration the habits of the peoples, is probably higher even than in England itself. Pauperism systematized and subsidized as it is in England is unknown in Burma. Mendicancy, a crime in England, is an honourable profession in Burma. Those who know the country-folk will bear witness to their ready hospitality to any stranger. Much of the well-known Burman insouciance is due to the fact that he knows that whatever may befall him he cannot starve. There is besides very little difference in the food eaten by beggar and prince; hence a rise in price of food does not affect the birth-rate in Lower Burma as it does in other less favoured countries. Moreover, our vital statistics are not sufficiently accurate for us to state with confidence that the fluctuations were due to the price of food-stuffs.

Annual Returns of Vital Statistics.

35. From the Annual Statistical Reports the following returns of births and deaths have been extracted. It must be recollected, however, that Northern Arakan and Salween were omitted from the operations for the collection of vital statistics in 1881 and thus only the returns of 3,692,263 persons were collected for that year. In 1882 further exclusions of the remoter villages and hill tracts in the Hanthawaddy, Tharrawaddy, Prome, and Bassein districts were made, so that the returns of births and deaths for that and the subsequent years are to be received as affecting only 3,663,923 souls and 77,500 square miles. It may be added that the number of the persons so excluded only amounted to 72,848; and whereas the average population to the square mile in the registration tracts was a trifle over 47, in the excluded tracts the average population barely exceeds 7. Hence the exclusion of these tracts has no appreciable effect on the returns of the whole province. Taking then the figures for the population for which these vital statistics were collected as being 3,663,923, we find that the following table shows that the natural growth by excess of births over deaths is only 185,537, or an increase at the rate of 5·06 per cent.

Births and Deaths, Lower Burma.

Year.	Births.			Deaths.			Net increase.		Total increase.
	Male.	Female.	Total.	Male.	Female.	Total.	Male.	Female.	
1881 ...	38,012	35,742	73,754	31,966	26,170	58,136	6,046	9,572	15,618
1882 ...	41,781	39,067	80,848	32,509	26,637	59,146	9,272	12,430	21,702
1883 ...	43,066	40,669	83,735	29,931	23,652	53,583	13,135	17,017	30,152
1884 ...	42,747	40,036	82,783	39,079	30,155	69,234	3,668	9,881	13,549
1885 ...	48,059	45,163	93,222	40,539	32,133	72,672	7,520	13,030	20,550
1886 ...	42,459	40,005	82,464	31,609	25,174	56,783	10,850	14,831	25,681
1887 ...	41,102	38,318	79,420	32,678	26,437	59,115	8,424	11,881	20,305
1888 ...	45,216	42,134	87,350	47,032	38,454	85,486	— 1,816	3,680	1,864
1889 ...	39,903	37,393	77,296	34,875	27,483	62,358	5,028	9,910	14,938
1890 ...	43,918	40,851	84,769	36,091	27,500	63,591	7,827	13,351	21,178
Total ...	**426,263**	**399,378**	**825,641**	**356,309**	**283,795**	**640,104**	**69,954**	**115,583**	**185,537**

The natural increment, if these returns be true, is exceedingly small and quite disproportionate to the total growth of the population. Mr. Copleston, in paragraph 69 of his report on the Census of 1881, calculated that—

"The natural increase since the enumeration of 1872 amounted to 605,110 or 22 per cent. The births would amount to 1,010,500 and the deaths to 405,390. In ten years, at the above rate, the natural growth would amount to about 26 per cent. The birth-rate would average about 36·7 and the death-rate 14·7 per mille of the total mean population. The above figures have, it must be admitted, little statistical value, but they are perhaps worth recording as representing an approximation to facts."

Considering how few data were at his disposal, it is indeed somewhat remarkable that the results of the present census have to a great extent corroborated the truth of Mr. Copleston's calculations. In the return of birth-place, which will be more fully discussed in Chapter IX, we find that the schedules showed that 4,032,739 persons were enumerated as having been born in Lower Burma. There were also 6,236 persons who were enumerated in India and who returned Burma as their birth-place, some of whom no doubt were born in the lower province. Out of the 4,658,627 persons enumerated in Lower Burma, 4,015,451 were enumerated as being born in Lower Burma. The balance of those born in Lower Burma, 17,269, were enumerated in Upper Burma. Turning to the birth-place returns of the last census, we find that 3,195,028 persons were enumerated as being born in Lower Burma. Accordingly we find an increase of 820,423 or 21·9 per cent. Here we have the exact amount of the natural increment if our birth-place returns are true. Without going further into the discussion of this question, which belongs to a separate chapter, it will be sufficient here to note that the birth-place returns of 1891 correspond very closely with those of 1881. In the report of 1881 we find the following passage:—

"It is worth noting" writes Mr. Copleston, "that the returns of birth-place, Form X, prove that 541,743 persons or nearly one-seventh of the total population resident in British Burma at the time of the census were born outside the province, and that of these 316,000 were natives of Upper Burma."

In the present returns we find that, out of every 10,000 persons resident in Lower Burma, only 8,619 were born in the province and 1,381, or not far short of one-seventh, were born outside of it. Accordingly we may take it that the returns of birth-place are correct and they denote that the natural increment, though not quite so high as was at first inferred, reaches the unusually high rate of 21·9 for the decade. As, however, the rate was assumed to be still higher, it will be necessary to give the reasons why the previous estimate was too high.

In the first place it must be remembered that the abnormal increase of 36·02, which we now find was due in part to defective enumeration in 1872, had to be explained away. Secondly, returns of births and deaths had not been kept for the whole of the previous intercensal period, and Mr. Copleston had apparently only the returns of one year by which to guide himself. It is true that nearly all adult males and females in Burma marry and that the unions are generally productive. On the other hand large families, such as are common in England, are almost unknown in Burma, the barbarous midwifery practised in Burma is no doubt partly responsible for this. Moreover, the mortality amongst infants is very high. It is true that among the upper and middle classes in England marriages are gradually becoming less common, but motives of economy or prudence have not in times past weighed much in the minds of the less thrifty poorer class. How little motives of prudence affect the lower orders in England may be judged from the fact that the last census report records that the average number of illegitimate births "registered as such" in 1880, 1881, and 1882 was 42,916 per annum.

In England, where the registration of births and deaths is carefully carried out, it was found that "the natural increment of the people showed an increase of 15·09 per cent. on the population of 1871" within the intercensal period of 1871—1881.

We can better understand the full meaning of this high rate of natural increment of 26 per cent. when we find, if Mr Copleston has gauged it aright, a single married couple living in the year 1256 A.D. on this hypothesis would have produced the whole of the population of Lower Burma living in 1881, and that if this rate were maintained the population of Lower Burma independent of all gains from immigration would amount to 100,000,000 in the year A.D. 2053.

An increase of 26 per cent. for a decennium is equivalent to an annual increase at the rate of 2·338 per cent. This we find is a very high rate of increase and far exceeds the annual rate of increase of any European country, and almost equals the admittedly rapid rate of growth of the United States where the population is annually recruited by large swarms of immigrants.

The following table gives the correct annual rate per cent. of increase for the following countries :—

State and Colonial Unit.	Annual rate.	Intercensal period.
England and Wales	1·108	1881—1891.
England and Wales	1·35	1871—1881.
United States	2·9	1871—1881.
Germany	1·0	1875—1880.
Prussia	1·2	1875—1880.
France	0·4	1877—1881.
Bombay	0·1	1872—1881.
Madras	0·2	1872—1881.
Bengal	1·2	1872—1881.
North-Western Provinces	0·6	1872—1881.
Punjab	0·6	1868—1881.
Lower Burma	3·68	1872—1881.
Bombay	1·36	1881—1891.
Madras	1·46	1881—1891.
North-Western Provinces	0·61	1881—1891.
Punjab	1·03	1881—1891.
Lower Burma	2·23	1881—1891.
Bengal	0·69	1881—1891.
Assam	1·15	1881—1891.

A comparison of the returns of births and deaths in the statement given above with the population will show that both births and deaths have been incorrectly registered and many deaths and probably more births have escaped being recorded. The highest birth-rate per mille, 25·51, was recorded in 1885, and the lowest, 19·98, in 1891. We might have expected from the fact that no allowance was made for the growth of the population that the average birth-rate would be higher towards the end of the intercensal period, but the difference is very slight. The mean annual birth-rate from 1871—1881 was 35·35 in England.

This was the highest birth-rate ever recorded. Mr. Copleston in placing the rate of natural increment as high as 26 per cent. for the intercensal period thought that the birth-rate per mille should be about 36·7 per mille. This rate is higher than the highest record in England, and though marriage is commoner amongst the Burmans than the English, yet on the other hand it must be remembered that we have a large proportion of Indian male immigrants who are generally celibate during their stay in Burma, and that the Burmese are far less prolific than the English and Welsh. If, however, we accept Mr. Copleston's estimate for the birth-rate we find that his estimate of the death-rate at 14·7 per mille is shown to be actually below even the admittedly incomplete record of deaths kept by our registrars. The lowest death-rate was 14·67 per mille in the healthiest year of the decade 1883. In 1881 and 1882, when the returns of the last census were just available and the death-rates could have been accurately calculated, the rates were 16·41 and 16·14 per mille. It is clear, therefore, that Mr. Copleston placed the death-rate far too low.

The following table gives the death-rate in Rangoon for the years 1881—1891 :—

Table showing the number of deaths according to sexes during the last 10 years in the Rangoon Municipality.

Year.	Male.	Female.	Total.	Rate per 1,000.	Ratio per 1,000 of the corrected population.
1881	2,503	1,157	3,660	27·28	...
1882	2,094	981	3,075	22·92	22·25
1883	2,677	1,014	3,691	27·51	25·92
1884	3,665	1,445	5,110	38·08	34·85
1885	2,432	925	3,357	25·01	22·22
1886	2,482	1,088	3,570	26·61	22·95
1887	2,478	1,162	3,640	27·13	22·72
1888	3,284	1,290	4,574	34·09	27·71
1889	3,818	1,758	5,576	41·56	32·80
1890	4,966	2,153	7,119	53·06	40·66
Total of decade ...	**30,399**	**12,973**	**43,372**	...	...
1891	4,414	2,274	6,688	49·92	36·93

It will be seen that the rate is exceedingly high and even when based on the recent figures of the census of 1891 the rate reached 36·93 per mille. These figures will be more fully discussed hereafter. They are quoted here to show that Mr. Copleston's estimate was somewhat too low. But it is not only in Rangoon that the death-rate is high; the death-rate in the towns of the Pegu division ranged as high as 34·67 per mille, in the towns of the Irrawaddy division as high as 25·95 per mille, and 29·74 per mille was the average death-rate for the 20 chief towns of Burma during the past year, which was considered fairly healthy, and was marked by an absence of any cholera epidemic. These returns are based on the corrected population according to the census of 1891. Lastly, we have the opinion of the Sanitary Commissioner in his report on the returns of 1884. Dr. Sinclair states :

"The registered rural death-rate per 1,000 is only 16·61. There is, however, every reason for supposing that the actual rate should at all events equal the urban, namely, 36·65. With this we get 118,000 deaths in place of 53,629 as per returns which with the 15,605 town deaths gives an aggregate slightly in excess of that estimated for births."

The actual birth-rate for that year it may be noted was only 22·58 per mille. The Chief Commissioner in his resolution "hesitated to accept the conclusion that the true death-rate exceeds the true birth-rate." He also demurred to the view taken that the rural death-rate at all events equals the urban. No doubt the Sanitary Commissioner drew his picture in colours too dark, yet we may safely assume that the death-rate far exceeds the rate estimated in the last census report. In England the mean annual death-rate between 1861 and 1871 was 22·50 and between 1871 and 1881 this rate had sunk to the lowest recorded, namely, 21·27 per mille. There is every reason therefore to suppose that the true death-rate for the whole of Burma, though it of course does not exceed the birth-rate, is too high to allow of a natural increment of 26 per cent. in the decennium. On the other hand the recorded natural increment is probably far too low. The mean between these two extremes is more likely to be correct, and we shall not be far wrong if judging by statistics recorded we fix the average birth-rate at 37 and the death rate at 18·02. Allowing for an annual increase of the population at the rate of 2·23 per annum as a basis of calculation we shall find that at the birth-rate given above 1,529,924 persons were born in Lower Burma within the last decade. Of these 820,423 still survived according to our birth-place returns. Leaving out the few who were enumerated in other provinces of India as being counterbalanced by a similar number absent from Burma in 1881, we find there must have been 709,501 deaths, which on the corrected returns of the population means an annual death-rate of 18·02 per mille. These estimates will be found to be fairly correct.

Increase due to excess of immigrants over emigrants.

36. The natural increment of the population only accounts for 21·9 of the total growth. We have a surplus of 101,433 or an increase at the rate of 2·77 per cent. for which we have still to account. This increase could only have been caused in two ways: either by better enumeration or by excess of immigrants over emigrants. We may dismiss the first of these as the enumeration of 1881, except in the remoter tracts where the population is exceedingly sparse, gave an accurate return of the inhabitants of Lower Burma. The excess then can only be due to excess of immigrants over emigrants. There is no difficulty in accepting the latter explanation. Indeed it would at first sight appear that the share due to immigration has been under-estimated and that of the natural increment has been exaggerated. The whole position will be found carefully reviewed in Chapter IX, Birth-place, to which the discussion of these details belong. It will be sufficient here to state briefly the main reasons why the returns of birth-place are accepted. In the first place when contrasted with the returns of 1881, and with the totals of the population distributed by religions and languages, the returns of the present census correspond with those of 1881. In the second place, although large swarms of immigrants arrive every year, the majority of them return so soon as the working season is over. Of those that do not return a very considerable proportion swell the death-rate of our large towns. Lastly, but by no means leastly, till the scarcity of the present year once more set the tide of emigration flowing from Upper into Lower Burma, the annexation of the kingdom of Ava, as the Revenue Administration Report bears witness, undoubtedly checked the movement of the population from Upper into Lower Burma. Not only was the tide checked, but it had begun to set the other way. The Financial Commissioner in a passage in his report already quoted at page 28 mentions that this is one of the causes assigned for the increase of the thathameda in Upper Burma. That there is probably some truth in this explanation may be inferred from the fact that the official estimate of the population of Upper Burma in 1890 was only 2,193,562, being 869,864 less than the actual population discovered there in February 1891. There were 17,269 persons who returned Lower Burma as their birth-place found in Upper Burma. Moreover the annexation of Ava has opened a new outlet for our Indian immigrants, and although barely 5 years had elapsed since the annexation, there were found in Upper Burma 43,073 who returned one of the Indian provinces as their birth-place. The great part of these must have found their way thither after the annexation through Lower Burma. These figures will explain why the number of immigrants into Lower Burma is responsible for only 11 per cent. of the total increase. The enormous increase of Indian immigrants in 1881 over 1872 is due, as was pointed out, to the fact that the census of 1872 was taken at a time when nearly the whole of our Indian coolies had returned to their homes.

37. Having dealt with the movement of the population caused by natural increment and by additions from outside the province, it now remains to deal with the variations caused by these movements in the various parts of the province.

Movement of the population within the province.

This can be discussed from two different points of view—

(*a*) The movement of population from rural to urban areas or *vice versâ*.

(*b*) The movement from district to district.

Here our discussion is perforce limited to the lower province as we have only the returns of the last census to guide us.

The question of the movement of population from rural to urban areas may be first considered. This point has already been briefly touched on in Chapter I. All of our towns, with the exception of Pantanaw and Ramree, have grown and some show large increases. These two towns are decaying. In the case of the former the cause is purely physical, namely, the silting of the river-bed. In the latter case no especial cause is given, but the paucity of males points to emigration as the cause of the decrease. The townspeople themselves have complained that trade is passing away from the town. If we analyse the returns of the 20 chief towns of which separate figures were furnished at the last census we find the result will fall into the accompanying statement.

This statement is extracted from Imperial Tables IV and V of the present report and Final Form XX of the report of 1881. The returns are analysed by religions, and though no doubt a return of towns by races would have been even better, yet in Burma, as nearly all Burmans are Buddhists, the return by religions is sufficiently accurate and more convenient. I have omitted two towns from the comparative statement—Allanmyo, because a reference to the returns of 1872 shows that the returns of 1881 must have been carelessly collected, and of Pantanaw, because the town is decaying and hence it is self-evident that population is not flowing into it.

Town.	Percentage of increase.	Percentage of increase due to Buddhism.	Percentage of increase due to other religions.	Percentage of increase amongst Buddhists on returns of Buddhists, 1881.	Percentage of increase on returns of other religions.
Akyab	11	34	66	10	12
Rangoon	34	28	72	14	49
Pegu	80	65	35	59	295
Prome	4	26	74	1	42
Shwedaung	5	*	*	— 2	134
Paungdè	52	91	9	48	169
Yandoon	59	79	21	49	213
Bassein	7	3	97	3	23
Lemyethna	4	34	66	1	371
Henzada	18	51	49	9	179
Myanaung	1	†	†	— 1	61
Kyangin	7	81	19	6	62
Thayetmyo	6	210‡	‡	21	— 18
Moulmein	5	56	44	5	10
Tavoy	12	93	7	12	14
Mergui	17	78	22	16	24
Shwegyin	16	84	16	15	23
Toungoo	11	69	31	11	13
Total of all above towns ...	20	43	57	13	33

* There is a decrease of 292 Buddhists on the returns of 1881 or 2 per cent. in Shwedaung town. The increase in the number of those professing other religions not only makes this loss up, but shows the slight total increase that the returns exhibit.

† There is an actual decrease in the Buddhist population of 84 or 1 per cent. in the returns of Myanaung town. The increase in the number of those professing other religions not only makes this loss up, but is responsible for the slight increase in the population.

‡ There is a decrease of 1,111 or 18 per cent. in the number of those professing other religions. In Thayetmyo town the increase in the number of Buddhists not only makes up for this decrease, but constitutes the whole of the actual increase in the total population.

The above statement shows at a glance the rate of increase of the 18 towns for which this statement could be prepared. It further shows how much of this increase is due to Buddhism, which may be taken in towns to represent adequately the Burmese population and how much to all other religions which in towns are professed by the foreign population. Column 3 shows how much Buddhists have increased compared with the total number of Buddhists in each town, and column 4 shows the rate of increase in other religions. In Pegu the great increase in the Buddhist population is due to the inclusion of the Burmese village of Zaingganaing within Municipal limits. The still greater proportionate increase of foreigners is due to the influx of population after the opening of the railways. In Yandoon and Paungdè the increase of the Burmese population is due to the influx of Burmese. These are the only two towns in which the Burmese element has increased more rapidly than the general rate of Buddhists throughout the province which is returned at 24·35, hence it is clear that to these towns there has been a steady influx of Burmese as well as foreigners. There are no other towns which show a higher percentage of increase amongst the Buddhists than the normal rate of natural increment. In Thayetmyo, Mergui, and Shwegyin we find the next largest increases in the Buddhist population, and in each of these cases the increase shown is partly due to more careful enumeration in 1891. In all of these towns the arrangements that were made were well carried out and were carefully supervised by the local Officers. The decrease in the foreign element in Thayetmyo is due to the decrease of the heavy garrison that was maintained there in 1881. In Rangoon, Akyab, Tavoy, and Toungoo the increase in the Buddhist element does not keep pace with the natural increment of the population, and falls far behind the general rate of increase amongst Buddhists generally throughout the lower province. In the remaining towns, Henzada, Prome, Bassein, Kyangin, Myanaung, and Moulmein, it is clear that the Burmese element is not keeping pace with the normal growth of the population, and that so far as the Buddhists are concerned the rural tracts have gained at the expense of these towns, or what is more probable the surplus population has gone to other towns. The total urban population of these 18 towns exhibits an increase of only 20 per cent. as compared with 24·67 per cent., which is the rate of growth of the total population; and whether we take the growth of the towns in detail or in the aggregate we see that the population of the rural tracts is on the whole growing more quickly than that of the towns. This of course is due to the fact that with exception of the timber and rice mills we have no large manufacturing industries in the province. The rice-husking mills are only worked for the half-year succeeding the harvest, and do not supply work all the year round to the mill hands. The saw mills employ comparatively speaking but few hands, and thus we have not, as in Europe, large manufacturing centres which can supply a steady output of work for a resident population. Moreover, the Burmans find that the demand for rice has raised the price of paddy so high that the cultivator is handsomely repaid for his labour. Land may be had without payment of rent by those who choose to clear it and have it allotted to them. Our occupation returns show that out of 1,434,017 males of over 15 years of age who work at agricultural pursuits 713,146 or 49·6 per cent. "occupy" themselves the land they till. Any one who has dwelt amongst the countryfolk of Lower Burma and who compares them with the farm labourers in England will readily admit that the Burman is better off. Every Burman ploughman wears a silk gaungbaung and has a silk paso or waist cloth for high days and holidays. Moreover, the Burman dislikes the steady monotonous labour of a mill hand and leaves the coolie work to be done by the immigrants from India. It is quite possible, therefore, that the next census will show the foreign element to be still stronger in the towns than it is at present. The towns, however, will continue to attract the immigrants from India. The accompanying statement is an attempt at a forecast of the probable population of these 18 towns in 1901 based on the annual rate of progression in the last decade.

Statement showing probable population of the towns of Lower Burma in 1901.

Akyab ...	42,345
Rangoon ...	242,343
Pegu ...	19,123
Prome ...	31,281
Shwedaung ...	12,475
Paungdè ...	15,566
Yandoon ...	32,309
Bassein ...	32,353
Lemyethna ...	5,885

Statement showing probable population of the towns of Lower Burma in 1901—concld.

Henzada	22,865
Myanaung	5,563
Kyangin	8,707
Thayetmyo	18,167
Moulmein	58,598
Tavoy	17,049
Mergui	11,903
Shwegyin	10,191
Toungoo	17,840

The census of 1901 will show how far these forecasts are correct. For reasons already stated I greatly doubt whether Pegu, Paungdè, and Mergui will show this amount of increase because the increase in the last decade is due to extraneous causes.

Growth of the population in the rural tracts.

38. The returns of the urban population prove that the greatest expansion of the population has taken place not in urban but in the rural tracts. The comparative table of district variations on page 36 bears out this view. Turning to this table we notice first that there has been a proportionally though not an actually greater increase in the number of females than of males. Without going into the remoter causes which affect the distribution of the population by sex, which belongs to the chapter devoted to that subject, we may notice that the following districts, Rangoon, Thôngwa, Mergui, Shwegyin, Salween, Henzada, and Northern Arakan, are the sole exceptions to the general rule that the increase among females is greater proportionately than the increase among males. In Northern Arakan, Salween, and Henzada the disparity is so slight that it is not noticeable. In Mergui the better enumeration of the Chinese amongst whom females are few is probably the cause of the growth both in the population and in the number of males. The Chinaman unless well managed resents any interference from the smaller Burmese officials, and the abnormal increase in the number of Chinamen in Burma is probably due to the fact that on this occasion the Chinese Elders both in Mergui and in Rangoon, in which districts Chinamen are most numerous, were themselves enlisted as Census Officials. The increase in Rangoon and in Thôngwa is, however, due not to petty causes, but to the fact that the population of these places is largely swollen by immigration. Rangoon will be dealt with separately at the end of this chapter. As regards Thôngwa here as in every country which has received immigrants the first settlers are almost invariably men and not women; men come for work whether it be to dig for gold or to plough paddy-fields. Thôngwa owes its rapid expansion to the vast extension of cultivation which has taken place within the last decade. The low-lying swamps of the delta of the Irrawaddy in which Thôngwa is situated are almost all under the level of the highest flood tide. A series of reclamation bunds have been erected and the area under cultivation has increased from 262,452 acres in 1881 to 536,708 in 1891, being an increment at the rate of 104·5 per cent.

The accompanying table of variation in the area under cultivation in districts of Lower Burma is perhaps the best commentary on the comparative table of district variations.

District.	Cultivated area in acres.		Increase per cent.
	1881.	1891.	
Akyab	368,407	560,655	+ 52·18
Northern Arakan	6,384	9,218	+ 44·39
Kyaukpyu	106,327	121,438	+ 14·21
Sandoway	46,555	55,251	+ 18·68
Arakan Division ...	527,673	746,562	+ 41·48
Rangoon	4,005	1,478	— 63·10
Hanthawaddy ... ... } Pegu ... ... }	* 914,048	*1,291,701*	+ *41·31*
Tharrawaddy	184,523	343,174	+ 85·98
Prome	225,891	316,712	+ 40·21
Pegu Division ...	1,328,467	1,953,065	+ 47·01

* As Hanthawaddy and Pegu had not yet been separated into two districts in 1881, separate figures of the area under cultivation are not available. The area under cultivation in Hanthawaddy is 499,734 and in Pegu 791,967.

District.	Cultivated area in acres.		Increase per cent.
	1881.	1891.	
Thôngwa	262,452	536,708	+ 104·50
Bassein	393,544	607,277	+ 54·31
Henzada	253,643	428,054	+ 68·76
Thayetmyo	112,597	117,512	+ 4·37
Irrawaddy Division ...	**1,022,236**	**1,689,551**	**+ 65·28**
Amherst	361,920	431,502	+ 19·22
Tavoy	74,880	86,201	+ 15·12
Mergui	51,840	60,462	+ 16·63
Shwegyin	48,000	96,494	+ 101·03
Toungoo	111,360	213,957	+ 92·13
Salween	13,440	13,620	+ 1·34
Tenasserim Division ...	**661,440**	**902,236**	**+ 36·41**
Total Lower Burma ...	**3,539,816**	**5,291,414**	**+ 49·48**

This will show how remarkable has been the extension of cultivation, but the whole of this apparent increase is not to be credited solely to this cause. Since 1881 the Cadastral Survey of India has been at work in the districts of Akyab, Bassein, Hanthawaddy, Pegu, Tharrawaddy, Henzada, and Thôngwa, and the result has been that the under-estimated areas based in great measure on the imperfect returns of the local thugyis have, in some cases, been largely increased. Much trouble has been taken in attempting to obtain the exact share of this increase, that is due to better measurement and more accurate survey, but as the calculation involves the necessity of distinguishing between the amount due to remeasurements by the cadastral and supplementary surveys and by the thugyis themselves, it has been found impossible to give anything but the approximate gain due to the better measurement of the areas already under cultivation. It has been calculated that in the Bassein district, where the thugyis in anticipation of the coming of the survey increased the returns of the areas of their circles, the remeasurement by the Survey of India showed a decrease of 10·5 on the areas surveyed by them; this is equivalent to a decrease of 6·82 per cent. on the whole of the cultivation. Hence in Bassein the increase of 54 per cent. does not really cover the total increase of cultivation. So far as has been ascertained, in Hanthawaddy 1·5 of the increase shown is due to better remeasurement. In Pegu, Henzada, Tharrawaddy, Akyab, Prome, and Thôngwa the respective increases due to this cause are, 15·2 per cent. in the case of Pegu, 8 per cent. in Henzada, 15 per cent. in Tharrawaddy, 20 per cent. in Prome, 15 per cent. in Akyab, and only 5 per cent. in Thôngwa. But even if we allow a deduction from all these districts, the increase of acreage which is due to extension of cultivation is sufficiently startling. We cannot, when looking at this table, be surprised that Thôngwa shows such an enormous increase in its population or that the growth of the rural tracts still outstrips that of our towns. The excess of the growth of males in Thôngwa then is undoubtedly due to the immigration of men who came there for employment. They will in due time be followed by women and we may expect that the returns of the next census will show in Thôngwa that the increase in females is proportionately greater than that of males, because of the comparatively few females there now. It is to this cause rather than to faulty enumeration in 1881 that the increase in the number of females is proportionately but not actually greater in the majority of districts. Immigrants from Upper Burma when they do come come accompanied by their families. Next to Thôngwa in the growth of its population comes Thayetmyo. The table of areas under cultivation does not help us here because the Upper Burma portion of the Thayetmyo district is under a different revenue system and is accordingly not included in the areas on which land revenue is assessed. As this area has not yet been surveyed it is impossible to show it in the table. But in our census returns the population of these three Upper Burma townships is included in the returns of the Thayetmyo district. Without this addition the population of Thayetmyo would be only

194,637 and the increase would fall to 17·5 per cent. This increase is very large when we consider that the population in 1881 was swollen by the large garrison which was then stationed in Thayetmyo. Besides Thôngwa, Rangoon, and Thayetmyo the following districts—Hanthawaddy, Pegu, Tharrawaddy, Mergui, and Toungoo—show a growth in excess of the average rate of increase. In all of these districts except Mergui the increase amongst the females outstrips the increase in the number of the other sex. In the case of Thayetmyo and Toungoo this is partly due tò a decrease in the garrison which was unusually large in 1881 on account of anticipated troubles in Upper Burma. In Hanthawaddy, Tharrawaddy, and Pegu the greater increase of females is due to the fact that in these districts the first rush of male settlers is over, and that the male pioneers having established themselves have gotten themselves wives and families. In Burma as in most countries an examination of the statistics of age and sex shows that unless there be external disturbing causes, although more males are born, females, owing to the greater mortality amongst male children, soon outnumber the males and continue to do so increasingly at each successive age period. Hence when once the in-rush of male settlers is over the tendency of females to outnumber the males comes into operation, and owing to the previous disparity in the numbers, an actually smaller increase in the number of females shows a larger proportionate increase. In Mergui the cause of growth has already been noted.

There are four more districts which, though they do not advance at the same quick rate as the general rate of progression, yet keep pace with the rate of natural increment. These districts are Sandoway, Bassein, Henzada, and Shwegyin. In the two latter the extension of the cultivated area is the explanation of their increase. In the case of Sandoway the improvement is due rather to better enumeration. The schedule books showed that the census work in Sandoway was as well done as in any district in Burma, and the Deputy Commissioner took a warm interest in his work. Of the remaining districts Amherst and Akyab may be classed as being progressive districts, though their progress is not so rapid as that of those already mentioned.

Stationary districts.

39. None of our Burmese districts can be called retrógressive, but when we compare the growth of the population in Kyaukpyu, Prome, Tavoy, Salween, and Northern Arakan with the rapid advances made elsewhere these districts may be classed as stationary. Salween and Northern Arakan Hill Tracts indeed deserve this name. They are, however, not regularly constituted districts, inasmuch as they are hill tracts under the charge of Superintendents of Police who exercise the powers of Deputy Commissioners. In the other districts, Tavoy, Prome, and Kyaukpyu, it will be noticed that though they show but poor progress compared to the more fortunate districts, yet they would in other Indian provinces be considered as progressive districts.

40. The following table gives the corrected rate of annual increase, which is one-tenth of the logarithmic difference between the two data:—

District.	Corrected rate of annual increase.
LOWER BURMA.	
ARAKAN DIVISION—	
Akyab	1·472
Northern Arakan	·0887
Kyaukpyu	·933
Sandoway	1·883
Total ...	1·351
PEGU DIVISION—	
Rangoon Town	3·000
Hanthawaddy	2·227
Pegu	3·149
Tharrawaddy	2·249
Prome	1·118
Total ...	2·223

District.	Corrected rate of annual increase.
LOWER BURMA—*concluded.*	
IRRAWADDY DIVISION—	
Thôngwa	4·616
Bassein	2·222
Henzada.	1·819
Thayetmyo	3·965
Total ...	2·944
TENASSERIM DIVISION—	
Amherst	1·654
Tavoy	1·130
Mergui	2·689
Toungoo	2·324
Shwegyin	1·889
Salween	·366
Total ...	1·789
Total Lower Burma ...	2·233

It would, perhaps, be rash to attempt to forecast the probable population in 1901. Successive years of drought in Upper Burma may denude the upper province and swell the returns of the deltaic districts. Famine in India and the gradual disappearance of the prejudice against sea-journeys felt by the bulk of the inhabitants of the plains of Bengal may flood Burma within the next intercensal period with settlers from Behar and Oudh.

41. In reviewing the growth of the districts and towns of Burma, Rangoon was purposely omitted as it deserves special attention. We have, moreover, better means of estimating the value of the returns owing to the more careful registration of the vital statistics. Yet this same registration has for years past given trouble and dissatisfaction to the Municipal authorities. In the report on the working of the Municipality in the year 1875-76 the President writes:

Rangoon.

"The registration of births and deaths in this city has hitherto been conducted with so little system that the figures returned are nearly worthless."

A new system was accordingly inaugurated. Next year's report merely mentions that the registration of vital statistics was still unsatisfactory. In 1883-84 another new system from which much was expected was introduced, but in the following year again the Health Officer reported that there was no improvement in the registration of births. As late as 1888 the President is still forced to admit: "The system of registration which is still in force is very defective and renders the returns unreliable."

There is a reason which in a great measure explains the difficulty experienced in Rangoon. Rangoon is a polyglot city, and the registrars instead of being men with the rank of police sergeants ought to be men knowing at least three languages, who would require wages which the Municipality would hesitate to pay. In the next place it must be remembered that in Rangoon we have a very large temporary population, whose presence renders the consideration of the returns exceedingly complex. Lastly, if we examine the returns we are startled to find that while the death-rate varies from 22 to 53, the birth-rate ranges from 10·71 to 19·30 per mille. This is on the face of it sufficiently perplexing, and the returns would appear to be what the Health Officer once designated them to be "simply ridiculous." Before passing judgment on these statistics it is but fair that we should take into consideration that the birth-rate depends not on the total gross population, but the number of females at the reproductive age, while the death-rate depends on the gross population, and when we find that there are only 55,557 females in the whole of Rangoon, that is to say, only on an average 445 females to every 1,000 males, the surprise at these abnormal returns is materially lessened. If we take the proportion of females to males in the years during which females are reproductive, which we may roughly fix as beginning about the 15th and ending at the 44th year, we find that the relative population of females to 1,000 males at the successive quinquennial periods of 15-19, 20-24, 25-29, 30-34, 35-39, 40-44 were 532, 326, 270, 270, 286, and 320 respectively. I have fixed the reproductive age limit for women rather later in life for Rangoon than what would be the limit for the province generally as there is a larger proportion of Europeans in Rangoon. Accordingly, on taking the whole age period together, we find that from 15—44 there were only 322·8 women to every 1,000 men. Naturally then the birth-rate would be rather less than one-third of what the normal birth-rate would be if the sexes were evenly distributed. Looked at from this point of view the birth returns are by no means abnormal. The death-rate, however, is unusually high; unfortunately, like the birth-rates, it is based on the uncorrected totals of the last census, and accordingly we can only look on the vital statistics of the last year and of 1882 as being fairly accurate. I append the statement of births with the rates given in the official report and the rates as they should be according to the return of the corrected population during the intercensal period. A similar return of deaths in Rangoon was given on page 40.

Table showing the number of births according to sexes during the last 10 years in the Rangoon Municipality.

Year.	Male.	Female.	Total	Ratio per 1,000.	Ratio per 1,000 of the corrected population.
1881	734	703	1,437	10·71	10·71
1882	803	783	1,586	11·82	11·47
1883	886	735	1,621	12·08	11·38
1884	818	671	1,489	11·01	10·15
1885	989	921	1,910	14·24	12·64
1886	997	946	1,943	14·48	12.49
1887	1,119	913	2,032	15·15	12·68
1888	1,178	1,031	2,209	16·46	13·38
1889	1,370	1,232	2,602	19·39	15·30
1890	1,317	1,171	2,488	18·54	14·21
Total ...	10,211	9,106	19,317	...	...
1891	1,417	1,210	2,627	19·58	14·51

In the decade if these returns be true there was an actual loss of 24,055 by "natural decrease." Instead of this there was an increase of 46,148. Turning to the table of birth-place we find that there were in Rangoon only 60,727 out of the total population who were born there, and altogether there were in the province 91,692 who gave Rangoon as their birth-place. In 1881 the figures must be received with some caution, because of the recent abolition of the Rangoon district, which included the present districts of Hanthawaddy, Pegu, and part of Thôngwa. Thus, if a person were asked where he was born, he would be more likely to reply Rangoon, meaning Rangoon district and not Rangoon town. In 1881, though there were in Rangoon itself only 48,856 persons who returned themselves as being born in Rangoon, there were in the Hanthawaddy or the old Rangoon district 24,842 who returned themselves as being born in Rangoon out of the total of 94,266 persons who returned "Rangoon" as their birth-place. In 1891 there were in the Hanthawaddy and Pegu districts only 9,180 persons who returned Rangoon as their birth-place. There is no doubt, therefore, that both enumerators and enumerated in 1881 were misled by the recent official change in the district's name and hence no reliance is to be placed on the return of those outside Rangoon who returned Rangoon as their birth-place. There is not, however, the same likelihood of error in the return made by those living in the town of Rangoon itself. We find that the number of those born in Rangoon and living in Rangoon has risen at the rate of 24 per cent.

The statement of births and deaths in detail by religions was kindly furnished by the Health Officer of Rangoon, and taking the return of 1890 in detail the following comparative statement has been prepared;—

Number professing each religion.	Number professing it in Rangoon.	Birth-rate per mille.	Death-rate per mille.
Buddhists	79,857	22·75	41·87
Hindus	57,845	3·83	40·00
Musalmans	28,836	10·68	34·88
Christians	12,678	11·04	12·77

I have not attempted to give the birth and death rate in detail for more than one year, 1890, as though this was an easy task of itself, I found that in working out the corrected population for each year, when the population was divided into the various religious denominations the possibility of errors was greatly enhanced by accidental causes, such as an increase or decrease of our garrison or jail population, which was abnormally large in 1888-89. These accidental variations would have a proportionately greater effect when the population was divided into these smaller groups than when the whole population was taken together. Moreover, 1890 will serve as an example, as it shows how in every class there is a loss. It is true that 1890 was an unusually unhealthy year and the disparity between births and deaths is therefore accentuated. Leaving Hindus, Musalmans, and Christians out of the calculation, we are still forced to believe that the registration of births is very defective, as it falls so far below the return of the rural tracts. This agrees with what the President of the Municipality himself said. Deaths, he believes, are accurately reported. There are so many people, including the police and the undertaker, who must know about every death that occurs, and there is also the body to be disposed of. Moreover, a funeral in Burma is quite a social function, and there is no rite to correspond to Christian christening except the ear-boring, which is not celebrated till the child is some years old and many children die before their ears are pierced. But any Burmese loafer will walk miles to be present at a funeral, which is generally celebrated with music and dancing and a general feast, if the means of the relations of the deceased will permit of it. Changes that have occurred since 1881 in the registration area render any comparison of the returns of vital statistics by circles an impossibility. It is difficult therefore, with doubtful returns both in birth-place and in vital statistics, to ascertain what is the rate of natural increment or of decrease since 1881. If we compare the returns of the various religions we find that Buddhists have risen from 67,131 to 79,857, an increase of 18·95 per cent.; Mahomedans from 21,169 to 28,836, an increase of 36·21 per cent.; Hindus from 35,871 to 57,845, an increase of 61·25 per cent.; and Christians from 9,741 to 12,678, an increase of 30·15 per cent., in spite of the heavy loss shown by excess of deaths over births. It is impossible, therefore, to accept the vital statistics of Rangoon as even approaching accuracy so far as births are concerned.

The reclamation schemes which have been approved for the filling up of the swamps in the Botataung, Yegyaw, and Theinbyu quarters will change the face of the town and reduce its death-rate. The present distribution of the population will be entirely altered by the opening of these new building-sites. Any attempts then to forecast the future population of any of the quarters of Rangoon, based on the figures of past enumerations, will necessarily be futile. All that can be inferred is the probable gross population, which, if the present rate of increase be maintained, will amount to 242,343 in 1901, 325,694 in 1911, 437,713 in 1921, and 588,258 in 1931. The accompanying statement of the corrected population is added for the convenience of the Registration Department.

1892	185,733
1893	191,305
1894	197,044
1895	202,956
1896	209,044
1897	215,316
1898	221,775
1899	228,429
1900	235,281
1901	242,343

CHAPTER III.

RELIGION.

Comparative statements showing the strength of the various religions in Burma. Comparative statement of the chief religions distributed by race. Buddhism the religion of the great mass of the people. The Buddhism of the Burmese laity contrasted with the Buddhism of the Sacred books. Nat-worship or Shamanism formerly the prevailing religion. Mahomedanism and Hinduism. Christianity. The sects of Christians; their history in Burma. Christianity among the Karens. Other religions.

Authorities consulted.

Asiatic Studies, by Sir Alfred Lyall, K.C.B. Murray.
The life or legend of Gaudama, by the Right Reverend Bishop Bigandet. Trübner, 1881, 3rd edition.
Buddhism, by Sir Monier Williams, K.C.I.E. John Murray, 1889.
Buddhism, by E. J. Eitel. London, Trübner, 1873.
Buddhism, by Rhys Davids.
Buddhism in China, by Reverend S. Beal, 1884.
Buddha Ghôsa, by the Reverend T. Foulkes, *Indian Antiquary*, Volume XIX, Part CCXXXIII. Bombay, 1890.
The Burman, by Shwe Yeo.
An Outline of the History of the Catholic Burmese Mission. Rangoon, 1887.
Account of the Burman Empire, by Father San Germano.
Hinduism, by Sir Monier Williams, K.C.I.E. London, 1877.
Confucianism and Taoism, by Professor R. K. Douglas, S.P.C.K. London, 1889.
The Golden Bough, by J. G. Frazer. Macmillan, 1890.
Notes on the spirit basis of Belief and Custom, by J. T. Campbell (unpublished).
Imperial Gazetteer of India, by Sir William Hunter, K.C.S.I.
British Burma Gazetteer, by Colonel H. Spearman.

42. In the Imperial Tables V, VI, VII, VIII, and XVI will be found the census returns of the population classified by the religion they profess. In Western Europe the return of religion practically relates to the strength of the various sects of one religion,—Christianity. In Burma, however, there is no such uniformity, and though nearly nine-tenths of the population return themselves as Buddhists, the remaining tenth is evenly divided between four very different kinds of faith—Hinduism, Islamism, Animistic or Nat-worship, and last, but not least, Christianity. Besides these we have a few who belong to the Sikh, Parsi, or Zoroastrian and Jewish forms of belief. In a few cases people returned themselves as having no religion. Others again were returned as professing some undecipherable and unrecognizable religion. These were, however, very few. Both of these classes were shown as Not returned; there were only 49 of them altogether.

In the Supplementary Imperial Tables **A** and **B** the sects of Christians are tabulated by race and age periods, but, with this exception, no attempt has been made on the occasion of this census to procure returns of any religion by sect or age.

In the accompanying table will be shown the number of those returned as belonging to the various religions throughout the province and their proportionate strength as compared with the total population.

Religion.	Number returned professing it.	Ratio per 10,000 of the total population.
Buddhists	6,888,075	9,056·63
Nat-worshippers	168,449	221·49
Hindus	171,577	225·59
Musalmans	253,031	332·69
Christians	120,768	158·79
Sikhs	3,164	4·16
Jews	351	·46
Parsis	96	·13
Not returned	49	·06

The total population given in this statement, namely, 7,605,560, is less than the return made of the total population in the general statement, because it was found to be impossible to enumerate the people by their religions in the Shan States and certain outlying tracts. Accordingly the population of these tracts is not taken into consideration in this chapter. From enquiries made it has been ascertained that the persons thus excluded are all either Buddhists or Nat-worshippers.

43. The following tables show the strength of the various religions returned in the Census schedule, and their relative position to the population of each district throughout the province :—

COMPARATIVE TABLE OF RELIGIONS.

Relative distribution of each Religion per 10,000 of the total population (a) *of district,* (b) *of those professing the religion.*

District.	Buddhists.		Nat-worshippers.		Mahomedans.		Hindus.		Christians.		Sikhs.		Jews.		Parsis.		Not returned.	
	a	b	a	b	a	b	a	b	a	b	a	b	a	b	a	b	a	b
LOWER BURMA.																		
ARAKAN DIVISION—																		
Akyab ...	6,204	375	678	1,675	2,862	4,709	234	569	21	74	·02	3	·33	399	...	...	...	...
Northern Arakan ...	823	2	8,914	774	12	1	250	22	·68	·07	...	...	...	...	...	...	...	...
Kyaukpyu ...	8,864	211	847	824	263	170	18	17	8	11	...	...	...	...	...	...	...	...
Sandoway ...	8,814	98	708	324	405	123	23	10	50	32	...	...	...	...	...	...	...	...
Total ...	**7,035**	**686**	**902**	**3,597**	**1,884**	**5,003**	**157**	**618**	**21**	**117**	**·01**	**3**	**·2**	**399**	...	...	...	...
PEGU DIVISION—																		
Rangoon Town ...	4,428	116	27	29	1,599	1,140	3,208	3,371	703	1,050	20	1,172	12	6,239	2	3,438	·05	204
Hanthawaddy ...	9,309	361	40	63	175	185	319	497	156	344	·03	3	...	...	...	...	...	...
Pegu ...	9,286	406	38	67	111	133	395	694	165	412	3	310	...	...	·96	3,021	·59	3,674
Tharrawaddy ...	9,725	491	53	110	48	66	82	166	91	262	·83	92	...	...	...	...	...	...
Prome ...	9,617	503	237	506	63	90	66	139	17	51	...	...	...	...	...	...	...	...
Total ...	**8,876**	**1,877**	**90**	**775**	**280**	**1,614**	**573**	**4,867**	**176**	**2,119**	**3**	**1,577**	**1·5**	**6,239**	**·42**	**6,459**	**·13**	**3,878**
IRRAWADDY DIVISION—																		
Thôngwa ...	9,505	616	27	71	83	146	87	227	298	1,102	...	...	...	...	...	...	...	...
Bassein ...	9,141	630	35	98	122	229	138	383	563	2,216	·02	3	·23	313	...	...	...	...
Henzada ...	9,682	535	2	5	57	86	71	158	187	591	...	...	·21	228	·15	625	...	...
Thayetmyo ...	9,063	329	690	1,025	86	85	101	147	59	121	·63	51	·03	29	·28	729	...	...
Total ...	**9,366**	**2,110**	**130**	**1,199**	**89**	**546**	**101**	**915**	**313**	**4,030**	**·1**	**54**	**·12**	**570**	**·08**	**1,354**	...	...
TENASSERIM DIVISION—																		
Amherst ...	8,624	523	193	479	453	747	584	1,421	145	502	·11	16	·26	313	·02	104	...	...
Tavoy ...	9,751	134	10	6	84	31	34	19	121	95	...	...	...	...	...	...	...	...
Mergui ...	8,583	92	256	112	717	209	116	50	328	200	...	...	...	...	...	...	...	...
Toungoo ...	7,610	179	547	527	157	101	189	178	1,495	2,008	·61	32	·24	114	·67	1,146	...	...
Shwegyin ...	9,115	263	482	568	84	66	198	229	119	196	2	129	...	...	...	...	...	...
Salween ...	1,375	6	8,485	1,584	67	8	55	10	18	5	...	...	...	...	...	...	...	...
Total ...	**8,429**	**1,197**	**564**	**3,276**	**301**	**1,162**	**334**	**1,907**	**371**	**3,006**	**·57**	**177**	**·17**	**427**	**·12**	**1,250**	...	...

COMPARATIVE TABLE OF RELIGIONS.

Relative distribution of each Religion per 10,000 of the total population (a) *of district,* (b) *of those professing the religion*—concluded.

District.	Buddhists.		Nat-worshippers.		Mahomedans.		Hindus.		Christians.		Sikhs.		Jews.		Parsis.		Not returned.	
	a	*b*	*a*	*b*	*a*	*b*	*a*	*b*	*a*	*b*	*a*	*b*	*a*	*b*	*a*	*b*	*a*	*b*
UPPER BURMA.																		
NORTHERN DIVISION—																		
Mandalay ...	9,113	495	40	89	495	731	257	561	82	254	12	1,498	1	969	...	...	...	...
Bhamo ...	8,430	66	601	193	174	37	636	201	151	68	8	142	...	...	...	...	...	...
Katha ...	9,569	83	23	8	151	35	188	65	12	6	57	1,072	...	...	...	...	...	...
Ruby Mines ...	8,981	34	488	76	116	12	297	45	103	22	9	76	...	...	1	312	5	2,857
Shwebo ...	9,517	187	6	5	251	134	155	122	58	64	13	575	...	...	...	...	...	...
Total ...	9,177	865	96	371	370	949	263	994	77	414	16	3,363	·52	969	·04	312	·21	2,857
CENTRAL DIVISION—																		
Ye-u ...	9,842	132	1	·47	43	16	46	25	54	42	14	417	...	...	...	...	...	...
Sagaing ...	9,846	355	2	2	62	61	53	76	32	66	5	405	...	...	...	...	...	...
Lower Chindwin ...	9,950	336	2	2	18	17	16	22	2	3	12	882	...	...	...	...	...	...
Upper Chindwin ...	9,642	106	123	56	63	19	147	65	10	6	15	357	...	...	...	...	...	...
Total ...	9,858	929	16	61	44	113	50	188	22	117	10	2,061	...	...	...	...	...	...
SOUTHERN DIVISION—																		
Myingyan ...	9,902	505	6	13	35	48	39	81	17	49	1	114	...	...	...	...	...	...
Pakôkku ...	9,769	431	122	220	43	52	59	105	6	17	·16	16	·03	29	·03	104	...	...
Minbu ...	9,668	315	249	332	31	27	43	57	6	11	3	199	...	...	...	...	...	...
Magwe ...	9,897	315	18	24	33	29	33	41	11	20	7	505	1	484	...	...	...	...
Total ...	9,816	1,566	90	589	36	156	44	284	11	97	2	834	·16	513	·009	104	...	...
EASTERN DIVISION—																		
Kyauksè ...	9,690	178	3	2	247	124	42	31	15	16	2	66	·39	142·5	...	...	...	...
Meiktila ...	9,863	296	5	7	62	50	54	64	15	27	·04	3	...	...	·19	417	...	...
Yamèthin ...	9,542	222	27	26	329	209	76	71	12	16	12	623	1	598	...	...	·06	204
Pyinmana ...	9,030	74	289	97	333	74	187	61	88	41	69	1,239	·88	142·5	·17	104	3	3,061
Total ...	9,644	770	41	132	210	457	71	227	22	100	11	1,931	·53	883	·09	521	·29	3,265
Total Lower Burma ...	8,680	5,870	320	8,847	452	8,325	306	8,307	240	9,272	1	1,811	·57	7,635	·18	9,063	·04	3,878
Total Upper Burma ...	9,652	4,130	66	1,153	144	1,675	98	1,693	30	728	9	8,189	·28	2,365	·03	937	·10	6,122
GRAND TOTAL BURMA ...	9,057	...	221	...	333	...	225	...	159	...	4	...	·46	...	·12	...	·06	...

This table, which is extracted from Imperial Table No. VI, is self-explanatory. The best commentary on it is the following comparative statement, which shows the strength of each religion amongst the various races and nationalities inhabiting Burma. The distribution of these religions by races into the districts of the province was found to be not only far too cumbrous for insertion, but the strength of some of the religions was so infinitesimal that nothing was gained by going into too great detail. The statement shows the relative strength of each race and religion to 10,000 of the total population of Burma. This statement is extracted from Imperial Table No. XVI.

44. The following comparative statement shows the relative strength of the various chief races throughout the eight administrative divisions in Upper and Lower Burma divided among the four chief religions distributed by 10,000 of the total population of the whole province :—

Amongst the Burmese it will be seen that the vast majority are Buddhists. There are, however, a few Christians—not quite 2 in every 1,000 ; a few Mahomedans, and, strangest of all, a sprinkling of Nat-worshippers. The Christians are those Burmans who have been converted to Christianity or the descendants of converts. That Christianity has progressed but slowly amongst the Burmese in comparison with the rapid progress made amongst the Karens is a fact admitted by the missionaries themselves. The Mahomedan Burmese are found amongst the Arakanese and amongst the Zerbadis or the descendants of Mahomedan fathers and Burmese mothers, who dress like the Burmese, speak Burmese, and who are often highly offended if not considered to be Burmese. But the sprinkling of Nat-worshippers requires some further explanation.

So far as could be ascertained, these Burmese Nat-worshippers are chiefly the children of Burmese fathers and Karen mothers, who returned themselves as being Burmans by race, but who clung to the religion of their mothers. There were, however, a very few cases of pure-bred Burmans who returned themselves as Nat-worshippers.

The Talaings have kept more constant to the Buddhist faith. The few Nat-worshippers found amongst them are the sons of stray Talaings who have settled down in nat-worshipping Karen villages.

The Karens are divided into three clans. Of these the Pwo are the most numerous. It will be seen that though the majority of them are Buddhists, Christianity has almost outstripped in numbers those who still return themselves under their formerly national religion of Nat-worship. But it is amongst the Sgau Karens that Christianity has made proportionately more converts than amongst the Pwo. The Bwès or Karennis are numerically insignificant, but it is amongst those Karennis living in English territory that we find the highest proportion of Christian converts. The Chins are chiefly Nat-worshippers. The Chinese are nearly evenly divided between Buddhism and Nat-worship. This is due to the fact that the Burmese enumerators refused to accept the Taoist Chinaman as a true Buddhist, and the return is a striking commentary on those writers who would class all Chinamen as Buddhists. A few Europeans and Eurasians returned themselves as Buddhists.

Comparative statement showing the strength of Races and Religions in every 10,000 of the total population distributed throughout the eight divisions of the province.

Divisions.	Burmese.				Talaings.				Shan.				Karen (Pwo).				Karen (Sgau).			
	Buddhists.	Nat-worshippers.	Musalmans.	Christians.	Buddhists.	Nat-worshippers.	Musalmans.	Christians.	Buddhists.	Nat-worshippers.	Musalmans.	Christians.	Buddhists.	Nat-worshippers.	Musalmans.	Christians.	Buddhists.	Nat-worshippers.	Musalmans.	Christians.
1	2	3	4	5	6	7	8	9	10	11	12	13	14	15	16	17	18	19	20	21
LOWER BURMA.																				
Arakan	613·2	·6	·4	·1	·03	...	...	...	·7	...	...	...	·06	·05	...	·02	·05	...	...	·005
Pegu	1,404·4	...	·6	3·4	109·8	...	...	·1	85·5	...	...	·08	29·08	2·2	...	1·9	51·4	·3	...	10·5
Irrawaddy	1,508·2	...	3·3	5·1	39·2	...	...	·7	6·4	...	...	·3	212·5	·8	·01	22·2	128·2	·06	·007	30·8
Tenasserim	455·6	1·7	·4	3·4	459·2	1·2	...	·1	51·6	·06	·06	·1	54·1	53·07	...	29·1	55·4	7·5	...	9·09
Total ...	3,981·6	2·3	4·8	12·2	610·8	1·2	...	·9	144·2	·06	·06	·5	295·8	56·2	·01	53·4	235·2	8·004	·007	50·4
UPPER BURMA.																				
Northern	686·3	2·4	1·02	·9	·8	...	...	·01	76·8	·3	...	·001	·06	·07	...	·06	·01	·01	...	1·
Central	810·6	·001	·08	1·4	·7	...	...	·001	27·5	...	...	...	·01	·002	...	·005	...	...	...	·001
Southern	1,397·1	...	·2	·1	·3	...	...	·007	4·1	...	...	...	·009	·009	...	·1	...	...	...	·009
Eastern	685·8	·02	3·3	·1	·02	...	...	·002	11·009	·006	·007	·003	·4	1·6	...	·4	·1	·3	...	...
Total ...	3,580·05	2·4	4·8	2·6	2·02	...	...	·02	119·5	·3	·007	·005	·5	1·6	...	·6	·1	·4	...	·1
GRAND TOTAL BURMA ...	7,561·7	4·9	9·6	14·9	612·9	1·2	...	·9	263·7	·4	·07	·5	296·4	57·9	·01	54·06	235·3	8·4	·007	50.5

Comparative statement showing the strength of Races and Religions in every 10,000 of the total population distributed throughout the eight divisions of the province—concluded.

Divisions.	Karennis.				Chins.				Chinese.				Europeans.				Eurasians.				Others.				
	Buddhists.	Nat-worshippers.	Musalmans.	Christians.	Buddhists.	Nat-worshippers.	Musalmans.	Christians.	Buddhists.	Nat-worshippers.	Musalmans.	Christians.	Buddhists.	Nat-worshippers.	Musalmans.	Christians.	Buddhists.	Nat-worshippers.	Musalmans.	Christians.	Buddhists.	Nat-worshippers.	Musalmans.	Christians.	Others.
1	22	23	24	25	26	27	28	29	30	31	32	33	34	35	36	37	38	39	40	41	42	43	44	45	46
LOWER BURMA.																									
Arakan	...	...	...	...	3·3	77·2	...	·4	·4	1·6	...	·01	...	...	...	·9	...	...	...	·08	3·4	·001	165·9	·1	13·9
Pegu	·3	·001	...	·02	1·1	7·1	...	·04	13·7	7·3	...	·05	...	...	...	6·3	·005	...	...	5·6	1·3	...	53·1	4·6	110·8
Irrawaddy	·7	·04	...	·03	8·9	22·05	...	·2	4·8	3·5	...	·3	...	...	...	1·8	...	...	...	·6	2·1	...	14·8	1·4	20·7
Tenasserim	·1	·06	...	·7	·3	·1	...	...	6·8	6·3	...	...	...	...	...	2·2	...	...	...	1·8	·3	2·1	38·1	·8	43·1
Total ...	1·3	·1	...	·8	13·7	106·6	...	·7	25·9	18·9	...	·3	...	...	...	11·4	·005	...	...	8·3	7·3	2·1	272·1	7·04	188·6
UPPER BURMA.																									
Northern	·01	·04	...	...	·4	1·2	...	·06	·7	3·6	...	·005	·003	...	...	3·2	...	...	...	·5	17·6	·4	30·5	2·3	23·8
Central	·001	...	...	...	·01	1·1	...	...	·1	·2	...	...	·001	...	...	·3	...	...	...	·06	1·9	...	3·5	·03	5·1
Southern	...	...	...	...	15·9	9·7	...	...	·6	3·3	...	...	...	...	...	·8	...	...	...	·1	·005	...	4·8	·2	6·7
Eastern	·003	...	...	...	...	·08	...	...	·1	·7	...	...	...	...	...	·5	...	...	...	·1	·4	·005	10·4	·3	6·003
Total ...	·02	·04	...	...	16·4	12·1	...	·06	1·6	7·9	...	·005	·005	...	...	4·9	...	...	...	·8	20·06	·4	50·7	2·9	41·7
GRAND TOTAL BURMA ...	1·3	·1	...	·8	30·1	118·8	...	·8	27·5	26·9	...	·3	·005	...	...	16·4	·005	...	...	9·1	27·3	2·6	323·03	9·9	230·4

The consideration of the return of races belongs to Chapter X. It will suffice here to point out that amongst the indigenous races of Burmese, Talaings, Shans, and Karens, by far the greater number return themselves as Buddhists. The Chins are, as might be expected, chiefly Nat-worshippers.

As the Hindus are restricted to those who have immigrated into Burma from India, and they have no converts among the indigenous races, there is nothing to be gained by showing them separately in this statement.

The number of Burmese Christians is larger than might have been expected. This is in some measure due to the inclusion of the Christian descendants of the Portuguese settlers of Syriam, deported to the old Burmese Tabayin Myo now included in the Ye-u district. These Christians, whose history and origin will be dealt with hereafter, returned themselves as Burmese, and the large number of Pwo, Sgau and Bghai (or Karenni) Karens returned as Christians is also very noticeable. Large as the proportion is, it may be anticipated to be still larger in 1901.

It will be seen that Buddhism is the religion of the vast majority of the population in Lower as well as in Upper Burma, but that in Lower Burma Buddhists form only 86·79 per cent. of the population, while in the newly acquired upper province the population rises to 96·52 per cent. of the population.

Buddhism.

45. So much has of late years been written on the subject of Buddhism that at first sight any discussion of the subject in this report would appear to be superfluous. But the Buddhism of the sacred books is not the Buddhism of the Burmese laity, and, although a detailed account of Buddhism is out of place in a census report, some explanation is necessary how far those who return themselves as Buddhists may be rightly so called.

Buddhism may be briefly described as an off-shoot from Brahmanism. It bears very much the same position to the latter creed that Christianity holds towards Judaism. It is from the purely religious point of view a reaction from the Pantheism which underlies Brahmanism, but at the same time it was a social as well as a religious movement. The yoke of a hereditary priesthood was gradually settling down on the necks of the warrior caste of India, and Buddhism was as much a political as a religious revolt against the power which the Brahmans were gradually arrogating to themselves. Buddhism acknowledges no supreme being as the ruler of the universe. Man is ultimately the master of his own destiny. Sacrifices and prayers are of themselves of no avail. It is the apotheosis of pessimism in that it teaches that life itself is not worth living. From a religious point of view Buddhism is inert and is rather a system of philosophy than a religion. The secret of the spread of its doctrines so far and wide in spite of the negative nature of its dogma is to be found in the fact that, as already stated above, it was a social as well as a religious movement. In India Buddhism spread far and fast because it was eagerly welcomed by the Kshatryas as the reinstatement of themselves in the position they formerly held. In Burma and China it was received as a welcome relief from the terrorism of Shamanism or spirit-worship. Research has shown that the earliest form of belief that prevailed in almost every country was a sort of Fetichism or deprecation of the powers of evil. The universe was ruled by good and evil spirits. The gratitude of the savage is proverbial as being the expectation of favours to come. His religion consists in attempting to avert the malevolence of evil spirits. Traces of this worship still linger even in England in the 19th century. To this Fetichism Buddhism, which is the assertion of man's independence, gave a welcome relief. This will explain why, in spite of its inert nature, Buddhism has spread so widely.

Although at the beginning of the present century before the labours of Csoma Körösi, the Hungarian, and Brian Hodgson had paved the way for future students, nothing absolutely was known of Buddhism; yet of late years so much attention has been paid by scholars to this newly discovered religion that Buddhism now has a literature of its own. It has become the latest fad in the way of fashionable religions. I do not therefore propose to attempt to describe Buddhism, its rise, its growth, and its present position. But a careful study of the numerous works cited in the beginning of this chapter will show that though there is no lack of eloquent descriptions of what the Buddhism of the sacred books is, no distinct attempt has yet been made to show what is the Buddhism professed by those in Burma who call themselves Buddhists. Merely to take census returns and say that so many millions return themselves as Buddhists would be vague if not absolutely misleading. Any one who is acquainted with the Burmese and has attempted to enquire into their customs and folklore is struck with the very vague notion which the ordinary Burman layman has about the religion he professes. This is a matter which directly affects the value of our returns, and it is on this point that further elucidation appears to be necessary.

Captain Forbes and Mr. Scott, especially the latter, in their interesting accounts of Burma, have dwelt on the superstitions and strange beliefs of the Burmans, which have no part of Buddhism in them. But I venture to think that even Mr. Scott has hardly gone far enough in pointing out how little Buddhism there really is in the religion the country-folk profess. But before venturing to put down my opinions I consulted several officers of the Commission and such well known Burman scholars as the Right Reverend Bishop Bigandet and Dr. Marks, as well as some of the leading Burmese gentlemen of Rangoon, and I have had on several occasions the privilege of discussing the points hereafter mentioned with them, and it is to them, as well as to the authors whose names I have cited, that I am indebted for anything of value that may be found in this portion of the present chapter.

46. The question whether Buddhism is merely a system of philosophy or a religion is one that is often raised. The Right Reverend Bishop Claughton says in a paper read before the Victoria Institute:

> "It must be kept in mind that Buddhism is rather a system of philosophy than a creed, and whilst it has a priesthood remarkable for their learning and the strictness of their rules of living, it does not profess to set before its followers an object of worship or encourage them to place reliance on such acts of religious observance as it permits rather than requires of them."

Such a religion, if religion it may be called, is on the face of it not one that is readily understood or obeyed by the mass of its followers, and notwithstanding the fact that Burmans are deeply attached to their religion and, as Bishop Bigandet has pointed out, are much under the influence of their religious orders, if we look into their customs and the belief which influences their conduct, we find that Buddhism pure and simple plays but a small part in their inner life. It is true that the Buddhist monks are universally held in great veneration notwithstanding the fact that they seldom interfere in political or social matters. It is true that Christianity has obtained but few converts from Buddhism. Nor is Buddhism as yet a moribund faith, for it is still attracting to it the Shamanist or Nat-worshipping Karens that have not fallen within the influences of the Christian missionaries.

But this attachment to Buddhism and veneration for the members of its religious order is due to the fact that the education of the young was almost entirely in the hands of the religious order. Moreover, the almost universal custom of sending a boy, when he attained puberty, to live in a pôngyi kyaung and to wear the yellow dress, if only for a few days, has had the effect of popularizing the religion and has created a strong sentimental attachment to the national religion throughout all those who profess its tenets. To this popularizing of Buddhism, as much as to the noble and high-minded character of the religion itself, may be traced the strong hold that Buddhism possesses over its votaries in Burma.

47. Notwithstanding all this sentimental attachment there is but very little true Buddhism to be found in the mass of superstitious beliefs which go to make up the religion of the common people. Any one who has read Shwe Yoe's account of the Burman, his life, and notions, or Captain Forbes's books on Burma, and who has studied the character of the Burmese, cannot but fail to see how little real influence Buddhism has over a Burman's life. The reason is not far to seek. As Bishop Claughton says in the passage above quoted, Buddhism is rather a system of philosophy than a creed. Such a movement as the crusades in Europe or a jihad in Arabia could never be excited by Buddhist monks. Religion, as the etymology of the word proves, means a tie or bond, but Buddhism possesses but little of this power in Burma. There is a reli ion underlying and inter-

mingled with Buddhism—a religion of Shamanism or Nat-worship—which was the creed of the people before the introduction of Buddhism. Buddhism, instead of displacing, adopted and modified this animistic worship, and the Buddhism of Burma at the present day is but a thin veneer of philosophy laid over the main structure of Shamanistic belief. In his report on the census of 1881 Mr. Copleston observes :—

"The Burmans frequently make offerings to nats, and regard the spirit-world with an awe not called for by the creed of Buddha. The belief in nats has remained underlying their thoughts and religion ever since they were converted to Buddhism, a relic of the ancient cult which is still preserved intact among the wilder Karens, Chins, and other hill races."

Mr. Copleston's view of the position of Buddhism and Nat-worship is undoubtedly correct, except that he has hardly insisted enough on the fact that the main basis of the religious feelings of the laity, and especially of the country-folk, is Nat-worship and not Buddhism. There is still going on a steady process of absorption into Buddhism of those who were formerly returned as Nat-worshippers. Buddhism is so tolerant, and the yoke of its observances presses so lightly on the laity, that we need not wonder that in spite of there being now no overt attempts to proselytize, year by year large numbers of the wild tribes are attracted into joining it. The same process is going on in India, where the aboriginal tribes are becoming Hinduised. The fact that no open attempt at proselytism is attempted by the Buddhist clergy is perhaps an inducement to the uncultured to join them. The savage looks on the missionary with suspicion. He cannot readily understand that the missionary's motives are disinterested, whereas he sees the advantage of joining such a religion as Buddhism as it raises him in the social scale. Moreover, he need not abandon his tutelary gods. It is this easy tolerance that has facilitated the spread of Buddhism. It may be taken as an axiom that the more thorough a conversion from one religion to another is, the more difficult it becomes to obtain converts. But this easy tolerance of Buddhism has led to its becoming adulterated in the process of absorption of the wilder creeds.

Sir William Hunter, in Chapter V of Volume VI of his *Imperial Gazetteer*, writes :—

"Buddhism readily coalesced with the pre-existing religions of primitive races. Thus among the hill-tribes of Eastern Bengal we see the Kyaungthas, or children of the river, passing into Buddhism without giving up their aboriginal rites. They still offer rice and fruits and flowers to the spirits of hill and stream ; and the Buddhist priests, although condemning the practice as unorthodox, do not very violently oppose it."

All this is perfectly true, but Sir William Hunter might have applied the words to the Burman himself. He does not go far enough. There are today to be found in many of the Burmese houses in Rangoon itself offerings of flowers put up to the Nat U Yin Gyi. These worshippers of U Yin Gyi go to the pagoda and they and their forefathers for generations back have been called Buddhists. There are also other Nats worshipped in Rangoon. In the house of nearly every Burman in Rangoon may be seen a cocoanut hung up as an offering to the Nat or spirit who guards his house. So soon as the milk of the cocoanut is dried up, that is to say, so soon as the spirit has drunk it up, a fresh cocoanut is hung up, and the reason given for these offerings is that, unless these cocoanuts be duly offered, the nat of the house will punish the householder by letting him or his wife fall ill. This is pure Shamanism. But it might be urged that these are mere customs which have been kept up and have not yet become unmeaning, such as our Harvest-home "cries" in Devonshire and the May-pole dance and the Jack-in-the-green of the 1st May. Such, however, cannot be the case where human sacrifices are made to appease the wrath of the spirits or to win their favour. There was an old custom that when a new capital was founded a deep pit should be dug in the foundations into which a victim was publicly cast and buried alive. His spirit became the guardian nat of the town. This nat is commonly called the မြို့စတေး (Myosade), which is a corruption of မြို့ကိုအစာကျွေးသည် (Myo go asa chwe the) which means "that which feeds the city." When Rangoon was founded by Alompra in 1755 A.D., a public sacrifice of a Talaing prince took place. The spirit of this victim, which is known as the Sule Nat Gyi, the မြို့စတေး of Rangoon, is still worshipped in Rangoon. It is but right to add that though this is the common legend, Burmese scholars trace the origin of the Sule Nat Gyi to Chula, a Hindu deity, but the fact that the Talaing prince was sacrificed is not denied. When Mandalay was founded in 1857, the late Mindôn Min, who has generally been supposed to be remarkable for his orthodoxy in religion as well as his comparative readiness to adapt himself to modern ideas, consulted, it is said, not the learned and pious amongst his Buddhist monks, but a famous fortune-teller, and in accordance with his advice a pregnant woman was slain at night in order that her spirit might become the guardian nat of the city. It is true that the greater influence that Buddhism has gained is admitted by the fact that the alleged human sacrifice is said to have been made by night. But whether this inhuman act was perpetrated or not, I have the authority of Colonel Cooke, the present Commissioner of the Northern Division, for saying that there is no doubt but that offerings of fruit and food were openly made by the king in the palace to the spirit of the dead woman, which was supposed to have taken the shape of a snake. This last point is interesting, as it connects this rite with the serpent-worship which is well known to be one of the commonest forms of animistic worship.

The village-folk are all the world over always more superstitious than the townspeople, and throughout Burma we find that in all the more important events of his life the Burman rustic still strives to appease the spirits of the unseen world. When he builds his house he offers fruits to the nats. When his son is born offerings are made to the nat of the house. When a plague breaks out offerings are made to U Yin Gyi or the local nat, whoever he may be. Though in pure Buddhist doctrine sacrifices and prayer are unavailing, the influence of this spirit-worship has made itself felt, and offerings are now made to Buddha through the monks at funerals and on any great calamity. Even among the better educated towns-folk this veneration for the nats is almost universal. They will deny worshipping these nats, and they profess to distinguish between this cult and the purer worship of Shin Gaudama. The country-folk worship the nats and Buddha alike. The nats, while they have no power to do good, have power to do evil, and must therefore be propitiated. The pôngyis alone do not join in this worship of the nats. The monks have so far yielded to this desire of the laity to make offerings, that though not permitted to possess property, they yet allow their pôngyi kyaungs to be stored up with the miscellaneous votive offerings of the laity. This Nat-worship, which underlies the Buddhism of Burma, is the religion that obtained in Burma before the advent of Buddhism. Nat-worship is nothing but a form of the spirit or devil worship which is now generally known as Shamanism or animistic religion. What this religion is, and the form it takes in Burma, is a question dealt with more fully later on.

48. Although these superstitions are not acknowledged by Burmese Buddhists to form part of their creed, there can be no possible doubt that the Buddhism of the Burmese laymen is thoroughly impregnated with the Shamanistic worship that formerly prevailed before the advent of Buddhist missionaries. A Burman would indignantly deny that he was anything but a pure Buddhist, but at the same time nearly all the real religion that he has, that is to say, those religious notions which compel him to any class of conduct, belong not to Buddhist but Shamanistic belief. It is from fear of displeasing the nats that the Burman ordinarily does one thing or refrains from doing another. Bishop Bigandet, to whose criticism the view now advanced has been submitted, has not only endorsed this opinion, but has gone even further, and I feel I cannot conclude this topic better than by quoting the opinion with which he has favoured me on the Buddhism of the Burman—

"The Buddhism of the people forms little or no part of their daily life. The hold that Buddhism has is the hold that a cold, somewhat cynical theosophical system has over the imagination and sentiments of the better educated amongst the people. This hold, and the influence the pòngyis exert, is created and strengthened by political and chiefly social ties. Every boy must go to a monastic school and wear the yellow robe. He thus becomes "free" of the faith and is early taught to look favourably on its professors, but in his everyday life, from the day of his birth to his marriage, and even when he lies on his death-bed, all the rites and forms that he observes are to be traced to animistic and not to Buddhist sources. If calamity overtakes him, he considers it to be the work of his nats, and when he wishes to commence any important undertaking, he propitiates these nats, who are the direct representatives of the old animistic worship. Even the pôngyis themselves are often directly influenced by the strong undercurrent of animistic religion which underlies their faith in Buddhism. This dual worship, which is still more clearly marked in China, is the explanation of the very slight connection between State and society on the one hand and religion on the other which is so noticeable in Burma."

Hitherto it has been the custom to preface every account of Buddhism with the statement that it numbered more adherents than any other religion in the world. The first who openly denied this was Sir Monier Williams, Boden Professor of Sanskrit, in the postscript of his work on Buddhism published in 1889. He enters his protest against this error—

"Since writing the foregoing prefatory remarks I have observed with much concern that a prevalent error, in regard to Buddhism, is still persistently propagated. It is categorically stated in a newspaper report of a quite recent lecture, that out of the world's population of about 1,500 millions, at least 500 millions are Buddhists, and that Buddhism numbers more adherents than any other religion on the surface of the globe. Almost every European writer on Buddhism, of late years, has assisted in giving currency to this utterly erroneous calculation, and it is high time that an attempt should be made to dissipate a serious misconception.

" It is forgotten that mere sympathizers with Buddhism, who occasionally conform to Buddhistic practices, are not true Buddhists. In China the great majority are first of all Confucianists, and then either Taoists, or Buddhists, or both. In Japan Confucianism and Shintoism co-exist with Buddhism. In some other Buddhist countries a kind of Shamanism is practically dominant."

49. Buddhism is divided into two schools, the northern and southern. This division is unknown to the Buddhists themselves. The Buddhists of Burma belong to the southern school and the sacred books are written, not in Sanskrit, but Pali, and were, it is acknowledged, brought from Ceylon.

The date of the introduction of Buddhism is only vaguely and indirectly mentioned in the Burmese chronicles. No direct admission is ever made that the Burmans ever had any other belief but Buddhism. The usual fanciful myths about the origin of the Burmese race are gravely recorded in the Maha Yaza Win or Royal chronicles, and the lineage even of the dynasty of Alompra is traced back to the Kshatrya princes. In Chapters VIII and X, which deal with the languages spoken and the races inhabiting Burma, the subject of the origin of the Burmese race is more fully discussed, but I may here state it is now generally admitted that the Burmans belong to that branch formerly designated Lohitic and now known as Tibeto-Burman. The labours of Brian Hodgson first cleared the ground for the proof of the undoubted connection between Burmese and Tibetan, and subsequent enquiries have shown that Burmese, Chin, Lushai, and Tibetan languages are really less dissimilar than the English of today and the English of the Song of Beowulf. The Burmese are not, as their language proves, descendants of the exile princes of Kapilavastu, and they were established in Burma even before Buddha was born. They could not then have brought Buddhism with them when they left Tibet. The Buddhists of Tibet belong to the northern school; their rites and ceremonies are widely different from Burmese Buddhism. The Sacred Buddhist Books of Burma are written in Pali, those of Tibet in Sanskrit. The question remains how then was Buddhism introduced into Burma?

The evidence that Buddhism was introduced to the Burmese direct from India through the exiles or missionaries who came through Manipur rests on the discovery of certain bricks in the ruins of Tagaung, which is said to have been the seat of the Indo-Burmese dynasty. These bricks are said to bear the effigy of Buddha and Pali inscriptions such as were found at Gaya in Bengal. Owing to the death of Dr. Forchhammer, who was engaged in the archæological survey of the ruins of Burma, no authoritative decision regarding these inscriptions has yet been published. It is asserted that Buddhist missionaries came from India to Burma in Asoka's times, but no proof of the assertion is forthcoming. We have of course the statements of the Maha Yaza Win above mentioned, but no more weight should be attached to the credibility of these chronicles than to the flattering poems of the Augustan poets, who were wont to trace the lineage of Cæsar back through Æneas to Venus herself. On the other hand, there is proof positive to show that the Buddhism of Burma, belonging as it does to the Southern or Ceylon school, was first brought over by missionaries to the Talaings of Thatôn in B. C. 241, and that thence the missionaries worked their way northwards into

Burma and eastwards into Siam and the Shan States. Not only have we the Talaing legends, but we have the acknowledged fact that in the 5th century, according to Rhys Davids, Buddha Ghôsa brought over the Buddhist Scriptures to Thatôn. Buddha Ghôsa was, according to Bishop Bigandet, a Pônna or Brahman of Thatôn. He sailed to Ceylon about the year 400 A.D. He there transcribed the scriptures and then brought them back with him to Thatôn. At this time Kyaung Dayit was reigning at Pagan, and it is stated that scriptures or copies of them were brought to him. At any rate it is an acknowledged fact that nearly 600 years after this date Anôrahtâ, King of Pagan, made war on Thatôn for the possession of these scriptures, and, conquering the town, he took the sacred books away with him. The courtly Burmese historians conveniently forgot that Buddhism was probably introduced along with its sacred books, but they incidentally mention the existence of Naga or serpent-worship, which in Syria, as well as in China, was one of the earliest known forms of animistic worship. Any reference to Buddha Ghôsa would be incomplete that did not mention the interesting monograph on the legend regarding Buddha Ghôsa, the St. Chrysostom of the Buddhists, by the Reverend. T. Foulkes which appeared in the *Indian Antiquary* of April 1890. Mr. Foulkes has analysed and compared the Burmese and Ceylonese legends. He finds that there are so many variations in these legends, and that they are so contradictory, that until a fuller acquaintance with the whole range of literature of Buddhism has been obtained, the time has not yet arrived when any final solution of the Buddha Ghôsa paradoxes can be properly attempted. "It may be," says Mr. Foulkes, "that the personality of the legendary Buddha Ghôsa "is destined to recede from view, gradually dissolving before new facts and "under the increasing light of the new criticism. It may be that the name of "Buddha Ghôsa, when it had once become famous, was attached as a matter of "literary policy to the works which had hitherto been regarded as his own com- "position." The very name Buddha Ghôsa, or the voice of Buddha, may explain how the myth, if myth it be, has been originated. Mr. Taw Sein Ko, who is engaged in editing Dr. Forchhammer's Archæological Notes, takes a very strong view as to the introduction of Buddhism amongst the Burmans being very recent. He says in a note not yet published—

"Tradition relates that after the Third Council, Moggaliputta, its president, sent missionaries to various countries to propagate the Buddhist religion, and that he sent the Theras Sona (Thawna) and Uttara (Ôktaya) to Suvannabhumi (Thuwunnabônmi Thatôn). From 244 B.C. to 450 A.D. is a long period, and it seems strange that it was only in the latter year a complete set of the Buddhist scriptures was brought to Burma by Buddha Ghôsa, a Brahman from Buddha Gaya, who translated the whole of the Buddhist canon from Sinhalese into Pali, and who wrote the celebrated works the Visuddhimagga and the Atthasalini. The advent of Buddha Ghôsa marks an important era in the history of Buddhism in Burma, as it gave an impetus to the study of the Buddhist scriptures and to the propagation of the religion itself in the Talaing Kingdoms of Kuthein (now changed to Putheen or Bassein), Hanthawaddy, and Môktama (probably Martaban). Buddhism, however, was not established in the upper valley of the Irrawaddy till 1058 A.D., when Nawratazau, King of Pagan, conquered Thatôn and carried away with him, among other spoils and captives of war, 32 elephant-loads of the Buddhist scriptures and 1,000 monks.

"In the latter part of the 12th century a brisk intercourse was maintained between Ceylon and Burma. Burmese monks went over to Ceylon to study Buddhism, and Sinhalese monks, imbued with missionary zeal, accompanied their brethren to Burma and took up their residence at Pagan. Owing to the difference of the teachings of the Sinhalese monks from those of their Burmese brethren, a number of sects sprang up for the first time on Burmese soil.

"When Ava became the capital of Burma in 1364 A.D., Buddhism found its seat there and continued to be the recognized religion of the people."

Orthodox Burmese Buddhists deny that Buddha Ghôsa translated the whole of the canon, and assert he translated only the Attagatas, Atthakathâ or Commentaries. The weight of evidence, however, is strongly in favour of the view that whether Buddha Ghôsa ever existed or not, Buddhism is of comparatively recent introduction into Burma, and that it was introduced by missionaries from Ceylon amongst the Talaings, and from them gradually spread over to the valley of the Upper Irrawaddy, but that until Thatôn was conquered by Nawratazau (or Anôrahtâ), the Buddhism of the Burmese was of doubtful orthodoxy.

50. If further proof of this were wanting, it might be found in the fact that between the Buddhists of Burma and Tibet lie the nat-worshipping Lushai and Naga tribes, amongst whom there are no traces to be found of any previous knowledge of the Buddhist faith. The possibility of the relapse to the lower form of spirit or Fetich worship from the enlightened religion of Buddhism is disproven not only by the still continued advance of Buddhism among the nat-worshipping Karens, Chins, and Shans, but by the fact that such a relapse is contrary to the generally accepted theory of the gradual evolution of revealed religion, such as Buddhism, from the Fetichism of the older spirit-worship. If Buddhism came through Manipur and the Naga Hills, or if the Burmans were Buddhists when they came to Burma, we should expect to find traces not only of Buddhist relics, but of Buddhist customs on the track by which Buddhism came into Burma.

This comparatively recent introduction of Buddhism will partly account for the mass of the superstitions and beliefs of the laity being still Animistic. But the main reason why Buddhism in taking root in Burma has not entirely displaced the religion it found flourishing here before its arrival is to be found in the well-known tolerance of Buddhism itself. Buddhism, like the Latitudinarianism of the present day, is almost wide enough to include an honest disavowal of itself. The tares of animistic worship have been allowed to grow up with the wheat. This duality of religion is strongly marked in China, and we even find it in the Hinduism of the present day. Major Temple says:

"This dual form of religion is equally strong in India, but in the converse form. There the superstitions and the rites are due to Brahmanical teaching and the profession of faith is due to the mediæval-reformers Kabir, Nanak, Ramananda, and others. Nor is this phenomenon unknown in Europe at the present time. The Buddhism of Burma, as understood by the laity, may be well compared to the Christianity of the Russian Moujik. In both of these countries the imported civilized religion has not yet succeeded in completely ousting the uncivilized Shamanism that preceded it."

51. Buddhist tolerance is proven by the fact that there are in Burma no Buddhist sects such as we find both in the Christian and Mahomedan religions. Schisms there are and have been since the foundation of Buddhism by Gaudama. It would appear that even during his lifetime attempts were made by his disciples to evade the rigid observance of the rules imposed on them, but these attempts were mainly directed against rules and rubrics rather than against dogmas. It was to prevent the spread of dissent that the three Buddhist councils were held in Northern India to settle the canon of the so-called Southern Church, namely, in 543 B.C., 443 B.C., and 244 B.C. But though there are no sects amongst the Buddhists in the sense that the word sect is now used, and all worship alike at the same shrines, there are two schools or main divisions amongst the Buddhists of Burma. These two divisions bear different names in different parts of Burma, but they are practically the same. In Rangoon they are called Sulagandi and Mahagandi, that is to say, the school of the Short and of the Great Exposition. In Bassein the Sulagandis are called Dwaya and the Mahagandis Kan. In Shwegyin and Mandalay they are known by the names Thudama-gaing and Shwegyin-gaing, and in Toungoo by the names of Shwenyandaw and Khanda. How little these differences affect the outer life of the people may be inferred from the fact that the late King Mindôn Min, at the last Convocation, took the side of the Shwegyin or Kan school and his chief Queen that of the Thudama or Dwaya, but no serious quarrel or public scandal ensued.

The difference of the two schools is in doctrine as well as in vestments, and they correspond in some way to the High and Low Church parties in the Anglican Church. The Sulagandis or Dwayas correspond to the High Church in being more careful of their ritual and more strict in the observance of the rules of their religious order. In doctrine the difference is that the Dwayas hold that all knowledge of the external world is conveyed by consciousness through the organs of sense, and that a sentient being is endowed with free will in accepting such knowledge. The meaning of the word Dwaya is literally "hole" or metaphorically "organ;" hence dwaya in this connection denotes on the "means" by which an act of worship is performed, and this connotes the volition of the worshipper. The doctrine of the Kan school is that there is no free will, but that everything is brought about by Karma, which may be taken to mean the influence caused by good or ill doing in previous states of existence, and which is manifested in determining the conditions of one's present life. The Kan school teaches that Karma (or, as the Burmans write it, Kamma) is created by any good act we may perform, whatever be the intent of the doer; the Dwaya school that the virtue of the good deed depends on the intent of the doer. To carry out the parallel before mentioned between the Buddhist religion and the Christian church, the Dwaya school would correspond to the followers of Tertullian and the Kan to those of St. Augustine.

Religious fervour on abstruse points of doctrine is not to be expected. It is true that in past times, in the reign of Bodawpaya, the rival schools of the "Tôngaing" and "Yôngaing," which corresponded to some extent with the Dwaya and Kan of the present time, discussed their variances in public convocation before the king. The end of the conference, though dramatic, was not attended with bloodshed. The king espoused the cause of the Yôngaing and ordered the leader of the opposite school to be disfrocked and to be publicly drummed out of the church. Serious bickerings regarding these opposing doctrines are almost unknown. Any quarrel between the schools is generally originated by some difficulty regarding the disposal of church property. The Sulagandi Kyaungtaga (a term that corresponds to our churchwarden) objects to his pôngyi being succeeded by a follower of the Mahagandi school. The villagers sometimes take sides and ill-feeling and quarrelling ensue. But so little do the laity care for these things that it would puzzle most ordinary Buddhist laymen to say whether the present Thathanabaing, the head of the Buddhist faith, belonged to the Sulagandi or Mahagandi party. As before related, Mindôn Min and his chief Queen took different sides on this question, but the king recognized his consort's right to freedom of conscience in religious matters and they agreed to differ. It necessarily follows that any attempt to enumerate the followers of these parties would have been futile. The only purpose such an enumeration could serve would be to accentuate a division which at present is only lightly regarded by the laity.

52. Buddhism, in spite of the efforts of the missionaries, still continues to be the religion of the great mass, not only of the Burmans, but of their kindred races. The form which Buddhism has assumed in Burma, or rather the form to which the intermixture of spirit-worship on the one hand and the natural characteristics of the people themselves on the other have reduced the pure Buddhism of the sacred books, admirably suits the temperament of the Burmans. Its tolerance agrees with their easy-going good nature, its doctrine of Karma with the fatalism which they share with other Eastern races, and the absence of a supreme deity—which is the peculiar feature of Buddhism—makes it none the less acceptable to a race whose previous spirit-worship supplies a ready-made divine "machinery" of nats, which Buddhism with characteristic tolerance has accepted wholesale. In Upper and Lower Burma 6,888,075 persons are returned as Buddhists. In other words, out of every 10,000 persons in Burma we find that 9,056 persons belong to this religion. In Upper Burma the proportion is still greater, as of every 10,000 persons enumerated 9,652 were put down as Buddhists. In Lower Burma the proportion is not so great, as only 8,679 out of every 10,000 are returned as belonging to this creed. This is due, not to the conversion of Buddhists, but to the presence of a much larger number of Hindus, Musalmans, and Christians. In 1872 there were 2,447,831 returned as Buddhists out of the total population, which was given as 2,747,148; in other words, out of every 10,000 persons 8,910 were Buddhists. The subjoined table exhibits the proportion of Buddhists to the total population in the various divisions in 1872, 1881, and 1891:—

Number of persons returned as Buddhists per 10,000 of the total population of divisions.

Division.	1872.	1881.	1891.
Arakan	7,515	7,189	7,035
Pegu	9,362 (Pegu and Irrawaddy)	9,171 (Pegu and Irrawaddy)	8,876
Irrawaddy			9,366
Tenasserim	8,787	8,457	8,429
Northern	...	...	9,177
Central	...	...	9,858
Southern	...	...	9,816
Eastern	...	...	9,644

Everywhere, except in the Irrawaddy division, the proportionate strength of those professing Buddhism to the total population shows a slight decline. This is due not to a defection from the number of Buddhists, but to the increase of the non-Buddhist population by immigration of Hindus and Musalmans from India and Chinamen from the Straits, for the orthodox Burman Buddhist refuses to confuse the Taoist Chinamen with those who profess the Buddhist faith.

53. There were in the whole of Burma 15,371 monasteries or one to every 93·08 houses, or to every 1·87 village or town. Of these 15,371 monasteries, by far the greater number were in Upper Burma. There were 10,488 monasteries, or nearly one for every town and village in the upper province, and every 53·55 houses on an average had a monastery to themselves. In Lower Burma there were only 4,883 monasteries, so that on an average 3·64 towns and villages and 177·99 houses shared a monastery between them. In Lower Burma in 1881 there were 4,279 monasteries or one to every 158 houses or 3·7 villages and towns. It is clear therefore that Lower Burma has not suddenly become irreligious as compared with the upper province. The real cause of the difference lies deeper.

After the war in 1854, when Lower Burma was annexed, not only the monks but the country people fled, or in some cases were driven by their ywathugyis to Upper Burma, where their king still reigned. Contemporary reports speak of the depopulation of the lower province. Many of the pôngyis who had not fled naturally followed their kyaungtagas or supporters on whose alms they lived. Hence many of the existing monasteries fell quickly into disrepair. By degrees the country people came back, and with them, but more slowly, have come back some of the clergy. But in the meanwhile the monasteries being built of wood had fallen into ruin and have had to be rebuilt. This will account for there being so few in Lower Burma. The reason why there are so many in Upper Burma in proportion to the number of Buddhist population is not to be directly traced to the superior sanctity and orthodoxy of the up-country Burman. As most of our European cathedrals were built in the dark cruel times of the middle ages often by men who to balance a life of crime died leaving their estates "in mort main" to the church, so in the same way many a fine monastery in Upper Burma is the expiation of the crimes of a successful dacoit who, living on unpunished, has become respectable when he grew older. In Lower Burma the Indian Penal Code knows no sympathy for the repentant sinner, and the successful dacoit preferred to retire with his hard-earned gains to the upper province where he could live in peace. Again, many of the fine monasteries were founded either by princes of the blood royal or rich officials. There was not the same temptation in Upper Burma to lay up treasures which only exposed the possessor to extortion. Hence we have ample explanation for the difference in the number of religious buildings in Upper and Lower Burma without charging the Buddhists of the lower province with either illiberality or decay of their religious beliefs. It is alleged that the monks of Lower Burma are more ignorant than those in Upper Burma, and hence there are fewer monasteries founded for them; but it must be remembered that till lately a clever lad had not the same temptation to leave the kyaung "to become a man" in Upper as in Lower Burma, and hence the deterioration in the pôngyis of the lower province. That there has yet been no outward sign of the decay of Buddhism and of its hold on the people of the lower province we have the fact that the number of monasteries built and inhabited in the lower province are practically just as numerous in proportion to the number of Buddhists as they were in 1881.

54. As regards those who are entered in the schedules as belonging to the religious orders, we find from the Occupation returns that there were 13,613 pôngyis or monks, 6,668 upazins or probationers, and 13,571 koyins or acolytes in Lower Burma in 1891. No attempt was made to distinguish between Christian and Buddhist clergy in 1872, but in 1881 there were 6,498 pôngyis, 626 upazins, and 1,386 koyins. It will be seen that the increase since 1881 is very marked, there being 6,115 more pôngyis, 6,042 more upazins, and 12,185 more koyins. Comparing these returns with the returns of the male population, we find that in 1881 out of every 10,000 males 32 were pôngyis, 3 upazins, and 6 koyins, whereas in 1891 the proportions had risen to 55 pôngyis, 27 upazins, and 55 koyins. Mr.

Copleston remarked that in 1881 the number of upazins and koyins was no doubt understated. It is probable that the number of pôngyis was also understated, but even if we allow for some omissions in 1881, the census returns of 1891 certainly do not show that the popularity of the Great Religious Order has suffered any loss in the past, or, if we consider the immense increase in the number of koyins, is there any reason to apprehend any probable loss in the immediate future.

55. Between 1872 and 1881 the number of Buddhists in Lower Burma increased at the rate of 32·8 per cent., that is to say, about 3·12 less quickly than the rate of growth of the total population. Between 1881 and 1891 the increase was at the rate of 24·35 per cent., which is almost as great as the rate of growth of the whole population and greater than the rate of increase of the Burmese and Talaings. Accordingly, although the proportion of Buddhists to the gross population is slightly less, the falling off is evidently not due to any serious defection of the votaries of this religion in Burma. Buddhism, it is true, received a shock when the King of Ava, the temporal head of the religion, was captured and his kingdom annexed, but the wise abstention of most of the pôngyis from taking any actively adverse action against the British has fully justified the liberality and tolerance which the British Government from the first extended to Buddhism. From the doctrine they profess the Buddhist monks are bound to abstain from mundane affairs. Their self-respect, which stands out in such bright contrast to the quaint behaviour of Musalman faqirs and Hindu priests, has generally kept them from secret intrigues. The present Director of Public Instruction in Burma, Mr. Pope,—whose previous service in the Educational Department has been entirely spent in India, and who therefore is well able to contrast the religious orders of Burma and India, with both of which he has been brought into close contact,—speaks in the highest terms of the Burmese monastic orders. His work has thrown him into close contact with the pôngyis, and I shall have to refer to his remarks on them as an educational instrument in connection with Chapter VII, which deals with the education of the people; but with regard to the religious character of the pôngyis, his remarks are worthy of quotation here—

> "The Burman pôngyi is generally a gentleman who lives an honest, cleanly life, and tries to do his duty according to his lights. The pôngyi in Burma earns respect; the priest in India claims it. The pôngyi is a factor for good; the Indian priest decidedly a factor for evil."

In their hearts no doubt all Buddhists have deplored the loss of their king, the head of their religion, and in secret their sympathy was no doubt with his fallen fortunes, but most District Officers who have served in Upper as well as in Lower Burma will bear willing testimony of the fidelity of the Buddhist monks in general to their tenet of non-interference. Although there is little or no fanaticism in Buddhism such as would induce men to fling themselves on the bayonets of a British square, there is, as we have already seen, a strong leaven of old Shamanist superstitions, which readily induces the Burman to accept any wild tales of the power of certain medicine-men to make them invulnerable; so that had Buddhist monks consented to pervert the doctrines of the faith they profess, they would no doubt have easily worked on the credulity of the people. When the history of Buddhism in Burma is written, credit will be given to the religious orders for the self-restraint they showed in not playing on this credulity. It is true that there are a few well-known cases of so-called pôngyis not only exciting but taking an active part in the rebellions in the Shwegyin and Minbu districts, but in all of these cases these men were considered by all orthodox Buddhists to have renounced their vows as soon as they took any active part in the rising. Buddhism in Burma is not moribund. A new school is being formed amongst the monks with wider views and greater readiness to accept Western progress. It is true that the pôngyis themselves complain of the laxity and neglect of the laity, but the Buddhist monks are not the only clergy that raises its voice in this way. So long as the pôngyis fulfil the self-appointed task of keeping up schools for the young, so long will their influence last. The spirit of Buddhism, which ignores all claims of high birth, is much more in consonance with modern ideas than Hinduism, that would stereotype the human race for ever. Accordingly, notwithstanding the shock Buddhism sustained in the annexation of the upper province, and in spite of the spread of education and Western ideas amongst the people, there is every reason to believe that the next census will show that, though the proportion of Buddhist to the total population will most certainly have been reduced by the influx of Hindus and Musalmans from India, yet the rate of increase in its number will keep pace with the growth of the Burman and Talaing race.

56. It is but fair to state that this view of the Buddhism of the people of Burma, put forward in this chapter, is not the view entertained by most of the Burmans themselves. One of the leading Burmese scholars, and one of the most enlightened Buddhists in Rangoon, U Po Hmyin, has favoured me with his view of the case.

Buddhism is not pessimism ; life—that is to say a pure life—is worth living of itself, but Buddhism teaches that the truth is that nothing is permanent. Knowledge of the truth is the purest happiness. Buddhism is not inert. It is the most active religion. It is a religion inasmuch as it teaches piety, sanctity, and inculcates a high sense of moral obligation and a spirit of reverence to Buddha, Dhama (the law), and Sanga (the congregation or assembly). Buddhism is not a negative, but a positive religious system. The mistake of looking on it as a purely philosophical system is due to Western scholars taking the Abidhama, which was a metaphysical treatise, as a religious discourse. Although it is not denied that the pre-existing animistic worship has coloured the religious life and folklore of the people, Burmans do not worship nats. Old women all over the world cling to by-gone superstitions, and Maung Po Hmyin might, had he so chosen, have compared these relics of nat-worship to the belief in witchcraft, which is scarcely yet extinct in Europe. It is asserted that Buddhism was introduced into Burma long before the date of the conquest of Thatôn by Nawratazau. I have inserted these opinions as they are, I believe, generally held by the Burmans themselves. No doubt orthodox Buddhists and patriotic Burmans would look on the views advanced regarding the character and quality of the Buddhism of country-folk with as much horror as was felt when the ancient rites and customs formerly held to be significant of the holy days of the Christian Church were first asserted to be relics of animistic worship, which preceded Christianity in Europe. The Yule log and Christmas tree are still so generally regarded as part and parcel of the Christmas festival, that to trace their origin, though this cannot now be denied, to Pagan customs, would seem a sacrilege. Without therefore the slightest intent to hurt the religious feelings of the Burmans, and despite the views held by those who would vindicate the claims of the laity to be considered pure Buddhists, it is impossible to overlook the fact that the religion of the great mass of the Burmese country-folk is but little removed from animistic worship.

Nat-worship or Animistic Religion.

57. Nat-worship, or the worship of the spirits who control the material world, was the general belief of the people before their conversion to Buddhism. Of late years attention has been drawn to the existence of various customs, most of which have lost their meaning and which are now dying out in Europe. A comparison of these customs and the collection of the folklore of various races living far apart, and who have had for generations no communication with one another, has brought to light the fact that in nearly every country the original religion or cult of the people was a " deprecation of the powers of evil " rather than the worship of the spirit of Good or " God." Good and God are but different forms of the same word. This fetichism or devil-worship took various shapes according to the temperament of its worshippers, but it has some points in common, and perhaps the strangest of this is the creation of a spirit by the slaughter of a victim. Mr. Frazer, who has recently published a most interesting work, " The Golden Bough," on the subject of spirit-worship, has drawn attention to this paradoxical rite. He has, however, made the rite even more paradoxical than it really is by taking it for granted that the victim was always treated as a god before he was made a spirit by slaying him. He points to the various ceremonies that attended the sacrifice. The Burmese custom of creating guardian nats or demons by inhumanly burying a victim alive when laying the foundations of a town was

apparently not known to him. The real idea which underlies the slaughter of a victim was not the slaughter of a God, but the creation of a spirit of evil stronger and therefore better able to keep away other evil spirits. So long as this spirit of evil is appeased, so long are they protected by him. Votive offerings then may be called the blackmail paid to the power of evil. The deification of this power of evil and the sanctification of the victim destined to furnish him were ideas subsequently evolved and did not form, *pace* Mr. Frazer, any part of motion that underlay the original ceremony. In Burma, as already stated, we find that the Buddhism of the country is deeply tinged with animistic worship, which is alien to it. There are, however, a large number of persons who are still Nat-worshippers pure and simple, and in dealing with their returns some explanation of the term Nat-worship is necessary. Nat-worship in Burma is a decaying and despised religion. It is gradually yielding to Buddhism, but the conquest has not been effected without loss to the purity of the faith of the conquering religion. There is no connected theogony in Nat-worship. To enter into a description of its rites, and even to enumerate the names of its chief or most popular deities, would be out of place in a census report. That the religion is still living any one who has had any intercourse with the wild hill tribes could easily assert. It is even stated by the Burman that human sacrifice is not yet unknown amongst the Red Karens and wild Chins and Kadus.

Some of these nats worshipped by the Nat-worshippers are also worshipped by Buddhists. In the delta of the Irrawaddy the Nat U Yin Gyi, whose legend in some respects resembles the legend of Narcissus, is the common object of worship of Buddhists and Nat-worshippers alike. In the towns this Nat-worship is despised by the educated, but among the country-folk, even amongst Buddhists, U Yin Gyi is the popular object of worship. In the towns this Nat-worship takes sometimes the form of ancestor worship. The origin of the worship of the Eng Saung Nat (အိမ်စောင့်နတ်) or Min Ma Gayi (မင်မာဂရိ) is said to be derived from a corruption of the Pali words meaning that "mother and father are a rock of deliverance," and therefore, if this be true, this form of Nat-worship is allied to the ancestor worship of the Chinese. In fact what is known as Nat-worship in Burma is better known by the name of animistic religion or Shamanism.

Shamanism.

58. The term Shamanism is said to be derived from the Chinese "Shaman," which is the Sanskrit S'ramana in a Chinese form. S'ramana means "one in whom all passions have been calmed." Another and more plausible derivation is given by Yule, who, following Schmidt, derives it from a Tungusic word "Shaman," which means a wizard. The difference between Shamanism and Taoism is very slight. Taoism, the belief of the great majority of the Chinese nation, is the worship of the powers of nature and of ancestors. It is the basis of all Chinese beliefs, on to which Buddhism and Confucianism have been grafted. Nat-worship has in Burma no regular priesthood, but necromancers and soothsayers for their own ends profess power to cope with the spirits of evil. As we have seen before, even Buddhists perform its rites in addition to the requirements of the Buddhist creed. There is no settled ritual, for each tribe has its own ceremonies and each clan possesses its own Nat. Animistic worship was undoubtedly, if not the most ancient, at least the prevailing religion all the world over. In Syria it was the worship of Baal and Astarte, in Egypt of Isis and Osiris. In Bengal it still exists and human sacrifices were made up till comparatively recent times by the wild tribes of the Santal Pergunas. The religion of the Aztecs in Mexico probably belonged to this class of creeds. In Burma it is gradually losing ground, and in a few years will nominally become extinct. Allusions to the Nat-worship of the Kachins and Chins will be found in the interesting monographs written by Mr. E. C. S. George and Mr. Houghton for this report and which will be found in Chapter X.

No systematic attempt has as yet been made to collate the relics of this once prevalent worship and to compare the rites and customs of the various animistic tribes of Burma with one another. Such an attempt would be out of place here. Enough has been already said to show what is meant by the term Nat-worship and the hold it once possessed over the whole country. If further proof were wanted of this fact, it is to be found in the numerous cairns which travellers in the wild tracts of the province often come across. On these cairns of stones may be seen votive offerings to the nats. These cairns or natsingôns (နတ်စင်ကုံ) correspond to the hill altars or "high places" of the spirits which are found all the world over wherever animistic or spirit-worship has prevailed. It is more than probable that the Buddhist missionaries, when converting the inhabitants to Buddhism, utilized these sites for the foundation of their pagodas. Legends regarding the miraculous foundation of the Shwe Dagôn by the merchants Taphussa and Bhallika may be resolved into old legends of the spirit-worship which were modified and adopted by the original Buddhist missionaries. That this is no mere idle surmise may be gathered from the fact that Bishop Bigandet himself is inclined to believe it to be true.

59. In the whole of Burma, out of every 10,000 persons 221 returned themselves as Nat-worshippers. Owing to the fact that but few Karens, who form the bulk of those who return Nat-worship as their religion, are to be found in the upper province, the proportion is greater in Lower Burma, and out of every 10,000, 320 are Nat-worshippers.

The following table will give the distribution by the administrative divisions of Nat-worshippers shown in the ratio they bear to every 10,000 persons enumerated. The returns of Lower Burma for 1872 and 1881 are also added for the sake of comparison.

Division.	1872.	1881.	1891.
Arakan	1,087	821	902
Pegu	188	193	90
Irrawaddy			130
Tenasserim	443	620	564
Northern	...	...	96
Central	...	...	16
Southern	...	...	90
Eastern	...	...	41

There were in 1872 110,514 Nat-worshippers in Lower Burma, but under this head were included unspecified religions, such as Brahmos, Jains, Jews, and Parsis. These latter were probably not numerous, as even in 1881 they only in the aggregate amounted to 329 persons. In 1881 143,581 were returned as Nat-worshippers, an increase of 30·2 per cent. This increase in the face of the decrease of 10,000 or 33 per cent. in Akyab and 9,400 or about 60 per cent. in Prome, due to absorption of Nat-worshipping communities into the Buddhist religion, is due to the better enumeration of the Karens on the occasion of the census of 1881. The Karens in Lower Burma owed their increase to natural causes, and their numbers are not to any appreciable extent recruited by immigration, hence an increase of 56·2 per cent. in the 8½ years preceding the census of 1881 could only mean that, as was well known at the time, large numbers of Karens escaped enumeration in 1872. At that time a much larger proportion of the Karens were Nat-worshippers, and consequently there can be no doubt but that the number of Nat-worshippers is understated in the 1872 returns, hence the increase of 30·2 per cent. is much in excess of what the true return should be. In 1891 the number of Nat-worshippers had increased to 149,021, an increase of only 3·78 per cent., although in the meantime the Karens had increased by 21·706 per cent., the Chins by 25·09, the other Hill tribes by 15·95 per cent., the Shans by 57·77 per cent., and the Chinese by 139·77 per cent. It is amongst these races that those returned as Nat-worshippers are found. Although the increase between 1872 and 1881 is overstated, yet the great falling off in the rate of increase of Nat-worshippers in the last intercensal period calls for some further explanation. A careful examination of the schedules has shown that the enumeration is not to blame. The explanation is to be found in the fact that both Buddhism and Christianity have increased at the expense of Nat-worship. Buddhists have increased at the rate of 24·35 per cent., which is almost exactly the same rate as the growth of the gross population of the province, notwithstanding the fact that there were included with the latter more than 50,000 Hindu and Musalman immigrants in excess of the returns of 1881. The normal rate of increase from natural causes even in Burma, where the checks on reproduction are unusually slight, would not ordinarily exceed 21 or 22 per cent., hence the increase in Buddhists is due either to immigration from Upper Burma or to the conversion of Nat-worshippers into Buddhists. It is probable that both these causes had been in operation. The decrease in the return of Nat-worshippers in the Prome and Akyab districts between 1872 and 1881 is accounted for by Mr. Copleston by supposing that they were included in the return of Buddhists. He says—

"It is certain that these decreases are due to the fact which has been already mentioned, namely, the tendency of Nat-worshippers to call themselves Buddhists, and not to a real falling off in the races forming this religious class."

This tendency of the older and less civilized religion of animistic or nat-worship to be absorbed into newer and loftier creeds is traceable not only in Burma but in India.

In the passage from Sir William Hunter's Gazetteer already quoted on page 60 the tendency of Buddhism to coalesce with the pre-existing religions of primitive races has already been noted. Elsewhere in his chapter on the non-Aryan races of India Sir William Hunter says—

"A Hinduizing process is going on both among the aboriginal low castes in Hindu provinces and among the aboriginal tribes who border on such provinces. That the disappearance of the Indian aborigines is apparent and not real can be proved. The birth-rate among some of the aboriginal tribes is unusually high, and with exceptions the aboriginal tribes and castes are numerically increasing, although they are practically merging their separate identity in the Hindu community."

The same process is going on in Burma, and as communications are improved and the wild tribes become tame, the number of those who return themselves as Nat-worshippers will decrease. They will still remain Nat-worshippers, but will call themselves Buddhists, because they have sometimes attended pagoda festivals and conform outwardly to Buddhist rites. Every thing points therefore to an actual decrease in the number of Nat-worshippers in Lower Burma in the returns of the next census of 1901.

Mahomedanism.

60. Buddhism being the religion returned by far the greater part of the population, was dealt with first. Nat-worship, although not so strong in the number of its followers as some of the others, was taken up next, as it was the primitive religion of the people of the country. It now remains to examine the return of the religions which are of comparatively recent introduction. Of these, Mahomedanism in point of numbers is the most important.

In 1872 there were in Lower Burma 99,846 Musalmans, so that out of every 10,000 of the inhabitants 364 were found to profess this creed.

In 1881 the number of Musalmans in Lower Burma had risen to 168,881, and 451·9 out of every 10,000 inhabitants were returned as Musalmans. In 1891 the number of Musalmans in Lower Burma was 210,649, so that out of every 10,000 persons almost exactly the same number, 452, are given as belonging to this creed as was found to be the case in 1881. This of course naturally follows the fact that the number of Musalmans in 1881 has increased *pari passu* with the growth of the total population, that is to say, while Musalmans have increased at the rate of 24·73 per cent., the gross population of Lower Burma has grown at the rate of 24·67 per cent.

The following table gives the number of Musalmans out of every 10,000 of the population in the eight divisions of Burma, and in the case of the lower province the returns of 1872 and 1881 are added for the sake of comparison :—

Division.	1872.	1881.	1891.
Arakan	1,328	1,809	1,884
Pegu	} 111	162	{ 280 } 181
Irrawaddy			{ 89 }
Tenasserim	283	300	301
Total Lower Burma ...	**364**	**451·9**	**452**
Northern	...	...	370
Central	...	...	44
Southern	...	...	36
Eastern	...	...	210
Total Upper Burma ...	...	..	**143**
TOTAL BURMA ...	...	...	**332**

The only part of Lower Burma in which we find that the number of Mahomedans is increasing at a greater rate than the total population is the Arakan and Pegu Divisions. This is due to the influx of Chittagongian and Indian coolies, who every year in gradually increasing numbers flock down to work at the rice-mills in Akyab and Rangoon. Most of the men return home every year. The vast increase between 1872 and 1881 is simply due to the fact that the enumeration in 1872 was taken during the rains after the coolies had returned home, and in 1881 and 1891 in the height of the milling season. Hence the increase between 1881 and 1891 is comparatively speaking slight, though it has kept pace with the growth of the population.

Hinduism.

61. Next to Mahomedanism in the number of its votaries amongst those enumerated at the last census comes Hinduism. They now outnumber the Nat-worshippers. In 1872 there were only 36,658 Hindus returned. In 1881 they amounted to 88,177, an in crease at the rate of 140 per cent. In 1891 their numbers had risen to 171,577, of whom 142,522 lived in Lower Burma, being an increase of 61 per cent. Hinduism, unlike Mahomedanism, is an exotic religion and has taken no hold on the people of the country. The Mahomedans have to some extent intermarried with the Burmans, and their descendants, known by the name Zerbadis, are becoming a recognizable portion of the inhabitants of Burma; but Hinduism is still exotic and shows no signs of becoming a part of the religious life of the settled as opposed to the temporary inhabitants of the soil. The vast increase in the numbers in the intercensal period between the enumeration of 1872 and 1881 is due, as Mr. Copleston pointed out, to the fact that the former census was taken in August, when our "rice-milling" season is over, and the latter when our cooly barracks are swarming with the mill-hands who flock every year to Burma to earn money and to return. The following table exhibits the distribution of Hindus amongst the divisions of Burma out of every 10,000 of the total population of each division. The returns of 1872 and 1881 for Lower Burma are added for the sake of comparison.

Divisions.	1872.	1881.	1891.
Arakan	62	160	157
Pegu	} 114	239	{ 573 } 329
Irrawaddy			{ 101 }
Tenasserim	245	280	334
Total Lower Burma ...	**133**	**236**	**306**
Northern	...	...	263
Central	...	...	50
Southern	...	...	44
Eastern	...	...	71
Total Upper Burma ...	...	...	**98**
TOTAL BURMA ...	...	...	**225**

Very few Hindus ever settle down in the rural tracts and take to cultivating the soil for themselves. Those that do settle down very often become Burmanized and adopt Burman names, and no longer remain Hindus in the strict sense of the term. The Hindus as a rule prefer to stay in the chief towns. In Rangoon there were 57,845 Hindus, being more than one-third of the total number who returned themselves as Hindus in Burma. In 1872 there were only 14,108 Hindus in Rangoon, of whom a great part were found in the Native Infantry regiments. In 1881, owing no doubt, as the report of 1881 states, "to the taking of the census at a time when Madrassi coolies are especially numerous," their numbers had risen to 35,871; of these 6,026 or only 16 per cent. were women.

Christianity.

62. Next in point of numbers come the various Christian sects, which in the aggregate include amongst their followers 120,768 of the total population of Burma; of these 92 per cent. are in the lower province. Before considering the return of sects of Christianity in detail, it will be interesting to compare the strength of the Christian religion in the various provinces of India. The annexed table will show the ratio per 10,000 of the population and the total number of Christians in Burma compared with the returns of the other provinces of India in 1881 and of Madras and Assam in 1891. The returns of the other provinces for 1891 are not yet available.

Province.	1881.		1891.	
	Total number of Christians.	Ratio per 10,000 of the total population.	Total number of Christians.	Ratio per 10,000 of the total population.
Lower Burma	84,219	225	111,982	240
Upper Burma	...	...	8,786	30
United Province	...	...	120,768	159
Madras	711,072	228	865,528	242
Madras including feudatories	...	...	1,580,179	401
Coorg	3,152	176	...	...
Bombay	145,154	62	...	...
Bengal	128,135	18	...	...
Punjab	33,699	15	...	...
Assam	7,093	15	16,844	30
Nizam's Dominions	13,614	14	...	...
North-Western Provinces and Oudh	47,664	11	...	...
Central Provinces	11,973	10	...	...
Berar	1,335	5	...	...

Except in Madras and its feudatory States Christianity is evidently stronger in Lower Burma than in any other province of India. It would be unfair to take Upper Burma into our calculations, as it is only after the annexation of the kingdom of Ava that our missionaries have had free opportunities since Thebaw Min came to the throne. The six years that have elapsed since the proclamation of Lord Dufferin annexing the upper province have witnessed a wonderful extension of missionary work in various districts of the newly annexed province, and everything points to the probability that the returns of 1901 will reveal still greater progress.

63. Hinduism and Mahomedanism have been described as exotic religions in Burma. The former is certainly deserving of such an appellation, while the latter has yet only taken root in Arakan. Christianity in Burma had already taken root many years before the establishment of British rule here. It is not merely the religion of temporary settlers, but it has almost become the national religion of the Karens. The Right Rev. Bishop Bigandet and the Rev. Dr. Cushing have been good enough to supply materials for the short sketch of the Roman Catholic and American Baptist Missions. A mere comparative statement of census returns conveys but a faint impression of the real power possessed by Christianity in Burma, and of the influences that it has exercised and will hereafter

exercise even more strongly over the national character, not merely of Karens, but of Burmans as well. Hitherto but few Burmans have been converted to Christianity. It has, however, been confidently asserted, and there may be reason to believe, that since the fall of the kingdom of Ava Burmans have begun to show greater inclination to become Christians. The prestige of Buddhism has no doubt received a shock, and the next succeeding census will show whether Christianity amongst the Burmans has achieved the success anticipated. Moreover, other Missions besides the two already mentioned have been opened by other Christian sects, and, though European and Eurasian Christians are numerically too insignificant to affect the returns, Native Christians, in which term Burmans, Karens, and Natives of India are included, may be confidently expected to show a still greater increase during the present decade.

64. There were in Lower Burma in 1872 52,299 Christians of all sects. In 1881 the returns showed an increase at the rate of 61 per cent., and the total number returning themselves as Christians was 84,219. In 1891 the number of Christians had risen to 111,982, being a further increase at the rate of 32·9 per cent. In 1881 the number of Christians in Lower Burma was swelled by the heavy garrison then required on account of the threatening attitude of the Court of Ava. There were three regiments of European infantry and five batteries of artillery, in all 3,081 fighting men. In 1891 this garrison had been reduced to two batteries of artillery and parts of three regiments of British infantry, in all numbering 1,800 fighting men, a decrease of 1,281 men. This number is of course exclusive of the wives and children of the troops.

Even if we allow for these accidental variations, which swelled the increase in 1881 and diminished the increase in 1891, the returns would apparently show that Christianity advanced at a more rapid rate before than after 1881. If, however, we turn to the figures of 1881 we find that the increase was almost entirely to be found among the Karens. In 1872 the returns for the Karens were taken from the thugyis' rolls and were only approximate. The Christian Karen is still somewhat shy of the Burmese thugyi, and an enumeration of Karens left to such an agency could only be futile. It is not to be imagined therefore that the rate of converting the heathen Karens could on the one hand have been so rapid and so wholesale as the returns of 1872 and of 1881 would imply, or that missionary zeal has been less successful in the past decade. Mr. Copleston was not misled by the returns of 1872, for as if in anticipation of the present returns he said: "It is clear, however, that the previous enumerations of the Baptists must have been imperfect, for Toungoo has long been a centre of energetic and successful work carried on among the Karens by Dr. Mason and other American Missionaries." Notwithstanding the loss through the reduction of the garrison, the increase in the number of Christians in Lower Burma far exceeds the rate of progression of the total population.

The following table shows the number of Christians in every 10,000 of the total population distributed among the divisions of the province, together with the returns of 1872 and 1881, which are inserted for the sake of comparison:—

Division.	1872.	1881.	1891.
Arakan	8	21	21
Pegu	} 225	235	{ 176 } 246
Irrawaddy			{ 313 }
Tenasserim	242	343	371
Total Lower Burma ...	**190**	**225**	**240**
Northern	...	...	77
Central	...	...	22
Southern	...	...	11
Eastern	...	...	22
Total Upper Burma ...	...	...	**30**
GRAND TOTAL BURMA ...	...	...	159

65. Christianity, as already stated, is the only religion for which any return of sect was prescribed. No such return is attempted in the English or Welsh census schedule, but there appears to be no objection to making this return felt by any of the various denominations here represented. Imperial Supplementary Table **A** shows the distribution by race of the various sects in the various districts. The classification followed does not distinguish between the various native races. This classification was adopted by the Government of India to distinguish merely between Christians of Asiatic and European blood. It is impossible therefore to state how many of our Christian converts among the various races belong to the different Christian sects. A similar classification was adopted in 1881. It may in our next returns be advisable to further discriminate between the native races.

The following statement shows the distribution per 1,000 of those belonging to each denomination distributed by race and sex. This table is extracted from and is a summary of Supplementary Table **A**:—

Denomination of sects.	Foreign.		Eurasian.		Native.	
	Male.	Female.	Male.	Female.	Male.	Female.
Church of England	479	119	80	53	145	124
Roman Catholics	82	24	94	76	387	337
Baptists	10	5	5	4	498	478
Methodists	166	67	125	145	258	239
Wesleyans	609	168	37	37	130	19
Presbyterians	642	190	95	39	27	7
Lutherans	868	51	4	...	43	34
Armenians	91	25	368	260	244	12
Greeks	867	67	...	...	66	...
Unitarians	545	455	...	...	...	...
Plymouth Brethren	1,000	...	...	...	...	...
Episcopalians	1,000	...	...	...	...	...
Quakers	1,000	...	...	...	...	...
Sects not returned	58	44	41	6	452	399

From this table it is clear that with the exception of the Roman Catholics, Baptists, Anglicans, Armenians, and Methodists, the bulk of these Christian sects are to be found amongst those of foreign extraction. The great proselytizing religious bodies are the Baptists and Roman Catholics, and next to them comes the Church of England, for the Armenians and Wesleyans are so few that the smaller number of native converts numbered as belonging to them gives them a higher proportion of Native to Foreign and Eurasian members of their church.

66. The following table will show more clearly the relative strength of each sect. In every 10,000 of the population of both sexes in Upper and Lower Burma taken together 158,789 persons returned themselves as Christians. The distribution of these Christians among the various denominations is shown below:—

Denomination of sect.	Ratio per 10,000 of the total population.
Church of England	17·053
Roman Catholics	32·268
Baptists	107·009
Methodists	·545
Wesleyans	·211
Presbyterians	·579
Lutherans	·310
Armenians	·318
Greeks	·019
Unitarians	·014
Plymouth Brethren	·001
Episcopalians	·001
Quakers	·001
Sects not returned	·451

67. The accompanying statement is an interesting one as it exhibits the returns of the sects of Christian population of the lower province contrasted with the returns of the two previous enumerations.

Christian Sects.

Sect.	Total 1872, both sexes.	Total 1881, both sexes.	Variation per cent.	Total 1891, both sexes.	Variation per cent.
Church of England	10,639	9,980	— 6·2	9,812	— 1·68
Episcopalians	9	78	...	1	— 98·71
Roman Catholics	11,726	16,281	+ 38·8	20,828	+ 27·92
Baptists	20,907	55,874	+ 167	79,748	+ 42·72
Presbyterians	152	655	+ 331	329	— 49·78
Wesleyans	...	166	...	110	— 33·73
Methodists	...	72	...	413	+ 473·61
Lutherans	53	346	+ 552	234	— 32·37
Quakers	...	2	...	...	...
Unitarians	...	4	...	8	+ 100
Armenians	175	131	— 25	186	+ 42
Greeks	7	95	+ 12·57	13	— 86·31
Christians, sect not returned ...	8,631	535	— 93·8	300	— 43·92

To gauge, however, more correctly the actual progress made it is not sufficient alone to take these figures, but we should compare them with the growth of the population during each intercensal period. The accompanying table will therefore show the relative progress made by each denomination since 1872.

Comparative table showing the strength of each sect per 10,000 of the total population of Lower Burma in 1872, 1881 and 1891.

Denomination.	1872.	1881.	1891.
Church of England	38·727	26·707	21·062
Roman Catholics	42·684	43·569	44·708
Presbyterians	·553	1·752	·706
Baptists	76·104	149·524	171·183
Wesleyans	...	·444	·236
Armenians	·637	·350	·399
Methodists	...	·192	·886
Episcopalians*	·032	·208	·002
Lutherans	·192	·926	·502
Greeks	·025	·254	·027
Quakers	...	·005	...
Unitarians	...	·010	·017
Unspecified	31·418	1·430	·643

68. The Baptists have, as in the previous intercensal period, shown the greatest actual and proportionate increase. The Roman Catholics also have increased very rapidly. In both of these religious bodies the accession of Church members is in excess of the normal rate of natural increment, notwithstanding the fact that, especially in the case of the Roman Catholic Church, there is a large proportion of foreign celebate members, and the natural rate of increment is therefore necessarily lower than the provincial rate. It is quite clear that these increases are due to accessions by conversion. The Church of England again shows a slight actual decrease, though on this occasion it is very slight indeed. But the decrease is due, in the case of the return of the members of the Church of England and of the Presbyterians, to the fact already noticed that the garrison of Lower Burma, which furnished a large proportion of those returned under these two denominations in 1881, has been largely decreased by the reduction of one regiment of British infantry and three batteries of artillery. It is probable too that this reduction has helped to diminish the increase that the Roman Catholics would have furnished. But for this change the return of the members of the Anglican Church would have shown a distinct increase, for, as it turns out, notwithstanding this loss, the decrease now shown is merely nominal. The decrease of 6 per cent. between 1872 and 1881 is ascribed by Mr. Copleston to more accurate enumeration, as he was of opinion that some persons may have been wrongly included in the total of Angli-

cans in 1872. This, however, seems unlikely, because there apparently was no hesitation felt in 1872 in returning Christians without distinguishing the sect. The number so returned in 1872 was 8,631, and this fell to 535 in 1881 and to 300 in 1891. This fact alone shows that more care was taken in the enumeration of the sects returned notwithstanding that the total number of Christians in Lower Burma alone had grown at the rate of nearly 33 per cent. That there should be a steady decrease in the proportion of members of the Anglican Church is due to the fact that most of its members are foreigners who have not settled down in the country, and whose increase in numbers is limited by commercial, social, and political causes. The decrease in the number of Presbyterians may be found in the cause already assigned. It is possible, however, that both of these two great Protestant denominations may have lost numbers temporarily who have since joined the Methodist Episcopalian Church, which was established in Rangoon shortly before the last census. Wesleyans and Methodists have risen from 238 to 523. This increase of the Methodists may account for the decrease in the Lutherans. The Armenians have more than regained their former numbers, while there is a heavy decrease in the number of Greeks. The only cause which has been assigned for the decrease among the Greeks is one which applies equally to all religions. It has already, in page 33, been noticed that the returns of the port of Rangoon, notwithstanding the immense increase in the volume of trade, showed a heavy decrease both in the number of ships in the harbour and in the sailors enumerated on board of them. It is possible that the Port authorities, who in other respects successfully carried out the enumeration of the port, may have omitted a sailor here or there, though this is not likely; but a ship at anchor could not of course be omitted. I have therefore no hesitation in accepting as a correct explanation of the decrease of nearly 1,000 sailors in the returns of 1891, the statement that steam-ships have nearly driven sailing ships out of the rice trade. Far fewer steam-ships are required and their detention in port is for a short time only, so that at no time have we so many ships waiting for cargo as used formerly to be the case. The sailors on board these ships are nearly all Europeans and they returned themselves as Christians. This fact will help to account for the decreases above noted.

In dealing with the question of the different sects of Christianity I have endeavoured to record a short account of the foundation and progress of each denomination that is found in Burma. A mere return of the number of those who profess to belong to each sect conveys by itself but little meaning, nor does it show what hold each really possesses among the residents of the country. I have therefore endeavoured to state as shortly as possible the history of each sect, and I have been favoured with a note on the subject of the Anglican Church by the Right Reverend the Lord Bishop of Rangoon, while to the Right Reverend Bishop Bigandet I am indebted for the interesting account of the Roman Catholic Mission in Burma written by himself, and to the Reverend Dr. Cushing, Reverend A. F. Moir and Julius Smith for the history in Burma of the denominations to which they belong.

Church of England.

69. The following account of the Church of England was placed at my disposal by the Right Reverend Dr. Strachan, Lord Bishop of Rangoon:—

"*The Church of England in Burma.*—Although the English acquired a footing in Burma as early as the year 1687 by taking possession of Negrais, it was not until after the expedition of Sir Archibald Campbell in 1826 that Chaplains were appointed to minister to the British troops stationed in Burma; whilst the first Church of England missionary entered upon his work in this country in 1859.

"In 1855 Bishop Wilson, after visiting Akyab, landed in Rangoon on 15th November. Six days afterwards Lord Dalhousie, the Governor-General, arrived; and after consultation it was agreed to build three churches to cost Rs. 35,000 each; to have one church in Rangoon and burial-grounds at all European stations. From that date the Anglican Church in Burma has been under regular episcopal supervision.

"Chaplains were appointed to Rangoon, Moulmein, Thayetmyo, Toungoo, and Akyab, with the primary object of ministering to the British troops stationed in those towns; and it was not until the year 1856 that practical steps were taken for entering upon direct mission work in this country.

"*Church of England Missions in Burma.*—Principally through the exertions of the Reverend C. S. P. Parish, Government Chaplain at Moulmein, a sum of Rs. 7,000 was collected, and the Society for the Propagation of the Gospel in Foreign Parts, on being appealed to, resolved to commence the mission with two ordained missionaries and trained school-masters with headquarters at Moulmein.

"The Reverend C. A. Shears, M.A., of St. John's College, Cambridge, reached Moulmein at the end of April 1859. There was associated with him the Reverend T. A. Cockey, of Bishop's College, Calcutta, who had already spent some time in Burma. Mr. J. E. Marks arrived in 1860 and took charge of the Mission School, which, under his energetic management, soon advanced both in numbers and efficiency. In 1862 Mr. Shears's health having failed he returned to England, and the Reverend T. A. Cockey was transferred to Cawnpore. In November of the same year Mr. P. Marks joined his brother at Moulmein. During the absence of the latter in Calcutta for preparation for ordination, the Reverend R. W. Evans was placed in charge at Moulmein. The Reverend J. E. Marks returned with the Reverend H. B. Nichols, M.A., formerly a missionary in New Brunswick, who had been appointed to the Burma Mission. His term of service was short, for being attacked with brain fever he died on 10th December 1864. In the beginning of 1864 Mr. Cooper arrived and took over charge of the school, the Reverend R. W. Evans having again been in temporary charge. Mr. J. Fairclough, of St. Augustine's College, joined the Mission and was ordained deacon in the month of December 1866. At an early date in this history girls' schools for natives were opened both in Moulmein and Rangoon.

"*Rangoon.*—Chiefly through the urgent representations of the Reverend H. W. Crofton, Government Chaplain, the Society resolved in 1862 to establish a mission at Rangoon. In December 1863 a large and influential meeting was held to make known the wants of the mission; and as a result, within a few days a sum equivalent to £570 was contributed. Early in 1864 the mission was opened under the leadership of the Reverend J. E. Marks.

"*St. John's College.*—The foundation stone of this the largest S. P. G. School in the country was laid in March 1869 by General Fytche; and the school was opened for pupils on 26th October of the same year. Government contributed Rs. 2,000 towards the cost of building on condition that a similar sum was provided by the Society. About Rs. 2,000, which had been expended on another site, was allowed by Government to stand as part of this sum. The rest was supplied by the Calcutta S. P. G. Committee from funds in their holding, which had been chiefly collected in Burma. Large additions have been made to the premises since they were opened.

"*Kemmendine* was separated from Rangoon and made a distinct mission district in 1877 under the charge of the Reverend James A. Colbeck, and *Pazundaung*, to the east, was made a mission district under the Reverend T. Rickard in 1883.

"*Mandalay.*—In 1869 the Reverend J. E. Marks, on the invitation of the King, proceeded for a second time to Mandalay. The King built a school-room, clergy-house, and church for the mission; and for some time showed his favour towards it. Her Majesty Queen Victoria presented a fount to the church. This was consecrated by the Bishop of Calcutta on the 31st July 1873. The school proved highly successful, and Mr. Marks continued at Mandalay until January 1875, when the Reverend J. Fairclough took over charge until March 1877, being succeeded by the Reverend C. H. Chard. Towards the end of 1878 the mission was in the hands of the Reverend J. A Colbeck, who was compelled to leave Mandalay at the close of 1879 with the British Resident and the other Europeans. By the very first passenger vessel proceeding after the annexation the Reverend J. A. Colbeck returned to Mandalay and re-opened the mission.

"*Toungoo.*—Without entering into any detailed account of the causes which led up to the action of the Bishop of Calcutta and the S. P. G., it may suffice to say that a new mission was opened in Toungoo in 1873 by the appointment of the Reverend C. Warren to that sphere of labour. His arduous labours as Chaplain to the English and Missionary to the Burmese and Karens, and the loss of his young wife, led to the death of this devoted clergyman in 1875, and in the following year he was succeeded by the Reverend T. W. Windly, M.A.

"*Shwebo.*—A desirable site being secured, a new mission was opened in this important centre by the appointment of the Reverend Francis William Sutton (M.R.C.S., Eng.) in 1887. Mr. Sutton's health failing, he had to resign his appointment in 1889 and return to England, the Reverend H. M. Stockings taking over charge of the mission.

"*Pyinmana.*—A new mission was opened in this town by the appointment of the Reverend J. Tsan Baw in 1890.

"*Bishops.*—On St. Thomas's day, 1877, the Reverend J. H. Titcombe, D.D., was consecrated first Bishop of Rangoon. The Diocese is one of the two new Indian Dioceses founded after the death of Bishop Milman, seventh Bishop of Calcutta. Grants towards the endowment were made by the Society for Promoting Christian Knowledge, by the Society for the Propagation of the Gospel in Foreign Parts, and by the Colonial Bishopric Fund. A large portion of the endowment was raised in the Winchester diocese as the result of a meeting held at the house of Sir Walter Farquhar, Bart., on the 7th October

1875, when it was resolved that £10,000 should be raised for the purpose. As a perpetual memorial of this, part of the episcopal seal of Winchester appears in that of Rangoon.

"Bishop Titcombe worked indefatigably, though with impaired health and amidst much domestic afflictions, when on visitation in the Karen hills, he slipped over a rock, and received injuries from which he never recovered. He resigned the Bishopric early in 1882, and the present Bishop, the Right Reverend J. M. Strachan, was appointed, having been consecrated in Lambeth Palace Chapel on the 1st May 1882. In 1887 fresh Letters Patent were issued extending the boundaries of the diocese so as to include all additions made to the Empire by the annexation of Upper Burma.

"*Churches.*—The first English Church built in Burma was that of St. Mathew's at Moulmein. It was erected in 1832, and was replaced by a new and very handsome structure in 1890. St. John the Baptist's Church at Kyaukpyu, 1846; St. Mark's, Akyab, 1855; Christ Church, Thayetmyo, 1860; St. John the Evangelist, St. John's College, 1869; St. John's, Port Blair, 1870; Christ Church, Rangoon, 1859; Holy Trinity, Rangoon, 1864; St. John the Baptist, Toungoo, 1870; St. John the Evangelist, Bassein, 1870; Christ Church, Mandalay, 1873; Christ Church, Port Blair, 1872; Christ Church, Insein, 1882; St. Augustine's, Moulmein, 1882; St. Michael's School Chapel, Kemmendine, 1881; St. Gabriel's, Rangoon, 1881; St. James's, Tavoy, 1885; Christ Church, Tharrawaddy, 1885; St. Mark's, Prome, 1881; All Saints, Henzada, 1884; St. George's, Madaya, 1890; Meiktila, 1890; St. Luke's, Shwebo, 1887; Cantonment, 1890; St. Philip's, Rangoon, 1887; St. Paul's, Toungoo, 1887."

The Roman Catholics.

70. On turning to Imperial Table **A** Supplementary we find that the Native Christians in Upper Burma who belong to this church far outnumber the native adherents of all the other denominations put together, and that these Christians are found in villages in the Shwebo, Sagaing and Ye-u districts. The origin of these Christian settlements and the narration of the persevering efforts of successive missions to keep alive and to further spread Christianity in Burma form an interesting page in the history of the country. The following brief account is extracted from the outline of the History of the Catholic Burmese Mission written by the Right Reverend Bishop and kindly placed by him at my disposal

The so-called Native Christians found in the districts of Ye-u, Shwebo, and Lower Chindwin are the descendants of those Portuguese and Natives of India taken prisoners in 1614 when Philippe de Britto was captured and his colony at Syriam broken up. The bulk of his followers were transported to Ava and settled down in villages on the banks of the Mu. The tolerance of their Burman conquerors permitted them to retain their own religion. These Christians were recruited by other captives taken prisoners when Alaungpaya again conquered Syriam, and subsequently the capture of Yodia or Juthia, the Siamese capital, by Sinbyu Shin brought a further addition as the conquerors carried back with them the Vicar-Apostolic and part of his flock from the latter place. As Bishop Bigandet points out, the trace of their foreign extraction is still to be seen in the faces of these Native Christians.

Besides these Native Christians, since the date of the arrival of the first Barnabite Missionary Father Calchi, the Roman Catholic Church has steadily received additions by conversion, and hence we may divide the returns of those belonging to this church into three divisions :

(1) Foreign residents.
(2) Converts to Christianity and their descendants.
(3) The descendants of the old Portuguese settlers.

How the Christians fared after their transportation to Upper Burma we have but little information till in 1719 the first missionary of the Barnabite Mission arrived. He died in 1727 and was succeeded by Father Gallizia, who built a church in Syriam. In 1743 he returned to Burma as the first consecrated Bishop of Elisma *in partibus*. In the troublous times that followed the Bishop was killed, and when, after the capture of Syriam by the Burmans, the Christians living there were transported to Upper Burma, the missionaries still clung to their flocks, and Bishop Percoto, who succeeded, followed his people to Upper Burma and eventually died in Ava in 1776. Amongst the best known of the Barnabite Fathers was father San Germano, who arrived in Burma in 1783, where he remained till 1806.

The mission, in spite of many vicissitudes, still continued to flourish, but the French revolution and the consequent war in Europe and the heavy losses caused by death and disease among the ranks of the missionaries weakened the Order so much that the heads of the Society were forced to give up the Burmese Mission, which was made over to the Priests of the Propaganda. One of the earliest of the missionaries of this Order was Father Domingo Carolly, who died but recently in Myaungmya, where he had lived and laboured for more than 50 years. In 1840 the mission was made over to the Society of the Oblats of Turin. Political troubles in Italy finally caused the transfer of the mission to the Seminary of Foreign Missions in Paris in 1856. The conquest of Pegu by the British had widened the field of labour and the usefulness of the mission. The time had come for increasing the scope of the mission, and in 1856 the Right Reverend Bishop Bigandet was consecrated Bishop of Ramatha and took over charge of the Pegu and Ava Missions. The Census Report is not the place in which to dilate on the devotion of the missionaries who have helped to introduce Christianity into Burma, but the census returns are themselves eloquent witnesses of the work that has been done, and are a proof that Christianity has taken root in the country and has become part of the national life.

Presbyterians.

71. The return of the Presbyterians in Burma shows a decrease on the returns of 1881. In point of numbers the community is small and is affected by any change in the garrison of the military posts in Burma. The Reverend A. F. Moir has kindly furnished me with the materials for the following account of the Presbyterian Church. The church was first established in 1873 owing to the exertions of the Reverend G. Fordyce, and the present church was built in 1875. In 1884 the church was affiliated to the Presbyterian Church of England. In 1885 new ground was broken. Hitherto the church had not attempted any mission amongst the natives of the country, but in that year a mission to the Chinese was begun and has been attended with some success. In 1884 the minister of the Kirk was recognized as Acting Chaplain to the troops.

Baptists.

72. The following account of the American Baptist Mission is extracted from the authorized history of the Society, which has been kindly placed at my disposal by the Reverend Dr. Cushing. The history of the Karen race for the past 50 years is so intimately connected with the foundation and success of the American Baptist Mission that any account of the Karens and the Baptist Christians amongst them would be unintelligible without a brief narration of the efforts of these missionaries who have done so much for their moral and intellectual as well as their religious welfare. The American Baptist Mission has a long record of good work. The larger number of converts it can show are not the result of spasmodic effort which may at any time die away, but the Baptist Mission has now become an integral part of the religious life of a large and yearly increasing section of the population of the country, and no excuse is necessary for entering at some length into the history of a movement that has played so important a part in the national life of Burma.

To Marsden and Chater and the Baptist Mission of Serampur belongs the credit of establishing the first Protestant Mission to Burma. In 1807 they first reached Rangoon, where they found Roman Catholic Missions already established and were kindly received by the priests of the mission. Next year Dr. Carey's son joined the mission. In 1809 a Mission House was built, and in 1813 Dr. Carey went to Ava, starting just four days before the arrival of Messrs. Judson and Rice, to whom on his return Mr. Carey transferred the mission.

The American Baptist Mission was founded by Messrs. Judson and Rice, who, disappointed in their design of working in India, finally landed in Rangoon on the 14th July 1813. From the very first the missionaries met with opposition, but nothing daunted, the mission, now recruited by several new members, set up a printing press at Rangoon in 1816. Troublous times followed, but the tact of their Medical Missionary Dr. Price for a time brought them back into favour with the Burmese Court. In 1824 war between the British and the Burmese broke out and not altogether unreasonably, the Burmans could not distinguish between the British and Americans. Messrs. Hough and Wade, who were then living in Rangoon, were seized, but were rescued on the fall of the town into the hands of the British. Messrs. Judson and Rice, who were with their wives at Ava, were imprisoned and were finally used as intermediaries when the treaty of Yandabo was concluded in 1827. The annexation of Tenasserim and Arakan opened new fields of labour to the mission, and in 1825 a mission was started in Tavoy by Mr. Boardman. He it was who first turned his attention to the Karens. Hitherto, as might have been expected, the mission was purely to the Burmese. But the conquest of the Burmese had brought into prominence the hitherto down-trodden race of Karens. The success that attended the new departure at once pointed out to the missionaries where they could most readily find converts. Mr. Boardman died in 1831, but his work was carried on by Dr. Mason. In the same year the mission at Kyaukpyu was founded by Mr. Wade. In 1834 Mr. Judson finished his translation of the Bible into Burmese, but civil war and anarchy in Ava and the dread of a new war with the British induced the missionaries in Rangoon to transfer their schools to Moulmein, Akyab and Sandoway. Here other missions to the Karens were opened. But though their success was at the time great and Karens flocked across the passes of the Arakan Yomas to join their countrymen, who had already escaped from the tyranny of Burmese rule in Pegu, and readily became converts; the deadly climate of Arakan proved fatal to the missionaries, and one after the other succumbed and died. In 1852-53 the conquest of Pegu by the British once more opened the way to re-establishing the mission in Pegu. Missions were accordingly opened in Toungoo, Rangoon, and Bassein. From the very first the Karens flocked to the missions. In Toungoo especially the labours of Dr. Mason and his coadjutors met with astonishing success, and there were in 1891 22,313 Baptist Christians in Toungoo alone, of whom 21,957 were natives. In 1872 in this district the Christians of all denominations only amounted to 7,889. It is, however, quite certain that many were omitted. In 1881 the number of Christians had risen to 18,191, of whom only 11,510 were Baptists.

In Bassein in 1872, when no return of sects was made, there were 16,078 Christians. In 1881 of Baptists alone there were 18,704 and in 1891 24,298, of whom 30 only were of European descent. These figures speak more eloquently than words of the fast increasing hold Christianity is acquiring amongst the Karens, for at present in these two districts the majority of the converts belong to that race. But, as already stated, missions to the Burmese, though not so successful in their result, have been steadily maintained, nor have other races been neglected. For some years past Dr. Bunker has worked amongst the Red Karens and Dr. Cushing amongst the Shans. The last 30 years has consolidated the position of the mission, which is now to a great extent self-supported by the converts.

73. Before leaving the subject of the work of these two great missions in Burma, I shall have to refer to another side of their work in dealing with the statistics of the education of the people. Enough has here been said to show that Christianity, whether Protestant or Roman Catholic, is now no longer an exotic religion in Burma. Christianity here has revived and nationalised the Karens, a race that was fast decaying and which, but for the influence of missionaries, would have by this time been almost merged into the Burmese. As the Financial Commissioner, Mr. Smeaton, has already proved in his work on the Karens, the Queen has no more loyal subjects in Her Indian Empire than our Karen Christians, and it is to the labours of the missionaries that we owe this source of strength and the Karens their national identity.

Wesleyans and the Methodists.

74. The distinction between these two sects is so slight that it is possible that there may be some confusion in the return. It is more than probable that the few Episcopalians, of whom only one apparently survives, have been now shown as Methodists belonging to the Episcopalian Methodist Church of Rangoon. The following account of the origin of the Methodist Episcopal Church in Burma has been placed at my disposal by the Reverend Julius Smith, the Minister of the Church here :—

Methodist Episcopal Church in Burma.

"The advent of the Methodist Episcopal Church in Burma is comparatively recent. In June 1879 the Reverend J. M. Thoburn, D.D. (now Bishop Thoburn of Calcutta), came to Rangoon on an evangelistic tour and preached in the old Baptist Chapel since torn down. The chapel was freely offered for the purpose. The converts growing too great for the church, the city hall was secured, where at the end of his two weeks' services a church was organized. The site for a church and parsonage was immediately secured on Fraser and Phayre streets, and buildings immediately erected for church and parsonage, and which are still occupied for that purpose.

"The little organization there begun entered upon a career of great activity, which has been attended with very decided prosperity.

"Reverend R. E. Carter was appointed the first pastor of the church in June 1879 and remained one year. In June 1880 the Reverend J. E. Robinson became pastor and continued until March 1886. His pastorate was one of activity and success. He erected a commodious building in Lewis street for a girls' high school. This school and its beginning has had a good patronage and a career of usefulness. Mr. Robinson also started a work among the sailors and founded the 'Seamen's Rest,' which exists and carries on the work of its founder.

"Mission work has been begun in a small way among the Tamils, Telugus, and Burmese. Our missionary force in Burma, teachers, helpers, catechists, &c., numbers about 25."

Of Methodists and Wesleyans the bulk are residents of Rangoon, 243 of the former and 90 of the latter being enumerated there. There is also a small Wesleyan community in Mandalay, where the Reverend A. Bestall, who is in charge of the mission, has opened a home for lepers.

75. Of the remaining sects, the Lutherans and Armenians also call for notice. The Lutherans are found in three towns—Rangoon, Akyab, and Bassein. They are composed of the German merchants and their assistants who are engaged in the rice trade of the country. Of Native Christians only 18 are returned as Lutherans.

The Armenians are a wealthy community and are apparently increasing in numbers. The date of the founding of the church here has not been ascertained. It is known, however, that there was a comparatively speaking large Armenian community here in 1847, when the Armenian Church stood on the river bank near the site of the present Barr street jetty. The Armenian Church is under the Armenian Bishop of Persia. The Armenian and Greek Church are in no way connected, but in doctrine and in ceremonial they are somewhat similar. Very few Armenians are found outside the neighbourhood of Rangcon town, where they are a wealthy and powerful community.

The remaining sects are too numerically insignificant to call for further notice here.

Sikhism.

76. There were no Sikhs returned in either of the two previous enumerations. There were in all 3,164 persons returned as Sikhs in 1891, but it is possible that many who are Sikhs by religion have been included amongst the Hindus. Only 140 out of this number were females, and with but very few exceptions all the Sikhs are military policemen or belong to the newly formed Burma regiments.

The subject, Sikhism, has been so thoroughly threshed out in the census report of the Punjab that no description is necessary here. Sikhs are divided into two sects, the Singh or Govindi Sikh and the Nanak Panthi. It is quite possible that some of the Nanak Panthi Sikhs have not been included in the return of Sikhs as they are not regarded as true Sikhs by orthodox Govindi Sikh. In the same way the Muzbi Sikhs are not regarded as Sikhs. Even the son of a Sikh, until he is initiated, is not a Sikh, but a Mona. Sikhism is sprung from Hinduism, and Sikh and Hindu castes often bear the same name and may have been treated as Hindus. Indeed, as Mr. Ibbetson points out, a man may be a Sikh and yet be a Hindu and return himself as such :—

"Sirdar Gurdial Singh points out," says Mr. Ibbetson, "that the word Hinduism is commonly used by the people themselves in precisely this sense, and that a true Sikh, if asked whether he is a Hindu or a Musalman, will answer that he is a Hindu." The Sirdar further writes "when I filled up the census schedule for my camp, my sweeper (Chuhra) was at a loss how to describe his religion. After some hesitation he said that he was not a Musalman and therefore must be a Hindu."

Under these circumstances it would not be wonderful if here in Burma some true Sikhs may have been returned as Hindus. There should have been no mistake, as special arrangements were made to secure an accurate return. The schedule books were filled up by the Native battalion clerks and checked by the commissioned and non-commissioned officers of the battalions.

Jews.

77. No separate return of Jews was made in 1872. In 1881 there were 204 of them in Lower Burma and in 1891 their number had risen to 268 in Lower Burma, while 83 were enumerated in the upper province. They chiefly congregate in the large towns; ·81 per cent. of those dwelling in Lower Burma live in Rangoon.

Parsis.

78. In 1881 there were 83 Parsis in Lower Burma and in 1891 there were 87 in the same province, while there were nine in Upper Burma. The slight increase is not wonderful considering how few females there are in Burma who return this religion. The Parsis have been established in Burma for many years past, probably before the annexation of Pegu. There are two sects among them—the Kudmees and the Sahansai—but no attempt was made to show this distinction.

Not returned.

79. Under this head are included only those who either state they had no religion, or who left the column for religion blank. There were also a few whose religion was undecipherable. Of these there were 30 in Upper Burma. In 1872 Nat-worshippers, Jews, Parsis, and those professing any other religion than Christianity, Hinduism, Mahomedanism, and Buddhism were included under the term "Others.". In 1881 the term "Others" was abandoned and "Others" were included under the heading of Nat-worshippers. This was a somewhat cynical classification for those who returned themselves as Agnostics. Hence we are unable to state how many cases there were in 1881 of those who either returned themselves as possessing no religion or whose returns were undecipherable. There were in 1891 only 49 persons grouped under the head of "Not returned." Considering the large number of entries, the comparatively few cases of undecipherable returns is eloquent testimony of the careful way in which the schedules were filled up.

CHAPTER IV.

SEX AND AGE.

General aspect of the question. Distribution of population by sex in Upper and Lower Burma. Diagram illustrating proportionate strength of the sexes at various age periods in Burma and England. Comparative Table showing relative distribution by sex in various countries Distribution by sex in the various religions, castes and races. Examination of the causes of the variations observed. Relative proportion of sexes at the various age periods throughout the districts of Burma. Diagram illustrating number of males and females in Upper and Lower Burma at various age periods. Comparison with result of last census and with Provinces of India and countries of Europe. Distribution of population by age and sex. Error in return of children. Comparison with other countries. Revised age periods by Sheet XII. Number of reproductive males and females. Mean age of the population.

General review of the scope of the chapter.

80. In Chapters I, II, and III the census returns have been discussed from the static, dynamic, and religious points of view. In this present chapter, which deals with the information collected in columns 6 and 7 of the Enumeration schedule, we have to deal with the physiological side of the question. In Burma, however, the consideration of the natural tendencies which govern the relative strength of the sexes to each other and the "expectation of life or mean after-lifetime" of each child that is born in Burma is seriously hampered by the fact that 374,253 persons are returned as having been born in the Shan States, Karenni, in the various provinces of India, and other places outside of Burma. Of these, 296,760 are males and 77,493 are females. Most of the males and females do not reach the province till they have arrived at maturity. Age statistics even in England are of doubtful value, partly because of the ignorance of some persons as regards their exact age, and partly because of the deliberate falsification of the return by females between the ages of 15 and 30. In the English census report the Commissioners admit that these returns were falsified. In Burma, although the average Burman is better educated than the average Indian peasant, he is careless and forgetful of his own age and his children's ages as our returns show. Thus while the return of the population by sex may be relied on as being accurate, the age returns, except when taken in aggregates, show great and inexplicable variations from year to year.

The first point to be noticed is that owing to the Wuntho rising the census schedule books of Wuntho and of the neighbouring townships of Kawlin, Uyu, and the returns of the Katha excluded tracts were destroyed. Fortunately the Deputy Commissioner had obtained the return of the total population, but the return by sex had not been secured. Accordingly our sex returns only cover 7,627,568 of the total population of the country. The loss of the returns of these townships is not of great moment, as they are remote, sparsely peopled tracts, and their loss does not affect the conclusions which may be drawn from the statistics for the rest of Burma.

Distribution by sexes in Upper and Lower Burma compared with other countries.

81. The accompanying Diagram **A** shows the distribution of the sexes at the various age periods. It gives the number of females to every 1,000 males for Upper and Lower Burma apart and taken together. It will be seen that the diagram starts with the completion of the first half-year because census statistics do not give the number of births in any single year, but only deal with those living on the night of the 26th February 1891. We find

that in Lower Burma as in other countries the vital statistical returns show that more boys than girls are born into the world. In England and Wales the disparity is less marked than in other European countries, yet even there the proportion of males to females among infants born in the years 1871 to 1880 was 963 of the latter to 1,000 of the former, and although the ratio is never exactly the same in every country, yet the general rule is that because the father is usually older than the mother more boys are born than girls. This original predominance of the male sex is soon lost in Burma as well as in England as the diagram shows.

82. Our vital statistical returns of births, though incomplete, preserve in all probability the proportion of births of males and females. We find that in Lower Burma on an average 936 girls are born for every 1,000 boys. No birth returns are available, however, for Upper Burma, and accordingly for the sake of uniformity I have commenced from the middle of the first year of life for both provinces.

Birth-rate of males and females.

The following table will show how general is this preponderance in the births of male children :—

Country.	Average number of male births to 1,000 female births.	Average number of male deaths to 1,000 female deaths.
Lower Burma	1,067	1,251
United Kingdom	1,048	1,026
Sweden	1,047	1,032
Bavaria	1,056	1,043
Switzerland	1,045	...
Spain	1,066	1,068
Holland	1,058	1,016
Prussia	1,050	1,074
France	1,051	1,011
Italy	1,064	...
Denmark	1,051	1,051

This interesting table will serve a double purpose. In the first place it shows that throughout Europe there is a preponderance of male over female births. In the second place it shows that there is, as might be expected, a preponderance of deaths of males over deaths of females, but then we find a strange diversity. We should expect that the deaths of males would correspond to the number of births, but whereas in England the deaths are fewer in proportion to the births, in Burma the deaths are far more numerous. The explanation of this is that in England a larger number of males than of females emigrate and die elsewhere. In Burma just the reverse is the case. We receive a much larger number of male than of female immigrants. In France the cause of the disparity is probably to be traced to the fact that a large number of weakly males had already been killed during the war of 1870 and only the stronger males survived.

In Burma there were, if we exclude the townships for which the sex returns were not available, 3,887,156 males and 3,740,412 females, that is to say, there were 962 females for every 1,000 males. In Lower Burma the disparity between males and females is even more strongly marked as there are only 891 females for every 1,000 of the opposite sex. In 1881 there were in Lower Burma 1,991,005 males and 1,745,766 females, so that there were only 877 females to every 1,000 males. In 1872 the return showed 914 females to 1,000 males. In Upper Burma the females out-number the males, and we find 1,084 women for every 1,000 men. Before we proceed to examine these variations, it would be interesting to compare the returns of the proportionate strength of the sexes in Burma at the various age periods with the returns of other provinces of India and other countries.

Average number of Females to 1,000 Males at each age period.

Age.	Burma, 1891.	Upper Burma, 1891.	Lower Burma, 1891.	Lower Burma, 1881.	India, 1881.	Assam, 1881.	Bengal, 1881.	Bombay, 1881.	Madras, 1881.	England and Wales, 1881.	Ireland, 1881.	Germany, 1881.	Victoria, 1881.	South Australia, 1881.	New Zealand, 1881.
Under 1 year	1,063	1,116	1,024	1,007	1,004	1,082	1,017	1,005	975	998	962	983	979	966	980
1 year	1,033	1,038	1,030	1,005	1,036	1,032	1,073	1,048	1,056	1,004	953	996	975	955	1,003
2 years	1,021	1,030	1,017	1,012	1,072	1,064	1,111	1,067	1,071	1,003	973	999	971	985	968
3 do.	1,007	1,033	992	994	1,070	1,076	1,102	1,096	1,097	1,006	999	1,001	973	992	966
4 do.	1,016	1,022	1,013	1,000	992	997	1,010	1,006	1,042	1,004	963	996	980	1,018	993
Total under five years ...	**1,027**	**1,051**	**1,014**	**1,003**	**1,034**	**1,048**	**1,065**	**1,042**	**1,057**	**1,003**	**971**	**995**	**976**	**982**	**981**
5—9 years	996	1,029	978	965	926	886	938	942	1,004	1,006	977	999	994	997	983
10—14 do.	926	999	883	860	795	802	801	806	879	997	957	1,000	994	991	978
15—19 do.	1,078	1,165	1,029	1,048	922	1,027	1,019	914	934	1,008	1,040	1,014	1,037	1,013	1,026
20—24 do.	962	1,065	907	850	1,088	1,052	1,195	1,059	1,218	1,093	1,060	1,036	1,069	819	994
25—29 do.	881	1,052	798	761	991	1,065	1,071	943	1,080	1,087	1,120	1,048	984	678	816
30—34 do.	823	1,053	708	696	955	874	1,006	948	1,066	1,077	1,161	1,047	972	701	714
35—39 do.	816	992	702	709	861	822	886	854	847	1,069	1,128	1,061	922	692	731
40—44 do.	893	1,082	780	783	964	866	1,015	877	1,041	1,079	1,128	1,065	820	823	682
45—49 do.	883	1,020	797	789	885	818	906	1,010	990	1,103	1,047	1,078	687	873	573
50—54 do.	1,035	1,188	943	900	1,021	954	1,092	1,071	1,168	1,104	1,095	1,098	580	790	548
55—59 do.	1,003	1,151	913	877	936	861	1,027	997	922	1,111	1,058	1,137	572	807	559
60 and over	1,160	1,415	945	987	1,195	1,163	1,352	1,223	1,240	1,187	1,075	1,171	623	841	692
Total ...	**962**	**1,084**	**891**	**877**	**959**	**948**	**1,011**	**955**	**1,024**	**1,055**	**1,043**	**1,043**	**909**	**872**	**856**

The fluctuations in the figures here shown may be due to either or both of the two following causes—

(1) the natural cause;

(2) artificial distribution of the sex brought about by migration of the population.

The latter cause can only affect the returns of countries when taken separately, but would not interfere with a general return of the sex for the whole world if such a return were possible.

Cause of the disproportion between the strength of the sexes.

The natural causes which determine the preponderance of either sex at any given period of life have already been well threshed out in previous census reports. They may be said to depend—

(1) on the proportion of male to female children that are born;

(2) on the longevity of the sexes.

83. If we could in Burma and in England depend on the absolute accuracy of our returns, we might then be in a position to criticize and compare the figures to some purpose. The returns of age, however, are notoriously doubtful even in England, and consequently any comparison between the strength of the sexes in Burma at any particular year is open to the objection that the returns of age of either sex may be influenced by some cause unknown, and our deductions will be valueless. A glance at the table on page 87 will show what is meant. In the returns of nearly every one of the countries in that statement it will be seen that females in the quinquennium 10—14 are much fewer in proportion to males than in either the prior quinquennium 5—9 or in the latter period of 15 to 19. The next quinquennium 15—19 shows a very great preponderance of females over males, and in Lower Burma this is the more remarkable, because in this quinquennium alone the females outnumber the males over the age of 5 years. The reason that is given for this irregularity in the returns in England, is that young girls try to make themselves older than they are up to 15, and younger than they are after 25. In England young women under 15 return themselves as being older than they really are because they are often employed largely in domestic service, where youth is a disqualification. Moreover, sweet seventeen is a favourite age for spinsters who have arrived at years of discretion, and the Registrar-General of England is forced to admit that there is no doubt as to the frequent falsification of the age returns of females between ages of 15 and 30. The question of the value of these age returns will be dealt with more fully hereafter. It will be sufficient to state here that the comparative strength of these sexes at various age periods cannot be accepted except in large aggregates of years. The next cause which operates in disturbing the relative strength of the sexes is the artificial cause of the unequal migration of males and females from one country to another. Males are more mobile than females even in England. The disparity between male and female immigrants into Burma is very strongly marked amongst our Hindu and Musalman immigrants. Before the annexation the same remark, though to a less extent, was true about immigration into Lower from Upper Burma, owing to the fact that the Upper Burma officials naturally looked with disfavour on the migration of their fellow-subjects into Lower Burma as the emigration of a household meant a diminution of the household tax, the "thathameda," and thereby indirectly they themselves were out of pocket. This artificial interference with the balance of sexes is easily discernible in the case of all "immigration" countries, and by inspecting the sex returns we can easily distinguish the "immigration" from the "emigration" countries. Burma then, especially Lower Burma, falls into the category of immigration countries. But we find one difference which marks off Burma as a unique specimen of its class, for whereas in the rest of the immigration countries, the preponderance of males is continued to the last age periods, in Lower Burma after 40 the females once more tend to regain equality. This is due not so much to the undoubtedly greater longevity of woman as to the fact that many of our immigrants are not permanent settlers, but merely temporary visitors who return home after having amassed a competence.

84. If we compare the returns of the present with those of the last preceding census as exhibited in the figures of the lower province, we find that in the first

three years of life the disparity in favour of the females is still more strongly marked in 1891 than in 1881. After the third completed year, the males are in the ascendant, but the females are once more in the majority in the last year of the first quinquennium. After this, with the exception of the fourth quinquennium, every age period shows a preponderance of males. This preponderance, however, is not so marked in 1891 as in 1881. The reason of this levelling up of the sexes is undoubtedly due directly to the annexation of Upper Burma. Before the annexation, large numbers of agricultural labourers came down every year to help to reap the harvest in Lower Burma; they were not allowed to take their wives and families except with the connivance of the officials, because, as already stated, every household that emigrated meant a diminished power of paying the thathameda, which is a tax assessed on the number of households in each village. It was to the village thugyi's interest to keep his village intact. When Lower Burma was annexed in 1852-53, the ywathugyis took their villagers north with them into the King's territory and founded villages there. Partly through compulsion and partly by raising the fears of the country-folk the officials succeeded in stripping a great part of the Pegu division of its inhabitants. A perusal of the reports of local officers written shortly after the annexation will show how deserted the country was. Gradually as Pegu was reduced to order and the country-folk found that the British had made up their minds to stay, and not as in 1826 to leave their "friendlies" to the tender mercies of the Burmese, the villagers began to find their way back, but when the effect of this emigration was felt in Upper Burma, every effort was made to stop it. Men were allowed to go down south, but were not allowed to take their families with them. Accordingly the bulk of the immigrants from Upper Burma were men, and hence the depletion of men in Upper and the excess of men in Lower Burma. Since the annexation men have found their way back to Upper Burma to establish their claims to the lands and property they had left behind. The recent scarcity, however, has no doubt driven many down south, but since the annexation the immigrants from Upper Burma are accompanied by their families and thus the proportionate strength of the sexes is not disturbed.

Proportionate strength of the sexes at various ages.

85. Taking Burma as a united province, we find that while the number of girls exceed that of boys for the first five years of life, in the second and third quinquennia it sinks below that of boys. In the fourth quinquennial period the number of females rises above that of males and then again falls below till we reach the 50th year of life, when we once more find that the females outnumber the males and continue to do so. Taking Upper and Lower Burma apart we find that with the exception of the third and eighth quinquennial periods the females invariably outnumber the males in Upper Burma. Strange to say we find a very close correspondence in the returns of England and Wales. In England and Wales in the third quinquennial period the males outnumber the females, and though in the eighth quinquennium the females still outnumber the males, the disparity between them is less than in any other quinquennium subsequent to the fifth. In Lower Burma, except in the first and fourth quinquennia the males invariably outnumber the females. The returns of sex of our Australian Colonies correspond closely with the returns of Lower Burma. England and Wales are countries in which the natural proportion between males and females is interfered with owing to the excess of male over female emigrants. In our Australian Colonies the natural proportion between the sexes is disturbed by the influx of a larger number of male than female colonists. Guided by this table alone then we could infer that while Lower Burma had received a large number of male immigrants, Upper Burma had been parting with a large proportion of its male inhabitants. But there is one more fact to be learnt from this table. The last three age periods of the Lower Burma returns differ from those of our Australian Colonies in that the females once more tend to regain equality. This is an unequivocal indication of the fact that Lower Burma surrenders the majority of its male colonists and that the bulk of the immigrants are temporary sojourners and not settlers.

The foregoing comparative statement showed that Upper and Lower Burma belong to two different categories when viewed from the point of view of the balance of the sexes. But in order to pursue the cause of the disturbance of the normal equilibrium to its ultimate source we shall find that the distribution of the sexes varies with the religions professed. The Buddhist may be taken as indicating the indigenous population, while Hinduism, Mahomedanism, and Christianity, being the religions professed by the foreign immigrants, we can, if we resolve the return of the sexes by the religions they profess, be better able to trace out the extent of the disturbing influence to which reference has been made.

Comparative strength of the sexes in Burma distributed by religions and age periods.

86. The accompanying comparative statement shows the average number of females to 1,000 males at each age period by the religions they profess.

Average number of females to 1,000 males at each age period distributed by religions.

Age.	Total population.	Buddhists.	Nat-worshippers.	Hindus.	Musalmans.	Christians.
Under 1 year	1,063	1,068	974	993	991	1,009
1 year	1,033	1,031	1,023	1,117	1,064	1,060
2 years	1,021	1,025	999	1,060	958	978
3 do.	1,007	1,010	917	954	1,007	1,013
4 do.	1,016	1,017	967	1,017	1,013	1,016
Total under 5 years ...	**1,027**	**1,030**	**971**	**1,017**	**1,004**	**1,011**
5—9	996	1,001	944	901	944	941
10—14	926	938	847	437	761	864
15—19	1,078	1,129	1,009	216	651	1,057
20—24	962	1,097	1,012	129	393	758
25—29	881	1,025	874	118	331	673
30—34	823	947	673	118	342	651
35—39	816	890	652	122	343	636
40—44	893	976	742	140	410	744
45—49	883	925	685	184	461	753
50—54	1,035	1,090	806	217	628	903
55—59	1,003	1,033	755	303	629	751
60 and over	1,160	1,194	829	352	722	866
Total ...	**962**	**1,019**	**858**	**190**	**561**	**829**

Buddhists.

Taking Buddhists first we find that females are in the ascendant till we reach the third quinquennium. Here the males outnumber the females, though in the three next quinquennia the females once more regain the preponderance. The decrease in the number between 14 and 15 years of age is probably due to the fact that Burmese girls are anxious to make themselves out older than 15. The Burmese girl, who not unfrequently elopes with her future husband without the leave of her parents, is liable to be brought back and her would-be Romeo is rendered liable to fine and imprisonment under the provision of the Indian Penal Code unless the girl is over 16 years of age. Hence it is not surprising to find that Burmese girls at this time of life add a few years to their age. This will account too for the abnormally large proportion of women to men in the next quinquennium. Between 30 and 50, however, we find the males outnumber the females, and then again after 50 the females once more outnumber the males. It is easy to understand why the females after 50 should outnumber the males, because the mean duration of female life is longer than that of males, and this is more marked after the "change in life" which occurs in women between the years of 40 and 50. But at first sight there seems to be some difficulty in understanding why men should outnumber women amongst the Buddhists between the years of 30 and 50. One reason is no doubt the reluctance that the Burmese woman shares with her English sister in returning herself as middle-aged. The Burmese matron declines to return herself older than she looks. But feminine vanity will not account for all of the difference. The main cause is one which lies deeper below the surface and is to be found in the barbarous midwifery practised in Burma. Any one who has read Shwe Yoe's account of the tortures through which the Burmese mother has to pass will not wonder that the mortality amongst women during their reproductive period is very heavy. The drain is felt by the falling off in the fifth and sixth quinquennia and in the seventh and eighth it reaches its lowest point. Burmese women rarely bear children after 40 years of age, and hence, as we might expect, the proportion of females to males immediately begins to rise. The apparent decrease in the period 45—49 is due to the well known tendency to return ages in multiples of 10 to which women are even more prone than men. The Dufferin Hospital in Burma, and its energetic Honorary Secretary, Dr. Pedley, are doing a great work in Burma. Trained midwives are now being sent to nearly every district of Burma, and the Burmans are gradually weaning themselves from their inhuman and barbarous methods. How far successful these efforts will be may perhaps be seen in our next census reports.

Nat-worshippers.

Among Nat-worshippers we find that, notwithstanding the great mortality amongst the male infants, they still exceed the number of females at the end of the first year. The females then exceed the males, but till we reach the fourth quinquennium the males exceed the females. Then for the 10 years from 15 to 24 we find the females in excess, but after that age the males once more outnumber them. The return of Nat-worshippers cannot be accepted as a normal return for two reasons,—firstly, because the return of males is swollen by the male Chinese immigrants who, being almost invariably Taoists, are classed as Nat-worshippers, and by the Shans and hill tribesmen, some of whom are Nat-worshippers, who immigrate into Burma and sometimes come without their families. But there is a further reason why the males should outnumber the females, which is not generally known, but which has no doubt some effect on our returns. The immigrant Chinaman, who is generally unmarried, takes to himself a Burmese wife. His sons, if he has any, he brings up as Chinamen; the girls wear Burmese clothes and intermarry with Burmans and remain Buddhists. As there are now 41,751 Chinamen in Burma, and as nearly half of them are returned as Nat-worshippers, their presence in the country is naturally proportionately more felt in the comparatively small numbers now returned as Nat-worshippers, and this custom of theirs of bringing up only their sons that are born to them by their Burmese wives as Chinamen further accentuates the disparity between the sexes that their immigration into the country has created.

Hindus and Musalmans.

Hindus and Musalmans we may consider together. Amongst the children born of Hindu and Musalman parents there is not much difference in the proportion of the sexes to each other from the normal returns, but as soon as we get to the third quinquennium there is a sudden drop in the number of females, which culminates in the sixth quinquennium. This disparity is more marked amongst the Hindus for two reasons, firstly—because, as we have seen, Mahomedanism has taken root amongst the Arakanese as one of the religions of the country, and secondly, because the Musalmans oftener take to themselves wives amongst the Burmese and the children they beget are brought up as Mahomedans and are known locally as Zerbadies. The Hindus, on the contrary, are forbidden by their caste to intermarry with alien races. Those who do intermarry are "outcastes" and often become Burmanized and their children are brought up as Buddhists. Their strong-willed, energetic Burmese wives, who offer such a contrast to the veiled Hindu women, obtain such a mastery over their whilom Hindu husbands that, if a Hindu does take unto himself a Burmese wife, he becomes Burmanized himself. The chief reason is the enormous influx of male Hindus who work as coolies in our rice-mills, and as few of them can afford to bring their wives over, the startling disparity in the returns is only what we might expect. The disparity is lessened later in life as the celebate Hindu never settles in Burma, whereas the married Hindu, who is probably well off, stays later to amass more money.

Christians.

The return of Christian sects occupies a midway position between the foreign religions on the one hand and Buddhism on the other. Its returns correspond most closely to the figures given by the Nat-worshippers. The same causes are in fact at work. We have a large section of Karen Christians whose returns, uninfluenced by immigration, may be taken as normal. These form the majority of the Christian community. Then we have as well the Eurasian community; these being domiciled in the country, do not interfere with the returns. But in addition to these two classes we have a large number of adult European Christians who have come into the country either in the military or civil services or as merchants and their assistants. Only a small proportion of these are married and have children, and of those who are married and have children many send their families home and work out here by themselves. This will explain the disparity between males and females between the years of 20 and 49.

87. The accompanying comparative statement exhibits the proportion borne by females to 1,000 males at every age period in every district throughout Upper and Lower Burma.

Comparative Statement showing Relative Distribution of Population by Sex and Age—A (Sex).

District.	Average number of Females to 1,000 Males of the same age in all districts of Burma.																		
	Under 1 year (infants).	1 year.	2 years.	3 years.	4 years.	Total 0—4.	5—9.	10—14.	15—19.	20—24.	25—29.	30—34.	35—39.	40—44.	45—49.	50—54.	55—60.	60 and over.	Of all ages. 1891.	Of all ages. 1881.
1	2	3	4	5	6	7	8	9	10	11	12	13	14	15	16	17	18	19	20	21
LOWER BURMA.																				
Arakan Division—																				
Akyab	989	1,027	989	1,002	1,002	1,002	954	859	905	784	681	614	594	680	700	834	845	852	806	778
Northern Arakan	978	1,264	1,007	1,005	714	939	1,048	942	1,122	1,151	1,004	785	850	807	724	694	768	767	924	941
Kyaukpyu	960	1,061	1,035	1,030	999	1,021	971	916	1,132	1,228	1,081	1,060	965	1,081	1,037	1,152	1,081	1,139	1,049	1,004
Sandoway	971	1,049	1,005	917	972	978	989	892	1,097	1,172	954	868	867	928	889	1,035	1,043	994	978	957
Total	**980**	**1,040**	**1,002**	**998**	**991**	**1,002**	**964**	**879**	**982**	**917**	**792**	**725**	**703**	**789**	**800**	**919**	**930**	**944**	**882**	**848**
Pegu Division—																				
Rangoon Town	927	1,042	995	1,009	1,036	998	1,005	738	532	326	270	270	286	320	428	515	624	822	445	466
Hanthawaddy	1,014	1,021	991	977	1,035	1,005	1,005	885	1,031	848	732	655	605	675	686	852	813	910	848	789
Pegu	1,014	1,040	1,021	1,035	1,000	1,022	984	861	946	685	642	559	601	625	686	882	890	913	799	...
Tharrawaddy	1,019	1,018	1,032	971	1,050	1,017	965	891	1,142	1,067	962	851	868	932	891	1,123	1,001	1,026	982	939
Prome	1,043	1,070	1,066	992	1,016	1,034	1,016	938	1,096	1,113	1,042	957	1,000	1,012	976	1,105	986	1,129	1,031	996
Total	**1,017**	**1,037**	**1,027**	**994**	**1,027**	**1,019**	**993**	**883**	**978**	**783**	**686**	**615**	**640**	**706**	**764**	**929**	**905**	**993**	**845**	**829**
Irrawaddy Division—																				
Thòngwa	1,055	1,055	1,037	1,007	1,027	1,035	978	875	995	841	767	695	665	713	740	905	864	896	866	892
Bassein	1,076	1,014	1,008	985	1,023	1,023	980	883	1,127	1,014	882	771	751	873	845	971	924	954	939	918
Henzada	1,033	989	1,010	997	1,007	1,008	997	915	1,117	1,103	967	891	853	929	889	1,094	1,031	1,020	990	993
Thayetmyo	1,020	1,063	1,087	1,031	1,027	1,044	993	919	1,117	1,001	958	871	878	958	947	1,069	957	1,141	993	942
Total	**1,051**	**71,02**	**1,028**	**1,001**	**1,021**	**1,025**	**986**	**894**	**1,084**	**977**	**875**	**786**	**763**	**848**	**843**	**997**	**939**	**986**	**938**	**935**
Tenasserim Division—																				
Amherst	999	1,031	984	973	982	989	944	872	1,039	951	807	669	638	722	699	801	774	699	855	879
Tavoy	955	1,038	1,024	978	1,028	1,007	971	908	1,067	1,245	1,143	1,071	972	1,062	988	1,274	1,162	1,621	1,039	1,033
Mergui	975	1,137	991	966	944	993	941	885	1,057	967	884	793	748	835	779	834	896	812	900	929
Toungoo	1,002	1,006	1,015	971	1,033	1,003	977	848	1,111	1,098	960	789	779	869	867	973	920	933	941	881
Shwegyin	1,051	1,010	993	981	993	1,004	964	859	1,040	1,012	899	704	667	799	768	912	875	805	892	908
Salween	1,049	1,029	959	929	1,107	1,005	940	841	1,134	1,248	998	678	666	767	701	764	757	735	902	934
Total	**1,008**	**1,022**	**994**	**973**	**997**	**957**	**955**	**869**	**1,057**	**1,021**	**890**	**734**	**706**	**789**	**774**	**891**	**871**	**804**	**898**	**885**

Comparative Statement showing Relative Distribution of Population by Sex and Age—A (Sex)—concluded.

District.	Under 1 year (infants).	1 year.	2 years.	3 years.	4 years.	Total 0—4.	5—9.	10—14.	15—19.	20—24.	25—29.	30—34.	35—39.	40—44.	45—49.	50—54.	55—60.	60 and over.	Of all ages 1891.	Of all ages 1881.
	Average number of Females to 1,000 Males of the same age in all districts of Burma.																			
1	2	3	4	5	6	7	8	9	10	11	12	13	14	15	16	17	18	19	20	21
UPPER BURMA.																				
Northern Division—																				
Mandalay	1,110	1,067	1,045	1,024	1,025	1,057	1,044	980	1,074	908	891	940	941	1,039	1,032	1,201	1,211	1,413	1,032	...
Bhamo	1,141	978	971	1,006	1,047	1,034	1,016	970	903	575	582	560	621	743	837	928	899	1,260	792	...
Katha	1,023	959	1,061	1,051	1,056	1,031	1,050	984	1,032	775	896	850	825	897	772	972	977	1,185	943	...
Ruby Mines	1,024	1,117	1,030	1,069	1,035	1,051	971	852	652	377	352	354	325	450	409	512	620	809	534	...
Shwebo	1,173	1,114	1,104	1,082	1,052	1,108	1,066	1,032	1,113	1,102	1,080	1,020	968	1,078	1,150	1,172	1,147	1,350	1,087	...
Total ...	**1,164**	**1,058**	**1,051**	**1,039**	**1,036**	**1,063**	**1,045**	**987**	**1,043**	**847**	**847**	**854**	**872**	**968**	**961**	**1,110**	**1,131**	**1,351**	**987**	...
Central Division—																				
Ye-u	1,149	1,037	1,005	1,138	1,126	1,099	1,172	1,059	1,201	1,283	1,361	1,295	1,049	1,166	971	1,165	1,067	1,297	1,166	...
Sagaing	1,117	1,021	1,015	1,057	1,014	1,051	1,037	1,010	1,242	1,239	1,170	1,191	1,096	1,183	1,120	1,334	1,207	1,417	1,152	...
Lower Chindwin	1,246	1,081	1,034	1,045	1,063	1,094	1,059	1,091	1,403	1,459	1,574	1,471	1,285	1,414	1,195	1,441	1,375	1,579	1,292	...
Upper Chindwin	1,119	1,109	1,042	1,059	1,054	1,076	1,044	1,007	1,069	875	954	898	825	896	886	1,103	985	1,257	997	...
Total ...	**1,165**	**1,055**	**1,023**	**1,063**	**1,049**	**1,075**	**1,063**	**1,046**	**1,065**	**1,247**	**1,293**	**1,244**	**1,112**	**1,221**	**1,094**	**1,318**	**1,219**	**1,451**	**1,175**	...
Southern Division—																				
Myingyan	1,068	1,001	1,034	996	990	1,022	1,030	1,009	1,252	1,215	1,141	1,176	1,070	1,144	1,060	1,285	1,245	1,509	1,134	...
Pakokku	1,127	1,005	1,020	1,016	1,019	1,040	1,022	981	1,156	1,135	1,140	1,110	1,062	1,158	1,088	1,274	1,232	1,528	1,118	...
Minbu	1,060	1,035	1,074	995	1,001	1,049	1,010	981	1,177	1,118	1,111	1,124	1,037	1,131	1,028	1,214	1,118	1,444	1,106	...
Magwe	1,086	1,004	1,002	1,002	993	1,018	994	976	1,155	1,070	1,031	1,022	965	1,028	956	1,082	1,059	1,285	1,042	...
Total ...	**1,084**	**1,009**	**1,032**	**1,003**	**1,017**	**1,032**	**1,016**	**988**	**1,189**	**1,142**	**1,112**	**1,116**	**1,040**	**1,121**	**1,039**	**1,225**	**1,176**	**1,460**	**1,105**	...
Eastern Division—																				
Kyauksè	1,057	1,016	1,019	1,056	1,018	1,037	1,015	934	1,077	1,086	996	982	929	975	953	1,015	970	1,266	1,017	...
Meiktila	1,125	1,073	970	1,048	996	1,047	102	1,017	1,239	1,201	1,211	1,208	1,027	1,125	1,053	1,178	1,156	1,418	1,131	...
Yamèthin	1,224	1,073	1,040	1,085	981	1,091	1,005	988	1,133	1,038	1,038	1,063	944	1,091	941	1,042	1,014	1,343	1,048	...
Pyinmana	988	1,076	1,049	979	918	998	943	905	975	757	710	776	740	845	835	989	885	1,142	877	...
Total ...	**1,126**	**1,062**	**1,008**	**1,054**	**987**	**1,054**	**1,006**	**980**	**1,157**	**1,064**	**1,040**	**1,047**	**945**	**1,011**	**970**	**1,072**	**1,039**	**1,345**	**1,052**	...
Total Upper Burma ...	**1,116**	**1,038**	**1,030**	**1,033**	**1,022**	**1,051**	**1,029**	**999**	**1,165**	**1,065**	**1,052**	**1,053**	**992**	**1,082**	**1,020**	**1,188**	**1,151**	**1,415**	**1,083**	...
Total Lower Burma ...	**1,024**	**1,030**	**1,017**	**992**	**1,013**	**1,014**	**978**	**883**	**1,029**	**907**	**798**	**708**	**702**	**780**	**797**	**943**	**913**	**945**	**891**	...
Total Burma ...	**1,063**	**1,033**	**1,021**	**1,007**	**1,016**	**1,027**	**996**	**926**	**1,078**	**962**	**881**	**823**	**816**	**893**	**883**	**1,035**	**1,003**	**1,160**	**962**	...
Total Lower Burma, 1881 ...	**1,007**	**1,004**	**1,012**	**994**	**1,000**	**1,003**	**965**	**937**	**1,048**	**850**	**761**	**696**	**709**	**783**	**789**	**900**	**876**	**987**	...	**877**
Variation ...	+ 17	+ 26	+ 5	− 2	+ 13	+ 11	+ 13	− 54	− 19	+ 57	+ 37	+ 12	− 7	− 3	+ 8	+ 43	+ 37	− 42	+ 14	...

Proportionate strength of the sexes at the various age periods throughout the whole of Burma.

The variation of the proportionate strength in the returns of 1881 and 1891 at the various age periods is also shown. The proportionate strength of the female and male population in the districts of Lower Burma are also contrasted. The table requires little comment as it explains itself. The variation between the returns of Lower Burma in 1881 and 1891 are best shown by diagram **A** opposite page 85. It will be seen that the returns of 1891 are a nearer approach to the normal proportion between the sexes. For the sake of contrast the diagram shows the proportion between the sexes that obtains in England according to the returns of 1881.

It has been found impossible to construct a diagram showing the variation by districts. A comparison of the figures, however, will show that.

In every division of Lower Burma the females have increased in proportion to the number of males. In Rangoon Town, Thôngwa, Henzada, Amherst, Mergui, Shwegyin, Northern Arakan and Salween districts the males have increased in proportion more quickly than the females. The remaining 10 districts, which were in existence in 1881, show that females have outstripped the males in their rate of increase.

These tables show that with the exception of Rangoon, Akyab, Amherst, Pegu, and Thôngwa there is a remarkable coincidence in the variations which mark the distribution of males and females at the various age periods in different districts of each division. Such a coincidence cannot be accidental, but must point either to the general truthfulness of the returns when taken in aggregate of years or to the fact that those enumerated were influenced by the same motives when making their returns of ages. This coincidence in the variations is still more marked in Upper Burma. That it is more marked is due to the fact that the proportion of immigrants to the total population is very small.

Comparison with the returns of 1872 impossible.

88. I have not attempted to compare the returns of 1872 with the returns of the past or present census by districts, because it was pointed out in 1881 that the census of 1872 was taken under very different conditions. In the first place the enumeration was in some districts confessedly inaccurate, and, secondly, it was taken at a time when our working season was over and the bulk of our coolies had returned. To go then into detail of comparing district by district and age period by age period would be of little use, and no attempt was made to do this even in 1881. Moreover, our districts have suffered so many changes since 1872 that comparison would not only be very difficult, but the result would be misleading. The main objection, and one which no doubt prevented the comparison of the sexes by age periods in 1881 with those of 1872, is the fact that the age periods in 1872 do not correspond with our present age periods, and, in order to obtain the figure of 1872, the ages would have to be obtained by interpolation, which would not give a satisfactory result.

89. The following statement shows the returns of sexes of the divisions of Lower Burma in 1872 and 1881 and 1891 contrasted:—

Average number of females to every 1,000 males.

Division.	1872.	1881.	1891.	Remarks.
Arakan	906	848	882	
Pegu *	922	881	892	* Old Pegu, including Pegu and Irrawaddy.
Pegu	...	829	845	
Irrawaddy	...	935	938	
Tenasserim	897	885	898	
Total Lower Burma ...	913	877	891	

This comparative table is an interesting comment on the inferences drawn in the report of 1881. Taken together with our birth-place table, the irresistible conclusion to be drawn is that the population in the last intercensal period has been recruited proportionately less by male immigrants seeking for work in Burma

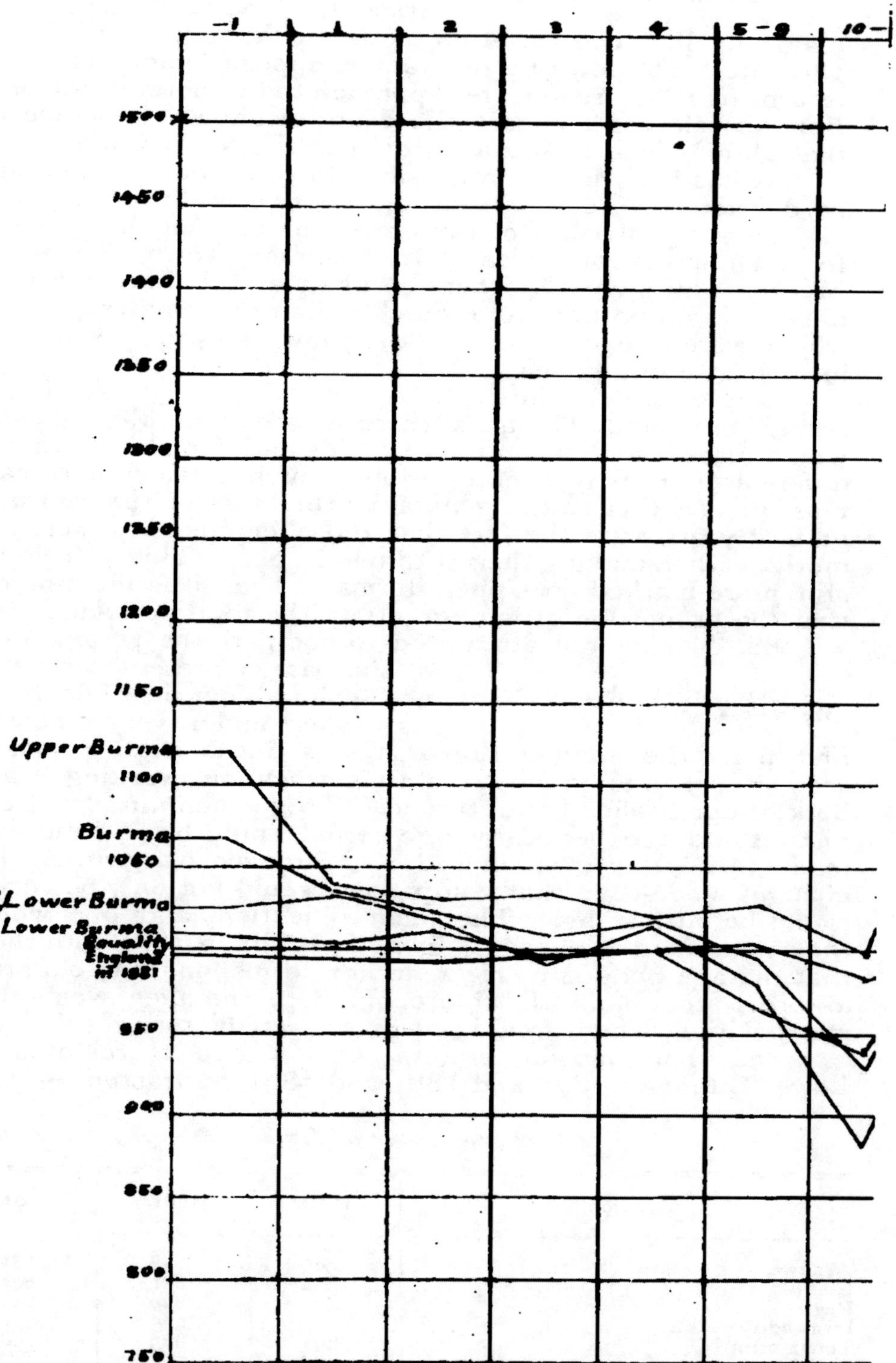

-1
1
2
3
4
5-9
10-
1500
1450
1400
1350
1300
1250
1200
1150
Upper Burma
1100
Burma
1050
1891, Lower Burma
1881, Lower Burma
Equality
England in 1881
950
900
850
800
750
700

Diagram A

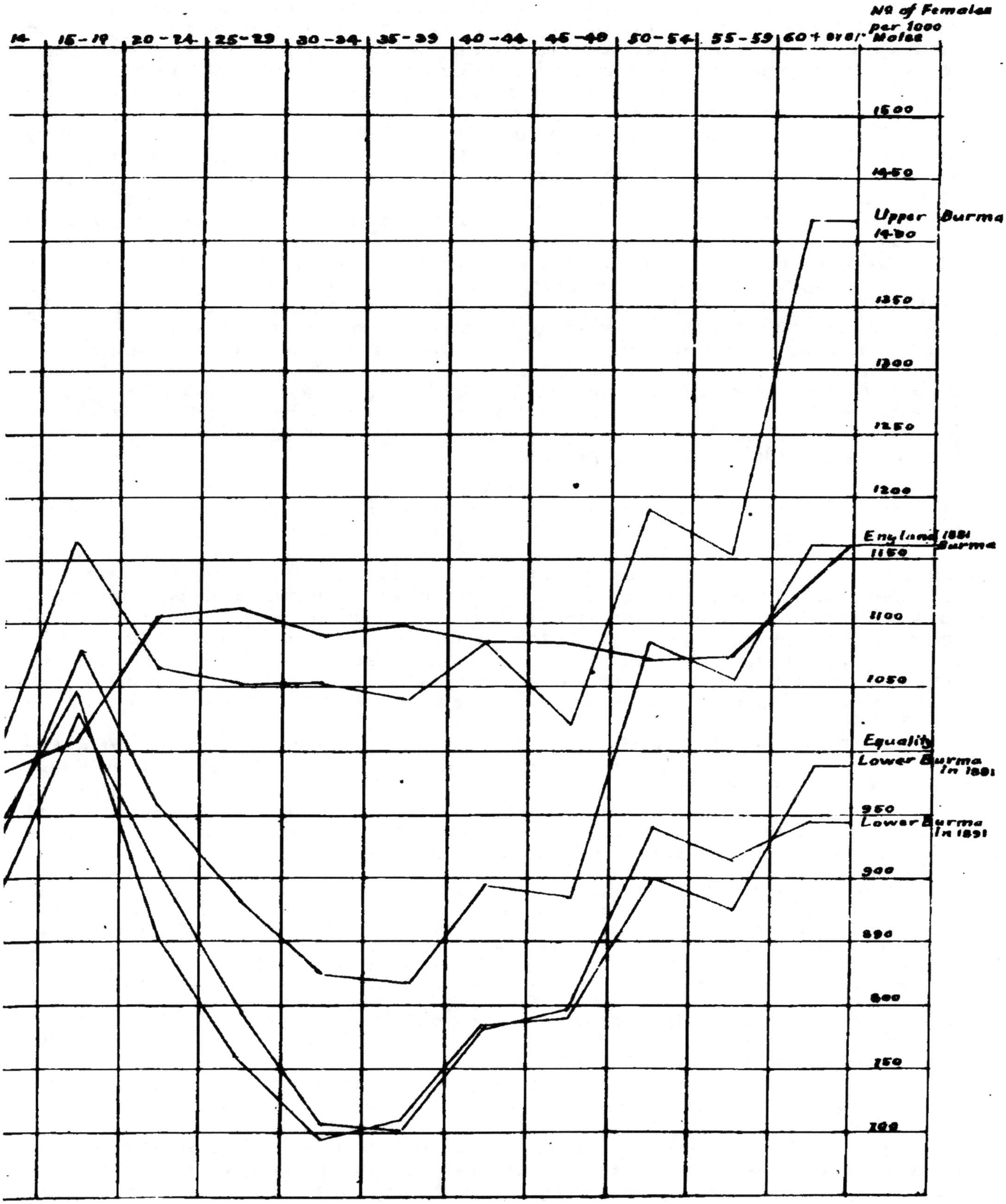

14
15-19
20-24
25-29
30-34
35-39
40-44
45-49
50-54
55-59
60 + over
No. of Females per 1000 Males
1500
1450
Upper Burma
1400
1350
1300
1250
1200
England 1881
Burma
1150
1100
1050
Equality
Lower Burma in 1881
950
Lower Burma in 1891
900
850
800
750
700

than by natural increment and by settlers who brought their families with them. The disparity between males and females in Burma is in no way influenced by any reluctance of the head of the house to give the names or sex of the dwellers in it.

90. Turning to the returns of birth-place we find that 4,015,461 persons, or a little over 86 per cent. of the population, were born in, and nearly 14 per cent. were born out of, Lower Burma. Of these 369,744 persons or 7·9 per cent. of the total population were recruited from Upper Burma and the Shan States and 237,589 persons or 5·1 per cent. from Indian provinces. Of those who came from Upper Burma there were 694 females for every 1,000 males, and amongst our Indian immigrants the proportion is still less, being only 230 females to every 1,000 male immigrants. That there should be a disparity in the strength of the sexes in Lower Burma is therefore not remarkable. The returns of the census of 1881 show that there were only 240 females to every 1,000 males of Indian origin. The proportion of women to men amongst the arrivals from Upper Burma before 1881 were 598 women to every 1,000 males. These figures bear out what was aforesaid regarding the difficulty experienced prior to the annexation by would-be emigrants from Upper Burma in bringing away with them their wives and families. The prohibition was no doubt more stringently enforced during the first half of the last decade owing to the strained relations between the British Government and the Court of Ava. Accordingly the fact that the proportion of female to male immigrants should have risen from 598 to 694 points to the inference that since the annexation the proportion of female and male immigrants from Upper Burma must have of late years nearly approached equality. The proportion of those enumerated in the province who were born outside it is slightly greater, being a little under 14 per cent.

Age.

The age returns.

91. The age periods adopted for the compilation of the Imperial tables are the same as those used in 1881. The first five years are shown separately and the following years in quinquennia up to 59, and all those over 60 are put in one group by themselves. It is unnecessary to explain the reasons on which this classification is founded, as this classification is now generally adopted. In addition to this return a special return was made for 10 per cent. of the population of Burma by every year from 1 to 100. This return was made for two reasons, firstly, as a check on the general return by the age period by quinquennia; secondly, because it obviated the necessity of having recourse to interpolation in order to ascertain the mean age of the population.

The general inaccuracy of all age returns.

92. The compilation of the returns of the population by ages is one of the most difficult as well as one of the most interesting operations in the whole census work. In every country the calculation of these returns is rendered exceedingly difficult owing to the inaccuracy of the ages returned. Even in England the Commissioners are obliged to say—

"But no sooner do we pass to the question of ages, or of occupations, or of other particulars dealt with in the third volume, than we find ourselves on very uncertain ground and must proceed with much care and circumspection. As regard ages there can be no doubt that the returns made by individuals are in a very considerable proportion of cases more or less inaccurate. In the first place very many persons, especially among the illiterate classes, do not know what their precise age may be; they keep their date of birth in mind for the earlier parts of their life up to 20 years or so, but after this lose reckoning and can only make an approximate statement. Such persons have a strong tendency to return their age at some exact multiple of 10, 30, 40, 50, 60, &c. * * * *

"There is also a similar tendency, though in a far less degree, to return the unknown age as 45, 55, or other uneven multiple of five."

I have quoted this at length because these remarks apply exactly to the returns of Burma as the statement on page 109, which is extracted from Sheet XII, will show.

But in Burma we have a still greater difficulty to meet. In Lower Burma, as we have already seen, nearly 14 per cent. of the total population was born outside the province. In Upper Burma the reverse has taken place, and we find that, whereas 3,196,719 persons were returned as born in Upper Burma, the population is 2,946,933 persons only. It is clear, therefore, that the returns of Upper and Lower Burma, will not yield to the same treatment in order to get a correct return of age by interpolation. Last, but by no means least, we have the fact that in Lower Burma exemption from capitation-tax is granted on all men below and above certain ages. There is therefore a direct inducement to return the age wrongly, especially as the circle supervisor of census was in most instances the tax-collector of the revenue circle. Under these circumstances it will be hopeless to expect accuracy, and any calculations based on these returns are therefore necessarily doubtful. But we find in the aggregate of years that the ages returned are fairly correct, and more we cannot expect.

Explanation of Diagram B.

93. The accompanying Diagram **B** exhibits the distribution by ages of 10,000 of each sex. It will be seen that no attempt has been made in this diagram to give the fluctuations of the population between the ages of under one year old and four years old. This question will be dealt with separately. Starting with the mean population of the first age period we find that females are far more regular in their distribution than males up to the age of 50 and that an inexplicable rise then takes place. This increase is noticeable in 31 out of the 36 districts and in all the eight divisions of Burma. The only explanation that has been offered of this anomaly is that the women, till they reach old age, which may, amongst the Burmese women, be said to begin at 40, return themselves as being younger than they are, but once they resign themselves to old age, they do not hesitate to return themselves as old as they are. Hence we have but few middle-aged women. The same thing to a certain extent is true of the men. Moreover, when once old, the temptation to the villagers is to return themselves as older than they are with a view to obtaining exemption from the capitation-tax.

Explanation of Diagram C.

94. Diagram **C** gives the distribution of 10,000 of the total population, showing the proportionate strength of the population, professing each of the chief religions at each of the age periods. This diagram illustrates the fact before mentioned that the foreign element is mainly responsible for the anomalous returns of ages in Burma. The population is shown divided by religions and not by races or castes, as the return of the castes and races was far too voluminous to render possible any return by age periods. Religions in Burma are still sufficiently coincident with nationality and race to render this distribution a fairly good index of the foreign element in the population of the country. The diagram requires some explanation. The line of life rises after the 59th year is passed because the rest of the population is shown under one age period 60 and over, and those thus included are more numerous (especially amongst the Buddhists, who form the indigenous population) than the population at any of the last three preceding age periods. That this difference is not so marked amongst those professing other religions is due to the return to their own countries of many of the immigrants. The attempt to work out by interpolation the remaining age periods would have been for these comparatively small aggregates of figures an exceedingly difficult and probably useless task.

It would be of some advantage if, before we examined this comparative statement of ages in Burma in detail, we were to compare the returns of Upper and Lower Burma with the returns of Lower Burma in 1881 and with similar returns of other provinces of India.

Comparative Statement showing the distribution by age periods of the population of the chief provinces of India in 1881, and Upper and Lower Burma in 1891. The distribution is calculated on 10,000 persons of each sex.

Age.	Burma.		Upper Burma.		Lower Burma.		Lower Burma, 1881.		India.		Assam.		Bengal.	
	Male.	Female.	Male.	Female.	Male.	Female.	Male.	Female.	Male.	Female.	Male.	Female.	Male.	Female.
1	2	3	4	5	6	7	8	9	10	11	12	13	14	15
Under 1 year	281	310	325	335	255	203	223	256	263	275	262	299	234	235
1 year	211	226	208	199	212	245	244	279	220	237	281	306	234	248
2 years	270	287	252	240	280	319	284	328	243	271	345	387	292	321
3 do.	312	326	310	295	314	349	313	356	295	329	366	415	350	381
4 do.	253	268	232	219	265	302	285	325	297	308	398	418	320	320
Total under 5 years ...	1,327	1,417	1,327	1,288	1,326	1,508	1,349	1,544	1,318	1,420	1,652	1,825	1,430	1,505
5—9 years	1,248	1,294	1,229	1,168	1,259	1,381	1,340	1,475	1,432	1,383	1,485	1,387	1,549	1,438
10—14 do.	1,194	1,149	1,199	1,105	1,190	1,179	1,213	1,189	1,214	1,006	1,053	891	1,139	902
15—19 do.	912	1,022	887	954	927	1,070	867	1,037	811	779	735	796	757	763
20—24 do.	910	910	859	845	939	956	888	861	799	905	764	847	711	840
25—29 do.	879	806	789	766	931	833	882	766	896	925	929	1,043	882	935
30—34 do.	799	683	728	708	839	667	844	670	885	881	828	762	859	856
35—39 do.	635	539	684	626	607	477	647	523	587	527	648	562	631	554
40—44 do.	553	514	568	567	545	477	570	509	642	645	535	488	631	634
45—49 do.	389	357	410	385	378	338	394	354	344	317	387	334	356	319
50—54 do.	365	393	378	414	358	379	351	360	436	464	336	338	409	442
55—59 do.	222	232	230	244	218	223	206	206	161	157	214	195	165	168
60 and over	567	684	712	930	483	512	449	506	475	591	434	532	481	644

Comparative Statement showing the distribution by age periods of the population of the chief provinces of India in 1881, and Upper and Lower Burma in 1891. The distribution is calculated on 10,000 persons of each sex—concluded.

Age.	Bombay Presidency division.		Central Provinces.		Madras.		North-Western Provinces.		Oudh.		Punjab.	
	Male.	Female.	Male.	Female.	Male.	Female.	Male.	Female.	Male.	Female.	Male.	Female.
1	16	17	18	19	20	21	22	23	24	25	26	27
Under 1 year	265	279	281	289	301	301	261	280	264	280	317	356
1 year	199	218	284	305	201	207	216	236	266	283	175	197
2 years	233	260	305	338	212	222	189	218	200	221	212	242
3 do.	243	279	354	394	261	280	263	299	275	302	257	292
4 do.	281	296	333	341	271	276	283	294	267	270	277	299
Total under 5 years ...	1,221	1,332	1,557	1,667	1,246	1,286	1,212	1,327	1,272	1,356	1,238	1,386
5—9 years	1,438	1,418	1,483	1,462	1,380	1,353	1,339	1,288	1,331	1,243	1,394	1,386
10—14 do.	1,275	1,077	1,102	906	1,319	1,132	1,262	1,011	1,207	969	1,217	1,064
15—19 do.	816	781	703	686	875	798	804	726	813	701	887	856
20—24 do.	828	917	759	913	891	975	869	937	789	854	847	911
25—29 do.	974	961	898	966	827	873	952	954	869	921	847	874
30—34 do.	889	878	968	908	893	928	934	930	872	917	845	867
35—39 do.	654	585	508	462	590	488	533	529	525	514	505	485
40—44 do.	505	463	728	661	650	660	687	722	718	779	644	689
45—49 do.	429	454	253	225	329	290	321	309	343	315	340	313
50—54 do.	403	451	455	455	416	474	482	525	538	571	485	463
55—59 do.	186	194	99	103	168	152	147	146	158	141	165	141
60 and over	383	489	487	624	488	591	458	596	565	719	579	565

Consideration of the comparative statement of age periods on the various provinces of India.

95. The first most noticeable point is that in five out of the eight provinces of India, counting North-Western Provinces and Oudh apart, in 1881 there was an increase in numbers which is almost progressive for the first four years of life. This is of course anomalous. It is a natural law in every country, except those in which the population is rapidly decreasing or increasing, where there is a very small indigenous and a very large immigrant population, that the numbers of the inhabitants born in any year should in successive years show a decrease as they gradually die off. The abnormal nature of these returns attracted the notice of Mr. Copleston in Burma, and as he finished his report long before the other Superintendents had begun to review their returns, he had not the advantage of comparing his returns with those of other provinces, and apparently the returns of previous enumerations in other provinces were not available. Had he seen how common the error was he would have been less exercised in mind and more ready to admit that the explanation lay in the fact that the census schedules do not give a correct return of the ages of the population. He was naturally loath to admit that the returns were wrong. The experiences of other provinces in 1881 and the returns of 1891 show that absolute accuracy as to the return year by year is not to be expected.

In the Punjab the returns of children's ages were most absurd; for, not only were the returns for separate years in the first 5 years abnormal, but the children in the second age period 5—9 outnumbered those under that age. Mr. Ibbetson attempted to explain these returns by supposing that a general wave of infecundity swept over India. Mr. Bourdillon's explanation that the returns were erroneously made is the only true explanation. A wave of infecundity which lasts 5 years is an explanation which hardly needs discussion.

Dissatisfied with the age returns, Mr. Copleston proposed two methods by which they might be tested. The first method was to have a test enumeration by age and sex, such as the Deputy Commissioner of Sandoway made for me, and the other was that in 1891 to compile the returns of the years 10 to 13 and compare them with the figures of 1881. If the ages were correctly returned in 1881 "in 1891," says Mr. Copleston, "the persons then 10 years old will be but few in number, while there will be many of 13 years of age." The figures for these years have been taken and the result shows that those 10 years of age are far more numerous than those of any of the next four succeeding years. If these returns are true, then the age returns of 1881 for the first five years must be wrong. Ten years of age was, however, an unfortunate year, for, as it has already been noted, multiples of 10 are favourite numbers for the return of ages to those who are either too ignorant or too careless to make a true return.

The causes of these anomalous returns of the age of children.

96. There are four possible ways in which these anomalous returns of ages might be made. Either they are true and have been rightly returned and rightly compiled, or they have been wrongly returned to the enumerators by the parents of the children, or the enumerators may have been careless, or, lastly, the mistake may have been in the compilation of these figures. Taking these four contingencies, we may at once dismiss the last, because warned as I was by the experience of the last census, special care was taken and special checks were provided to guard against error in the compilation of these returns. Not only were doubtful returns re-abstracted, but in Burma, as in the rest of India, a special abstraction sheet was provided, and I feel sure that the Census Commissioner for India will agree in believing that the age returns have been carefully and correctly compiled. That the figures represent the true facts of the case, I think we may disbelieve without going into details of birth and death statistics. A glance at the comparative statement will prove this. There are then only two possible ways in which the error may have arisen either in the carelessness of the enumerator or by misstatement on the part of the parents of the children. In a matter of age returns it must be remembered that the enumerator is to a certain extent at the mercy of those whom he enumerates. On all other points a man's answers may be corroborated by questioning his neighbours; but few know the exact ages of their next door neighbours. Even in England the Commissioners found people who did not know their own ages. Instead of trying to explain away the mistake,

for such I believe it to be, I have tried to find out where the mistake lay. I have written to several of the Deputy Commissioners in whose districts these returns assumed the most anomalous shapes. The Deputy Commissioner of Sandoway answered the question in the best possible way by holding a trial census by skilled enumerators in Sandoway town. He writes :—

"The figures in this return being *primâ facie* inexplicable, I had a small age census taken of a portion of Sandoway town, the result being shown in the accompanying statement.* Close on 1,000 persons were examined and the enumerators being all clerks, the results ought to be fairly correct, but in effect it partially supports the figures of the regular census. That the latter are wrong hardly admits a doubt, though it is not by any means easy to say where the error comes in. Nobody here seems to be able to put forward any theory on the subject. After some hesitation the only explanation I can give as to the anomalous results of the figures in your table is that the ages of the children are wrongly given by the parents. The Burman mind is not prone to exactness in anything, and except when it is a case of being exempted from the capitation-tax he does not trouble himself to state the age of himself or progeny with any nicety. For example, at this last enumeration, I hear that a young girl when asked her age gave it as 21 and, on being questioned as to that of her mother, stated it to be 25! It is hardly fair to blame the enumerators for the incorrectness of the children's ages as they had no reason to suppose that they would be given wrongly, and in any case could hardly be expected to cross-examine their parents in each case. The fault lies with the peculiar idiosyncracy of the average Burman and it shows that a new meaning may be given to the adage 'There is nothing more deceptive than facts except figures.'"

* Not printed.

Mr. Houghton's view is supported by the replies I have received from other Deputy Commissioners. It will be noticed that the returns of 1891, especially in Upper Burma, compare very favourably not only with the returns of Lower Burma in 1881, but with the returns of other provinces. The returns of Upper Burma are remarkably good. It will be further noticed that three is the favourite figure, and the explanation given is that the enumerator when he asks a child's age is often answered at random : "Oh he or she is about two or three years old (nahnit thôn hnit lauk she thee)." It will be interesting to compare the remarks made by Mr. Bourdillon in the Bengal Census Report of 1881, page 116 : "When it was decided that each of the first five years of infant life should be shown separately, much stress was laid on the argument that every mother knows the age of her young children, and it was urged that these figures above all must be absolutely correct. But this argument did not take sufficiently into account the inaccuracy of the ignorant mind and expected that maternal tenderness would supply the deficiencies of an untrained memory. Just as in speaking of later periods of life the tendency of the native is to use round numbers with a preference for describing the age of all adults as 25, so the most common phrase for expressing the age of a child is '3 or 4 years old.'" It is strange that the replies of the officers consulted should coincide so closely with the experience of the Census Superintendent of Bengal.

Of course the model enumerator should not have rested satisfied with such a vague reply, but should have pressed for something more definite, and as a Burman has no objection to tell his age, there is no reason to prevent a better return in 1901. It will be seen that our figures, especially in Upper Burma, are an improvement on the returns of Lower Burma in 1881. The returns of 1881 were so anomalous that my attention was naturally drawn to them and I had the advantage of my predecessor's advice on the subject. In that year the mistake of attempting too much was made. The enumerators were ordered to ascertain and record how many months old each child under one year of age was. No use was made of the information so acquired, and owing, as it was supposed, to the omission of the word month, a child of 10 months was often shown as 10 years old. In 1891 the return was simplified. It was supposed that the introduction of the word infant and the omission of the word month would work a change for the better, and this result has been partially achieved; but I feel sure that now we know where the mistake originates we shall be better able to guard against it. In 1891 we tried to impress the enumerators with the necessity of being careful; in 1901 we must try to make those enumerated to answer more correctly, and I feel confident that we shall get better results.

97. The accompanying comparative statement shows the distribution by age periods of 10,000 of the population of each sex in every district and division in Burma.

District.	Infants.		1		2		3		4		0 to 4 years.	
	Male.	Female.	Male.	Female.	Male.	Female.	Male.	Female.	Male.	Female.	Male.	Female.
LOWER BURMA.												
Arakan Division—												
Akyab	169	208	203	259	251	308	303	376	241	299	1,167	1,450
Northern Arakan ...	125	132	90	122	184	201	247	269	282	218	928	942
Kyaukpyu	175	161	239	242	257	253	345	338	268	255	1,284	1,249
Sandoway	234	233	248	266	299	308	365	342	312	310	1,458	1,459
Total ...	**177**	**197**	**214**	**252**	**256**	**291**	**318**	**360**	**255**	**286**	**1,220**	**1,386**
Pegu Division—												
Rangoon	110	230	63	147	110	247	127	287	106	246	516	1,157
Hanthawaddy	256	306	191	230	285	333	300	345	256	312	1,288	1,526
Pegu	253	321	191	250	273	348	290	375	249	310	1,255	1,605
Tharrawaddy	325	338	241	249	318	335	333	329	293	313	1,510	1,564
Prome	307	310	198	205	292	302	326	314	295	291	1,418	1,422
Total ...	**259**	**312**	**183**	**225**	**264**	**321**	**284**	**334**	**247**	**301**	**1,237**	**1,493**
Irrawaddy Division—												
Thôngwa	282	344	202	245	272	326	309	359	256	304	1,321	1,578
Bassein	288	330	235	253	311	333	334	351	287	313	1,455	1,580
Henzada	295	308	235	235	316	322	335	338	290	295	1,471	1,498
Thayetmyo	294	302	217	232	276	302	294	306	288	298	1,369	1,440
Total ...	**289**	**323**	**222**	**243**	**295**	**324**	**321**	**343**	**279**	**303**	**1,406**	**1,536**
Tenasserim Division—												
Amherst	217	254	266	315	302	348	341	388	287	330	1,413	1,635
Tavoy	210	193	278	278	301	297	341	321	308	304	1,438	1,393
Mergui	231	250	197	249	262	288	357	383	287	300	1,334	1,470
Toungoo	325	346	173	185	272	293	343	354	266	292	1,379	1,470
Shwegyin	273	322	251	284	317	353	345	380	265	295	1,451	1,634
Salween	340	395	166	190	315	334	367	378	237	291	1,425	1,588
Total ...	**250**	**281**	**241**	**274**	**298**	**329**	**344**	**373**	**279**	**310**	**1,412**	**1,567**
UPPER BURMA.												
Northern Division—												
Mandalay	293	314	178	184	221	224	266	264	182	180	1,140	1,166
Bhamo	255	367	155	192	219	268	258	327	175	230	1,062	1,384
Katha	255	277	220	224	257	289	295	328	199	222	1,226	1,340
Ruby Mines	142	273	90	188	133	257	136	271	116	225	617	1,214
Shwebo	297	320	188	193	225	228	299	297	203	197	1,212	1,235
Total ...	**279**	**315**	**177**	**190**	**220**	**235**	**268**	**282**	**184**	**193**	**1,128**	**1,215**
Central Division—												
Ye-u	351	346	188	167	250	215	326	318	182	176	1,297	1,222
Sagaing	340	329	224	198	267	235	350	322	241	213	1,422	1,297
Lower Chindwin	307	296	219	183	270	216	392	317	242	199	1,430	1,211
Upper Chindwin	231	261	215	241	220	231	291	311	198	212	1,155	1,256
Total ...	**316**	**312**	**216**	**193**	**259**	**225**	**354**	**318**	**228**	**202**	**1,373**	**1,250**
Southern Division—												
Myingyan	407	383	228	202	284	259	332	292	274	239	1,525	1,375
Pakôkku	328	330	263	237	294	268	362	329	249	227	1,496	1,391
Minbu	345	331	228	213	287	278	327	294	254	251	1,441	1,367
Magwe	286	298	221	212	262	252	289	278	277	264	1,335	1,304
Total ...	**348**	**341**	**236**	**216**	**283**	**264**	**330**	**300**	**264**	**243**	**1,461**	**1,364**
Eastern Division—												
Kyauksè	283	294	145	145	162	163	193	201	152	152	935	954
Meiktila	378	376	198	187	253	217	314	291	280	247	1,423	1,318
Yamèthin	362	423	193	197	247	245	294	305	269	252	1,365	1,422
Pyinmana	346	390	166	203	190	227	237	264	184	192	1,123	1,276
Total ...	**348**	**372**	**180**	**182**	**223**	**214**	**272**	**272**	**236**	**222**	**1,259**	**1,262**
Total Lower Burma ...	**255**	**293**	**212**	**245**	**280**	**319**	**314**	**349**	**265**	**302**	**1,326**	**1,508**
Total Upper Burma ...	**325**	**335**	**208**	**199**	**252**	**240**	**310**	**295**	**232**	**219**	**1,327**	**1,288**
Total Burma ...	**281**	**310**	**211**	**226**	**270**	**287**	**312**	**326**	**253**	**268**	**1,327**	**1,417**

5 to 9 years.		10 to 14 years.		15 to 19 years.		20 to 24 years.		25 to 29 years.		30 to 34 years.		35 to 39 years.	
Male.	Female.	Male.	Female.	Male.	Female.	Male.	Female.	Male.	Female.	Male.	Female.	Male.	Female.
1,218	1,441	1,095	1,167	920	1,033	945	919	1,014	857	968	737	687	507
1,080	1,225	1,007	1,026	825	1,002	970	1,208	934	1,015	1,210	1,029	579	532
1,378	1,275	1,262	1,103	942	1,016	780	913	841	867	756	764	624	576
1,447	1,464	1,331	1,214	969	1,087	773	927	814	795	722	641	518	460
1,276	**1,395**	**1,156**	**1,152**	**928**	**1,034**	**890**	**925**	**952**	**856**	**899**	**739**	**652**	**520**
512	1,156	569	943	915	1,095	1,555	1,141	1,725	1,050	1,451	882	877	563
1,183	1,402	1,159	1,209	881	1,071	957	957	968	835	879	678	700	494
1,142	1,407	1,122	1,210	910	1,078	1,077	924	1,057	850	937	656	683	514
1,412	1,388	1,335	1,212	975	1,132	893	971	837	821	687	596	459	406
1,331	1,312	1,258	1,145	999	1,063	903	975	799	808	625	580	443	429
1,152	**1,325**	**1,119**	**1,170**	**940**	**1,088**	**1,051**	**984**	**1,040**	**845**	**882**	**653**	**612**	**463**
1,228	1,387	1,179	1,191	921	1,057	984	954	917	813	828	663	634	487
1,314	1,371	1,281	1,205	907	1,093	899	972	865	812	794	652	558	446
1,332	1,342	1,311	1,212	975	1,101	875	975	802	783	695	626	519	447
1,323	1,322	1,225	1,134	957	1,077	929	937	798	769	666	583	513	453
1,294	**1,360**	**1,249**	**1,191**	**936**	**1,082**	**924**	**962**	**855**	**799**	**760**	**637**	**564**	**459**
1,376	1,520	1,221	1,246	878	1,067	834	929	872	823	879	688	633	473
1,431	1,337	1,333	1,165	990	1,016	757	907	761	838	669	690	643	602
1,363	1,424	1,189	1,168	861	1,009	907	974	904	887	820	722	643	534
1,305	1,354	1,270	1,144	859	1,013	808	942	864	881	864	724	634	525
1,342	1,451	1,223	1,178	905	1,055	836	950	870	877	862	681	617	461
1,212	1,262	952	887	896	1,125	778	1,075	1,027	1,136	1,097	825	714	527
1,356	**1,443**	**1,229**	**1,189**	**890**	**1,048**	**827**	**941**	**868**	**860**	**857**	**700**	**634**	**499**
983	994	1,014	962	909	945	996	876	943	814	820	747	788	717
858	1,099	762	933	743	846	1,344	975	1,247	916	1,158	819	719	564
1,127	1,254	988	1,030	832	909	1,028	845	970	921	938	848	732	640
615	1,118	675	1,077	866	1,058	1,479	1,044	1,426	939	1,361	902	881	536
1,136	1,114	1,196	1,135	881	902	854	865	860	854	840	788	784	698
996	**1,055**	**1,006**	**1,007**	**879**	**928**	**1,028**	**883**	**983**	**844**	**895**	**775**	**780**	**690**
1,114	1,119	1,360	1,234	864	890	674	741	658	768	716	795	763	687
1,219	1,096	1,198	1,050	896	965	779	837	733	744	634	656	673	640
1,376	1,128	1,256	1,061	811	882	648	732	574	700	617	702	655	652
1,115	1,177	1,078	1,098	899	972	1,016	898	932	899	901	818	739	616
1,244	**1,120**	**1,226**	**1,086**	**863**	**924**	**749**	**791**	**694**	**748**	**674**	**710**	**688**	**648**
1,362	1,236	1,264	1,124	903	996	801	858	742	745	652	676	613	578
1,328	1,214	1,231	1,080	899	930	809	821	683	696	669	664	619	588
1,283	1,171	1,177	1,043	871	926	818	827	722	727	651	662	606	568
1,376	1,313	1,342	1,256	972	1,077	880	903	750	742	650	637	592	548
1,340	**1,232**	**1,253**	**1,121**	**910**	**979**	**823**	**850**	**723**	**727**	**657**	**662**	**607**	**573**
1,010	1,008	1,129	1,036	837	886	823	878	885	866	837	808	872	797
1,405	1,267	1,380	1,242	861	981	792	841	727	778	666	711	657	596
1,402	1,344	1,385	1,305	925	998	845	836	724	717	666	663	640	576
1,149	1,234	1,154	1,190	933	1,036	1,077	928	961	776	838	741	693	584
1,283	**1,228**	**1,297**	**1,209**	**882**	**970**	**847**	**856**	**789**	**780**	**725**	**722**	**706**	**635**
1,259	**1,381**	**1,190**	**1,179**	**927**	**1,070**	**939**	**956**	**931**	**833**	**839**	**667**	**607**	**477**
1,229	**1,168**	**1,199**	**1,105**	**887**	**954**	**859**	**845**	**789**	**766**	**728**	**708**	**684**	**626**
1,248	**1,294**	**1,194**	**1,149**	**912**	**1,022**	**910**	**910**	**879**	**806**	**799**	**683**	**635**	**539**

District.	40 to 44 years. Male.	40 to 44 years. Female.	45 to 49 years. Male.	45 to 49 years. Female.	50 to 54 years. Male.	50 to 54 years. Female.	55 to 59 years. Male.	55 to 59 years. Female.	60 years and over. Male.	60 years and over. Female.
LOWER BURMA.										
ARAKAN DIVISION—										
Akyab	575	485	396	344	371	383	219	229	425	448
Northern Arakan ...	812	708	363	284	550	413	199	165	543	451
Kyaukpyu	504	520	419	415	362	398	288	296	560	608
Sandoway	482	457	382	347	344	364	248	264	512	521
Total ...	**554**	**496**	**399**	**362**	**370**	**385**	**237**	**250**	**467**	**500**
PEGU DIVISION—										
Rangoon	765	552	335	323	357	414	127	178	296	546
Hanthawaddy	552	439	407	331	359	360	231	230	436	468
Pegu	547	428	373	320	313	346	186	208	398	454
Tharrawaddy	479	455	360	327	341	390	219	223	493	515
Prome	508	499	416	394	422	452	294	281	584	640
Total ...	**559**	**477**	**381**	**344**	**359**	**395**	**216**	**232**	**452**	**531**
IRRAWADDY DIVISION—										
Thôngwa	562	463	366	313	356	372	209	209	495	513
Bassein	506	470	349	314	368	381	206	198	498	506
Henzada	493	463	369	332	356	394	224	233	578	594
Thayetmyo	552	532	429	409	403	434	273	263	563	647
Total ...	**527**	**476**	**372**	**334**	**367**	**390**	**220**	**221**	**526**	**553**
TENASSERIM DIVISION—										
Amherst	538	455	364	298	323	302	204	184	465	380
avoy	465	475	378	359	272	334	261	292	602	592
Mergui	506	469	415	359	361	335	222	220	475	429
Toungoo	587	542	375	346	377	390	203	198	475	471
Shwegyin	560	470	357	307	340	347	175	172	462	417
Salween	693	589	327	254	393	333	135	113	351	286
Total ...	**546**	**480**	**368**	**318**	**336**	**333**	**202**	**196**	**475**	**426**
UPPER BURMA.										
NORTHERN DIVISION—										
Mandalay	623	627	439	439	390	454	245	287	710	972
Bhamo	661	619	374	395	401	470	193	219	478	761
Katha	602	572	402	329	418	431	208	216	529	665
Ruby Mines	721	608	365	280	401	385	168	195	425	644
Shwebo	571	566	401	374	373	402	213	224	679	843
Total ...	**619**	**607**	**418**	**407**	**391**	**439**	**226**	**259**	**651**	**891**
CENTRAL DIVISION—										
Ye-u	604	604	479	399	389	388	260	238	822	915
Sagaing	556	571	420	409	367	425	251	263	852	1,047
Lower Chindwin	555	608	444	411	397	442	259	276	978	1,195
Upper Chindwin	602	556	418	374	370	412	224	223	551	701
Total ...	**569**	**588**	**437**	**404**	**380**	**425**	**251**	**260**	**852**	**1,046**
SOUTHERN DIVISION—										
Myingyan	508	512	372	347	345	391	223	245	690	917
Pakôkku	539	559	400	389	373	425	224	246	730	997
Minbu	546	558	412	383	396	435	246	249	831	1,084
Magwe	522	515	395	362	365	379	216	219	605	745
Total ...	**527**	**535**	**393**	**369**	**367**	**407**	**227**	**241**	**712**	**940**
EASTERN DIVISION—										
Kyaukse	725	695	506	475	468	467	280	267	693	862
Meiktila	510	508	369	343	339	353	209	214	662	848
Yamèthin	542	513	367	330	355	353	194	187	590	756
Pyinmana	630	606	388	369	379	427	168	174	507	659
Total ...	**583**	**561**	**403**	**371**	**378**	**386**	**217**	**214**	**631**	**806**
Total Lower Burma ...	**545**	**477**	**378**	**338**	**358**	**379**	**218**	**223**	**483**	**512**
Total Upper Burma ...	**568**	**567**	**410**	**385**	**378**	**414**	**230**	**244**	**712**	**930**
Total Burma ...	**553**	**514**	**389**	**357**	**365**	**393**	**222**	**232**	**567**	**684**

Of course with so large a proportion of grown up male immigrants, there is some excuse for fluctuating returns from 20 to 44 years; but we might have expected to find the ages of children correct. We find that the districts in which the age periods are best returned are the districts of Myingyan, Minbu, and Magwe.

Comparative table showing degree of accuracy in the return of children's ages in the various districts.

98. The subjoined statement is taken from the report of 1881. It shows the order in which the return of ages was made. I have, however, slightly altered the method employed. The normal return of course is that children should be most numerous in the first year of life and that their number should lessen year by year, hence out of five years I have put the numbers (1) as denoting the highest number living, (2) the next highest, and so on. Accordingly the numbers should run 1, 2, 3, 4, and 5. Moreover, there is no gain in showing the return of religions by these age periods of 0—4 by districts as we receive but very few immigrants of Hindu and Mahomedan religions of this age.

District.	Under one year.	One year.	Two years.	Three years.	Four years.
LOWER BURMA.					
Akyab	5	4	2	1	3
Northern Arakan	4	5	3	1	2
Kyaukpyu	5	4	3	1	2
Sandoway	5	4	3	1	2
Rangoon Town	4	5	2	1	3
Hanthawaddy	4	5	2	1	3
Pegu	3	5	2	1	4
Tharrawaddy	1	5	3	2	4
Prome	2	5	3	1	4
Thôngwa	2	5	3	1	4
Bassein	3	5	2	1	4
Henzada	3	5	2	1	4
Thayetmyo	2	5	4	1	3
Amherst	5	4	2	1	3
Tavoy	5	4	3	1	2
Mergui	4	5	3	1	2
Toungoo	2	5	3	1	4
Shwegyin	3	5	2	1	4
Salween	2	5	3	1	4
Total ...	4	5	2	1	3
UPPER BURMA.					
Mandalay	1	5	3	2	4
Bhamo	1	5	3	2	4
Katha	3	4	2	1	5
Ruby Mines	1	5	3	2	4
Shwebo	1	5	3	2	4
Ye-u	1	5	3	2	4
Sagaing	2	5	3	1	4
Lower Chindwin	2	5	3	1	4
Upper Chindwin	2	3	4	1	5
Myingyan	1	5	3	2	4
Pakôkku	2	4	3	1	5
Minbu	1	5	3	2	4
Magwe	1	5	4	2	3
Kyauksè	1	5	3	2	4
Meiktila	1	5	4	2	3
Yamèthin	1	5	4	2	3
Pyinmana	1	5	3	2	4
Total ...	1	5	3	2	4
GRAND TOTAL ...	2	5	3	1	4

The next statement shows the return of the population distributed by religions for the first 5 years of life for Upper and Lower Burma together, and then separately for Lower and Upper Burma. The returns of 1881 are inserted for comparison.

Religion.	Burma, 1891.					Lower Burma, 1891.					Upper Burma, 1891.					Lower Burma, 1881.				
	Under one year.	One year.	Two years.	Three years.	Four years.	Under one year.	One year.	Two years.	Three years.	Four years.	Under one year.	One year.	Two years.	Three years.	Four years.	Under one year.	One year.	Two years.	Three years.	Four years.
Buddhists ...	2	5	3	1	4	4	5	2	1	3	1	5	3	2	4	5	4	3	1	2
Nat-worshippers	4	5	2	1	3	4	5	2	1	3	2	5	3	1	4	5	4	2	1	3
Hindus ...	2	5	3	1	4	2	5	3	1	4	1	5	3	2	4	3	5	2	1	4
Musalmans ...	5	4	2	1	3	5	4	2	1	3	2	5	3	1	4	5	4	3	1	2
Christians ...	3	5	2	1	4	3	5	2	1	4	1	5	2	3	4	5	4	1	2	3
Total ...	2	5	3	1	4	4	5	2	1	3	1	5	3	2	4	5	4	2	1	3

It will be noticed that the returns by ages in Upper Burma are undoubtedly more accurate than those in Lower Burma, and that our returns in 1891 show an improvement on 1881. The only cause which I can assign for the figures being better in Upper Burma is that as a rule the officers in Upper Burma generally took greater interest in their work and that they and their subordinate officers exert a more active influence throughout their districts. The results here tabulated agree with the observations I made on my tour throughout various districts of the province regarding the quality of the work done, and it is for this reason that I feel sure that any attempt to explain away the figures by natural cause would be useless.

Comparison of age periods in aggregates of 10 and 20 years.

99. Enough has been said to show that until we improve the accuracy of our enumeration we cannot hope to make any real use of our figures, except by taking them in aggregates. The following returns show the distribution of the population by age periods of 10 and 20 years respectively, compared with the returns of Lower Burma in 1881, and with the returns of England, Scotland, and Germany :—

Ratio of the population at each period of 10 years to 10,000 of the total population of each sex.

	Lower Burma.		Upper Burma.		Burma.		Lower Burma, 1881.		England and Wales, 1881.		Scotland, 1881.		Germany, 1885.	
	Males.	Females.	Males.	Females,	Males.	Females.	Males.	Females.	Males.	Females.	Males.	Females.	Males.	Females.
0—9	2,585	2,889	2,556	2,456	2,575	2,711	2,689	3,019	2,632	2,506	2,702	2,450	2,528	2,416
10—19	2,117	2,249	2,086	2,059	2,106	2,171	2,080	2,226	2,112	2,007	2,197	2,003	2,049	1,978
20—29	1,870	1,789	1,648	1,611	1,789	1,716	1,770	1,627	1,656	1,712	1,688	1,697	1,507	1,604
30—39	1,446	1,144	1,412	1,334	1,434	1,222	1,491	1,193	1,254	1,276	1,167	1,234	1,262	1,274
40—49	923	815	978	952	942	871	964	863	966	998	913	1,004	1,043	1,071
50—59	576	602	608	658	587	625	557	566	687	721	653	740	746	798
60 and over	483	512	712	930	567	684	449	506	693	780	680	872	865	859

Ratio of the population at each age period of 20 years to 10,000 of the population of each sex.

	Lower Burma.		Upper Burma.		Burma.		Lower Burma, 1881.		England and Wales, 1881.		Scotland, 1881.		Germany, 1885.	
	Males.	Females.	Males.	Females.	Males.	Females.	Males.	Females.	Males.	Females.	Males.	Females.	Males.	Females.
0—19	4,702	5,138	4,642	4,515	4,681	4,882	4,769	5,245	4,744	4,513	4,899	4,453	4,577	4,394
20—39	3,316	2,933	3,060	2,945	3,223	2,938	3,261	2,820	2,910	2,988	2,855	2,931	2,769	2,878
40—59	1,499	1,417	1,586	1,610	1,529	1,496	1,521	1,429	1,653	1,719	1,566	1,744	1,789	1,869
60 and over	483	512	712	930	567	684	449	506	693	780	680	872	865	859

The age at which the population is evenly divided.

100. In these tables, errors due to accidental mistakes in the statements of those enumerated are, as Mr. Copleston pointed out, practically lost. These tables, which may be therefore taken as correct, point out first, that average length of life or mean age is greater in England than in Burma and is greater in Lower Burma in 1891 than in 1881. This is shown by the more even distribution of the population, and there being fewer in the earlier and more in the later age periods. The population of Burma is divided into half at the age of 20 years and 2 months. This means that half of the population of Burma is found to be under, and the other half to be over, that age. Taking the sexes apart, we find that males are divided at 20 years and 9 months and females at 19 years and 8 months.

The following table shows at what age the population of Upper and Lower Burma distributed by religions is equally divided :—

Table showing at what age the population of Upper and Lower Burma, distributed by sex and religions, is equally divided.

Religion.	Burma.			Upper Burma.			Lower Burma.		
	Total.	Male.	Female.	Total.	Male.	Female.	Total.	Male.	Female.
Buddhists ...	19·71	19·71	19·71	21·24	20·47	21·88	18·77	19·26	18·33
Nat-worshippers ...	20·79	22·11	19·49	23·80	25·54	20·90	20·38	21·50	19·35
Hindus	27·08	27·56	23·01	25·90	26·06	23·38	27·38	27·97	22·95
Musalmans ...	22·28	24·17	17·39	22·24	24·08	21·19	21·93	24·19	16·66
Christians ...	19·89	21.32	18·06	24·04	24·61	20·78	19·15	20·37	17·94

The reason why the age at which Hindus are divided is so high is to be found in the fact that a very large proportion, especially of the males, are immigrants. If we contrast the ages of Christians in Upper Burma, where they are nearly all immigrants, with the ages of those in Lower Burma, where there is a large indigenous Christian population, we at once see that immigrants who are generally adults raise the age at which the population is equally divided.

It is not easy to understand why the "dividing" age of Buddhists in Upper should be higher than in Lower Burma. If we turn to the mean age table at page 110 we find that the mean age is correspondingly slightly higher. I am inclined to think that judging by the age returns of infants, the returns of Upper Burma are more probably correct than those of Lower Burma. This I may add is borne out by the criticism of the Census Commissioner on the mean ages returned in 1881, which he is inclined to think were "pitched" too low.

In Lower Burma in 1881 half the total population was below the age of 20 and half above that age, while males were divided at the age of 21¼ and females at 18¼.

101. Guided by the experience of 1881 and in order to simplify our calculations of mean age and to assist in preparing the return of those ages which do not coincide with the quinquennia of the age table, a special return of 10 per cent. of the population by every year of life was prepared. The accompanying table shows this return.

Diagram B.

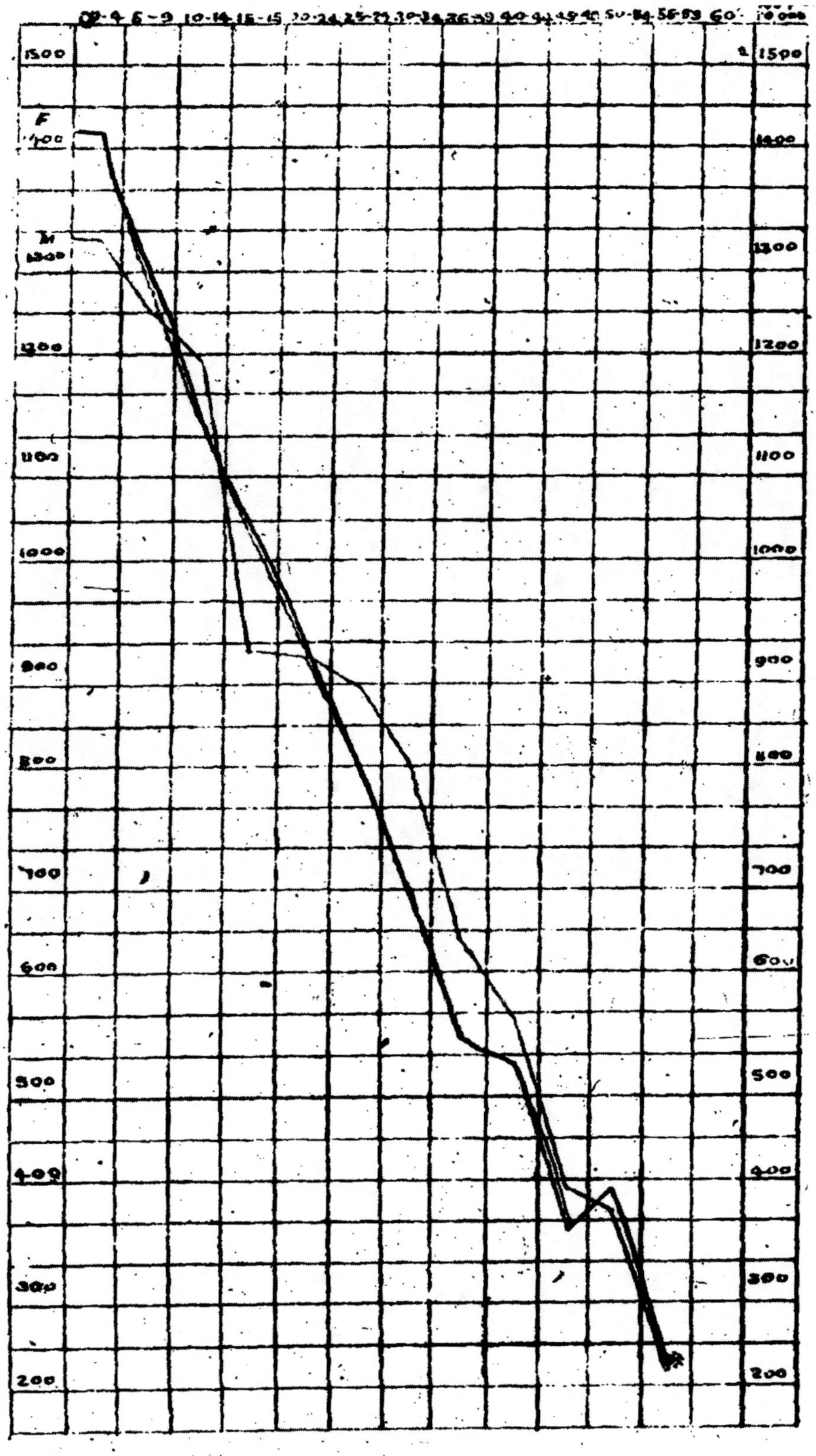

The balance is on 6a% over.

Table showing ages of the population by sexes in every year of their life per 10,000 of the total population of each sex, excluding the population of Rangoon Town.

Age.	Males.	Females.	Age.	Males.	Females.
Infant	296·7	312·7	58	58·1	33·6
1	205·3	213·4	59	19·2	22·6
2	263·4	266·1	60	129·2	160·4
3	303·8	390·7	61	31·6	31·6
4	252·2	285·2	62	33·8	33·3
5	296·7	307·5	63	33·5	31·5
6	267·4	280·4	64	27·3	22·6
7	231·1	267·8	65	48·4	69·2
8	272·7	294·6	66	20·5	16·1
9	177	175·9	67	22	22·6
10	338·3	335·3	68	11·8	9·6
11	164	172·3	69	6·8	6·4
12	270·6	259·7	70	60·2	112·8
13	231·7	212·8	71	8·6	11·9
14	175·5	181·7	72	7·7	8·7
15	256	268·1	73	7·1	11·3
16	206·6	199·5	74	5·2	6·7
17	178·9	188·8	75	19·8	25·8
18	193·5	226·7	76	5·2	8
19	152·2	152	77	30·1	6·1
20	372·8	388·4	78	27·3	5·8
21	116·8	119·6	79	27	4·5
22	141	128·4	80	17·7	30·4
23	133·2	147·1	81	·9	3·2
24	127	170	82	2·7	1·9
25	336·1	314·7	83	1·2	1·6
26	149·7	120·6	84	......	1·9
27	132	130·9	85	4·6	3·8
28	142·9	126·7	86	·6	·6
29	83·5	97·6	87	1·2	1·6
30	395·8	336·3	88	·3	·6
31	87·9	79·5	89	·3	·9
32	114	108·6	90	1·8	5·4
33	95	83·4	91	·3	·6
34	81·7	69·8	92	......	......
35	266·8	191·1	93	·6	......
36	108·1	89·2	94	......	·3
37	103·1	82·1	95	·3	1·6
38	107·7	107	96	·3	·3
39	66·1	61·1	97	......	......
40	266·5	242·2	98	......	......
41	66·7	59·5	99	......	·3
42	78·6	85	100	·6	·3
43	70·5	62·1	101		
44	41·6	54·3	102		
45	176·4	158·4	103		
46	64	64·3	104		
47	63	54·9	105		
48	55·9	57·2	106		
49	33·5	27·4	107		
50	166·2	193·4	108		
51	45	39·4	109		
52	53·4	52	110		
53	38·2	45·6	111		
54	33·2	32	112		
55	83·2	82·1	113		
56	50	59·8	114		
57	41·3	29·1	......		

Age returns in Rangoon.

102. The return of ages in Rangoon is so anomalous that a special diagram D has been prepared showing the variation of the returns of age from year to year. In Chapter II the disparity in the number of females and males and its effect on the birth-rate would prepare us to find that owing to immigration the number of middle-aged persons might easily outnumber the children of any given year, but the diagram not only shows this, but illustrates better than words can the tendency already noticed to return multiples of 5 instead of the intervening years.

Proportionate strength of population within the reproductive age period.

103. In trying to find out the number of reproductive males and females it is necessary to fix the limit between which both sexes are reproductive. The limit in England, where both males and females arrive at puberty much later in life, is taken as beginning at 15 and ending at 45. The Census Commissioner, admitting the difficulty of fixing an age, proposed 18 to 59 as the limits for men and 15 to 44 for women. These periods may be correct for Indian provinces, but they do not obtain in Burma. For men 18 seems too late, as it is not uncommon to find Burman lads of that age who have children. I should feel inclined to fix the age at 15 as in England. On the other hand, 59 is much too old. From enquiries I have made I find that very few cases are known of men in Burma begetting children when they are past 50. I should therefore feel inclined to reduce the age by 5 years and fix the limits at 15 and 54. As regards women the limits of 15 to 44 err in prolonging the period of productiveness. Owing to the barbarous system of midwifery practised in Burma, the reproductive age rarely extends to 40 years. From enquiries made I have discovered that few Burmese women over 40 years of age ever bear children. There is a Burmese phrase to the effect that the fertility of women is exhausted at 40 years of age (မိမ္မတို့ဝမ္မထာအသက်၄၀ဝသွေးဆိုးရာ။). The reproductive age for women would therefore be from 15 to 39. Taking these ages we find that out of 10,000 of each sex 5,443 males and 3,900 females may be classed as being reproductive.

The mean age of the population.

104. With a large immigrant population there is some difficulty in calculating the mean age of the people. The mean age in Burma depends on four things, (1) the proportion of children to the total population, (2) the proportion of immigrants and emigrants to the local population, (3) the length of residence made in the country by the immigrants, (4) and lastly the longevity of the indigenous population. It may not readily be understood why the number of children should affect the mean age, but if we reflect we must see that a disproportionately large number of children born in any year must reduce the mean age, for then the numbers at advanced ages are proportionately fewer.

The following table gives the mean age of the population compared with the return of other provinces:—

Statement showing mean age of the population in Upper and Lower Burma and of the other provinces of India and of England.

Province or State.	Total.	Male.	Female.
Burma	24·54	24·57	24·51
Upper Burma	26·01	25·37	26·59
Lower Burma, 1891	23·62	24·11	23·07
Lower Burma, 1881	23·24	23·71	23·70
England	26·4	26·	26·8
Bombay	24·5	...	...
Bengal	24·99	24·49	25·49
Madras	...	...	...
Assam	23·7	23·76	23·63
Central Provinccs	24·07	...	...
North-Western Provinces	...	24·9	..

The figures for other provinces are extracted from the reports of the respective Deputy Superintendents.

The figures for Burma have been obtained from Imperial Table VII corrected as far as possible by the results of Sheet XII. In 1881 the figures were considered as being probably placed too low. In preparing a table of this sort from the doubtful age returns and the still more doubtful vital statistics we possess and with no return of ages at which deaths were recorded to act as a check, the results can only be looked on as being approximately correct, though much trouble has been taken to secure right return.

CHAPTER V.

CIVIL CONDITION.

The causes which determine the tendency to marriage. Divorce. Returns showing the comparative strength of the tendency to marriage in both sexes in Burma compared with the returns of other States and provinces. Relative proportion of the sexes in each condition by age and religion. The age at which the tendency to marriage develops itself in Burma and in other countries. The tendency to early marriage shown by the numbers of the various religions enumerated.

105. In this present chapter we deal with the relations which exist between the two sexes. Except in so far as the natural conditions are disturbed and the proportions between the sexes affected by immigration from other countries, longevity and the proportional strength of males and females at birth are matters not directly affected by the volition of the population. But marriage, by which we mean the legalized union of the sexes, depends entirely on moral and religious grounds. The coition of the sexes of human beings is by the introduction of marriage lifted out of the sphere of mere physiological enquiry. In Burma, marriage, as a distinct civil condition of rights on the one hand and duties and obligations on the other, is found to exist even amongst the wildest tribes. These marriage customs will be briefly noticed hereafter. In Burma marriage amongst the indigenous races is easily contracted, and is almost as easily annulled. Mere cohabitation, if it be openly practised, is one of the ways in which marriage may be contracted. The facility with which the tie may be contracted and annulled, however much it may at first shock the susceptibilities of those who are accustomed to the stricter code of Western civilization, has this one compensating advantage, that proportionately fewer illegitimate children are born into the world in Burma than in most of the countries generally considered civilized. In comparing the results obtained from the schedule books, there will be no necessity to enter into a discussion or comparison of the figures of one district with another. Marriage customs do not necessarily vary with administrative divisions, and nothing can be inferred from the results of small groups of figures, as they possess in regard to civil condition no statistical value whatsoever.

Marriage.

106. Before entering into a consideration of the returns, the question of divorce and the method in which divorced persons were enumerated must be mentioned. In Burma, where, as already stated, divorce is easily obtained, in fact more easily than in any other country, the number of divorced persons is necessarily high. On the occasion of the last census 18,563 persons, 8,027 of whom were males, were returned as divorced. As Mr. Copleston pointed out, this return could not be looked on as accurate. The value of the return may be gauged from the fact that while 3,389 persons were in 1881 returned as divorced in Prome, only 43 were so returned in the adjoining district of Tharrawaddy out of a population almost equally large. This variation was of course due to the fact that the instructions regarding the entry of divorced persons, were not understood by the enumerators. Moreover the return is made more complex by the fact that re-marriages between the *ex*-husband and *ex*-wife are not uncommon, while if the divorced couple do not re-marry each other, almost invariably each seeks a fresh partner, and it is only amongst the middle-aged and old that we find persons remaining unwed, because they have been separated from their former partners. Unless then the term "divorced" were to be made to include all who have ever been divorced, the return would not show the real number of persons who had been divorced, or how frequent divorces were. On the other hand, such a return as divorced and re-married would not only be cumbersome, but would be evaded as the previous divorce would not

Divorce.

be mentioned except in cases where the enumerator knew the past life of those whom he enumerates. On these grounds no attempt to return "divorced" was made. Those who returned themselves as divorced were, according to the instruction of the Government of India, included amongst widowed as was done on the last occasion in Burma. The inclusion of divorced persons amongst the unmarried, which is the practice in England, would render difficult in the East the ascertainment of the age at which marriage takes place, as the age of divorced people should be on an average higher than that of the married.

The returns of civil condition were not of course collected in the tracts excluded from regular census operations, and accordingly the total population regarding whom the subjoined tables are prepared, numbers 7,605,560 souls.

In dealing with this question, I propose to divide it into three parts, first, the general tendency in the province towards marriage compared with the tendency in other provinces and countries; secondly, the age at which this tendency develops itself in Burma; and, thirdly, the comparison of the strength of this tendency shown by those professing the chief religions found in Burma.

Comparison of the strength of the tendency to marriage in Burma and in other countries.

107. The accompanying table exhibits the returns of the total population of Burma distributed in the ratio of 10,000 of each sex by civil condition compared with the returns of Lower Burma in 1881, of the various provinces of India, of the countries of Europe, and of our chief Colonies:—

Province or country.	Sex.	Single.	Married.	Widowed.
Burma	Males	5,578	3,945	477
	Females	5,059	3,782	1,159
Upper Burma	Males	5,603	3,884	513
	Females	4,947	3,573	1,479
Lower Burma, 1891 ...	Males	5,564	3,980	456
	Females	5,136	3,927	937
Lower Burma, 1881 ...	Males	5,791	3,818	391
	Females	5,191	3,892	917
India	Males	4,841	4,670	489
	Females	3,232	4,895	1,873
Assam	Males	5,400	4,249	351
	Females	4,115	4,275	1,610
Bengal	Males	4,651	4,946	403
	Females	2,937	4,913	2,150
Bombay	Males	4,587	4,888	525
	Females	3,026	5,143	1,831
Central Provinces ...	Males	4,631	4,939	430
	Females	3,439	5,080	1,481
Madras	Males	5,471	4,146	383
	Females	3,641	4,232	2,127
North-Western Provinces ...	Males	4,495	4,847	658
	Females	2,992	5,291	1,717
Oudh	Males	4,603	4,851	546
	Females	3,079	5,234	1,687
Punjab	Males	5,242	4,150	608
	Females	3,622	4,952	1,426
England and Wales ...	Males	6,193	3,463	344
	Females	5,928	3,314	758
Scotland	Males	6,628	3,044	328
	Females	6,285	2,896	819
Ireland	Males	6,871	2,750	379
	Females	6,344	2,698	958
New South Wales ...	Males	7,064	2,694	242
	Females	6,354	3,173	473
Victoria	Males	6,958	2,757	285
	Females	6,398	3,072	530
France	Males	5,513	3,954	533
	Females	5,041	3,934	1,025
German Empire ...	Males	6,213	3,449	338
	Females	5,809	3,321	870

The first thing that is noticeable in the above table is that marriage is more common in the other provinces of the Indian Empire than in Burma, and that marriage is more common in Burma than in our colonies and in most of the countries of Europe. It would also appear that marriage has in Lower Burma become more common within the last decade. The next noticeable point is that in Lower Burma the number of widowed females is much less than in Upper

Burma. This is probably due chiefly to the emigration of able-bodied males to Lower Burma before the annexation when penal laws prohibited the emigration of the entire families. Men sometimes left their wives and never returned, having found a home in Lower Burma. It is also in part due to the loss of male lives in Upper Burma in the recent disturbances. The dacoits, who at one time comprised a very large proportion of the available male population capable of bearing arms, suffered heavily both in encounters with the Military and still more from fever and exposure. Their wives stayed at home and hence suffered less. The disparity, therefore, is easily explained. But the disparity between widowed females in Burma and widowed females in India is due to the fact that widows in Burma are allowed to re-marry and often do re-marry, whereas widows in India in certain castes are prohibited from re-marrying.

108. The reason why married people are less numerous in Burma than in India is due, not so much to the fact that real marriages are so much fewer, as to the absence of child marriage amongst the Buddhists and Nat-worshippers who compose the bulk of the population. In India, children are married, or rather betrothed, and are returned as married; a certain proportion of these of course die before they reach the age at which in Burma or in England they would think of marrying. Under these circumstances, in order to compare the number of married people and the real strength of the tendency to marriage, we must exclude from our calculations all children who have not yet attained puberty, although in India a large number of them are returned as married. Marriage is of course more common in Burma than in England. The tie is so easily undone by divorce, and a wife is so often a means of support instead of being a burden to a husband, that few Burmans reach the age of 23 without being married. In Burma, moreover, generally, and in Lower Burma in particular, there is so wide a margin between the ordinary style of living and the bare means of existence that, except in the larger towns, no Burman is ever prevented by motives of prudence alone from entering into the married state.

Civil condition of the population by age.

109. We have now to compare the returns which show the period of age at which the tendency to marriage develops itself in Burma with the results of previous enumerations in other provinces of India and in Europe.

The accompanying table shows the returns of civil condition of the population in the ratio of 10,000 of each sex at each age period distributed according to the proportionate strength of each condition.

Comparative statement showing the distribution of the population by 10,000 of each sex at each age period into the three civil conditions.

Province.		0—14		15—24		25—39		40—49		50 AND OVER.	
		Males.	Females.	Males.	Females.	Males.	Females.	Males.	Females.	Males.	Females.
Burma ...	Single ...	9,996	9,984	7,344	5,063	1,624	739	516	353	424	354
	Married ...	4	15	2,498	4,528	7,841	8,231	8,595	7,527	7,492	4,401
	Widowed ...	...	1	158	409	535	1,030	889	2,120	2,084	5,245
Upper Burma...	Single ...	9,997	9,989	7,672	5,791	1,742	1,040	569	550	527	491
	Married ...	3	10	2,188	3,757	7,739	7,689	8,621	7,033	7,236	3,841
	Widowed ...	...	1	140	452	519	1,271	810	2,417	2,237	5,668
Lower Burma...	Single ...	9,995	9,981	7,167	4,612	1,562	515	483	193	350	219
	Married ...	5	17	2,664	5,006	7,895	8,634	8,579	7,930	7,675	4,957
	Widowed ...	...	2	169	382	343	851	938	1,877	1,975	4,824
Lower Burma, 1881.	Single ...	9,996	9,978	7,511	4,561	1,978	463	633	180	416	197
	Married ...	4	21	2,364	5,115	7,561	8,766	8,536	8,017	7,797	4,686
	Widowed ...	...	1	125	324	461	711	831	1,803	1,787	5,117
India ...	Single ...	9,348	8,061	4,875	4,916	1,160	123	433	79	341	61
	Married ...	630	1,872	4,916	8,671	8,231	8,055	8,359	5,563	7,545	2,526
	Widowed ...	22	67	209	603	519	1,822	978	4,358	2,114	7,413

Comparative statement showing the distribution of the population by 10,000 of each sex at each age period into the three civil conditions—concluded.

Province.		0—14 Males.	0—14 Females.	15—24 Males.	15—24 Females.	25—39 Males.	25—39 Females.	40—49 Males.	40—49 Females.	50 and over. Males.	50 and over. Females.
Bengal	Single ...	9,165	7,454	4,377	290	823	69	233	39	159	30
	Married ...	810	2,438	5,437	8,872	8,753	7,686	8,979	4,976	8,074	2,212
	Widowed ...	25	108	186	838	424	2,245	788	4,985	1,767	7,758
Madras	Single ...	9,820	8,801	7,112	1,376	1,512	234	292	169	192	125
	Married ...	174	1,144	2,810	7,885	8,103	7,481	8,910	4,783	7,941	1,910
	Widowed ...	6	55	78	739	385	2,285	798	5,048	1,867	7,965
Scotland	Single ...	10,000	10,000	9,275	8,623	3,431	3,274	1,457	2,001	1,140	1,961
	Married ...	...	...	716	1,360	6,366	6,339	8,016	6,680	7,069	4,282
	Widowed ...	...	...	9	17	203	387	527	1,319	1,791	3,757
German Empire	Single ...	10,000	10,000	9,649	8,754	3,148	2,411	944	1,134	765	1,092
	Married ...	...	...	348	1,231	6,735	7,241	8,712	7,632	7,400	4,896
	Widowed ...	...	...	3	15	117	348	344	1,234	1,835	4,012
Victoria	Single ...	10,000	10,000	9,452	8,371	4,235	2,044	2,776	597	2,414	448
	Married ...	...	...	539	1,588	5,598	7,459	6,760	8,075	6,241	6,426
	Widowed ...	...	...	9	41	167	497	464	1,328	1,345	3,126

Notwithstanding the large proportion of Indian immigrants, there are but very few returned as married under 15 years of age in Burma. Nor does the tendency to marriage attain its full development till the third age period 25—39. The last feature which distinguishes the return in Burma is the comparative scarcity of widows. There are of course more widows than widowers, but this is not, as in India, due to the prohibition of re-marriage, but because, as in England, unless a widow possesses a jointure, which few in Burma do, she stands a poor chance of marrying again, for though well in the van of progress in marriage law, women in Burma have not yet assumed the privilege supposed to be permitted to women in Europe in Leap Year. Something deeper than mere accidental causes is at the bottom of this divergence in the returns of Burma and India.

Polygamy comparatively rare in Burma.

110. The Burmese Marriage Law must not be looked at from the standpoint of the elaborate foreign legislation found in the Damathats. Mr. Coryton, a former Recorder of Moulmein, wrote that polygamy was practically obsolete, and that the law relating to it had fallen into disuse. Mr. Coryton has perhaps overstated his case, but his remarks are worthy of being reproduced as not only are they forcibly if somewhat picturesquely expressed, but he quotes in corroboration of his own views the opinion of Mr. Macrae, now Deputy Commissioner of Hanthawaddy, and the oldest member of the Burma Commission. The only point on which I think there is any reason to differ from Mr. Coryton is the statement from which it might be inferred that these laws were ever anything but foreign legal dissertations in Burma. If Buddhism, as Mr. Taw Sein Ko asserts, is comparatively of recent origin, it stands to reason that this supposed divinely grown law is also of recent introduction.

Polygamy in Burma.

That it would have been impossible at the present day to have given the sanction of law to the maxims of the Damathat pure and simple is, I think, evident when one considers the essential difference between the modern and ancient state of society among the Burmese. The ancient Burmese were slave-owners and polygamists, and seem to have drawn a line of considerable nicety between polygamy and concubinage. What fearful complications must at times have arisen in the administration of the law we may gather from the details into which the great Lawgiver thought it necessary to go. In the 48th Chapter of the third volume of the Dhamathat (Richardson's translation, page 93) we have "the two Laws when a man has a head wife and a lesser"—enactments as to "the six kinds of concubines,"—the "eight kinds of debts contracted by these without the knowledge of the head of the family," and—"the five kinds of wives and the five ways of paying debts." In the preceding chapter we find "the law when the husband contracts debts without the knowledge of the two wives and six concubines." Jeremy Bentham, what a mess!

It is scarcely stating a fact too broadly to say that polygamy no longer exists in British Burma. Major Brigges, some time Deputy Commissioner of Tenasserim, in the work I have before referred to, thus notices its decadence. Most Burmans have only one wife and few more than two. The first, or head wife, is usually the choice of the husband in his youth, and when she ceases to have children she often assists in the choice of a young wife who is bound to obey her.

The tendency towards monogamy has, since Major Brigges wrote, become stronger still. Among Moulmein Burmese polygamy may be said to have ceased to exist. My friend, Mr. J. K. Macrae, probably the most popular and most experienced Magistrate Moulmein has had, was obliging enough to give me when I was writing my report for 1866 the following note on the subject:—

"Polygamy is so very rare among the Burman inhabitants of this town that in all my "experience I have never been called on to deal with a case arising out of it. Women here "are so independent that they will not put up with the position of lesser wife, and a man "already burdened with a wife, if desirous of taking another, finds himself almost invariably "obliged to part with the first. The terms of separation are arranged and settled by elders "chosen by the parties and are in accordance with their own Burman ideas based on the "rules contained in the 12th volume of the Laws of Menu (the Damathat.)"

The portions of the Code especially referring to divorce as it affects the person and property of the wife are these. By section 35 (based on the Damathat, Volume I, Chapter 12) it is provided that when a husband and wife mutually agree to separate, each party is entitled to take out his or her separate property, and the joint property shall be divided equally between them. Of the children, the father is entitled to take the son, the mother the daughter; and if the sons are too young to be taken from their mother, they shall be left with her until they attain the age of seven years.

By section 36 it is provided that when the husband wishes to separate, and the wife does not, or *vice versâ*, supposing that no sufficient cause for separation can be established, the one who wishes for the divorce is entitled to take his or her property only, all the rest of the property and all the children shall remain with the party unwilling to be divorced, save and except that if the wife is the party wishing for the divorce, she has a right to take with her her loom, with all the implements belonging to it, and the unfinished web in it.

Divorce, I may mention, is very rare, a fact attributable equally perhaps to the high position occupied by women in Burmese society, the care with which marriage contracts are entered into, and the extreme evenness of temper which characterizes both sexes.

111. The fact that polygamy no longer exists amongst the Buddhists to any appreciable extent is clearly proven by the fact that the numbers of married males and females almost exactly balance each other. There are exactly 1,306,722 husbands to 1,307,292 wives, and the disparity is easily accounted for when we consider the number of dacoits who have been deported within the last 5 years; many of whom were no doubt married, but were not accompanied into transportation by their wives. The fact is that in Burma women taking on themselves a fair share of the duty of supporting their household, have gradually acquired a position of independence after marriage which has only by recent legislation been introduced into England. Within the last few months the Judicial Commissioner of Lower Burma, after consulting every available authority on law and custom, ruled that a husband cannot alienate the property acquired jointly by himself and wife after marriage without his wife's consent.* We have still something to learn from Burma in marriage law. The independence thus acquired by women has given them equal rights in divorce, and it is but fair to both Burmese men and women to state that though custom, which is laxer than the written law, permits almost absolute freedom in this matter, the privilege is not generally abused. Here again the safeguard is not merely public opinion, which would at once condemn a man who married and divorced his wives too freely, but the self-respect of the woman, for such a man would not easily find a wife if it became known that he had been in the habit of ill-treating his previous wives. With such independence of character and self-respect amongst the women it is not wonderful that, as Mr. Copleston remarked in 1881, child marriage is unknown amongst the indigenous races. No doubt our returns show that marriage is contracted more freely and earlier in life in Burma than in Europe, but this is due to the fact that destitution is almost unknown and the wants of life in the temperate

* *Ma Thu, appellant, v. Ma Bu, defendant—Civil 2nd appeal No. 16 of 1891.*

climate of Burma are more easily satisfied than in the colder countries of Northern Europe. A young Burmese couple can start house-keeping with a da (or Burmese knife) and a cooking pot. The universal bamboo supplies materials both for building his house, lighting the fire, carrying the water from the well and even may help to compose the dinner itself. Moreover, a Burman wife is often cleverer than her husband, and is a source of income rather than of expenditure. Last but perhaps not least the facility for obtaining a divorce renders the entrance into matrimony a less serious and irrevocable step.

The mean age of married persons in Burma.

112. As might be expected from the foregoing table, the mean age of married persons is higher in Burma than in India and lower than in European countries. The accompanying table exhibits the mean age of single, married, and widowed by sexes in Upper and Lower Burma apart and taken together, and also of the mean age of married persons distributed by the four chief religions.

	Single.		Married.		Widowed.	
	Male.	Female.	Male.	Female.	Male.	Female.
Lower Burma	11·8	9·4	38·5	34·2	47·5	50·5
Upper Burma	12·3	11·4	40·6	36·6	51·9	52·7
Burma	12·02	10·2	39·3	35·2	49·2	51·7

Religion.	Male.	Female.	Total.
Buddhist	39·98	35·47	36·73
Hindu	33·18	30·21	32·73
Musalman	35·5	30·65	33·98
Christian	38	33·35	35·51

A discussion of the marriage rites and ceremonies of the Burmese is rendered unnecessary here as it has already been adequately dealt with elsewhere by Mr. Scott (Shwe Yeo) and others. The marriage customs of the semi-civilized tribes on our frontiers will be briefly dealt with in Chapter X. It only remains to contrast the returns of civil condition of the population of Burma distributed by religions.

The tendency to marriage among those professing the different religions returned.

113. The accompanying statement shows the proportion borne by the numbers returned by each sex under each of the three civil conditions out of every 10,000 of the population according to the religion they profess.

Religion.	Civil condition.	Distribution of 10,000 persons of each religion by sex.		
		Both sexes.	Males.	Females.
Total of all religions ...	Unmarried	5,323	5,578	5,059
	Married	3,865	3,945	3,782
	Widowed	812	477	1,159
Buddhists ...	Unmarried	5,372	5,680	5,070
	Married	3,795	3,832	3,759
	Widowed	833	488	1,171
Nat-worshippers ...	Unmarried	5,239	5,463	4,979
	Married	4,032	4,004	4,066
	Widowed	729	533	955
Hindus	Unmarried	3,882	3,928	3,644
	Married	5,651	5,717	5,302
	Widowed	467	355	1,054

Religion.	Civil condition.	Distribution of 10,000 persons of each religion by sex.		
		Both sexes.	Males.	Females.
Musalmans ...	Unmarried	4,804	4,757	4,889
	Married	4,544	4,869	3,965
	Widowed	652	374	1,146
Christians... ...	Unmarried	5,816	6,135	5,433
	Married	3,633	3,526	3,763
	Widowed	551	339	804
Sikhs	Unmarried	4,617	4,716	2,500
	Married	5,060	4,951	7,428
	Widowed	323	333	72
Jews	Unmarried	4,929	4,848	5,033
	Married	4,586	4,799	4,313
	Widowed	485	353	654
Parsis	Unmarried	4,063	3,780	5,714
	Married	5,625	5,854	4,286
	Widowed	312	366	......
Not returned ...	Unmarried	3,674	3,256	6,667
	Married	5,918	6,279	3,333
	Widowed	408	465	......

In this statement all the religions of the province are shown irrespective of age periods. Before comparing these returns, it must be recollected that the large number of unmarried is due to the fact that 37·68 per cent. of the males and 38·59 of the females are under 14 years of age, and that they are not in Buddhist or Christian eyes fit for marriage. Next must be remembered that large numbers of the Hindus, Mahomedans, and Christians do not reach the country till they have passed this period, and are therefore marriageable. On the other hand, amongst those who profess these religions, the females are few in proportion to the males as the returns of age and sex (Chapter IV) have already shown. Moreover, a large number professing these religions do not stay as settlers in the country, and hence the number of widowed amongst them is comparatively small.

114. Sikhs, Jews, and Parsis are so few in number that there is no advantage gained by taking these returns distributed by age periods, but for those professing the other religions it is clear that in order to gauge the value of these returns the true strength of the tendency to marriage can only be observed when the population is distributed by the age periods as in the annexed tables.

Comparative statement showing the distribution of the population by civil condition in every 10,000 of the population at each age period according to the religion professed.

Religion and condition.		0—14		15—24		25—39		40—49		50 and over.	
		Males.	Females.	Males.	Females.	Males.	Females.	Males.	Females.	Males.	Females.
Total of all Religions.	Single ...	9,996	9,984	7,344	5,063	1,624	739	516	353	424	354
	Married ...	4	15	2,498	4,528	7,841	8,231	8,595	7,527	7,492	4,401
	Widowed ...	...	1	158	409	535	1,030	889	2,120	2,084	5,245
Buddhists ...	Single ...	9,997	9,989	7,450	5,172	1,476	751	484	359	420	358
	Married ...	3	10	2,387	4,414	7,954	8,211	8,619	7,550	7,475	4,413
	Widowed ...	...	1	163	414	570	1,038	897	2,091	2,105	5,229
Nat-worshippers.	Single ...	9,989	9,969	7,421	4,542	1,921	566	542	243	337	333
	Married ...	10	30	2,385	5,166	7,466	8,542	8,351	7,538	7,529	4,622
	Widowed ...	1	1	194	292	613	892	1,107	2,219	2,134	5,045
Hindus ...	Single ...	9,911	9,857	6,211	1,743	2,690	476	1,140	278	950	294
	Married ...	83	138	3,674	7,935	7,011	8,711	8,149	6,896	7,296	3,754
	Widowed ...	6	5	115	322	299	813	711	2,826	1,754	5,952
Musalmans ...	Single ...	9,986	9,870	6,508	2,531	1,632	445	506	251	321	230
	Married ...	12	125	3,348	6,977	7,987	8,448	8,723	6,776	7,897	3,591
	Widowed ...	2	5	144	492	381	1,107	771	2,973	1,782	6,179
Christians ...	Single ...	9,995	9,982	8,244	5,172	2,908	855	598	305	305	292
	Married ...	4	17	1,677	4,635	6,714	8,340	8,511	7,308	7,862	4,708
	Widowed ...	1	1	79	193	378	805	891	2,387	1,833	5,000

This table is a companion table to the comparative statement on page 113 in which the tendency to marriage in the provinces of India is compared with the tendency disclosed by the returns of Burma. We here see that in the first age period the tendency to marriage is almost confined to Hindus, Musalmans, and Nat-worshippers. Early marriages are apparently more common amongst Christians than among Buddhists, but the former, it must be remembered, contain 66·4 per cent. of Karens, many of whom are comparatively recent converts to Christianity. We find, however, that above the age of 25 there are proportionately fewer unmarried males amongst Buddhists than even amongst Hindus and Musalmans. This is no doubt due to the fact that a large number of our Hindu and Musalman immigrants have emigrated to Burma as they were too poor in India to support themselves, much less a wife. Again we find that among Hindus and Musalmans the number of widows is much larger than amongst other religions, and this might be expected, inasmuch as the proportionate strength of widows is much larger in India. On the other hand, we see that, probably influenced by their environment, the tendency to child marriage amongst Hindus and Musalmans is far less prominent in Burma than the returns of Indian provinces would lead us to expect, and the same cause may account for the proportionate decrease in the number of widows.

115. The annexed statement shows the distribution of 10,000 of each sex and of each condition by age periods.

Religion and condition.		0—14		15—24		25—39		40—49		50 AND OVER.	
		Males.	Females.	Males.	Females.	Males.	Females.	Males.	Females.	Males.	Females.
All conditions distributed by age period.		3,768	3,859	1,823	1,933	2,313	2,028	942	871	·1,154	1,309
Total of all religions	Single ...	6,752	7,617	2,399	1,934	674	296	87	61	88	92
	Married ...	4	15	1,154	2,314	4,597	4,414	2,053	1,734	2,192	1,523
	Widowed	2	4	606	681	2,592	1,801	1,757	1,593	5,043	5,921
Buddhists ...	Single ...	6,966	7,583	2,309	1,962	556	299	80	62	89	94
	Married ...	3	10	1,096	2,259	4,443	4,400	2,108	1,763	2,350	1,568
	Widowed.	1	3	587	680	2,499	1,785	1,722	1,567	5,191	5,965
Nat-worshippers ...	Single ...	6,612	7,808	2,314	1,831	905	252	104	43	65	66
	Married ...	9	29	1,015	2,549	4,800	4,659	2,180	1,630	1,996	1,133
	Widowed.	10	5	618	614	2,958	2,072	2,170	2,043	4,244	5,266
Hindus ...	Single ...	1,951	8,347	4,255	1,122	3,340	398	315	66	139	67
	Married ...	11	80	1,729	3,201	5,982	5,009	1,546	1,124	732	586
	Widowed.	14	14	872	652	4,111	2,349	2,171	2,314	2,832	4,671
Musalmans ...	Single ...	5.581	8,694	3,138	1,042	1,124	180	100	37	57	47
	Married ...	7	135	1,577	3,543	5,375	4,203	1,680	1,219	1,361	900
	Widowed.	13	19	881	864	3,340	1,907	1,933	1,852	3,833	5,358
Christians ...	Single ...	5,882	7,536	2,678	2,031	1,321	348	80	41	39	44
	Married ...	4	19	948	2,629	5,306	4,898	1,971	1,429	1,771	1,025
	Widowed.	13	4	464	511	3,099	2,211	2,140	2,183	4,284	5,091

Here as might be expected we find that the bulk of the unmarried are found in the earlier age periods, and that in the total of all Burma there is except in the last age period, which of course contains a large number of persons as the period is more extended, a gradual decrease in the number of the unwed. In the case of the married there are but few up to the end of the 1st period and the bulk of them are found in middle life. The widowed and divorced are few up to 24 years of age, they then increase only to fall again in the 4th age period (40—49), and are naturally most numerous in the last age period. This variation in the 3rd and 4th age periods is due to the fact that the 3rd age period covers 15 and the 4th age period only 10 years. Even if the age periods were equally divided we should still find that the widowers are more numerous between 30 and 40 than in each of the next two decades. On referring to the returns of widowed for Lower Burma in 1881 we find that the same anomaly was then noticeable.

Turning to the returns of the population distributed by religions we find that this apparent anomaly is to be found most marked in the case of Hindus and Musalmans. It is difficult to assign a reason for this except that in the case of Buddhists re-marriage of widowers is common and that amongst our Indian immigrants those who have lost their wives are more ready to emigrate because less hampered. The decrease in the following decade is caused by their return to their native country.

Taking the sexes apart this table shows that in all religions alike women marry earlier than men and that fewer women than men remain unmarried except in the case of Mahomedans where the numbers are nearly evenly balanced. In the case of Buddhists the overwhelming preponderance in the number of widows makes up for the deficiency in the number of the married. It is noticeable that while the number of married males is in excess of the females both in Upper and Lower Burma, which is due no doubt to the presence of a large number of married immigrants who have come to Burma without their wives, the number of widows in Upper Burma is more than thrice as great as the number of widowers, or 3,126 widows to every 1,000 widowers. This is partly due to the fact before mentioned that widows find it more difficult to re-marry. Referring to the returns of Lower Burma we find that there are only 1,831 widows for every 1,000 widowers. The excess in Upper Burma is in part due to the fact that in years past before the annexation Upper Burma had been depleted of its male population. As an illustration of this we may take the case of Victoria, the disparity between widows and widowers is less marked than in England, whence the bulk of the Victorian immigrants come. But we have also another cause which has already been noticed in Chapter IV, and that is the fact that the anarchy and consequent trouble inflicted a heavier proportionate loss on the males than on the females. How much of this preponderance of widows is due to either cause there are no possible means of determining now.

The reproductive age period.

116. Taking 15—39 to be the limits of the reproductive age amongst women, we find that 39·6 per cent. of the total number of women are found to be between these ages, and that 948,881 or 64·2 per cent. of these women are married. Amongst men we find that allowing 15—49 as being the reproductive age, 50·7 per cent. of the male population is included in this period and that 1,193,467 or 60·6 per cent. of them are married. It is of course impossible to say how many of these reproductive husbands and wives are married to partners who are not within the productive age limits.

CHAPTER VI.

INFIRMITIES.

Comparative Statements A, B, C, D, E, F, G and H. Insanity; its definition; reasons assigned for the variance observed in the return of lunatics in Eastern and Western Countries; the causes of insanity; its local distribution; the greater prevalence of insanity amongst females in Upper Burma; lunatics distributed by religion and race. Deaf-mutism; its definition; local distribution by sex, age, religion, and race. Blindness; noticeable decrease in the number of those so returned in the three successive enumerations; the disproportionately large return of the blind in Upper Burma; the causes of blindness; the increasing tendency to develop this affliction in the later years of life; the return of the blind distributed by age, sex, race, and religion. Leprosy; the definition adopted; decrease in the return of the present Census in Lower Burma compared with the return of 1881; disparity between the return of those thus afflicted in Upper and Lower Burma; Comparative Statements C and D tend to prove that leprosy is contagious; distribution of lepers by sex, religion, and race.

117. As on the occasion of the last two enumerations, the returns of the four chief infirmities only were compiled. These four infirmities are Insanity, Deaf-mutism, Blindness, and Leprosy. The information abstracted from the schedules is, however, much fuller. In the first place the age periods are in groups of five years throughout, and not as in 1881 by decennia after the completion of the 19th year. In the next place the return of Infirmities by Caste and Race has never been attempted before in Burma. The following comparative statements of all htese four infirmities have been prepared for reference and are here inserted, as not only does this arrangement save much space, but there is some advantage in contrasting the prevalence of these infirmities. The infirmities themselves will be discussed *seriatim* afterwards. The classification of infirmities and the definitions adopted are exactly the same as those used in 1881.

A.—COMPARATIVE STATEMENT OF INFIRMITIES.

Province or country.	Comparative Statement showing in 10,000 persons of each sex the average number who are									
	Insane.		*Deaf-mute.*		*Blind.*		*Leper.*		*Total afflicted.*	
	Male.	Female.	Male.	Female.	Male.	Female.	Male.	Female.	Male.	Female.
Burma	10	8	5	5	17	23	12	5	44	41
Upper Burma	12	13	8	7	32	41	16	8	68	69
Lower Burma	8	5	4	3	9	10	9	3	30	21
Lower Burma, 1881 ...	11	8	7	5	15	16	10	3	43	32
India, „ ...	5	3	11	7	23	25	9	3	48	38
Assam, „ ...	4	2	6	4	7	6	9	4	26	16
Bengal, „ ...	5	4	15	9	14	15	12	4	46	32
Bombay, „ ...	6	3	8	6	24	29	9	3	47	41
Madras, „ ...	4	3	6	5	15	17	7	2	32	27
North-Western Provinces, „ ...	2	1	8	5	27	32	6	2	43	40
Punjab, „ ...	6	4	13	9	48	54	5	2	72	69
England and Wales	31	33	6	5	9	8	...	...	46	46
Scotland	38	39	3	2	9	8	...	...	50	49
Ireland	38	34	8	7	11	12	...	...	57	53
Germany	...	...	...	...	8	8	...	...	...	...
Italy	8	6	6	5	8	7	...	...	22	18
Austria	22	19	15	11	10	8	...	...	47	38
Portugal	23	17	3	2	21	19	...	...	47	38
Ceylon	13	9	2	1	24	18	...	...	39	28
Victoria	37	31	4	3	11	6	...	...	52	40
New Zealand	33	32	2	3	4	3	...	...	39	38
United States of America ...	35	32	7	6	10	9	...	...	52	47

B.—COMPARATIVE STATEMENT OF INFIRMITIES.

Distribution by sex and locality.

District, &c.	Local distribution of 1,000 of total number afflicted.				Average number of persons amongst whom is found one afflicted.				Average number of females per 100 males afflicted.			
	Insane.	Deaf-mute.	Blind.	Leper.	Insane.	Deaf-mute.	Blind.	Leper.	Insane.	Deaf-mute.	Blind.	Leper.
LOWER BURMA.												
ARAKAN DIVISION—												
Akyab	54	51	15	17	1,116	2,081	1,810	3,890	70	51	74	64
Northern Arakan ...	4	2	2	6	541	2,089	406	356	42	250	89	70
Kyaukpyu ...	22	13	5	8	1,070	3,212	2,275	3.276	61	142	89	42
Sandoway ...	10	8	3	1	1,071	2,410	1,606	9,641	71	60	92	33
Total ...	**90**	**74**	**25**	**32**	**1,075**	**2,316**	**1,740**	**3,261**	**66**	**65**	**80**	**58**
PEGU DIVISION—												
Rangoon Town ...	41	7	4	10	634	6,440	2,908	2,691	10	47	58	34
Hanthawaddy ...	17	24	14	36	2,282	2,840	1,236	1,161	42	64	92	22
Pegu ...	22	26	19	48	2,036	3,014	1,065	978	37	66	66	19
Tharrawaddy ...	39	46	31	35	1,296	1,919	736	1,523	54	79	128	27
Prome ...	41	54	42	32	1,277	1,723	559	1,748	69	84	120	27
Total ...	**160**	**157**	**110**	**161**	**1,325**	**2,379**	**868**	**1,401**	**40**	**74**	**104**	**24**
IRRAWADDY DIVISION—												
Thôngwa ...	28	42	25	71	2,347	2,719	1,189	965	69	78	93	32
Bassein ...	35	40	20	62	1,970	3,064	1,588	1,178	53	50	91	27
Henzada ...	36	39	29	50	1,536	2,489	861	1,183	69	109	89	30
Thayetmyo ...	27	17	24	25	1,330	3,678	668	1,525	70	172	156	29
Total ...	**126**	**138**	**98**	**208**	**1,790**	**2,874**	**1,041**	**1,148**	**65**	**84**	**104**	**30**
TENASSERIM DIVISION—												
Amherst ...	30	22	12	17	2,055	4,796	2,208	3,900	57	47	53	28
Tavoy ...	8	7	5	2	1,757	3,273	1,157	5.932	54	38	127	33
Mergui ...	8	6	4	5	1,271	2,949	1,293	2,107	81	47	83	29
Toungoo ...	17	23	18	15	1,374	1,781	600	1,671	63	54	106	31
Shwegyin ...	18	20	14	15	1,575	2,578	963	2,046	57	63	80	29
Salween ...	4	6	1	2	1,257	1,429	1,849	2,619	177	57	183	100
Total ...	**85**	**84**	**54**	**56**	**1,674**	**2,954**	**1,191**	**2,687**	**60**	**52**	**86**	**31**
UPPER BURMA.												
NORTHERN DIVISION—												
Mandalay ...	63	65	92	93	859	1,478	266	625	87	96	129	61
Bhamo ...	6	8	12	3	1,391	1,750	308	2,712	105	121	155	66
Katha ...	6	11	10	5	1,412	1,379	390	1,977	90	86	153	66
Ruby Mines ...	2	3	2	2	2,010	2,177	746	2,010	116	50	169	30
Shwebo ...	23	19	27	17	861	1,852	333	1,252	153	121	140	54
Total ...	**100**	**106**	**143**	**120**	**946**	**1,575**	**298**	**843**	**101**	**99**	**135**	**60**
CENTRAL DIVISION—												
Ye-u ...	19	23	29	14	723	1,039	206	995	106	78	148	55
Sagaing ...	48	42	76	66	745	1,513	213	585	128	105	149	53
Lower Chindwin ...	54	54	84	55	624	1,111	181	648	100	113	160	55
Upper Chindwin ...	17	25	14	9	631	757	347	1,284	106	88	100	55
Total ...	**138**	**144**	**203**	**144**	**680**	**1,154**	**208**	**694**	**110**	**100**	**149**	**54**
SOUTHERN DIVISION—												
Myingyan ...	57	67	89	82	903	1,346	259	659	131	89	149	59
Pakôkku ...	57	75	76	42	774	1,043	262	1,120	111	85	137	54
Minbu ...	56	45	56	42	587	1,275	265	831	134	83	148	51
Magwe ...	43	34	42	39	738	1,635	341	880	113	63	139	44
Total ...	**213**	**221**	**263**	**205**	**752**	**1,274**	**274**	**830**	**122**	**82**	**143**	**54**
EASTERN DIVISION—												
Kyauksè ...	21	16	23	17	873	2,009	358	1,140	88	80	107	42
Meiktila ...	37	34	46	36	820	1,553	296	898	111	114	178	63
Yamèthin ...	22	19	26	15	1,043	2,200	413	1,622	94	65	112	41
Pyinmana ...	8	7	9	6	971	2,167	402	1,482	93	100	118	31
Total ...	**88**	**76**	**104**	**74**	**903**	**1,865**	**348**	**1,151**	**99**	**91**	**136**	**50**
Total Lower Burma ...	**461**	**453**	**287**	**457**	**1,467**	**3,971**	**1,065**	**1,573**	**55**	**71**	**98**	**29**
Total Upper Burma ...	**539**	**547**	**713**	**543**	**794**	**1,382**	**271**	**841**	**111**	**91**	**142**	**54**
GRAND TOTAL ...	**1,000**	**1,000**	**1,000**	**1,000**	**1,104**	**1,948**	**499**	**1,176**	**81**	**81**	**128**	**42**
Total Lower Burma of 1881	...	...	...	...	1,002	1,646	638	1,443	64	58	93	58

C.—Comparative Statement of Infirmities.

Distribution of 1,000 afflicted persons of each sex by age periods.

Infirmity.	0—4		5—9		10—14		15—19		20—24		25—29		30—34		35—39		40—44		45—49		50—54		55—59		60 and over.	
	M.	F.	M.	F.	M.	F.	M.	F.	M.	F.	M.	F.	M.	F.	M.	F.	M.	F.	M.	F.	M.	F.	M.	F.	M.	F.
Insane ...	6	8	20	22	57	48	91	81	118	100	117	92	130	110	101	91	108	107	59	72	65	92	39	42	89	135
Deaf-mute ...	31	35	101	95	133	107	109	88	117	107	75	72	80	91	83	74	46	64	42	44	43	48	23	38	117	137
Blind ...	27	13	36	18	48	26	44	29	43	29	39	29	51	40	52	36	62	54	63	45	78	82	66	76	391	523
Leper ...	3	5	8	9	37	39	72	94	94	118	110	108	125	123	134	94	128	112	83	62	78	79	42	46	86	111

D.—Comparative Statement of Infirmities.

Distribution of those afflicted per 10,000 of population at each age period.

Infirmity.	0—4		5—9		10—14		15—19		20—24		25—29		30—34		35—39		40—44		45—49		50—54		55—59		60 and over.	
	M.	F.	M.	F.	M.	F.	M.	F.	M.	F.	M.	F.	M.	F.	M.	F.	M.	F.	M.	F.	M.	F.	M.	F.	M.	F.
Insane ...	·4	·4	1	1	4	3	9	6	12	9	13	9	15	13	15	14	19	17	14	16	17	19	17	14	15	16
Deaf-mute ...	1	1	4	3	6	4	6	4	7	5	4	4	5	6	7	6	4	5	6	5	6	5	5	7	11	9
Blind ...	3	2	5	3	6	5	8	6	8	7	7	8	11	13	14	15	19	24	27	29	36	48	51	74	118	175
Leper ...	·2	·1	·7	·3	3	1	9	4	12	6	14	6	18	9	24	8	27	11	24	9	25	10	22	10	17	8

E.—Comparative Statement of Infirmities.

Distribution of 1,000 Afflicted Males and 1,000 Afflicted Females by Castes, Tribes, or Races.

Infirmity.	Burmese.		Karens.		Talaings.		Chins.		Shans.		Mahomedan tribes.		Hindu castes.		Europeans, Eurasians, and Armenians.		Others.	
	M.	F.	M.	F.	M.	F.	M.	F.	M.	F.	M.	F.	M.	F.	M.	F.	M.	F.
Insane	833	878	61	46	18	15	23	18	14	12	18	12	23	9	1	1	9	9
Deaf-mute	834	856	55	47	22	18	25	21	26	26	17	14	14	10	1	...	6	8
Blind	911	933	27	18	11	6	10	10	23	18	7	4	5	5	...	...	6	6
Leper	851	871	71	54	15	9	18	21	18	21	12	13	9	5	...	...	6	6
1,000 of each sex of the total population distributed by castes, tribes, or races.	728	791	74	67	60	64	15	15	26	22	41	22	37	7	4	2	15	10

F.—Comparative Statement of Infirmities.

Distribution of 1,000 Afflicted Males and 1,000 Afflicted Females by Religions.

Infirmity.	Religion.											
	Buddhists.		*Nat-worshippers.*		*Hindus.*		*Mahomedans.*		*Christians.*		*Others.*	
	M.	F.	M.	F.	M.	F.	M.	F.	M.	F.	M.	F.
Insane	889	923	55	38	22	10	27	22	7	7	...	...
Deaf-mutes	907	919	51	42	15	10	22	21	5	8	...	...
Blind	953	966	29	20	6	6	7	4	5	4	...	...
Leper	930	934	38	34	10	6	14	16	8	10	...	...
1,000 of each sex of the total population distributed by religions.	880	933	24	21	37	7	42	24	17	15	*	*

* There are so few professing other religions that the total of the males is less than ·05 per cent. and the total of the females less than ·005 per cent. of the total population of each sex.

G.—Comparative Statement of Infirmities.

Proportion of Females to 100 Males afflicted at each age period.

Age period.	Insane.	Deaf-mute.	Blind.	Leper.
0—4	108·3	92·5	63·3	66·6
5—9	92·0	77·3	63·6	48·5
10—14	68·8	65·5	68·4	43·7
15—19	71·7	65·8	83·2	55·1
20—24	68·7	74·5	86·9	53·2
25—29	63·9	77·7	96·5	41·4
30—34	68·7	93·5	98·8	41·6
35—39	73·6	73·0	88·4	29·5
40—44	80·0	114·1	111·5	37·0
45—49	100·0	84·6	92·3	31·8
50—54	114·9	91·3	134·7	42·8
55—59	87·1	132·0	145·7	45·8
60 and over	124·0	95·2	171·4	55·0

H.—Comparative Statement of Infirmities.

Proportion of Females to 100 Males afflicted by Castes, Tribes, or Races.

Caste, tribe, or race.	Insane.	Deaf-mute.	Blind.	Leper.
Burmese	85·7	83·6	131·0	43·2
Karens	61·	70·3	83·4	31·9
Talaings	66·6	68·0	72·0	25·3
Chins	63·9	66·6	122·3	50·0
Shans	70·3	82·1	104·6	50·0
Mahomedan tribes	56·7	69·4	71·1	48·1
Hindu castes	31·0	58·0	118·9	22·5
Europeans, Eurasians, and Armenians ...	100·0	...	...	...
Others	82·8	100·0	144·7	36·6

Insanity.

The various forms of insanity.

118. No distinction was made between idiots, lunatics, and imbeciles. The first term is generally used to denote congenital mental deficiency and the last to denote persons who in later life have fallen into habitual or chronic dementia. The term lunacy is used with some vagueness, but is generally confined to those afflicted with the more acute forms of the disease. Any attempt to make such distinctive returns would have been rendered fruitless, because it would have involved probably more discriminative faculty than is possessed by the ordinary village enumerator. The Burmese term "yuthutthu" connotes all forms of mental disease.

Comparative prevalence of insanity in Burma, India, and Europe.

119. Referring to Comparative Statement A it will be seen that insanity is apparently more common in Burma than in any province of India, but is nevertheless far less prevalent than in Great Britain, our English colonies, and in European countries. In the province itself we find that, whereas in Lower Burma there are fewer insanes than in 1881, in Upper Burma we have a larger proportion of those afflicted with this infirmity. It seems strange, on the one hand, why Burma should so far exceed the average of India and fall so far below the returns of more-civilized countries. There has been a continuous decline in the proportionate number of insanes to the total population since the first enumeration of 1872. In that year there were in Lower Burma 2,677 male and 1,576 female lunatics, that is to say, there were 18 male and 12 female insanes out of every 10,000 of the total population of each sex. This disparity was explained in 1881 to be due to defective enumeration in 1872. It is noticeable that in 1872, both in England and in Burma, idiots and insanes were compiled separately, but in 1881 this distinction was abandoned. The explanation of the difference in the returns of England and India made by Surgeon-Major Deakin, who reviewed the returns of 1881 in the North-Western Provinces, is worthy of consideration. He said :

"In comparing the number of insanes in India with those in European countries, it must be borne in mind that in Europe the fact of insanity is usually testified to by medical experts, while in India the data given in the census reports are mostly collected by non-professional persons. I have little doubt that thus many persons who have suffered from harmless manifestations of mental disease, or whose attacks are periodical, have not been returned as insane, although they would have been so considered in Europe."

120. The explanation given by Dr. Deakin does not put the solution of the question in the proper light. The real cause probably lies in the fact that in a highly civilized community humanity on the one hand demands that people of unsound mind shall be properly cared for, and on the other the artificiality of life in our great towns, which have absorbed by far the greater part of our population, forbids the *laissez faire* system in vogue in the East and in country villages. Wordsworth's "Idiot Boy" would not have been allowed to wander about at large had he lived in London at the end of the 19th century. The hurry and stress of civilization enforces the seclusion of those who cannot take care of themselves; hence no form of insanity can easily escape the notice of the public in our crowded population, and therefore more cases are brought before our experts and naturally the number of detected cases of true insanity are proportionately greater. But admitting that insanity is more closely scrutinized in civilized countries, it is possible that this alone is not responsible for the disparity in the returns. The greater mental strain of civilized life may be in part responsible for this large number of the insane. Drink and debauchery are admitted causes of insanity. On the other hand, the English Census Commissioners recorded their opinion that agricultural districts produce proportionately more idiots and imbeciles than are found in the great industrial centres. The explanation of this apparent anomaly is that the strongest, healthiest, and most intelligent of the country-folk seek employment in the towns.

Causes of insanity.

121. The causes of insanity in Burma, as elsewhere, may be divided into two classes, physical and moral. Among physical causes the most prominent are hereditary taint and the use of intoxicants. On referring to the annual report of 1890 on the only lunatic asylum in Burma, we find that the Superintendent does not disguise the fact that the statement in which the alleged causes are noted is admittedly unsatisfactory and untrustworthy. In almost every case no history is given, and, if data be forthcoming, it is generally meagre. Gunja-smoking, opium-smoking, spirit-drinking, fever, and epilepsy appear to be the most common of the physical causes of insanity. It is noticeable that whereas opium-smoking appears to induce insanity, not a single case is traceable to opium-eating; only 76 or 21·4 per cent. out of the 354 cases under observation in the asylum are traceable to physical causes; of the remainder 97 are traceable to moral causes, of which grief seems to be by far the most common; loss of property and domestic trouble and fright are also mentioned as frequently causing insanity. But, while only in 173 cases are the causes known, in 181 no cause is assigned. The report remarks that "few or any deductions can be drawn from this statement." One thing, however, is worthy of notice, and that is, while there are 315 males, there are only 39 females confined in the asylum, being in the ratio of 12·3 females to every 100 male insanes. This would tend to show that the more pronounced cases of madness are less common amongst women than amongst men. As women in Burma do not indulge in intoxicating drugs and are better treated and more independent than in most countries, we might expect that not only would there be fewer cases of madness amongst women as compared with men in Burma but as compared with women in other countries.

It is impossible to give any returns of the numbers of those eating opium, but the fact that the number of opium shops in Lower Burma is smaller now than in 1881 may be significant in connection with the smaller proportionate return of insanes. Against this we have the fact that insanes are more numerous in Upper Burma, where there are fewer opium shops. One cause may account for the paucity of the return in Lower Burma and in India and the higher proportion in Upper Burma. To the Eastern mind generally madness is a manifestation of divine power. To lock up and confine the mad is, therefore, repugnant to their sentimental notions as well as to their passive or rather apathetic habit of mind. In Upper Burma lunatic asylums are as yet unknown; hence there is less inclination to screen the imbecile from the view of the Government official. That Burmans often object to their mad relatives being sent to a lunatic asylum is well known to those who have the management of the Rangoon Lunatic Asylum, where constant applications are made by the relatives of the insanes to be allowed to give security and take care of those who have been sent thither by the Magistracy for confinement. Dr. Pedley thinks that the greater prevalence of insanity in Burma is not merely due to the caprice of the enumerator, but may be traced to the fact that in average mental development the Burmans are ahead of the bulk of Indian races, at the same time they are more indulgent to their passions, more excitable, and more liable to fits of frenzy.

Local distribution of insanes.

122. In Statement **B** will be found the distribution of insanes throughout the tricts and divisions of Burma. Rangoon, where the Provincial Lunatic Asylum is located, naturally possesses a large proportion of insanes to the total population. It is, however, exceeded by the Northern Arakan Hill Tracts. Here the enumeration was carried out by the Deputy Commissioner, the Myoôk, and the Inspectors of Police themselves, who, owing to the sparsity and illiteracy of the population, could not entrust the work to the ordinary village enumerator. Here with more skilled enumeration we find the highest proportion of insanity. On the other hand, it must be recollected that the district contains but 14,628 inhabitants altogether, and that annually able-bodied men emigrate from it and settle in the plains, and naturally the proportion of the infirm who would be left behind is higher here. Moreover, fever, which is notoriously prevalent in these hills, is frequently assigned in Burma as a cause of imbecility. In Upper Burma districts generally we find a large proportion of insanes, and the proportion of female in these districts is almost invariably greater than that of male lunatics. Nor can the suggestion that the return was swelled in Upper Burma by the inclusion of those who hope to get remission of revenue by pleading infirmity account for the difference in the return of the two provinces, for the same cause should be equally operative in Lower Burma, where lunacy is equally efficacious as an excuse for remission of the capitation-tax. The preponderance of the females over the males in Upper Burma has already been explained in Chapter IV as being due to the emigration of males from Upper Burma before the annexation of the kingdom of Ava and to the greater loss of male life in the troubled times that immediately succeeded the annexation. The same cause may account for the larger number of insane folk found in the upper province.

The last interesting return in the Statement **B** is the local distribution of the proportionate strength of female and male imbeciles. In Lower Burma on an average there are 100 insane males to every 55 insane females, but in Upper Burma there are 111 females to every 100 males afflicted with the same infirmity. It is difficult to assign a reason for this unless it be that the troublous times succeeding the annexation, while it caused loss of male life, left its mark amongst the women by increasing the number of insanes.

Distribution of insanes by age periods.

123. Turning to Table **C** we find that, notwithstanding the greater proportionate strength of the population in the earlier age periods, the number of the insane gradually increases with scarcely a check up to the 7th age period, 30—34. After this the number of insanes decreases, but the decrease is due to the gradual decrease of the population. As a fact the insanes show a gradual proportional increase up to the 9th quinquennial age period, which corresponds in women to the "change in life." Table **D**, which should be read along with **C**, shows the proportion of insanes to the total population at each age period. The reason why there are so few found in the first age period may be assigned to one of the three following causes,—(1) that congenital insanity is uncommon; (2) that the parents cannot naturally detect signs of insanity in the undeveloped minds of their young children; (3) to the natural disinclination of the parents to admit that the imbecile child is anything but a "little backward." Still the gradual increase in each successive age period is strongly in favour of the explanation that there is but little congenital insanity in Burma. District Officers will testify that idiot children are exceedingly rare in Burma.

124. Statement **E** is extracted from the table of infirmities distributed by caste and race. From the statement we find that insanity is proportionately more prevalent among the Burmans and Chins and less prevalent amongst the other races. That insanity should be less common among our immigrant population is just what might be expected, but the comparative immunity of the Talaings is certainly remarkable. Whether this is due to the idiosyncracies of the enumerators, or whether these figures actually represent the facts, we have no means of finding out now, as this is the first census in Burma in which the return of infirmities distributed by caste and race has been attempted. The Talaing, or Môns as they call themselves, are naturally quieter and more placid in disposition than the Burmese, and we should naturally expect that insanity would be less prevalent amongst them; but that the disparity in the returns between Burman and Talaing insanes should actually be so great is a fact that can only be verified by comparison with the figures obtained at the next forthcoming census. It is noticeable that amongst Hindu males the proportion of insanes is very low and among females the proportion is very high. This disparity is due to the fact that among females the proportion of those born in the country is far higher than among the males. Explanation of this fact is discussed at length in Chapter IX. There are fewer females, and the adults are all married; their children are begotten in the normal proportion of females and males. Hence the number of female children is greater in proportion to the total Hindu female population than that of the male children to the total Hindu male population. Hence among the females we might expect the return of infirmities to be more normal than amongst the males. For among the latter we include a large proportion of sepoys and able-bodied coolies, who naturally may be expected to be exceptionally free from this and other infirmities. The return of the Mahomedan tribes bears out these deductions.

Insanes distributed by religions they profess.

125. Statement **F** is a similar statement to Statement **E**. Here we have the average number of insanes in Burma found in every 1,000 persons of each sex distributed by the chief religions in Burma. We find that Buddhists have their fair share of insane persons, Nat-worshippers have more than their fair share, Christians, both male and female, possess far fewer insanes than their share. Amongst Hindus, while there are few male insanes, their women possess more than the proportionate number of those thus afflicted. The same thing is noticeable among the Musalman men, while even their women are less proportionately afflicted than the average of women in Burma.

Distribution by sex.

126. In considering Statement **G** we must remember that in Burma the number of men exceeds that of women. What the proportion is, may be ascertained by referring to Diagram **A** in Chapter IV. Accordingly we are prepared to find that except in the first quinquennium, the male insanes exceed the females in every age period up to the 10th. Here, though males still outnumber females in the total population, the fact that women have at this age period passed through their change of life, and that this change, as in England, is attended with danger to women's constitution and sanity, is demonstrated by the sudden rise in the proportion of female insanes. This is more marked in the next age period, when women for the first time outnumber the men; then in the next age period the male once more outnumber the female insanes. In the last age period women decisively outnumber men in the total population, and they still have more than their proportional number of insanes.

127. In Statement **H** the tendency to insanity amongst males and females is discussed from another standpoint, namely, that of caste and race. Here we find that, as in most European countries, insanity is more common amongst males in every race except, strange to say, the European, Eurasian, and Armenian community, in which males and females show exactly equal liability to this disease. As, however, this agrees with the English return of 1881, we may accept it as being correct.

Deaf-mutism.

128. The definition of a deaf-mute was the same as that adopted in England. Only those who were deaf and dumb from their birth were included in the return.

In 1872, out of every 10,000 of either sex, 16 males and 10 females were returned as being both deaf and dumb. In 1881 these figures had sunk to 7 and 5, respectively, "owing no doubt," as Mr. Copleston remarked, "to the inclusion in 1872 of many persons who were not dumb as well as deaf." In 1881 there was a further decrease recorded, and now in Lower Burma the return of deaf-mutes is lower than in any province of India. The improvement is again due to more careful enumeration. At the enumeration of 1881 a zealous enumerator insisted on returning all the children too young to speak as being deaf-mutes. The reduction in the proportion of deaf-mutes is therefore due to more careful instruction by the District Officers and greater accuracy on the part of the enumerators.

Local distribution of deaf-mutes.

129. In Comparative Statement **A** we see that Upper Burma contained a much larger proportion of deaf-mutes than we find in Lower Burma. The cause of this variation may be traced to the fact that in Lower Burma our birth-place returns show that nearly 14 per cent. of our population in the lower province consist of immigrants from India or Upper Burma. Deaf-mutes are not usually found abounding among immigrants, and hence, while Upper Burma sent sound men to Lower Burma, it kept its infirm ones at home. Pakôkku, Myingyan, and Mandalay possessed the greatest number of deaf-mutes. Mandalay, abounding as it does in pôngyi kyaungs, is the natural home of those afflicted who have to live on charity, but no reason can be put forward to explain the excess of deaf-mutes in the two other districts. These districts probably furnished a larger number of emigrants to Lower Burma. The excess is probably due to less careful exclusion of those who were deaf only. When the number of deaf-mutes is so small, it would be unsafe to hazard any reasonable explanation of the excess of deaf-mutes in any district. The manner in which the deductions of longevity amongst those thus afflicted—which had been carefully prepared in preceding enumerations in England—were completely "masked" by the returns of 1881, proves that it is dangerous to generalise when the field of observation is so narrow. In the list of districts graded according to the proportionate number of those thus afflicted Toungoo, which in 1881 stood first, now stands but third, and Northern Arakan, which stood second in 1881, now stands sixth. Amherst, which stood third, now stands last but one out of the districts of Lower Burma. The affliction seems to be more evenly distributed between the two sexes both in Lower and Upper Burma than was the case in the former province in 1881. The greater prevalence of this infirmity amongst males was noticed in England and in the United States. Mr. Copleston thought this disparity was due to women being weaker and dying off in larger numbers in early life. Unfortunately for this theory, we find that males die off more rapidly than females. The reason given in the English report is probably more correct. Deaf-mutism, like idiocy, is congenital, and "congenital defects, as a rule, are much more common among males than among females."

Cause of variance in the return of deaf-mutes.

130. In Statement **C** at first it seems somewhat anomalous that deaf-mutism, which is congenital, should not be most noticeable in the earliest age period. Exactly the same anomaly is present in the last four successive enumerations in England. There is no reason to suppose that the returns either in England or Burma were vitiated by distinctly wilful omissions. The omissions are due to the fact that parents are often not aware of the existence of the infirmity, as with children of a few months old the infirmity is naturally not easily recognizable. The number of deaf-mutes increases up to 14 years of age and then gradually declines. This increase is anomalous and is probably due to mis-return of ages by the enumerated. In Statement **D** we see the comparative longevity of deaf-mutes as compared with the rest of the population. If this return be correct, deaf-mutes are no weaker or feebler than ordinary folk. These returns agree with the returns of the English Census of 1881.

131. Taking the distribution of deaf-mutes by their caste or race, we find that, as in the case of insanity, the Burmans and Chins possess more than their proportionate number of those thus afflicted. But the Shans and Hindus also possess slightly more than their right proportion of female deaf-mutes. The

other races show proportionately fewer thus afflicted. The number of deaf-mutes amongst the Talaings is remarkably small. The proportionate preponderance of deaf-mutes among the females of the Mahomedan tribes and Hindu castes may be traced to the same causes as those given for the proportionate excess of female insanes in these two classes of the population. Comparing the returns of those afflicted with this infirmity distributed according to the religions professed, we find that, as might be expected, the indigenous religions show the heaviest proportion of afflicted. It is strange that, though amongst the males professing Hinduism and Mahomedanism the proportion is low, yet amongst females it is above the average. This proves two things, first that few immigrants—for the bulk of the immigrants are men—are thus afflicted, and, secondly, that as the number of women belonging to these religions is very few, the proportion of those born in Burma is higher; hence, while the bulk of our adult Hindus and Musalmans are males, the children they bear are more equally divided as our age returns show, and hence the proportion of those born in the country to the total number of those professing these religions is greater amongst females than amongst males. Deaf-mutism being congenital, and, if the returns of the Census of 1881 are correct, being more common in India than in Burma, we should naturally expect, if our returns were true, that a large proportion of the women would be afflicted as we find to be really the case. The above will also explain why Buddhists and Nat-worshippers have more than their share of deaf-mutes.

Distribution of deaf-mutes by religions.

Statement G is useful as it proves the truth of the opinion before expressed that few of our Indian immigrants are deaf-mutes, though no doubt their children exhibit the average tendency observable in the countries whence their parents came.

Blindness.

The comparative prevalence of blindness.

132. The definition of blindness in the printed instructions ought to have left no doubt in the minds of the enumerator. Yet we find that, while in Lower Burma there is a satisfactory decrease in the return of those blind as compared with the figures of 1881, the return of Upper Burma is much heavier than the return of the lower province. In 1872 there were 24 males and 18 females returned as blind out of every 10,000 of either sex. In 1881 the ratios had fallen to 15 and 16 respectively. Mr. Copleston rightly inferred that the improvement was due to more careful exclusion of those who were but partially blind. Turning to the English figures we find that the Census Commissioners report that "the proportion of the blind to the population has decreased with each successive enumeration since 1851, in which year account was taken of them for the first time." In England the improvement is supposed to be due to improved surgery and diminished prevalence of smallpox; in Lower Burma the spread of vaccination and the increase in the number of civil dispensaries have greatly decreased the ravages of smallpox. The inspection of the books of any civil dispensary will show how many cases of eye-disease are treated. Contagious conjunctivitis or ophthalmia is exceedingly prevalent in all hot dry countries, and this disease, if left untreated, is apt to become chronic and give rise to ulcerations of the cornea and to develop an increasing tendency to blindness with advancing years. Since 1881 the number of civil dispensaries in Lower Burma has been increased from 29 to 35. The establishment of the Dufferin Hospital and the education of the native midwives may also have helped to remove one of the most fruitful causes of eye-disease in children, conjunctivitis, acquired at birth by the new-born child. Taken together these causes will account in great measure for the diminution in the number of the blind in Lower Burma within the last decade and for the disparity between the returns of the lower and upper province. But the variation is too great to be accounted for by these causes alone. Mr. Copleston's explanation in 1881 is undoubtedly true in 1891. The returns of Upper Burma, where no census was ever held before, show that in all probability persons but partially blind were entered as blind. The next census will probably show that a smaller proportion of the population in Upper Burma is thus afflicted.

Moreover, it must be remembered that, unless care be taken, persons anxious to gain remission of tax on account of infirmity, when partially thus afflicted often assert they are totally blind, and verification in such a case can only be obtained by an expert. Leprosy is recognizable by most Burmans. Insanity and deaf-mutism cannot be put forward by the sufferers themselves as a ground for exemption, but blindness, involving no inherent shame, is not unfrequently urged as an excuse for exemption. "None are so blind as those who do not wish to see." Accordingly, in 1901 especial care should be taken to ensure a correct return, and, when the people understand there is no connection between the enumeration and taxation, we may hope for more accurate returns.

Cause of blindness.

133. The figures of Lower Burma may be taken as being correct; they are much lower than the average of India. So little is at present known about the tendency of elderly people to become blind more quickly in certain places than in others, that any dogmatic assertion would be out of place. In the Bombay Census Report Mr. Baines, after comparing the returns of the various districts, suggests that "Other conditions being equal, it seems as if heat, drought, and the absence of sea air were determining factors in the prevalence of blindness." The German specialist, Dr. Mayer, is quoted in the Bombay Report as being of opinion that climate and race to a certain extent influence this tendency. Leaving Upper Burma out of our calculations, though of course the greater prevalence of blindness there might be taken in support of Mr. Baines' theory, even if we confine ourselves to Lower Burma, we find that in the Arakan and Tenasserim divisions, which are chiefly "littoral tracts," the lowest proportion of blind persons to the total population is found. That this variance is not accidental may be inferred from the fact that in the two deltaic divisions except in Rangoon, blindness is far less common in the littoral districts than in the inland districts of Prome, Thayetmyo, Henzada, and Tharrawaddy. In Rangoon the number of blind beggars who live on charity at the Rangoon pagodas entirely vitiates the value of the return.

From Comparative Statements **C** and **D** it is quite clear that the number of the blind increases actually as well as proportionately through each age period and is commonest in old age.

134. Considering that a large proportion of our immigrant Indian population only visit Burma while in the prime of life, notwithstanding the fact that blindness appears to be more prevalent in India than in Burma, we are prepared to find that both in the return of castes and races and of religions the Indians show a smaller percentage of those who suffer from this disease. The most fruitful causes of blindness are purulent ophthalmia and cataract. The latter is most noticeable in old age, and to the former children are most liable. Moreover, as in the case of other infirmities, we might expect to find fewer blind persons amongst those who have the courage to leave their own country and seek employment in another. Accordingly, it is rather a matter for astonishment that we should find so many than that we should find so few blind persons amongst Indian races and castes.

135. In every other infirmity males are oftener afflicted than females. In blindness alone do we find that there is a distinct tendency, which is found in almost every age period for women, to show a gradually increasing proportion of those afflicted with blindness. This becomes very marked after women have passed "the menopause" or "change of life." The explanation that has been offered of this phenomenon, which has been observed to exist in India, is that the smoke of the cook-room hurts the eyes of the women who cook in them. Both sexes suffer alike from the usual cause of blindness—smallpox and fever. Cataract is usually the cause of blindness that comes on with old age. But the explanation of the kitchen smoke being injurious to the eyes of women does not possess the same force in Burma as in India, for the Burmans do not burn cowdung as fuel, and, except in the rainy season, the cooking is generally carried on in the open air. Another and more probable cause may be the fact that purulent ophthalmia is very contagious, and as women would naturally more often than the men attend upon the sufferers from this disease, their ignorance of precautionary measures would render them very liable to contract the disease themselves.

136. Before attempting to discuss this point further, it would be as well to note the comparative prevalence of blindness in the sexes distributed by races. Here we find that amongst the Burmese the number of females far exceeds the number of the males. Amongst Mahomedan tribes, Karens, and Talaings, blindness is commoner amongst the men. Taking the population distributed by races, blindness appears to be most common amongst the Burmans, and taking the population distributed by religions, we find that amongst the Buddhists this affliction is most prevalent. This may in part be due to the fact that the blind are generally beggars dependent on charity, who live by the alms of the Buddhist frequenters of the shrines, and who would naturally, to excite sympathy amongst the most numerous class, profess to be of the same religion and of the same race.

The prevalence of blindness amongst the female Hindus seems at first sight to be absurdly high considering how few the females are, but this disparity is readily understood when we take into consideration the fact that a very large proportion of the males are temporary immigrants of middle age, and who are sepoys and mill-coolies and consequently do not include blind men, who would be useless for such employment.

Leprosy.

137. The returns of leprosy made at the present census will be scrutinized more closely than those of any other infirmity. So much interest of recent years has been felt regarding this disease that a Special Commission has been engaged in investigating the facts connected with the origin and extent of leprosy. Leprosy is not included amongst the infirmities enumerated in the returns of the European countries whose figures are set forth in Statement **A.** No mention is made of it in the English Report of 1881. Dr. Pedley has very kindly examined the returns of infirmities, and especially those of leprosy, and the tables annexed to this chapter and the discussion of the points noticeable therein have had the benefit of his criticism, and it is to him that I am indebted for much valuable assistance and advice.

Comparative prevalence of leprosy.

138. In the returns of Indian provinces Lower Burma shows a slightly less proportionate return than in 1881. But in Upper Burma leprosy is more prevalent than in any other Indian province. Turning to the figures of 1872, we find that the returns showed 16 males and 7 females suffering from this disease out of every 10,000 persons of each sex. The explanation of this high rate, suggested tentatively by Mr. MacIvor, was that the people live on ngapi, or what he called putrescent fish. The smell of ngapi is sufficiently offensive, but there seems to be no ground for imputing to it any share in the prevalence of leprosy. Mr. Copleston remarked that the decrease noticeable in 1881 is due to a more rigid exclusion of those not afflicted with true leprosy. Leucoderma or "Kayu thin" is known by a separate name from true leprosy, which is known as "nu nga," and more careful instructions in successive enumerations have produced more accurate returns in Lower Burma. We may then expect in 1901 to find the high percentage of lepers in Upper Burma reduced to less alarming proportions.

Local distribution of leprosy.

139. Leprosy appears to be most prevalent in the small district of Northern Arakan. Indeed, if the figures are to be trusted, this petty district, with a population of less than 15,000 souls, has far more than its right proportion of lepers, blind, and insanes. But, as Mr. Copleston remarked in 1881, little weight can be attached to such small aggregates of figures. Next in rank comes Mandalay, which not only contains the greatest number of lepers, but lepers are more common here in proportion to the total population of the district than in any district in Burma, except Sagaing and Northern Arakan. Mandalay was and is still a refuge for the maimed, halt, and blind, and there is now a Lepers' Home established by the Rev. A. Bestall, who has devoted himself to the noble task of striving to alleviate the sufferings of those afflicted with this most terrible of all infirmities. In the same way as the Lunatic Asylum in Rangoon raises the proportion of lunatics in that town, it might be supposed that the Home at Mandalay no doubt had attracted to Man-

dalay lepers from other districts. I am informed that this is not the true explanation. The Home has been recruited hitherto from the lepers residing in Mandalay. Mandalay, however, is a mushroom city not yet 35 years old, and the presence of the leper community is due to the fact that the afflicted resorted to the numerous monasteries and pagodas in it for the alms of the charitable and the largesses of the Burmese officials. The proportionate strength varies so much from district to district in Upper Burma that we may safely conclude that many who would not have been classed as lepers in one district were so included in another. In Lower Burma, of the large districts, Pegu and Thôngwa show the highest ratios.

140. The Deputy Commissioner of Pegu thinks that the prevalence of leprosy in his district may be due to venereal disease. Though there is no connection established between these two forms of disease, it is more than probable that the enumerators have mistaken the one for the other. Rangoon town shows a remarkable decrease in this disease. In 1881 there was one leper out of every 1,656 persons ; in 1891 there was one leper out of every 2,691. The actual number of lepers decreased from 81 to 67. It is to be feared that this decrease does not represent the fact that there are fewer lepers in the province, but that they are wisely no longer permitted to infest our streets and beg for charity. The gradual accumulation of those suffering from this loathsome disease, and the open way in which they infested the Pagoda entrance and Pagoda road, became at last such a public nuisance, that steps had to be taken, and thanks to the action of the police and of the Pagoda Trustees, some abatement of this nuisance has been effected within the last 15 months, many of the afflicted having been induced to return to their own towns and villages. They have probably emigrated to Pegu and Thôngwa and swollen the returns there. It would seem that leprosy attacks men more frequently than women. In no district do female outnumber the male sufferers. In only one district, Salween, is the disease equally prevalent in either sex.

Distribution of those afflicted with leprosy by age periods.

141. The returns of Statements **C** and **D** are, if true, strong testimony in favour of the theory that leprosy is a contagious disease, and that it is one which, if inherited, is not developed in infancy. Unlike any of the three other infirmities, leprosy, if the disease be fully developed, is as distinguishable in the young infant as in the grown man. Lepers are most numerous in middle age, and that their longevity is not so great as that of the rest of the population may be inferred from the fact that there are proportionately fewer in the two last age periods.

142. Statements **E** and **F** show that, as might be expected, the indigenous races and religions claim more than their share of those tainted with leprosy. Amongst the hill tribes leprosy appears to be far more common. Of course the number of these is relatively so small that it would not be right to base any argument on these figures unless the field of observation were widened. The prevalence of leprosy among the Chins may, if leprosy be a contagious disease, be due to the absence of proper precautions against contagion. The high proportion of lepers who return themselves as Burmans is probably due, as in the case of those afflicted with other infirmities, to the desire of those afflicted to claim kin with the most numerous and charitable of the races of Burma. The Christians who are shown as lepers are chiefly Christian Karens. No Europeans are returned as suffering from this infirmity. At all ages and in all races leprosy seems to be far more prevalent amongst men than amongst women.

143. Taking all infirmities together, the return of Lower Burma in 1891 is far below the returns recorded here in 1881, which were in their turn below the average figures for the whole of India. Except in Assam, the present return of Lower Burma is lower than any recorded in India in 1881. In Upper Burma infirm people are commoner than in any province except the Punjab. In Upper and Lower Burma taken together there is almost exactly the same proportion of infirm males as there was in Lower Burma at the last enumeration, but the disparity is greater amongst the females. The returns of infirmities in the upper province lose much of their significance because we have no previous data with

which to compare them. Under the Burmese rule, lepers were rigorously segregated, and the advisability of enforcing this seclusion is strongly urged by those who believe in the disease being contagious. Not the least interesting part of the report of the next succeeding census will be the chapter that deals with the statistics of infirmities. Judging from the figures of previous enumerations, we may expect a large decrease in the returns of all four infirmities in the upper province, and especially in the returns of the blind and of lepers. That the returns of Lower Burma should in 1901 show a like decrease is perhaps more than may be expected, as, from a careful scrutiny of the schedules, it would appear that the experience of previous enumerations had not been wasted and more care and scrutiny had been bestowed in making the return of those afflicted.

CHAPTER VII.

EDUCATION.

Classification of the population into Illiterates, Learners, and Literates. Proposed distribution into two classes of Illiterates and Literates. Education in Burma, in other provinces of India, and in other countries. The returns of 1881 and 1891 in Lower Burma contrasted. Causes of the relatively wide spread of education in Burma. The returns of Illiterates, Learners, and Literates distributed by Religions. Education in Upper Burma. The attitude of the Pôngyis. Explanation of the comparatively low degree of education amongst women. Comparative statements showing the spread of education amongst males and females throughout the districts of Burma. The future prospects of education in Burma.

The scope of the census returns.

144. The information obtained from those enumerated regarding the spread of education is necessarily confined to the narrowest limits. The enumerated were divided into three classes,—literate, meaning those who could both read and write; learners, meaning those under instruction; and illiterate, meaning those who could not both read and write. It will be seen that this division, though it has now been adopted for two successive enumerations, is not very clear. The division between learner and literate is unsatisfactory, as, according to this classification, an undergraduate reading for honours is classed as under instruction, and an ignorant villager, who can just read and write, ranks above him as literate. We have in India a special department of public instruction to which might with advantage be left the task of dealing with those under instruction, and the census returns might be directed to preserve the distinction of literate and illiterate alone. It might be urged that those under instruction, who could read and write, should return themselves as literates, returning as learners only those who could not yet read and write; but the practical effect of this would be that nearly all those under instruction would be lost in the return of literates. Moreover, there might be some disadvantage in attempting to draw the line between the school-boy who is still "learning" and his fellow class mate who is "literate."

Proposal to restrict return to literates and illiterates.

145. If any further proof were wanted of the difficulty of obtaining this return of "learners," a perusal of the returns of the last census would supply it. We find that though the returns compiled by the Director of Public Instruction gave the total number of those under instruction in 1881 as 88,553, yet the census returns of that year gave 215,237 males alone as being under instruction. Unfortunately no return of literates, illiterates, and learners by age periods was attempted in 1881, but a reference to the Age table will show that between the ages of 5—14 there were then in the province only 508,284 boys altogether, being 2,553 out of 10,000 males of all ages, while 1,081 out of every 10,000 males of all ages were under instruction, that is to say 42·3 per cent. of the boys between 5—14 were under instruction. As a rule Burman boys do not go to school till they are 7 or 8 years old and leave when they are 15 years old; hence the proportion of scholars to the actual population is really even higher than these figures would indicate. A perusal of the returns in detail showed that the Nat-worshippers in Kyaukpyu, a notoriously illiterate race, made some astonishing returns, which Mr. Copleston pointed out were palpably erroneous. It is true that on the present occasion the returns of the census correspond more closely with the returns of the Director of Public Instruction, but as in Burma nearly every school is visited by the Deputy Inspectors of Schools and is thus brought under the notice of the Educational Department, any wide divergence between the returns must necessarily imply that some mistake must

exist in either one or other of the returns. The returns of the Educational Department show that the number of scholars of both sexes in 1891 in schools in Lower Burma under the supervision of the department was 115,297 and in 1890 there were 129,007 scholars. The census returns show that there were in Lower Burma on the night of 26th February 1891 128,269 males and 14,853 females, or 143,122 of both sexes returned as under instruction. Under the circumstances it is probable that our returns in 1891 are more correct than the return of learners in 1881, but the fact that the returns of the Educational Department so nearly cover the whole ground of education in Lower Burma shows that there exists no necessity for obtaining any return under this head in the census schedule.

As in the case of the returns of age, civil condition, birth-place, and infirmities, no attempt was made to acquire information regarding the state of education of the inhabitants of the excluded tracts, and accordingly the returns of the state of education were only prepared for 7,605,560 of the inhabitants of Burma and 2,992 persons living in the tract of the Shan States where the census was taken synchronously.

Comparison of the state of education in Burma with that of other provinces and countries.

146. Compared with other Indian provinces, and even with some of the countries of Europe, Burma takes a very high place in the returns of those able both to read and write. Taking the sexes apart, it will be seen that, although owing to causes which will be referred to hereafter, women fall far behind men in Burma in the matter of education, still women are better educated in Burma than in the rest of India, though compared with the returns of European countries they fall far behind.

The following comparative statement shows the average number of literates and illiterates in 1,000 of each sex in Burma, in the other provinces of India, and in various European countries and English colonies. For the purpose of this return, those under instruction are classed with literates, as the distinction between learners and literates is not preserved in most countries outside of India :—

Province or country.	Learning and literate.		Illiterate.	
	Male.	Female.	Male.	Female.
Burma	450	29	550	971
Upper Burma	462	15	538	985
Lower Burma, 1891	443	38	557	962
Lower Burma, 1881	461	36	539	964
Assam	47	1	953	999
Bengal	87	3	913	997
Bombay	112	7	888	993
Central Provinces	47	2	953	998
North-Western Provinces and Oudh	58	2	942	998
Madras	138	9	862	991
Punjab	63	2	937	998
India	91	4	909	996
Ireland	554	501	446	499
Italy	377	236	623	764
Austria	521	467	479	533
Ceylon	269	29	731	971
Victoria	755	755	245	245
New South Wales	688	667	312	333

The returns of literates and illiterates are not included in the English and Scotch census schedules.

Educational returns of 1881 and 1891 in Lower Burma contrasted.

147. It will be seen that Burma holds a high place in this table, and that apparently there has been a retrogression in the education of the inhabitants of Lower Burma since 1881, and that, so far as males are concerned, Upper Burma is more literate than Lower Burma. If, however, we show literate and learning apart, we find that the high position held in 1881 by Lower Burma is in great measure due to the astonishing returns of those "under instruction." The following statement shows the number of males and females in 1,000 of each sex in

Upper and Lower Burma divided into the three classes of learning, literate, and illiterate in 1891 contrasted with the returns of 1881 in Lower Burma:—

Province.	Learning.		Literate.		Illiterate.	
	Male.	Female.	Male.	Female.	Male.	Female.
Burma, 1891	59	5	391	24	550	971
Upper Burma, 1891	70	2	392	13	538	985
Lower Burma, 1891	52	7	391	31	557	962
Lower Burma, 1881	108	18	353	18	539	964

We have only to turn to the report of 1881 to find out that the return of those under instruction was admittedly incorrect, and this is confirmed as much by the disproportion in the return between learning and literate in 1881 as by the return of 1891. For instance, we find that female scholars in 1881 were most numerous in the Kyaukpyu district, yet the ratio of 396 females under instruction out of every 10,000 enumerated is, as Mr. Copleston remarks, curious, since there were only 69 out of the same number who could read and write. The explanation given was that the words "under instruction" were understood to mean that the parents of the child "intended at some time or other to send the infant to a school or monastery." In comparing the state of education prevailing in Lower Burma at the beginning and end of the last intercensal period we must, therefore, exclude from our calculations those returned as learning and restrict ourselves to the return of literates.

Causes of position held by Burma.

148. Before discussing in detail the returns in Burma of education distributed by age periods and religions, it may be considered necessary to explain why Burma should hold the position it does in regard to the literacy of its inhabitants. Although Upper Burma has been so recently annexed, and although it has been brought under the control of the Director of Public Instruction within the last two years, a perusal of the Imperial Table IX shows that, though in female education it is slightly behind, yet, as regards the number of males under instruction and able to read and write, it ranks higher than Lower Burma.

On this point Mr. Copleston's report contains a very interesting comment:

"It is worth noting perhaps that it is in the districts which (the Birth-place tables show) receive large number of immigrants from Upper Burma that the proportion of males able to read and write is greatest. Thôngwa and Thayetmyo stand second and third if the districts are arranged either by the proportion of educated men to the total males or by that of persons born in Upper Burma to the total population. It is possible that the natives of the kingdom of Ava, where the pôngyis maintain their hold with a firmer grasp than they do here, are already on the average better educated than the Burmese of the English province."

Our present census shows how shrewd this remark was. But Mr. Copleston omitted to take into consideration the fact that the greater proportion of immigrants from India which is to be found in the lower province is undoubtedly one of the causes of the general state of education in Lower Burma not being much higher than that of the upper province. Most of our Hindu coolies are illiterate, and the birth-place returns of 1891 show that while in Lower Burma there were 237,589 persons born in India, there were only 40,423 persons in Upper Burma who made a similar return. Still the fact that Upper Burma can boast of so many males who are literate or are under instruction proves that there must be a large number of indigenous schools there. If we leave out of our calculation the number of children under 5 years of age who are perforce too young to be literate, we find that in Lower Burma 510 are either literate or learning and 490 are illiterate out of every 1,000 males, while in Upper Burma 532 are either literate or learning and 468 are illiterate. Here the divergence is still wider and more in favour of Upper Burma. The explanation of these figures must be sought in the returns of the uneducated, distributed by the religions they profess.

149. The annexed comparative statement shows the degree of education prevailing amongst every 1,000 persons of each sex who profess one of the five chief religions of the province. A deduction is allowable of all those who are under 5 years of age from the total, as children of this age may be presumed in Burma at least to be mostly, if not entirely, below school age. They are of course included in the return of illiterate; accordingly in making the comparative statement shown below, in the case of the illiterate the number under 5 years of age is subtracted from the divisor as well as the dividend, and in the case of learning and literate, from the divisor only.

Education and Religion.

Religion.	Illiterate.		Learning.		Literate.	
	Male.	Female.	Male.	Female.	Male.	Female.
Buddhists	443	970	74	5	483	25
Nat-worshippers	922	997	6	1	72	2
Hindus	757	960	13	8	230	32
Musalmans	746	961	25	9	229	30
Christians	471	723	79	51	450	226

Amongst males Buddhists are on the whole better educated than any of those who profess the other religions shown in this table. The Nat-worshippers, as might be expected, are the most illiterate. Christians, who include many Karens who have but recently been converted from Nat-worship, rank lower than Buddhists in males, but show a decided improvement in the number of females under instruction and literate. Hindus and Musalmans are next to Nat-worshippers the worst educated, but they show proportionately a higher degree of education than is found in any of the provinces of India. This is due in the case of Musalmans especially, to the large numbers of native Arakanese that have been returned as belonging to this faith. But the chief reason is no doubt the fact that a large proportion both of Hindu and Musalman immigrants is drawn from the trading classes. It stands to reason that voluntary immigrants in most cases are not the least enterprising and least intelligent part of the community from which they come. Referring to the census report of Lower Burma in 1881 we find that the same improvement is noticeable, so that there is every reason to believe that this difference in the literacy of our Indian immigrants is not due to the vagaries of enumerators or to the misstatements of the enumerated.

150. The fact that in Upper Burma the proportion of literates is nearly as high as, and the proportion of those under instruction even higher than, that of the corresponding classes in Lower Burma, is a clear proof that in primary education at least, the credit for the superiority of the Burman over the Native of India is due to indigenous schools. The Director of Public Instruction speaks in terms of the highest praise of the Upper Burman pôngyi. How liberal-minded and enlightened some of these worthy monks are may be judged from the fact that U Ayeindama, a pôngyi of Sagaing, "made his upazin (or probationer) "become a layman in order to undergo training in the Moulmein Vernacular "Normal school and afterwards, when he had obtained a teacher's certificate, to "re-assume the yellow robe and re-enter the monastery as a trained teacher." Nor is U Ayeindama the only example of this liberal-mindedness and zeal: "U "Naka, Gaingdauk or Abbot of Ava, was found teaching himself English, and "teaching in addition to his pupils that language as fast as he proceeded with it. "U Gunama, of Nabet, and U Adeissa, of Alagappa, of their own accord procured "copies of Stilson's Arithmetic and pressed the Deputy Inspector to remain in "their kyaung a few days in order to give them lessons in fractions."

Education in Upper Burma and attitude of the pôngyis.

Note.—These quotations are from the exceedingly interesting Report on Public Instruction for the year 1890-91.

It must not be supposed that no difficulty was felt by these tolerant pôngyis in overcoming not only the prejudices of their fellows but their own natural distrust of innovations. A few influential pôngyis, resident at Mandalay, have shown hostility to this movement. There are of course two schools, one composed of men who distrust the introduction of new studies that may wean the minds of their pupils to follow the new-fashioned ideas. The feeling of the pôngyi towards the certificated teacher who teaches a system of geography hitherto unknown to Buddhist minds, is not without a parallel in England even in the 19th century. On the other hand, the average pôngyi is not merely an honest ascetic; he is, considering his education and environment generally, a shrewd observer. There is therefore another school to which men like U Ayeindama belong. To quote Mr. Pope's words: "the pôngyis see clearly that in their own interests "and in the interests of their religion their only hope of retaining their power of "moulding the minds of the young and of preventing the people of the future "growing up more or less without a faith lies in taking advantage of the system "of education held out to them in common with laymen by the Government in "the Educational Department."

Though this party is as yet not so influential as the other, there are good reasons for expecting that it will ultimately get the upper hand. Patience and tact will gradually overcome the not unnatural prejudices of the old-fashioned school. Time itself is on the side of the advanced school, and if no attempt be made to force the system of education on those unwilling to receive it, the sooner will they turn round and ask for what they now reject. There is perhaps no more hopeful sign of the future of the country than this admirable foresight which the pôngyis in Lower Burma have shown before and which is shown at the present day by the pôngyis of Upper Burma. The worst service the conquerors of Burma could render the conquered is to take away their religion and give them instead nothing but a smattering of English and a Calcutta degree. It is true that in Burma we have but few Burman Bachelors of Arts, but thanks to the pôngyis and to the tact of our previous and present Directors of Public Instruction, there is little fear that the pôngyis who have in times past done so much to raise the tone of their fellow countrymen will be supplanted in their self-imposed task.

State of education in the different districts of Burma.

151. To enter into details of the distribution of the population divided into literate, learning, and illiterate throughout the districts of Burma is the next task before us. The accompanying statements must be read together. In Statement **A** the distribution per mille of the total population of every district and division is shown under the three heads mentioned above. As this return does not show the ages of the population, Statement **B** is added as a contrast, as in this latter statement children under the age of 5 are deducted. The district in which amongst the males enumerated the largest proportion of literates is found is, strange to say, the Upper Chindwin district. This is due to the fact that the Shan States of Kalè, Taungthut, and Kanti were excluded from the regular census, otherwise, had the illiterate inhabitants of these States been included, the return of literates would have been proportionately much lower. The districts in which education is at its lowest ebb are, as in 1881, the Northern Arakan Hill Tracts and Salween. This is only what was to be expected, as the proportion of Burmans is lowest in these districts. The tables show two things, first, that education, so far as males are concerned, is very generally spread over the country, and, next, that few females outside of Rangoon are found among the literates. The cause of this want of education amongst women in a country where they are well known to take an active share in the work of their husbands, not merely as farm labourers, but as traders and even as brokers, is only to be explained by the fact that since the mass of those who learn to read and write have acquired their education at the monasteries, girls, who are not allowed to attend these schools, are consequently debarred from enjoying the same facilities for education as are possessed by their brothers.

Female education in Burma is still almost entirely confined to schools managed either by Government teachers or Christian Missionaries. It is, however, satisfactory to see that, whereas in 1881 there were only 18 women returned as literate out of every 1,000, the proportion in Lower Burma has risen to 31. The Burmans are becoming aware that education is good for women as well as for men, and there is every reason to believe that the number of literates amongst women will be much increased at the forthcoming census of 1901.

STATEMENT A.—*Comparative Table showing the number returned as Learning, Literate, and Illiterate out of every 1,000 persons of each sex in every district and division in Burma.*

District.	Learning. Male.	Learning. Female.	Literate. Male.	Literate. Female.	Illiterate. Male.	Illiterate. Female.	Grade of district and division arranged by proportion of male literates.	Grade of district and division arranged by proportion of female literates.
Arakan—								
Akyab	25	2	267	17	708	981	29	17
Northern Arakan	...	...	49	...	951	1,000	35	36
Kyaukpyu	38	3	346	15	616	982	23	18
Sandoway	35	3	298	11	667	986	28	21
Total ...	**28**	**2**	**284**	**16**	**688**	**982**	VIII	V
Pegu—								
Rangoon	48	32	370	151	582	817	21	1
Hanthawaddy	52	6	459	37	489	957	7	5
Pegu	63	12	492	50	445	938	2	2
Tharrawaddy	84	5	462	28	454	967	6	9
Prome	93	13	464	24	443	963	4	12
Total ...	**70**	**11**	**454**	**43**	**476**	**946**	I	I
Irrawaddy—								
Thôngwa	45	6	479	40	476	954	3	4
Bassein	39	8	376	30	585	962	18	8
Henzada	67	4	455	27	478	969	8	11
Thayetmyo	74	3	464	19	462	978	4	15
Total ...	**53**	**5**	**439**	**30**	**508**	**965**	II	II
Tenasserim—								
Amherst	30	5	261	28	709	967	31	9
Tavoy	41	5	329	21	630	974	26	13
Mergui	27	3	266	19	707	978	30	15
Toungoo	76	10	342	35	582	955	24	6
Shwegyin	43	5	348	31	609	964	22	7
Salween	4	...	46	5	950	995	36	33
Total ...	**40**	**5**	**291**	**28**	**669**	**967**	VII	III
Northern Division—								
Mandalay	52	6	430	41	518	453	12	3
Bhamo	43	2	167	5	790	993	34	33
Katha	44	4	317	14	639	982	27	19
Ruby Mines	29	1	223	9	748	990	33	26
Shwebo	75	2	422	8	503	990	14	27
Total ...	**54**	**5**	**383**	**27**	**563**	**968**	V	IV
Central Division—								
Ye-u	113	...	455	5	432	995	8	33
Sagaing	56	2	408	12	536	986	15	20
Lower Chindwin	73	1	371	7	556	992	19	31
Upper Chindwin	84	1	541	10	375	989	1	24
Total ...	**74**	**1**	**419**	**9**	**507**	**990**	III	VII
Southern Division—								
Myingyan	70	1	384	10	546	989	16	24
Pakôkku	68	1	371	7	561	992	19	31
Minbu	88	2	455	11	457	987	8	21
Magwe	93	2	449	11	458	987	11	21
Total ...	**78**	**1**	**408**	**10**	**514**	**989**	IV	VI
Eastern Division—								
Kyauksè	57	1	254	8	689	991	32	27
Meiktila	82	1	377	8	541	991	17	27
Yamèthin	74	3	331	8	595	989	25	27
Pyinmana	62	3	424	20	514	977	13	14
Total ...	**72**	**2**	**340**	**9**	**588**	**989**	VI	VII
Lower Burma	**52**	7	**391**	31	**557**	**962**	...	...
Upper Burma	**70**	**2**	**392**	13	**538**	**985**	...	...
Burma	59	5	**391**	**24**	550	**971**	...	...
Lower Burma in 1881	108	18	353	18	539	964	...	...

Education amongst males.

152. In Statement **A** the districts are graded in the order, firstly, those in which there are proportionately most male and next those in which there are most female literates. Upper Chindwin holds the first place in the former grade because the non-Burman element in the district was not included in the regular census. Pegu, Thôngwa, Prome, and Thayetmyo rank next; then come Tharrawaddy, Hanthawaddy, Henzada, Minbu, and Ye-u. There are 15 districts, eight of which are in Upper Burma, which contain more than 400 literates out of every 1,000 males. There are 33 out of the 36 districts of Burma which contain more than 20 per cent. of literates out of the total male population. The remaining three districts are Bhamo and the Hill Tracts of Northern Arakan and Salween, where the proportion of Buddhists to the total population is very low. It may be said that Buddhism and male education go hand-in-hand, and the number of male literates found in a district depends on the number of Buddhists as compared with other religions.

Education amongst females.

153. In female education we find that Rangoon, which, owing to the number of illiterate Hindu cooly immigrants in it, only ranks 21st on the list of male literates, is easily first in the list of female literates. This is due to the following reason. There are comparatively speaking few women in Rangoon, and a very large proportion of these are Christians, amongst whom female education is more common than in any other religion. Moulmein, which was first in 1881, is no longer ranked as a district, its identity being lost in Amherst. Pegu holds the proud position of being second, alike in the extent of female as of male education. This is due to the efforts of the missionaries, who have laboured here very successfully. Mandalay ranks next, owing its place no doubt to the large European community. In Thôngwa, Hanthawaddy, Toungoo, Shwegyin, Bassein, and Tharrawaddy the presence of Christian missions explains the position held by these districts.

The accompanying Statement **B** is a variation of Statement **A** in that it shows the proportion of literates, learning, and illiterates distributed by 1,000 of the population of each sex after deducting all children under 5 years of age who may be supposed in Burma at least to be under the age at which they are sent to school. No such return was prepared in 1881, hence no comparison can be instituted.

STATEMENT B.—*Comparative Table showing the number returned as Learning, Literate, and Illiterate out of every 1,000 persons of each sex in every district and division in Burma deducting those who are under 5 years.*

District.	Learning.		Literate.		Illiterate.	
	Male.	Female.	Male.	Female.	Male.	Female.
Arakan—						
Akyab	28	2	302	20	670	978
Northern Arakan	...	...	54	1	946	999
Kyaukpyu	44	4	397	17	559	979
Sandoway	41	4	349	13	610	983
Total ...	**32**	**3**	**323**	**18**	**645**	**979**
Pegu—						
Rangoon Town	51	36	390	171	559	793
Hanthawaddy	59	8	527	43	414	949
Pegu	72	15	563	59	365	926
Tharrawaddy	98	6	545	33	357	961
Prome	108	15	540	28	352	957
Total ...	**80**	**13**	**518**	**51**	**402**	**936**
Irrawaddy—						
Thôngwa	52	8	552	47	396	945
Bassein	46	8	440	36	514	956
Henzada	78	5	534	32	388	963
Thayetmyo	86	4	537	22	377	974
Total ...	**62**	**7**	**511**	**36**	**427**	**957**
Tenasserim—						
Amherst	35	6	304	34	661	960
Tavoy	47	6	385	25	568	969
Mergui	32	4	306	22	662	974
Toungoo	88	11	397	42	515	947
Shwegyin	50	6	407	37	543	957
Salween	5	...	53	5	942	995
Total ...	**47**	**7**	**339**	**33**	**614**	**960**
Northern Division—						
Mandalay	58	7	486	46	456	947
Bhamo	48	2	187	6	765	992
Katha	50	4	361	17	589	979
Ruby Mines	31	1	238	10	731	989
Shwebo	86	2	480	9	434	989
Total ...	**60**	**5**	**432**	**31**	**508**	**964**
Central Division—						
Ye-u	130	1	523	5	347	994
Sagaing	66	2	475	14	459	984
Lower Chindwin	85	1	433	8	482	991
Upper Chindwin	95	2	612	11	293	987
Total ...	**86**	**2**	**486**	**10**	**428**	**988**
Southern Division—						
Myingyan	83	1	452	12	465	987
Pakôkku	80	1	436	9	484	990
Minbu	103	3	531	12	366	985
Magwe	107	3	519	12	374	985
Total ...	**91**	**2**	**478**	**11**	**431**	**987**
Eastern Division—						
Kyauksè	63	2	280	8	657	990
Meiktila	96	1	439	9	465	990
Yamèthin	86	3	383	9	531	988
Pyinmana	70	3	478	23	452	974
Total ...	**82**	**2**	**389**	**10**	**529**	**988**
Total Lower Burma ...	**60**	**8**	**450**	**37**	**490**	**955**
Total Upper Burma ...	**81**	**3**	**451**	**15**	**468**	**982**
Total Burma ...	**68**	**6**	**450**	**28**	**482**	**966**

154. The accompanying statement is a development of the idea which underlies Statement **B.** As we have already discussed and laid out in detail the extent of education in the various districts of Burma, there is no necessity to go into such local detail in this statement. Accordingly the population is taken by divisions and not by districts.

Education in relation to age.

STATEMENT C.—*Comparative Table showing number of those returned as Learning, Literate and Illiterate out of every 1,000 persons of each sex at each age period.*

By divisions.	0–14						15–24						25 and over.					
	LEARNING.		LITERATE.		ILLITERATE.		LEARNING.		LITERATE.		ILLITERATE.		LEARNING.		LITERATE.		ILLITERATE.	
	Male.	Female.	Male.	Female.	Male.	Female.	Male.	Female.	Male.	Female.	Male.	Female.	Male.	Female.	Male.	Female.	Male.	Female.
Arakan ...	64	5	41	5	895	990	24	1	369	22	607	977	2	...	445	22	553	978
Pegu ...	177	25	81	20	742	955	36	4	626	89	338	907	1	1	668	43	331	956
Irrawaddy ...	119	12	78	12	803	976	31	3	629	65	340	932	1	...	696	32	303	968
Tenasserim ...	83	11	51	12	866	977	33	3	423	53	544	944	2	...	463	33	535	967
Northern ...	143	12	61	9	796	979	44	2	475	45	481	953	1	1	551	33	448	966
Central ...	165	3	59	3	776	994	60	1	564	15	376	984	1	...	672	11	327	989
Southern ...	155	3	43	4	802	993	79	1	576	20	345	979	2	...	691	11	307	989
Eastern ...	159	4	37	3	804	993	58	1	474	17	468	982	1	...	550	10	449	990
Total Lower Burma...	121	15	67	13	823	972	33	3	553	64	416	933	1	...	601	34	398	966
Total Upper Burma...	156	5	48	5	796	990	63	1	529	24	408	975	2	...	625	16	373	984
Total Burma ...	134	11	60	10	806	979	43	2	544	49	413	949	1	...	610	26	389	974

155. Amongst males we find that learners and illiterates, as might be expected, are most numerous in the 1st age period. In the 2nd age period everywhere, except in Arakan and Tenasserim in Lower Burma and the Northern and Eastern divisions of Upper Burma, literates are in the ascendant and learners had already begun to dwindle. In the 3rd age period, while illiterates are nearly as numerous as in the 2nd age period, literates, reinforced by those who were learners in the previous age period, are now still more numerous. The fact that there are still a few learners over 25 years of age is one that will call for explanation. This anomaly was noticed during the abstraction of the figures from the census schedules and the entries were accordingly verified as far as possible. The return of learners over 25 years of age was due to the fact that those entered as such were either grown men or women in Mission schools, or upazins in monasteries, who, with somewhat unnecessary modesty, had returned themselves as under instruction.

Education amongst men.

156. Amongst women the course of education follows the same lines as regards age periods as that followed by male education. The table is interesting as it shows that, if we deduct the inmates of Missions and the probationers in monasteries, education in Burma usually ceases soon after the end of the 1st age period, 0—14.

Education amongst women.

157. Mr. Copleston, in his report of 1881, closes his chapter on education with the following suggestive remarks :—

"It is impossible to decide whether the education of the people as a whole is declining or advancing. In some parts of the country the former would appear to be the case. The influence of the pôngyis is undoubtedly decaying, and probably with this weakening of their hold on the people will come a falling off in the attendance of the boys at the kyaung for instruction. If the Burmese are to continue as well educated as they are at present, the Government schools and lay schools will have to grow in numbers to make up for the loss of monastic teaching."

The future prospects of education in Burma.

* * * * *

The following comparative statement, which exhibits the number of Buddhists returned as learning, literate, and illiterate out of every 1,000 of each sex of the population in Lower Burma is the best answer to this question :—

	Learning.		Literate.		Illiterate.	
	Male.	Female.	Male.	Female.	Male.	Female.
1881 ...	.119	17	382	16	499	967
1891 ...	58	6	429	29	513	965

If we make allowance for the mistake in the return of those under instruction in 1881, or, better still, confine our attention to the return of literates, it will be seen that education is not retrograding amongst the Buddhists of Burma. It is clear that, even if the pôngyis are losing their influence, their place is being taken by lay schools. We may then rest assured that, when the returns of the census of 1901 are compiled, we shall find that Burma, instead of having lost ground, will have advanced still further, and that a still larger proportion, both of males and females, will be found amongst the returns of the literate.

CHAPTER VIII.

LANGUAGES.

Parent-tongue, its definition. Classification of languages. Group A, languages of Burma. Variation in the returns of Lower Burma in 1881 and 1891. Other dialects of the Tibeto-Burman family. The Môn-Annam language. The Shan language. Group B, languages of India. Group C, the languages of Asia beyond India and Burma. Group D, languages of Europe and Africa. Mr. Cust's classification of languages. Discussion of the different classifications; new classification proposed. Reasons advanced for adopting it. Polytonic and Monotonic languages. Classification of the languages of Eastern Asia. Dr. Cushing's opinion. Burmese and its dialects. Arakanese an archaic form of Burmese. Mr. Houghton's note on the language of the Southern Chins. The Kachin-Naga group. The Karen dialects; the Môn or Talaing language. Increase in the number of those who were returned as speaking Môn explained. The Taic Shan group. Dr. Cushing's monograph. The Selung language.

Authorities consulted.

1. The Science of Language, by Abel Hovelacque. Chapman and Hall, 1877.
2. Life and growth of Language, by W. D. Whitney. London : Kegan Paul Trench and Co., 1877.
3. Language and the study of Language, by W. D. Whitney. London : Trübner.
4. Linguistic Essays, by Carl Abel. Trübner, 1882.
5. Languages of China before the Chinese, by Terrien de la Couperie.
6. China's Place in Philology, by J. Edkins. London : Trübner.
7. Cradle of the Shan Race, by Terrien de la Couperie.
8. Journal of the American Oriental Society, Proceedings, October 1885. The Lepcha Language, by J. Avery.
9. Linguistic and Oriental Essays, by R. N. Cust. London : Trübner.
10. A Sketch of the Modern Languages of the East Indies, by R. N. Cust. Trübner, 1878.
11. Lectures on the Science of Language, by Max Müller, M.A. London, 1862.
12. Chips from a German Workshop, by Max Müller, M.A. London, 1868.
13. Burma, by Rev. F. Mason, D.D. Rangoon, 1860.
14. The Selungs of the Mergui Archipelago, by J. Anderson. London : Trübner, 1890.
15. Specimens of the Languages of India. Calcutta, 1874.
16. The Language, Literature, and Religion of Nepal and Thibet, by Brian Hodgson. London : Trübner and Co., 1874.
17. Comparative Grammar of the Languages of Further India, by Captain C. J. F. S. Forbes. London : Allen and Co., 1881.
18. Thibetan Grammar, by H. A. Jäschke. Trübner, 1883.
19. Comparative Vocabulary of the Burma-Malayan and their Languages. Serampore, 1810.
20. Colloquial Exercises in the Lushai Dialect of the Dzo or Kuki Language, by Captain Lewin. Calcutta, 1874.
21. Manual of Malay Language, by the Honorable W. E. Maxwell. Second edition.
22. Essay on the Language of the Southern Chins and its Affinities, by Bernard Houghton, C.S. Rangoon, 1892.
23. Notes on the Languages and Dialects spoken in British Burma. Rangoon, 1884.

Substitution of parent-tongue for mother-tongue as the term used for denoting the language spoken.

158. Imperial Table X gives in detail, district by district, the distribution of the population by sex and parent-tongue. And here it may be as well to notice that the term parent-tongue was substituted for mother-tongue. The return of languages in the census schedule is made in order to find out the language which is commonly spoken by a person in his own home. In Burma, where there are many languages spoken and much admixture of race, there is naturally more difficulty experienced in making this return than in European countries, where nationality and language are more often coincident than in the Indian Empire. The term mother-tongue, though clear enough to English ears, when translated is apt to mean the language spoken by the enumeratee's mother, which in Burma certainly does not invariably mean the language generally spoken by the person himself. If a Burman were to marry a Shan woman, his children would probably speak Burmese. If a Chinaman were to marry a Burmese woman, the boys would in every case be brought up as Chinamen and be taught to speak Chinese and would invariably return themselves as Chinese. Accordingly, the term mother-

tongue was changed to parent-tongue and the definition of parent-tongue was the language usually spoken in his parents' household.

It must next be noted that as no attempt was made to obtain the languages spoken by those living in the excluded tracts, and as the schedule books of the Kawlin and Uyu townships were burnt, no return of parent-tongue could be prepared for 116,493 persons out of the total population of Burma. The returns received, therefore, only affect 7,605,560 of the inhabitants of Burma. Subsequent enquiry, however, has shown that the people whose returns were not obtained are Burmese, Shans, Kadus, and Kachins, but the actual number speaking each language and dialect could not be ascertained.

Classification of languages.

159. There are two ways in which languages may be grouped. The first method is the more or less arbitrary method of grouping languages by their geographical position. The other and more scientific method is to group languages linguistically according to the affinity they bear to the various families of speech. The former method, if less scientific, is the more useful for imperial purposes. Accordingly, in Imperial Table X the languages returned in the schedules are divided into four groups:—

A. Vernaculars of Burma.
B. Vernaculars of India.
C. Vernaculars of Asiatic countries beyond India.
D. European and other languages.

The classification originally proposed was to include the languages spoken in Burma in Group **A** along with the Indian vernaculars.

From the scientific and purely linguistic point of view this grouping is misleading, as Burmese, Talaing, and Karen, which are the three chief vernaculars spoken in Burma, belong to the Tibeto-Burman, Môn-Annam, and Sinitic groups of languages, which are returned in Group **C** and not with the languages in Group **B** to which they have no affinity.

I have therefore included all the vernaculars of Burma under Group **A**, classifying the vernaculars of India in Group **B**, and the other languages of Asia in Group **C**. This classification is useful for the comparison of our returns, and in accordance with the instructions of the Government of India the scientific grouping of these languages can be discussed hereafter.

But this classification, however useful it may be for the purpose of comparing the proportionate strength of those who speak these languages, is obviously incomplete. The annexation of Upper Burma has so much enlarged the field of enquiry that we now have better scope and fairer opportunities than have ever been before possessed. In a census report language forms but one of the many topics that have to be considered, and neither space nor time worthy of the discussion is possible in one brief chapter. I have, however, been able to enlist the aid not only of several members of the Burma Commission, but of Dr. Cushing, who has been of the very greatest help to me in the attempt to classify the languages of the Indo-Chinese Peninsula. I would not have attempted to grapple with this task but for the fact that there is at present no final arrangement generally accepted, and the census returns, coupled with the interesting monographs furnished me by Dr. Cushing, Mr. Houghton and Mr. George, have placed materials at my disposal hitherto unpublished.

Group **A**, Languages of Burma. (*a*) Burmese and its dialects.

160. In Group **A** we find 30 vernaculars that are returned as being spoken in Burma against 20 mentioned in the Imperial Tables of 1881. Of these 30 vernaculars the first seven are grouped together as being but different forms or dialects of one language—Burmese.

1. Burmese spoken by	5,554,572	or	7,303·00	Per 10,000 of the total population.
2. Arakanese spoken by	344,848	or	453·41	
3. Chaungtha spoken by	271	or	·35	
4. Tavoy spoken by	972	or	1·29	
5. Danu spoken by	1,160	or	1·53	
6. Kadu spoken by	114	or	·15	
7. Yaw spoken by	57	or	·07	
Total of those speaking these languages	5,901,994	or	7,760·10	

These seven vernaculars have, with the approval of Dr. Cushing, who is undoubtedly the greatest living authority on the languages of the Shan States and

Burma, been grouped together as dialects of Burmese. It will be sufficient here to allude to Mr. Houghton's opinion that the language returned in the schedules as Kadu should be written Kudo. He thinks that it belongs to the group of Kachin-Naga dialects. Nothing certain is as yet known about the language. It contains a large number of Shan vocables, but that by the Burmans themselves this language is considered to be a dialect of Burmese may be inferred from the fact that the Burmese enumerators in the Katha district, where most of these Kudos (or Kadus) were enumerated, invariably returned them as speaking Burmese as their parent-tongue. I think that Mr. Houghton will probably be able to establish the truth of his statement, but until he himself is quite satisfied on this point I do not feel justified in altering the usually accepted classification. This point incidentally shows the difficulty to be grappled with in attempting to classify the languages of Burma. At the last census Mr. Copleston adopted the same classification, with this difference, that Kadu and Danu not being amongst the languages enumerated, did not find a place in his table, while he included Yabein, which perhaps belongs to the same group of dialects, but which is not mentioned in our present tables as not a single person has returned it as his parent-tongue. At the last census 436 persons were returned as speaking Yabein. Mr. Copleston remarked regarding the Yabein language: "It would seem if "they ever had a language it is now extinct or has become modified into a mere "dialect of Burmese." The census returns prove that Mr. Copleston's augury was correct. The circumstances leading to this extinction will be dealt with more fully hereafter.

161. The following table compares the returns under these dialects for Lower Burma in 1891 with the returns of the previous census:—

Languages.	1881.	1891.	Variation.	
			Increase per cent.	Decrease per cent.
Burmese	2,245,125	2,818,306	25·53	...
Arakanese	362,988	344,519	...	5·08
Tavoy	1,343	972	...	27·62
Chaungtha	2,341	271	...	88·42
Yaw	41	26	...	36·58

The inclusion of the Danus and Kadus in this group will be discussed more fully hereafter. The Kadus are only found in Upper Burma, and of the Danus only 194 were returned as living in Lower Burma, and they may probably be lately arrived immigrants. This will explain their not being found in the return of the census of 1881.

162. The next group of the vernaculars of Burma are the hill dialects. These are known to the Burmese by the generic name of Chin. Unfortunately this term is sometimes used ambiguously to denote a tribe of the Chins as well as to connote the whole race. Mr. Houghton agrees in thinking that the term Chin might be used to connote the whole group of languages, and the present dialect known as Chin be in future termed Southern Chin.

The Chin dialects.

These dialects are—

Southern Chin spoken by	95,499 or	125·56	Per 10,000 of the total population.
Kun spoken by	32 or	0·04	
Pallaing spoken by	23 or	0·03	
Daignet spoken by	856 or	1·13	
Sak or Thet spoken by	152 or	0·20	
An or Anu, which is a dialect of Southern Chin, spoken by ...	298 or	0·39	
Mro spoken by	15,891 or	20·90	
Kami or Kwemi spoken by	14,126 or	18·57	
Total ...	126,877 or	166·82	

Of these, Southern Chin, Kun, Daignet, Sak (or Thet), Mro, and Kwemi find place in the returns of the last census of Lower Burma.

The following statement compares the returns of the two enumerations in Lower Burma :—

Language.	1881.	1891.	Variation.	
			Increase per cent.	Decrease per cent.
Chin	55,015	68,822	25·09	...
Daignet	1,995	856	...	57·09
Sak (or Thet)	69	152	120·29	...
Mro	11,021	15,891	44·18	...
Kwemi	13,773	14,126	2·56	...
Kun	11	32	190·90	...

The increase in the number of those termed Chin is due probably as much to better enumeration as to the actual natural increment. It may be due to the immigration of Chin septs into British territory from the as yet comparatively unexplored tract known as the Chin Hills. The same causes probably underlie the increase of the numbers of the Sak, Mro, and Kun clans. The decrease in the Daignets may be due to the absorption of these into the Burmese-speaking races or to their being returned as Chins.

The Kuki dialects.

163. The next group is the Taungthu or Kuki group, of which there are two representatives known in Burma,—the Shandu spoken by 7 persons and the Kyaw by 79 only. At the last census 71 were returned as speaking Shandu or Shendu and 587 as speaking Kyaw (or Chaw). The decrease in both cases is due to the absorption of the clansmen into Burmese races.

The Chingpaw and Lishaw dialects.

164. The next group includes the Kachin, sometimes styled the Singpho or Chingpaw dialects spoken by 2,642 persons in the Bhamo and Katha districts, whose returns were collected on the regular census schedule. Of course, this does not give any real indication of the strength of this race, as in the Bhamo district only the riverine tracts could be included within the scope of the regular census operations. Of the Lishaws and their language but little is known : 1,099 persons in the Ruby Mines district returned this vernacular as their parent-tongue. The Deputy Commissioner states that they have a language of their own and originally came from the hills bordering the western frontier of the Chinese province of Sechuan (Syetchuen). It will probably be found that the so-called Lishaws are the Leso or Letcho mentioned by Pere Desgodens, who has prepared a vocabulary of 107 words of their language. Letcho merely means a man and is the name which these mountaineers have given to themselves. They were also met by Dr. Anderson. Their language is said to belong to the Tibeto-Burman family of speech. It is probably cognate to the Kachin.

The Môn-Annam dialects.

165. The Môn-Annam dialects known by the Burmans as Talaing, Palaung, and Khamu were only represented at the last census by Talaing. In 1872 the number of those returned as belonging to the Talaing race amounted to 181,602 ; in 1881 the number of those who gave Talaing as their mother-tongue was only 154,553, a decrease of 27,049 or 14 per cent. Mr. Copleston's remarks are well worth quoting.

* * * * *

"215. There are in British Burma 154,553 pure Talaings and 177,939 persons of mixed Burmese and Talaing parentage, or Talaings who speak only Burmese. * * * * The term Talaing in 1872 included many of that race whose language was Burmese, or who were not pure Talaing by race. The returns show 181,602 of them. Of the pure Talaings recorded at this census more than half, or 85,616, are in the Amherst district. Hanthawaddy, once the stronghold of the Talaing Kingdom, has but 25,986, and probably many of these habitually speak Burmese. Of the remainder, 22,282 are found in Shwegyin. The language is fast dying out, and probably the census in 1870 will show a great decrease in the numbers of persons speaking the Môn language."

* * * * *

Accordingly in 1891—for 1870 is a manifest misprint—we should have expected to find a decrease; on the contrary, somewhat unexpectedly, we find the number thus returned in Lower Burma was 226,304, an increase of 46 per cent. Thus 297 persons out of every 10,000 of the total population return Talaing as their parent-tongue. This increase is apparent rather than real and is due to more careful enumeration in 1891. I shall recur to this subject hereafter.

To the Môn-Annam stock belong two languages that have for the first time appeared in our schedules, the Palaung dialect, which is spoken by 2,821 persons in the Ruby Mines, 23 in the Kyauksè, and 3 in the Myingyan district, and the Khamu dialect returned by 8 persons in the Salween district. Palaung is a true Môn dialect and is classed as such by de la Couperie and Dr. Cushing. Khamu is a dialect spoken in Cambodia, and the few Khamus who speak it must be immigrants.

166. The next two groups are the Karen and Taic Shan. The former includes:

Pwo Karen spoken by	408,475 or 537·07	Out of every 10,000 of the total population.
Sgau Karen spoken by	225,193 or 296·09	
Bghai Karen (or Karenni) spoken by	16 or ·02	
Taungthu spoken by	41,115 or 54·06	
Total ...	674,799 or 887·24	

The following table compares the returns made of those speaking these languages in Lower Burma in 1881 and 1891:—

Language.	1881.	1891.	Variation. Increase per cent.	Variation. Decrease per cent.
Pwo	514,495 (Pwo and Sgau)	405,966	22·58 (Pwo and Sgau)	...
Sgau		224,738		
Taungthu	35,554	35,220	...	·93

No attempt was made either at the last preceding or the present census to return the subdivisions of the three chief Karen races to which Dr. Mason devoted so much attention, as these divisions are rapidly being obliterated and were mere tribal distinctions.

167. The Taic Shan group finds the following representatives amongst our census returns:—

Shan spoken by	172,644 or 226·99	Out of every 10,000 of the total population.
Lü spoken by	77 or 0·10	
Meungsa or Maingtha spoken by	1,243 or 1·64	
Total ...	173,964 or 228·73	

The Lüs and Meungsas were not mentioned in the 1881 report. While in 1881 there were in Lower Burma 59,723 who gave Shan as their mother-tongue, in 1891 the number of Shans in Lower Burma had risen to 94,226, an increase of 57·77 per cent. This increase, as will afterwards be explained, does not denote the increase of the Shan race in Lower Burma.

The Maingthas as they are called by the Burmans, or Meungsas as they call themselves, and the Lüs belong to the Taic Shan race; the former to the number of 1,209 men and 17 women were found in the Ruby Mines district, whither they annually resort for work. They are not settlers, but mere labourers who earn their wage and depart. The Lüs consist of a small community of 77 persons in all who live in the hills that divide Amherst from Siam.

168. The last of the languages included in Group **A** is the Selung or Selôn dialect. It is spoken by 1,628 persons living in the Mergui district, being an increase of 82 per cent. over the returns of 1881. This, of course, is an abnormal increase due to greater care being taken by the local officers in carrying out the census operations, and also in great measure to the ready assistance granted by Mr. Hughes of the Geological Survey of India. The Selung language and race will be noticed more fully hereafter. In all of these vernaculars of Burma the males and females are fairly evenly distributed.

169. In Group B, Languages of India, there are altogether 18 dialects that are returned by persons enumerated in Burma. Here, as might be expected, in every case amongst those who return these languages, the males far outnumber the females. The accompanying statement compares the returns of the present with those of the last enumeration in Lower Burma :—

Group B, Languages of India.

Language.	1881.			1891.			Variation.	
	Males.	Females.	Total.	Males.	Females.	Total.	Increase per cent.	Decrease per cent.
Bengali ...	68,320	31,425	99,745	105,828	57,337	163,165	63·58	...
Urdu ...	Not shown.			5,146	2,681	7,827	...	...
Hindi ...	53,290	19,700	72,990	47,431	14,640	62,071	...	14·98
Uriya ...	780	82	862	2,053	80	2,133	147·44	...
Khasia ...	...	...	...	2	...	2	...	...
Assamese ...	...	...	...	1	...	1	...	...
Gurmukhi ...	8	6	14	950	185	1,135	8,007·14	...
Nepali ...	59	19	78	220	72	292	274·32	...
Tamil ...	27,483	7,575	35,058	42,646	13,807	56,453	61·02	...
Telugu ...	28,609	5,106	33,715	51,261	9,978	61,239	81·63	...
Kanarese ...	3	2	5	2	1	3	...	40·00
Malayalam ...	25	3	28	6	...	6	...	78·57
Guzerathi ...	163	43	206	424	173	597	189·80	...
Mahrathi ...	21	3	24	287	206	493	1,954·16	...
Goanese ...	7	3	10	10	...	10	...	...
Deccani ...	...	...	...	3	6	9	...	...
Panka ...	...	...	...	3	...	3	...	...
Singhalese ...	1	...	1	15	...	15	1,400·00	...

In 1881 there were 11 persons shown as speaking Tipperah, of whom none have been found in our present returns. These have probably been shown either as Manipuris or Bengalis.

In the same way the Surati language mentioned in the returns of 1881 has disappeared, and those who were returned as speaking it are now shown rightly as speaking Guzerathi, or perhaps they have gone to swell the return of those who give Persian as their parent-tongue. The language of the Laccadive Islands, spoken in 1881 by 9 persons, has also disappeared. Nine persons are returned as speaking Deccani. There is no such lauguage as Deccani. In all probability the language spoken was Kanarese or Telugu, but as it was impossible to ascertain which was meant, the return was accepted.

170. The third group of languages, C, consists of those spoken in countries of Asia outside India and Burma. There are 12 languages in this group; of these Hebrew, which was returned both in the census of 1881 and 1891, is probably Syriac, and not pure Hebrew. Doubting the truth of the return I instituted fresh inquiries, but the Jews who made the return stuck to their assertion that Hebrew and not Syriac was their parent-tongue, and I was not in a position to dispute their statement. Of the 683 who return Persian, only a few really own it as their parent-tongue. It was, however, found that except in a few cases there was no possibility of finding out whether the return meant Urdu or true Persian. There is a colony of Persians in Burma, though by no means so numerous as the return of parent-tongue would seem to indicate. The Manipuri of 1881 is represented by two dialects of the language of Manipur, Kathe and Pônna. The existence of these two separate dialects is doubted. Primrose makes no mention of them in his Manipuri Grammar. I have been, however, assured that the two dialects do as a fact differ from each other. The difference, if it really exists, may be due to the fact that Kathe represents the dialect of the captives deported by Shin Byu Shin in 1764 A.D., which would naturally be purer and less adulterated with Burmese vocables than the language of the Pônnas or Manipuri Brahmans who had previously settled in Burma. The number returning these dialects shows a marked decrease in Lower Burma, due to the rapid absorption of those who returned it into the Burman population

Group C, Languages of Asia beyond India and Burma.

among whom they dwell. Siamese and Laos are but branches of the Taic Shan race. But both are now different languages, and a Siamese of Bangkok would find some difficulty in making himself understood in the Northern Shan States. The Laos or Yun, like the Siamese, belong to the Southern Group and must not be confounded with the Lüs of Kainghung, who belong to the Intermediate group and who have therefore been included in the vernaculars of Burma. There was no return made of the "Panthè" language. There were 10 who returned it in 1881. In 1881 the Panthè rebellion had been but recently quelled. Since then 10 years only have intervened, and it is probable that the Panthès are now not so eager to distinguish themselves from the other Chinese. Mr. J. G. Scott, "Shwe Yeo," regarding these Panthès, writes:

"There is a considerable probability that the so-called Panthès (the Hui Hui of the Chinese) are Shans, or, at any rate, largely filled with Shan blood. Very little is, however, really known about their origin."

The accompanying statement exhibits the returns of 1881 compared with those of Lower Burma obtained at the present census:—

Language.	1881.			1891.			Variation.	
	Males.	Females.	Total.	Males.	Females.	Total.	Increase per cent.	Decrease per cent.
Kathe / Pônna } Manipuri.	1,246	1,278	2,524	757	621	1,378	...	45·40
Siamese ...		Not shown.		48	13	61	...	...
Laos ...		Not shown.		6	7	13	...	...
Persian ...	132	66	198	407	198	605	205·55	...
Arabic ...	43	17	60	392	16	408	580·	...
Hebrew ...	96	75	171	215	117	332	94·22	...
Armenian ...	269	197	466	112	93	205	...	56·00
Chinese ...	11,473	1,489	12,962	23,108	7,971	31,079	139·77	...
Japanese ...		Not shown.		9	33	42	...	...
Malay ...	968	764	1,732.	1,148	1,003	2,151	24·19	...

Group D, Languages of Europe and Africa.

171. Group D embraces the languages of Europe, and as there is but one African language returned, Egyptian, and only two persons who speak it, I have widened the classification so as to include this stray African language. From inquiries I have made I am inclined to believe that the so-called Egyptian language is Arabic.

The accompanying statement compares the returns of Lower Burma in 1881 and 1891:—

Language.	1881.			1891.			Variation.	
	Males.	Females.	Total.	Males.	Females.	Total.	Increase per cent.	Decrease per cent.
English ...	7,714	2,658	10,372	8,701	4,475	13,176	27·03	...
Welsh ...	146	...	146	...	...	...	...	...
Gaelic ...	4	...	4	...	...	...	...	...
German ...	310	29	339	277	56	333	...	1·76
French ...	91	20	111	67	30	97	...	12·61
Italian ...	333	20	353	144	5	149	...	57·79
Portuguese ...	134	26	160	80	18	98	...	38·75
Norwegian ...	256	...	256	77	...	77	...	69·92
Austrian ...		Not shown.		5	1	6	...	...
Maltese ...	24	...	24	1	...	1	...	95·83
Egyptian ...	3	1	4	2	...	2	...	50·00
Swiss ...		Not shown.		5	2	7	...	...
Fin ...	5	...	5	5	...	5	...	...
Danish ...	13	...	13	23	1	24	84·61	...
Dutch ...	18	2	20	17	3	20	...	...
Turkish ...	1	...	1	6	...	6	500·00	...
Russian ...	11	2	13	16	...	16	23·07	...
Spanish ...	21	...	21	12	2	14	...	33·33
Greek ...	28	2	30	12	2	14	...	53·33
Swedish ...	151	...	151	69	1	70	...	53·64

It will be seen that there is a decrease in the return of those speaking Italian, German, Norwegian, Greek, Swedish, French, Portuguese, Welsh, and Gaelic. As there were only four persons in 1881 who spoke Gaelic and the return was probably made on the spur of the moment by four enthusiastic Highlanders, the omission of the language is not difficult of explanation. The disappearance of the Welsh is due, no doubt, to the fact that they have been returned as English-speaking. Indeed, the presence of as many as 146 persons who gave Welsh as their mother-tongue in 1881 is somewhat astonishing of itself, considering how small the whole of the European community is. But the decrease of those returning Italian, German, and the other important European languages is one that required careful investigation. It is a well known fact that the wealthy German community in Rangoon has been increased in the last intercensal period. From enquiries that have been made it has been ascertained that the decrease in the number of large sailing ships that used to be engaged in the rice trade was felt in the decrease of the population of the Port of Rangoon that has already been noticed. The Vice-Chairman of the Port Commissioners reported—

"I have seen as many as 40 ships lying up in the Pegu river during the months of January and February in the old days, where now we hardly see one, because the bulk of the carrying trade has passed into the hands of the steamship companies."

The decrease explained.

These ships were manned by English, Swedish, Norwegian, Italian, and German crews, and their absence now not only explains the decrease shown under the returns of parent-tongue, but has been noticed as a cause of the diminution in the return of certain Christian sects. The only large increase is under the head of English. It must be remembered that this increase would have been much larger if the English garrison of Lower Burma had not been reduced since the pacification of Upper Burma. The increase in the number of English-speaking people is therefore all the more remarkable and it is due partly to natural increment and partly also to the expansion of trade and the increase in the number of Government officials. The returns for the remaining countries call for no further comment, except that the return of a so-called Austrian language has been entered as returned, as the persons who made it are not Germans and probably meant Magyar instead of Austrian. It has, however, been impossible to verify the entry.

172. The languages have now been dealt with under the geographical classification prescribed by the Government of India. This classification makes no pretence of being of any scientific value and was utilized merely as the most practicable form of comparing the returns. I have, however, to a small extent followed the scientific method in classifying the various languages that are grouped under the name of languages of Burma. It now remains to discuss the right method of classification, the consideration of which was commended to the Provincial Superintendents as belonging to the critical rather than the statistical portion of the census work.

Mr. Cust classifies the languages of India somewhat in the following way:

- Aryan Family ...
  - Eranic Branch.
  - Indic ... ...
    - Pure.
    - Mixed Dravidian.
    - Mixed Kolarian.
    - Mixed Tibetan.
- Dravidian Family...
  - Southern.
  - Northern.
- Tibeto-Burman ...
  - Himalayan Branch.
  - Nipal Branch.
  - Assam Branch.
  - Eastern Frontier Branch.
  - Burmese Branch.
- Khasi Family.
- Tai or Shan Family.
- Malay and Andamanese Family.

Mr. Cust in following Professor Max Müller's lead is tempted to go astray. The classification we find in Max Müller's works is not merely fanciful and useless but actually misleading, at any rate so far as they relate to the languages of Burma. The branches here mentioned are then divided into languages, dialects, and sub-dialects; for instance, Karen is classed as a Tibeto-Burman language; Singpho or Kachin as Tibeto-Assam; Sak as Tibeto-Manipuri; Tunghlu, which is not traceable as such, is shown as Tibeto-Burman, and Selung or Selôn as Tibeto-Burman.

Mr. Cust's classification of languages.

Such a classification, however correct it may be as regards the Indian families of speech, is not only incomplete, but incorrect when it is extended to the languages of Burma and the Indo-Chinese Peninsula. How valueless this classification is may be judged from the fact that it includes a language which does not exist and groups the various vernaculars of Burma in the most haphazard manner. But before I go further I must admit most fully my debt to Mr. Cust. When he confines himself to the languages with which he is personally acquainted his remarks are shrewd and suggestive. He only errs when he follows the lead of others who had not the same personal acquaintance with the languages of the East.

173. Professor Max Müller divides the languages of Asia and Europe into three great families: the Aryan, the Semitic, and the Turanian. With the first two we have in Burma but little to do as neither has established itself, except as a foreign element, and both are still traceable as such. For instance, the Pali element in Burmese is just as distinguishable from the Burmese element as the Latin from the Saxon element in English. But as regards the Turanian family we find that Max Müller has placed our vernaculars in the Lohitic class of the Southern Division of that family. This classification has been severely criticised by M. Hovelacque and has been disregarded by M. de la Couperie. The whole value of this classification is lost when we find that it is based on an erroneous idea of the form of speech—I purposely avoid the word family—to which Burmese and its cognate languages belong, for Max Müller classifies them under the agglutinative group. It is true that some of them show traces of approaching agglutination, but this alone will not justify their inclusion among agglutinative languages. We must then reject this classification. Hovelacque does not attempt to classify these languages. He styles Chinese, Burmese, and Karen alike independent; such a classification though better than a misleading one is unsuggestive. De la Couperie classifies the Tibeto-Burman family under the Turano-Scythian stock and in the Kuenlunic family to which belong Chinese and Karen. Shan and Môn dialects he classifies in the Indo-Chinese division of the Pacific stock of languages. With such variance in those who take the lead it is by no means easy to select whom to follow. In this difficulty I had recourse to Dr. Cushing, who has the most intimate knowledge of these languages of any man living. To him I am indebted for what may be of any value in the following remarks. I have thought it better, instead of working downwards from a hypothetical classification, to work up to it, choosing as a vehicle that language which is best known to us in Burma, namely, Burmese.

174. Burmese is now generally classed as belonging to the "Isolating Form" of speech. By Professor Max Müller it is placed in the Lohitic class of the Southern Division of the Turanian Family. Mons. Hovelacque rejects this imaginary classification of various totally independent languages under the supposititious patriarchal name of Tur. Hovelacque's arguments appear to be unanswerable, and of late years the Turanian theory has dropped into disfavour. Hovelacque declines to attempt to classify these languages. Mr. Cust following the lead of Brian Hodgson, places Burmese in the Tibeto-Burman family. Captain Forbes, whose death was a great loss to the advance of philology in Burma, adopted this name and was in favour of abandoning the meaningless term of "Lohitic." Mons. Terrien de la Couperie, though he has not directly discussed the origin of Burmese, has by his researches thrown a strong side-light on the matter. In the present imperfect state of our knowledge any classification of languages is a matter of danger. When a learned scholar of

Discussion of the classifications already made.

world-wide renown like Professor Max Müller has gone astray simply because, as Captain Forbes points out, he was absolutely unacquainted with the name of a language which he calls Tunghlu and which he boldly classified as Lohitic and which is not a language but merely a dialect of Pwo Karen, any attempt to classify our languages would seem to be a presumptuous task. Still, as the work must be done, with the help of Dr. Cushing, the pioneer of our knowledge of the Taic Shan dialects, and Mr. Houghton, Deputy Commissioner of Sandoway, the first man who has attempted to deal scientifically with the Chin group of languages, an attempt has been made to grapple with the subject.

And here, before going further, I think it but right to point out that nothing so ill becomes an explorer in philology as a light-hearted derision of the mistakes of his predecessors. Dr. Mason, than whom no one has done more service in the cause of scientific research in Burma in philology, botany, and ethnology, is frequently held up to derision for conjectures that he made which, by the light of recent research, appear to be absurd. But when we find a man of whose unequalled ability in philological research there can be no doubt—I mean Professor Max Müller—falling into what to us in Burma is a palpable mistake, more leniency might be shown to Dr. Mason, who worked with wonderful acumen and shrewdness, though unguided by the knowledge gained by recent inquiry. The moral to be learnt then is that nothing is so unsafe as to hazard any conjecture unsupported by evidence, however plausible it may seem. Luckily, however, the labours of Brian Hodgson in Nepal, of Mason and Forbes in Burma, and the short but useful vocabularies prepared by the Government of India of the languages of the aboriginal tribes of Bengal, published in 1874, together with the vocabulary of the Lushai dialect of the Kuki language of Captain Lewin and the Chin, Shandu, and Kami vocabulary prepared by Mr. Davis have to some extent prepared the way for future research. A comparison of these vocabularies shows that Tibetan and Burmese both belong to the same family. It would not be going on unsafe ground to state that from Tibet to Burma the tribes known as the Singphos (Chingpaws) or Kachins, the Nagas, the Kukis, the Shandus, and Chins all belong to the same Tibeto-Burman family. The variation in their vocabularies is not wonderful considering that, as Max Müller says, "among the wild illiterate tribes of Siberia, "Africa, and Siam two or three generations are sufficient to change the whole "aspect of their dialects." Further on in writing on the same subject of dialectical regeneration Max Müller says:

"We hear the same observations everywhere where the rank growth of dialects has been watched by intelligent observers. If we turn our eyes to Burma, we find that there the Burmese has produced a considerable literature, and is the recognized medium of communication not only in Burma, but likewise in Pegu and Arakan. But the intricate mountain ranges of the peninsula of the Irrawaddy afford a safe refuge to many independent tribes, speaking their own independent dialects, and in the neighbourhood of Manipur alone Captain Gordon collected no less than twelve dialects. 'Some of them' he says, 'are spoken by no more than 30 or 40 families, yet so different from the rest as to be unintelligible to the nearest neighbourhood.' Brown, the excellent American Missionary who spent his whole life in preaching the Gospel in that part of the world, tells us that some tribes who left their native village to settle in another valley, became unintelligible to their forefathers in two or three generations."

Terrien de la Couperie's classification.

175. Mons. Terrien de la Couperie groups Tibeto-Burman, Karen, and the Chinese languages under the name of Kuenlunic and assigns them to the so-called Turano-Scythian stock of languages. The Môn Taic, Môn Khmer, and Taic Shan groups he separates from the Turano-Scythian group and calls them Indo-Chinese. The term Turano-Scythian perpetuates the fallacy of the Turanian theory of a common origin and is at best an unlovely compound word. The word Sinitic might be used to denote this family, not because the languages are descended from Chinese, but because Chinese is the most famous and widely spoken of the languages of this group. Perhaps the best or rather the least misleading name for this class or stock of languages would be some name such as Isolating or Polytonic, which would serve to mark the radical distinction between them and the Aryan and Semitic families of speech. The name Indo-Chinese is misleading because it has a geographical as well as a linguistic meaning. It is the name pro-

posed by M. Terrien de la Couperie for the three groups of the "Môn Taic," "Môn Khmer," and "Taic Shan" languages. But, as he himself points out, these languages are pre-Chinese and have nothing Indian about them. Dr. Cushing, who is very cautious in advancing theories which in the present imperfect state of our knowledge of these dialects are not only unsusceptible of proof, though true, but which may, though plausible, be erroneous, is inclined to think that the Chinese group of languages, the Tai or Shan group and the Karen group, are all descended from some common tongue no longer in existence and of which we have no literature. It is possible that the Tibeto-Burman group is also descended from this common stock. All of these languages are in character monosyllabic or isolating. It is true that Max Müller has classed Burmese and Shan among the agglutinative languages, but as this is a palpable error it is clear that he knew nothing about these languages, and it is therefore needless to discuss his classification further. In the second place, these languages possess the peculiarity of employing tones to vary the mere weight and value and meaning of a sound, and thus to make two or more words out of what to an unpractised ear appears to be but a single sound. In English and in all Aryan languages words, except when spoken in anger, surprise, or interrogation, are of uniform tone. The use of accents in French is merely a convention for giving a different sound to a vowel which has to do duty in English for sometimes three sounds. In Burmese, Shan, and Chinese tones are employed, not to eke out an inadequate alphabet, but to eke out an inadequate vocabulary. These Polytonic languages belong to an earlier form of speech than the Monotonic languages. If, as is averred, human speech has been gradually evolved from the inarticulate sounds which animals and children alike make to express their emotions, then these Polytonic languages are an earlier and stereotyped form evolved out of the inarticulate language of primeval man.

176. This subject has been discussed by Professor Max Müller in his essay on the Science of Language. He has investigated what he calls the Bow-wow and Pooh-pooh theories. Starting with the idea that no animal thinks and no animal speaks except man, it is but logical that he should believe that "Man in his primitive and perfect state was not only endowed like the brute with the power of expressing his sensations by interjections, and perceptions by onomatopœa. He possessed likewise the faculty of giving more articulate expression to the rational conceptions of his mind." Yet Professor Max Müller admits that languages may have passed from the radical through the agglutinative into the inflectional stage. The value of tones used instead of consonantal sounds has, however, not been fully appreciated by him. In some Chinese dialects the consonantal sound is immaterial so long as the tone is preserved. It might be argued that the keenness of ear necessary to denote change of tone is against the use of a tonic as opposed to an inflectional language. Against this we have the acknowledged fact that the language which employs tones more freely than any other is the earliest that became stereotyped, namely, Chinese. Moreover, it is admitted that the sense of hearing is far more highly developed among savages and among some of the lower animals than among civilized men. If it be true that the earlier forms of speech employed tones more freely than the later and more inflectional, then there is every reason to believe that human speech was evolved from the power of imitating noises and of making "interjectional" sounds. Professor Max Müller would have us believe that the human race started its existence equipped with phonetic types. Unacquainted with any but a comparatively limited number of languages, he boldly argues and generalizes from insufficient data regarding the phonetic types from which all languages according to him must have sprung. All these theories must in time be abandoned. It seems almost absurd to go further back than what we see before our own eyes. The evolution of the faculty of speech amongst mankind in general finds an almost exact parallel in the laborious and gradual acquisition of the power of speech by an infant. That the process is not quite the same is due to the fact that the tuition of the infant's parents assists the child to acquire a special form of speech, whereas no such tuition was of course possible in the history of the evolution of articulate speech of mankind in general.

Max Müller's theory regarding the origin of speech.

177. But leaving a subject which is at present undecided, we may assert that the progress of speech is marked by the evolution of the power of articulation out of the power of ejaculation, that is to say, man has gradually acquired the power of articulating, *i.e.*, putting or joining together sounds instead of being compelled to get as many tones as he can out of a single sound. To use a simile which exactly conveys our meaning, the savage having but few sounds was forced to make as many words as he could out of the sounds he possessed by uttering the sounds in different tones like Paganini, who could play on one string of his violin. The reason of this incapacity to create new sounds is due to the fact that vowels are naturally more easily pronounced than the consonants. The latter require the use of tongue or of lips, while the true vowel may be ejaculated. In order to prove this we must show that languages which are known to be polytonic gradually tend to lose this characteristic. This we find actually the case in the dialects of the wild tribes of the Malay Peninsula. Even in the Talaing or Môn language the use of tones is falling into abeyance, although as will be shown hereafter the existence of them is distinctly proven. The same tendency is shown in Chinese and Burmese when, for the sake of additional clearness, a synonym is used. Max Müller, ignoring the fact that sounds may have various meanings depending on the tone employed, mentions this peculiarity incidentally. "The "fact is," he says, "that in Chinese every sound has "numerous meanings, and in order to avoid ambiguity, "one word is frequently followed by another which "agrees with it in that particular meaning." The use of these synonyms is more readily understood by those who have been compelled to learn and use a tonic language. In Burmese, as in Chinese, the tendency is to rely less on tones and more on synonyms, and the first step to the agglutinative stage is the use of synonyms to help the failing power of the ear.

The evolution of articulate language out of ejaculation.

Variation in tone used to denote variation of meaning.

178. The use of tones, then, seems to mark the radical stage through which all languages have passed or in which those that are still tonic have become stereotyped. In all humility I would then suggest that those languages which still more or less preserve the polytonic character should be classed together, and those which are inflectional or polysyllabic and hence have lost their original polytonic character and have become monotonic be classified apart. The principle which underlies this classification is that languages are to be classified not on mere accidental similarity of vocables or even of accidence, but the main division should be based on the stage of development to which they have arrived. We might then dispense with the imaginary patriarchal name of Turanian or the unlovely compound term of Turano-Scythian suggested by de la Couperie, and designate the languages of Eastern Asia that make use of this peculiarity as the Polytonic group.

The term Polytonic proposed.

179. It may be urged why not adhere to the terms isolating, monosyllabic, or independent? The reasons to be advanced against these names are as follows. Isolating is of itself an awkward name. It refers to the mental process undergone in formulating speech. In reality the meaning conveyed is not actually expressed. The use of the term would seem to convey the idea that these languages are intentionally isolating, whereas in fact the tendency of all languages is to become agglutinative and then inflectional. Moreover, as Mr. Houghton points out, the process is so gradual that in some cases great difficulty is experienced in assigning a language to either class. Against the term monosyllabic there is the strong objection that it is not sufficiently distinctive. Every language possesses a large number of monosyllables. Independent is an unsatisfactory term. It was used by Hovelacque as a protest against the false grouping under the name Turanian. It has served its purpose. In itself it is unmeaning, insomuch as all languages uninfluenced by others are independent. It is, however, too early for us to say that Chinese, Shan, and Burmese are independent. On the contrary, Mons. de la Couperie has shown that the languages of the Indo-Chinese Peninsula have influenced each other. In favour of adopting this new nomenclature, it may be argued that since the use of tones distinctly marks a stage in

Reasons advanced for adopting the term Polytonic.

the development of speech, the term Polytonic is peculiarly suitable as a class name for those languages which still preserve this characteristic. Again, it may be urged supposing this classification of polytonic and monotonic is preferable to the less distinctive names of monosyllabic, independent, and isolating, what is the gain in adopting it? The answer to this objection is of course that logical classification is a distinct help in the acquisition of fresh knowledge, while wrong classification is directly misleading.

As Professor Whitney remarks—

"The only way to cast light upon it (the history of the development of language) is by a careful induction from the change and growth which are seen to have been going on in the recent periods for which we have recorded evidence or which are going on at the present time."

Any classification then based on such inductions must be better than an obsolete and misleading terminology.

"To account for the great and striking differences of structure among human languages is," says Professor Whitney, "beyond the power of the linguistic student and will doubtless remain so."

Is it not possible that this barrenness is due to the unscientific treatment of the subject? Dr. Carl Abel in his interesting but inconclusive lecture on the origin of language notices what he terms the unintelligibility of ancient Egyptian. "In early Teutonic" he says "things totally dissimilar were confused and denoted by a single sound. The Gothic root liub stands for faith, love, and hope; the Gothic word leik both for carcass and body; if we suppose that in addition to these meanings liub and leik could have a great variety of other significations having no apparent connection with each other, and that many, if not all, other Gothic words were equally multifarious in meanings, we shall have conceived an epoch in the history of speech which, judging it by modern standards, may be described as unintelligible."

He then goes on to give us specimens of homonyms in ancient Egyptian.

But we are in Burma in exactly the same position as the one Dr. Carl Abel describes. "Judging from modern standards" in Dr. Abel's mind evidently means "judging from the words as they appear written" and "judging from the narrow view of limiting sound to one tone of the voice." If this sort of "judging from modern standards" is the only method, then Dr. Abel is right in supposing ancient languages were unintelligible; but if we, following what we see is still a living method of expression in China, Burma, and Tibet, use this knowledge as a key to the supposed unintelligibility of ancient languages, does not the new classification help us in doing what Mr. Whitney says is "the as yet unachieved end of the linguistic student?" Mr. Cust, whose essays are most suggestive when he does not allow himself to be led astray by others who do not possess the same intimate colloquial knowledge of Eastern languages that he himself possesses, has hit the mark when he says—

"In monosyllabic languages the colloquial medium is limited. On a new object being presented to the mind a new name was wanted, and the possibility of uniting two words to form a new word never occurred. A monosyllable already in use must therefore be made use of again, but differentiated by a tone adding force, length or rapidity of pronunciation."

This is exactly what occurred, but all languages were as is now generally admitted evolved from the "root" or monosyllabic stage. Some have as yet not left it. It may be asked is it not extraordinary that these languages should remain thus stereotyped? Not more so than the fact that we have still tribes in the Indian Empire not yet emancipated from the stone age. Language is after all but an instrument. In some countries it is a perfected instrument; in others the advancement has through circumstances been checked and the form of speech has become stereotyped. We see the same thing in the arts of the East. The Aryan languages cast aside the use of tones; the Sinitic clung to and elaborated their tones.

The definition of the term tone.

180. But it may be asked what is meant by a tone? If we read the works of Professor Max Müller and several other learned philologists, we cannot help seeing that the use or existence of tones as a mode of speech is unknown to them. This is because they write learnedly of languages they cannot speak. How does Dr. Abel know that

the Egyptians were unintelligible? He supposes it because he has seen only the fossilized remains of their language, and fashions his ideas thereon according to his preconceived notions derived from speaking Aryan languages. But for this open ignoring, I had almost written ignorance, of the existence of tones, I would not have thought it necessary to define what a tone was.

Mr. Roby in his Latin Grammar* very nearly hit the mark, but his opening sentence shows that he does not appreciate that the use of the accent which is in reality tone and not accent in our modern sense was used to differentiate not merely the sound of one syllable from another, but the word from other words, *i.e.*, to mark the difference of the sound.

"Accent is the elevation of voice with which one syllable of a word is pronounced, in comparison with the more subdued tone with which the other syllables are pronounced.

"This subdued tone is called by grammarians the grave accent. The principal rules of Latin accentuation are given by Quintilian, 1-5, 22-31.

"It is the habit in modern times to understand by accent in Latin (as in English) only stress or greater stress on one syllable relatively to other syllables, and to denote this by loudness or greater loudness of voice. There are, however, some grounds for thinking that the Romans meant by accent musical pitch, and pronounced acutely accented syllables in a higher pitch, but not with greater stress or force or loudness.

"Monosyllables always have the accent. Dissyllables have the accent on the penultimate syllable, unless they are enclitic. Words of more than two syllables have the accent on the ante-penultimate if the penultimate syllable is short; on the penultimate if it is long."

If Mr. Roby is right in supposing that the accent in Latin was an inflection of the musical pitch, then the Latin "accent" and the Eastern "tones" are one and the same thing. The word tone denotes an inflection in the pitch of the voice while a sound is uttered. Accents in modern use are merely conventional methods used in French to distinguish between the sound of vowels which have but one sign to denote them both. Uttering then two words written alike but which have different tones, we utter different sounds just as much as when in singing we utter different notes. It would be going too far afield here to attempt to trace the connection between spoken sound which we call speech and tonic sound which we call singing. No doubt at one time speech was more tonic and singing was confined to recitative.

181. That tones may exist in a language unknown to those who are supposed to be able to write learnedly about it may be deduced from the fact that the existence of tones in the dialects of the wild tribes of the Malay Peninsula was unknown. They were discovered quite recently. Moreover, the adoption of synonyms to help to distinguish the meaning of the various tones is a significant fact, as it points out the approaching disuse of tones.

182. Leaving then the consideration of the Burmese language alone, we may now attempt to formulate a system of classification of the languages on the principle we have just evolved.

The classification of the languages.

I. *Polytonic.*—This includes the languages of China, the Tibeto-Burman and the pre-Chinese languages—the Taic Shan, Môn Taic, Môn Khmer and Karen, which de la Couperie classifies as pre-Chinese.

II. *Monotonic,* which will include the Aryan, Semitic, and Dravidian family.

Of monotonic languages the only one which we need mention as belonging distinctively to Burma is the Selung or Selôn, which is a dialect of Malay. The other languages of India have already been discussed and nothing furtherneed be said here.

The polytonic stock then falls into six great divisions—

(1) The Pre-Chinese dialects of the hill tribes on our north-east frontier which are called by Mons. de la Couperie the Môn Taic group.

(2) Môn Khmer, which Mr. Houghton prefers to call Môn-Annam, which includes Talaing or Peguan, Palaung, and Khamu.

---

* Latin Grammar, by Roby. London: MacMillan and Co., 1890.

(3) The Taic Shan, which includes the Shan and Siamese dialects and the Ahom language which is now extinct.
(4) The Chinese family.
(5) The Karen.
(6) The Tibeto-Burman.

Of course there are many other Polytonic languages, but as they do not occur in Burma, to attempt to classify them would be an unnecessary as well as a presumptuous undertaking.

Dr. Cushing's opinion.

183. Dr. Cushing is of opinion that modern Chinese, Shan, and Karen are sister or (perhaps if still further separated) cousin languages. He thinks that they may have all been derived from a common stock, and Tibeto-Burman may perhaps be traced to the same origin. I am inclined to think, with all due deference to his authority, that the common origin of such a family is a point which not only can never be proved, but which it is unnecessary to presuppose. If as there is every reason to believe languages have been gradually evolved from inarticulate ejaculations in which the evolutions of the speaker were reproduced and denoted by variance in the pitch of his voice, they have been evolved so gradually that among the earlier forms of speech the date at which they developed their own distinctive characteristics would depend so much on local circumstances as to render speculation hopeless. It is only when languages have passed through the polytonic into the monotonic stage and have become agglutinative, that we have any power of judging of the date when any offshoot was thrown off from the parent stock. Tones are too vague and too apt to change to give any firm ground to the feet of the explorer.

In classifying the dialects of the Chin, Lushai, and Kachin-Naga groups I have followed the grouping suggested by Mr. Houghton, except that I have left Kudo in the group of Burmese dialects. For while I am inclined to believe that Mr. Houghton is right as to the origin and descent of the tribe, yet there is reason to believe that their language, as in the case of the Yabeins, has become so influenced by their environment as to lose its distinctive features.

184. The languages of Burma then, arranged on the classification proposed above, would fall thus:

Polytonic languages ...
- (I) Môn Khmer or Môn-Annam group.
  - Talaing or Peguan.
  - Palaung.
  - Khamu.
- (II) Taic Shan ...
  - Northern ...
    - Ahom.
    - Khamti.
    - Chinese Shans, Maingtha.
    - Burmese Shans.
  - Intermediate ...
    - Khun.
    - Lü.
  - Southern ...
    - Laos or Yun.
    - Siamese.
- (III) The Karen ...
  - Sgau.
  - Pwo, including Taungthu.
  - Bghai or Bwè.
- (IV) Tibeto-Burman ...
  - (1) Burmese ...
    - Burmese.
    - Arakanese.
    - Tavoy.
    - Chaungtha.
    - Yau.
    - Kadu or Kudo.
    - Danu.
  - (2) Chin Lushai or Chin.
    - Southern Chin.
    - Pallaing.
    - Kun.
    - Daignet.
    - Thet.
    - An.
    - Mro.
    - Kami.
    - Haka or Baungshe.
    - Siyin.
    - Shandu.
    - Kyau.
    - Lushai.
  - (3) Kachin Naga ...
    - Kachin.
    - Lishaw.
    - Sak or Thet.

Burmese and its dialects.

185. To return once more to the Burmese language. We find that while in structure, ideology, and vocabulary Burmese is non-Aryan and belongs to the Polytonic division of speech, it has borrowed its alphabet and mode of writing that alphabet from Sanskrit through the Pali scriptures which were brought over from Ceylon. The Burmese alphabet bears internal evidence of its foreign origin. The Burmese language possesses two kinds of literature. The first which is foreign consists of translations of sacred books into Burmese and of more or less, chiefly less, truthful annals of the Burmese nation, and the other which is indigenous but untaught and almost unrecognized as literature, is represented by the songs and lyrics composed by various obscure poets and singers. The existence of this literature is almost unknown, but some of these lyrics are of considerable merit and show true poetic feeling. This national literature is as different as possible from the stilted unnatural style of the Court historians. Shwe Yeo has drawn attention to them in his account of Burma and his eulogy is well deserved. That there is a strong lyric and dramatic power of expression in the Burmese language is readily acknowledged by those who have heard a Burmese singer improvise a song.

Arakanese.

186. In addition to Burmese itself there are six dialects returned by those who are included in the Imperial return as Burmese-speaking. Of these by far the most important as well as the most interesting from a linguistic point of view is Arakanese. Although in the instructions issued no attempt was made to obtain the various dialects of Burmese, 344,848 persons voluntarily returned Arakanese as their parent-tongue. On the occasion of the census of 1872 319,364 persons were returned as Arakanese (not merely those who speak Arakanese be it noted). In the Arakan division alone they formed 65·9 per cent. of the total population of Arakan, and with 12,084 persons and others who were returned as Arakanese in the rest of Burma, they made up a total 331,448 or 12 per cent. of the total population of Lower Burma. In 1881 the number returned as speaking Arakanese as a mother-tongue was 358,559 or 61 per cent. of the total population of the Arakan division, which was returned as amounting to 587,518 persons. The slight decrease in the proportionate strength of the Arakanese in 1881 was due partly to the fact that at the second census the return was not by the birth but by the language spoken, and that many who were returned as Arakanese by birth in 1872 were returned as speaking Burmese, Hindustani, or Bengali in 1881 ; but most probably this decrease of their strength in proportion to the total population of Arakan, was due to the influx of Chittagongian coolies who, though they rarely settle in the country, swarm down in the harvest and rice-milling season, during which period the census of 1881 was taken, whereas they would have all returned to their homes by August, the month in which the census of 1872 was taken. From this it is clear that if the census of 1881 had been taken in August instead of in February the proportion of those returned as speaking Arakanese as compared to the total population of Arakan would have been considerably greater. The decrease in the last intercensal period is undoubtedly due to the fact that according to the instructions of the Government of India no return of dialects was enforced. The choice of returning either Arakanese or Burmese was left to the enumerated. Enumerators were not, however, ordered to enter those who returned Arakanese as their parent-tongue as speaking Burmese as this might hurt the susceptibilities of the Arakanese needlessly. Arakanese is an older and more archaic form of Burmese. It bears the same position to Burmese that lowland Scotch, *i.e.*, the English spoken south of the Highlands, bears to the English of today. It contains the rougher sounds unsmoothed down and old archaic words and phrases which have fallen into disuse. It bears a closer resemblance to the Burmese spoken when the Burmans first forced their way down the valley of the Irrawaddy and across the passes of the Arakan Yoma.

Tavoy.

187. The next dialect of Burmese is Tavoy. The number of those who returned it is already given, and the remarks just made about the return of the Arakanese dialect apply with equal force to Tavoy. At the next census there will probably be no gain in allowing the enumerator to enter either of these dialects, and he might be directed

to enter Burmese instead, as the result of the last two returns has shown that the dialects of Burma are gradually being absorbed into Burmese. Tavoy, as Mr. Copleston remarks, is the language of an Arakanese colony planted in Tavoy long before the conquest of Pegu by the Burmans.

Yaws.

188. The figures quoted in the first part of this chapter show that the Yaw dialect is rapidly dying out. In the Pakôkku district, whence they are supposed to come, we find that they have all returned themselves as Burmans. The dialect like Yabein was probably a mixture of Burmese and the original hill dialect spoken by the Yaws, who as they became assimilated to the Burmans gradually merged their language in Burmese as well. Maung Ba Tu, Assistant Commissioner, informs me that the legend of the Yaws traces their descent from a clan of the Palaungs called Parawga or Payawga. This in time was shortened to Yawga and then to Yaw. There are still to be found Parawga Sayas or "Wizards" who are considered adepts in witchcraft. They use the Burman alphabet and their language is very closely related to Burmese. The common folk say that the reason why their dialect sounds different from Burmese is because they used to drink the water of the mountain torrents.

Chaungtha.

189. It is generally admitted that the Chaungtha dialect is but a sub-dialect of Arakanese. They are rapidly decreasing and it is probable that both they and the Yaws will have disappeared in 1901. In 1872 there were 9,634 who were returned as Chaungthas, and in 1881 the number had fallen to 2,341, while now there are but 271 who returned Chaungtha as their parent-tongue. Mr. Copleston says again:

"It would appear therefore that as they reach the plains they adopt Arakanese habits and cease to call themselves Chaungthas. As regards the word Chaungtha, I am inclined to doubt the truth of the Burmese derivation, 'sons of the river,' being correct. Chaungtha is probably, like Maingtha, a corruption of the real name, but as it happens to resemble the two Burmese words for creek and son, the derivation above given seemed so plausible that it was at once adopted."

Kudo or Kadu and Danu dialects.

190. The Kadu or Kudo language spoken by the so-called Kadu is not a pure language, but merely a hybrid dialect spoken by hybrid Shans and Burmans. As before stated Mr. Houghton would prefer to place it in the Kachin-Naga group. From an analysis of a list of vocables which has been furnished to him, Mr. Houghton is inclined to believe that this dialect belongs to the Kachin-Naga sub-group. I think that he will probably establish the descent of the Kudo language from this group, but the dialect, I am informed, has now practically become a hybrid. The Danu language is said to be a dialect of Burmese spoken by a colony of Burmans who settled formerly in the Shan States. They must not, so Mr. Hildebrand says, be confused with the Dunaws who live in the Pindaga lake. The latter are rapidly becoming extinct and their language is said to be similar to Taungthu. The Danu dialect is probably like Kadu but a mere hybrid of Burmese and Shan.

The Yabein dialect.

191. The Yabeins, or, as Dr. Mason calls them, the Yebeins formerly had a language of their own, which has died out. The name Yabein is said to be a corruption of the word Zabein. It is probable they are not of pure Burmese race, but are one of the broken tribes forced southward by the pressure of the advancing Chinese power. The Yabein dialect was nothing but a corrupt form of Burmese mingled with this now extinct language. The fact that Yabein was a separate language is proved by Captain Forbes. Notwithstanding that the Burmans themselves claim them as belonging to the wilder clans of their race, the view held by Captain Forbes tallies with de la Couperie's statement that the Chinese gradually drove down southward the broken tribes they found in the hill ranges south of the Middle kingdom.

The Chin-Lushai group.

192. There are several hill dialects spoken by hill tribes in Burma which belong to the generic name of Chin. Of these the Kwemi or Kami, Pallaing, An or Anu, Mro or Myo, Daignet, and Kun are found in the western side of the Arakan Yoma. On the eastern slopes we have the Siyin, the Haka, the Baungshe, and the Chinbôk. The term Chin is used in a double meaning and it is therefore somewhat

ambiguous. It is the term applied by the Burmese to all of these hill tribes, and it is better perhaps to use the name as the generic name of the race and not the specific name of any particular clan. Chin belongs to the Tibeto-Burman group of languages. It is related on the one hand to Burmese and on the other to Tibetan. It is still more closely connected with the Lushai dialect of the Kuki language. It will be sufficient to note here that the connection between Burman and Chin to which the structure of the language and their vocabularies bear testimony is admitted both in Burmese and Chin legends. The following interesting account of the Chin language is extracted from a monograph on the tame Chins with which Mr. Houghton has been kind enough to furnish me:

Language.

The Chin language is copious enough for all the wants of a half-savage people, and it is a mistake to suppose, with Colonel Hughes, that it is exceedingly poor. The statement of that writer that the name of the Chief is used for that of the village, "probably owing to the extreme poverty of the language," is certainly quite unsustainable. One reason why the language has been supposed to be poor is the habit of Chins when questioned off-hand as to their language to give, probably through nervousness, Burmese words in many cases where they possess a true Chin one. Like most savage people in contact with others considerably more civilized than themselves they do not manufacture Chin words to express things and ideas known only to civilized people, but adopt for such the Burmese words. This does not, however, prevent them from having Chin words and idioms for everything that can be known to people living in small villages amongst mountainous jungles.

The grammar and construction of the Chin language are more or less similar to those of the Burmese. The language varies somewhat from place to place, particularly in the matter of the vowels, which are seldom clearly pronounced. Indeed distinct articulation is not by any means affected by the Chins as might be inferred from the occurrence in the language of the obscure initial nasals *n* and *m* which are found in so many African languages and I believe also in Kachin. The Chin language, like the hill dialects allied to it, also delights in modified vowels similar to those which exist in German. All words in Chin must terminate with a vowel, nasal or aspirate, the only exceptions being a few words which end in *k* or *t*. The result is that the language is a very soft-sounding one.

The language has some years ago been reduced to writing by the Baptist missionaries, the system employed being a modification of the Pwo Karen alphabet. These characters are open to the objection of being complicated and not well adapted to the language.

The system I have employed in writing it is identical with that which was lately proposed independently by Mr. Shaw, C.S., for the writing of Kachin names, and it is a system which seems open to no objection. (I omit the subject of tones in Chin as this is at present contentious matter.)

A few peculiarities of the grammar may here be noticed. Numeral adjectives are placed between the noun and the number, and not last of all as in Burmese.

Thus ak'laung pün-t'ün = man-body-three = three persons.

The comparative degree (like all Turanian languages Chin has no true adjectives) is formed by adding the verb hèk to the root.

Thus, ni' ak'laung-t'á ayánü p'oi-hè-kü = He is better than this man.

The pronoun is sometimes reduplicated before the verb.

There is a dual, both in nouns, pronouns, and verbs.

The negative voice is formed by various terminations and not by prefixing a word (ma) as in Burmese. Further, certain classes of roots are inflected to form the negative voice, and also in the regular conjugation.

A trace of the harmonic sequence so noticeable in other languages of the Turanian family may be seen,—thus *ló* (to come) makes ló-wó in the present tense instead of adding *ü*, the regular affix.

Appended are two examples of inflection in the Chin verb—

English.	Present tense.	Past tense.	Future.	Imperative.	Negative.
I look ...	Ka 'sawkü ...	Ka 'sawniü ...	Ka'sawkaih	ka'só ...	Ka zónü
I fall ...	Ka klaukü ...	Ka klauniü ...	Ka klaukaih	klau ...	Ka glónü

The first example is an irregular and the second a regular verb of the second conjugation. No roots in the first conjugation undergo inflection.

The conditional particle *ná* used in Chin is the same as in Thibetan. A kind of reflective verb similar to that in use in the Dravidian languages is formed by the addition of *è* (to eat) to the verbal root.

The poetical language used in Chin songs differs to a certain extent from that used in ordinary life.

All Chins have a Chin name as well as a Burman one, the latter often being a translation of the former. The prefixes used before the names of males are Ta and N, and before those of women Pa and Si.

Examples (of males) names N'Gán, N'Ló-i, and Ta Lan; (of females) Pa' Sá Pa Dawn.

The names of the months in Chin are generally the same as the Burman or rather Arakanese ones (for the Chin in such words keeps the older or Arkanese form of pronunciation); exceptions are Kazón, Nayón, Wázó, and Wágaung, which are called respectively Maw, N'Gau, Klóndün, and Klónüu.

It may be noted here that the Chins call themselves Ashö and the Burmans Wó.

I append a table of nouns showing the relations in vocabulary of Chin and Burmese respectively to Thibetan (written). The latter is extracted from Hodgson's Comparative Vocabularies, whilst the Burmese words are transliterated as they are spelt and not as they are pronounced.

The non-radical portions of the words are *italicized*.

English.	Thibetan.	Chin.	Burmese.*	Remarks.
Air ...	Lung*ma* ...	Klí *or* Kló ...	Lé.	
Arrow ...	*M*dah ...	*A*t'aw ...	Mya.	
Bird ...	Byu ...	Payó ...	Hngak ...	*cf.* Burmese, pyan.
Bone ...	Rus*pa* ...	Yó ...	Ró.	
Day ...	Nyin*myo* ...	Nút ...	Ne*yet*.	
Dog ...	Khyi ...	Ui ...	Khwé ...	*cf.* coll. Thibetan, u-yo.
Ear ...	Ná ...	'Nó ...	Ná*khaung*.	
Eye ...	Mig ...	Ami ...	Mrak.	
Father ...	Phâ ...	Ap'ó ...	Aphé.	
Fire ...	Mé ...	Mé ...	Mi.	
Fish ...	Nya ...	Ngo ...	Ngá.	
Hand ...	Lagpa ...	Lagpa† ...	Lak.	
Hog ...	Phag ...	Wo ...	Wak ...	*cf.* Magar, wak.
House ...	Khyin ...	In ...	Im ...	*cf.* Limbu, him.
Leaf ...	Ló*ma* ...	Law ...	Rwak.	
Moon ...	*Lá*va ...	Kló ...	La.	
Mother ...	Amá ...	Anü ...	Amé.	
Month ...	Khà ...	*Wawk*'ó ...	Khant*wang*.	
Name ...	Ming ...	*A*mín ...	*A*man.	
Night ...	Shan*mo* ...	Sayan ...	Nya.	
Road ...	Lam ...	Lawn ...	Lam.	
Salt ...	Tsha ...	Zí ...	Chhá.	
Sky ...	*Nam*khah ...	K'ó ...	Mò.	
Snake ...	Brul ...	P'aw ...	Mrwe ...	*cf.* Bhuta, bo.
Star ...	*S*karma ...	A'sí ...	Kray.	
Sun ...	Nyi*ma* ...	*K'o*ní ...	Né.	
Tree ...	*Lfon*shing ...	T'én ...	Thasbang.	

It will be seen that of the Thibetan roots in this table the Chin language preserves rather more than the Burmese. The word "anü," mother, is a striking exception. In the Chin "wo" and "ami" the final vowel is short consequent on the elision of the terminal *k*.

A comparison of the Chin in this district with vocabularies of wild Chin, Shandu, and Kami given in "Hughes' Hill Tracts of Arakan" shows it is equally closely related to each of these dialects, the resemblance being as is usual in these languages much closer in the nouns than in the verbs. These vocabularies are not, however, drawn up according to any recognized alphabetical system, and in the Chin one at least there are several obvious mistakes.

The relationship of Chin with the Kuki and the Naga languages, which is close and interesting, cannot be entered into here. It will suffice to state that its relationship with the former language is apparently very intimate.

Of the Himalayan languages it may be noted that Limbu (spoken by a tribe of Gurkhas), shows a markedly stronger affinity with Chin than with Burmese.

193. We have in Burma two more representatives of the Chin-Lushai group, Shandu or Shendu and Kyau or Chaw. These dialects have hitherto been classified as dialects of the Naga group. From a statistical point of view they are insignificant, but from the philological point of view they are important as they serve as a link between the Burmese and Chins of Burma and the Nagas of Assam, to which tribe they were supposed to belong. From Brian Hodgson's and Colonel Lewin's books mentioned amongst the authorities consulted, it is easy to trace the connection of Burmese and Kuki on the one hand and between Kuki and Tibetan on the other. The Shandus are, as Mr. Copleston states, a newly arrived tribe, who have been preceded by the Chin clans. There is not, I think, any evidence to justify the assertion that the hill tribes of Arakan seem to have

* It will be noticed that Mr. Houghton has not used the system of transliteration adopted by Government. For instance the word သစ်ပင်, which according to the Government system would be transliterated as "thitbin," Mr. Houghton transliterates as "thasbang." The Government system much more nearly reproduces the true pronunciation.

† Poetical. Ordinary Chin kút.

formed an earlier wave of the great Mramma family and to have arrived in the hills of Northern Arakan and the neighbourhood before the appearance of the Arakanese. This question, however, belongs rather to the ethnological than to the philological side of the enquiry.

The Kachin-Naga group.

194. The Kachins, who are generally known by the name Singpho, or, as Mr. George more correctly terms them, Chingpaw, which is a corruption of the Nam Chin Phaw, inhabit the hills that divide the Bhamo district from the Chinese province of Yünan. An interesting account of them, their ethnology, descent, and customs, written by Mr. E. C. S. George, Deputy Commissioner of Bhamo, will be found in Appendix A to this report "On the tracts excluded from census operations." In this present chapter we are confined to a discussion of the Chingpaw language. There are many dialects. Mr. George mentions the three main groups—

I. The true Kachins.

II. The second group consists of three tribes, who, though not true Chingpaws, are certainly connected with them—

(1) The Marus. | (2) The Lishaws or Yawyins.
(3) The Lashis.

These three have distinct languages of their own, and are found on our extreme frontier to the south of the Tapin river. Of these three tribes I have been unable to trace the Marus, but the Lishaws are evidently the same as the Liso or Letcho mentioned by de la Couperie, and the Lashis are probably the Lutze clan which was settled in Shan Si in the 6th century B.C.

III. The third group consists of six tribes less closely connected with the Kachins—

(1) Khangs.
(2) Kaphawks.
(3) Kaluns.
(4) Kumôns.
(5) Kumans.
(6) Tarens or Meungsa, called by the Burmans Maingthas.

Mr. George remarks that these last have a language and customs of their own. Dr. Cushing is inclined to class them not with the Kachin race, but under the Tai family. Mr. George says that the only two other branches of the Chingpaw stock that have a distinct language of their own are the 'Szis and the Kawris. These two clans are branches of the Lapai tribes.

Too little is known of these tribes and of the dialects they speak to allow an attempt at any final arrangement at present. Mr. George not unnaturally deals more with the ethnological than the linguistic side of the question.

The Kachin language is classified by Mons. de la Couperie and Dr. Cushing as belonging to the Tibeto-Burman group. Dr. Cushing states that at present there is but little known of the various dialects, but he makes the classification on the strength of the fact that in structure the Kachin language resembles both Burmese and Tibetan. Forbes points out that all their lingual affinities are with the Burma-Naga languages. It has been asserted that the Kachins are allied to the Karens, but there is no evidence to support this, and it is probable that this classification is a mere conjecture.

The Karen dialects.

195. The next most important group of languages is the Karen group. This group belongs, according to de la Couperie, to the Kuenlunic group of the Turano-Scythian family, of which Chinese and Tibeto-Burmese are also members. Karen legends relate how the Karens came from the river of rolling sand, which may be identified with the desert of Gobi. Dr. Cushing agrees in thinking that the Karen languages are in some way connected with, but not descended from, Chinese. Dr. Cross of the American Baptist Mission at Toungoo claims for the Karens that they are the aborigines and have been driven to the hills by the later Burmese settlers. This theory is discussed in Chapter X as it belongs rather to the ethnological than to the philological side of the controversy. Following de la Couperie we find that he divides the Karens into the Northern Pre-Chinese branch and the Southern or Burma branch. The existence of the Northern branch we need not discuss; of the Southern there are three well-marked divisions, the Pwo or Talaing Karen, the

Sgau or Burman Karen, and the Bghai or Red Karen. Dr. Mason divided the Karens into various tribes such as "Pant" Bghai, Tunic Bghai, &c., on account of various differences he noticed in their customs and dress as well as in the dialects they spoke. The question of their division into tribes by their dress and customs does not concern the present discussion which relates to their language alone. There are really only three divisions before named. These are—

(1) The Sgau, which includes the Sgau clan, Maunhepaku and the Wewa. Here again we have the unfortunate and ambiguous use of a term in the generic as well as the specific sense, but the mistake is scarcely worth rectifying as the distinction between these clans is fast disappearing under the increasing influence of Christianity, education, and good government. The multiplication of petty clans is of itself an indication of lawlessness which induces men to band themselves together in petty communities for mutual protection from internecine warfare.

(2) The Pwo, which includes Pwo, Shangkhipho, Mopgha, Taru, and Taungthu. Taungthu is from its vocabulary evidently composed chiefly of Pwo words with an admixture of other vocables. The Taungthus, however, do not seem to be very closely connected with the other Karens in their customs or legendary history.

(3) The Bwè, or, as Dr. Mason calls them, the Bghai tribes. Dr. Mason, who knew them well, divided them into a number of somewhat fanciful divisions. Practically there are but two divisions, the Red Karens and the Bghais. The disintegration of the language follows the breaking up of the clans owing to the centrifugal movement before noticed, which induces the clans to throw off swarms which re-form themselves into separate clans.

The Sgau dialect will, so Dr. Cushing thinks, gain the mastery. It differs from Pwo in that, like Bghai, it has no final consonants. Bghai, which includes the language spoken by the Red Karens, differs most noticeably in its system of numeration. It somewhat resembles Sgau, but possesses a large number of separate roots. It is spoken chiefly in the Toungoo district. With the exception of the Taungthu dialect we may put aside the elaborate classification of the Pwo dialects suggested by Dr. Mason. Mopgha is really only a sub-dialect or variation of Northern Pwo. In fact the difference between Southern, Northern, and Mopgha may be disregarded as they differ less each from the other than Yorkshire, Somerset, and Sussex dialects do in English. No return of these dialects was made. But the Taungthu dialect is often regarded as a separate language. We have seen how Professor Max Müller, dignifying it with the name of Tunghlu, classes it as a Lohitic language. Mr. Copleston pointed out in 1881 that the language was very closely connected with Pwo Karen. It is therefore rather for ethnological than for philological reasons that the Taungthus are classed separately. In 1872 there were 24,923 belonging to this clan enumerated in Burma. This number had risen to 35,554 in 1881. The increase of 42 per cent. was due probably to better enumeration in 1881. In 1891, when no attempt was made to obtain the dialects, the number of persons returned in Lower Burma as Taungthus sunk to 35,220. This decrease is due solely to the fact that the Taungthus are becoming Burmanized. Indeed this process is, so Dr. Cushing states, becoming general with the whole Pwo race.

No attempt was made to show the Sgau and Pwo dialects of the Karen language apart either in 1881 or 1872, although somewhat illogically the sub-dialect of Red Karen, which is a sub-dialect of Bghai, and Taungthu, which is a dialect of Pwo Karen, are distinguished. Accordingly there are no means of comparing the returns of the three censuses together. Moreover, the comparison is rendered difficult in that the return was made by race in 1872, and by language or mother-tongue and birth-place in 1881. On the occasion of the present census, however, we have made the return both by race and nationality as well as by parent-tongue and birth-place.

Taking the Karens, Taungthus, and Karennis together, we find that in 1872 there were 356,629 returned as speaking these dialects of the Karen language. In 1881 the number returned was 553,848, being an increase at the rate of 55 per cent. In 1891 the total number of Karens and Taungthus in Lower Burma was 630,704 of the former and 35,220 of the latter, or 665,924 altogether, being an increase of 20·2 per cent. If we refer to the Upper Burma returns we find that there were only 2,964 Karens and 5,895 Taungthus returned as residing in that province, so that it is clear that, as was remarked in the Administration Report of 1881, there was not much room for the increase of the Karens by recruiting their number with immigrants from Upper Burma.

The Census schedule allowed no column for dialect, and hence the return of those speaking Pwo or Sgau is not of itself to be taken as indisputable, but in columns 4 and 5 of the schedule instructions were given for the submission of returns of race and nationality, and it is in this way we have on this occasion been able to supplement the return of parent-tongue. The question of the probability of the Pwo Karen being merged in the Burman or Sgau Karen is one that belongs rather to ethnology than to language and will be discussed there.

Môn or Talaing.

196. The origin of the term Talaing is one that is now happily settled, not on a chance coincidence of sound, but according to the rules of etymology. It was supposed that Talaing and Telingana were the same words, and on the ground of this coincidence of sound and of a supposed agreement of the roots of vocables with the roots of the aboriginal Kolarian language spoken by the Kols in India, it was supposed that the Talaings brought their language over from India. Captain Forbes and Dr. Forchhammer have disposed of this theory once for all. The refutation of the theory, however, lay in the name Talaing itself, which is never used by the Talaings to distinguish themselves. They always call themselves Môns. Talaing was a term of reproach forced on them by the conquering Burmans just as the conquering Saxons called the Britons, whom they conquered, Welch or in Devonshire "Gubbings." Captain Forbes proves that a mere accidental coincidence in the sound of vocables is over-balanced by the overwhelming evidence of a totally different grammatical structure. Sir George Campbell in his preface to the specimens of the languages of India notes this curious affinity, but does not discuss it. The resemblance, however, if we take the trouble to wade through the whole vocabulary, is confined to a few words, and this resemblance fades away when the words are taken as they are really pronounced and not as in Talaing, at least, they are often phonetically misrepresented. The Talaing vocabulary does not pretend to be scientifically transliterated, and the Talaing words are written down often according to English convention as to the manner in which a sound is to be phonetically spelt.

197. The rapid disappearance of the Môn language is due in the first place to the proscription of its use by the Burmese conquerors. It was discouraged by them after Alaungpaya had captured Pegu in 1757 and after the Môns had made common cause with the British in 1824. On the departure of the British forces, the Môns were oppressed and their language was "furiously proscribed." The Môn language had therefore already become partly displaced before the final annexation of Pegu in 1852-53 by the British, and since that date, though so long proscribed, it has fallen gradually into further disuse. Notwithstanding this steady decay which was noticed in the last report we find that there is apparently a great increase of 32 per cent. since 1881 in the number of those who return Talaing as their parent-tongue. This increase is due partly to more careful enumeration, but chiefly to the fact that since the kingdom of Ava has been finally conquered by the British the terror of once more being ground down by their Burman masters has been for ever dispelled, and the Môns are less afraid to acknowledge their nationality and less eager to enrol themselves amongst the Burmans. The increase is shown in the district of Pegu where the number of Talaings rose to 54,422, though in 1881 in Pegu and Hanthawaddy, which were then one district, there were only 25,986, and in Amherst and Moulmein, where the number rose from 88,326 in 1881 to 139,955 in 1891. These abnormal increases could only be due to one of the causes before mentioned. The Talaing language is now still being taught in the village school in Amherst, though the pôngyis do not teach it. Whether the Môn language will or will not eventually die out in the Amherst district it is yet too early to prophesy, but the language is fast disappearing in most of the districts of the Pegu and Irrawaddy divisions. The process of decay in the delta at any rate has, I believe, advanced too far to be checked by any transient

revival of national feeling. The fall of Ava has come too late to save the Môn language in Pegu, and the return of the next census will probably show that those who return Talaing as their parent-tongue are far fewer than in 1891.

198. Maung Ba Tu, Assistant Commissioner of Paungdè, himself of pure Talaing descent, has favoured me with a short note in Burmese about the Talaings. He derives the name Môn from a Môn word meaning "first, or original;" hence the Môns were "the first amongst men." He does not, however, enter into a discussion concerning the Môn language or whence it was derived. He, however, has proved conclusively that Talaing or Môn is a Polytonic language. This was asserted by Mr. Copleston in his report in 1881, but as this fact has been doubted, I referred the point to Maung Ba Tu and he has set the question at rest by supplying me with lists of words in Môn showing that tones are used as in Burmese, Shan, and Chinese to denote different vocables.

The Môn-Annam language to which Talaing or Môn belongs is classed by de la Couperie as one of the Môn-Khmer group of the Indo-Chinese family. There can be no doubt, as Captain Forbes has pointed out, that Môn and Cambodian were formerly one and the same language. Though now divided one from the other by the intrusive Siamese language, their structure and vocabulary clearly prove their common origin. The Siamese language has no affinity with either Cambodian or Môn, but like a stratum of intrusive rock the appearance of this language corroborates what the Shan legends assert regarding the descent of the Shans along the valley of the Mekong.

199. The Môn-Annam kingdom not only embraced, as Captain Forbes inferred, the deltas of the great rivers of the Indo-Chinese Peninsula, the Irrawaddy, Salween, Mekong, and Menam, but investigations into the languages spoken by the wild tribes of the Malay Peninsula show that Môn influence and the Môn language had penetrated there. Mr. Blagden, of the Straits Settlements Civil Service, to whom I am indebted for this information, is unable yet to say how far this influence was felt, but if his views are proved to be correct we shall have independent and conclusive testimony of the existence of an extensive Môn empire which has been invaded and broken up by Burmese, Tai, and Malay intruders. The Palaungs belong to the Môn family. Dr. Mason wrongly classified them as one of the Shan tribes. They are chiefly found in the Ruby Mines district. De la Couperie states that they were settled in Yünan where they were conquered by the Chinese, and some of them have found their way southward. A vocabulary has been prepared of their language by Bishop Bigandet. Their language contains a great admixture of Shan words, but the structure of their language proclaims its affinity to the Môn-Khmer group. The Khamus are identified by Dr. Cushing as being probably a few stragglers from the Khamu tribe which is settled on the other side of the Mekong river. They belong to the Môn-Annam family.

Shan or Tai dialect.

200. The Shan language is the language spoken by the people who call themselves Tai or in the case of the Siamese Htai or "the free." The Taic group is classified by de la Couperie among the pre-Chinese languages belonging to the Indo-Chinese family of speech. The reason already given for this classification of the Indo-Chinese family is peculiarly unsuited to the Tai family, who are described by de la Couperie as being driven away from China by the Chinese and who have nothing Indian about them or their language. The Tai language, of which there are numerous dialects, is essentially a Polytonic language. It contains five tones, and in some of the combinations of vowels and consonants there are three series of these, tones so that in such cases there are 15 possible different pronunciations of a single syllable. It is true that as a matter of fact the complete series of 15 is never actually found in common use, but still those that we do find in ordinary use show that 15 combinations are possible. Hovelacque classes the Tai language in the independent group, and he states that it belongs to the isolating form of speech.

I have been favoured by the Rev. Dr. Cushing with the following note on the Shan or Tai languages. The note deals with the history as well as with the language of the Shan race. In this chapter I have therefore introduced that part of the note that bears on the Shan language; the rest of the note will be found in

Chapter X, which deals with races and their ethnology. I may add that not only has Dr. Cushing favoured me with this monograph, but that the rough notes of this chapter were submitted to his kindly criticisms before I ventured on the difficult task of classifying the languages spoken in Burma.

Extent of the race.

The Tai or Shan race in its different branches is perhaps the most widely spread of any race in the Indo-Chinese Peninsula. Beginning with the network of mountains towards the source of the Irrawaddy river, the race sweeps south-eastward along the broad belt of mountainous country between Burma Proper and China, thence southward over the broad plains between the Salween and Cambodia rivers to the Gulf of Siam. It overlaps the Cambodia river in the Hsip Hsawng Panna and other districts on the southern borders of Yünnan and in the regions east of Luang Prabang. The Pai'y and some of the other peoples of South-Western China are parts of the Shan race. One branch, the Ahom, which conquered Assam, has entirely lost its visibility by becoming merged in the people of that country. Formerly the Shan was the dominant race west of the Upper Irrawaddy, but where it has not been displaced by the pressure of other races it has been reduced to a remnant of its former self as in Wuntho and the adjacent regions.

Divisions of the race.

There are ten divisions of the race differing more or less widely from each other. These may be formed into three groups, two of which are widely dissimilar and are connected by an intermediate group possessing not a few of the peculiarities of both the other groups. The ten divisions may be arranged thus:—

Tai family.

Northern group.	*Intermediate group.*	*Southern group.*
Ahom (extinct).	Khün (Kaingtung).	Laos or Yûn.
Khamti.	Lü (Kainghung).	Law.
Chinese-Shans.	Hsip Hsawng Panna (east of Cambodia river).	Siamese.
Burmese-Shans.		

Divisions of race in British territory.

Of these divisions the Khamti, a small section of the Chinese-Shans or Tai Mau, the Burmese-Shans, the Khün, and the Lü dwell in British territory. The Khamti occupy the extreme northern part of Burma towards the headwaters of the Irrawaddy river. The Chinese-Shans are found in the region bordering on the Shan territory tributary to China. The Burmese-Shans are the main population of the tributary principalities west of the Salween extending from Theinni southward to Mobyè. Half-way between the Salween and the Cambodia rivers are the Khün with Kaingtung as a centre, whilst the Lü border the Cambodia river with Kainghung as their principal town. The Khün and Lü dialects seem to be the natural link between the Northern and Southern groups of the Tai family, although they have more characteristics of the latter group than of the former group.

Name of race.

The signification of the word Tai used by all branches of the Shans except the Siamese is unknown. The Siamese aspirate the first letter, pronouncing the word Htai and giving it the signification of *free*. This is doubtless a modification of the original form of the word to commemorate some prominent event in their early history as Bishop Pallegoix has indicated.

Essential identity of the language.

It is an interesting fact that notwithstanding the great distance between the regions occupied by some of the divisions of the Tai family so much remains of the common original forms of speech that members of one division can easily understand much which members of another division may say and may also attain fluency in the use of another dialect in a few months. This fact is the more remarkable when we consider the great variety of languages of the peoples who surround them or dwell in the same regions. This marked identity makes it very probable that the language of the Tai people had become essentially fixed before their migration to their present homes took place. It seems to indicate that in their original home they were a compact organized body of people. The remains of so much homogeneity are a strong witness of a united social and political life in ancient times, powerful enough to cast the speech of the people in such a firm mould that the migrations, dispersions, and mixture with other races during subsequent centuries have marred only but not destroyed its essential oneness.

Rise of present diversity in language.

It is not improbable that there were slight and unimportant dialectic differences before the successive great migrations began, but localisms of word and grammatical structure were sure to spring up quietly after each branch of the family settled by itself. The influence of the languages of surrounding races could not fail to be felt. Thus any one who studies the traditions and speech of the Laos or Zimmè Shans cannot fail to see how sensibly the language of that branch of the Tai family has been affected by the influence of the aboriginal Lewa population, a remnant of which is still found in a few wretched villages of the Mainglôngyi district. The Northern Shans obtained their alphabet and books from the Burmans, the Laos from the Môns, and the Siamese from the Cambodians. Each of these divisions in a marked but different form shows the results of this close connection in life and literature. It is not impossible that the more southern divisions which were the later ones to migrate were subjected to influences from the invading and conquering Chinese before starting on their march southward, which the more northern divisions escaped. My opinion is that more of the original form of the Shan speech is found in the northern division of the Shan people, but the full proof of this and a clear understanding of the character and amount of the modifying influences in each division require much more philological investigation than has been given to the subject.

Alphabets and literature.

The Burmese-Shans derived their alphabet from the Burmans, and the alphabets of the Chinese-Shans and Khamti seem to be mere local modifications of it, not an essential change in form. Burmese-Shan tradition says that about 300 years ago after the establishment or more probably the revival of Buddhism, a Shan priest went down into the Burman country, learned Pali and Burmese, devised the present Shan alphabet, and translated religious books into Shan. The literature of the Shans of Burma is considerable, but it is chiefly religious. Some medical and historical works exist. All of these are written in a rhythmical or poetical style often of an intricate construction, familiarity with which can be gained only by special study.

I may here add that Dr. Cushing, though he does not touch on the subject of the classification of the Tai group under any heading, informs me that he is inclined to think that the Karen, Tai, and Chinese groups are all cognate. He does not agree with the use of the term Turanian and admits that the term Indo-Chinese is in some respects inapplicable as a general name for the family.

201. Mr. J. G. Scott, Superintendent of the Northern Shan States, whose opinion is of much value, writes :—

"Linguistically the Shans may be divided into at least five branches—

(1) The British Shans.
(2) The Tai Mow and Tai Nö.
(3) The Lu and Keing Hung Shans, with whom may be associated the Khon of Keing Tung.
(4) The Lao Shans of the Siamese Shan States.
(5) The Siamese.

"The British Shans have a character of their own, probably the simplest of all, certainly with the fewest characters. The Tai Mow use the same alphabet and characters, but form them in a diamond shape instead of rounding them. Any one acquainted with what we call Shan, can after a little practice read this diamond character. The Lu and Khon use the same character, quite different from our Shan, with a much larger alphabet and indicating the open and closed tones by signs, which is not done in British Shan.

"The Lao's written character differs much less from that of the Lu than from that of the British Shan, but is yet so different that it cannot be read by a Lu scholar, though the spoken languages offer much fewer differences than do Lu and British Shan or Lao and British Shan.

"Siamese has been very much affected by outside influences. The character is absolutely distinct from that of all the other branches of the race, and though many of the words are identical, yet the general differences are so great as to make the learning of Siamese really the learning of a new language to a 'Shan' scholar."

Of the Shan family the following dialects are spoken in Burma: Meungsa, Lü, and Hpun. The first is classed by Mr. George as a Kachin tribe otherwise called the Taren. It is possible that the Maingtha or Meungsa dialect has adopted Kachin words, but the balance of testimony is in favour of including it in the Tai Shan family. The Hpuns correspond to the Burmese-Shans mentioned by Dr. Cushing. The name Hpun is not, however, a Shan name. Mr. George's interesting note on them will be found in Appendix A. The Ahom language is now extinct. It was the dialect spoken by the Shans who invaded Assam and established the Ahom kingdom there. An interesting account is given by Mr. George in explanation of their presence in the Bhamo district.

The Lü of Kainghung and the Laos are found in the tributary Shan States. The former belong to the Intermediate and the latter to the Southern school. A few Lüs were enumerated in the Amherst district. The Shans of Tavoy and Mergui are really Siamese of the Southern group.

The Selung or Selôn language.

202. The last of the vernaculars of Burma is the Selôn or Selung language as Dr. Anderson more accurately calls it. Selôn is the Burmese pronunciation of the name. It is now

generally admitted that Selung is a distinct Malayan language. The Selungs are in fact the northernmost of the Orung Laut or Sea tribes of the Malay race. The dialect is unwritten. An interesting pamphlet by Dr. Anderson gives a long vocabulary of Selung words. I have also been favoured with interesting accounts of these people by Colonel Butler and Mr. Merrifield and the venerable missionary Mr. Brayton who was one of the very first who worked amongst them. Mr. Merrifield very kindly collected a short list of Selung words. This list, with Dr. Anderson's vocabulary, were revised for me by Mr. Blagden, of the Straits Settlements Civil Service, who has supplemented the list of Malay words given by them and has lent additional corroboration to the inferences they drew. The publication of Dr. Anderson's interesting monograph has anticipated my intention of reproducing here the shorter but still interesting descriptions written by the officers I have named above. There is but one point that need be noticed here with regard to what Dr. Rost says on this Selung language. "The Selung is a distinct "Malay language, not a dialect of any of the Malay languages. It has a number "of characteristic features in morphologya which distinguish it from all its sisters. "It has, however, a greater resemblance to the languages of Sumatra than to "other Malayan languages." Mr. Blagden who, it may be noted, has the advantage of possessing a colloquial knowledge of the Malay dialects is more cautious. In his opinion Selung and Malay are cognate languages, but Selung has adopted into the language a number of words which are not Malayan.

CHAPTER IX.

BIRTH-PLACE.

The objects of the enquiry into the birth-place of the population. Divisions of the enquiry. Comparative mobility of the population in India and Burma. Comparison with the returns of 1881. The excess of immigrants over emigrants. The two classes of the latter. The birth-place returns compared with the returns of religion and parent-tongue. The returns of immigrants and emigrants under the Native Passenger Ships Act. Movement of the population between Upper and Lower Burma. Movement of the population from district to district. Comparative Statements A, B, and C explained. The statistics of immigration and emigration in the districts of Burma.

The objects of the enquiry into birth-place.

203. In 1881, for the first time in India was any enquiry made into the birth-places of the enumerated. The principal object then in view, in Lower Burma especially, was by combining these returns with the returns of mother-tongue to find out the nationality of each person. On the present occasion a separate table has been prepared showing the nationality or caste of every person in the province. These returns of birth-place, even when combined with mother-tongue, cannot pretend to define nationality so accurately as this direct statement. But the table of birth-place still remains one of the most important and interesting of the statements prepared from the census schedule. On this occasion a separate chapter for the discussion of the problems connected with the return of birth-place has been prescribed by the Census Commissioner. In Chapter II, which deals with the movement of the people, I have briefly touched generally on the question of birth-place, and, as a fact, before writing that chapter I was obliged to review the returns of birth-place and note the results of the present enquiry in connection with the movement of the people. In that chapter the enquiry is devoted to the causes of the movement, causes which are partly political and partly economical. In this present chapter the extent and direction of the movement is considered in detail. The division of the enquiry into two sections or chapters is perhaps an advantage.

204. No return of birth-place could be collected in the tracts excluded from the regular census, but in the synchronous census tract in the Shan States the returns were duly filled in, and the total population for which this return has been made amounts to 7,608,552 souls. The synchronous census tract of the Shan States, though isolated from Burma, has for the purposes of this enquiry been treated as a district of Burma, for otherwise the number of immigrants from India and other places outside the province would not have been complete. The term "province" is here used in its widest sense and includes the whole of the tributary Shan States and Chin Hills, as, although this return was not made for the excluded tracts, yet from one point it would be wrong not to include those born in those parts of the province amongst the home, as compared with the foreign, born population. In the same way, though no return of birth-place was made in the Chin Hills itself, those who gave the Chin Hills as their birth-place were included as having been born within the province. Another reason for not showing the return of birth-place in the regular census tract apart from the excluded tracts in column 1 of the table was the impossibility of discriminating between those born in and those born outside the regular census area in Bhamo and Katha as well as in the Shan States. A perusal of the table will show that no inconvenience arises from the arrangement adopted, because in no case does the total population of a district ever agree with the number of those enumerated as being born in it.

The annexed table is a summary of Imperial Table XI, and is here inserted for ready reference.

SUMMARY OF TABLE

Province or agency.	Total population.			Classification by birth-places. A			B		
	Total.	Male.	Female.	Total.	Male.	Female.	Total.	Male.	Female.
1	2	3	4	5	6	7	8	9	10
LOWER BURMA.									
Akyab	416,305	230,414	185,891	344,962	177,346	167,616	62,369	45,524	16,845
Northern Arakan	14,628	7,600	7,028	13,941	7,047	6,894	442	357	85
Kyaukpyu	163,832	79,943	83,889	159,084	76,769	82,315	3,309	1,953	1,356
Sandoway	77,134	38,994	38,140	71,263	35,472	35,791	5,173	3,000	2,173
Rangoon Town	180,324	124,767	55,557	60,727	30,104	30,623	1,387	1,090	297
Hanthawaddy	267,039	144,441	122,598	201,811	101,694	100,117	11,029	6,388	4,641
Pegu	301,420	167,538	133,882	196,562	99,158	97,404	11,226	5,988	5,238
Tharrawaddy	347,454	175,293	172,161	288,232	141,926	146,306	20,064	10,871	9,193
Prome	360,252	177,349	182,903	318,375	153,790	164,585	17,053	9,031	8,022
Thôngwa	446,076	238,958	207,118	299,481	150,918	148,563	27,781	15,416	12,365
Bassein	475,002	244,895	230,107	428,051	213,877	214,174	8,944	5,152	3,792
Henzada	380,927	191,403	189,524	318,607	156,467	162,140	11,622	6,382	5,240
Thayetmyo	250,161	125,474	124,687	231,819	114,029	117,790	8,634	4,772	3,862
Amherst	417,312	224,964	192,348	374,567	192,372	182,195	4,803	2,987	1,816
Tavoy	94,921	46,542	48,379	93,592	45,556	48,036	386	248	138
Mergui	73,748	38,789	34,959	65,115	32,864	32,251	5,480	3,199	2,281
Toungoo	162,132	83,496	78,636	121,656	60,645	61,011	22,541	11,381	11,160
Shwegyin	198,521	104,915	93,606	175,467	89,445	86,022	7,196	3,997	3,199
Salween	31,439	16,521	14,918	27,521	13,968	13,553	3,314	2,112	1,202
Total Lower Burma ...	4,658,627	2,462,296	2,196,331	3,790,833	1,893,447	1,897,386	232,753	139,848	92,905
UPPER BURMA.									
Mandalay	374,060	184,000	190,060	303,932	142,951	160,981	30,265	15,150	15,115
Bhamo	54,257	30,261	23,996	44,441	22,135	22,306	4,103	2,965	1,138
Katha	59,329	30,520	28,809	55,049	27,173	27,876	1,353	905	448
Ruby Mines	26,134	17,032	9,102	13,002	6,242	5,760	7,221	4,761	2,460
Shwebo	135,255	64,778	70,477	128,299	59,479	68,820	2,278	1,250	1,028
Ye-u	92,549	42,712	49,837	89,352	40,690	48,662	1,932	985	947
Sagaing	248,207	115,293	132,914	242,526	111,618	130,908	3,121	1,642	1,479
Lower Chindwin	232,245	101,324	130,921	229,552	99,350	130,202	887	538	349
Upper Chindwin	75,785	38,093	37,692	69,924	34,221	35,703	3,837	2,031	1,806
Myingyan	351,411	164,596	186,815	339,511	156,716	182,795	4,870	2,675	2,195
Pakôkku	303,753	143,376	160,377	296,559	138,208	158,351	2,568	1,420	1,148
Minbu	224,475	106,557	117,918	215,565	101,256	114,309	6,088	3,159	2,929
Magwe	219,190	107,307	111,883	212,380	102,577	109,803	3,186	1,912	1,274
Kyauksè	126,622	62,763	63,859	113,502	55,557	57,945	10,705	5,471	5,234
Meiktila	206,650	96,963	109,687	201,205	93,193	108,012	2,315	1,278	1,037
Yamèthin	160,662	78,424	82,238	144,894	69,490	75,404	9,049	4,400	4,649
Pyinmana	56,349	30,006	26,343	36,539	18,565	17,974	12,763	6,738	6,025
Total Upper Burma ...	2,946,933	1,414,005	1,532,928	2,736,232	1,280,421	1,455,811	106,541	57,280	49,261
Shan States	2,992	2,882	110	72	31	41	141	137	4
GRAND TOTAL ...	7,608,552	3,879,183	3,729,369	6,527,137	3,173,899	3,353,238	339,435	197,265	142,170

(*A*) District of enumeration.
(*B*) Districts in Burma and in neighbouring provinces of India contiguous to the district of enumeration.
(*C*) Remote districts, &c., of same province.
(*D*) Provinces, &c., of India, excluding districts contiguous to Burma which are included in *B*.

No. XI.—*(Imperial)*.

CLASSIFICATION BY BIRTH-PLACES—concluded.

C			*D*			*E*			*F*			*G*			*H*		
Total.	Male.	Female.	Total.	Male.	Female.	Total.	Male.	Female.	Total.	Male.	Female.	Total.	Male.	Female.	Total.	Male.	Female.
11	12	13	14	15	16	17	18	19	20	21	22	23	24	25	26	27	28
1,151	735	416	6,421	5,553	868	807	695	112	517	501	16	1	...	1	77	60	17
14	5	9	46	32	14	184	158	26	1	1	...	...	...	...	...	...	...
425	308	117	953	860	93	29	24	5	20	19	1	...	...	...	12	10	2
296	239	57	393	275	118	4	3	1	4	4	...	...	...	...	1	1	...
26,441	16,904	9,537	83,052	69,174	13,878	5,569	4,861	708	2,865	2,413	452	13	9	4	270	212	58
42,503	26,557	15,946	9,958	8,394	1,564	1,691	1,377	314	46	30	16	...	...	...	1	1	...
77,826	49,286	28,540	13,876	11,417	2,459	1,857	1,638	219	39	24	15	...	...	...	34	27	7
34,848	18,772	16,076	3,471	3,010	461	739	639	100	32	25	7	...	...	...	68	50	18
20,477	11,056	9,421	3,733	2,978	755	540	442	98	30	22	8	...	...	...	44	30	14
111,254	65,541	45,713	6,088	5,710	378	1,427	1,344	83	25	18	7	...	...	...	20	11	9
26,127	15,729	10,398	10,200	8,670	1,530	1,251	1,081	170	377	354	23	...	...	...	52	32	20
46,198	24,580	21,618	3,810	3,451	359	538	395	143	97	88	9	...	...	...	55	40	15
5,108	2,989	2,119	3,485	2,736	749	160	140	20	651	618	33	...	...	...	304	190	114
8,315	5,622	2,693	26,371	21,273	5,098	2,010	1,638	372	279	209	70	...	...	...	967	863	104
312	237	75	444	370	74	168	118	50	10	7	3	...	...	...	9	6	3
591	379	212	1,119	1,058	61	1,394	1,247	147	41	34	7	...	...	...	8	8	...
12,731	7,056	5,675	4,073	3,424	649	447	381	66	642	580	62	...	...	...	42	29	13
10,110	6,386	3,724	4,991	4,468	523	715	591	124	19	10	9	...	...	...	23	18	5
316	185	131	219	206	13	66	47	19	3	3	...	...	...	...	...	...	...
425,043	**252,566**	**172,477**	**182,703**	**153,059**	**29,644**	**19,596**	**16,819**	**2,777**	**5,698**	**4,960**	**738**	**14**	**9**	**5**	**1,987**	**1,588**	**399**
25,039	13,410	11,629	11,679	9,862	1,817	1,854	1,511	343	1,086	976	110	...	...	...	205	140	65
1,073	776	297	3,067	2,988	79	1,066	987	79	296	282	14	...	...	...	211	128	83
889	554	335	1,849	1,758	91	157	102	55	30	28	2	...	...	...	2	...	2
2,443	1,710	733	769	744	25	2,430	2,366	64	154	154	...	...	...	...	115	55	60
573	401	172	3,348	3,064	284	126	122	4	331	301	30	...	...	...	300	161	139
505	302	203	743	719	24	12	12	...	4	3	1	...	...	...	1	1	...
817	429	388	1,664	1,536	128	51	44	7	28	24	4	...	...	...	...	...	...
792	471	321	910	862	48	68	68	...	2	2	...	...	...	...	34	33	1
407	287	120	1,404	1,351	53	146	140	6	22	19	3	...	...	...	45	44	1
4,070	2,465	1,605	2,282	2,095	187	301	293	8	322	314	8	...	...	...	55	38	17
1,844	1,055	789	2,664	2,579	85	83	82	1	29	26	3	...	...	...	6	6	...
1,113	591	522	1,489	1,360	129	190	171	19	22	16	6	...	...	...	8	4	4
1,898	1,186	712	1,587	1,503	84	69	66	3	52	45	7	...	...	...	18	18	...
1,339	760	579	1,024	949	75	47	21	26	5	5	...	...	...	...	...	...	...
1,177	681	496	1,530	1,404	126	142	142	...	215	208	7	...	...	...	66	57	9
4,076	2,161	1,915	2,422	2,199	223'	149	125	24	39	29	10	...	...	...	33	20	13
4,812	2,695	2,117	1,935	1,774	161	219	202	17	36	30	6	...	...	...	45	2	43
52,867	**29,934**	**22,933**	**40,366**	**36,747**	**3,619**	**7,110**	**6,454**	**656**	**2,673**	**2,462**	**211**	...	...	...	**1,144**	**707**	**437**
26	11	15	2,707	2,663	44	8	8	...	9	7	2	...	...	...	29	25	4
477,936	**282,511**	**195,425**	**225,776**	**192,469**	**33,307**	**26,714**	**23,281**	**3,433**	**8,380**	**7,429**	**951**	**14**	**9**	**5**	**3,160**	**2,320**	**840**

(*E*) Other Asiatic countries.
(*F*) Other continents.
(*G*) At sea.
(*H*) Unspecified.

205. The best way of treating this enquiry will be to consider (1) the immigration into and emigration from the province as a whole, and (2) the migration within the province.

Divisions of the enquiry.

This latter division may be sub-divided into (*a*) the migration from Upper into Lower and Lower into Upper Burma, (*b*) the migration from the Shan States into both provinces (there is practically no migration into the Shan States from Burma), (*c*) the migration from district to district.

206. Taking the province then as a whole, we find that 7,282,213 persons were enumerated in Lower Burma and in the "regular census" tract of Upper Burma and the Shan States as having been born in the province. This means that out of every 10,000 persons 9,571 were born within the jurisdiction of the Chief Commissioner of Burma. If we exclude the Chin Hills and the Shan States entirely, the total population for which this return is made is 7,605,560, and treating the Chin Hills, Karenni, and Shan States as outside Burma, the total number born in Burma is 7,231,307 persons or 9,508 out of every 10,000. The following statement compares the returns of Burma with those of the other Indian provinces:—

Comparative mobility of the population in India and Burma.

	Number born in the province out of every 10,000 persons.
Burma	9,508
Burma with tributary States	9,571
Bengal	9,886
North-Western Provinces	9,821
Hyderabad	9,774
Bombay	9,708
Punjab	9,657
Madras	9,611
Rajputana	9,588
Mysore	9,583
Central Provinces	9,524
Assam	9,425

The significance of these figures is only perceived when we consider that Burma is the only place to which the majority of immigrants must go by sea and when it is realized that since the annexation of Upper Burma the inclusion of Upper Burmans as immigrants into Lower Burma is not preserved in this present return.

207. In 1881 out of every 10,000 persons only 8,550 were born in Lower Burma. Of the 1,450 persons born outside Lower Burma, 494 came from India, and of the remainder, 846 came from Upper Burma and 51 from the Shan States. In 1891 we have, in order to preserve the comparison, to include in the number of those born in Indian provinces those who returned Nepal as their birthplace. Nepal is in 1891 no longer considered an Indian province; but, on the other hand, Manipur, which was excluded in 1881, is now included. Accordingly, if we leave out the 212 persons born in Manipur and add the 294 persons born in Nepal for the purpose of comparison with the returns of 1881, we find that the total number of persons born in India and enumerated in Lower Burma on the occasion of the census of 1891 was 237,671 persons, being 510 out of every 10,000 souls. For reason already explained in Chapter II, the immigration from Upper into Lower Burma received a check after the annexation of the kingdom of Ava, and thus, though the total number of immigrants increased to 339,315, the proportionate strength for every 10,000 persons fell to 728. If the immigrants from the Shan States were included, the total number of immigrants out of every 10,000 persons enumerated in Lower Burma would be 793 from Upper Burma and the Shan States taken together and 65 from the Shan States alone. Of persons born in Lower Burma, 8,619 out of every 10,000 were born in the province, and the balance outside. Thus, notwithstanding the fact that 43,130 persons born in India—in which definition Manipur is now included and Nepal excluded—were enumerated in Upper Burma and the Shan States—all of whom must have come through Lower Burma, and some of whom no doubt would have remained there but for the superior attractions in the shape of work and pay in the upper province—the proportion of Indian-born to Lower Burma-born is higher in 1891 than in 1881. Lower Burma thus practically maintains the position it held in 1881.

Comparison with the returns of 1881.

208. By the courtesy of the Provincial Superintendents of Census in India, I am enabled to prepare the following statement of persons enumerated in India who gave Burma as their birth-place :—

Return of Burmese emigrants enumerated in other provinces.

Province.	Male.	Female.	Total.
Bombay	378	151	529
Berar	4	...	4
North-Western Provinces	1,391	128	1,519
Native States	7	9	16
Punjab	60	66	126
Central Provinces	344	30	374
Bengal	558	280	838
Assam	44	23	67
Andamans	662	41	703
Ajmere	2	2	4
Madras	1,465	578	2,043
Native States	3	4	7
Coorg	5	1	6
Total ...	**4,923**	**1,313**	**6,236**

If we deduct the 6,236 persons born in Burma, but found in India, we find the province has obtained a net gain of 274,483 on the exchange. In 1881, 3,107 persons were enumerated in India and returned as being born in Burma, by which was meant Lower Burma, being 8 out of every 10,000 persons. Unfortunately the returns now furnished do not discriminate between those born in Upper and those in Lower Burma. Altogether there were 9 persons out of every 10,000 who emigrated from Burma to India. If we analyze the returns of those who went to India, we find that the males far outnumber the females. The employments of these emigrants are not stated, but the Superintendents of Census in the North-Western and the Central Provinces inform me that approximately 1,099 out of the 1,391 males found in the North-Western Provinces are convicts in jail, and that nearly all of those in the Central Provinces answer to the same description.

The two classes of emigrants from Burma.

209. There are two classes of emigrants from Burma—those of Burmese blood, and those who, though of foreign extraction, were born while their parents were in Burma. As the return gives the sexes apart, and as in Burma female convicts are few and far between and serious crime amongst women is practically unknown, we may set down the women, who number 1,313, as being free emigrants. If we allow an equal number of men to be free emigrants, we shall not be far from the truth if we take the remaining 3,610 men to be convicts in the different jails of India. If this seems a high proportion, it must be remembered that dacoity was rife in Upper and Lower Burma in 1886, 1887, and 1888, and even before that date was not entirely unknown. Our jails in Lower Burma were naturally unable to keep pace with the volume of crime, swollen as it was by the disturbances of the newly annexed province.

210. The following table shows the number of emigrants out of every 10,000 persons of both sexes born in each of the chief provinces of India in 1881 :—

Province		Province	
Rajputana	768	Bombay	251
Mysore	427	Bengal	89
Central Provinces	379	Assam	84
North-Western Provinces ...	242	Lower Burma, 1881 ...	8
Madras	124	Burma, 1891	9
Punjab	89		

Comparison of the returns of birth-place, religion, and parent-tongue.

211. Before we leave the subject of the exchange in population between Burma and India, it would be interesting to compare the returns of birth-place, religion, and parent-tongue in Lower Burma in 1881 and 1891, and if possible see whether the returns correspond. This will be useful as a check on our figures. Unfortunately no return of caste or race was prepared in 1881. Lastly, we have the returns prepared under the Native Passenger Ships Act, X of 1887, and the returns independently compiled in the office of the Chief Collector of Customs, Rangoon. Taking the returns of 1881 and 1891, we find that in Lower

Burma out of every 10,000 persons, in 1891, 510 were returned as born in India as against 494 in 1881. Seven hundred and fifty-nine out of every 10,000 of the population in 1891 returned either Hinduism, Sikhism, or Mahomedanism as their religion as against 688 in 1881, and in parent-tongue 765 persons as against 659 who were returned as speaking Indian vernaculars in 1881. If we compare these figures with each other in another way, in 1881 we find that only 72 per cent. of those who returned one of the Indian religions, and 75 per cent. of those who returned an Indian vernacular as their mother-tongue, were actually born in India. In 1891 the number of those born in India was 67 per cent. of those who returned one of the religions of India and 66 per cent. of those who returned themselves as speaking an Indian vernacular as their parent-tongue.

Explanation of the disparity.

212. That there should be a disparity between the returns of birth-place, religion, and parent-tongue was to be expected, because we have in Rangoon and in most of our large towns Indian colonists who preserve their language and religion, and who have settled down in Burma. Besides this it is an undoubted fact that Mahomedanism claims a number of Burman-speaking Burman-born followers. Mahomedanism is now professed by a large and increasing number of Arakanese. The figures of 1881 and 1891 would tend to prove that there is established in Burma a large and increasing colony of natives of India and their descendants. As the returns of 1881 and 1891 correspond so closely, there would appear to be good reason for accepting them as correct.

The immigration and emigration statistics collected in the ports of Burma.

213. We have, however, one other method of criticizing these figures by comparing the returns of immigrants and emigrants compiled under the provisions of Act X of 1887 in the office of the Port Officer and in the office of the Chief Collector of Customs, Rangoon. These returns are interesting; but when they were furnished to me I was informed that their statistical value was problematical. In the first place they do not agree : this disagreement may be due to the method of compilation. Moreover, the returns furnished by the Port Officer are compiled, not for the purpose of ascertaining the movement of the population, but as a check on the steam-ship companies. So long as the number of persons carried on each ship does not exceed the number permissible under the Act, the requirements of the Act are satisfied. Accordingly, no return is made of passengers from the Straits Settlements, because those ports are not under the Indian Government Acts. As an index of the actual gain to the province by excess of immigrants over emigrants these returns are disappointing. An attempt has been made for some years past by the Chief Collector of Customs to ascertain the number of immigrants and emigrants who land in Rangoon. This return is made under no legislative sanction. In comparing the returns made under Act X of 1887 with those of the Chief Collector of Customs, after making allowance for deductions for those sailing from the other ports of the province, I find that there is a discrepancy of 1,367 between the returns of those who left the port of Rangoon in 1890. No returns before 1887-88 were made by the Port Officer, and before that date the collection of these returns by the Custom House was made while the ship was at the wharf. As coolies are in the habit of crowding on board up to the very last minute, the accuracy of returns of emigrants made in this manner may be more easily imagined than calculated. The immigration and emigration figures of Akyab are worthless for reasons explained by Mr. Copleston : "Numerous "immigrants from Chittagong and Bengal enter Akyab district penniless and on "foot, but at the close of the season, with full purses, return by steamer to their "homes." With the exception of Akyab, Rangoon is practically the only port in direct steam-ship communication with Indian ports. We may therefore confine our enquiries to Rangoon.

Mr. Copleston noted that—

"There are no trustworthy statistics of immigration or emigration ; but as an instance of the way in which floating population fluctuates, the following facts furnished by the Port Commissioners of Rangoon may be quoted. Between the 15th of February 1880 and the 15th of February 1881, 39,341 natives of India landed in Rangoon, while only 17,370 sailed for their own countries, leaving a balance of nearly 22,000 souls."

214. If these figures were correct and 1880-81 were not an exceptional year, the intercensal period between 1872 and 1881 would account for the whole Indian-born population in Burma in 1881. The figures for the years 1881—1886 are not available in the Port Commissioners' office, but the Deputy Chairman has kindly furnished me with the return for the past five years, of which the subjoined table is a summary :—

Return of immigrants and emigrants, showing the arrivals and departures in each month of the year from 1887 to 1891.

Months.	Immigrants.	Emigrants.
January	38,071	17,170
February	30,945	24,445
March	24,935	36,130
April	24,343	47,453
May	23,623	43,610
June	30,125	28,483
July	28,219	20,032
August	26,820	21,031
September	38,561	18,102
October	49,462	18,664
November	76,180	19,227
December	66,839	17,864
Total ...	558,123	312,211

The total net gain for the past five years, according to these returns, averaged 29,182 persons every year. It must be remembered that these years are subsequent to the annexation of Upper Burma, and a large proportion of these arrivals were natives of India enlisted for the Upper Burma military police. The net gain, moreover, is proportionately far less than in the year 1880-81 quoted by Mr. Copleston, when over 55 per cent. of those who landed apparently stayed on in the country, whereas in the five years, notwithstanding the fact that the bulk of our military police have been stationed permanently in the country, the proportion of those who remained to those who landed in the country is only 31 per cent. This shows that the late returns are more correct, but it shows also how unreliable any deductions drawn from such statistics must necessarily be. But though this return may understate the emigrants, it may be taken as a fairly correct statement of the immigrants, and it is interesting because it shows the strength of the current of immigration and at what time it ebbs and flows.

Cause of the discrepancy in the returns.

215. One cause of the apparent discrepancy of these immigration and emigration returns and those of the census is to be found in the fearfully high mortality amongst our Indian, and especially amongst our Hindu cooly immigrants. The death-returns of Rangoon town show that within the last 10 years 14,965 deaths were recorded amongst these coolies, and that the deaths exceed the births by 13,164. It is clear therefore that many of our Indian immigrants do not return because they die in Burma. Crowded together in insanitary lodging-houses, they swell the death-rates of our chief town. In his report for the year 1890-91 the President of the Rangoon Municipality states :—

"It will be seen that death finds its victims in a higher ratio among the Hindu than amongst any other people, and this is not surprising when the conditions of their existence are borne in mind. They are mostly imported coolies and thousands of them live in the veriest hovels in the suburban swamps, with the most disgusting filth piled up in heaps or fermenting in pools at their very doors. The water they drink is, owing to the belief of their class as to water, often diluted with sewage, and they live as poorly as possible in order to save money to take or send to India."

* * * * *

"Out of a total of 167 cases of smallpox, 108 were Hindus; also 57 Hindus died of cholera out of a total mortality from this disease of 98, and of the total of 976 deaths from bowel-complaints, Hindus contributed 572. Although the correct returns of the population are not available, it is well known that Hindus are not nearly as numerous as the Burmese, therefore these figures are a startling illustration of the fact that Rangoon owes most of its cholera and smallpox, as well as its high death-rate, to the imported coolies."

It is unnecessary to pursue the enquiry further, as the officers from whom I obtained these returns would not vouch for their accuracy, and informed me I should be rash to place much reliance on them although at that time the figures had not been scrutinized. The figures have been carefully examined, and the results of the examination have been noted here more to emphasize the necessity of having in future some regular official record of the immigrants and emigrants at each port, and to show how useful such a record would be as a check on our census figures than as an inquiry into the accuracy of returns which were already discredited.

Movement of the population between Upper Burma, Lower Burma, and the Shan States.

216. In Lower Burma there were, as already recorded, out of every 10,000 of the inhabitants 728 persons born in Upper Burma and 65 in the Shan States. In Upper Burma 17,269 persons born in Lower Burma were found, being 58 out of every 10,000 persons, while of those born in the Shan States the proportion is almost exactly the same as in Lower Burma, being rather more than 65 out of every 10,000 persons. As the return of birth-place was only taken in a very small tract in the Shan States and was included for the sake of those born out of Burma, no return can be made giving the total number or proportion to the total population of immigrants from Burma. There are, however, practically no Burmans in the Shan States except the few who are employed in an official character. The return of the synchronous census tract, where Burmans might be expected to be comparatively numerous, shows that there were but 19 born in Lower and 147 born in Upper Burma as against 1,249 born in the Madras Presidency and 1,435 born in the Punjab out of a total of 2,992 souls. We may safely conclude that there are but few of those born in Burma to be found in the Shan States.

The returns show that while in Lower Burma out of every 10,000 persons there are 1,381 who were born outside and have immigrated into the province, in Upper Burma, though 3,196,719 persons were returned as having been born there, only 3,063,426 were found there. If we include the whole population of the excluded tracts in Upper Burma for which no returns of birth-place were made as being all born in Upper Burma, we should find the number of those born in Upper Burma would be 3,313,212 and the disparity would be still greater, being 249,786. The disparity is made still greater if we deduct from the population of Upper Burma the 19,336 persons returned as being born in the Shan States, the 17,269 persons returned as being born in Lower Burma, and the 40,423 persons born in India. Lastly, if we deduct all those born in other Asiatic States and in countries of Europe, we find that out of the total of those returned as being born in Upper Burma, which is returned as 3,313,212, only 2,973,750 were found there, so that out of every 10,000 persons born in Upper Burma, only 8,975 were enumerated there, that is to say, the total number of those born in Upper Burma and found outside of it is more than 10 per cent. of the total number of those born in the upper province.

Causes of this movement of the population.

217. It is perhaps yet too early to assign its due share in the exodus to the three chief causes, but these three causes were undoubtedly the true ones. As before noted, the exodus of Burmans northward after the annexation of Pegu left the deltaic districts partially denuded of inhabitants. After Lower Burma had been pacified and the countryfolk were assured the British intended to stay the pressure of the superabundant population in the kingdom of Ava, the desire to return to and cultivate their deserted homesteads caused a great portion of the unwilling exiles to return gradually to Lower Burma. Up to 1885, when the kingdom of Ava was annexed, numbers of up-country Burmans emigrated yearly into Lower Burma to escape the exactions of the subordinate Burmese officials. If asked his reasons, after some hesitation the up-country man would often reply that it was "te pu thi," *i.e.*, "very warm," or, more forcibly, a bit too warm for him. These causes are now removed. The third cause was the liability to drought and consequent scarcity from which the inland districts of Upper Burma are accustomed to suffer. Whether this migration from the upper to the lower province will continue depends on the recurrence of these droughts and to the success of our engineers in improving the irrigation works already in existence and in devising new schemes.

Diagram C.

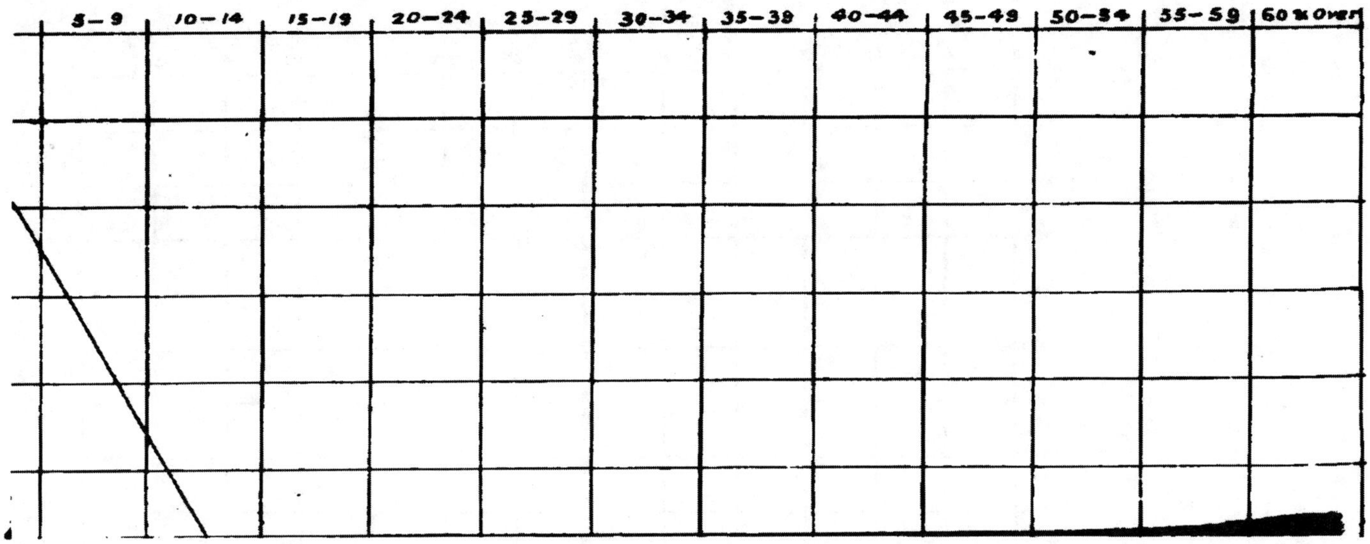

Diagram D.

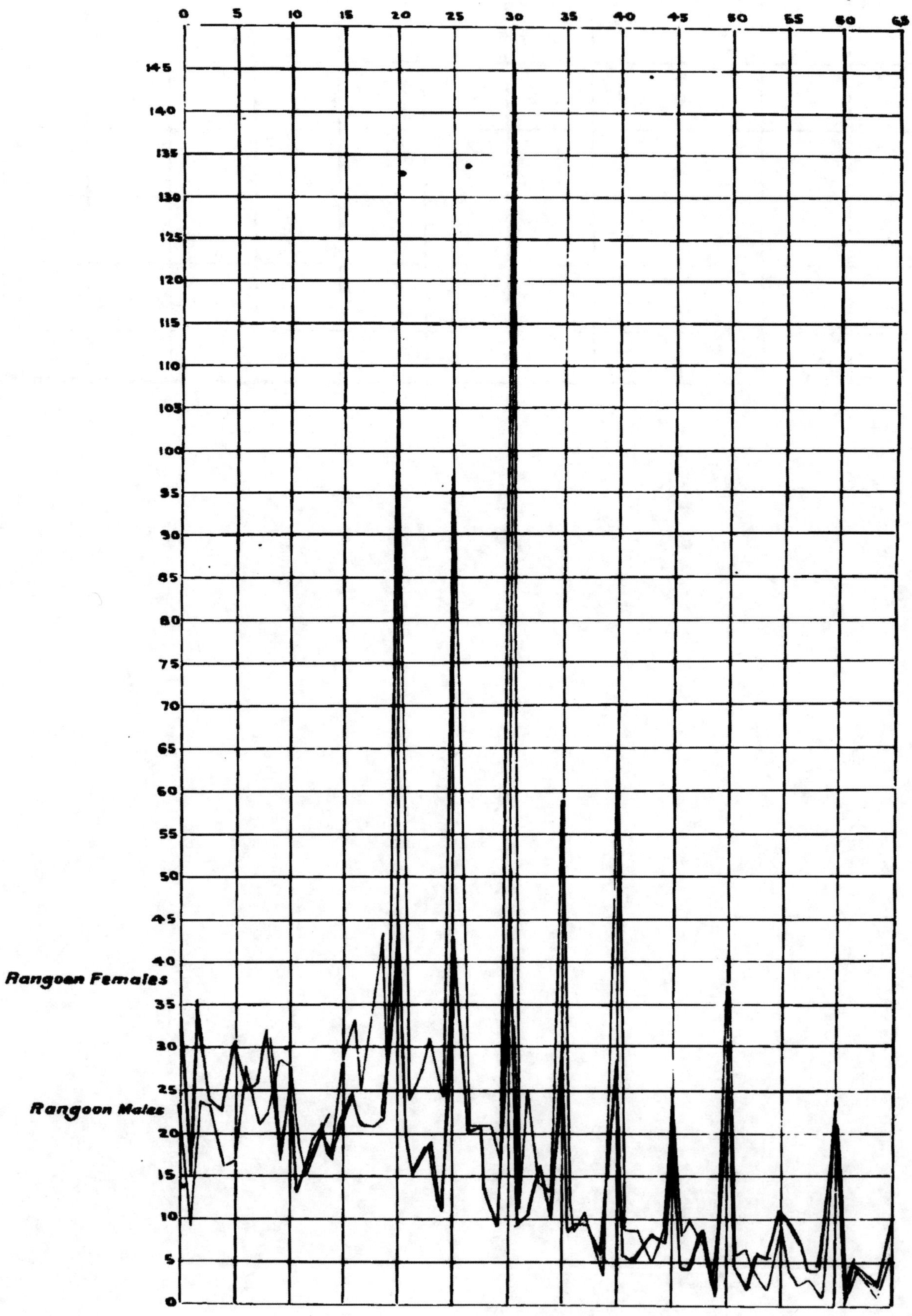

0
5
10
15
20
25
30
35
40
45
50
55
60
65
145
140
135
130
125
120
115
110
105
100
95
90
85
80
75
70
65
60
55
50
45
40
35
30
25
20
15
10
5
0
Rangoon Females
Rangoon Males

(Read vertically this table shows the distribution of 10,000 of the popula

Birth-place.	Akyab.	Northern Arakan.	Kyaukpyu.	Sandoway.	Rangoon Town.	Hanthawaddy.	Pegu.	Tharrawaddy.	Prome.	Thôngwa.	Bassein.
Akyab	8,286	190	75	17	13	3	2	1	3	5	5
Northern Arakan	...	9,530	...	...	...	...	...	...	...	...	...
Kyaukpyu	181	8	9,710	420	4	...	...	...	...	...	39

Movement of the population from district to district.

218. In order to facilitate the discussion of this somewhat intricate question, the three comparative statements herewith annexed have been prepared. Comparative Statement *A* shows the distribution of the 10,000 of both sexes in each district according to birth-place read in vertical columns. The antique type which runs diagonally from left to right shows the total number of the indigenous population of each district. Comparative Statement *B* is to be read in horizontal lines and shows 10,000 persons born in each district distributed according to the districts in which they were found when the enumeration took place. For instance in Statement *A*, if we take Rangoon Town, we find that out of every 10,000 persons enumerated in Rangoon only 3,367 were born in Rangoon itself. In Statement *B* we find that out of every 10,000 persons born in Rangoon 6,622 were found there. The reason of this divergence of course is that the number of those born in Rangoon is far less than the total population. Read diagonally from the top left-hand corner Statement *B* shows the exact proportion of those who have stayed in the district of their birth out of every 10,000 born in it. The balance of the 10,000 persons in each district in Statement *B* is composed of those who are born out of the province and not in one of the districts of the province. Statement *C* is a profit and loss account between each district in the province, discriminating between males and females, the males to the right and the females to the left of the diagonal line.

This table should be read in the following way. If we take Kyaukpyu and wish to find how it has fared in its exchange with other districts, we read horizontally and we find under the vertical column headed "Rangoon" that it has received 22 males born in Rangoon and that it has sent 75 males who were born in Kyaukpyu thither, and the balance against it is 53 males.

219. The Census Commissioner for India, in his report on the 1881 census, remarked :—

> "The Indian population is in no instance a people that desires to leave its home, and so long as it can obtain a fair amount of subsistence in its own village lands it never migrates."

That this is true of India generally is undoubted, but these statements show his remarks do not apply with the same force to Burma.

Comparative mobility of the population in the districts of Burma —Immigration.

220. Statement *A* shows the proportion of those born in the district to those found in it on 26th February, and thus negatively shows how much the district has gained by immigration. Rangoon of course comes first, 66·33 per cent. of the total population being immigrants. For those who know Rangoon these figures require no explanation. Next on this list we find the Ruby Mines district. The explanation of the position held by this district is not far to seek. In the first place, the district contains but 26,134 inhabitants, and of these a large proportion is employed in working the ruby mines. Next in order comes Pyinmana in Upper Burma, and Pegu and Thôngwa in Lower Burma. Pyinmana is a very small district, containing but 56,349 inhabitants altogether, 12,926 of whom live in Pyinmana town. Of these a very large proportion consists of military police, railway officials, and servants of the Bombay Burma Trading Corporation, many of whose foresters are Karens, and accordingly the circumstances of the district are so abnormal and the total population so small that the high percentage of the immigrants to the total population is easily understood. Pegu and Thôngwa are large and populous districts, and the explanation in their case is to be found in the marvellous extension in the area of land under cultivation. In Toungoo, which comes next, Statement *A* shows that it owes its position partly to the foreign garrison, consisting of British and Native troops, but chiefly to large immigration from Pyinmana, Shan States, Meiktila, and Yamèthin. Hanthawaddy, Akyab, Tharrawaddy, and Henzada, which come next in order in Lower Burma in the high proportion of their immigrant population, are rapidly progressive districts. Mandalay, the old capital of Upper Burma, naturally attached to itself a large number of the inhabitants of other districts, who were drawn there by the court and by the various exemptions from taxation with which the inhabitants of this city were favoured. Moreover, as 36 years have not elapsed since Mandalay city was founded, we might naturally

expect a large influx of immigrants. In Bhamo the population is so small that the large military and police force there stationed have a preponderating effect. In Kyauksè to the fertility of the soil and its immunity from drought, due to the system of irrigation canals, is to be attributed the large proportion of immigrants.

As a rule the Upper Burma districts naturally show a large proportion of emigrants and a smaller proportion of immigrants. Whether this will continue or not will depend on the success or failure of the crops and the measures adopted to prevent the latter contingency.

Comparison with the returns of districts in Indian provinces. Emigration.

221. Table *B* shows the number who have emigrated from the district of their birth into other districts of the province. The proportion of emigrants varies from 33·78 per cent. in Rangoon to 22·46 per cent. in Mandalay and 21·7 per cent. in Shwebo. In paragraph 206 of this chapter I have already compared the mobility of the population of Burma with that of Indian provinces. If we take the migration in detail by districts, it will be seen that the superiority is maintained. The returns of the Bombay census show that in no case did the percentage of emigrants from a district even exceed 15·1 per cent., which is the proportion borne by emigrants to the number of persons who returned Rutnagiri as their birth-place. This is further emphasized by the fact that this emigration was not counterbalanced by any immigration, because the 84·9 per cent. of those born in Rutnagiri constituted 97·7 per cent. of the total population of the district. In the Punjab the percentage of emigrants to the total number born in each district varies from 20 per cent. in Gurgaon, where distress had been acute, and 24 per cent. in Simla, where the returns are admittedly abnormal owing to the physical conditions of the district, to 17 per cent. in Delhi and 14 per cent. in Karnal and Rohtak.

In Lower Burma, at any rate, except in the Hill Tract districts of Northern Arakan and Salween, the Burman can almost always obtain a fair amount of subsistence in the land surrounding his own village, so that there is no absolute necessity for him to rove. Moreover, our districts in Burma are so large that a man may satisfy his crave for wandering without crossing the borders of the district he was born in. On the other hand, the Burman is naturally fond of roving and is not fettered by caste restrictions.

222. Comparing the returns of the present and the last preceding census, we find that much that was true then is equally true now. The proportion of those born in Rangoon and found there in 1881 was 36; it is now 33 per cent. In Akyab there is a larger percentage of home-born population now than in 1881, when only 76 per cent. of the total population was born there. Hanthawaddy, which then comprised Pegu as well as the present district of Hanthawaddy, possessed the largest population of foreigners. We now see that it was to the Pegu and not to the Hanthawaddy section of the district that this pre-eminence was due.

An examination of Table *C* shows that within the province itself women are almost as mobile as the male population. This is not astonishing when the well-known activity and independence of character of the women is considered. In short it may be asserted that while in India the population is, in the face of successive famines and the narrow "margin" which divides their ordinary means of subsistence from actual want, and notwithstanding a vast improvement in the means of communications, still essentially immobile, the Burmans, in spite of the absence of any necessity to leave their homes in search of work, are from temperament and disposition a roving people.

CHAPTER X.

CASTE OR RACE.

The return of Caste and Race. Parent-tongue and Birth-place an inadequate substitute. Reasons for attempting to make the return in Burma. The Imperial classification unsuited to Burma. Imperial Table XVI. The relative strength of Hindu Castes and Musalman Tribes to the total population of Burma. The Provincial classification by Races. The Burmese. The subdivisions of the Burmese race. The origin and history of the Burmese. The Arakanese, Tavoyers, Kudos, Yaws, Yabeins, Chaungthas, Danaws and Danus; the Chins; the Taungthas or Kukis; the Kachins; the Shans, Dr. Cushing's monograph on the Shans; the Ahoms; the Môns or Talaings; the Karens; the Taungthus, Mr. Hildebrand's note on the Taungthus; the Malays; the Selungs, Mr. Merrifield's note on the Selungs; the Chinese; the Panthès; the Musalman Tribes. Note on the Tamil, Choliar, and Telugu Races by the Bishop of Rangoon. Hindu Castes. Comparative statement showing the distribution of Hindu Castes. Europeans and Eurasians.

Authorities consulted.

1. Sir W. Hunter's *Gazetteer of India*. London: Trübner and Co., 1886.
2. Journal of the American Oriental Society, Thirteenth Note, Social and Military Position of the Ruling Caste in Ancient India, by Edward W. Hopkins.
3. Burma, by Captain C. J. F. S. Forbes.
4. Legendary History of Burma and Arakan, by Captain Forbes. Rangoon, 1882.
5. The Burman, by Shwe Yeo.
6. The Selungs of the Mergui Archipelago, by John Anderson, M.D.
7. The *British Burma Gazetteer*, by Colonel Horace Spearman.
8. Mason's Burma. Rangoon: Ranney, 1860.
9. Amongst the Shans, by A. Colquhoun. Field and Freer, 1885.
10. De la Couperie's Introduction to Amongst the Shans by A. Colquhoun.
11. Mandalay to Momein, by J. Anderson, M.D. Macmillan, 1876.
12. The Kingdom and People of Siam, by Sir J. Bowring. London, 1851.
13. An Ethnographical Handbook for the North-Western Provinces and Oudh, by W. Crooke. Allahabad, 1890.
14. The History of Burma, by Sir Arthur P. Phayre. London: Trübner, 1884.
15. The Language of the Southern Chins and its Affinities by B. Houghton. Rangoon, 1892.

The present Census Report is the first one that contains any return of caste.

223. In the previous enumerations of 1872 and 1881 no attempt was made in Burma to obtain a return of caste, and at the Agra Conference, Mr. Copleston, who represented Burma, was authorized to state that, so far as Burma was concerned, there existed no necessity for attempting this return. The details for race could, it was urged, as in the Census of 1881, be obtained by collating and comparing the returns of parent-tongue and birth-place. In 1872 a return was made of races, but not of castes. In 1881 Mr. Copleston made no attempt to return caste. Referring to Imperial Final Form VIII prescribed for the return of caste, he wrote—

"This form is blank for British Burma, since it was determined to be useless, with Burmese enumerators, to attempt to record Hindu castes or Mahomedan tribes, and since, as I have noted, the form is not required for aboriginal tribes."

In dealing with the question of races he remarks as follows:—

"At the recent Census, the mother-tongues and birth-places of the people were taken as the best tests of nationality or race."

On the occasion of the Census of 1891 it was decided that in Burma the races at least should be returned, even if caste were not practicable. Parent-tongue and birth-place cannot be taken as a satisfactory test of nationality or race, and experience has shown that the two columns added to the present schedule, Race and Nationality, have helped to clear away the ambiguity caused by an immigrant population and consequent confusion of tongues.

224. At the best, the returns of birth-place and parent-tongue are untrustworthy data from which to infer the race of the enumerated. Indeed, it is quite plain that as time goes on and our Indian colonists increase and multiply, birth-place —which, of course, is useless to distinguish between the indigenous races—will become altogether misleading as an index of the race even of Hindus and Musalman tribes. Parent-tongue is, of course, a better index of race; but even here the hard-and-fast lines are becoming obliterated. In Lower Burma we find that out of every 10,000 persons of both sexes, 6,532 returned themselves as Burmans, and it is clear from internal evidence that a few of these were not true Burmans, but half-bred Shans and Karens and hill tribesmen, while 6,792 persons out of every 10,000 returned themselves as speaking Burmese. Of course the birth-place return of 8,619 out of every 10,000 persons cannot therefore be accepted as an index of the number of Burmans in Burma, while the return of Buddhists, which rises to 8,680 out of every 10,000, shows that religion is no test of race. If we turn to the Karens, we find that the returns of birth-place are, of course, useless to distinguish between Karen and Burman. Religion amongst the Karens is even less useful than amongst the Burmans as a guide, for we find that out of the 536,237 who returned themselves as Karens, 405,441 returned themselves as Buddhists, 80,213 as Christians, 50,563 as Nat-worshippers, and 20 as Musalmans. The number of those who returned Karen as their parent-tongue was 633,684. This variance was partly due, as the schedule books showed, to those of mixed parentage returning the language of their mother, who was a Karen, as their parent-tongue. But the chief cause is, no doubt, the fact that many Karens, especially those who have become Buddhists, desire to sink their despised Karen origin and return themselves as Burmese, but are betrayed by the language they speak. Here the language return is undoubtedly the truer indication of those of Karen blood, but, for political purposes, it would be plainly misleading to count as Karens those who denied their Karen origin, and hence the race return is, for practical purposes, the more useful. It is quite clear, therefore, that the return of race in Burma is a useful and even a necessary return.

Parent-tongue and birth-place as a substitute for the return of race.

225. The question of the return of caste was left open till the arrival of the Census Commissioner. The Burmese translation of the schedule was so made, that, if necessary, an attempt might be made to return caste. After due consideration, it was decided that an attempt to return caste should be made. The reasons for taking this step were—

Reasons for making the return of caste and race.

(1) That the numbers of immigrants into Burma from India are now so great that they form a not inconsiderable part of the total population not only of Burma, but of the Indian Empire.

(2) That it might, for Imperial as well as Provincial reasons, be important to ascertain which castes are most strongly represented amongst our immigrant population.

(3) That the bulk of these immigrants reside either in towns or are employed in gangs on public works, or are enlisted in the native army and military police, and accordingly, if proper instructions were issued, a return of some value might be obtained.

(4) And lastly, that the return was required to complete, as well as to act as a check on, the caste returns of the other provinces.

If the return proved worthless, no second attempt need ever be made; if successful, information of some value would be available regarding the castes that most readily availed themselves of the benefits of immigration into Burma. It would also be more easy to ascertain what effect this migration had on the restrictions of caste itself, and whether these restrictions were enforced in Burma. The steps that were taken will be more fully dealt with in the chapter on Census operations. The schedule books show that a much fuller and more accurate return was obtained than was ever expected. A list of castes was prepared and submitted to the Census Commissioner, and this list was revised at the Simla Conference by the Superintendents of the other provinces of India. It was then finally determined that Imperial Table XVI should be prepared. It is, perhaps, just as well that the experiment was made on this occasion. It is more than probable that caste will not be again attempted at another census, and, had not the trial been made now, it would never have been made at all.

Imperial and Provincial classifications.

226. There are two ways of dealing with the question of caste and race—

(1) The Imperial point of view, which is embodied in Imperial Table XVI, in which caste and race are classified by their traditional occupations.
(2) The Provincial.

In the former the Burmese and Karens and other races are treated as castes, and are classed, for Imperial purposes, by their traditional occupations. Among the races of Group F no such traditional occupations exist. The nearest approach to traditional occupation or caste that we have amongst the indigenous population is found in—

(1) the Yabeins, who are rearers of silkworms;
(2) the Manipuri or Ponna settlers in Mandalay, who were formerly the King of Ava's silk-weavers, and who are the descendants of Manipuri captives who were deported from their native country when it was conquered by the Burmese; and
(3) the pagoda slaves, who were captives taken in war.

But none of these three are of pure Burmese race, and their isolation is due rather to political than to social causes. Besides these there are the hereditary militia of the king, who live chiefly in the Shwebo and Meiktila districts. They held their land by military tenure, but this distinction was one of rank rather than of caste, for all Burmans were compelled to serve as soldiers when called on, and the Shwebo men had special favours granted to them because Alaungpaya was thugyi of Shwebo and they were naturally his staunchest adherents.

The Imperial classification is unsuited to Burma.

227. Accordingly, so far as the indigenous races of Burma are concerned, the Imperial classification is just as meaningless as it would be in England itself. Moreover, as regards our Indian population, the classification by traditional occupation has already lost much of its significance. I am informed by Major Temple that the scavengers of Rangoon are recruited from the Chamar caste, and they prefer to pocket their pride in order to pocket the sweeper's pay. The Indian immigrant, especially if he belongs to a low caste, often settles down in the country and marries one of the daughters of Heth and gives up all caste restrictions, except when he wants an excuse for getting himself off an uncongenial task.

Then, again, as to the accuracy of the returns, it must be remembered that there are not the same difficulties in the way of a Hindu in Burma returning himself in a caste higher than his real one. Many men of inferior caste, if asked casually to what caste they belong, boldly reply Brahmans if they think their interrogator is likely to be ignorant of the nice distinctions of Hindu caste, and if there is no one present who could set him right. It is possible, indeed it is probable, that several of those who have been returned in our schedule books have thus given themselves "brevet" rank.

As caste is an exotic institution in Burma, and as its origin and definition have been exhaustively dealt with in previous Census Reports, notably in Mr. Ibbetson's Report of the Census of 1881 in the Punjab, there is no need to repeat here what has already been threshed out. A glance at Imperial Table XVI will show that, however necessary the arrangement, in which castes are treated on an equality with nationalities which are grouped together under Class F, may be in India, such an arrangement is not suitable in Burma, where out of a total population of 7,605,560, only 103,298 persons, or 136 out of every 10,000 of the total population, belong to these castes. So far, then, as Burma is concerned, it is needless to dilate on the castes of India.

But though caste does not concern us, the races of Burma, especially since the annexation of the Upper Province has doubled the area to be reviewed, form a most interesting field of labour from the purely ethnographical point of view.

228. The first point to be dealt with is the classification of the races. In Burma the Provincial classification, disregarding the question of caste and traditional occupations, treats of the different races and nationalities found in Burma and groups them by their ethnical affinities. In Chapter VIII, Languages, an attempt has been made to classify the languages spoken according to the latest information available. In Burma this classification holds good from an ethnographical as well as from a philological point of view, as, with the exception of the Yabeins, Danaws, Danus, and Taungyos, no recognized tribes have as yet entirely lost their parent-tongue. It is true that a process of assimilation to Burmese has till lately been rapidly reducing Talaing and Pwo-Karen to the position of dead languages, but at present we are only emerging from the method of classification which recently prevailed of treating every dialect as a separate language, and the people who spoke it as a distinct race. Max Müller's remarks on the tendency of languages to throw off separate dialects have been already quoted. Ethnographically speaking, we may broadly disregard dialects unless they are accompanied by variety in dress, customs or religion.

229. Imperial Table XVI is so lengthy that the following table, which is a summary of it, is here inserted in order that we may better understand it before proceeding to analyse the figures therein contained.

STATEMENT A.—*Summary of Imperial Table No. XVI, "Caste, Tribe or Race by Nationality or Traditional Occupation."*

Class.	Group.	Populatiou.	Proportionate strength per 10,000 of the total population.
A.—Agricultural ...	1. Military and dominant	21,020	27·64
	2. Minor agricultural	34,444	45·29
	3. Foreign recruits	...	...
	4. Forest and hill tribes	700	·92
	Total Class A ...	**56,164**	**73·85**
B.—Professional ...	5. Priests	11,630	15·29
	6. Devotees	629	·82
	7. Temple-servants	11,652	15·32
	8. Genealogists	45	·05
	9. Writers	4,602	6·05
	10. Astrologers	58	·07
	11. Musicians and ballad-reciters	8	·01
	12. Dancers and singers	58	·07
	13. Actors and mimics	...	...
	Total Class B ...	**28,682**	**37·71**
C.—Commercial ...	14. Traders	6,689	8·79
	15. Pedlars	...	...
	16. Carriers	...	...
	Total Class C ...	**6,689**	**8·79**
D.—Artizans and village menials.	17. Goldsmiths	280	·36
	18. Barbers	540	·71
	19. Blacksmiths	210	·27
	20. Carpenters and turners	121	·15
	21. Brass and copper smiths	...	...
	22. Tailors	66	·08
	23. Weavers, calenderers, and dyers... ...	837	1·10
	24. Washermen	1,559	2·04
	25. Cotton-cleaners	1	·001
	26. Shepherds and wool-weavers	1,768	2·32
	27. Oil-pressers	833	1·09
	28. Potters	381	·50
	29. Glass-workers	388	·51
	30. Salt, &c., workers	7	·009

STATEMENT A.—*Summary of Imperial Table No. XVI, "Caste, Tribe or Race by Nationality or Traditional Occupation"*—concluded.

Class.	Group.	Population.	Proportionate strength per 10,000 of the total population.
D.—Artizans and village menials—*concld.*	31. Lime-burners	...	...
	32. Goldsmith's refuse collectors	...	...
	33. Gold-washers	...	...
	34. Iron-smelters	...	...
	35. Fishermen, boatmen. palki-bearers, cooks, &c.	1,688	2·22
	36. Distillers and toddy-drawers	355	·46
	37. Butchers	...	...
	38. Leather-workers	753	·99
	39. Scavengers	399	·52
	Total Class D ...	10,186	13·39
E.—Vagrants, minor artizans, and performers, &c.	40. Grindstone-makers and stone-quarriers ...	...	...
	41. Earthwork and stone dressers	56	·07
	42. Knife-grinders	...	...
	43. Mat-makers and cane-splitters	201	·26
	44. Hunters, fowlers, &c.	5	·006
	45. Miscellaneous and disreputable livers ...	1,313	1·72
	46. Tumblers and acrobats	2	·002
	47. Jugglers, snake-charmers, and animal exhibitors.	...	...
	Total Class E ...	1,577	2·07
F.—Races and nationalities.	48. Non-Indian Asiatic races	7,291,356	9,586·86
	49. Mixed Asiatic races	19,106	25·12
	50. Non-Asiatic races	11,723	15·41
	51. Eurasians	6,978	9·17
	52. Christian converts	97,351	127·99
	Total Class F ...	7,426,514	9,764·58
G.—Not returned ...	53. Unspecified	75,748	99·59

230. Of how little value this Imperial classification is from the purely Provincial point of view may be inferred from the subjoined statements, **B** and **C**, which show the relative strength of the various races found in Burma. Table **B** is interesting for its own sake, as it shows at a glance the distribution of the population amongst the various nationalities found in the province.

STATEMENT **B**.—This comparative table shows the relative strength of the various indigenous races, Hindu and Mahomedan tribes, per 10,000 of the total population.

Division.	Burmese.	Talaing.	Shan.	Karen (Pwo).	Karen (Sgau).	Karenni.	Chin.	Chinese.	Hindu castes.	Musalman tribes.	Sikh.	Kachins.
Arakan ...	614·6	·03	·7	·1	·06	...	81·05	2·1	13·9	165·9	·001	...
Pegu ...	1,408·5	112·5	84·1	33·3	62·3	·4	8·3	21·1	109·8	53·1	·6	·004
Irrawaddy ...	1,516·8	39·9	6·8	235·6	159·1	·8	31·2	8·7	20·6	14·7	·02	...
Tenasserim ...	461·3	460·6	49·6	136·4	72·05	·9	·5	13·2	43·02	35·4	·07	·146
Total Lower Burma.	4,001·2	613·1	141·3	405·5	293·7	2·2	121·1	45·3	187·3	269·3	·7	·15
Northern ...	688·2	·9	54·9	·2	·1	·06	1·7	4·4	22·4	30·5	1·4	2·7
Central ...	812·1	·7	27·5	·02	·001	·001	1·1	·3	4·2	3·6	·8	...
Southern ...	1,397·6	·3	2·1	·1	·009	...	25·6	3·9	6·4	4·8	·3	...
Eastern ...	689·5	·03	10·5	2·4	·5	·003	·08	·8	5·1	11·8	·8	...
Total Upper Burma.	3,587·4	2·05	95·05	2·8	·7	·06	28·6	9·5	38·2	50·8	3·4	2·7
Total Province...	7,588·6	615·1	236·4	408·4	294·3	2·2	149·8	54·8	225·6	320·2	4·1	2·85

Table **C** is not merely an expansion of the foregoing statement, but it views the races found in Burma from a different standpoint. In this statement Hindus and Musalman tribesmen and numerically insignificant indigenous clans such as Kachins and Manipuris are included in the term "Others" and the distribution of the races by religion is shown. This table has been prepared in order to show this distribution, as the influence of religion in modifying national customs and even in obliterating racial characteristics is felt even in Burma. But as in this chapter the distinction of nationality and race is the most important factor, I have restricted the definition of "Burmese" to those who are admittedly of Burmese origin, omitting the Kachins, although some of them are Buddhists and have become Burmanized, who are shown separately, for though of cognate race, they are not Burmese.

STATEMENT C.—This table shows the chief races found in the eight administrative divisions of Burma distributed by religions.

Divisions.	Burmese.				Talaings.				Shans.				Karens (Pwo).				Karens (Sgau).			
	Buddhists.	Nat-worshippers.	Musalmans.	Christians.	Buddhists.	Nat-worshippers.	Musalmans.	Christians.	Buddhists.	Nat-worshippers.	Musalmans.	Christians.	Buddhists.	Nat-worshippers.	Musalmans.	Christians.	Buddhists.	Nat-worshippers.	Musalmans.	Christians.
1	2	3	4	5	6	7	8	9	10	11	12	13	14	15	16	17	18	19	20	21
LOWER BURMA.																				
Arakan	466,390	529	378	111	30	...	...	...	592	...	...	...	53	41	...	21	42	...	...	4
Pegu	1,068,170	...	467	2,651	85,521	...	...	78	63,889	...	...	60	22,124	1,733	...	1,496	39,095	282	...	8,004
Irrawaddy	1,147,144	...	2,524	3,951	29,815	...	...	550	4,925	...	...	272	161,630	619	14	16,935	97,570	51	6	23,445
Tenasserim	346,563	1,357	318	2,614	349,248	974	...	108	37,598	58	50	62	41,219	40,370	...	22,199	42,127	5,755	...	6,921
Total ...	3,028,267	1,886	3,687	9,327	464,614	974	...	736	107,004	58	50	394	225,026	42,763	14	40,651	178,834	6,088	6	38,374
UPPER BURMA.																				
Northern	521,923	...	777	736	683	...	...	8	41,763	27	...	1	50	54	...	53	11	14	...	95
Central	616,512	1	65	1,090	603	...	...	1	20,919	...	...	...	12	2	...	4	...	...	...	1
Southern	1,062,630	...	227	115	235	...	...	6	1,577	...	...	...	7	7	...	93	...	...	...	7
Eastern	521,658	22	2,582	89	22	...	...	2	7,989	5	6	3	349	1,221	...	317	133	302	...	...
Total ...	2,722,723	23	3,651	2,030	1,543	...	...	17	72,248	32	6	4	418	1,284	...	67	144	316	...	70,137
TOTAL PROVINCE ...	5,750,990	1,909	7,338	11,357	466,157	974	...	753	179,252	90	56	398	225,444	44,047	14	41,118	178,978	6,404	6	83

Divisions.	Karennis.				Chins.				Chinese.				Europeans.				Eurasians.				Others.				
	Buddhists.	Nat-worshippers.	Musalmans.	Christians.	Buddhists.	Nat-worshippers.	Musalmans.	Christians.	Buddhists.	Nat-worshippers.	Musalmans.	Christians.	Buddhists.	Nat-worshippers.	Musalmans.	Christians.	Buddhists.	Nat-worshippers.	Musalmans.	Christians.	Buddhists.	Nat-worshippers.	Musalmans.	Christians.	Others.
1	22	23	24	25	26	27	28	29	30	31	32	33	34	35	36	37	38	39	40	41	42	43	44	45	46
LOWER BURMA.																									
Arakan	...	...	...	...	2,578	58,750	...	320	373	1,277	...	12	...	...	...	740	...	...	...	61	2,616	1	126,226	146	10,608
Pegu	304	1	...	19	867	5,448	...	35	10,480	5,589	...	44	...	...	...	4,795	4	...	...	4,269	2,243	2	40,361	4,149	84,309
Irrawaddy	582	34	...	27	6,776	16,774	...	224	3,691	2,714	...	234	...	...	...	1,441	...	...	...	525	1,615	...	11,266	1,065	15,747
Tenasserim	116	41	...	572	238	149	...	...	5,218	4,828	...	...	...	...	...	1,726	...	...	...	1,437	2,060	1,644	29,039	659	32,805
Total ...	1,002	76	...	618	10,459	81,121	...	579	19,762	14,408	...	290	...	...	...	8,702	4	...	...	6,292	8,534	1,647	206,892	6,019	143,469
UPPER BURMA.																									
Northern	13	36	...	...	340	947	...	53	592	2,783	...	4	3	...	...	2,445	...	...	...	388	30,212	2,397	23,244	1,220	18,163
Central	1	...	...	...	14	866	...	...	90	153	...	...	1	...	...	247	...	...	...	47	1,470	...	2,777	28	3,882
Southern	...	...	...	...	12,152	7,382	...	...	459	2,530	...	...	...	...	...	644	...	...	...	126	1,578	...	3,720	178	5,156
Eastern	3	...	...	...	...	66	...	...	84	596	...	...	...	...	...	453	...	...	...	121	481	17	8,984	211	4,567
Total ...	17	36	...	...	12,506	9,261	...	53	1,225	6,062	...	4	4	...	...	3,789	...	...	...	682	33,741	2,414	38,725	1,637	31,768
Total Province ...	1,019	112	...	618	22,965	90,382	...	632	20,987	20,470	...	294	4	...	...	12,491	4	...	...	6,974	42,275	4,061	245,617	7,656	175,237

231. Before proceeding to discuss the returns *seriatim* by nationality and race, it will be interesting to compare the result of the enumeration of 1872 with that of 1891. Table D will show the strength of the various races inhabiting Lower Burma at these two dates. In 1881 the strength of the various races was calculated on the returns of mother-tongue and birth-place, but as no reliance can be placed on the deductions thus obtained, I have omitted the returns of 1881 from this table.

STATEMENT D.—*Comparative Table showing the actual and relative strength of the chief Nationalities enumerated in Lower Burma in 1872 and 1891.*

Name of nationality.	1872.	Ratio per 1,000 inhabitants.	1891.	Ratio per 1,000 inhabitants.
Burmese	1,583,801	577	2,682,879	576
Arakanese	331,448	121	354,599	76
Chaungthas	9,634	3	3,492	1
Yabeins	5,436	2	2,197	1
Chins	51,117	19	60,383	13
Daingnets	3,548	1	1,910	·4
Mros	7,875	3	15,666	3
Kwemis	18,969	7	14,200	3
Kathès	1,845	1	1,775	·3
Talaings	181,602	66	466,324	100
Karens	331,255	121	531,756	114
Karennis	451	·1	1,696	·3
Taungthus	24,923	9	2,732	1
Shans	36,029	13	107,506	23
Chinese	12,109	4	34,462	7
Hindu castes	35,230	13	142,522	30
Mahomedan tribes	95,683	35	206,890	44
European nationalities	5,154	2	8,702	2
Eurasians	4,023	1	6,296	2
Others	7,016	2	12,640	3
Total ...	**2,747,148**	**1,000**	**4,658,627**	**1,000**

232. Out of the 7,605,560 persons in Burma for whom this return of race was prepared, 5,771,594 are returned as either Burmese or under the names given of the Burmese tribes. No separate instructions were issued enforcing the return of these subdivisions of the Burmese race. In every case—except perhaps that of the Tavoyers—they have been willingly returned. Moreover, there was still some uncertainty regarding the classification of the smaller tribes, and, accordingly, it was left to the Burmese enumerator to judge of the truth of the return made to him without hampering him with too many rules. The classification of the languages of Burma has already been considered at some length in Chapter VIII, Language or Parent-tongue. Language, though not an infallible guide in the case of individuals, is yet a certain index of the origin, and sometimes of the history, of the race that claims it as its own. The classification of languages and races has been submitted to the criticism of the ablest scholars in Burma, and though, of course, to hope that it is final would be vain, it may be taken as sufficient for the present purpose of discussing the returns of race and nationality. It may, perhaps, be as well to note that the terms "Race" and "Nationality" are used in the sense of genus and species.

The Burmese.

The following table shows the strength of each of the tribes included in the Burmese race:—

		Ratio per 10,000 of total population.
Burmese	5,405,727	7,107·60
Arakanese	354,900	466·63
Chaungtha	3,492	4·59
Tavoyer	744	0·98
Danu	547	0·72
Kadu	3,617	4·76
Yaw	370	0·48
Yabein	2,197	2·89

233. The most important of these, indeed, the most important of all the nationalities of Burma, are the Burmese. In physique and appearance they resemble the mountaineers of the

The Burmese.

Himalayas, and the similarity of their language to Tibetan may therefore be taken as proof that, in descent as well as in language, they belong to the same stock. Indeed, the links of the chain that connect them with Tibet are still unbroken, for further acquaintance with the Naga, Chin, and Lushai tribes has proved that they all belong to the same family. The Burmese legends, which trace back the Burman race to be exiles of Oudh and Kapilavastu, are as worthy of credit as the legends of Æneas' arrival in Wales. It may very possibly be true that a few exiles or missionaries did force their way across the Naga hills, just as a few Phœnician merchantmen may have come to Cornwall to look for tin. But the descent of the Kings of Ava or Pagan from an Indian prince of the blood-royal is the invention of the court historian. There is, it may be mentioned, one argument against the probability of this legend of the migration of the royal Kshatriya tribes which has hitherto not been mentioned, and that is that there is no trace in Indian history of any such migration to Burma.

There are, however, in Burmese legends, as well as in the legends of the founding of Prome, probably some grains of truth with the usual admixture of falsehood. In stating that the first capital of the Burmese and their first settlement in Burma was at Tagaung, Burmese history is probably in accordance with the real history of the advent of the Burmese. The Burman Mahayazawin states that Tagaung was first founded, and that subsequently the kingdoms of Prome and Pagan were established. This agrees with the theory that the Burmese belong to the Tibeto-Burman race, and that they have moved south-eastward.

Abandoning these legends, we may take it for granted that the Burmese were an offshoot of the same ethnic race as the mountaineers of the Himalayas, and gradually spread themselves from valley to valley till they struck the sources of the Chindwin. They then came down the Chindwin and worked their way across to the Irrawaddy, which they struck near the ruins of their first capital, Tagaung. We have negative proof of this in the fact that north of Katha there is but a very slight admixture of pure Burmese blood to be found even in the riverine villages. The researches of later times have shown that it is very probable that these Burmese were neither Hindus nor Buddhists, but merely Nat-worshippers. The date of the introduction of Buddhism into Burma has already been fully discussed in Chapter III of this report. Hence, if any other argument were wanted to disprove the fanciful derivation of the word Burma from Brahma, which was formerly gravely asserted, we have not only a philological, but we have here a direct historical contradiction of this theory. The word မြမ္မာ (Myamma) is the vulgar way of writing မြန်မာ, and Bishop Bigandet has conclusively shown that this မြန်မာ or Myanma is derived from the word Mian, meaning man.

Under the head of Myanma or Burmese may be included the Arakanese, Tavoyers, Chaungtha, and Yaw, for, as Mr. Copleston says, "though similarity of "language is no sure proof of identity of race, there can yet be no doubt but that "these races belong to the same stock."

The essential facts of Burman history.

234. As the Burmese gradually worked their way down the valley of the Irrawaddy, it is most probable that they found no aborigines to oppose them till they met, and were probably driven back by, the Môns or Talaings whom they found settled in the delta of the river. On receiving this check, the unexpended energy of the immigrants found a fresh outlet in the conquest of Arakan, which quickly succumbed. The legendary account of the dragons slain in Arakan probably refers to the slaughter of the aboriginal tribes, and the fact that there is no record of monsters being slain till the Burmese reached Wettigan in the Prome district, where they first encountered the outlying villages of the Talaings, is negative proof in favour of the statement before made, that on their way down they encountered little or no opposition from aborigines. The history of the various kingdoms of Burma and their vicissitudes are already written at full length in Sir Arthur Phayre's History. The more or less true chronicles of Burma have already been carefully edited by him, and it is needless to touch on the fortunes of the various petty kingdoms and their perpetual internecine warfare. The only facts that stand out prominently are that the Burmese race split up into several

kingdoms—Pagan, Prome, Toungoo, and Arakan—and that, so long as this division continued, the progress of the race was checked. Consequently we find the Môns able to make headway against the Burmans, and even at times to take their capital. The other noticeable point is that the Burmans, notwithstanding their dissensions, still possessed enough energy to repel the hordes of what are called in Burmese history the Chinese invaders. The first irruption of these so-called Tarôks or Tarets was the invasion which culminated in the destruction of the Burmese kingdom of Tagaung. The date given in the Mahayazawin of this irruption is said to fall within the lifetime of Buddha. This date is of course uncertain, but the fact that the date is so fixed by the Burmese themselves shows that they had been long established in Burma before Buddhism arose in the person of Buddha, and hence that they could not have been Buddhists when they arrived in Burma, but must have been converted afterwards. This irruption is clearly proved to have been made, not by the Chinese, but by the Tai or Shans. The Shans by this invasion gained a footing in Burma. It was this Shan race that founded the Shan or Ahom kingdom of Assam. The date of this irruption of the Shans probably coincides with the return of Buddha Gôsha to Thatôn in the 4th century A.D., and it is possible that the chroniclers have mixed up the details of the life of the disciple with the great founder of their religion. The next invasion from the north-east was in the latter end of the 13th century, when the Emperor of China enforced his claim to receive homage and tribute from Burma by overrunning the country right up to the frontier of the Talaing kingdom. The effort exhausted the power of the invaders, and the Burmans once more drove them out. But the weakening of the Burmese power is proved by the fact that subsequently Shan kings reigned both in Ava and Sagaing. After a while the power of the Shans waned and the Burmese reasserted themselves. Meanwhile another invasion by the Chinese, it is said, was made in the beginning of the 15th century, but with no result. Again, in 1651, another invasion by the Chinese was decisively repulsed under the walls of Ava. These irruptions were all probably the work of Shan Tayôks or Tarôks and not made by regular Chinese troops. But in 1765-67, in the reign of Shenbyu Shin, third king in the Alaungpaya dynasty, the Chinese troops made four successive invasions, which were all finally repulsed.

Its temporary disintegration into petty kingdoms.

The repulse of foreign invaders.

The re-consolidation of the Burmese race under Alaungpaya.

The importance of the repulse of the Chinese invasions in the 18th century.

235. The tenacity with which the Burmese repelled each successive attack of the Shans prevented the spread of the Tai race over the lower valley of the Irrawaddy. These attacks, however, were probably the irruption of uncivilized hordes, and it is not remarkable that the more civilized Burmans beat them back. But the invasion by the Chinese in the last century is more worthy of notice, firstly, because it proves that the semi-civilized power of the Chinese had already begun to force its way south of the mountains of Yunnan, and secondly, because its result proved that Burmese unity and the spirit of national pride and patriotism created by the obscure dacoit Chief Alaungpaya had enabled a small kingdom to stop the advance of the Chinese to the shores of the Indian Ocean. But apart from these outside troubles, Burma was torn with perpetual warfare. Burman fought with Burman and Burman fought with Môn with varying success, till in 1740 the Môns got the upper hand, and the history of the Burmese races seemed to be at the point of extinction. It was when their fortunes were at their lowest ebb that the robber or dacoit Bo of Shwebo village raised a gathering of a few desperate men and surprised the Môn outpost, and, going on from success to success, soon found himself at the head of a force of fighting men ashore and a fleet of war boats on the Irrawaddy. Local traditions still relate how off Kyaukmyaung he met and signally defeated the Môn flotilla, and in a very short space of time he had completely turned the tables on the Talaing invaders. He followed up his victories by attacking and destroying Pegu, and, unlike previous conquerors, he not only destroyed, but he created, for he founded the town of Rangoon, and thus distinguished himself from the ruck of mere wanton conquerors. The effect of his conquests, and his undoubted courage, was to reawaken the spirit of Burmese unity and patriotism, and the most important and lasting result thereby

achieved was not the temporary grandeur and sudden expansion of the Burmese power over the Indo-Chinese peninsula, but the fact that his example nerved the Burmans to successfully resist the onward march of the Chinese. Had the Burmans succumbed in 1765 to the Chinese, the whole valley of the Irrawaddy and of the Mekong would have become part of the Chinese Empire and the inhabitants would rapidly have become Sinicized. The ultimate result, of course, would have been that Burma would not now belong to the British Empire. It is needless to trace the course of Burmese history beyond the final repulse of the Chinese in 1767. Nor is it, fortunately, necessary to expatiate on the Burmese character: Lieutenant-General Horace Browne, Shwe Yeo (Mr. Scott), and Captain Forbes have rendered such a task unnecessary. There is, however, one point in the national character which the census returns have illustrated, and which, perhaps, is not so fully noticed as it deserves, and that is, the faculty which the Burman, like the Celtic races of Europe, possesses to a high degree—the faculty of assimilating and absorbing the lesser tribes and nationalities with which they are brought into contact. This faculty the Irish and French possess and the Burman possesses it also. This will explain the gradual disappearance of the Talaings, Yabeins, Kadus, Danaws, and Danus into the main body of the Burmese race.

236. This reintegrating force is going on amongst the Burmans and is undoing the evil of the disintegration and disunion which is so prevalent in hill tribes, to which category the Burmans at one time belonged. This power of assimilation is well worthy of attention. So long as the Burmese nation possesses vitality and clings to its religion, it may be expected to falsify the prediction which is gaining ground, that in time the race will disappear. Between the Europeanizing force of the British rulers on the one hand, and the admixture of foreign Chinese and Indian blood on the other, it is generally believed that the Burmese race will become gradually extinguished. Rangoon, it is said, is no longer a Burmese town, and in time the country as well as the town will become Indianized. These fears, though there may be some ground for them, greatly exaggerate the danger. The Burmese race is absorbing the wild hill tribes, and even some of the Indian settlers themselves become Burmanized. By settlers, men who merely come to earn money and then return to their own country are not meant—their influence is little felt and they are not affected in their turn. The natives of India who settle down in the country, and not in the towns, gradually give up their Indian and adopt Burmese customs and Burmese names. It is true that in Rangoon and the large towns the secret influence of caste and religion keeps the Indian settler from becoming Burmanized, and amongst the wealthy and better educated the influence of the higher European civilization tends to correct this subtle Burmanizing influence. But in the rural tracts the isolated Indian settler loses touch of his brotherhood, and those who know the districts will readily admit that the casual native of India often becomes in dress and language a Burman. The Chinaman, proud of his superiority to the Burman, invariably preserves his national dress and customs. If he marries a Burmese woman, his sons become Chinamen, his daughters remain Burmans. With all its faults, the Burmese character is in many respects much to be admired. Notwithstanding the fact that Burma has now become an integral part of the British Empire—indeed, perhaps, because the whole Burmese race is now included in the roll of nations under the British flag—let us hope the Burmese race will preserve its identity and its distinctive national characteristics.

The figures of the census of 1891 show that the proportion of Burmans to the rest of the population of Lower Burma is as 18·8 is to 10. In 1872 the proportion was greater, being as 23·6 is to 10. The difference, as has already been shown, is due partly to better enumeration of the Karens and partly to the influx of foreign immigrants.

The main divisions of the Burmese race are the Arakanese, Tavoyers, Yaws, Chaungthas, and Pyus. Besides these there are the Burmanized Yabeins, Danaws, Danus, Taungyo and Talaings, most of whom are now hardly distinguishable from the ordinary Burmese.

The Arakanese.

237. The Arakanese are not all of pure Burmese race. They are the descendants of the Burmese invaders who conquered Arakan soon after the arrival of the main body in the valley of

the Irrawaddy. They include under the term Arakanese many who style themselves as such, though not of pure Burmese stock. Mr. Chan Toon has kindly, from time to time, favoured me with his views on the Arakanese. Mr. Chan Toon is himself of pure Arakanese descent, and takes great interest in the matter. He is himself as yet undecided as to the origin of the Arakanese race, but he has collected the views of some of the ablest Arakanese and has placed them at my disposal. There are three theories advanced: the first, which Maung Saw Hla Pru has put forward, agrees with the view of Sir Arthur Phayre, that the Burmans are descended from the Kshatriya tribe of India; that they founded Tagaung and then crossed the Yomas and conquered Arakan; the second is put forward by Maung San Hla Baw, Extra Assistant Commissioner, who believes that the main body of the Arakanese came from India, but mentions the legend of the irruption of a Tibetan horde into the valley of the Irrawaddy, and that these invaders crossed the Yoma and founded their capital at Kyaukpadaung long before the era of Gaudama. The third theory, of Maung Mra U, Extra Assistant Commissioner of Akyab, is the one that finds most favour with the elders of Arakan. It is that the Arakanese derive their name of Mughs from the fact that they came from Magadha and are descendants of the Kshatriya princes who came straight to Arakan without first going to Tagaung.

All these theories are founded on national Arakan legends and must therefore be received with a due amount of caution. The fact that the Arakanese language belongs to the Tibeto-Burman family, and that the Arakanese still preserve in their physique and features, as well as in their customs, traces of the similarity to the original stock, proves that they are descended from a common source. As regards the term Mugh, since the Arakanese do not know themselves by this name and have never adopted it, there is no need to attempt to deduce their descent from the Magadha princes through a name which is unknown to them. Mr. Chan Toon thinks that the name Mugh and the admixture of Bengali or Indian blood may be due to the fact that a large body of Arakanese about 200 years ago established themselves for a time in the districts of the Gangetic delta, where they settled down temporarily, and where their descendants may still be found. After some time the Arakanese power was broken and large numbers of these Arakanese returned to Arakan. While in Bengal they were called Mughs by the Bengalis, and by this name they are still known by the Bengalis. In a very short space of time this migration has probably become mixed up with the mythical migration of the Kshatriya princes. The origin of the word Arakan is given by Sir Arthur Phayre. He states that it is derived from Rekkaik, a corruption of the Pali word Yekkha, a demon, and Arakan therefore means the "Land of demons." This agrees with the derivation given by Maung San Hla Baw, who says that amongst the Bengalis Arakan was formerly known as "Rubehapori," the town or country of Rubehas or demons.

This derivation is probably a fanciful one, and the name Arakan is probably a corruption of the aboriginal name of the country. Much more important than mythical history, and the more or less correct derivation of their name, is the character of the Arakanese people. In some respects they resemble the Burmans, but they have not the same fascinating character that has attracted the sympathy and admiration of all who of recent years have written about Burma. The Arakanese, it is said, approximate more closely to Hindu and Musalman customs in secluding their women. They are cleverer and more persevering than the Burmese generally. They are less fond of extravagant show. In the opinion of some the Arakanese are a decaying race, but this opinion is strongly combated by others, who believe that the Arakan branch will outlive the Burman.

Tavoyer.

238. The Tavoyers are nothing but an offshoot of the Arakanese branch of the Burmese stock. They have become isolated by being cut off from their parent stem, and have developed provincialisms in their dialect; but in their customs and dress they are still purely Burmese. Strange to say, few Tavoyers are shown in the Tavoy district. This anomaly is simply due to the fact that the Tavoyer declines to call himself anything but a Burman, and it is only out of Tavoy that he is returned as a Tavoyer by the enumerator, who is not himself a Tavoyer. We find that the same peculiarity is traceable in English surnames: English or Inglis is not an uncom-

mon surname in Scotland, and French or Ffrench is a fairly common name in Ireland. The improvement in communications since the conquest of Burma by the British is rapidly undoing the work of centuries of segregation. The Tavoyers who were returned as speaking Tavoy in 1881 were 1,343. There were only 972 who returned Tavoy as their parent-tongue in 1891, and of these but 744 would admit they were Tavoyers by birth.

Kudo.

239. The Kudos or Kadus are believed to be Burmese and Shan half-breeds. They certainly abound in those places where the Shan invaders have entered on Burmese territory, but Mr. Houghton, as I have already noted in Chapter VIII, is against this classification. He classifies them under the Kachin-Naga group as a separate tribe. I am inclined to believe that Mr. Houghton is right. Nothing certain, however, is known of their origin and history, and it will require a keen student of ethnography to ascertain their right position amongst the tribes of Burma, as it would appear that they have adopted many of the customs and part of the language of their Shan and Burmese neighbours. If the theory of their Shan descent be true, it will be found that they are probably one of the broken Shan tribes who invaded Upper Burma, and who crossed the Irrawaddy and founded the Shan dynasty of which Sagaing was the capital.

Yaw.

240. Dr. Mason classes the Yaws as a Burmese tribe. In this he is followed by Dr. Cushing. Mr. Houghton is inclined to doubt the accuracy of this classification. It is probable that the Yaws are one of "the broken" tribes belonging to the Tibeto-Burman race that are being gradually absorbed by the Burmans. They are described by Yule as a tribe of hucksters and pedlars. These are the civilized Yaws. The rude uncivilized Yaws live in the Yaw valley subdivision of the Pakôkku district. How far the Yaw legend is true that they are descended from the Palaungs, or, as they call the tribe themselves, Parawga or Payaorga (Mason), is uncertain. The derivation of the name Yaw has been already noted. They are scarcely a pure-bred race now. Our tables show that of Yaws of unmixed blood there were but 370 who returned themselves as such in the province. These all returned themselves as Buddhists. There were but 65 of them in Lower Burma as against 41 in 1881 and 9 in 1872. It is noticeable that the Yaws of Pakôkku, like the Tavoyers, have called themselves Burmans, and it is only the wandering Yaws found among the Burmans who were returned as Yaws by the Burmese enumerator, just as, no doubt, the Samaritans would have returned themselves as Israelites.

Yabeins.

241. Of Yabeins there were but 2,197, all of whom were found in Lower Burma. Mr. Wilson, Deputy Commissioner of the Shwegyin district, states that their name was originally (စဘိန်) Sabein, and that this name was softened into Yabein or Yebein as Dr. Mason calls them. Mr. Wilson is inclined to believe that the Yabeins are not a distinct race. Only 436 persons were returned in 1881 as talking Yabein, but the language has now entirely disappeared from our census schedules. Indeed, as has already been noticed, Mr. Copleston foretold its complete extinction. He is inclined to believe that there is some truth in the apparently fanciful story of the origin of this tribe, that certain people took to the rearing of silkworms and thus incurred, through the destruction of the silkworm chrysalises, in the eyes of their more orthodox Buddhist neighbours, not only a danger of future punishment after death, but contempt and dislike in their present life. But the pecuniary reward of their toil outweighed other considerations, and they gradually disassociated themselves from the other villagers and founded villages of their own, where they could pursue their calling in peace. Gradually they came to differ in language and customs, and were treated as an outcast race by the Burmans. That races disintegrate into tribes is of course a well known fact, and Captain Forbes' discovery of different numerals may prove nothing more than that the Yabeins have partially retained an archaic system of numeration given up by their more civilized kindred races. Inquiries into the languages of the Malay peninsula have shown that a change in the names of numerals is not uncommon, and that a tribe will, when brought in contact with more civilized races, abandon its own system if the newer system be palpably more easily managed. Even in English

we still count by scores as well as by tens. It may have been that the Yabein tribe was only founded when the introduction of Buddhism gave the silk-worm rearers a choice between losing their livelihood or the respect of the orthodox. Silkworm-rearing is carried on in out-of-the-way villages, and is the work of women as well as of men; hence the argument that hunters and fishermen, who follow equally reprehensible callings, have not become a separate race, is not a certain proof that the Burmese and Yabein legend is untrue. Soldiers as well as hunters and fishermen should have become outcasts, but they have held their place. In their case the fact that hunting is often the sport of the Burmese official, and not a profession merely, and the natural love of sport implanted in the Burmans, may have prevented the separation of hunters and fishermen into separate communities. The real reason, however, probably is that hunters and fishermen were too powerful a community to be lightly treated with disrespect. Of course it is possible that the Yabeins are the relics of "a broken clan," but I have not cast aside as utterly vain the account of the origin of this race given by Burmans and Yabeins without discussing the possibility of its being true.

Chaungthas.

242. There are but 3,492 Chaungthas, and all of them live in the Akyab district or Northern Arakan Hill Tracts. Mr. Copleston has given a possible, but not probable, account of their origin. Far more probable is it that they have disassociated themselves from some Chin hill tribe, and, becoming more civilized, have adopted the language and dress of their neighbours, the Arakanese. In 1872 there were 9,634 Chaungthas, so that the race is dying out as a separate one. This process of Burmanizing has been noticed by Sir William Hunter.

Danus and Danaws.

243. Of Danus there were but 547 found in Burma, while no return is made of Danaws. Dr. Cushing is inclined to believe that the Danus are a hybrid race. They talk Burmese, but their dialect is not pure Burmese. They wear the Kachin tunic. They are by some said to be branches of the same clan, but Mr. Hildebrand, C.I.E., Superintendent of the Southern Shan States, divides the Danus from the Danaws. The former, he states, are a Burmese colony who emigrated from Burma some hundreds of years ago. The Danaws, however, were quite a distinct tribe. The Danaw language resembles Taungthu, and they dress like the Taungthus, but in customs and religion they resemble the Danus.

Chins.

244. The term Chin is used in two senses. It is sometimes wrongfully confined to some particular tribes of the Chin family, and sometimes to the group of tribes which the Burmans designate by the name of Chin. The Chins or Khyins are a group of hill tribes, all talking various dialects of the same Tibeto-Burman speech, and calling themselves by various names. All of these tribes are known to the Burmans by the generic name of Chins. Hence to apply this Burmese name to one tribe only is manifestly wrong. The derivation of the name Chin is unknown; it is probably the corruption of some Burmese equivalent of some Chin name. The Chins call themselves Asho. De la Couperie identifies them with the Hui or Shu tribes that formerly lived near the Tunglung lake between the Yangtze and Han rivers, who were driven southward by the Taru tribe in the 11th century B.C. But the affinity of their language to the Kuki dialects on the one hand, and their kinship to the Burmese on the other, is strongly against de la Couperie's theory, for which indeed he advances insufficient proof.

There are several clans or dzos amongst the Chins. The following list does not pretend to be exhaustive. It is merely based on the returns made in the schedules. The chief tribes are—

(1) The Kwemis or Kamis.
(2) The Saks or Thets.
(3) The Mros.
(4) The Kuns.
(5) The Siyins.
(6) The Hakkas or The Baungshès divided into the—
 a. Welaungs.
 b. Chinbôks.
(7) The Chinbôns.
(8) The Yindus.
(9) The Lagats.
(10) The Yonans.
(11) The Khaings.
(12) The Kunsaw Pus.
(13) The Pusaws.
(14) The Lusaws.
(15) The Pos.
(16) The Hlwasaws.
(17) The Yebôns.

Mr. Houghton and Lieutenant Macnabb are doing valuable work in preparing handbooks of the various dialects of the Chin group of languages. Till all the various dialects are thoroughly examined, it will be impossible to assert what is the relative position they hold one to the other. It is probable that the last nine clans are mere subdivisions of one tribe, and that the process of disintegration is still going on.

An interesting account of the Chins and their customs is to be found in the *Gazetteer of the Thayetmyo District* by Major (now Lieutenant-General) Horace Browne. The quaint Chin customs to which Sir W. Hunter alludes are now embodied in the Chin Dammathat edited by Maung Tet Pyo. A most interesting account of the Southern Chins has been written by Mr. Houghton and has lately been published, and it will therefore be unnecessary to reproduce here what Mr. Houghton says.

Taungthas or Kukis.

245. Following the classification recommended by Dr. Cushing, I have shown the Taungthas or Kukis as being of a separate and distinct branch of the Tibeto-Burman family. Respect for Dr. Cushing's opinion has led me to adopt this classification. The Taungthas, as they are known by the Burmans, or the Kukis as they are sometimes called, belong to the same race as the Chins and Nagas, and are the connecting link between them. Indeed, after studying the vocabulary of the Kuki language published by Captain Lewin, I am inclined to think that the Kukis, with their subdivisions the Shandus and Kyaws, are equally with the Chin tribes but one branch of the Tibeto-Burman family. The Burmese know all of these tribes—the Kyaws, Shandus, Mros, Kamis—by the generic name of Chin, and I am inclined to believe that the Burmese classification, founded on their knowledge of these tribes, with whom after all they are akin, is probably correct.

Kachins.

246. The name Kachin, by which the tribes on our northern borders are known, is not the name by which they call themselves. Their proper name is Chingpaw, corrupted into the better known form of Singpho. Yule states that they call themselves Kakus. They are found on the borders of Assam, Yunnan, and Burma. Their language, of which but little is known at present, is believed to belong to the Tibeto-Burman stock, but it is said to contain an admixture of Karen vocables. Dr. Anderson, who wrote the account of the Mission to Yunnan in 1868, Colonel Sladen in his Note on the Trade through Burma and China (Glasgow, 1870), Colonel (now Lieutenant-General) Horace Browne in his report on the Mission to Yunnan, 1874-75 (Eyre and Spottiswood, 1876), and Mr. Strettell in his account of his wanderings in search of the *Ficus elastica* (Rangoon, Government Press, 1876), have all mentioned the Kakhyens, as they term them. But it was not till after the annexation of Upper Burma that our officers were brought into close contact with these mountaineers.

Mr. E. C. S. George, C.S., the Officiating Deputy Commissioner of Bhamo, has favoured me with an exceedingly interesting monograph on these Kachin tribes, and as it contains much that is entirely new, and as it is by far the fullest and most scientific account of these mountaineers, I have reproduced it *in extenso* in Appendix **A** of this report which deals with the enumeration of those living in the excluded tracts. As but few Kachins live within the area comprised in the regular census tract, I have reserved this monograph for the appendix to which it belongs.

Dr. Mason mentions the account given by Captain Hannay and Mr. Kincaid. The latter was the first to identify the Kachins with the Singphos.

Dr. Anderson has written on these Kachins, but his experience of them was limited to the short time the embassies he was engaged on were passing through their country. Mr. George has had the advantage of Dr. Anderson's work as a basis, and his experience of them as Deputy Commissioner has given him opportunities such as Dr. Anderson never possessed.

Shans.

247. The Shans, or, as they call themselves, the Htai or Freemen, fall into three groups politically as well as linguistically. The three linguistic divisions have already been noted in

Chapter VIII, and the political divisions to a great extent coincide with this linguistic division. These three political divisions are (1) the Chinese or Northern Shans, (2) the Intermediate Shans, who fell under the sway of the Burmans, and now of the British, who have succeeded to the heritage of Alaungpaya, and (3) the Siamese Shans or Southern Branch. It may not be generally known that the form Siam is nothing but a corruption of the French method of writing Shan or "Sciam." In adopting the French method of spelling the word, we mispronounce the name because we make two syllables of the word. This mispronunciation, however, has become generally accepted, and to call the Shans of Bangkok anything but Siamese would be needlessly misleading as well as pedantic. Moreover, the difference in the name is now useful, as it marks off the southern branch of the Tai or Htai race. It will not be necessary here to reproduce anything that has been already published about this interesting people. The part of the monograph on the Tai Shans by Dr. Cushing that relates to their language has already been reproduced in Chapter VIII, and the remainder, relating to their history and ethnography, is now published for the first time. Dr. Cushing is so well known as the authority on the Shan race that any criticism or addition to his note on my part would be unnecessary. The grouping of the Tai Shan languages and the classification of the races will be found in Chapter VIII and it will be unnecessary to reproduce them here.

Original seat.

South-Western China was the original home of the Tai people, or, rather, was the region where they attained to a marked separate development as a people. There are many indications that they had anciently a close connection with the Chinese before settling in Setchuan and the country south of the Yangtsekiang river. Dim traditions of such a connection still exist among them. From Chinese history it appears that until about B.C. 250 the Chinese rule had not extended itself permanently south of the Yangtsekiang river, and the Chinese kingdom had not that compact character which we have been accustomed to attribute to it. From that time, however, the empire began to solidify by the decay of feudalism and grow by slow advances of conquest, during which, notwithstanding occasional reverses, it made tributary many non-Chinese princelings, who bore the Tai title of Chaw or Saw (pronounced like *ow* in how). These Chiefs, with their people, were undoubtedly of the Tai race. The title of Chaw or Saw is still universally retained as the title of a prince by all the divisions of the Tai family. It is certain, however, that centuries elapsed before all Yunnan yielded to Chinese rule. As early as the first half of the 7th century of the Christian era, we find the strong Tai State of Nanchao existing in Western Yunnan, which long maintained itself as the kingdom of Tali until its final conquest by Kublai Khan in the 13th century. Probably the pressure of the Chinese advance southward was the principal cause of the gradual growth and consolidation of this Tai kingdom. For a long time before it comes to our notice historically, Burman history tells us of two great military expeditions from Yunnan into Burma by *Taróks*, one not long before the Christian era and the other about A.D. 241. These could not have been the Chinese, for the Chinese did not have any connection with the Burmans until after the conquest of Yunnan by Kublai Khan in A.D. 1253. These Tarôks must have been of the Tai race, who were at the time the predominant people in Yunnan, and their invasions of Burma seem to indicate the presence at those early dates of a strong Tai kingdom or kingdoms in Yunnan, whence they were sent. More than this, the great homogeneity of the different divisions can be accounted for only by the existence of one or more strong Tai States in South-Western China for a considerable time before the first historical notice of Nanchao. Of that State or those States Nanchao, by its peculiar situation, was probably the only part to maintain its independence. Only by the early existence of such a State or States could the remarkable unification of the Tai people have taken place, as it must have done before the migration of the present divisions began. The existence of the Tai kingdom of Nanchao in the 7th century is a fact of too late a date to account for the striking homogeneity of the Tai peoples, which has so wonderfully withstood centuries of separation and the strong influences of alien races and diverse political connections. It should also be noted that the Pai'y and some other tribes in the south and west of Yunnan are undoubtedly the remnants of the Tai people stranded on the borders of the ancient home of their race. Their language and customs bear indubitable proof of their descent.

All these indications point to South-Western China not only as the home of the Tai race, but as the region in which the various tribes of which they doubtless consisted originally, were welded together into a united and essentially homogeneous body. They also suggest the existence of powerful political organizations as the natural condition under whose influence the unifying process would take place. How far that political organization was spontaneous and natural, or grew out of the necessity of resistance to the known pressure of the Chinese from the north by making union for common defence a necessity, is a matter of conjecture.

Migrations.

The migrations of the Tai into Burma probably began about 2,000 years ago, although Shan and Burman tradition place the time several centuries earlier. At first they may have been small in number of persons, due partly to that restlessness of nature which has always characterized the Tai and led to frequent change of residence, and partly to the military expeditions from Yunnan, of which we have an instance in the destruction of ancient Tagaung. Later, larger and more important migrations were due to the pressure of Chinese invasion and conquest, by which the Tai of Eastern and Southern Yunnan were driven westward and southward.

Shan legend says that in the middle of the 6th century of our era, two brothers descended from heaven and took up their abode in the valley of the Shweli, where they found a race which at once acknowledged their sway. This is probably the mythological statement of what is a historical fact. A great wave of Tai migration descended in the 6th century of the Christian era from the mountains of Southern Yunnan into the Shweli valley and the adjacent regions, and through it that valley became the centre of Shan political power. Tradition with little variation asserts that the Shweli valley is the first home of the Shans in Upper Burma. It is not improbable that this wave of migration followed the path already traversed by earlier Tai colonists, who had sought a home in that region, but had attained no political importance. From the Shweli valley the Shans spread south-east into Theinni and the adjacent principalities, north into the present Khamti region, and west of the Irrawaddy river into all the region between that river, the Khyindwin river and Assam, centuries later overrunning and conquering Assam itself. Not only does tradition assert that these Shans of Upper Burma are the oldest branch of the Tai family, but they are always spoken of by other branches as the Tai Long or Great Tai, while the other branches call themselves Tai Noi or Little Tai. It is time that the Siamese call themselves Htai Noi or Little Htai, and the Laos, from whom they say that they sprang, Htai Nyai (the equivalent of Tai Long) Great Htai. But the Laos in turn call themselves Tai Noi and acknowledge the Northern Shans of Burma to be the Tai Long. The Chinese-Shans who occupy the principal highway pursued by Shan migration into Burma, share in the name Tai Long. The appellation of Tai Long may also be due in part to the fact that the earliest strong political centre was established by the northern branch of the family. The term forms a very strong recognition of the precedence of that branch in age and power.

In due time other branches moved southward from Yunnan, joining the Laos, Lau, and Siamese peoples. It was not until into the 14th century that the Siamese pressed down into the great delta of the Menam between Cambodia and the Môn country. This latest movement was most likely the more or less direct result of the conquest of the Shan kingdom of Tali by Kublai Khan in A.D. 1253, by which large numbers of the inhabitants, unwilling to submit to Chinese rule, gradually moved southward and formed the present Siamese monarchy.

History.

The early history of the Shans in Burma is very obscure. There is little doubt that a powerful Shan kingdom called Möng Maw grew up in the north, with its capital at Möng Maw Lông on the Shweli river. The Indian classical name was Kosambi, corrupted in later times to Koshanpyi. The silence of Burman history with reference to their kingdom seems strange. In the Manipur chronicles it is referred to as the kingdom of Pong. Shan history indicates that this kingdom began in the 7th century of our era, and maintained itself with varying degrees of prosperity until the rise of Anawratta, the King of Pagan. During this period one dynasty above that of Kham-sip-hpa held power for 322 years. New kings sometimes chose new sites for capitals, but always in the Shweli valley. Anawratta restored the power of the Burman monarchy and gained ascendency in much of the territory over which the Shans held sway. On his return from his military expedition to Yunnan, he married a daughter of the king of Möng Maw. The chronicles of Möng Maw, according to Ney Elias, say that that sovereign "gave his daughter to the Pagan monarch, though it is "also stated that he never went to the Pagan court, as a true vassal must have done." But whether he became a real vassal of Anawratta or not, after Anawratta's reign came to an end in A.D. 1052, the Möng Maw princes were left in independence until A.D. 1210, when, on the death of the reigning sovereign, a prince of a collateral branch of the royal house came to the throne. This prince had two sons, San Khan Hpa, who came to the throne, and the distinguished Sam Lông Hpa, who evinced decided military genius in his extensive conquests. In A.D. 1220, five years before San Khan Hpa ascended the throne, Sam Lông Hpa became the Sawbwa of Mogaung, where he built a new city and established a new line of powerful princes tributary to Möng Maw. The four military campaigns which he undertook were remarkably successful and the dominion of the Möng Maw Government was extended over an area of territory greater than at any other time in its history. He caused the suzerainty of the Möng Maw king to be acknowledged as far as Moulmein and Kainghung on the east. He extended the Maw dominions westward by overrunning Arakan and destroying its capital and by invading Manipur. Assam was subjugated by him in A.D. 1229 and passed under the rule of the Shans, who were henceforth styled Ahone in that country. It is claimed that even the Tai kingdom of Tali acknowledged allegiance to the Maw king before its fall under the conquering hand of Kublai Khan in A.D. 1253, but the relation of Tali may have been rather one of alliance than subordination. For nearly thirty years after the conquest of Yunnan by the Mongol-Chinese army, the Chinese hovered on the frontier. In A.D. 1284 a Mongol-Chinese army swept down to Pagan and overthrew the Burman monarchy. This expedition does not seem to have seriously injured the Maw kingdom. It could hardly have passed through without doing so if the Maw sovereign were hostile, and the presumption is that there was more or less agreement of feeling if not political alliance. A new capital called Möng Maw was established in A. D. 1285 near the site of the present town of Bhamo. This last recorded change of capital occurring just at this time may have had some unexplained connection with the invasion. The weakening of the Burman power was favourable to the prosperity of the Maw kingdom, and it is claimed that the Maw territories were increased by the conquest of the Menam valley to Ayuthia and of the Yunsalen and Tavoy. It is probable that there is much exaggeration in the historical statements of the extent of the Maw dominions, and that the distant members of the kingdom were tributary States rather than integral parts of the realm.

The fall of the Pagan-Burman dynasty gave an opportunity for Shan men, who had already risen to distinction and power in the Burman kingdom by royal favour, to gratify their ambition; they seized the government and established the Shan dynasty, which for a while ruled over a part of the old Burman territory independently of the Maw kings.

The prosperity of the Maw kingdom began to wane soon after it had attained its greatest area of territory. From the 14th to the 16th centuries there was a gradual decadence. The Siamese and Laos dependencies became a separate kingdom under the head of Siam. Wars with Burma and China were frequent. The invasions of the Chinese were a cause of great loss. On one occasion the capital was burned and the king, San Ngam Hpa (A.D. 1445), fled to Ava, where he took poison and died, a fact mentioned by Burman historians. The Chinese continued their attacks, evidently from a determination to assert the right of suzerainty over the Northern Shans. Constant wars weakened the central power, and the various principalities, among which Mogaung was the most powerful, gained a semi-independence. It is alleged that San Hum Hpa, the last Maw king, reigned 88 years, dying A.D. 1604, and that his kingdom attained a prosperity never before realized. Such a prosperity was impossible, for Bureng Naung, the ambitious and successful King of Pegu, brought that prince under his victorious sway as a vassal in A.D. 1562. Subsequently there were Chinese invasions in A.D. 1582 and in A.D. 1604, when the royal line of the Möng Maw ended. Although Mogaung maintained a semi-independence until its final conquest by Alaungpaya a century and-a-half later, from A.D. 1604 Shan history merges in Burmese history, and the Shan principalities, although always restive under Burmese rule and given to frequent rebellions and intestine wars, never threw off the yoke of the Burmans, and passed, as a part of King Thebaw's kingdom, under the control of the English Crown.

One of the most interesting but not altogether trustworthy narratives of Shan history is that of a Shan manuscript which Captain Pemberton obtained and had translated during his mission to Manipur in 1835. This manuscript was given by him to the Rev. Natham Brown, D.D., of the Baptist Mission, in the same year and apparently has been lost. The kingdom was known to the Manipuris as the kingdom of Pong. This name is foreign to the Shans, but is most probably derived from *hpong*, which in Burmese signifies "glory," and was doubtless used by the Shans as an honorific title in describing their kingdom.

Chinese affinities.

The Chinese affinities of the Shans show themselves in their physical characteristics and language. Time will prove, I think, that these affinities are not the result of mere accidental neighbourhood and intercourse in former centuries, but are due to a more ancient and closer race relationship, by which both the Tai and Chinese belong to a family of which the Chinese is the representative branch. The Shans have a Chinese type of face, which is perhaps more marked in the various divisions of Shans tributary to Burma and China than in the Laos and Siamese. The complexion is light and the eyes are almond-shaped.

True race descent and transmission of language are not always correllative, but there are marked resemblances between the Tai speech and that of the Chinese. There is space for only a few illustrations. In Edkin's *Chinese Characters,* among some lists of Chinese words in which their ancient and modern forms are compared, I found fifteen words in their ancient form identical with Shan words. M. de la Couperie in *Languages of China before the Chinese,* in stating "the equivalents of most frequent occurrence between the Taïc languages and the Mandarin or standard Chinese," says that "the proportion of their respective loan words reaches a total of 325 out of one thousand words which I have compared." A comparison of Chinese and Shan numerals shows the close similarity of six out of ten. The Tai languages are noted for their couplets or words of related meanings used together. They have also phonetic couplets in which one word has an inherent meaning and the other word seems to be a shadow word used for the sake of euphony. These shadow words are probably words emptied of their ancient signification, for some of them are found to be in use in Chinese dialects, where they have the same meaning as the substantial word in the Shan phonetic couplet. Thus *ka* in Shan means "to be shiny" and the phonetic couplet is *ka, ki, ki,* having no meaning apparently, whereas in Chinese *ki* has the meaning "to be shiny." The grammatical structure of sentences in Shan is very different from the Tibeto-Burman family, but quite the same as in Chinese. Thus the place of the object of the verb and of the possessive are identical with the Chinese. The elaborate tonal system, so similar to the Chinese, by which the language abounds in homonyms, although not necessarily a proof of relationship to Chinese, is a strong presumptive proof. The time is not far distant, it is to be hoped, when thorough scientific philological research will throw full light on the relation of the Tai and Chinese.

Decadence of the race in Burma.

The Shans occupy no longer that prominence in area of territory, political power or population, which they formerly did. The Kachins have pressed south-eastward and driven them from much of the country between Burma Proper and China as far south as Northern Theinni. Shan names of mountains and villages are the only remaining witnesses of former occupation. Intestine war, Burman aggression and rapacity have reduced many principalities to utter insignificance. The once powerful principalities west of the Salween possess only a meagre and much Burmanized population, while the border principalities east of the Irrawaddy river from Thônzè to Nyaungywè have suffered in the same way from the deliberate policy of the Burman kings. Theinni with its 48 districts, once a powerful princedom embracing a far larger area than any other Shan State, has been broken into several small principalities, and large parts of it depopulated by the convulsions of the last 50 years. It is doubtful whether the Shan principalities will recover under English suzerainty the prosperity of the older time as long as the princes are left to control the taxation and other internal matters without any special supervision and direction of the English Government. Large numbers of Shans emigrated to Lower Burma while the upper country was still under Burman rule, but the emigration still continues under the English rule on account of the exorbitant taxation by the Sawbwas.

Race qualities.

The Shans are a thrifty people. Being the inhabitants of a mountainous region, the necessaries of life are not so easily obtained as in the fertile deltas of the Irrawaddy and Menam. They are good agriculturists, but excel in trading, by which they supply themselves with food and merchandise not obtainable in their own country. The houses of the better class exhibit a cleanliness and comfort not found among Burmans of the same rank. They have much independence of character, but are given to jealousies and personal dislikes which have kept them divided politically and socially. In warfare they are often cruel and vindictive, not only seeking to put to the sword all men of a hostile region, but often slaughtering the male children which fall into their hands. In time of peace they are cheerful, hospitable, and ready to render help to one another. An innate restlessness gives rise to frequent change of residence in the Shan country itself, so that often a good percentage of the population in a principality is not native born to that principality. This would doubtless cease to a considerable degree under the peaceful rule of a wise government which secured to the people a reasonable taxation and security in the possession and enjoyment of property.

Introduction of Buddhism.

It is uncertain when Buddhism was introduced among the Shans of Burma. The current legends in regard to it are manifestly untrustworthy. Probably a long time elapsed after its introduction into Thatôn by Buddha Gôsha, about A.D. 400, before it reached the Shans in the north. If the Buddhist religion at the time of Anawratta's succession to the throne of Pagan was so corrupt in doctrine and lax in practice in his kingdom, it was probably in an equally bad, if not worse, condition in the still more northern kingdom. Naga or dragon worship was mixed up with Buddhism in the Pagan kingdom and followed extensively. Ancient spirit-worship also, which continues to the present time, had a strong hold on the people. Anawratta became a zealous religious reformer, and, as he married into the Maw royal family, doubtless he made his religious influence felt in that direction. But Buddhism must have remained more or less corrupt and inert, for in A.D. 1562 Bureng Naung, as an ardent defender of the faith, introduced extensive religious reforms among the Shans in his northern conquests. It is a fact that when Burman influence among the Shans has been greatest, Buddhism has its strongest hold on them. The Buddhism of the principalities west of the Salween present no such laxity of practice on the part of the pôngyis as it does east of the Salween.

The Ahoms or Assamese.

248. The Ahoms or Ahams of Assam are a branch of the Taic-Shan race; their language is now extinct and they have lost much of the national characteristics of the Shans; they numbered 179,283 souls according to the Census Report of Assam in 1881. They were at one time the dominant race in the upper valley of the Brahmaputra. From 1228, the date of their conquest, till 1654, when they were converted to Hindusim, the Aham kings, in exchange for a fictitious genealogy, surrendered their Shan names. Their name still survives in the name of the province Assam, but Sir William Hunter, from whose Gazetteer as well as from the Assam Census Report, the above account of the Ahams has been taken, doubts the truth of this derivation. A colony of these Ahoms or Assamese is settled in the Koywa circle near Mogaung. A note on the Ahoms, written by Mr. Symington and sent to me by Mr. George, is herewith attached. The extract is exceedingly interesting, as it gives an account of the manner in which members of a Shan race that had become Hinduized have reverted unconsciously, by change of environment, back to their original religion and customs. It would appear from the note that Mr. Symington was not aware, or, if he is aware, is not a believer in the Shan descent of the Ahoms, and this fact makes his testimony the more remarkable :—

When Podaw Shwebo Min (Bodau Paya) ruled in Burma, Sindaraw Kan (Chandra Kanta) was King in Assam. Sindaraw Kan's prime minister was one Mingyi Baragohai (Boora Gohain), but he was unable to agree with one of the members of council known as the Malauk Wun (Bor Phokan). In a quarrel that occurred the Malauk Wun was worsted, and, to revenge himself, went to Bengal to try and raise an army. Failing in this, he presented himself at the Burmese Court and persuaded Shwebo to send an army against Assam. This was commanded by Maha Bandula. The army marched north to Mogaung, and thence followed the Mankông chaung, and passing through the amber mines, eventually entered Assam at Rongpu town. Sindaraw Kan, on being attacked, immediately fled to the British for protection.

The Burmese then placed one Jaris Singh on the throne of Assam thus precipitately vacated. However, Jaris Singh's mother, accompanied by her daughter and two sons, returned with the victorious army to Burma. The daughter was given in marriage to the Burmese King, who conferred on her the name and title of Bhamo Mepara (Mipaya). The elder of the two sons, Tabaungyasa, was appointed Sawbwa of Mogaung as his headquarters. He brought over 500 Assamese sepoys with their families and quartered them in Mogaung. They had barracks at the south of the Shwe-in quarter. There seems to have been no appointment for Mawlu Min, the younger son. When Tabaungyasa had been Sawbwa for three years, he decided to join his sister Bhamo Mepara at the palace, and on arrival there was granted the title of Mintha.

But when Tabaungyasa left Mogaung, the Assamese sepoys, finding their pay not forthcoming and no one to look after them, began to build villages and cultivate for themselves. When they first came from Assam they rigorously observed the rites of their caste, but from continually and freely mixing with the Shans, they seem to have gradually dropped all their caste prejudices, and only a few now adhere religiously to their caste and follow the Brahman religion, although they have all adopted Burmese customs and can only be recognized by their Assamese features.

At present there are around Mogaung the following Assamese villages, while a considerable number are to be found mixed up among all the other villages and in Mogaung itself:—Mahaung, Ywathit, Kyaingale, Lwèsun, and Nankaiktaw.

The Tabaungyasa established a small Assamese village north of Bhamo. There is also a small village called Saungalan (Zingalein) to the east of Amarapura, which was founded by the Assamese followers of Bhamo Mepara. Up to lately they seem only to have married amongst themselves, and at present the majority seem still to continue to do so, though many have married with Shans. When the Burmese capital was changed to Mandalay the Assamese had three courts,—Bhamo Mepara, Tabaungyasa, Mawlu Mintha. Each court consisted of about 40 houses, all revenue collected from the Assamese princes and princesses. The Mawlu Mintha lived in the capital with his mother and his sister Bhamo Mepara, who had no children. Tabaungyasa and Mawlu Mintha brought their wives over with them from Assam ; the former had five sons—Maung Gyi, Maung Mintha, Maung Lat, Maung Galè, and Maung Sôn. In Burmese times Maung Gyi and Maung Lat held the office of Myinmu Mintha, and Maung Galè was Wun of Mawlu, Kaungtôn, and Manlè (Katha district). Maung Sôn had no official position and is the only one now living, but his residence is not known to the Assamese here. Tabaungyasa's daughter was Madaya Mepaya, wife to Mindôn Min, and the other two were maids of honour "Apyodaws." Mi Mi Glè is still alive and resides in Mandalay.

The Kachin occasionally kidnapped Assamese, but never to any great extent. They were usually sold to the Assamese settlers in Burma. The Assamese in Burma are therefore the descendants of the followers of the court and not captives of war as usually believed.

249. The Mons or Talaings. The Môns, Peguans or Talaings as they are now generally called, were the masters of the delta of the Irrawaddy until they were finally conquered by the Burmese under Alaungpaya. How victory inclined now to the Burmans and now to the Môns in the

internecine strife that had been waged for centuries is too well known to need notice here. But the origin and former greatness of the Môn kingdom, and its intimate connection with the kingdom of Cambodia, has been established only in comparatively recent years. That Môn conquests were extended and the influence of Môn civilization was felt even as far as the Straits of Malacca is not, however, yet generally known. There is reason to believe that the deltas of the four great rivers of the Indo-Chinese Peninsula were occupied by branches of the Môn races, and the traces of Môn vocables that have recently been discovered in the Malayan dialects point to the probability of the inclusion of the peninsula within the sphere of Môn influence. Mr. D. Wilson, C.S., and Maung Ba Tu have collected all the information they could acquire of the legends of the Talaings regarding their previous history. I have also been fortunate enough to obtain a manuscript, but as these legends merely reproduce the usual fanciful fairy tales of the mythical history of the Môns, I have not reproduced them here. Mr. Wilson reports that the Talaings are becoming rapidly Burmanized, and that in the Shwegyin district at any rate the language is dying out. In Chapter VIII the affinities of the Môn or Talaing language have already been traced. After the surprising increase in the number of those who returned Talaing as their parent-tongue to predict the future self-effacement of this race may seem rash. Still, notwithstanding the fact that there is much more national life amongst the Talaings than most of us have believed, yet I fear that the returns of 1901 will show that the Talaings are becoming merged into and indistinguishable from their former conquerors, the Burmans. There were 466,324 Talaings in Lower Burma, of whom there were 315,749 in the Amherst district alone. Next to Amherst comes Pegu, where was the ancient capital of the Môn kingdom. There were 63,935 who returned themselves as Talaings here. In Shwegyin there were 32,257, in Thôngwa there were 24,550, and in Hanthawaddy 19,506. In the other districts the number of Talaings is comparatively insignificant. The number of Talaings in Upper Burma is naturally very small. In Lower Burma 1,001 out of every 10,000 of both sexes returned themselves as Talaings, while the corresponding number in Upper Burma is 5 only.

The Irrawaddy, the Salween, Mekong, and Menam.

250. Of the Karen race but little remains to be written: Dr. Mason, General McMahon and Mr. Copleston have left little to be said regarding them. But as regards the origin of the race the researches of M. de la Couperie point to the belief now generally entertained that the Karens were one of the pre-Chinese races driven southwards by the pressure of the Chinese, and that they were not, as Dr. Cross supposes, the aboriginal inhabitants of Burma. Mr. Houghton is, however, not sure that Karen is not a Tibeto-Burman tongue; but the general consensus of opinion is in favour of the view that Karen belongs to the Sinitic group. Mr. Copleston says that further enquiry may establish a close connection between the Karens and the Myawke (Maosi) or wild tribes of China. The Taungthus are in all probability nothing but a tribe of Karens. Of Karens, including the Taungthus, there were in 1891 540,927 of both sexes; of these there were 536,184 in Lower Burma as against 546,065 who returned Karen and Taungthu as their mother-tongue in 1881 and 331,255 in 1872. No return of race was made in 1881, and, as we have seen already, the return of language is, as regards the Karens, probably a surer test of the numbers who belong, either in whole or in part, to that race. There are three great divisions of the Karen race—the Sgau, Pwo, and Bghai or Bwè Karens. The latter are commonly known as the Red Karens. Dr. Mason, the pioneer of ethnography in Burma, has subdivided these three tribes into several clans, but the distinguishing features on which he based his careful and perhaps over elaborated classification are already being fast obliterated. The tendency to disintegrate has been of late years changed into a steady process of assimilation, and Dr. Mason's quaint divisions of the Red Karens into Tunic and Pant Bghais and of the Sgaus into Maunepghas and Wewas are almost lost. Not only has the disintegrating tendency been checked, but the spread of Christianity among the Karens has had an unforeseen result in checking the Burmanizing of the Karens. Up to the conquest

Karens.

of Pegu in 1852-53 the Karens were treated with harshness by their Burmese conquerors, and no assimilation was probably allowed by the Burmans themselves. After the annexation, when Pegu was nearly depopulated by the emigration of the Burmans in large numbers northwards, the comparatively few Burmans left, their pride being now humbled, no longer dared to treat the Karens with the same open contempt. Although the Missionaries with just cause often complained that the Burmans oppressed the Karens and obtained the favour of the English district officers, yet the fact that the Burmans did so by diplomacy and cunning showed that they no longer dared openly oppress the Karens. Treated now more on terms of equality, a Burmanizing process was commenced—a process which may still be felt to be going on among the Karens of the plains. But the introduction of Christianity, the instinct of self-respect, and the spread of education introduced by the Missionaries, has re-infused new life into the Karen language and into the Karen nationality. A Karen is now no longer ashamed of belonging to his once despised down-trodden race; indeed, those officers who have been on duty with Karens against Burman dacoits will bear witness to a very different feeling. The Karen now in his turn looks down on the Burman, and this feeling of national pride, though strongest amongst the Christian Karens, is not without its effect on the others. In time the Pwo Karen may disappear: some will become Burmanized and some will be merged into the Sgau. The Pwo Missionaries, proud of their flocks, may probably deny this; time will show if the Pwos will retain their individuality.

The Taungthus.

251. So much has already been published regarding the Pwos, Sgaus, and Bwès that there is no need to enlarge further on their ethnology and history. As regards the Taungthus, however, the annexation of Upper Burma has extended the field of our knowledge regarding this people. It was formerly supposed that the Taungthus came from Thatôn in the Shan States, but Mr. Hildebrand, the Superintendent of the Southern Shan States, is inclined to believe that just the very contrary was the case, and that the Taungthus in the Shan States came from Thatôn in the Amherst district. Mr. Hildebrand has very kindly put the following notes at my service:—

Legend.

In the year 419 B.E. (957 A.D.) the Taungthu king of Thatôn, Manuha, invited a Buddhist priest to visit his country for the purpose of spreading the Buddhist religion. This priest came and brought with him thirty sets of the Buddhistic scriptures named Pitakat (ပိဋကတ်). The neighbouring king of Pagan, named Nawrata Minsaw, hearing of this and being desirous of obtaining one set, sent an Amat with a letter to the Taungthu king Manuha asking for one set of the scriptures. The king of Thatôn, on reading the letter sent back an insolent reply that the subjects of the king of Pagan were so exceedingly ignorant and wild, that even if he sent a copy, his subjects would not be able to understand them, and therefore refused to part with one. The Amat returned to Pagan and communicated the reply of the Taungthu king Manuha, which so incensed Nawrata Minsaw that he at once gave orders for the equipment of a large army, to proceed both by water and land, against Thatôn, and headed the water force in person. The numbers of the forces employed are so exaggerated that it would be absurd if I mentioned them here. Thatôn was attacked and captured, and king Manuha and his wife and family taken prisoners; the scriptures were also seized and placed on eight white elephants and taken in triumph to Pagan. *Ex*-King Manuha of Thatôn and his family were made over as offerings as pagoda slaves to the Shwe Sigôn Pagoda at Pagan. It is apparent that the inhabitants of the kingdom of Pagan had some knowledge of Buddhism, otherwise this pagoda could not have been built, and I am told that this king, Nawrata Minsaw, had obtained one of Gaudama's teeth from China, and that this pagoda was built in honour thereof. It is also said that this king had an inscription cut on a marble slab relating his conquest of Thatôn, &c., and fixed it on this pagoda (I do not know whether such an inscription has ever been found). After the conquest of Thatôn and the carrying off of their Taungthu king, the inhabitants of the country immigrated towards the north in large numbers, and founded a colony in the Shan States, which they named after their old country Thatôn. Taungthus are to be found all over the Shan States, and I have always heard the same story regarding their origin, and think there must be some truth in it.

Language.—I am somewhat acquainted with the Taungthu language, both written and spoken, and it is apparent that there are very few words of either Burmese or Shan origin to be found in it, and I may almost say there are none. The alphabet is composed of the same number of consonants, vowels, &c., as the Burmese, and the letters are exactly similar.

Customs.—This custom is very similar to that prevalent in Burma, and is as follows.

Marriage. When two parties have fallen in love with one another, the consent of their parents to their marriage is asked, and, if obtained, a day is fixed for the event, and the bridegroom, on the arrival of the day fixed, buys fruits, letpet and betel, and, accompanied by a number of villagers, proceeds to the bride's house, where a feast which has been prepared is eaten. The bridegroom and bride have to each eat letpet before the lugyis of the village, and the ceremony is over. The bridegroom, when the evening comes, has to hire a villager to partition off a small room in the house of the bride's mother, and the fee of this service is invariably four annas (why, I cannot find out). Divorce very seldom takes place.

Birth. The custom is exactly similar to that prevalent in Burma, only the navel string must be buried in the ground just in front of the steps leading down from the house. A short time after the birth, the midwife who has assisted is invited to the house, and her hands washed by the parents, and then dismissed with a small piece of silver.

Naming of the child. A name is given to the child by its parents shortly after birth, but this name is changed after the child, if a boy, has served in a monastery, by the pôngyi of that monastery. The custom of naming after a letter allotted for each day of the week is exactly the same as that practised by Burmans.

Death. The same as in Burma. The only peculiarity that I can discover is the following. Should a woman die in child-birth, her body is invariably beaten with sticks and ropes in the hope that, if the woman has only swooned away, she will return to consciousness.

Spirits. It is a peculiar custom that whenever a Taungthu roofs his house, which is invariably done once a year in the month of Kason or Nayon, the "Ein-nat" or house spirit must be propitiated by an offering of food, one of the ingredients of which must be fish. Should the householder be unable to obtain fish, his family are unlucky in anything they may do throughout the year. The offering must be always placed on the east or west side of the house: never south or north. This offering is also made to the "Ein-nat" by the parents of any young couple just married, so that they will have luck during their married life. It is also a peculiar custom that no property made over to a Taungthu for custody can be accepted without petitioning and making offerings to this all-powerful spirit; should the practice of offerings or petitioning be omitted, and the guardianship of the property accepted, the household has no luck whatever. Another peculiar custom is that, on the death of a person, the nearest relative of the deceased measures the body of the dead person from head to feet with a piece of twisted cotton, and then, throwing the cotton on the dead body, states that the soul of the deceased person is released. Again, just before a dead body is to be consigned to the grave, the nearest relative of the deceased has to wash the face of the dead person. This is always done when the body has arrived at the cemetery.

Other customs. A Taungthu will never sell paddy in the month of Pyatho; before the arrival of this month the householder puts aside a sufficient quantity of paddy for the consumption of his family during the month, the rest, being put by, is not allowed to be touched.

The ashes from the fire-place are also never brushed up or collected during this month, but on the first Lasan of Tabodwè they are collected and thrown away.

Dress. The dress of men is exactly the same as the Shan, namely, the ordinary coat, either black or white, and Chinese black or white trousers, and gaungbaung.

Women.—Their dress is quite distinct.

Head dress.—A black cloth or tabet is wound round the head, very much in the manner of a gaungbaung, but this head-dress is ornamented with coloured tassels. A silver band is placed round the "sado," and above this is fixed a large silver spike to keep the band and hair in place, and wound round the head is a silver rope or cord about 6 feet in length and about one-eighth in breadth. Earrings are worn; they are very long and drooping, of silver, and remind me of the earrings worn years ago at home.

The women wear a black "thindaing," which, in the case of the better classes, is sometimes embroidered and otherwise ornamented; under this is worn a short tamein, which reaches the knee; a kind of leggings, black or white, is also worn. Round the legs, just below the knee, cotton dyed black is encircled, much in the same manner as Intha women. The forearm is also covered with parti-coloured velvet or flannel, green and purple being much affected. Large hollow bracelets are also worn.

Malays. 252. There were 2,129 Malays in Burma, nearly all of whom were enumerated in Mergui. The derivation of this name is traced by Mr. Maxwell to the Sanskrit name of a mountain mentioned in the Puranas, and is supposed to have been used as a designation of the rude tribes of Sumatra and the peninsula with whom the early Sanskrit-speaking adventurers from India came into contact. The other and hitherto commonly received derivation is from Melayu or the "swift-flowing river," which was the name given to a tributary of a river called the Tatang. The Malays in physique and physiognomy resemble the Talaing type, and their primitive dialect still shows traces of the use of tones. That there should be such a resemblance is remarkable, but what is more strange is that recent enquiries by Mr. Blagden, an Officer of the Straits Settlements Civil Service, have elicited the fact that among the wild tribes of the Malay peninsula we find dialects, especially the Bisisi, that possess vocables that correspond very closely to words of the same meaning in Talaing. Mr. Blagden himself is the first to admit that this resemblance may, though that is unlikely, be superficial, but he is inclined to think that if this fact of the identity of the vocables be established, the explanation may be sought for in the existence of the Môn kingdom that once dominated the mouths of the Irrawaddy, Mekhong, and Menam. The Môns probably traded and, perhaps, partially conquered the wild aboriginal tribes. The identity in type between the aboriginal Malay tribes and the Môns would point to a close relationship, and it is possible, and even probable, that the wild Malay tribes are of Môn descent. The Malay of the sea-coast is a hybrid creature, partly Malay, partly Arab, partly Hindu, and our preconceived notions of the Malay differ widely from the type found prevailing among the pure-blooded Malays in the interior of the peninsula. Besides these Malays who are returned as such, we have the Selungs, or, as they are known in Burma, the Selôns, a true Malay race. The Selôns talk a dialect of Malay, and to all intents and purposes are Malays. They are a tribe of sea-gypsies living amongst the islands of the Mergui archipelago. So much has been written on the subject already that with reluctance I am unable to reproduce an interesting monograph written by Colonel Butler, as a pamphlet by Dr. Anderson has been recently published and covers the same ground. Mr. Merrifield, however, has struck out a new path for himself, and I extract the following remarks from his very interesting report :—

The Selaungs, a nomadic race inhabiting the Mergui archipelago and adjacent islands, range in their boats—in which they almost entirely live—from Junkseylon in the south to Mergui itself. Although now somewhat mixed in many instances with other races near them, they still constitute a distinct people, though the time cannot be far distant when they will be either obliterated or absorbed. This race is one of presumably high antiquity. There are reasons for believing that the Selaungs are the present representatives of a race that, prior to the arrival of the tribes of the great Htai family upon the coast and their spread down the peninsula, lived on the mainland as well. Their own traditions and those of their neighbours point to their having formerly constituted a fairly numerous and thriving community. Buried in the jungles of Kisseraing are the ruins of an old town that legend calls their capital; and it is evident that at some time, whether by Selaungs or others, this part of the world was much more thickly populated than at present.

The Selaungs present marked affinities in appearance, language, and even in certain customs—these might have been acquired by imitation—to some of the more backward Malay communities of the Siamese States. I am inclined to think, indeed, that a good deal of the blood of the primitive race from which I consider the Selaungs are descended, survives, though masked, throughout the peninsula. Among themselves the Selaungs use a language of their own; this has a tendency to absorb words from surrounding languages. In the north Burmese has enlarged the Selaung vocabulary to a very large extent, while in the south Malay and Siamese have performed the same office. The underlying Selaung language, however, bears a marked resemblance in vocabulary, structure, and idiom to primitive Malay, that is, I fancy that both Malay and Selaung, stripped of their accretions and tested by the ordinary methods of comparative philology, will be found to descend from a common *Ursprache,* or, at least, from a group of kindred tongues.

The manners and customs of the Selaungs might be easily summed up in the words of the midshipman asked to report on another race: "They have no manners and their customs are beastly." In private life they wear few or no clothes, and, as both sexes of all ages pack themselves together in their boats, denuding themselves of almost everything, when, as is apt to occur in the hot weather, the breeze dies away and it gets hot, their ideas of modesty may be classed as low. Their notions of cleanliness are equally rudimentary: though in and out of the water perpetually, they never seem to wash themselves, their clothes, or their boats, which are generally filthy. They suffer from a very unpleasant skin disease, locally known as Selaung itch, and are altogether an unlovely people.

Missionaries, who are apt to find traces of a primitive revealed religion and the Deluge among all races, have discovered that the Selaungs believe in a great beneficent spirit; otherwise I should be inclined to consider—not having heard of this great beneficent spirit myself—that they have no religion, as the term is generally understood, but are nat-worshippers of a very low type. They have certain ceremonies, chief of which seem eating a pig and getting drunk—in which, were this not a regular habit of all savage races, one might trace an analogy with the Chins—in connection with marriages and funerals; they have also certain superstitions connected with births. Offerings of a propitiatory nature are made to nats of a malignant type. If the Selaungs do not believe in God, they most assuredly do in the devil, and in not only one, but many, while omens are the cause of much searching of hearts. Though timid to a singular degree and shy of strangers, like many other backward races they occasionally commit startlingly savage crimes. On the whole, however, they are peaceable and inoffensive, giving little or no trouble. They frequently visit the ports, but they conduct their business entirely with a few traders who have won their confidence by means that do not altogether commend themselves to approval, as they seem to include raw opium and spirits, which can hardly be good for these children of nature. These favoured traders obtain by barter at ridiculously low rates the various articles of island trade; but were strangers to offer higher prices, the Selaungs would not trade with them, and a few men enjoy a practical monopoly.

In the neighbourhood of Kopah inlet a few Selaungs seem to have settled down. About a year back a dozen families settled near Victoria Point, building little houses like dog-kennels on posts: these were not boat Selaungs, but long-shore people from Kopah. They made taungya for one season, but have left on being requested to pay taxes. The majority of Selaungs proper live in boats made of a dug-out with about a foot of gunwale made of hpaw (cork-cane) and rattan. They carry with them a folded attap mat, which they use as a tilth in case of rain or sunshine. Some of the better boats have a permanent roof like those on Siamese boats. They sail these with a peaked lug. In rowing they use a short oar and squat to their work like Malays, whereas Siamese stand facing the direction in which they are going and push their sweeps. These boats make fairly good weather and travel fast with the wind aft. In them they live all the year round, visiting the outer islands in fine weather, and running under lee of the big inner islands in the south-west monsoon. Though confining themselves to no particular locality, they usually are to be found sheltering under the same group of islands every year, and are thus divided into Radet Selaungs, Domel Selaungs, &c., according to the group they chiefly affect. As, too, they usually intermarry only in their own group, these groups are to a certain extent mutually related. As a matter of fact, however, the Selaungs do not seem to have attained any idea of communal life: each boat constitutes a separate despotism regulated by the headman. Outside their own particular boat relationship counts for little; and it is currently reported that in bad seasons both useless pensioners and surplus babies are turned adrift to take their chance. At the same time, as they usually travel for mutual protection and assistance in little fleets of from four to ten boats, generally owned by people from the same group, they may be classed as gregarious if not as possessing the blessings of communal existence.

These people maintain themselves by trading in fish, which they barter with the fish-curers in the season, pearl-shell, bêche-de-mer, achaw, honey, wax—of the two latter articles great quantities are found, but the honey is generally too dirty for eating—and a gigantic kind of whelk (Bur. *thadee*), of which the shell is exported for manufacture into an inferior mother-o'-pearl, while the inhabiting animal is dried for export to China, where it is esteemed a delicacy. The only industry of the islanders is the manufacture of a peculiarly soft grass matting, in the making of which they display considerable skill and taste. Of the same matting, which is largely used for sleeping-mats, they also make tobacco-pouches of neat design; these articles are extensively purchased and used by the Siamese.

On all occasions when I have questioned the Selaungs I have found them apparently contented with their lot. They have only expressed one wish,—that we would assist them with rice in bad seasons; otherwise, I fancy they would prefer to be left alone. Whether we can, both in their interest and our own, leave them much longer to the ministrations and civilizing influences of Chinese and Malay traders, who, in the absence of control, seem to do exactly what they like in the islands, is another matter.

The increase in Selaungs in the present census I attribute to two causes (to say nothing of more careful enumeration): the pearl-fishing near Bôkpyin, which has already attracted many of them, and, secondly, the fact that many Siamese Selaungs have lately migrated north and settled down in our islands, where they are left somewhat severely alone.

Though it might be expected the physical condition of a people so low in the social scale would be bad, the contrary is the fact. Their physique is good, and they generally look, barring skin-complaints and dirt, in good condition. Their life is active, and the struggle for existence under hard conditions necessarily eliminates the weakly. Many of them attain a patriarchal age in spite of hardship and exposure. In appearance they are hardly to be distinguished from the Malays about here, though some of them have crimped hair (not like that of the Andamanese in tufts), on account of which the Malays pretend to divide them into two classes, those with straight and those with crimped hair, a distinction to which importance does not necessarily attach, as the same peculiarity is not uncommon among the local Siamese.

My reasons for considering the Selaungs to be of very considerable antiquity are—

(1) The local tradition throughout Mergui points to their having existed pretty much as at present for a long time prior to Alompra's invasion. It is true this tradition—in this agreeing with their own—says that anterior to the great invasion they were more numerous, perhaps more comfortable; while they had some form of government administered by an officer with head-quarters at Myohaung on Kisseraing and paying the Selaung tribute through Mergui.

(2) The Selaung tradition describes the destruction of Myohaung and the cruelties of the Burmese invaders as comparatively recent events, almost within the memory of man. But it represents them as a distinct race, inhabiting the islands from time immemorial.

(3) The Siamese, whose records and tradition are more continuous and credible, represent the "*Chow nam*" as a distinct race that has always existed on the islands in a wild state, probably from before the arrival of the Siamese themselves. At what time the Htai invaders reached the western shores of the peninsula I do not know, but it must have been early.

(4) The Malays always consider the *Orang laut* as a distinct people, who, as far as they know, have always existed on the island. They repudiate all connection with these wild men. Now the Malay and Arab traders have been navigating these seas for centuries, and if the Selaungs were a race of comparatively recent arrival, some tradition of their migration would be sure to exist somewhere.

(5) The Malays have been followers of Islam since at least the 9th century. Had the Selaungs at that time been a sub-Malayan tribe inhabiting the peninsula, I fail to see how (*a*) they could have escaped the somewhat forcible methods of conversion then in vogue, or (*b*) acquiring by contact some of the customs, &c., pertaining to Mahomedanism.

(6) Their customs, however, point to no such connection. If they are a sub-Malayan tribe, they must have split off the parent stock and differentiated into a distinct race prior to the general spread of Islam. The few *Arabic*-Malay words now existing in their vocabulary are probably of recent absorption.

(7) The invasion of the Western States of Siam by Malays is comparatively recent. I am inclined to think that, except by sea, there can have been little personal contact between the Malays and the Selaungs from the time of the great Htai settlement to the wars of the 15th century, when the Malays again swept northward.

(8) The customs of the Selaungs point to their constituting a tribe that was separated from the rest of the world in an extremely backward and primitive condition. This leads me to think their separation must have taken place when neighbouring races were no more advanced than themselves, or they must have attained and retained a higher degree of civilization. For the rest of the population of the peninsula, the Talmes, the Siamese, and the Malays attained a fair standard at an early date.

(9) I am not prepared to accept the theory that the Selaungs have become wild only since Alompra's time, say, from the middle of the last century. This is flatly contradicted by their own traditions and those of their neighbours. This most extraordinary and impossible theory is probably founded on a misconception of the cessation of all control over the islanders after the destruction of Myohaung,—a very different matter.

(10) Nor can I accept the theory that they are the descendants of a sub-Malayan tribe driven north by the Malays, for the very simple reason that the Selaungs seem to have been where or what they are before the Mahomedans swept northward. My own theory, founded on a personal examination of the race, its customs, and language, is that it represents an aboriginal or semi-aboriginal race formerly connected with the (then) non-Mahomedan stock, inhabiting considerable portions of the peninsula, perhaps as far north as the present frontier. From their congeners they must have become isolated, probably by the arrival of the Siamese. Later on, while the Selaungs themselves sought an asylum in the islands of the Mergui archipelago, their relatives, driven south by the new invaders, embraced Mahomedanism, intermarried with other races, accepted a Sumatran domination, and evolved the present Malay race.

253. Burma draws its supply of Chinese immigrants from three sources. In the north, in Bhamo, the Chinese settlers are emigrants from Yunnan. In the south our immigrants come either from China direct or from Singapore and Sumatra. The Chinese descended from marriages between Chinese and the Burmese or Talaing women are known locally as Babas. After some consideration it was decided not to attempt to make any separate return of Chinese of pure descent and of those from mixed stocks. The Babas, or "Ship yit tem" as the Chinese term them, are very jealous of being considered true Chinamen, and, as they dress and consider themselves as apart from the natives of the country, it is possible that the return might have been very ineffectual. It will be seen from our language returns that the number of Chinese-speaking persons has increased enormously in the past decade; this was partly due to the willing co-operation of Chinamen on the occasion of the last census. In order to secure this, it was necessary to avoid wounding their prejudices. At the next census a return of Chinese of mixed and of pure blood may be attempted, but there will be, I much fear, great reason to doubt the accuracy of the return. Perhaps the best way of arriving at an approximation to the figures will be to deduct from the total number of Chinamên the number of those returned as speaking Chinese, and the residue, amounting to 5,203 persons, may be taken to represent fairly the number of persons of both sexes of mixed Chinese and foreign blood. For reasons already stated, the girls of these mixed unions are rarely brought up as Chinese, but they adopt the dress, customs, and religion, as well as the language, of their mothers. The term Baba, sometimes pronounced Bawa, is a corruption of the Malay word Wawa, which means a "half-breed."

Chinese.

254. Panthès only numbered 23 persons. The derivation of their name has already been discussed in Chapter VIII. Their history has been already brought into prominence by the Panthè rebellion and further notice of them here is unnecessary.

Panthès.

255. Orders were received to class Musalman tribes under heading of No. 48, Non-Indian Asiatic races. Of Musalman tribes and races we have a very varied assortment in Burma. In the first place we have the Burmese, Arakanese, Panthès, and Shan-Mahomedans; we have then those who return themselves as Moghul, Shaikh, Sayad, and Pathan, the four great divisions into which the Musalmans of India are usually classed. Of these no notice beyond what is contained in the Imperial tables is necessary, as all the information to be obtained about them in Burma is obviously at second hand. There are 5,053 Moghuls, 3,405 Sayads, 15,689 Pathans, and 204,846 Shaikhs in Burma. The Shaikh Musalman is practically but very little different from the Hindu. The Pathans are numerous owing to the number of them employed in the military police.

Musalman tribes.

256. The following brief account of our Indian immigrants from Southern India has been kindly put at my disposal by the Right Reverend Dr. Strachan, Bishop of Rangoon:—

The great majority of our fellow-subjects who come over from South India either to make their permanent home in Burma, or, as is more generally the case, to stop for a time and then return to their villages, are Tamils, Telugus, and people from Orissa. Of these the chief, both as to numbers, intelligence and wealth, are the Tamils.

Tamil.—This ought to be spelt with a final *r*—Tamir. The derivation of the word is doubtful; possibly it may be from the Sanskrit Dravida. Dr. Caldwell thus traces the changes. The oldest form of Dravida appears to have been Dramida. Through the change of *d* into *l*, the Dramidas were called Dramilas. "In the Pali of the Mahâwanso the "form used is Damilo, the derivative of which is Dâmilo; and as initial *d* becomes *t* by rule "in Tamil, we now reach the ordinary Tamil mode of writing the word, Tamir or Tamil."

Tamil is spoken by 14,500,000 persons, who are found occupying the Carnatic from a little north of Madras to Cape Comorin, and from the Western Ghâts to the Bay of Bengal. Tamil is also spoken in some parts of the State of Travancore and in the north of Ceylon. It consists of two dialects, which are quite distinct,—the Kodun Tamil, the common or colloquial form; and the Shen Tamil, the classical or poetical form. The language is rich in valuable and complete grammars written both by Native and European scholars, whilst the indigenous literature is of a very high order. There are also many treatises translated from the Sanskrit. The chief works are the Kural, which treats of (1) virtue, (2) royalty, (3) sensual pleasure; the Chintamani, declared to be the finest Tamil composition extant, which gives the history of King Sivajan; and the Ramâyana of Kamban. Some of the writings are ancient; but the chief epoch of literary vigour and excellence seems to have been from the 8th century A.D. to the 13th century A.D. Since the British occupation, there have been large additions made to Tamil literature, being chiefly translations of European works.

There are several other languages, cultivated and uncultivated, cognate to Tamil, and which are spoken principally throughout South India. The chief of these are Telugu, Canarese and Malayâlam. The Telugu is spoken by 15,500,000 in the country which is surrounded on the north by Uriya, on the north-west by Mârathi, on the south-west by Canarese, and on the south by Tamil. Canarese is spoken by 9,250,000 in Mysore, in part of the district of Canara, and in part of the Nizam's territories. Malayâlam is spoken by 3,750,000 people on the western side of South India from Mangalore to Trevandrum.

These, with some uncultivated dialects, have, as a matter of convenience, been grouped together under the name of Dravidian (Tamilian), Tamil being the chief member of the group. The origin of this South Indian group has not been determined. On the one hand, it is considered that it has a strong affinity to Sanskrit, whilst others, with whom is Dr. Caldwell, are of opinion, after careful examination of the grammatical structure, that these languages are independent of Sanskrit and ought to be grouped with the Scythian.

The Dravidians have occupied South India from a very remote period. Like all ancient Indian history, the facts connected with their advent are veiled in impenetrable obscurity. Dr. Caldwell writes: "We may, indeed, with tolerable safety regard the Dravi-"dians as the earliest inhabitants of India, or, at least, as the earliest race that entered from "the north-west; but it is not so easy to determine whether they were the people whom "the Aryans found in possession and conquered, or whether they had already, before the "arrival of the Aryans, moved on southwards out of the northern provinces, or been expelled "from their provinces by the prehistoric irruption of another race."

Of all the races in India, the Tamils are the most enterprizing. Under the pressure of want arising from bad seasons, they readily cross the sea, and are now to be found in large numbers in Burma, the Straits Settlements (where they and the Telugus are called Klings, from Calingapatam), Mauritius, British Guiana, and some of the West Indian Islands. Unfortunately, the female relatives, out of fear and ignorance, decline to share the risks incurred in emigration, so that the majority of emigrants return to their native soil with their well-earned savings. To this is owing the fluctuating character of the "Kala"* or foreign population of Rangoon, and, indeed, of Lower Burma generally. Large numbers come over for the harvest, when the wages are exceptionally high, and then return to their homes at the end of the season.

Besides those who come over from South India for cooly work, others come as merchants and money-lenders. The chief of these are the *Chetties*. They belong to the well-known Hindu caste, and come from the Madura and Tanjore zillahs or from Madras itself. Some of them grow very wealthy in Burma. There are some *Vellalars* too from the same zillahs, who engage successfully in the same occupations.

The *Choliar* (சோழியர்) come over in great numbers. The name is to be traced back to an ancient and powerful dynasty, the Chola, which seems to have included in its limits in the 11th century the whole of the Tamil people. The seat of government was at Uriyur, which was probably close to where Trichinopoly now stands, but the seat of government was finally moved to Tanjore. By distributing the waters of the Kâveri by means of anicuts and canals, the Chola authorities converted the Tanjore district into one of the most, if not the most, fertile district in all India. Cholamangalam was one of the 56 countries of Hindu geography and extended along part of the coast, hence the name Coromandel coast.

The Choliar are Mahomedans, but they do not speak Hindustani, their colloquial being Tamil. They are all taught the Koran indeed, but the language in which it is written is foreign to them, and many understand very imperfectly what they are taught. The *Labbais*, who are also Mahomedans, may be here mentioned. They are on the Coromandel coast what the Moplahs are on the western coast, the descendants of Arab traders and the women of the country. The Labbais are teachers to the Choliar. They are not fond of work, are to be found lingering about the precincts of mosques, and get a little money by ceremoniously cutting the throats of fowls and sheep and goats accompanied by prayer.

Telugu, of all the Dravidian group, is spoken most largely. It was at one time called by Europeans Gentoo, from the Portuguese word signifying heathen. The derivation of the term has not been ascertained. "The favourite derivation of Telugu pandits for

* *Kala*.—The popular idea of the Burmans is that this word is simply made up of the two words which form it and which mean "to come across." But it is in reality a Pali word (ကုလား) which means a race. It has now the meaning of the word Gentile and is applied to people who belong to countries west of Burma who are not of Sinitic or Burmese origin.

"Telugu or Telungu, the ordinary name of their language, is from Trilinga 'the language "of the three lingas,' that is, as they represent, of the country of which three celebrated "linga-temples constituted the boundaries." But this explanation has been rejected by competent scholars, and the derivation remains in doubt. The Mahomedans called the Telugu country Telingana. The Telugu language differs considerably from the Tamil. It is reckoned as the most mellifluous and sweet of the whole Dravidian group. The Telugu people are not so migratory as the Tamil, but the recent census shows that large numbers have come over to Burma. It is not necessary to speak here of Canarese and Malayâlam, as the people speaking these languages do not come over to Burma.

There is one other race to which allusion must be made, of which large numbers embark every year from Gopalpur for Rangoon, namely, the Ooriyas. These aborigines, like so many other hill tribes, have retained much of the simplicity and inanity of their primitive religion. "They are fearless, independent, and remarkably truthful; live on fruits, "nuts, wild honey, flesh, and are fond of intoxicating drinks; they worship a deity which "is generally invisible, though sometimes they have gods of wood and stone; their worship "is usually accompanied with bloody sacrifices. The practice of human sacrifices was very "general amongst them; and, notwithstanding the repressive measures of the British Gov-"ernment, it is to be feared that the hideous practice has not even yet died out. Amongst "these sacrifices were made—

"*1st*.—Annually to propitiate Tarri Pennu, the earth-goddess, to favour agriculture. After the victim is slain, his blood and pieces of the flesh are distributed among the bystanders to be strewed over the fields.

"*2nd*.—Whenever the health of the society is seriously affected, as in the case of cholera or smallpox.

"*3rd*.—Whenever any sudden calamity affects the patriarch or his family."

The following table of virtues and vices shows that these hill-tribes possess in a striking degree a sort of savage nobility. The chief sins are—

(1) To refuse hospitality or abandon a guest.
(2) To break an oath or promise, or to deny a gift.
(3) To speak falsely, except to save a guest.
(4) To break a solemn pledge of friendship.
(5) To break an old law or custom.
(6) To commit incest.
(7) To contract debts.
(8) To skulk in time of war.
(9) To betray a public secret.

The virtues are—

(1) To kill a foe in public battle.
(2) To fall in public battle.
(3) To be a priest.
(4) To be a victim to the earth-goddess. (*Vide* Journal, Royal Asiatic Society, Volume XIII, Part 2, page 229.)

Some will be tempted to think that these rude tribes have a truer sense of right and wrong than the more astute and civilized denizens of the plains in India.

Hindu Castes.

257. Of those who returned themselves as belonging to one of the recognized Indian castes there were but 103,298 persons in Burma, and they compose but 1·36 per cent. of the total population of the province. Of these 103,298 persons 99,998 are Hindus and 3,164 are Sikhs. Of the remaining 136 persons 132 are Musalmans and 4 are Buddhists who, notwithstanding they are no longer Hindus, have still retained their caste names. In the appendix to this chapter will be found a list of the castes returned, classified according to the directions of the Government of India by their hereditary occupations.

The following table will show at a glance how the Hindu and Sikh population of Burma is distributed. It must be recollected that 70,196, or 92·29 out of every 10,000 persons or nearly one-half of the total Hindu population, and ·9229 per cent. of the total population of Burma, made no return of caste at all, or the enumerators were unable to understand and transliterate the name of the caste. Under the circumstances, the fact that, in a foreign country where caste is unknown, and where a large number of the Hindu immigrants have practically no caste at all, any return at all should have been made is creditable to the enumerators. The only way in which this return was obtained was by employing Hindu enumerators, and, where none were available, the Burmese enumerators were instructed to prepare lists of castes recorded in the preliminary record; these lists were checked, and hence we have been able to make the present return.

Comparative statement of the distribution of Hindus and Sikhs by main caste per 10,000 of the population of the province.

Class.	Group.	Burma.	Lower Burma.	Upper Burma.
A. Agricultural ...	1. Military and dominant	23·516	15·127	8·389
	1. Sikh ditto	*4·132*	*·753*	*3·379*
	2. Minor agricultural	45·287	41·523	3·764
	4. Forest and hill tribes	·920	·919	·001
	Total ...	**73·845**	**58·290**	**15·555**
B. Professional ...	5. Priests	15·291	9·230	6·061
	6. Devotees	·816	·777	·039
	7. Temple servants	15·319	14·068	1·251
	8. Genealogists	·058	·053	·005
	9. Writers	6·051	5·848	·203
	10. Astrologers	·076	·076	...
	11. Musicians and ballad reciters	·010	·010	...
	12. Dancers and singers	·075	·049	·026
	Total ..	**37·714**	**30·117**	**7·597**
C. Commercial ...	14. Traders	8·722	7·579	1·143
	Total ...	**8·722**	**7·579**	**1·143**
D. Artizan and village menials.	17. Goldsmiths	·367	·311	·056
	18. Barbers	·709	·631	·078
	19. Blacksmiths	·247	·224	·023
	19. Sikh do.	·027	...	·027
	20. Carpenters and turners	·158	·135	·023
	22. Tailors	·086	...	·086
	23. Weavers, calenders and dyers	1·096	·941	·155
	24. Washermen...	1·964	1·704	·260
	25. Cotton cleaners	·001	·001	...
	26. Shepherds and wool-weavers	2·324	1·913	·411
	27. Oil pressers	1·095	1·053	·042
	28. Potters	·500	·102	·398
	29. Glass workers	·511	·265	·246
	30. Salt, &c., workers	·009	·009	...
	35. Fishermen, boatmen, palki-bearers, books, &c.	2·218	15·76	·642
	36. Distillers and toddy-drawers	·466	·160	·306
	38. Leather workers	·988	·794	·194
	39. Scavengers	·523	·403	·120
	Total ...	**13·297**	**10·210**	**3·087**
E. Vagrants, minor artizans, and performers, &c.	41. Earthwork and stone dressers	·073	·073	...
	43. Mat makers, cane splitters	·264	·203	·061
	44. Hunters, fowlers, &c.	·006	·006	...
	45. Miscellaneous and disreputable livers ...	1·725	1·512	·213
	46. Tumblers and acrobats	·002	·002	...
	Total ...	**2·070**	**1·796**	**·274**
	GRAND TOTAL ...	**135·504**	**106·722**	**28·782**

258. The majority of the 70,196 who did not return caste or whose return was wholly unintelligible was found among the low-caste coolies in Amherst. There are, moreover, large colonies of Hindus who have settled down in the Moulmein and Amherst districts who practically have no caste; but for them and the coolies working on the mills, many of whom either would not or could not give their caste, the proportion of "Not returned" would have been far lower. It will be seen that the most numerous of the castes returned are the military and dominant and the minor agricultural. These were found in the ranks of the military police battalions, the returns of which were generally prepared with great care and precision. No attempt to go into the question of caste, or to discuss its various phases, is necessary in Burma, as this task has already been satisfactorily dealt with in the previous Census Reports of the Punjab and North-Western Provinces. Moreover, the observances of caste are unknown amongst the indigenous races, and the

journey by sea and their new environment has succeeded in weakening the hold of caste over those who in their own country are bound by it. An alphabetical index of the castes enumerated in the province will be found in Appendix **B** of this report.

The European nationalities.

259. The return of European nationalities in Imperial Table No. XVI requires but little explanation. Out of the 11,723 persons returned as Europeans in Burma, 8,702 were enumerated in Lower Burma. Accordingly, in Lower Burma 18 persons out of every 10,000 of both sexes are either Europeans or of European parentage. The absence of any return of race and nationality in 1881 renders any comparisons of the strength of the various nationalities represented impossible. The return of "Mother-tongues" in 1881 is delusive, as we find that while 11,873 returned themselves as speaking European languages, the return of Christian sects gave only 7,866 Europeans and Americans taken together. Taking all Europeans and Americans together we find that their numbers have increased at the rate of over 16 per cent. Comparing the figures given for the sexes apart we find that the return of European British subjects in 1881 must have been construed so as to include Eurasians; for while there were nominally 6,843 European British subjects, other Europeans and Americans in 1881, there were only 6,494 male Europeans in Lower Burma in 1891. The census reports of other provinces besides Burma in 1881 show that the selection of the term European British subject, which is borrowed from the Criminal Procedure Code, was particularly unfortunate, for it includes those who are known as Eurasians as well as Europeans of pure blood. Hence any comparison of the returns of the two enumerations would be unfruitful. Although it is probable that some persons who should have been classed as Eurasians still returned themselves as Europeans, yet the table shows clearly that the returns of 1891 are far more trustworthy. There are only 340 females to every 1,000 male Europeans in Lower Burma. This alone would show that Europeans are not a domiciled race. The majority of Europeans are to be found in the British regiments, in the professional and mercantile classes, and in the civil servants of Government.

Eurasians.

260. The returns of mixed races, Final Form No. VIII-A of the Census Report of 1881, gave only 762 persons of both sexes who were returned as of mixed European and Burman race, but from the return of Christian Sects III-A, it was found that there were 4,998 Eurasian Christians. In 1891 there were in Lower Burma 6,296 Eurasians, of whom 6,292 were Christians and 4 were Buddhists. Thus the number of Eurasians increased at the rate of almost 26 per cent. during the last decade. If we take the sexes apart, we find that the sexes are much more evenly distributed amongst them than amongst Europeans. In 1881 there were 810 females to every 1,000 male Eurasians. In 1891 in Lower Burma there were 801 females to every 1,000 males. But for reasons already stated when discussing the return of Europeans, any comparison with the returns of 1881 is necessarily of little value owing to the change in the definition of European. Owing to the annexation of the kingdom of Ava a large number of the Eurasian population of Lower Burma has found its way northward, and an increase of 26 per cent. within one decade in the number of Eurasians in Lower Burma is therefore somewhat improbable. It is possible therefore that some who returned themselves as European British subjects in 1881 have returned themselves as Eurasians in 1891. The history of Eurasians in India is a melancholy one, and the prospect of their ever exerting any influence over the course of Indian politics seems to be somewhat remote. In Burma the absence of caste prejudice and the tolerance that marks the Buddhist religion is more favourable for the growth of self-respect amongst those of mixed blood. On the other hand, this very tolerance and good feeling has the effect of diminishing the number of those returned as Eurasians, as children of mixed marriages often adopt the Burmese dress and return themselves as Burmans. Moreover, this matter is so mixed up with social, religious and political questions, that any discussion as to the future history of the Eurasians in Burma can scarcely lie within the scope of a census report.

CHAPTER XI.

OCCUPATIONS.

Method of abstraction, tabulation, and compilation of the returns of occupations and the difficulties experienced. The change in the method of classification. Classification of occupations into 7 classes, 24 orders, 77 groups, and 479 items or headings. The consequent difficulties experienced in comparing the returns of the present with those of previous enumerations. The classification of agriculturists proposed by the Financial Commissioner. The three abstract statements prepared. Distribution of population by occupation, sex and age, by districts and divisions, and by urban and rural tracts. Comparison of the returns with those of previous enumerations.

Variety in the occupations returned and the method of compilation.

261. The Census Commissioners, in their report on the English and Welsh census of 1881, stated that "the most laborious, the most costly, and, after all, the least satisfactory part of the census is that which is concerned with the occupations of the people." The same words will apply, with almost equal force, to the census of Burma. It is true that we have not the same complexity or subdivision of the various branches of labour, but even in Burma the variety of the returns found in the schedules was far greater than any one unacquainted with the wearisome task of compiling these returns could imagine to be possible. Added to this was the difficulty, unknown in England, of translating and identifying obscure terms and local phrases, which often proved to be beyond the power of the ordinary Burman clerks. The term "thwe thaukgyi" or "great blood-drinker" is now known to be an official title, but most officers would be puzzled to know what an "ekkaya" was. A "nauk taing" or "back sitter" is not at once recognizable as the humble follower who sits back to back with the first violin of a Burmese band and gives the musician something to lean against when he is tired. Nor would it at once be supposed that in Burma demonology and spiritualism would have gone so far as to separate between the raiser of spirits, Hmaw Saya, and the spirit medium or Nat thangè. In the census schedules an immense number of entries was found, and by the order of the Census Commissioner these entries were reproduced exactly as entered in the schedules by the abstraction clerks. It was manifestly too dangerous to allow the clerks any discretion in the matter either of translating or classifying the entries. Accordingly, before any entries were tabulated, all of these entries had to be collated from the abstraction sheets and compiled under the 479 authorized headings. This task was done under my own immediate direction, and the entries in the abstraction sheets were numbered by a few select clerks under the number of the heading to which each entry was assigned. In the tabulation register the number of each occupation, and not its name, was entered. The work thus left to the tabulation clerks was purely mechanical, and not only was the work done very much more quickly and accurately in this way, but I was enabled to employ a cheaper class of men for the work. The immense amount of work that had to be done, notwithstanding the collation and compilation of the quaintly named and diverse occupations into only 479 headings, may be judged from the fact that a district of the average size and population required over 30 volumes of the occupation register. When it is recollected that on this occasion, for the first time, were persons shown distributed by age periods as well as by sex, the enormous number of entries required may be easily conceived. The mere addition of the three age periods increased the work in geometrical and not mere arithmetical progression.

The Imperial Tables XVII A and B.

262. Imperial Table XVII-A gives the population of Burma outside of the excluded tracts divided into two great divisions—Urban and Rural. The population is here shown distributed by sex and age periods. The age periods, which were selected by the Government of India are 0—4, 5—14, 15 and over. The first and second age periods correspond very closely with the first two periods in life, when the individual is wholly and partially dependent on others, and the last age period, 15 and over, covers the time when a man or woman becomes self-supporting. In Imperial Table XVII-B the distinction of age periods was perforce abandoned because, though the results had already been worked out for the summary in Table XVII-A, to have reproduced this distribution in the district table would have rendered Table B, already sufficiently cumbersome, completely unwieldy.

263. In the census schedule the enumerators were ordered to show dependents under the head of the employment of the person on whom they depended, adding the word "dependent" thereto. Even this distinction could not be maintained in preparing the Imperial tables, as this would have just doubled the number of headings, and consequently the size of the registers would have been doubled, while the size and cost of the Imperial tables would have been enormously increased. In India, where the vast majority of the women are either employed in domestic and family duties or are *purda nashins*, or, if they have work, are employed as assistants to their husbands, little is lost by not preserving this distinction. All children under 5 and most females over that age may be ranked as dependents. Accordingly the orders issued to the census enumerators that the occupation of the parent or supporter was to be entered for the dependent, but that the word "dependent" was to be added, were not intended for use in the compilation of the returns, but rather as a guide and help to the enumerator himself, and to smooth away the seeming eccentricity of the returns and at the same time to draw his attention to the fact that the employment of the supporter, and not necessarily that of the dependent's parent or caste, was to be entered. Practically the end aimed at by the return of occupations, that is to say, the number supported by any handicraft or occupation, and not merely the actual number of the workers, is thus gained.

264. In Burma, where women even after marriage preserve a freedom unknown in any other eastern country and, perhaps, in the world, the danger lay in the fact that the enumerator might be tempted to return the husband's and not the wife's own occupation. Theoretically, it is impossible sometimes to draw the line between the woman who works with her husband at the same occupation, as, for instance, in agricultural work, and the dependent but useful domestic drudge. Practically, however, the problem has been satisfactorily solved by the enumerators themselves, who, being Burmans, were the best judges whether the woman was dependent or independent and earning a separate livelihood from her husband. Turning to the tables, we see that in those occupations, such as weaving and in the vending of various articles of consumption, the women far outnumber the men, and in these cases, by comparing the returns of age periods, the number of women who are independent workers can be gauged with some approximation to the truth.

The classification adopted.

265. The classification hitherto adopted in the compilation of the occupation tables was based more or less closely on the English system, which is generally known as Dr. Farr's system, but which Dr. Farr himself borrowed from German sources. A study of the reports of 1881 and 1872 will show how unsuitable this classification is to the more primitive industries of India. Even as it stands the arrangement and terminology adopted at the last census by the Government of India was unscientific as well as misleading. Every Superintendent of Census who went thoroughly into his returns, complained with more or less vehemence of the unsuitableness of this classification. In the suggestive chapter on occupations in the Bombay report, it is interesting to note the first draft of the classification now adopted. In some ways it agrees outwardly with Dr. Farr's system. That system attempted to show the number of those actually engaged in each of the recognized occupations. If the list of occupations could by any means be made exhaustive, and if the line

could be sharply drawn, as before stated, between the dependent who occasionally helps, and the assistant who earns his or her livelihood, then such a system as that of Dr. Farr's might be accepted as definite and exhaustive. The present classification which accepts the impossibility of discriminating between worker and dependent merely seeks to show the actual number of persons dependent for their livelihood, directly or indirectly, on any occupation. This aim, though less ambitious, is more easily attainable, and more valuable after it has been attained, than the results obtained under the English system. In Dr. Farr's system all children under 5 years of age and all those of indefinite occupation are included in the unproductive class. By this arrangement it becomes manifestly impossible to ascertain the exact number of persons affected by losses confined to any particular occupation.

Comparison of the two classifications.

266. The goodness of a classification rests on the object to be gained by the census. If this is meant to ascertain the exact number of workers at each particular occupation, then Dr. Farr's system is preferable; if, however, the object sought is to divide the population according to the various occupations followed, and to show exactly the numbers affected by the course of trade, the decay of industries, and the failure of crops, then the present system introduced by the present Census Commissioner for India is undoubtedly superior.

In this classification we have seven great classes: **A**, administration, defence, and foreign and feudatory service; **B**, live-stock rearing and agriculture; **C**, personal and household service; **D**, preparation and supply of materials; **E**, commerce, transport, and storage; **F**, professions; **G**, indefinite and independent. Those whose means of livelihood have not been returned are grouped apart. There are, however, but very few in this group. Dr. Farr's classification is as follows: professional, domestic, commercial, agricultural, industrial, and unoccupied. The professional here covers classes **A** and **F** in our present classification, the domestic covers class **C**, the commercial, class **E**, the agricultural, class **B**, and the industrial, class **D**. The unoccupied class covered 5 per cent. of the total male population of England and Wales within the working period of life, and how misleading this term was, may be inferred from the somewhat naive admission of the English Census Commissioners that—

"Of the 182,282 males in the working period of life (20—65) without specific occupations, a large number doubtless were busily engaged in avocations which were none the less serious or less important because not recognized in our classification. They were managing their estates or property, directing charitable institutions, prosecuting literary or scientific research, or engaged in other of the multifarious channels by which unpaid energy finds vent."

The term "unoccupied" is therefore clearly misleading. On the whole it may be admitted that the classification adopted by the Census Commissioner for India is better suited to the requirements of a census in India than the system of Dr. Farr.

267. Unfortunately, however, Dr. Farr's system was the system adopted for the census of 1881, and accordingly the comparison of the various classes is rendered much more difficult by the adoption of the new system. This diversity is still more evident in the divisions and subdivisions of these classes. In 1881 there were 6 classes, 18 orders, and numerous sub-orders—so numerous that Mr. Copleston does not trouble to specify them. There were, as a fact, 82 sub-orders or groups and 806 occupations. In our present system there are 7 classes, 24 orders, 77 groups, 33 sub-groups and 479 items or occupations. A dictionary of the terms used has been prepared and submitted for incorporation in the Imperial Report of the Census Commissioner. It will not be necessary to enumerate them here again. It was found that practically the 479 items covered all our requirements. The only additions that have been made were introduced at the request of the Chief Commissioner. Religious mendicant, No. 404, was subdivided into 404*a* pôngyis or monks, 404*b* upazins or probationers, 404*c* maungyins or koyins or acolytes, 404*d* pothudaws and methila or religious mendicants who have not taken vows.

268. Owing to the change in the system now adopted, any comparison between class and class, order and order, group and sub-order, would be fruitless, and it is not

till we come to the actual separate occupations themselves that any comparison with the returns of previous enumerations is possible. The returns of 1872 are classified on a system which in some way resembles the present classification, whereas, in reality, it is based on Dr. Farr's system, so that even in 1881 no attempt at comparison was made. No attempt to compare even the returns under the separate occupations was made. Unfortunately, from an inspection of the returns of 1881 it is quite evident that, although orders were issued that all boys under 15 years of age should be returned as unproductive, a considerable number of lads under that age were included in the productive classes; hence a comparison even in the return of separate occupations is rendered of doubtful value. Such being the case, it is manifestly impossible to work out the proportional tables for the census of 1881 in order that they may be compared with the proportional statements of the present report. The only possible way would be by first interpolating the right figures, but as this would be after all mere guess work, I have been obliged to compare the actual figures of 1881 as given and confine the proportional statements to the returns of the present enumeration.

The arrangement of the classes.

269. Before analysing the returns, the arrangement of the classes calls for some explanation. The first class is the service of Government. That this is put first in order is not due, as the unkindly critics might urge, to the self-appreciation of the importance of their office by Government servants. Order is not only heaven's first law, but without security to life and property—to maintain which is the especial duty of the servants of the State—none of the occupations of civilized man could be carried on; hence those whose duty it is to watch over and maintain this security come first. Next we take each class of occupations in the natural order in which they were evolved. The pastoral and the agricultural pursuits therefore form class **B**, which is next analysed; then follow the domestic and household servants, class **C**, some of whom are hard to distinguish from the preceding class; after them comes class **D**, which comprises the handicraftsmen and manufacturers, who work the raw materials produced by class **B**. The division of labour next evolved the commercial and carrying classes, which are engaged in bartering the productions of classes **B** and **D**. It is not till the division of labour and the accumulation of capital have produced a leisured wealthy class that we find the professions rising into sufficient importance to be treated as a separate class. In the pastoral age the shepherd kings combined all these professions in themselves. Lastly, we have the indefinite and independent class. And here it would appear that these two might have been well separated. Order XXIII, Indefinite, might have been treated with advantage as a class and Order XXIV have been called the "Non-productive."

270. The Government of India decided that the distinction of age periods should not be maintained in the Imperial Table XVII-B, Occupations distributed by districts. The distribution by age periods was for reasons already given confined to the province distributed into Urban and Rural tracts. Consequently there has been in Burma no small difficulty experienced by me in obtaining the proper proportion of the population under each occupation, in Lower Burma alone, in order to compare the results of the present with that of past enumerations. The method followed is to obtain from Table XVII-B the total number of those engaged in or dependent on each occupation, and then by comparing the distribution by age periods for this particular occupation in Table XVII-A, to ascertain the approximate number of those returned under the occupation distributed by the three age periods given. It was assumed that in most occupations all persons under 14 years of age were either wholly or partially dependent and those over that age were considered in the case of males as working at the occupation. Of course in particular occupations such as money-lending or among the religious orders this rule does not hold good. In those cases the proportions followed were obtained from the Table VII, the population distributed by age periods. Of course the figures thus obtained can only be approximate, but it has been pointed out that, when we have to deal with large numbers, the figures are practically correct. Such calculations would not have been necessary had the Census Commissioner's proposal to show dependents separately under each occupation been

feasible or if the distribution by age periods been maintained in Table XVII-B. As a fact, however, the results thus obtained are, I believe, fairly accurate, and the incalculable advantage of not having nearly one-half of the population returned as dependent on no occupation must be taken to outweigh the loss of absolute accuracy in the attempts that have been made to compare the results of the present with those of past enumerations. Moreover any regret that may have been felt on this score is very considerably lessened by the fact that, though I have laboured hard to compare the figures, I find that the change in the system of classification has of itself nearly frustrated the best intentioned effort to effect a comparison. In criticising my figures, therefore, it must be remembered that, although they represent a very large amount of labour, I do not claim that the number of those shown as working at each occupation in Lower Burma can be anything but as close an approximation as is possible to the true figures. It is necessary to note that though the return of occupations in the synchronous census tract of the Shan States has been included in the Provincial total, I have excluded the figures when analysing and comparing the return of occupation in the following pages of this report. The inclusion of these figures, though they were necessary for imperial purposes, would only tend to obscure the relative positions of Upper and Lower Burma when considered from a purely provincial point of view.

271. Imperial Tables XVII-A and XVII-B are so bulky that perhaps, before proceeding to analyse, it may be as well to summarize them first. The following statement, Abstract **A**, gives the total number of persons of each sex in Upper and Lower Burma and in each Commissionership separately, distributed by the 8 classes and 24 orders :—

A.—*Abstract Table*

Class and order.	Total of province.		
	Total.	Male.	Female.
1	2	3	4
Class A.—Service of Government.			
Order I.—Administration.			
Services of the Imperial and Provincial, Local and Municipal bodies, and village services.	103,572	61,437	42,135
II.—Defence.			
Army, Navy, and Marine	31,158	29,165	1,993
III.—Foreign and Feudatory State service.			
Administrative Army and Marine services	192	53	139
Total, Class A ...	**134,922**	**90,655**	**44,267**
Class B.—Pasture and Agriculture.			
IV.—Live-stock.			
Stock breeding and dealing and subsidiary services to stock ...	52,753	32,630	20,123
V.—Agriculture.			
Interest in land, agricultural labourers, growers of special products and trees, and agricultural training and supervision.	4,826,737	2,437,823	2,388,914
Total, Class B ...	**4,879,490**	**2,470,453**	**2,409,037**
Class C.—Personal Services.			
VI.—Personal and household services.			
Personal and domestic services, non-domestic establishment, and personal and household services.	59,670	36,990	22,680
Total, Class C ...	**59,670**	**36,990**	**22,680**
Class D.—Preparation and supply of material substances.			
VII.—Food and drink.			
Food and drink, vegetable food and drink, condiments and narcotics.	755,386	342,800	412,586
VIII.—Light, firing, and forage.			
Lighting, fuel, and forage...	69,392	34,283	35,109
IX.—Buildings.			
Building materials and artificers in buildings	48,795	24,704	24,091
X.—Vehicles and vessels.			
Railway plant, cart, carriages, &c., and ships and boats ...	14,108	7,852	6,256
XI.—Supplementary requirements.			
Paper, &c.; books and prints, &c.; watches, clocks, and scientific instruments; carving, engraving, &c.; toys, curiosities, &c.; music and musical instruments; necklaces, bracelets, beads, sacred threads, &c.; furniture; harness; tools and machinery; and arms and ammunition.	32,667	16,144	16,523
XII.—Textile fabrics and dress.			
Wool and fur; silk; cotton; jute, flax, coir, &c., and dress ...	375,166	101,475	273,691

of Occupations.

Arakan division.			Pegu division.			Irrawaddy division.		
Total.	Male.	Female.	Total.	Male.	Female.	Total.	Male.	Female.
5	6	7	8	9	10	11	12	13
7,965	4,351	3,614	17,927	10,804	7,123	15,544	9,305	6,239
8	4	4	3,033	2,620	413	1,605	1,461	144
20	...	20	106	19	87	3	3	...
7,993	**4,355**	**3,638**	**21,066**	**13,443**	**7,623**	**17,152**	**10,769**	**6,383**
5,600	3,025	2,575	14,319	9,538	4,781	8,197	4,931	3,266
513,917	262,302	251,615	934,886	486,947	447,939	1,055,094	535,595	519,499
519,517	**265,327**	**254,190**	**949,205**	**496,485**	**452,720**	**1,063,291**	**540,526**	**522,765**
3,572	2,663	909	21,125	14,438	6,687	5,664	3,496	2,168
3,572	**2,663**	**909**	**21,125**	**14,438**	**6,687**	**5,664**	**3,496**	**2,168**
42,516	21,632	20,884	132,876	61,162	71,714	189,115	89,174	99,941
1,717	1,057	660	11,980	6,633	5,347	12,615	5,941	6,674
700	513	187	7,564	4,295	3,269	16,050	8,349	7,701
1,899	1,021	878	3,150	1,959	1,191	3,406	1,638	1,768
866	390	476	5,558	3,111	2,447	1,899	1,130	769
11,220	4,922	6,298	46,966	16,636	30,330	34,784	12,906	21,878

A.—*Abstract Table*

Class and order.	Tenasserim division.		
	Total.	Male.	Female.
1	14	15	16
Class A.—Service of Government.			
Order I.—Administration.			
Services of the Imperial and Provincial, Local and Municipal bodies, and village services.	13,846	9,263	4,583
II.—Defence.			
Army, Navy, and Marine	1,308	1,200	108
III.—Foreign and Feudatory State service.			
Administrative Army and Marine services	3	2	1
Total, Class A ...	**15,157**	**10,465**	**4,692**
Class B.—Pasture and Agriculture.			
IV.—Live-stock.			
Stock breeding and dealing and subsidiary services to stock ...	7,154	4,834	2,320
V.—Agriculture.			
Interest in land, agricultural labourers, growers of special products and trees, and agricultural training and supervision.	670,984	347,123	323,861
Total, Class B ...	**678,138**	**351,957**	**326,181**
Class C.—Personal Services.			
VI.—Personal and household services.			
Personal and domestic services, non-domestic establishment, and personal and household services.	7,572	4,749	2,823
Total, Class C ...	**7,572**	**4,749**	**2,823**
Class D.—Preparation and supply of material substances.			
VII.—Food and drink.			
Food and drink, vegetable food and drink, condiments and narcotics.	78,741	36,214	42,527
VIII.—Light, firing, and forage.			
Lighting, fuel, and forage	4,650	2,561	2,089
IX.—Buildings.			
Building materials and artificers in buildings	5,678	3,179	2,499
X.—Vehicles and vessels.			
Railway plant, cart, carriages, &c., and ships and boats ...	2,522	1,477	1,045
XI.—Supplementary requirements.			
Paper, &c.; books and prints, &c.; watches, clocks and scientific instruments; carving, engraving, &c.; toys, curiosities, &c.; music and musical instruments; necklaces, bracelets, beads, sacred threads, &c.; furniture; harness; tools and machinery; and arms and ammunition.	1,465	755	710
XII.—Textile fabrics and dress.			
Wool and fur; silk; cotton; jute, flax, coir, &c., and dress ...	35,639	9,272	26,367

of Occupations—continued.

Northern division.			Central division.			Southern division.		
Total.	Male.	Female.	Total.	Male.	Female.	Total.	Male.	Female.
17	18	19	20	21	22	23	24	25
13,230	8,019	5,211	9,249	5,231	4,018	15,160	8,321	6,839
11,683	11,146	537	2,390	2,294	96	6,274	5,747	527
13	1	12	...	...	...	...	...	...
24,926	**19,166**	**5,760**	**11,639**	**7,525**	**4,114**	**21,434**	**14,068**	**7,366**
3,782	2,473	1,309	4,467	2,465	2,002	6,381	3,763	2,618
242,715	117,186	125,529	378,157	177,527	200,630	676,823	335,838	340,985
246,497	**119,659**	**126,838**	**382,624**	**179,992**	**202,632**	**683,204**	**339,601**	**343,603**
9,129	5,122	4,007	3,268	1,672	1,596	5,612	2,466	3,146
9,129	**5,122**	**4,007**	**3,268**	**1,672**	**1,596**	**5,612**	**2,466**	**3,146**
76,971	33,926	43,045	63,419	27,059	36,360	124,448	54,165	70,283
17,341	8,592	8,749	6,253	2,984	3,269	10,213	4,362	5,851
5,369	2,906	2,463	4,363	1,940	2,423	6,158	2,307	3,851
770	448	322	434	263	171	1,155	654	501
7,080	3,647	3,433	4,339	1,694	2,645	10,170	4,819	5,351
69,369	22,573	46,796	52,835	9,991	42,844	94,016	18,178	75,838

A.—*Abstract Table*

Class and order.	Eastern division.		
	Total.	Male.	Female.
1	26	27	28
Class A.—Service of Government.			
Order I.—Administration.			
Services of the Imperial and Provincial, Local and Municipal bodies, and village services.	10,588	6,105	4,483
II.—Defence.			
Army, Navy, and Marine	2,896	2,769	127
III.—Foreign and Feudatory State service.			
Administrative Army and Marine services	47	28	19
Total, Class A ...	**13,531**	**8,902**	**4,629**
Class B.—Pasture and Agriculture.			
IV.—Live-stock.			
Stock breeding and dealing and subsidiary services to stock ..	2,853	1,601	1,252
V.—Agriculture.			
Interest in land, agricultural labourers, growers of special products and trees, and agricultural training and supervision.	354,158	175,303	178,855
Total, Class B ...	**357,011**	**176,904**	**180,107**
Class C.—Personal Services.			
VI.—Personal and household services.			
Personal and domestic services, non-domestic establishment, and personal and household services.	3,099	1,786	1,313
Total, Class C ...	**3,099**	**1,786**	**1,313**
Class D.—Preparation and supply of material substances.			
VII.—Food and drink.			
Food and drink, vegetable food and drink, condiments and narcotics.	47,292	19,460	27,832
VIII.—Light, firing, and forage.			
Lighting, fuel, and forage	4,623	2,153	2,470
IX.—Buildings.			
Building materials and artificers in buildings	2,913	1,215	1,698
X.—Vehicles and vessels.			
Railway plant, cart, carriages, &c., and ships and boats ...	772	392	380
XI.—Supplementary requirements.			
Paper, &c.; books and prints, &c.; watches, clocks, and scientific instruments; carving, engraving, &c.; toys, curiosities, &c.; music and musical instruments; necklaces, bracelets, beads, sacred threads, &c.; furniture; harness; tools and machinery; and arms and ammunition.	1,290	598	692
XII.—Textile fabrics and dress.			
Wool and fur; silk; cotton; jute, flax, coir, &c., and dress ...	30,334	6,994	23,340

of Occupations—continued.

Shan States synchronous census tract.			Total, Lower Burma.			Total, Upper Burma.		
Total.	Male.	Female.	Total.	Male.	Female.	Total.	Male.	Female.
29	30	31	32	33	34	35	36	37
63	38	25	55,282	33,723	21,559	48,227	27,676	20,551
1,961	1,924	37	5,954	5,285	669	23,243	21,956	1,287
...	...	...	132	24	108	60	29	31
2,024	**1,962**	**62**	**61,368**	**39,032**	**22,336**	**71,530**	**49,616**	**21,869**
...	...	...	35,270	22,328	12,942	17,483	10,302	7,181
3	2	1	3,174,881	1,631,967	1,542,914	1,651,853	805,854	845,999
3	**2**	**1**	**3,210,151**	**1,654,295**	**1,555,856**	**1,669,336**	**816,156**	**853,180**
629	598	31	37,933	25,346	12,587	21,108	11,046	10,062
629	**598**	**31**	**37,933**	**25,346**	**12,587**	**21,108**	**11,046**	**10,062**
8	8	...	443,248	208,182	235,066	312,130	134,610	177,520
...	...	...	30,962	16,192	14,770	38,430	18,091	20,339
...	...	...	29,992	16,336	13,656	18,803	8,368	10,435
...	...	...	10,977	6,095	4,882	3,131	1,757	1,374
...	...	...	9,788	5,386	4,402	22,879	10,758	12,121
3	3	...	128,609	43,736	84,873	246,554	57,736	188,818

A.—*Abstract Table*

Class and order.	Total of province.		
	Total.	Male.	Female.
1	2	3	4
Class D.—Preparation and supply of material substances—*concluded.*			
Order XIII.—Metals and precious stones.			
Gold, silver, and precious stones; brass, copper, and bell-metal; tin, zinc, mercury, and lead; and iron and steel.	69,348	40,007	29,341
XIV.—Glass, pottery, and stone ware.			
Glass and Chinaware and earthen and stone ware	38,195	16,670	21,525
XV.—Wood, cane, and leaves, &c.			
Timber and wood and cane-work, matting and leaves, &c. ...	217,327	119,539	97,788
XVI.—Drugs, gums, dyes, &c.			
Gums, wax, and similar forest produce, and drugs, dyes, pigments, &c.	11,044	5,537	5,507
XVII.—Leather, horns, bones, and grease.			
Leather, &c.	20,109	11,778	8,331
Total, Class D ...	**1,651,537**	**720,789**	**930,748**
Class E.—Commerce, Transport, Storage.			
XVIII.—Commerce.			
Dealers in money and securities, general merchandise, dealing unspecified, and middlemen, &c.	131,356	63,068	68,288
XIX.—Transport and storage.			
Railway, road, water, messages, and storage and weighing ...	193,107	132,512	60,595
Total, Class E ...	**324,463**	**195,580**	**128,883**
Class F.—Professions.			
XX.—Learned and artistic professions.			
Religion, education, literature, law, medicine, engineering, and surveying; other sciences, pictorial art and sculpture, and music, acting, dancing.	208,595	159,903	48,692
XXI.—Sports and amusements.			
Sport and exhibition and games	5,681	3,624	2,057
Total, Class F ...	**214,276**	**163,527**	**50,749**
Class G.—Indefinite and Independent.			
XXII.—Complex occupations.			
XXIII.—Indefinite.			
Unskilled labour and undefined, &c.	305,699	177,816	127,883
XXIV.—Independent of work.			
Property and alms and supported at the public charge ...	37,541	22,950	14,591
Total, Class G ...	**343,240**	**200,766**	**142,474**
Not returned	954	423	531
Total	**954**	**423**	**531**
Grand Total ...	**7,608,552**	**3,879,183**	**3,729,369**

of Occupations—continued.

Arakan division.			Pegu division.			Irrawaddy division.		
Total.	Male.	Female.	Total.	Male.	Female.	Total.	Male.	Female.
5	6	7	8	9	10	11	12	13
3,432	2,221	1,211	14,512	8,640	5,872	11,501	6,574	4,927
3,971	2,123	1,848	5,249	2,222	3,027	10,078	4,787	5,291
6,470	4,264	2,206	39,298	22,894	16,404	45,528	23,616	21,912
190	107	83	1,385	658	727	1,082	589	493
261	198	63	2,466	1,697	769	3,925	2,398	1,527
73,242	**38,448**	**34,794**	**271,004**	**129,907**	**141,097**	**329,983**	**157,102**	**172,881**
7,958	4,265	3,693	30,568	16,121	14,447	26,667	13,352	13,315
13,143	10,522	2,621	63,848	46,365	17,483	37,768	26,339	11,429
21,101	**14,787**	**6,314**	**94,416**	**62,486**	**31,930**	**64,435**	**39,691**	**24,744**
11,088	7,297	3,791	30,214	21,517	8,697	34,114	24,846	9,268
219	186	33	1,107	695	412	1,356	981	375
11,307	**7,483**	**3,824**	**31,321**	**22,212**	**9,109**	**35,470**	**25,827**	**9,643**
31,479	21,730	9,749	60,087	44,707	15,380	32,724	20,407	12,317
3,688	2,158	1,530	6,618	4,767	1,851	4,514	3,610	904
35,167	**23,888**	**11,279**	**66,705**	**49,474**	**17,231**	**37,238**	**24,017**	**13,221**
...	...	...	485	222	263	95	23	72
...	**...**	**...**	**485**	**222**	**263**	**95**	**23**	**72**
671,899	**356,951**	**314,948**	**1,455,327**	**788,667**	**666,660**	**1,553,328**	**801,451**	**751,877**

A.—*Abstract Table*

Class and order.	Tenasserim division. Total.	Male.	Female.
1	14	15	16
Class D.—Preparation and supply of material substances—*concluded.*			
XIII.—Metals and precious stones.			
Gold, silver, and precious stones; brass, copper and bell-metal; tin, zinc, mercury, and lead; and iron and steel.	8,753	5,420	3,333
XIV.—Glass, pottery, and stone ware.			
Glass and Chinaware and earthen and stone ware	3,744	1,584	2,160
XV.—Wood, cane, and leaves, &c.			
Timber and wood and cane-work, matting and leaves, &c. ...	30,128	17,684	12,444
XVI.—Drugs, gums, dyes, &c.			
Gums, wax, and similar forest produce, and drugs, dyes, pigments, &c.	1,063	554	509
XVII.—Leather, horns, bones, and grease.			
Leather, &c.	783	513	270
Total, Class D ...	**173,166**	**79,213**	**93,953**
Class E.—Commerce, Transport, Storage.			
XVIII.—Commerce.			
Dealers in money and securities, general merchandise, dealing unspecified, and middlemen, &c.	21,440	10,232	11,208
XIX.—Transport and storage.			
Railway, road, water, messages, and storage and weighing ...	24,995	16,583	8,412
Total, Class E ...	**46,435**	**26,815**	**19,620**
Class F.—Professions.			
XX.—Learned and artistic professions.			
Religion, education, literature, law, medicine, engineering, and surveying; other sciences, pictorial art and sculpture, and music, acting, dancing.	27,265	22,550	4,715
XXI.—Sports and amusements.			
Sport and exhibition and games	295	194	101
Total, Class F ...	**27,560**	**22,744**	**4,816**
G.—Indefinite and Independent.			
XXII.—Complex occupations.			
XXIII.—Indefinite.			
Unskilled labour and undefined, &c.	26,251	16,533	9,718
XXIV.—Independent of work.			
Property and alms and supported at the public charge ...	3,572	2,659	913
Total, Class G ...	**29,823**	**19,192**	**10,631**
Not returned	222	92	130
Total ...	**222**	**92**	**130**
Grand Total ...	**978,073**	**515,227**	**462,846**

of Occupations—continued.

Northern division.			Central division.			Southern division.		
Total.	Male.	Female.	Total.	Male.	Female.	Total.	Male.	Female.
17	18	19	20	21	22	23	24	25
15,606	8,785	6,821	4,508	2,518	1,990	7,838	4,150	3,688
3,770	1,539	2,231	3,582	1,061	2,521	5,343	2,258	3,085
24,940	14,199	10,741	21,493	10,829	10,664	26,277	13,735	12,542
1,915	973	942	2,692	1,111	1,581	1,264	732	532
5,943	3,311	2,632	3,010	1,682	1,328	2,537	1,331	1,206
229,074	**100,899**	**128,175**	**166,928**	**61,132**	**105,796**	**289,419**	**106,691**	**182,728**
15,200	6,760	8,440	8,584	3,718	4,866	13,766	5,380	8,386
17,900	11,076	6,824	10,665	6,230	4,435	16,690	9,936	6,754
33,100	**17,836**	**15,264**	**19,249**	**9,948**	**9,301**	**30,456**	**15,316**	**15,140**
31,563	23,234	8,329	25,555	20,416	5,139	32,841	27,224	5,617
703	329	374	980	602	378	714	445	269
32,266	**23,563**	**8,703**	**26,535**	**21,018**	**5,517**	**33,555**	**27,669**	**5,886**
68,794	37,208	31,586	34,126	14,310	19,816	28,905	12,604	16,301
5,190	3,109	2,081	4,388	1,802	2,586	6,227	3,414	2,813
73,984	**40,317**	**33,667**	**38,514**	**16,112**	**22,402**	**35,132**	**16,018**	**19,114**
59	29	30	29	23	6	17	7	10
59	**29**	**30**	**29**	**23**	**6**	**17**	**7**	**10**
649,035	**326,591**	**322,444**	**648,786**	**297,422**	**351,364**	**1,098,829**	**521,836**	**576,993**

A.—*Abstract Table*

Class and order.	EASTERN DIVISION.		
	Total.	Male.	Female.
1	26	27	28
CLASS D.—PREPARATION AND SUPPLY OF MATERIAL SUBSTANCES—*concluded.*			
Order XIII.—Metals and precious stones.			
Gold, silver, and precious stones; brass, copper and bell-metal; tin, zinc, mercury, and lead; and iron and steel.	3,198	1,699	1,499
XIV.—Glass, pottery, and stone ware.			
Glass and Chinaware and earthen and stone ware	2,458	1,096	1,362
XV.—Wood, cane, and leaves, &c.			
Timber and wood and cane-work, matting and leaves, &c. ...	23,189	12,316	10,873
XVI.—Drugs, gums, dyes, &c.			
Gums, wax, and similar forest produce, and drugs, dyes, pigments, &c.	1,453	813	640
XVII.—Leather, horns, bones, and grease.			
Leather, &c.	1,184	648	536
Total, Class D ...	**118,706**	**47,384**	**71,322**
CLASS E.—COMMERCE, TRANSPORT, STORAGE.			
XVIII.—Commerce.			
Dealers in money and securities, general merchandise, dealing unspecified, and middlemen, &c.	7,163	3,230	3,933
XIX.—Transport and storage.			
Railway, road, water, messages, and storage and weighing ...	8,092	5,436	2,636
Total, Class E ...	**15,235**	**8,666**	**6,569**
CLASS F.—PROFESSIONS.			
XX.—Learned and artistic professions.			
Religion, education, literature, law, medicine, engineering, and surveying; other sciences, pictorial art and sculpture, and music, acting, dancing.	15,936	12,800	3,136
XXI.—Sports and amusements.			
Sport and exhibition and games	307	192	115
Total, Class F ...	**16,243**	**12,992**	**3,251**
CLASS G.—INDEFINITE AND INDEPENDENT.			
XXII.—Complex occupations.			
XXIII.—Indefinite.			
Unskilled labour and undefined, &c.	23,067	10,064	13,003
XXIV.—Independent of work.			
Property and alms and supported at the public charge ...	3,344	1,431	1,913
Total, Class G ...	**26,411**	**11,495**	**14,916**
Not returned	47	27	20
Total ...	**47**	**27**	**20**
GRAND TOTAL ...	**550,283**	**268,156**	**822,127**

of Occupations—concluded.

Shan States synchronous census tract.			Total, Lower Burma.			Total, Upper Burma.		
Total.	Male.	Female.	Total.	Male.	Female.	Total.	Male.	Female.
29	30	31	32	33	34	35	36	37
...	...	...	38,198	22,855	15,343	31,150	17,152	13,998
...	...	...	23,042	10,716	12,326	15,153	5,954	9,199
4	2	2	121,424	68,458	52,966	95,899	51,079	44,820
...	...	...	3,720	1,908	1,812	7,324	3,629	3,695
...	...	...	7,435	4,806	2,629	12,674	6,972	5,702
15	**13**	**2**	**847,395**	**404,670**	**442,725**	**804,127**	**316,106**	**488,021**
10	10	...	86,633	43,970	42,663	44,713	19,088	25,620
26	25	1	139,754	99,809	39,945	53,327	32,678	20,649
36	**35**	**1**	**226,387**	**143,779**	**82,608**	**98,040**	**51,766**	**46,274**
19	19	...	102,681	76,210	26,471	105,895	83,674	22,221
...	...	...	2,977	2,056	921	2,704	1,568	1,136
19	**19**	...	**105,658**	**78,266**	**27,392**	**108,599**	**85,242**	**23,357**
266	253	13	150,541	103,377	47,164	154,892	74,186	80,706
...	...	...	18,392	13,194	5,198	19,149	9,756	9,393
266	**253**	**13**	**168,933**	**116,571**	**52,362**	**174,041**	**83,942**	**90,099**
...	...	...	802	337	465	152	86	66
...	...	...	**802**	**337**	**465**	**152**	**86**	**66**
2,992	**2,882**	**110**	**4,658,627**	**2,462,296**	**2,196,331**	**2,946,933**	**1,414,005**	**1,532,928**

272. Perhaps the best commentary on Abstract **A** is the following Statement **B** showing the proportional strength of those whose occupations are included in the classes, orders, and the 77 groups into which these classes and orders are divided and sub-divided. In this statement no attempt has been made to go into the detail of sex or age, but the groups are shown in their relative strength to the total population, the only distinction being that urban and rural tracts are shown apart. The next statement, Abstract **C**, advances one step further It was manifestly a waste of labour as well as of space to attempt to prepare a proportional statement showing the relative strength of those pursuing each of the 479 occupations given in detail district by district. I have therefore selected 48 of the most important occupations and analysed the returns. This statement gives the relative strength of the persons following or dependent on these occupations in every 10,000 persons of both sexes in the whole of Burma. This table is interesting as it is practically the key to the distribution of the population of Burma, district by district, amongst the occupations most generally followed. I have omitted all the items of Class **A**, Government service, as their distribution is already known officially, but all the chief occupations have been included, and the table gives a bird's-eye view, so to speak, of the occupations followed in each district.

The Abstracts **A**, **B**, and **C**.

ABSTRACT **B**, *showing the relative Strength and local Distribution between Urban and Rural Tracts of each Class, Order, and Group of Occupations.*

Class.	Order.		Sub-order or group.	Ratio per 10,000 of the total population. Total of Province.	Town.	Country.
A	I	1	Services of the Imperial and Provincial Governments.	114·1	37	77·1
		2	Services of Local and Municipal Bodies ...	6·5	4·8	1·7
		3	Village service	15·4	1·6	13·8
			Total I ...	**136·0**	**43·4**	**92·6**
	II	4	Army	37·9	16	21·9
		5	Navy and Marine	·4	·1	·3
			Total II ...	**38·3**	**16·1**	**22·2**
	III	6	Administrative service	·2	·16	·1
		7	Army and Marine	...	...	...
			Total III ...	...	...	...
			Total Class A ...	**·25**	**·16**	**·09**
B	IV	8	Stock breeding and dealing	67·9	7·6	60·3
		9	Subsidiary services to stock	1·3	·4	·9
			Total IV ...	**69·3**	**·8**	**61·3**
	V	10	Interest in land	4,300·5	67·5	4,233·
		11	Agricultural labourers	897·5	18·9	878·6
		12	Growers of special products and trees ...	1,148·2	25·9	1,122·3
		13	Agricultural training and supervision ...	...	...	...
			Total V ...	**6,346·3**	**112·3**	**6,234·**
			Total Class B ...	**6,415·6**	**120·3**	**6,295·3**

ABSTRACT B, *showing the relative Strength and local Distribution between Urban and Rural Tracts of each Class, Order, and Group of Occupations*—continued.

Class.	Order.		Sub-order or group.	Ratio per 10,000 of the total population. Total of Province.	Town.	Country.
C	VI	14	Personal and domestic services ...	65·4	41·1	24·3
		15	Non-domestic establishment	7·8	4	3·8
		16	Sanitation	4·3	3·3	1
			Total VI ...	**77·6**	**48·5**	**29·1**
			Total Class C ...	...	...	...
D	VII	17	Animal food	304·3	58·8	245·5
		18	Vegetable food	315·2	91·8	223·4
		19	Drinks, condiments, and narcotics ...	373·5	71·4	302·1
			Total VII ...	**993·2**	**222·2**	**771·**
	VIII	20	Lighting	49·1	15·2	33·9
		21	Fuel and forage	42	10·5	31·5
			Total VIII ...	**91·2**	**25·8**	**65·4**
	IX	22	Building materials	52·4	6·5	45·9
		23	Artificers in building	11·6	5	6·6
			Total IX ...	**64·1**	**11·5**	**52·6**
	X	24	Railway plant	·9	·1	·8
		25	Carts, carriages, &c.	5·7	1·5	4·2
		26	Ships and boats	11·8	1·5	10·3
			Total X ...	**18·5**	**3·2**	**15·3**
	XI	27	Papers, &c.	1·4	·7	·7
		28	Books and prints, &c.	3·8	3·2	·6
		29	Watches, clocks, and scientific instruments ...	·6	·5	·1
		30	Carving, engraving, &c.	18·2	10·4	7·8
		31	Toys, curiosities, &c.	·8	·5	·3
		32	Music and musical instruments	·3	·1	·2
		33	Necklaces, bracelets, beads, sacred threads, &c.	·9	5·2	3·8
		34	Furniture	·9	·7	·2
		35	Harness	·7	·2	·5
		36	Tools and machinery	6·4	2·6	3·8
		37	Arms and ammunition	·2	·1	·1
			Total XI ...	**42·9**	**24·5**	**18·4**

ABSTRACT B, *showing the relative Strength and local Distributioa between Urban and Rural Tracts of each Class, Order, and Group of Occupations*—continued.

Class.	Order.		Sub-order or group.	Ratio per 10,000 of the total population. Total of Province.	Town.	Country.
D—concluded.	XII	38	Wool and fur	·08	·07	·01
		39	Silk	32·8	18·7	14·1
		40	Cotton	335·3	55·3	280·
		41	Jute, flax, and coir, &c.	16·5	4·3	12·2
		42	Dress	108·3	64·7	43·6
			Total XII ...	493·2	143·2	350·
	XIII	43	Gold, silver, and precious stones ...	47·9	22·7	25·2
		44	Brass, copper, and bell-metal	5·6	3·5	2·1
		45	Tin, zinc, mercury, and lead	4·9	2·8	2·1
		46	Iron and steel	32·7	10·1	22·6
			Total XIII ...	91·2	39·1	52·1
	XIV	47	Glass, pottery, and stoneware	1·9	1·2	·7
		48	Earthenware and stone ware	48·2	8·8	39·4
			Total XIV ...	50·2	10·	40·2
	XV	49	Timber and wood	184·	61·5	122·5
		50	Canework, matting, and leaves, &c. ...	101·6	17·7	83·9
			Total XV ...	285·7	79·3	206·4
	XVI	51	Gums, wax and similar forest produce ...	5·2	·9	4·3
		52	Drugs, dyes, pigments, &c.	9·2	3·6	5·6
			Total XVI ...	14·5	4·6	9·9
	XVII	53	Leather, &c.	26·4	19·7	6·7
			Total XVII ...	26·4	19·7	6·7
			Total Class D ...	2,171·4	583·2	1,588·2
E	XVIII	54	Dealers in money and securities ...	7·1	2·7	4·4
		55	General merchandise	11·2	9·5	1·7
		56	Dealing unspecified	100·2	30·8	69·4
		57	Middlemen, &c.	54·1	22·	32·1
			Total XVIII ...	172·7	65·	107·7

ABSTRACT B, *showing the relative Strength and local Distribution between Urban and Rural Tracts of each Class, Order, and Group of Occupations*—concluded.

Class.	Order.		Sub-order or group.	Ratio per 10,000 of the total population. Total of Province.	Town.	Country.
E—*concluded.*	XIX	58	Railway	11·8	7·8	4·
		59	Road	78·2	31·1	47·1
		60	Water	148·5	53·6	94·9
		61	Messages	5·2	3·1	2·1
		62	Storage and weighing	10·	8·7	1·3
			Total XIX ...	**253·9**	**104·3**	**149·6**
			Total Class E ...	**426·6**	**169·3**	**257·3**
F	XX	63	Religion	148·3	27·	121·3
		64	Education	10·9	5·6	5·3
		65	Literature	3·7	·9	2·8
		66	Law	5·6	3·3	2·3
		67	Medicine	66·5	15·6	50·9
		68	Engineering and surveying	6·9	2·4	4·5
		69	Other sciences, &c.	2·7	1·1	1·6
		70	Pictorial art and sculpture	10·2	4·3	5·9
		71	Music, acting, and dancing	19·	6·4	12·6
			Total XX ...	**274·2**	**66·9**	**207·3**
	XXI	72	Sport	·6	·1	·5
		73	Exhibition and games	6·8	1·6	5·2
			Total XXI ...	**7·5**	**1·7**	**5·8**
			Total Class F ...	**281·7**	**68·6**	**213·1**
G	XXII	...	Complex occupations not shown in the Imperial Table.			
	XXIII	74	Unskilled labour	398·4	167·7	230·7
		75	Undefined, &c.	3·1	2·3	·8
			Total XXIII ...	**401·6**	**170·1**	**231·5**
	XXIV	76	Property and alms	31·	9·2	21·8
		77	Supported at the public charge	18·3	14·8	3·5
			Total XXIV ...	**49·3**	**24·**	**25·3**
			Total Class G ...	**450·9**	**194·1**	**256·8**
			Not returned occupation	1·2	...	...

ABSTRACT C, ***showing relative Strength***

Occupation.	Akyab.			Northern Arakan.		
	Total.	Male.	Female.	Total.	Male.	Female.
1	2	3	4	5	6	7
25. Cattle breeders and dealers and Commissariat farm establishment.	...	·736	·855	...	...	...
26. Herdsmen	...	1·539	·762	...	...	...
27. Buffalo breeders and dealers ...	...	·974	1·134	...	...	...
37. Land occupants not cultivating...	...	2·78	3·06	...	...	...
38. Land occupants cultivating ...	...	106·45	100·23	...	4·42	4·17
41. Tenants and sharers cultivating...	...	41·61	40·37	...	...	...
43. Field labourers and crop-watchers	...	41·61	31·17	...	...	...
44. Tea, coffee, tobacco, and cinchona planters and assistants, &c.	...	·009	·019	...	...	...
46. Betel-vine, sugarcane, and areca-nut growers.	...	1·23	1·32	...	·002	...
48. Cardamom, til-seed, and pepper growers.	...	...	·055	...	...	...
50. Fruit growers	...	1·753	2·057	...	...	...
51. Market gardeners (vegetable growers).	...	17·842	16·153	...	4·878	4·803
81. Fishermen and fish-curers ...	...	2·759	2·195	...	·047	...
82. Fish dealers	...	1·970	1·694	...	...	...
83. Grain dealers	...	3·484	1·013	...	...	...
89. Vegetable sellers	...	·535	·269	...	...	...
92. Confectioners and sweetmeat makers and sellers and cooks.	...	3·007	4·115	...	·005	·003
98. Toddy drawers and sellers ...	...	·603	·394	...	...	...
104. Molasses (jaggery, gur, &c.) makers and sellers.	...	·057	·007	...	...	...
109. Grocers and general condiment dealers.	...	·650	·241	...	...	...
111. Betel-leaf and areca-nut sellers...	...	3·943	4·267	...	...	...
117. Oil and salt sellers	...	·528	·301	...	...	...
121. Kerosine-oil dealers ...	...	·077	·028	...	...	...
135. Thatch dealers and thatchers ...	...	·117	·035	...	...	...
157. Press proprietors, lithographers, and printers.	...	·019	·014	...	...	...
169. Wood and ebony carvers ...	...	·003	·003	...	...	...
172. Turners and lacquerers ...	...	·059	·032	...	...	...
206. Looms and loom-comb makers and sellers.	...	·038	·044	...	...	...
226. Silkworm rearers and cocoon gatherers.	...	...	...	...	...	...
227. Silk carders and spinners ...	...	...	·001	...	...	...
228. Silk weavers and dealers ...	...	·043	·081	...	...	...
231. Cotton cleaners, pressers, and ginners.	...	·001	...	..	...	...
232. Cotton carpet and rug makers and sellers.	...	...	...	...	...	...
233. Cotton spinners, sizers, and yarn beaters.	...	·022	·022	...	...	...
234. Cotton weavers, mill owners and managers.	...	·779	3·151	...	...	...
244. Net makers and sellers ...	...	·575	·425	...	...	...
260. Gold and silver workers ...	...	1·458	·858	...	...	...
290. Blacksmiths	...	·491	·088	...	...	...
298. Potters and pot and pipe-bowl makers and sellers.	...	·886	·696	...	...	...
302. Timber, cutch, and bamboo agents and dealers.	...	·465	·287	...	...	...
383. Boat and barge owners ...	...	·865	·256	...	...	...
385. Boat and bargemen ...	...	7·064	·873	...	...	...
401. Priests, ministers, preachers, missionaries, &c.	...	·332	·210	...	...	...
404. Religious mendicants, inmates of monasteries, convents, &c.	...	·067	·105	...	...	...
404*a*. Pôngyis	...	·532	...	...	·002	...
404*b*. Upazins	...	·444	...	...	...	...
404*c*. Maungyin, koyin, scholars ...	...	·866	...	...	...	...
404*d*. Methila and pothudaw ...	...	·157	·180	...	...	·001

of the chief Occupations district by district.

Kyaukpyu.			Sandoway.			Rangoon.		
Total.	Male.	Female.	Total.	Male.	Female.	Total.	Male.	Female.
8	9	10	11	12	13	14	15	16
...	·134	·157	...	·103	·055	...	·256	·046
...	·063	·018	...	·044	·053	...	·320	·098
...	·117	·109	...	·180	·138	...	·003	...
...	·87	·99	...	·75	·68	...	·12	·106
...	54·46	59·501	...	27·01	26·80	...	1·70	·76
...	8·89	9·78	...	9·14	8·47	...	·007	·007
...	3·47	3·19	...	·65	·508	...	·78	·23
...	·71	·68	...	·026	·015	...	...	...
...	·293	·339	...	·205	·220	...	·142	·040
...	·003	·005	...	·001	...	...	·001	·002
...	·232	·286	...	·027	·030	...	·746	·466
...	11·381	10·790	...	4·465	5·002	...	·055	·049
...	2·208	2·105	...	·909	·794	...	1·122	·867
...	·516	·688	...	·153	·188	...	·607	·821
...	·157	·191	...	·109	·055	...	4·466	3·296
...	·049	·084	...	·049	·103	...	·871	1·088
...	1·040	1·998	...	·341	·866	...	1·517	1·330
...	·055	·049	...	·080	·074	...	·084	·073
...	·023	·002	...	·011	...	...	·065	·061
...	·127	·148	...	·006	·018	...	1·321	1·179
...	·326	·264	...	·223	·337	...	·364	·527
...	·132	·168	...	·002	·010	...	·673	·355
...	·090	·084	...	·105	·032	...	·056	·023
...	·030	·014	...	·034	·048	...	·110	·094
...	...	...	...	...	...	...	·937	·593
...	·002	·001	...	...	...	...	·103	·089
...	·088	·169	...	...	...	...	·072	·048
...	·015	·068	...	·019	·032	...	·001	...
...	...	...	...	...	...	...	...	...
...	...	...	...	...	...	...	...	...
...	·062	·094	...	...	...	...	·316	·155
...	...	...	...	...	...	...	·017	·015
...	...	...	...	...	...	...	...	...
...	·022	·094	...	...	...	...	·028	·013
...	3·944	1·861	...	·040	·232	...	·067	·170
...	·390	·177	...	·006	·021	...	·046	·005
...	·308	·237	...	·088	·060	...	1·626	·950
...	·210	·190	...	·055	·039	...	1·042	·465
...	1·171	1·259	...	·053	·060	...	·195	·132
...	·068	·057	...	·005	·013	...	·620	·516
...	·164	·145	...	·153	·074	...	·798	·474
...	1·589	1·187	...	·415	·120	...	8·162	1·504
...	·048	·017	...	·077	·031	...	·358	·140
...	...	·005	...	...	...	...	·299	·132
...	·374	...	...	·142	...	...	·414	...
...	·209	...	...	·043	...	...	·587	...
...	·773	...	...	·057	...	...	·812	...
...	·056	·065	...	·002	·034	...	·205	·401

ABSTRACT C, *showing relative Strength*

Occupation.	Hanthawaddy. Total.	Hanthawaddy. Male.	Hanthawaddy. Female.	Pegu. Total.	Pegu. Male.	Pegu. Female.
1	17	18	19	20	21	22
25. Cattle breeders and dealers and Commissariat farm establishment.	...	·712	·554	...	·867	·495
26. Herdsmen	...	2·032	1·393	...	4·140	1·104
27. Buffalo breeders and dealers ...	...	·197	·159	...	·239	·248
37. Land occupants not cultivating...	...	3·71	2·50	...	1·76	2·002
38. Land occupants cultivating ...	...	50·34	49·12	...	52·44	47·60
41. Tenants and sharers cultivating...	...	15·24	13·60	...	23·15	21·32
43. Field labourers and crop-watchers	...	44·97	37·86	...	73·63	50·66
44. Tea, coffee, tobacco, and cinchona planters and assistants, &c.	...	...	...	...	·047	·009
46. Betel-vine, sugarcane, and areca-nut growers.	...	1·120	1·114	...	·048	·031
48. Cardamom, til-seed, and pepper growers.	...	·081	·069	...	·006	...
50. Fruit growers	...	4·938	4·620	...	1·519	1·309
51. Market gardeners (vegetable growers).	...	5·150	5·017	...	2·139	2·215
81. Fishermen and fish-curers ...	...	3·756	2·916	...	2·060	1·505
82. Fish dealers	...	·924	·991	...	·474	·698
83. Grain dealers	...	2·859	2·508	...	2·496	2·219
89. Vegetable sellers	...	·364	·594	...	·479	·901
92. Confectioners and sweetmeat makers and sellers and cooks.	...	2·253	3·430	...	2·007	3·793
98. Toddy drawers and sellers ...	...	·107	·056	...	·099	·042
104. Molasses (jaggery, gur, &c.) makers and sellers.	...	·089	·136	...	·088	·153
109. Grocers and general condiment dealers.	...	1·627	1·821	...	2·111	2·699
111. Betel-leaf and areca-nut sellers ...	...	·703	·899	...	1·836	2·746
117. Oil and salt sellers	...	·507	·433	...	·837	·862
121. Kerosine-oil dealers ...	...	·056	·023	...	·048	·014
135. Thatch dealers and thatchers ...	...	·377	·610	...	·962	1·003
157. Press proprietors, lithographers, and printers.	...	·022	...	...	·009	·006
169. Wood and ebony carvers ...	...	·001	...	...	·006	·007
172. Turners and lacquerers ...	...	·103	·074	...	·080	·069
206. Looms and loom-comb makers and sellers.	...	·014	·026	...	·026	·002
226. Silkworm rearers and cocoon gatherers.	...	·003	...	...	...	...
227. Silk carders and spinners ...	...	...	...	...	...	...
228. Silk weavers and dealers ...	...	·007	·002	...	·076	·011
231. Cotton cleaners, pressers, and ginners.	...	·007	·019	...	·051	·038
232. Cotton carpet and rug makers and sellers.	...	...	...	...	...	...
233. Cotton spinners, sizers, and yarn beaters.	...	...	·010	...	·002	·002
234. Cotton weavers, mill owners and managers.	...	·415	2·611	...	·382	4·501
244. Net makers and sellers ...	...	·032	·024	...	·028	·042
260. Gold and silver workers ...	...	·599	·426	...	·670	·544
290. Blacksmiths	...	·853	·698	...	·518	·415
298. Potters and pot and pipe-bowl makers and sellers.	...	·557	·955	...	·291	·758
302. Timber, cutch, and bamboo agents and dealers.	...	·474	·335	...	1·935	1·354
383. Boat and barge owners ...	...	1·699	1·132	...	2·233	1·268
385. Boat and bargemen ...	...	8·297	2·542	...	7·873	2·615
401. Priests, ministers, preachers, missionaries, &c.	...	·102	·057	...	·057	·077
404. Religious mendicants, inmates of monasteries, convents, &c.	...	·001	...	...	·032	·007
404*a*. Pôngyis	...	·741	...	...	·089	...
404*b*. Upazins	...	·453	...	...	·817	...
404*c*. Maungyin, koyin, scholars ...	...	·817	...	...	1·207	...
404*d*. Methila and pothudaw ...	...	·024	·134	...	·078	·081

of the chief Occupations district by district—continued.

Tharrawaddy.			Prome.			Thongwa.		
Total.	Male.	Female.	Total.	Male.	Female.	Total.	Male.	Female.
23	24	25	26	27	28	29	30	31
...	·415	·340	...	·470	·276	...	·236	·172
...	·424	·078	...	·105	·019	...	·541	·256
...	·163	·226	...	·038	·056	...	·152	·130
...	·94	·88	...	2·05	2·84	...	2·02	1·84
...	88·73	88·96	...	123·21	116·89	...	105·108	108·64
...	17·65	17·38	...	14·97	14·19	...	31·54	29·30
...	42·08	38·65	...	12·58	14·19	...	34·81	26·72
...	4·25	4·603	...	·748	·796	...	·027	·024
...	1·32	1·170	...	2·318	2·508	...	5·626	1·418
...	10·949	11·094	...	·140	·128	...	·335	·324
...	1·944	2·757	...	5·168	5·493	...	8·562	6·787
...	10·228	10·577	...	16·113	15·145	...	10·443	8·389
...	6·100	5·858	...	4·824	5·601	...	23·712	18·219
...	2·235	2·917	...	·888	1·565	...	1·349	1·874
...	2·595	2·914	...	1·281	1·477	...	6·574	5·104
...	·311	·649	...	·235	1·157	...	1·079	1·287
...	2·023	3·845	...	2·420	4·014	...	4·766	7·102
...	·518	·394	...	2·093	1·679	...	·107	·134
...	·237	·404	...	·341	·548	...	·406	·404
...	1·537	2·098	...	1·054	1·454	...	5·457	5·856
...	1·074	1·861	...	1·827	2·719	...	1·493	1·689
...	·891	1·268	...	·474	·646	...	2·047	1·977
...	·031	·040	...	·097	·111	...	·152	·153
...	·320	·677	...	·049	·038	...	1·489	1·450
...	·003	...	...	...	·017	...	...	·006
...	·031	·013	...	·038	·032	...	·019	·014
...	·072	·068	...	·138	·169	...	·064	·069
...	·081	·174	...	·178	·244	...	·046	·048
...	·036	...	...	1·045	1·062	...	·001	...
...	...	·002	...	1·285	1·940	...	...	...
...	·056	·093	...	·873	1·782	...	·093	·022
...	·027	·033	...	·036	·060	...	·006	·007
...	...	...	...	...	...	...	·005	...
...	·013	·021	...	·063	·249	...	·040	·061
...	·437	3·084	...	1·608	9·738	...	·596	3·638
...	·160	·099	...	·385	·444	...	1·103	1·279
...	·784	·671	...	·599	·464	...	1·317	·820
...	·543	·351	...	·969	·500	...	·849	·629
...	·423	·611	...	·518	·597	...	·800	·805
...	1·337	1·159	...	1·709	1·262	...	·614	·481
...	·197	·241	...	·514	·189	...	1·756	1·281
...	1·571	·169	...	1·434	·408	...	11·187	1·302
...	·103	·040	...	·061	·042	...	·173	·102
...	...	...	...	·030	·011	...	·034	...
...	·644	...	...	·816	...	...	·965	...
...	·550	...	...	·742	...	...	·767	...
...	1·051	...	...	1·168	...	...	1·116	...
...	·018	·157	...	·026	·262	...	·048	·189

ABSTRACT **C**, *showing relative Strength*

Occupation.	Bassein. Total.	Bassein. Male.	Bassein. Female.	Henzada. Total.	Henzada. Male.	Henzada. Female.
1	32	33	34	35	36	37
25. Cattle breeders and dealers and Commissariat farm establishment.	...	1·112	·873	...	·617	·477
26. Herdsmen	...	·959	·523	...	·491	·082
27. Buffalo breeders and dealers ...	...	·529	·474	...	·160	·149
37. Land occupants not cultivating...	...	1·27	2·11	...	1·35	1·74
38. Land occupants cultivating ...	...	115·69	105·11	...	69·02	78·32
41. Tenants and sharers cultivating	...	31·43	30·75	...	27·29	29·34
43. Field labourers and crop-watchers	...	36·19	37·51	...	53·27	39·16
44. Tea, coffee, tobacco, and cinchona planters and assistants, &c.	...	·29	·29	...	3·32	2·92
46. Betel-vine, sugarcane, and areca-nut growers.	...	3·397	3·184	...	2·006	2·226
48. Cardamom, til-seed, and pepper growers.	...	·182	·177	...	3·632	1·993
50. Fruit growers	...	3·117	7·272	...	6·408	7·244
51. Market gardeners (vegetable growers).	...	12·363	14·234	...	15·036	15·582
81. Fishermen and fish-curers ...	...	11·112	10·204	...	4·492	4·004
82. Fish dealers	...	1·605	1·997	...	1·825	2·787
83. Grain dealers	...	7·920	8·124	...	3·168	4·797
89. Vegetable sellers	...	·508	·959	...	·293	·975
92. Confectioners and sweetmeat makers and sellers and cooks.	...	5·405	8·754	...	2·383	4·587
98. Toddy drawers and sellers	...	·298	·247	...	1·100	·790
104. Molasses (jaggery, gur, &c.) makers and sellers.	...	·324	·223	...	·481	·677
109. Grocers and general condiment dealers.	...	7·064	8·698	...	2·786	4·106
111. Betel-leaf and areca-nut sellers ...	...	1·029	1·644	...	5·14	·745
117. Oil and salt sellers	...	2·108	2·488	...	1·101	1·790
121. Kerosine-oil dealers ...	...	·067	·035	...	·084	·059
135. Thatch dealers and thatchers ...	...	2·590	2·750	...	2·485	3·472
157. Press proprietors, lithographers, and printers.	...	·014	·022	...	·005	...
169. Wood and ebony carvers ...	...	·006	·003	...	·034	·017
172. Turners and lacquerers ...	...	·064	·088	...	·101	·084
206. Looms and loom-comb makers and sellers.	...	·048	·052	...	·060	·086
226. Silkworm rearers and cocoon gatherers.	...	...	...	...	·027	...
227. Silk carders and spinners ...	...	...	...	...	...	...
228. Silk weavers and dealers ...	...	·055	·023	...	·236	·466
231. Cotton cleaners, pressers, and ginners.	...	...	...	...	·011	...
232. Cotton carpet and rug makers and sellers.	...	...	...	...	...	·001
233. Cotton spinners, sizers, and yarn beaters.	...	·002	·028	...	·028	·031
234. Cotton weavers, mill owners, and managers.	...	·729	4·136	...	·561	3·636
244. Net makers and sellers ...	...	·105	·073	...	1·346	1·366
260. Gold and silver workers ...	...	1·296	1·005	...	1·057	·606
290. Blacksmiths	...	·994	·798	...	·852	·581
298. Potters and pot and pipe-bowl makers and sellers.	...	2·265	2·646	...	·976	1·525
302. Timber, cutch, and bamboo agents and dealers.	...	3·070	2·449	...	·700	·612
383. Boat and barge owners ...	...	1·569	·992	...	·994	·815
385. Boat and bargemen ...	...	4·098	1·199	...	3·688	1·538
401. Priests, ministers, preachers, missionaries, &c.	...	·280	·257	...	·107	·086
404. Religious mendicants, inmates of monasteries, convents, &c.	...	·052	·019	...	·720	·064
404*a*. Pôngyis	...	·853	...	...	·669	...
404*b*. Upazins	...	·708	...	...	·617	...
404*c*. Maungyin, koyin, scholars ...	...	1·107	...	...	1·326	...
404*d*. Methila and pothudaw ...	...	·076	·218	...	·039	·248

of the chief Occupations district by district—continued.

Thayetmyo.			Amherst.			Tavoy.		
Total.	Male.	Female.	Total.	Male.	Female.	Total.	Male.	Female.
38	39	40	41	42	43	44	45	46
...	·506	·281	...	·986	·503	...	·023	·006
...	·061	·024	...	·949	·381	...	·205	·043
...	·007	·015	...	·561	·307	...	·034	·005
...	·32	·76	...	4·62	·94	...	·48	·43
...	76·84	63·23	...	93·13	105·49	...	19·89	17·48
...	4·91	8·26	...	14·57	14·70	...	6·18	4·65
...	5·25	6·007	...	36·14	30·09	...	8·709	5·79
...	·61	·56	...	·17	·23	...	·009	·007
...	...	·222	...	4·71	2·63	...	·111	·130
...	2·820	2·763	...	·003	·010	...	·010	...
...	·287	·332	...	8·184	7·911	...	1·468	1·458
...	28·686	37·953	...	28·435	19·350	...	5·393	4·841
...	2·861	4·223	...	2·688	1·823	...	2·417	2·352
...	·397	·508	...	·276	·362	...	·312	1·066
...	1·213	1·679	...	2·382	1·938	...	·155	·365
...	·402	·503	...	·418	1·149	...	·228	·765
...	·857	2·059	...	1·835	2·761	...	·272	·807
...	·784	·809	...	·945	·674	...	·261	·206
...	·147	·353	...	·550	·427	...	·018	·015
...	·301	·577	...	1·543	1·567	...	·048	·099
...	1·167	1·151	...	·836	·527	...	·061	·164
...	·160	·312	...	·261	·159	...	·051	·177
...	·022	·052	...	·056	·032	...	·011	·005
...	·067	·249	...	·820	·724	...	·594	·694
...	...	...	...	·051	·071	...	...	...
...	...	...	...	·024	·013	...	·001	...
...	·302	·026	...	·068	·077	...	·002	...
...	·014	·014	...	·003	·032	...	·001	·003
...	·048	·056	...	...	...	...	·002	...
...	·001	·002	...	...	...	...	...	...
...	·030	·024	...	·049	·046	...	·273	1·182
...	·007	·023	...	·005	·002	...	...	·001
...	...	...	...	...	...	...	...	·001
...	·030	·249	...	·015	·005	...	·009	·157
...	·426	2·989	...	·917	5·313	...	1·586	11·364
...	·156	·147	...	·038	·003	...	·103	·101
...	·468	·506	...	1·375	·965	...	·257	·184
...	·777	·521	...	1·174	·704	...	·155	·089
...	·414	·698	...	·880	1·086	...	·195	·428
...	2·037	2·565	...	1·667	1·384	...	·278	·188
...	·458	·213	...	1·136	·553	...	·144	·119
...	2·298	1·333	...	4·103	2·592	...	·824	·278
...	·076	·044	...	·201	·105	...	·433	·017
...	·048	·003	...	·027	·231	...	·022	·007
...	·574	...	...	9·976	...	...	·213	...
...	·703	...	...	·915	...	...	·257	...
...	2·350	...	...	2·516	...	...	·573	...
...	·068	·109	...	·118	·289	...	·028	.09

ABSTRACT C, *showing relative Strength*

Occupation.	Mergui. Total.	Mergui. Male.	Mergui. Female.	Toungoo. Total.	Toungoo. Male.	Toungoo. Female.
1	47	48	49	50	51	52
25. Cattle breeders and dealers and Commissariat farm establishment.	...	...	...	...	·314	·131
26. Herdsmen						
27. Buffalo breeders and dealers ...	...	·090	·013	...	·311	·073
37. Land occupants not cultivating ...	...	...	...	...	·021	·019
38. Land occupants cultivating ...	...	·05	·08	...	·66	·34
41. Tenants and sharers cultivating...	...	25·27	24·09	...	27·66	25·71
43. Field-labourers and crop watchers	...	1·76	1·71	...	12·49	13·76
44. Tea, coffee, tobacco, and cinchona planters and assistants, &c.	... ...	2·349 ·109	1·767 ·068	... ...	6·203 ·306	6·098 ·381
46. Betel-vine, sugarcane, and areca-nut growers.	...	·152	·133	...	1·479	1·439
48. Cardamom, til-seed, and pepper growers.	...	·003	·003	...	·688	·667
50. Fruit growers	...	1·349	1·247	...	·282	·230
51. Market gardeners (vegetable growers).	...	4·416	4·074	...	20·285	20·715
81. Fishermen and fish-curers ...	...	5·682	4·433	...	1·331	1·284
82. Fish dealers	...	·315	·518	...	·156	·333
83. Grain dealers	...	·326	·307	...	1·505	1·892
89. Vegetable sellers	...	·117	·213	...	·529	·823
92. Confectioners and sweetmeat makers and sellers and cooks.	...	·262	·564	...	1·017	1·735
98. Toddy drawers and sellers ...	...	·343	·404	...	·210	·114
104. Molasses (jaggery, gur, &c.) makers and sellers.	...	·023	·018	...	·181	·177
109. Grocers and general condiment dealers.	...	·059	·110	...	·410	·470
111. Betel-leaf and areca-nut sellers ...	...	·036	·046	...	1·847	2·077
117. Oil and salt sellers	...	·011	·043	...	·235	·327
121. Kerosine-oil dealers ...	...	·002	...	...	·031	·006
135. Thatch dealers and thatchers ...	...	·103	·049	...	·344	·381
157. Press proprietors, lithographers, and printers.	...	...	...	...	·009	·024
169. Wood and ebony carvers ...	...	·001	·001	...	·023	·021
172. Turners and lacquerers ...	...	·001	...	...	·028	·038
206. Looms and loom-comb makers and sellers.	...	...	·010	...	·032	·084
226. Silkworm rearers and cocoon gatherers.	...	...	...	...	·461	·558
227. Silk carders and spinners ...	...	·006	·056	...	...	·002
228. Silk weavers and dealers ...	...	...	·002	...	·164	·156
231. Cotton cleaners, pressers, and ginners.	...	...	...	...	·002	·005
232. Cotton carpet and rug makers and sellers.	...	...	...	...	...	...
233. Cotton spinners, sizers, and yarn beaters.	...	...	·002	...	·010	·030
234. Cotton weavers, mill owners and managers.	...	·099	·550	...	·579	3·941
244. Net makers and sellers ...	...	·059	·073	...	·002	·032
260. Gold and silver workers ...	...	·237	·170	...	·473	·177
290. Blacksmiths	...	·142	·098	...	·307	·184
298. Potters and pot and pipe-bowl makers and sellers.	...	·017	·024	...	·290	·453
302. Timber, cutch, and bamboo agents and dealers.	...	·070	·047	...	·532	·447
383. Boat and barge owners ...	...	·056	·045	...	·026	·024
385. Boat and bargemen ...	...	·436	·118	...	1·330	·629
401. Priests, ministers, preachers, missionaries, &c.	...	·006	·006	...	·289	·226
404. Religious mendicants, inmates of monasteries, convents, &c.	...	·001	·001	...	·009	·006
404*a*. Pôngyis	...	·107	...	...	·391	...
404*b*. Upazins	...	·132	...	...	·433	...
404*c*. Maungyin, koyin, scholars ...	...	·142	...	...	·820	...
404*d*. Methila and pothudaw ...	...	·001	·013	...	·027	·061

of the chief Occupations district by district—continued.

Shwegyin.			Salween.			Mandalay.		
Total.	Male.	Female.	Total.	Male.	Female.	Total.	Male.	Female.
53	54	55	56	57	58	59	60	61
...	·316	·102	...	·105	·047	...	·599	·361
...	·728	·348	...	·046	·014	...	·819	·312
...	·281	·290	...	·001	...	...	·293	·001
...	·608	·51	...	...	·001	...	·30	·44
...	53·57	46·66	...	2·14	1·83	...	17·78	21·72
...	8·44	7·35	...	·086	·080	...	10·25	10·39
...	12·11	10·21	...	·23	·22	...	6·53	8·304
...	·294	·324	...	...	...	...	·11	·134
...	4·988	4·868	...	·261	·154	...	1·493	1·327
...	4·378	4·044	...	...	...	...	·224	·127
...	2·590	2·396	...	·005	·006	...	2·880	2·450
...	12·141	11·791	...	16·134	15·459	...	17·687	15·530
...	2·872	2·483	...	·072	·052	...	7·961	8·346
...	·795	·879	...	·003	·001	...	1·360	2·371
...	1·191	1·529	...	·007	·009	...	2·423	3·697
...	·416	1·238	...	·014	·061	...	1·199	2·761
...	1·254	2·269	...	·060	·101	...	3·953	5·091
...	·072	·082	...	·002	...	...	·512	·491
...	·111	·135	...	·001	...	...	·269	·428
...	·946	1·097	...	·002	·001	...	1·964	3·026
...	2·603	3·425	...	·055	·011	...	·729	1·404
...	·268	·305	...	·024	·023	...	1·155	1·406
...	·035	·013	...	...	...	...	·333	·341
...	·095	·101	...	·022	·009	...	·629	1·076
...	...	...	...	...	...	...	·153	·031
...	·040	·006	...	...	...	...	·642	·441
...	·040	·034	...	...	...	...	·795	·711
...	...	·001	...	...	...	...	·160	·259
...	...	...	...	...	...	...	·002	...
...	...	...	...	...	...	...	2·783	6·184
...	·011	·005	...	...	...	...	1·601	2·438
...	...	...	...	...	...	...	·036	·043
...	·005	...	...	...	...	...	...	·106
...	·003	·005	...	...	...	...	·098	·758
...	·298	2·407	...	·023	·497	...	16·218	31·859
...	·160	·103	...	...	...	...	·107	·138
...	·520	·394	...	·034	·018	...	1·918	1·316
...	·781	·055	...	·047	·028	...	1·281	·884
...	·420	·535	...	·003	...	...	·997	1·583
...	·504	·382	...	·127	·078	...	1·145	1·200
...	·209	·126	...	·059	·006	...	·155	·057
...	1·045	·443	...	·297	·006	...	2·617	1·786
...	·047	·014	...	·003	...	...	·069	·088
...	·003	·009	...	...	...	...	·024	·002
...	·349	...	...	·039	...	...	2·757	...
...	·445	...	...	·023	...	...	2·949	...
...	1·007	...	...	·127	...	...	6·250	...
...	·049	·078	...	...	·005	...	·865	2·857

ABSTRACT C, *showing relative Strength*

Occupation.	Bhamo. Total.	Bhamo. Male.	Bhamo. Female.	Katha. Total.	Katha. Male.	Katha. Female.
1	62	63	64	65	66	67
25. Cattle breeders and dealers and Commissariat farm establishment.	...	·026	·003	...	·001	...
26. Herdsmen	...	·057	·001	...	·002	...
27. Buffalo breeders and dealers ...	...	...	...	...	·026	·022
37. Land occupants not cultivating ...	...	·01	·017	...	·001	·005
38. Land occupants cultivating ...	...	14·18	15·54	...	9·55	10·58
41. Tenants and sharers cultivating...	...	·53	·52	...	1·63	1·81
43. Field labourers and crop-watchers	...	1·14	·69	...	1·17	1·468
44. Tea, coffee, tobacco, and cinchona planters and assistants, &c.	...	1·007	1·058	...	1·032	1·095
46. Betel-vine, sugarcane, and areca-nut growers.	...	...	·003	...	...	...
48. Cardamom, til-seed, and pepper growers.	...	·032	·028	...	...	...
50. Fruit growers.	...	·460	·395	...	·002	...
51. Market gardeners (vegetable growers).	...	2·896	2·300	...	9·202	9·157
81. Fishermen and fish-curers ...	...	2·144	1·379	...	2·549	2·590
82. Fish dealers	...	·315	·404	...	·306	·295
83. Grain dealers	...	·656	·418	...	·176	·195
89. Vegetable sellers	...	·102	·177	...	...	·035
92. Confectioners and sweetmeat makers and sellers and cooks.	...	·206	·395	...	·136	·136
98. Toddy drawers and sellers ...	...	...	...	...	...	...
104. Molasses (jaggery, gur, &c.) makers and sellers.	...	0·78	·102	...	·026	·047
109. Grocers and general condiment dealers.	...	·039	·059	...	·018	·015
111. Betel-leaf and areca-nut sellers ...	...	·013	·019	...	·002	...
117. Oil and salt sellers	...	·105	·122	...	·084	·115
121. Kerosine-oil dealers	...	·001	·015	...	...	...
135. Thatch dealers and thatchers ...	...	·323	·184	...	·028	·046
157. Press proprietors, lithographers, and printers.	...	...	...	...	...	...
169. Wood and ebony carvers ...	...	...	...	...	...	...
172. Turners and lacquerers ...	...	·017	...	...	·007	·002
206. Looms and loom-comb makers and sellers.	...	·006	·001	...	·002	·003
226. Silkworm rearers and cocoon gatherers.	...	...	...	...	...	...
227. Silk carders and spinners ...	...	...	...	...	...	...
228. Silk weavers and dealers ...	...	·026	·032	...	...	·003
231. Cotton cleaners, pressers, and ginners.	...	·042	·014	...	·021	·42
232. Cotton carpet and rug makers and sellers.	...	...	...	...	...	...
233. Cotton spinners, sizers, and yarn beaters.	...	·001	·003	...	...	·001
234. Cotton weavers, mill owners and managers.	...	·095	·869	...	·127	·101
244. Net makers and sellers ...	...	·057	·047	...	·002	·021
260. Gold and silver workers ...	...	·094	·073	...	·061	·047
290. Blacksmiths	...	·103	·013	...	·122	·071
298. Potters and pot and pipe-bowl makers and sellers.	...	·067	·169	...	·026	·027
302. Timber, cutch, and bamboo agents and dealers.	...	·418	·290	...	·565	·519
383. Boat and barge owners ...	...	·005	·002	...	·013	·002
385. Boat and bargemen ...	...	·799	·386	...	·092	·053
401. Priests, ministers, preachers, missionaries, &c.	...	·073	·028	...	·013	·005
404. Religious mendicants, inmates of monasteries, convents, &c.	...	·017	·014	...	...	...
404*a*. Pôngyis	...	·310	...	...	·188	...
404*b*. Upazins	...	·224	...	...	·252	...
404*c*. Maungyin, koyin, scholars ...	...	·624	...	...	·558	...
404*d*. Methila and pothudaw ...	...	·024	·138	...	·023	·073

of the chief Occupations district by district—continued.

Ruby Mines.			Shwebo.			Ye-u.		
Total.	Male.	Female.	Total.	Male.	Female.	Total.	Male.	Female.
68	69	70	71	72	73	74	75	76
...	·230	·063	...	·055	·015	...	·002	...
...	·015	·002	...	·110	·084	...	·026	·005
...	·042	...	...	·009	·005	...	·002	·013
...	·002	...	...	·38	·79	...	·47	1·26
...	4·63	4·37	...	35·71	40·95	...	29·59	37·90
...	·01	·01	...	7·43	7·88	...	4·57	5·87
...	·13	·01	...	3·22	4·037	...	1·35	1·57
...	·082	·091	...	·023	·023	...	...	·001
...	·015	...	...	·317	...	...	·097	·131
...	...	·015	...	·334	·323	...	·022	·028
...	·185	·161	...	·019	·013	...	·032	·011
...	·905	·773	...	·387	·357	...	·085	·106
...	·544	·435	...	·971	1·739	...	·742	1·147
...	...	·034	...	·628	·802	...	·021	·032
...	·402	·188	...	·307	·503	...	·099	·210
...	·022	·038	...	·128	·343	...	·223	·182
...	·298	·307	...	·450	·817	...	·234	·443
...	·001	·002	...	1·615	1·059	...	·561	·376
...	...	...	...	·465	1·354	...	·172	·423
...	·172	·102	...	·255	·265	...	·987	·182
...	·065	·013	...	·274	·327	...	·201	·445
...	...	·019	...	·272	·347	...	·080	·057
...	...	...	...	·007	·006	...	·001	·005
...	·156	·093	...	·206	·491	...	·050	·080
...	...	...	...	...	...	...	...	...
...	...	...	...	·001	·003	...	·003	·006
...	...	...	...	·092	·090	...	·077	·056
...	...	...	...	·027	·044	...	·053	·093
...	...	...	...	·002	·006	...	...	...
...	...	...	...	...	...	...	...	...
...	·009	·001	...	·635	·820	...	·007	·019
...	...	...	...	·034	·017	...	·005	...
...	...	...	...	...	...	...	...	...
...	...	·001	...	·013	·222	...	·048	·185
...	·013	·065	...	·838	5·824	...	·504	2·662
...	...	...	...	·061	·076	...	·013	·010
...	·051	·032	...	·159	·127	...	·060	·049
...	·118	·002	...	·326	·328	...	·142	·106
...	·068	·072	...	·727	·940	...	·115	·235
...	·343	·214	...	·736	·598	...	·406	·290
...	...	...	...	·067	·059	...	·022	·023
...	·003	·006	...	·540	·326	...	·216	·099
...	·006	·001	...	·051	·010	...	·002	·003
...	...	...	...	·027	·001	...	·034	·023
...	·169	...	...	1·022	...	...	·039	...
...	·144	...	...	1·268	...	...	·725	...
...	·347	...	...	2·433	...	...	2·908	...
...	·010	·052	...	·111	·193	...	·074	·036

ABSTRACT C, *showing relative Strength*

Occupation.	Sagaing.			Lower Chindwin.		
	Total.	Male.	Female.	Total.	Male.	Female.
1	77	78	79	80	81	82
25. Cattle breeders and dealers and Commissariat farm establishment.	...	·179	·159	...	·056	·034
26. Herdsmen	...	1·518	·988	...	·448	·268
27. Buffalo breeders and dealers ...	...	·006	·009	...	...	...
37. Land occupants not cultivating...	...	1·45	2·00	...	3·47	4·01
38. Land occupants cultivating ...	...	36·81	38·95	...	42·82	54·07
41. Tenants and sharers cultivating...	...	19·32	19·58	...	24·39	25·22
43. Field labourers and crop-watchers	...	8·14	9·29	...	1·77	2·178
44. Tea, coffee, tobacco, and cinchona planters and assistants, &c.	...	·165	·194	...	·032	·043
46. Betel-vine, sugarcane, and areca-nut growers.	...	·264	·416	...	·256	·436
48. Cardamom, til-seed, and pepper growers.	...	2·574	2·257	...	·068	·063
50. Fruit growers	...	·817	1·216	...	·047	·040
51. Market gardeners (vegetable growers).	...	15·901	15·934	...	4·991	5·134
81. Fishermen and fish-curers ...	...	4·586	5·294	...	2·300	2·907
82. Fish dealers	...	1·139	2·072	...	·311	·641
83. Grain dealers	...	1·028	1·049	...	·823	1·375
89. Vegetable sellers	...	·458	1·054	...	·391	1·076
92. Confectioners and sweetmeat makers and sellers and cooks.	...	1·514	2·714	...	·804	1·882
98. Toddy drawers and sellers ...	...	5·081	4·250	...	3·873	3·674
104. Molasses (jaggery, gur, &c.) makers and sellers.	...	·502	1·596	...	·302	1·209
109. Grocers and general condiment dealers.	...	·661	1·207	...	·212	·389
111. Betel-leaf and areca-nut sellers ...	...	·252	·535	...	·663	·787
117. Oil and salt sellers	...	·357	·779	...	·844	·915
121. Kerosine-oil dealers	...	·135	·197	...	·028	·027
135. Thatch dealers and thatchers ...	...	·440	1·183	...	·308	·694
157. Press proprietors, lithographers, and printers.	...	...	...	...	...	...
169. Wood and ebony carvers ...	...	·003	·003	...	·003	...
172. Turners and lacquerers ...	...	·143	·101	...	·531	·547
206. Looms and loom-comb makers and sellers.	...	·082	·126	...	·099	·109
226. Silkworm rearers and cocoon gatherers.	...	...	·002	...	·003	·088
227. Silk carders and spinners ...	...	·007	·035	...	·015	·188
228. Silk weavers and dealers ...	...	·060	·177	...	·362	·316
231. Cotton cleaners, pressers, and ginners.	...	·637	·925	...	·385	1·333
232. Cotton carpet and rug makers and sellers.	...	...	...	...	...	...
233. Cotton spinners, sizers, and yarn beaters.	...	·273	2·106	...	·144	1·563
234. Cotton weavers, mill owners and managers.	...	2·659	17·840	...	4·108	24·404
244. Net makers and sellers ...	...	·168	·447	...	·046	·024
260. Gold and silver workers ...	...	·481	·245	...	·306	·240
290. Blacksmiths	...	·573	·315	...	·461	·397
298. Potters and pot and pipe-bowl makers and sellers.	...	·619	1·405	...	·393	1·179
302. Timber, cutch, and bamboo agents and dealers.	...	·437	·443	...	·366	·211
383. Boat and barge owners ...	...	·134	·188	...	·152	·138
385. Boat and bargemen	...	1·715	1·267	...	1·990	1·734
401. Priests, ministers, preachers, missionaries, &c.	...	·051	·027	...	·006	·005
404. Religious mendicants, inmates of monasteries, convents, &c. ...	...	1·291	·001	...	...	·001
404*a*. Pôngyis	...	1·510	...	...	1·539	...
404*b*. Upazins	...	1·564	...	...	1·702	...
404*c*. Maungyin, koyin, scholars ...	...	2·838	...	...	3·559	...
404*d*. Methila and pothudaw ...	...	·277	·646	...	·123	·295

of the chief Occupations district by district—continued.

Upper Chindwin.			Myingyan.			Pakôkku.		
Total.	Male.	Female.	Total.	Male.	Female.	Total.	Male.	Female.
83	84	85	86	87	88	89	90	91
...	·017	·017	...	·232	·202	...	·034	·015
...	·022	·024	...	·966	·679	...	1·093	·361
...	·042	·019	...	...	...	...	·015	·001
...	·22	·29	...	1·61	2·49	...	1·32	1·91
...	20·19	17·73	...	59·51	65·51	...	47·	40·04
...	7·54	8·72	...	16·74	19·81	...	34·93	23·83
...	3·907	5·267	...	6·507	6·204	...	8·317	7·65
...	·403	·514	...	·767	·806	...	2·72	1·49
...	·007	·003	...	·472	·440	...	·220	·777
...	...	·019	...	12·355	14·582	...	·153	·621
...	·007	·003	...	·725	·086	...	·059	·107
...	1·396	1·945	...	24·526	28·623	...	28·606	36·536
...	1·305	1·460	...	4·091	5·315	...	1·472	1·844
...	·084	·135	...	1·316	1·594	...	·290	·692
...	·515	·422	...	1·942	2·382	...	·781	1·618
...	·085	·126	...	·891	1·696	...	·149	·448
...	1·214	·397	...	1·508	3·467	...	1·696	1·604
...	·014	·028	...	15·057	11·492	...	13·607	13·312
...	·034	·021	...	·990	4·233	...	·433	3·856
...	·048	·064	...	·798	1·289	...	·645	·957
...	·061	·053	...	1·576	2·147	...	1·777	1·251
...	·161	·059	...	·540	·882	...	·311	·475
...	·010	·003	...	·127	·182	...	·043	·088
...	·145	·262	...	·452	·746	...	·594	1·466
...	·002	...	...	...	...	...	...	...
...	...	...	...	...	...	...	·036	·011
...	·017	·026	...	3·782	4·187	...	·046	·314
...	·013	·010	...	·043	·078	...	·461	·426
...	·002	·002	...	...	·005	...	·017	·024
...	...	...	...	...	...	...	·026	·128
...	·017	·010	...	·136	·134	...	·258	·308
...	·051	·060	...	2·281	3·417	...	·109	·544
...	...	...	...	·001	...	...	...	...
...	·002	·026	...	1·078	3·680	...	·401	4·369
...	·114	·720	...	3·515	19·631	...	4·361	33·979
...	...	...	...	·226	·351	...	·216	1·246
...	·076	·049	...	·691	·416	...	·422	·364
...	·082	·072	...	·882	·920	...	·789	·673
...	·117	·236	...	·713	·662	...	1·213	·916
...	·327	·316	...	·763	·807	...	·414	·299
...	·094	·010	...	·336	·466	...	·157	·107
...	·557	·487	...	1·964	1·132	...	1·333	1·915
...	·009	·023	...	·017	·007	...	·024	·018
...	·005	...	...	·002	·002	...	·006	·077
...	·347	...	...	1·719	...	...	1·314	...
...	·356	...	...	2·763	...	...	1·364	...
...	1·451	...	...	6·808	...	...	3·585	...
...	·043	·088	...	·084	191	...	·077	·180

ABSTRACT C,—*showing relative Strength*

Occupation.	Minbu.			Magwe.			
	Total.	Male.	Female.	Total.	Male.	Female.	Total.
1	92	93	94	95	96	97	98
25. Cattle breeders and dealers and Commissariat farm establishment.	...	·078	·067	...	·039	·151	...
26. Herdsmen	...	·140	·084	...	·919	·394	...
27. Buffalo breeders and dealers ...	...	·360	·006	...	·157	·168	...
37. Land occupants not cultivating...	...	·61	·84	...	1·24	1·16	...
38. Land occupants cultivating ...	...	25·1	24·05	...	40·94	40·03	...
41. Tenants and sharers cultivating...	...	43·88	44·	...	8·76	8·00	...
43. Field labourers and crop-watchers	...	2·678	2·72	...	3·688	3·905	...
44. Tea, coffee, tobacco, and cinchona planters and assistants, &c.	...	·552	·07	...	·626	·485	...
46. Betel-vine, sugarcane, and areca-nut growers.	...	1·285	1·945	...	·154	·097	...
48. Cardamom, til-seed, and pepper growers.	...	·544	·557	...	4·779	4·273	...
50. Fruit growers	...	·193	·202	...	·736	1·089	...
51. Market gardeners (vegetable growers).	...	18·887	21·135	...	39·789	41·486	...
81. Fishermen and fish-curers ...	...	2·211	2·837	...	1·354	2·094	...
82. Fish dealers	...	1·011	1·506	...	·431	·550	...
83. Grain dealers	...	·865	1·614	...	·470	·733	...
89. Vegetable sellers	...	·234	·737	...	·189	·427	...
92. Confectioners and sweetmeat makers and sellers and cooks.	...	1·292	2·553	...	·867	1·238	...
98. Toddy drawers and sellers ...	...	2·688	2·645	...	2·144	1·544	...
104. Molasses (jaggery, gur, &c.) makers and sellers.	...	·344	·937	...	·207	·896	...
109. Grocers and general condiment dealers.	...	·733	·965	...	·403	·537	...
111. Betel-leaf and areca-nut sellers...	...	1·070	1·851	...	1·258	1·810	...
117. Oil and salt sellers	...	·215	·161	...	·214	·410	...
121. Kerosine-oil dealers ...	...	·390	·111	...	1·109	1·105	...
135. Thatch dealers and thatchers ...	...	·230	1·263	...	·023	·018	...
157. Press proprietors, lithographers, and printers.	...	...	...	...	·001	...	...
169. Wood and ebony carvers ...	...	·005	·005	...	·002	...	...
172. Turners and lacquerers ...	...	·376	·390	...	·374	·332	...
206. Looms and loom-comb makers and sellers.	...	·356	·649	...	·034	·011	...
226. Silkworm rearers and cocoon gatherers.	...	...	...	...	·168	·198	...
227. Silk carders and spinners ...	...	·028	·082	...	...	...	...
228. Silk weavers and dealers ...	...	·097	·088	...	·285	·198	...
231. Cotton cleaners, pressers, and ginners.	...	·018	·206	...	·099	·092	...
232. Cotton carpet and rug makers and sellers.	...	·010	·015	...	...	...	...
233. Cotton spinners, sizers, and yarn beaters.	...	·510	1·241	...	·089	1·036	...
234. Cotton weavers, mill owners and managers.	...	1·782	10·199	...	1·725	11·586	...
244. Net makers and sellers ...	...	·076	·085	...	·207	·184	...
260. Gold and silver workers ...	...	·637	·444	...	·248	·193	...
290. Blacksmiths	...	·629	·592	...	·497	·337	...
298. Potters and pot and pipe-bowl makers and sellers.	...	·412	·905	...	·345	·828	...
302. Timber, cutch, and bamboo agents and dealers.	...	2·540	2·648	...	1·109	·784	...
383. Boat and barge owners ...	...	·166	·072	...	·453	·144	...
385. Boat and bargemen ...	...	·477	·356	...	·838	·435	...
401. Priests, ministers, preachers, missionaries, &c.	...	·028	·009	...	·014	·007	...
404. Religious mendicants, inmates of monasteries. convents, &c.	...	...	...	...	·149	...	...
404*a*. Pôngyis	...	1·180	...	...	1·103	...	...
404*b*. Upazins	...	1·089	...	..	1·243	...	...
404*c*. Maungyin, koyin, scholars ...	...	1·271	...	...	3·083	...	...
404*d*. Methila and pothudaw ...	...	·053	·130	...	·031	·065	...

of the chief Occupations district by district—concluded.

Kyaukse.		Meiktila.			Yamethin.			Pyinmana.		
Male.	Female.	Total.	Male.	Female.	Total.	Male.	Female.	Total.	Male.	Female.
99	100	101	102	103	104	105	106	107	108	109
·069	·049	...	·042	·026	...	·105	·086	...	·023	·009
·358	·184	...	·190	·063	...	·168	·021	...	·193	·061
·001	·001	...	...	·006	...	...	...	...	·005	·001
·201	·15	...	·97	1·26	...	·85	·807	...	·11	·18
21·47	20·64	...	70·60	76·78	...	40·34	43·07	...	8·91	8·94
6·85	5·84	...	7·13	8·09	...	21·36	21·21	...	4·19	3·65
12·39	11·23	...	5·42	3·97	...	2·84	2·908	...	·78	·78
...	·039	...	·001	...	...	·003	·002	...	·202	·176
1·427	·992	...	·027	·015	...	1·994	1·438	...	·366	·358
·859	1·142	...	·010	·022	...	2·124	1·868	...	1·930	1·861
·809	·834	...	·222	·030	...	·061	·057	...	·049	·028
4·137	4·153	...	7·503	7·874	...	2·892	2·909	...	1,477	1·685
·770	·097	...	1·327	1·945	...	·894	1·338	...	·678	·649
·194	·357	...	·094	·172	...	·098	·143	...	·056	·078
1·402	1·889	...	1·475	·581	...	·525	·631	...	·153	·389
·401	·944	...	·287	·461	...	·436	·539	...	·073	·155
·903	1·505	...	·925	1·851	...	·473	1·333	...	·362	·582
2·156	2·022	...	3·038	2·987	...	·255	·235	...	·038	·028
·205	·521	...	·216	·284	...	·072	·077	...	·073	·106
·319	·520	...	·435	·745	...	·260	·498	...	·044	·077
·528	1·063	...	·891	1·540	...	1·443	2·867	...	·740	·808
·335	·511	...	·145	·220	...	·265	·207	...	·102	·103
·065	·038	...	·092	·135	...	·064	·090	...	·007	·003
·312	·570	...	·243	·500	...	·115	·156	...	·127	·172
·001	...	...	...	...	...	...	...	...	...	...
...	...	...	·011	·011	...	...	...	...	...	...
·021	·009	...	·028	·023	...	·107	·101	...	·111	·067
·002	·002	...	·019	·031	...	·035	·031	...	...	...
...	...	...	...	...	...	...	·006	...	·253	·152
...	...	...	...	...	...	...	...	...	·001	·001
·038	·023	...	·110	·131	...	·144	·241	...	·032	·031
·126	·114	...	·358	·696	...	·002	·022	...	...	...
...	...	...	...	...	...	·005	·009	...	...	...
·015	·118	...	·172	·682	...	·022	·164	...	·007	·027
1·932	5·448	...	2·077	12·284	...	1·235	6·664	...	·203	·983
...	...	...	...	...	...	...	·002	...	...	...
·169	·157	...	·226	·049	...	·185	·172	...	·095	·067
·201	·168	...	·340	·331	...	·460	·385	...	·195	·157
·625	·638	...	·294	·512	...	·131	·306	...	·144	·140
·527	·509	...	·280	·247	...	1·175	·909	...	2·754	2·208
...	·003	...	...	...	...	...	...	...	·002	...
·631	·519	...	...	...	...	·019	·102	...	·124	·0920
·030	·010	...	·032	·030	...	·039	·031	...	·034	·009
...	·002	...	·006	·030	...	·013	...	...	...	...
·710	...	...	·781	...	...	·711	...	...	·218	...
·857	...	...	·862	...	...	1·034	...	...	·144	...
1·519	...	...	3·405	...	...	1·003	...	...	·159	...
·244	·180	...	·063	·086	...	·002	·093	...	·023	·03

Class A, Service of Government.

273. The first class is restricted to the servants of Government. This, in India, is a well-defined class, much more so than in England. There the service of Government is reckoned only one of many professions. Indeed, the highest servants of the Crown are just those whose pay is nominal. No one but a rich man can afford to hold any of the higher appointments. Moreover, the line is not so clearly defined. Our Judges in England are all recruited from the Bar, except the "great unpaid" magistracy. In India, on the contrary, the servants of the Crown are a well-defined body. Recruited generally while young, they usually become permanent servants of the State. Moreover, the learned professions do not out here naturally hold the same position in point of numbers to the same professions at home. In this respect India is still 300 years behind England. We have but few independent men belonging to these learned professions, for the simple reason that there is but a small demand for their labour. Government supplies its own medical and clerical men. We have no leisured or wealthy class to support such professions as music, painting, or literature. Hence in Burma these arts are still in a rudimentary stage. Accordingly the service of Government is treated as a separate service and not as one of the ordinary professions.

The returns of Class **A** require no explanation beyond that afforded by the Imperial Tables themselves and the comparative statements already prepared. The only noticeable item is No. 8. Here, of males over 14, headmen (not agriculturists) number 555 in towns. This is due to the fact that most of our smaller towns are mere overgrown villages or groups of villages which, although they have outgrown the status of villages, still maintain the machinery of rural administration. These men are naturally not agriculturists; hence the apparent disproportion of them to headmen not agriculturists in rural tracts. Of these there are only 3,478 males over the age of 14. Of course there are many more village headmen, but, being agriculturists, they were excluded from this class. In 1881, although no orders were issued to exclude headmen who were agriculturists, there were only 946 returned as kyedangyis, the name by which village headmen were then generally known in Lower Burma. Since then Upper Burma has been taken over and the number of villages largely increased, but if we make all allowances, it is clear that village headmen were understated in 1881.

The pastoral and agricultural Class B.

274. The pastoral and agricultural class comprises 6,415 out of every 10,000 persons of both sexes. This class is divided into two orders—stock-breeding and agriculture. The former order is comparatively unimportant. Live-stock in Burmese are restricted to draught-cattle and draught-buffaloes, a few ponies, goats, and pigs. Sheep, except in Government farms and in the hands of importers, are unknown. It seems strange that in a country apparently so well fitted for the breeding of live-stock so little attention should be paid to their rearing. But Burmans are Buddhists, and, as such, are averse to the systematic slaughter of living animals for food. The hunter and fisherman are looked on as not being quite respectable. A Burman will eat his bullock if it dies a natural death, but it may be safely said that no Burmese Buddhist will admit that he breeds or fattens cattle for the slaughter-house. He will sell his cattle to the Choliar or Chittagongian butcher. Comparatively few ponies are bred in Lower Burma, as, until the annexation of Upper Burma, the export of stallions was forbidden. There were but 1,618 persons either engaged or dependent on pony-breeding; of these but 716 were males over the age of 14. They are most numerous in Mandalay. Ruby Mines, Myingyan, Pakôkku, and Meiktila supply 882 persons, or more than half of those who live by this occupation.

Breeders of live-stock, Order IV.

Of cattle-breeders and Commissariat farm hands there are but 12,442 persons; of these 5,854 were found in the districts of Akyab, Hanthawaddy, Pegu, Bassein, and Amherst.

It would seem strange that whereas pony-breeding is commoner in Upper, cattle-breeding should be more popular in Lower Burma. That pony-breeding is more frequently found as an occupation in Upper Burma is due partly to political causes and partly because ponies breed better in the drier and more elevated parts of the province. We should expect that the same cause would lead to more cattle being bred in Upper Burma. It is probably true that agriculturists do breed more cattle in Upper than in Lower Burma, but there are few who devote themselves to cattle-breeding alone. Indeed, few Burmans can be said to breed cattle. They drive them out to their grazing-grounds, and they are allowed to breed at their own free will. In Lower Burma, however, there is in Akyab, Amherst, Hanthawaddy, Pegu, and Bassein a large and fairly wealthy class of Indians who are by caste cattle-breeders and milkmen. Then, again, some Karens have taken to cattle-breeding. Of Burmans alone there are probably fewer cattle-breeders in Lower than in Upper Burma. Low as these figures are, yet they far exceed the return of cattle-breeders in 1881, when only 449—a manifest under-statement—were found in the lower province.

The classification of herdsmen.

275. Herdsmen are entered in this order. Only 22,273 are returned as connected with this occupation; but, as herdsmen are generally the servants, not of the breeders, but of the cultivators, and as, indeed, there are few breeders who are not cultivators as well, the herdsman is generally only herdsman for part of the year and works as field-labourer or crop-watcher, and it is therefore probable that the return made is correct. Indeed, considering the fact that, as before stated, stock-farming is generally carried on as subservient and in addition to land cultivation, the inclusion of herdsmen in Order IV is in Burma open to objection. During the preparation of these returns the recent famine in Upper Burma rendered the preparation of the statistics of the agricultural population a matter of urgent importance. When the returns of occupations were revised, the Financial Commissioner asked that herdsmen might be included in the return of those employed in agricultural pursuits, and at the same time asked that Forest Officers and Forest Rangers, guards, and peons might be omitted. Of course, however suitable this arrangement might be for local purposes, it was manifestly impossible that it should interfere with the already arranged Imperial classification. Accordingly, I have followed the Census Commissioner's classification in my Imperial tables, and the Financial Commissioner's amended classification in the Provincial tables. It will be seen that this has led to a discrepancy in the Imperial and Provincial returns. This subject will be noticed more fully when Order V is considered.

Buffalo breeders and dealers, occupation No. 27, include but 6,349 persons. The majority of them are found in Lower Burma. Buffalo-breeding is not an uncommon occupation amongst Karens living in the jungle, and as there are but few Karens in Upper Burma, the number returned there under this heading is consequently very small, as the majority of Burman cultivators would no more think of returning themselves as buffalo-breeders—though most of their buffaloes are chanpauk or home-bred—than would the English farmer return himself as a poultry-breeder because of the poultry in his yard.

Elephant-catchers are but few, and we have no camel-breeders in Burma. The ass and mule breeders are also very few. They are found chiefly in Bhamo and Ruby Mines and are the Panthè transport men. Forty-eight were returned in Rangoon, whither, it is supposed, they had come on a visit.

Sheep and goat breeders are classed together. Nearly all of them must be goat-breeders, as the only sheep bred in the country are bred by the Commissariat, or by natives of India entrusted with the sheep. There are also a few sheep-dealers in Rangoon, but most of the 1,303 persons entered under this heading are probably breeders and dealers in goats and not sheep.

Pig-dealers are few because only Chinamen, Karens, and Chins breed pigs.

Order V.—Agriculture.

276. The importance of this order may be gauged from the fact that 63·46 per cent. of the total population is either directly or indirectly engaged in, or dependent on, one of the 22 occupations contained under it. The next most important order is No. VII, the preparation and supply of food, which comprises fishermen, butchers, grain-dealers, fruit and vegetable sellers, and a whole tribe of petty bazaar-sellers distributed amongst 40 separate occupations. This order absorbs 9·93 per cent.

only of the population. So far as can be ascertained from the return of 1881, about 56·68 per cent. of the males over 14 years of age were engaged in agriculture. Taking the return for the whole of Burma, we find that out of 2,418,639 males over 14 years of age, 1,434,017, or 59·29 per cent., were employed in agricultural pursuits. As the return by age periods was prescribed only for the province divided by urban and rural tracts, it is impossible to give the figures for Lower Burma. In the return of occupations irrespective of age, but distributed by districts, we find that while the return of the total province shows that this order absorbs 63·46 per cent. of the total population, in Lower Burma the percentage rises to 68·15, while in Upper Burma it sinks to 56·06, which is almost exactly the same as the return of Lower Burma in 1881. It is very certain that agriculture in Lower Burma, with its broad paddy-plains, must absorb a larger proportion of the population, and it is probable that a large number of farm hands were in 1881 classed as coolies, of whom there were 87,675, and who were shown in the Indefinite class. It is possible, however, that the extension of cultivation and the decay of the fisheries in more than one of the deltaic districts may account for the higher percentage of agricultural labourers shown in our Lower Burma returns. It is at least quite clear that agriculture has lost none of its attractions, and still absorbs as much, if not more, of the total working population.

Comparison of the results of the two classifications of agriculturists.

277. In dealing with the return of herdsmen, the classification recommended by the Financial Commissioner for the Provincial tables and for the Famine Report returns has already been noticed. The Financial Commissioner, for reasons already given, wished to include herdsmen as agriculturists, and to exclude persons engaged on forest work and land occupants not cultivating, who combined with the renting out of land some occupation which rendered them independent of their land rent. Of these we have in Burma but very few. Such people, he argued, should not be included amongst agriculturists. A separate list of these combined occupations, Imperial Table XVII-C, has been prepared and will be analysed later on. In Burma, however, these combined occupations are but few. The result of the reclassification by the Financial Commissioner is a slight increase in the number of those dependent on agriculture for their livelihood. The following comparative statement shows the result of the two classifications district by district in Burma, and this table should be borne in mind in considering the return of agriculturists in the Provincial tables :—

ABSTRACT **D** *showing the number of agriculturists per 10,000 of the total population of each district.*

District.	Agriculturists according to Census Commissioner's classification.	Agriculturists according to Financial Commissioner's classification.
Akyab	7,447	7,489
Northern Arakan	9,508	9,508
Kyaukpyu	7,695	7,699
Sandoway	8,285	8,295
Arakan division ...	**7,649**	**7,677**
Rangoon town	224	240
Hanthawaddy	6,841	6,927
Pegu	7,065	7,196
Tharrawaddy	7,758	7,765
Prome	7,375	7,375
Pegu division ...	**6,419**	**6,466**
Thôngwa	6,509	6,523
Bassein	6,482	6,505
Henzada	7,195	7,206
Thayetmyo	7,307	7,307
Irrawaddy division ...	**6,798**	**6,811**

ABSTRACT **D** *showing the number of agriculturists per 10,000 of the total population of each district*—concluded.

District.	Agriculturists according to Census Commissioner's classification.	Agriculturists according to Financial Commissioner's classification.
Amherst ...	6,782	6,797
Tavoy ...	6,174	6,193
Mergui ...	7,074	7,083
Toungoo ...	6,543	6,559
Shwegyin ...	7,214	7,252
Salween ...	8,874	8,884
Tenasserim division ...	**6,860**	**6,880**
Mandalay ...	2,395	2,417
Bhamo ...	5,749	5,750
Katha ...	5,995	5,992
Ruby Mines ...	3,324	3,329
Shwebo ...	5,750	5,760
Northern division ...	**3,740**	**3,754**
Ye-u ...	6,835	6,835
Sagaing ...	5,373	5,449
Lower Chindwin ...	5,579	5,600
Upper Chindwin ...	6,858	6,852
Central division ...	**5,829**	**5,865**
Myingyan ...	5,687	5,722
Pakôkku ...	5,922	5,958
Minbu ...	6,415	6,422
Magwe ...	6,987	7,031
Southern division ...	**6,159**	**6,191**
Kyauksè ...	5,606	5,638
Meiktila ...	6,981	6,990
Yamèthin ...	6,950	6,958
Pyinmana ...	4,839	4,858
Eastern division ...	**6,436**	**6,451**
Lower Burma ...	6,815	6,842
Upper Burma ...	5,606	5,631
Burma ...	**6,346**	**6,373**

278. Order V is divided into the following four groups:—

(*a*) Those with interest in the land cultivated.
(*b*) Agricultural labourers.
(*c*) Growers of special products.
(*d*) Agricultural training and supervision.

The first group contains landlords who let out their land, but do not work it. Of these there are but 58,771 including dependents, or, if we take males over 14 alone, then there are but 17,892 in Upper and Lower Burma together. In Lower Burma alone there were in 1881 12,886 males over 14 years of age returned as land proprietors who do not cultivate. Though we are not able to give this return separately for Lower Burma now owing to the way the Imperial table was classified, yet if we turn to Imperial Table XVII-B we see clearly that the number of persons who live on the rent of land is greater actually and proportionately in Upper Burma. There were of males of all ages in Lower Burma but 18,581 persons who lived on the rent of land. Calculating the due proportion of those who would be over 14 years of age, we find that there were 11,591 males over 14 years of age who depended for their livelihood on the rent of land in 1891 as against 12,886 in 1881. It is true that the definition in 1881 was merely "land proprietor" and "land proprietors cultivating" were not expressly excluded though a separate item was given for "paddy cultivators and land owners." It is more than probable that several land proprietors who were cultivators of other kinds of produce were returned land proprietors only in 1881. If, however, the figures of 1881 be correct, then the result is satisfactory in that it shows that cultivators are not selling their lands through debt, and that the land of Burma is still worked by its "peasant proprietors." The Revenue Administration Report of the years 1891-92 has pointed out the increase in the districts of Pegu, Bassein and Henzada in the number of land proprietors who rent out and do not work their land. The vast extent of culturable land in the delta hitherto unworked has alone prevented the full force of this tendency being felt. So long as fresh land may be had for the asking, the cultivator who sells his land through debt more often prefers to take up new land under a patta than to remain on as a tenant on his old holdings. Accordingly, those who remain obtain better terms from their landlords, and this, by diminishing the profits of land-holding, further checks the process of the alienation of the soil from the hands of those who work it. As the supply of culturable land still lying waste decreases, so the number of land proprietors not cultivating may be expected to increase.

Item 38, Land occupants cultivating.

279. Of land occupants cultivating, Item 38, there are 2,475,010 souls including dependents. This single occupation thus absorbs more than 32 per cent., or in round numbers nearly one-third of the total population of Burma. A comparison with the returns of 1881 is rendered more than usually difficult in this instance owing to the unnecessary detail in which the land occupants cultivating were then divided, namely, into wheat and rice growers. It would appear that there were about 363,142 males over 14 returned under this head against 713,146 males over 14 returned for the whole of Burma in 1891.

Allowing for the increase of the population in Lower Burma and for the addition of the inhabitants of Upper Burma, we find that, supposing that there is the same proportion of land occupants cultivating in both provinces, there are 482,277 males over 14 thus employed in Lower Burma now, being an increase of nearly 33 per cent.

Of tenants not cultivating, Item 40, we have very few, and 607 out of the 625 thus returned are women.

Item 41, Tenants and sharers.

280. Tenants and sharers cultivating, Item 41, are again another large section of the community. Of males over 14 years of age, 217,367 were thus returned. There were in 1881 but 40,893 returned as rice-cultivators who are tenants. The difference is in great measure due to the change in the wording. Our present definition includes sharers as well as tenants. Sharers were not shown separately in 1881, and were in all probability classed as land occupants cultivating or perhaps as land proprietors. Amongst the Karens this system of sharing is not uncommon. Then, again, the inclusion of Upper Burma has widened the area under review, and the increase of cultivation and of population must be taken into account. Still it would seem strange that while land occupants not cultivating have apparently decreased since 1881, tenants and sharers should have increased so rapidly, since their increase is at the rate of over 192 per cent. in Lower Burma alone. It is clear, therefore, that the excess is in great measure due to the inclusion of sharers.

It is unfortunate that the change in the definition prevents any weight being attached to this discrepancy. In Upper Burma the tenure of the land is very different to the simple uniform system of the lower province. In the former we have large stretches of "ledaw" or State land, on which the revenue up till lately was assessed by the king taking from one-fourth to one-tenth share of the produce. The workers of "ledaw" lands are not occupants in the sense of the Land Revenue Act, but tenants of the Crown.

Then, again, we find that we have in Upper Burma a wealthy class of landholders, men or the descendants of men who have received grants of land for services rendered to some Burmese king. Ancestral rights over land known as "bobabaing" and royal grants of "minmye" made to courtiers will account for there being more land occupants not cultivating and more tenants in Upper than in Lower Burma.

Group 11, Agricultural labourers.

281. The next Group 11 consists of two items—farm and field labourers and crop-watchers. There are but few farm labourers returned as such, whereas the item field labourer and crop-watcher absorbs 682,093 persons. Practically, in Burma, where the holdings are small, farm labourers are few, but field labourers and crop-watchers are hired by the job. Moreover, it is difficult to draw the line between the farm

labourer and the field labourer in Burma, where the division of labour is yet in a rudimentary state and high farming is unknown. In this subdivision at the last census there were four occupations returned—hired labourer, paddy planter, paddy reaper and extractor, and paddy watcher. It will probably be unnecessary to compile the occupations apart in future. Of both items, 42, Farm servants, and 43, Field labourers, there were 229,207 males over 14 years of age in all Burma as against 92,870 in Lower Burma alone in 1881. If we deduct the proportion of these workers living in Upper Burma, those thus employed were, after allowing for the increase in the total population, proportionably nearly twice as numerous in 1891 as they were in 1881.

Group 12, Growers of special produce.

282. In Group 12 the most important item is No. 51, Market gardeners or vegetable growers. Under this head were placed the taungya or "jhoom" cultivators of Burma. On this occupation there are 628,013 workers and dependents, or 8·25 per cent. of the total population. Of males over 14 there are 181,366 or 7·5 per cent. of the male population of that age thus employed. In 1881 there were only 70,952 males over 14 engaged on this occupation. Allowing for the increase of the population and for the annexation of Upper Burma, we find that there is an appreciable increase in the number of "ya" cultivators, as the percentage of "ya" cultivators was only 5·8 of the male working population in 1881, while in 1891 of "ya" cultivators there were in Lower Burma 100,618 males over 14 years of age, being 6·5 per cent. of the total male working population. Groups 10 and 11 with those included in this item comprise the great bulk of the producers of the staple food-grains of the country, which are rice, both "ya" and "le," Indian-corn, and the vegetables the country folk eat. The other items of Group 12 are mere accessories of the food. Taking these occupations of Group 12 together, we find that they absorb 11·482 per cent. of the total population. The following statement will, perhaps, be interesting as showing the proportionate strength of each of these items to one another in every district in Burma:—

ABSTRACT E, *showing the proportionate number working at the several agricultural occupations per 10,000 agriculturists, by districts, divisions, Lower and Upper Burma, and also for the whole province.*

District.	Land occupants not cultivating.	Land occupants cultivating.	Tenants not cultivating.	Tenants and sharers cultivating.	Field and farm labourers.	Growers of special products.
Akyab	144	5,070	...	2,011	1,781	994
Northern Arakan	...	4,705	...	...	...	5,295
Kyaukpyu	113	6,876	...	1,127	403	1,481
Sandoway	170	6,405	...	2,097	138	1,190
Arakan division ...	**135**	**5,671**	...	**1,750**	**1,190**	**1,254**
Rangoon	439	4,657	2	32	1,960	2,910
Hanthawaddy	259	4,142	...	1,201	3,450	948
Pegu	135	3,574	...	1,588	4,440	263
Tharrawaddy	52	5,014	...	988	2,278	1,668
Prome	140	6,874	...	835	758	1,393
Pegu division ...	**138**	**5,042**	**·01**	**1,119**	**2,565**	**1,135**
Thôngwa	101	5,599	...	1,587	1,614	1,099
Bassein	84	5,454	·09	1,536	1,824	1,101
Henzada	86	4,089	...	1,572	2,566	1,687
Thayetmyo	46	5,829	·1	548	468	3,108
Irrawaddy division ...	**83**	**5,204**	**·05**	**1,388**	**1,724**	**1,600**
Amherst	150	5,338	·07	787	1,784	1,940
Tavoy	118	4,851	...	1,404	1,882	1,745
Mergui	21	7,197	...	492	600	1,690
Toungoo	73	3,827	·7	1,882	881	3,336
Shwegyin	60	5,331	40	839	1,186	2,544
Salween	3	1,085	...	45	124	8,745
Tenasserim division ...	**99**	**5,023**	**9**	**971**	**1,362**	**2,536**
Lower Burma ...	**111**	**5,194**	**2**	**1,279**	**1,809**	**1,605**

ABSTRACT E, *showing the proportionate number working at the several agricultural occupations per 10,000 agriculturists, by districts, divisions, Lower and Upper Burma, and also for the whole province*—concluded.

District.	Land occupants not cultivating.	Land occupants cultivating.	Tenants not cultivating.	Tenants and sharers cultivating.	Field and farm labourers.	Growers of special products.
Mandalay	64	3,354	...	-1,753	1,260	3,569
Bhamo	7	7,272	...	260	450	2,011
Katha	2	4,306	...	738	566	4,388
Ruby Mines	4	7,885	2	21	132	1,956
Shwebo	116	7,497	2	1,497	710	178
Northern division ...	**62**	**5,485**	**·5**	**1,269**	**838**	**2,345**
Ye-u	209	8,115	...	1,257	352	67
Sagaing	198	4,321	...	2,219	995	2,267
Lower Chindwin	440	5,688	...	2,912	232	728
Upper Chindwin	77	5,551	...	2,380	1,343	649
Central division ...	**266**	**5,593**	...	**2,318**	**674**	**1,149**
Myingyan	156	4,759	...	1,392	485	3,208
Pakôkku	137	3,681	...	2,486	676	3,020
Minbu	77	2,597	...	4,642	286	2,398
Magwe	120	4,022	...	833	377	4,648
Southern division ...	**126**	**3,846**	**·02**	**2,247**	**469**	**3,311**
Kyauksè	38	4,512	...	1,361	2,533	1,556
Meiktila	118	7,771	·7	803	496	811
Yamèthin	113	5,683	...	2,900	392	912
Pyinmana	84	4,984	...	2,187	441	2,304
Eastern division ...	**98**	**6,245**	**·2**	**1,682**	**867**	**1,107**
Upper Burma ...	**142**	**5,001**	**·1**	**1,999**	**655**	**2,202**
LOWER AND UPPER BURMA ...	**122**	**5,127**	**1**	**1,527**	**1,414**	**1,809**

283. This table brings out clearly what was before stated, that in proportion to the total number of agriculturists, while there are fewer land occupants not cultivating in Lower Burma, there are more land occupants who cultivate their own fields, and proportionately fewer tenants and sharers. As a fact there are in Lower Burma 35,218 persons living by the former occupation as against 23,553 in Upper Burma, and 406,220 tenants and sharers in Lower Burma as against 330,158 of the same calling in the upper province. It may be noted that these abstracts were prepared some time before the appearance of the Revenue Administration Report of the year 1891-92. In paragraph 9 of the Chief Commissioner's resolution on this report, the Chief Commissioner remarks that "it appears that a landlord class is being gradually formed in Burma, that this class is "drawn for the most part from the agricultural population, but that a class of non-"agricultural landlords is also in process of formation, and that the process is more "rapid in Pegu than elsewhere." Owing to the fact that land in Burma is often rented out on the system of the landlords sharing in the profits, the method of classification adopted has to some extent masked the true number of the land occupants not cultivating, or "non-agricultural landlords" as they are termed in the report above quoted. It will be seen that it is possible that some landlords may have been returned as sharers. If, however, we turn to the figures that show the number of land occupants cultivating, we find that they are proportionately fewer in the Pegu district than in any other district in Lower Burma except Salween, where the majority of the cultivators are growers of special products. This coincidence of the census returns with those of the Financial Commissioner is an almost irresistible proof of the truth of the remarks above quoted.

The explanation of Abstract E.

284. Omitting Rangoon, where the number of agriculturists is very small and where the presence of a few visitors would vitiate the true proportion of the return, we find that outside of the Hanthawaddy district, in which a considerable quantity of land is held by non-cultivating proprietors, the bulk of the land is in the hands of the men who work it. In Pegu, where the holdings are largest, we find the largest number of farm and field labourers. Next after Pegu come

Hanthawaddy, Henzada, and Tharrawaddy, all large paddy-producing districts. The proportion of field labourers as compared with tenants and sharers cultivating is low in Thôngwa and Bassein owing to the custom of the Karens, who are numerous in these two districts, to work for each other in turn. In Upper Burma the proportion of tenants and sharers cultivating to the total number of agriculturists is far higher than in Lower Burma. If we take the two items of land occupants not cultivating and tenant and sharers cultivating, we find that for every 1,000 of the former in Lower Burma there are but 668·7 in Upper Burma, while for every 1,000 of the latter in Lower Burma there are 812·75 in Upper Burma. The only explanation of this disproportion is that the landlords in Upper Burma have large holdings or that the workers of State lands have returned themselves as tenants. Both explanations are probably correct.

In proportion to the total population we find that there are 7·5 land occupants not cultivating and 87 tenants and sharers cultivating out of every 1,000 persons in Lower Burma, and 7·9 land occupants not cultivating and 112 tenants and sharers in Upper Burma out of the same number.

Growers of special products.

285. Of the remaining occupations in this group, the most important are No. 44, Tea, coffee, tobacco, and cinchona planters; No. 46, Betel-vine, sugarcane, and areca-nut growers; No. 48, Cardamom, til-seed, and pepper growers; and No 50, Fruit growers. The first of these, No. 44, is composed chiefly of tobacco growers and their families. The Burman countryfolk do not drink tea, but eat the pickled leaves of one of the varieties of the tea plant. Tobacco-growing is chiefly carried on in the Tharrawaddy, Henzada, Thayetmyo, Katha, Myingyan, and Pakôkku districts, on the alluvial banks of the Irrawaddy, and in the numerous islands that are formed in that river in the dry weather.

In Item 46, Betel-vine, sugarcane, and areca-nut growers are all lumped together, and it is impossible to separate them except by referring to the district table. In Akyab, Hanthawaddy, Prome, Thôngwa, Bassein, and Henzada, the majority of those thus returned are betel-vine growers, with a few sugarcane growers; in Amherst, Toungoo, and Shwegyin, areca-nut palms and sugarcane are largely cultivated.

Item 48, Cardamom, til-seed, and pepper growers are a still more numerous body. Few earn a livelihood by growing cardamoms and pepper alone, but til-seed is grown in large quantities in Thayetmyo, Shwegyin, Sagaing, Magwe, and especially in Myingyan.

Item 50, Fruit-growers, have next to market gardeners, the most numerous following of any occupation in this group. Eighty-seven thousand and thirty-three persons live by their fruit trees. They are most numerous in the deltaic districts, such as Hanthawaddy, Pegu, Tharrawaddy, Thôngwa, Bassein, Henzada, Amherst, Tavoy, Mergui, and Shwegyin, and, except in Mandalay, there are but few in Upper Burma.

Class C, Personal and household service.

286. Class **C** includes all those who live by rendering personal or household service. It is divided into three groups: domestic servants and their dependents, who compose 49,755 of the total number, 59,041 belonging to this class; non-domestic establishment, a somewhat unfortunate term meant to express those who are engaged in providing accommodation for travellers, of whom there are 5,979; and, thirdly, sanitation, under which sanitary officers and sweepers are included. All of our sanitary officers of Government who combine the administration of sanitation with other duties have not unnaturally preferred to return themselves under their other designation.

Class D. The preparation and supply of material substances.

287. Class **D** includes the bulk of the various trades and handicrafts pursued in the country. It is divided into 11 orders, 37 groups, and 270 different heads, each denoting one and sometimes more than one occupation. The reason of this latter arrangement of placing what are often separate occupations under one head is that, in a comparatively rude state of civilization, the preparation and the supply, or the manufacture and the sale, of an article of commerce are both performed by the same man. This is because the function of sale or distribution

is now in civilized countries divided into two processes—wholesale and retail. Manufacturers do not now like to be classed in England with the tradesmen who sell their goods. This distinction vanishes in a country where the division of labour is yet not fully developed.

Group 17, The suppliers of animal food.

288. The first group deals with the suppliers of animal food. Of these there are 231,478 including dependents, being 3·04 per cent. of the total population. By far the most important of these occupations is that of fishermen and fish-curers. These form 2·2 per cent. of the total population. To show how impossible it is to compare the results of the present with those of the past census, it will be sufficient to note that fishermen were in 1881 included in the agricultural class, and were further subdivided into sea and trap fishermen, and the sellers of fish were divided into three heads and included in Class V, the Industrial. Even if we collect all these items, we find that there were but 24,535 males over 14 years of age engaged in this business in 1881, or 2·02 per cent. of the male population, as against 52,690 and 9,104 males of corresponding age under the heads into which these fishermen and fish-dealers are now shown in the employment table in the whole of Burma in 1891. On turning to Abstract C we find that but very few of this occupation are found in Upper Burma; indeed, we find that in Thôngwa district alone there are 34,244 souls dependent on this occupation, while there were in the whole of Upper Burma only 73,870 persons engaged in or dependent on these means of livelihood, being but 34 per cent. of the total population returned under these heads; so that we may safely conclude that out of the 61,794 fishermen and fish dealers before mentioned, 42,612 are found in Lower Burma. This is an increase of 73·67 per cent., which far outstrips the relative growth of the population. This increase, in the face of the well-known decay of fisheries owing to the extension of cultivation and the draining of water-logged swamps like the Pagaing plains north of Pegu, would have required some explanation. But Mr. Copleston has forestalled further enquiry by remarking in 1881 that "it can-"not be said that these figures (*i.e.*, those relating to the return of fishermen) "include all persons who are engaged in fishing."

The next group, No. 18, Preparers and sellers of vegetable food, calls for no notice.

Item 98, Toddy-drawers and sellers.

289. Group 19 is an important one. It is remarkable how many toddy-drawers and sellers there are. In 1891 we find 26,233 males over 14 engaged in this work as against 1,652 only in 1881. The comparative statement will show the cause of this enormous increase. It will be seen that just as the greater number of fishermen are found in the deltaic districts, so the majority of toddy-climbers are found in Upper Burma. In the districts of Shwebo, Sagaing, Lower Chindwin, Myingyan, Pakôkku, Minbu, Magwe, Kyauksè, and Meiktila toddy-drawers are most numerous. Indeed, Myingyan and Pakôkku alone contain 40,667 or almost half of those dependent on this industry. Comparison with the returns of 1881 is again difficult, as it is possible that many toddy-drawers combine this work with the work of preparing molasses and sugar. If, however, we make allowances for the number of those living in Upper Burma, we find that there were in 1891, 5,909 males living in Lower Burma, of whom 3,489 were males over 14 years of age. This gives an increase of over 111 per cent. on the returns of 1881. Part of this increase may probably be traced to the steady and increasing demand for jaggery, which is still imported from Madras into Burma. It is, however, very probable that the number of toddy-drawers was understated in 1881, as toddy-trees are subject to taxation, and in 1881 the people of Lower Burma were still afraid that the enumeration must mean increased taxation. Foreign wine and spirit-dealers are not represented in this group, because the importers and dealers of imported liquors generally combine this occupation with other trades, and are shown as general merchants and hotel-keepers. Brewers are evenly distributed between Pakôkku and Mandalay. It might seem strange that manufacturers and sellers of opium are absent when there are still so many opium farms in the province, but this heading is not meant for them; they will be found in Class E, Group 57 (*b*).

As regards the occupation of tea tasters and sellers, it must be recollected that this includes the sellers of pickled tea or "letpet." This is a variety of the tea plant not cultivated in Assam or China for the manufacture of tea for drinking; it is the variety known as the *Elæodendron orientale* (McClelland).

Dealers in oil.

290. In Group 20 there are three occupations that absorb nearly the whole of the population entered under this heading, oil-pressers and sellers, oil and salt sellers, and kerosine-oil dealers. The first two of these occupations are fairly evenly distributed throughout Burma. Even in those villages where til is not cultivated we find that some villager has a "si-son" or oil-press. It is at first sight difficult to understand why the oil-pressing industry should not be confined to places where the til-seed is produced, so that the cost of carriage might be saved. The only reason that can be assigned is that til-seed oil is much adulterated by the oil of the ground-nuts imported in large quantities for this very purpose from Madras. By pressing his own oil the villager can be sure of its purity. Among kerosine-oil sellers are included the workers of the petroleum-oil wells. As these wells are confined to the oil-fields of Yenangyaung in the Magwe district and to the Kyaukpyu fields, it is in these districts that we may expect to find kerosine-oil sellers most numerous in proportion to the population; indeed, 34·7 of the whole population included under this head is to be found in the Magwe district.

The next group relates to those who supply fuel and forage. Firewood and grass gatherers, firewood contractors, and charcoal-burners absorb 31,721 out of the 31,997 included in this group.

Order IX, Builders and dealers in building materials.

291. The next order, IX, deals with those employed in building, and, as might be expected, by far the most numerous are those who live by working in thatch. If thatch-dealers are included, there appears to be no reason why bamboo-cutters should not have been included also, as houses in Burma are often built and even roofed with bamboos. But bamboo-dealers and workers are included in Items 302 and 306 of Order XV. In Burma at least the bamboo-workers should most certainly have been included in Order IX. The number of masons appears to be small, being 9·775 in every 10,000 of the inhabitants, but the paucity of masons is due to the fact that most houses in Burma are built of wood or bamboo. I would not include wood-cutters in Group 22, Order IX, because wood is not used exclusively for building purposes.

Groups 25 and 26, Boat-builders and makers of vehicles.

292. In Order X, in Group 25, the only item of any practical importance is Item 146, which includes those who live by making or selling carts and carriages. The makers of carriages are found in Rangoon, Moulmein, and Mandalay. The returns of other districts are confined to cartwrights. These seem to be very evenly distributed, except that they seem to be very few in Akyab, Bassein, Tavoy, and Upper Chindwin, while none are returned under this head in Mergui, Bhamo, and Salween. It is possible that the cartwright is sometimes a carpenter as well, and is often returned under the more general term, as lethama, which we translate as carpenter, while in Burmese it literally means "the handy man." The next, Group 26, is, owing to the splendid waterways of the province, far more numerous and important than the sister groups devoted to the manufacture of carriages by land. Item 151, Canoe-diggers, alone contains 8,785 persons. Of these 2,212 are found in the Bassein district alone, but each district in Lower Burma, except the Northern Arakan Hill Tracts and Salween, is well supplied with canoe-makers. Under this heading, Item 151, are included all builders of native craft as opposed to shipwrights and boat-builders, who were restricted to the builders of boats and craft built on English lines.

Supplementary requirements.

293. Order XI contains a large number of miscellaneous employments. The first group calls for no particular notice, except that under Item 153 there were no paper-makers found and but few palm leaf-binders. The paper-sellers are found in nearly every bazaar, as paper is required for petitions in Court.

Press proprietors and printers.

294. Group 28 is an important group. The number of press proprietors, lithographers, and printers, Item 157, would at first sight appear to be large. There were 673 males over 14 years of age employed in this work or dependent on it for their support. This is, everything considered, a large number for the province, being 2·7 out of every 10,000 persons over that age. In England, of course, the proportion is much higher, but a comparison of the actual strength of these occupations is difficult, as in England a certain number of the printers and engravers are women. In proportion to the total population, there are out of 100,000 souls not quite 9 persons actually engaged in this occupation in Burma, while in England in 1881 there were 270 out of the same number. To understand Burma's position in this matter, it is not enough to show its weakness by comparing it with England. If we turn to the returns of India, in 1881 we find that there were but 10,960 males over 14 years of age employed on these occupations, being only 4 out of every 100,000 of the total population. If we take the figures of 1891 for Lower Burma only, we find that out of the 1,536 returned as dependent on and working at these occupations, 1,391 live in Lower Burma and 145 in Upper Burma. Of the 1,391 in Lower Burma, 1,164 live in Rangoon and 93 in Moulmein. Of the 145 in Upper Burma, 141 live in Mandalay. If we take the proportion of workers to be the same in Lower Burma as in the whole province, we may take it that out of the 673 males over 14 years of age employed on these occupations, 586 are found in Lower Burma. In 1881 there were only 364 so returned; thus there is an increase of nearly 61 per cent. The annexation of Upper Burma is still too recent to have allowed for much expansion in this direction, but if we confine ourselves to Lower Burma, we see how enormously the power of the press has advanced in the last decade. Of newspaper proprietors and managers, Item 160, there are but 10 males over 15 years of age, but some were returned as press proprietors. There were apparently only four publishers and press proprietors altogether in 1881. There were 307 males over 14 years of age who returned themselves as book-sellers and publishers, Item 159, and in this number are included several petty book-sellers, while, as before stated, some newspaper proprietors who owned presses returned themselves as press proprietors.

Wood-carvers and lacquerers.

295. The next group that calls for notice is Group 30, which is noteworthy, because it includes the wood-carving craft, Item 169, and turners and lacquerers, Item 172. Wood-carving and lacquer-work are well-known Burmese handicrafts. In wood-carving the Burmese excel, and the wealth of imagery and ornament which is found on some of the Burmese monasteries is perhaps unequalled in its own peculiar line throughout the world. In Mandalay more than 61 per cent. of the total number of wood-carvers were enumerated. They congregated to Mandalay, as in that capital of the old Burmese kingdom the artist found the best market for his labour. Next to Mandalay comes Rangoon, where 10 per cent. of the total number of carvers were found. In Prome, Henzada, Pakôkku, Tharrawaddy, and Shwegyin a few persons returned themselves as living by wood-carving alone. But the majority of wood-carvers—men who were not clever enough to live by wood-carving alone—have returned themselves as carpenters, furniture and box-makers. Of lacquerers and turners and their dependents there were 12,081. More than half of these were returned in the Myingyan district, which now includes Pagan, the headquarters of the lacquer-ware workers. In Mandalay they are also numerous and are also found in large numbers in the Lower Chindwin, Minbu, and Magwe districts.

Group 36, Tool-makers.

296. No other industry is worthy of especial mention till we come to Group 36, Tools and machinery. The ordinary tool of a Burman is his da, but the da-maker rarely confines himself to making das, and does any blacksmith's work. There is one industry which is dying hard. Notwithstanding the introduction of manufactured piece-goods, the rude but useful loom of the country is not yet driven out of the market. The loom-makers' industry therefore, though doomed, still lingers on. These loom-makers are most numerous in Minbu, Pakôkku, and Mandalay, but, except in Prome and Tharrawaddy, the industry is now almost extinct in Lower Burma. It

is impossible to compare the returns with those of the previous census in Lower Burma, as no mention is there made of the makers of loom-combs, an important part of the industry.

Order XII, Makers of textile fabrics.

297. In Order XII, Makers of textile fabrics, Group 38 calls for no remark. Group 39 is, however, important. Silkworm rearers and cocoon-gatherers number 3,229 of both sexes, and formerly this industry was solely followed by the Yabeins. The Burmese Buddhists look on the taking of life as a sin, and look down with contempt on the man who takes life habitually in the course of his occupation. The Yabeins are hereditary silkworm rearers from inclination, because it pays, not from force of custom or caste. Many Yabein villages have abandoned this industry and have, especially in the Pegu district, taken to agriculture instead. Silkworm rearers are most numerous in Prome, Toungoo, Pyinmana, and Magwe. But while the Yabeins have taken to agriculture, the Karens have in some cases taken to silkworm rearing. The silk carders and weavers are a numerous class; Mandalay and Prome are the headquarters of this industry. But this industry, too, is losing ground and Manchester piece-goods are driving the native product out of the market. Owing to the difference in the classification, it is impossible to compare with any accuracy the results of the present with those of the past census, and as the returns of the past census did not give the returns in detail by districts, it is impossible to verify the returns or draw inferences in this matter.

Group 40, Workers in cotton.

298. Group 40 comprehends the workers in cotton. It includes 335 out of every 10,000 of the total population. Cotton is grown largely in the Myingyan district, and in most of the Upper Burma districts a little cotton is produced, but we have no cotton-mills in the country, and, though a little cotton yarn may be made and consumed locally, nearly all the cotton yarn that is woven is imported. There are 229,185 persons engaged or dependent on this industry, of whom but 16,530 are males over 14 years of age, and but 39,142 males of all ages are included in this category of cotton-weavers, while 190,043 females are thus shown. We find that 38,797 weavers and their dependents live in the towns and 190,388 live in the country. Only 181 weavers and their dependents are to be found in Rangoon, and we may therefore conclude that weavers that are enumerated in towns are to be found in the smaller and remoter towns. On referring to Abstract C we find that weavers are comparatively few in Lower Burma and most numerous in Mandalay, Pakôkku, Lower Chindwin, Myingyan, and Sagaing. These figures also show that weaving is essentially an occupation pursued by females; that the few males shown are probably all dependents; that it is pursued in the rural tracts; and that, notwithstanding the excess of the population in Lower Burma, far fewer weavers are found there. Weaving in Lower Burma is the work of the young girls of the house. In the old days every woman plied her loom, and the loom is mentioned as being the woman's and not the man's property in the Burmese law books. Manchester goods have reduced weaving from the position of the chief industry of women to a secondary place. Instead of working at their looms at home, now that weaving is no longer lucrative, the Burmese girl prefers to keep a stall in the bazaar. The thrifty housewife in the rural tracts and smaller towns of Lower Burma still keeps her loom to employ her spare time and keep her daughters employed and out of mischief, but the loom is gradually falling more and more out of favour. The cloth woven is coarse but strong, and in Lower Burma it but just repays the weaver to weave for her own household, because she can profitably employ time which would otherwise be wasted. But weaving for a livelihood brings but a bare pittance to those who are solely dependent on it. It is useless to attempt to compare the return of the lower province with the figures of the 1881 census, for we find that only 3,475 women over 14 years of age were returned as being employed in this manner. This is palpably wrong. It is probable that many cotton-weavers were in 1881 returned as weavers not otherwise described, of whom there were 35,915.

Weavers.

299. If we take weavers of all kinds together, we find that in 1881 there were 40,797 women thus employed; but a comparison of these figures with the present returns is rendered

impossible because weaving is a handicraft which is followed by girls long before they attain the age of 15; and though it is clear that the number of females in Lower Burma who depend on weaving is fewer than in 1881, it is impossible to say how much of the decrease is due to a difference in the classification. As weavers and dealers are classed together, it is difficult to discriminate between them, but it has been calculated that 49,796 females are returned as weavers of some kind of textile fabric or as dependents. Allowing that no girls of under 10 years of age are returned as weavers, we find that the number of weavers amongst women in Lower Burma is only 35,412, a decrease of 13·19 per cent. The increase in the number of women within the last decade amounted to 25·8 per cent., and at this rate the number of women weavers should have amounted to 51,322. The decrease shown therefore is a clear proof that the native industry has been proportionately displaced by the increase in the importations of English piece-goods. But this decrease may also, in part, be caused by the increase in wealth and in luxuriousness of the people. Nearly every Burman wears a silk paso or waistcloth; hence the market for cotton goods is probably more limited. Taken from this point of view the decrease is not necessarily to be deplored.

Group 41, Workers in jute, coir, &c.

300. Group 41, Workers in flax, jute, coir, &c., is only important for the item of net makers and sellers. This is an important industry and is carried on either by fishermen themselves or their wives. In a country with such large fisheries, net-making might well be expected to have bulked even more largely, but the majority of Burmese fishermen use bamboo traps and screens and not nets for their work.

Group 42, Drapers and workers in articles of attire.

301. In the next group, 42, Dress, we find the usual proportion of tailors and darners and a very large number of piece-goods sellers. Out of the 41,926 tailors 28,423, or 67 per cent., are found in the towns; but the piece-goods sellers are more evenly divided, as nearly every village has its local pedlar. False plait-makers are included in this group. In England, where barbers are not domestic servants and would not be included in Item 59, which is confined to that class, we should expect false plait-makers to be entered in the same group as barbers. But a false plait-maker is not a domestic servant, and in India a barber is; this is a fair example of the difficulty of applying a classification suitable in England to the occupations pursued in the East. That there are as many as 251 false plait-makers and dependents is due not merely to the vanity of Burmese women, as might be supposed, for a Burmese youth, if his hair be short and thin, often secretly ekes it out with a false tress. Burmans, both men and women, usually have long and thick, if somewhat coarse, hair, which the man knots up into a round ball on the top of his head, and to have a good sized "yaung" or top-knot is a *sine quâ non* with the Burmese dandy.

Order XIII, Workers and dealers in precious metals and stones.

302. Order XIII, which deals with the workers and dealers in metals and precious stones, includes 0·91 per cent. of the total population. This fact alone would show that Burma was not a great mineral producing or manufacturing country, and when we deduct the 24,564 gold and silver workers, the residue is insignificant. There are four groups, the most important of which is Group 43, Workers and dealers in gold and silver and precious stones. Of these the goldsmiths and silversmiths form by far the most important part. The Burmese gold jewellery, though delicate in work, is not generally admired, but the silver work produced by Burmese artists is of original design and handsome workmanship. In 1881 there were 5,795 gold and silver smiths, in 1891 there were in Lower Burma exactly 10,000 males working at or dependent on this occupation. Boys of under 15 are not employed in delicate work of this kind, so that, allowing for the number of those under 15 years of age as being dependents, we may assume safely that there were 6,887 gold and silver workers in Lower Burma in 1891. This gives an increase of 18 per cent. But on comparing the two classifications, it will be found that the present classification discriminates between the smith and the dealer, but that no distinction was made in 1881, so that, in order to come to a fair comparison, we must include the gold and silver dealers and assayers and goldsmiths' dust washers. Even if we include these and

make allowance for dependents, we find that there is only an increase of 25·8 per cent. in the decade. Of ruby-workers and ruby-dealers Burma has its full share. Out of 1,368 ruby-workers and their dependents 1,359 live, as might be expected, in the Ruby Mines district. Of ruby and emerald dealers Mandalay is evidently the headquarters, and next comes the Ruby Mines district.

The group of brass and copper workers is unimportant. Unlike the natives of India, Burmans do not use brass or copper cooking vessels.

Tin workers and sellers, by which is generally meant workers in and sellers of tinned ware, are evidently evenly distributed throughout the districts of Lower Burma, but in Upper Burma they seem to congregate chiefly in Mandalay and Sagaing. In Mergui, where the tin-mines are, we find but very few returned, but if we turn to Item 287 in the same group, we find that out of the 644 lead and quicksilver workers, 506 live in Mergui. There is therefore reason to believe that the miners there, who mine for both tin and lead, returned themselves as lead-workers.

Blacksmiths.

303. The next group, No. 46, contains one important item—"Blacksmiths." Of these and their dependents there are 23,352. These, as might be expected, are distributed very evenly over the whole country. In 1881 there were 4,414 blacksmiths in Lower Burma; in 1891, after allowing for dependents, there were 5,490, an increase of 24 per cent. This shows that those returning this profession have increased at almost exactly the same rate as that at which the population has been increasing within the same time.

Item 298, Potters.

304. Potters, Item No. 298 in Group 48, is the next most important occupation on the list. There were 31,352 or 0·412 per cent. of the total population dependent on this occupation, and it is more frequently pursued in rural than in urban areas. The returns show that the distribution of potters is very evenly made throughout the districts of Burma. Bassein appears to be the place where potters most abound, and Bassein pottery ware is well known throughout the country. In 1881 there were 1,994 male potters, and, after making due allowance for dependents, there were 4,146 potters in Lower Burma in 1891, an increase of 108 per cent. This is an enormous increase. As pottery ware is not exported beyond the limits of the province, and the demand for pottery depends on the ordinary needs of the province and would perhaps, far less than most handicrafts, be liable to fluctuations, this large increase is unaccountable except on the ground that potters were understated in 1881 or overstated now. Turning to the figures of 1872, we find that there were 1,186 males over 14 years of age who returned themselves as potters. Notwithstanding that in 1881 some males under 15 were included, the increase of 68 per cent. over the return of 1872 is far less than in the succeeding decade. Hence it is probable that the return of potters in 1881 is understated.

Order XV, Workers in wood, cane, and leaves.

305. In Order XV is included one of the staple and best known industries of the province. Burmese teak and cutch are well known, and next to rice, timber is the most important commodity which Burma sends into the general exchange market of the world. Timber and cutch agents and dealers are an important class. As might be expected, they are chiefly to be found in rural and not urban areas. They are most numerous in the Bassein, Thayetmyo, Pegu, Amherst, Prome, Tharrawaddy, and Henzada districts in Lower Burma, and in the Minbu, Pyinmana, Mandalay, and Magwe districts in Upper Burma. Comparison with the returns of 1881 is difficult as teak timber-dealers were shown separately from timber-merchants, and it is possible that several now included as timber-merchants were shown in 1881 as saw-mill and saw-pit owners, while in our present classification cutch boilers and dealers are included. In fact as many of these forest occupations are worked at in turn by the same men, the figures are liable to what would appear to be inexplicable fluctuations. Wood-cutters sometimes work as sawyers, sometimes as cutch-boilers. If we take cutch boilers, dealers, and sellers, teak timber-dealers and timber-dealers, all of whom were shown apart in 1881, and compare their returns with the returns of 1891, we find that there were but 8,238 males of over 14 returned under this head in

1891 as against 14,220 returned in 1881 as working at the occupations above mentioned. This falling off in the number returned is probably to be traced to the contraction of the cutch-boiling industry, as out of the 14,220, 11,483 were cutch-boilers and 505 cutch-dealers. The Forest reports bear testimony to the wilful waste of cutch trees in times past, whereby this valuable tree was almost extirpated in Lower Burma. Moreover, the action of the Forest Department in reserving "cutch areas," while it preserves the industry from extinction, and will thus save a valuable source of income to the forest worker, and revenue to the State, has undoubtedly accentuated for a time the decrease in the number of those who live by cutch-boiling. That the cutch-boilers have not been ruthlessly cut off from obtaining a livelihood may be gathered from a comparison of the return of wood-cutters and sawyers, Item 303, with the return of wood-cutters and sawyers and log and post cutters combined in 1881. In 1891, after allowing for a due proportion of dependents, we may calculate that about 13,076 males were employed in Lower Burma on these occupations against 8,428 in 1881. These figures will in part account for the decrease in cutch-boilers, while some who formerly boiled cutch may now be found under the heading of firewood and grass gatherers and sellers and firewood dealers, who are shown in Group 21. Of firewood cutters and sellers in 1881 there were but 1,316, while of firewood and grass gatherers and dealers there were 3,565 males of working age. We may therefore assume that the cutch-boilers of 1881 have found congenial work.

Item 304, Carpenters.

306. The next item, "Carpenters," covers a host of minor occupations. The number of carpenters is evenly divided between urban and rural tracts as in 1881. Carpenters are evenly distributed amongst the districts of Burma. There were 11,502 returned in 1881 as working at this occupation in Lower Burma, and there were 13,913 males over 14 years of age returned under this description in 1891. This is an increase of 20·9 per cent., and it is probable that the superior profits made by agriculturists are responsible for the increase being less than the decennial rate of increase amongst the population.

Group 50, Bamboo-workers, &c.

307. In Group 50 we find three important occupations—Bamboo and rattan splitters, workers and sellers, basket weavers and mat makers. Here, again, as regards the first of these employments, comparison with the returns of 1881 is practically impossible as bamboo dealers have already been shown combined with other employments. Basket makers and sellers have increased from 2,478 in Lower Burma in 1881 to 3,577 males over 14 years of age employed in the trade in 1891 in the same province. It is a rural and rarely an urban trade, and in Lower Burma it is most popular in Thôngwa, Bassein, Prome, and Tharrawaddy, and in Myingyan, Mandalay, Sagaing, and Minbu in Upper Burma.

Mat makers and sellers were undoubtedly understated in 1881, for apparently only 543 were shown as thus employed out of the total male population, whereas under this heading the return of 1891 shows 3,856 males of 15 years and over. Mat-making is a favourite occupation of women. There were in 1881, 4,355 thus employed in Lower Burma; in 1891 their numbers had increased to 6,697 females 15 years of age and over who were employed on this means of livelihood. This increase of 53·7 per cent., though considerable, is not out of all proportion to the increase of population, while the increase in the number of male mat-makers is at the rate of 6·10 per cent. The occupation returns in 1891 were generally carefully filled in. There were fewer circulars and fewer contradictory orders issued by the Census Commissioner for India in 1891 owing to the fact that the scheme of classification had been settled, and the principles enunciated, before the task of instructing the enumerators was commenced. If, then, there is any question which of the returns should be accepted, the Deputy Superintendent of Census, 1881, would himself, I believe, more readily accept our occupation returns than those compiled in that year. There is reason therefore to suppose that the number of male mat-makers was understated in 1881.

There is one more important occupation in this group, the pith workers, Item 315, on which 9,380 persons are either employed or dependent. The pith is the pith of the Onnhe tree (ဩနှဲ) used by Burmans, who mix it up with tobacco and other herbs and then roll it into a long cheroot of gigantic proportions.

Order XVII, Workers in leather, horns, and bones.

308. Out of the 20,109 persons dependent on the various occupations devoted to working leather, 17,588 are shoe and sandal makers. Here, unfortunately, the classification is deceptive; the vast majority of Burmese shoes are made of wood (ခုံဖိနပ်, Kon binat, pronounced punnat), and not of leather. These wooden sandals are gradually yielding to the ပိန်းတန်းဖိနပ် peindan pannat or leather and felt sandals. There were but 1,708 shoe-makers in 1881, and after making allowance for males too young to work, there were 2,828 in 1891 in Lower Burma, an increase of 65·5 per cent. The use of leather shoes is spreading with English education, and one of the distinguishing marks of the man who prides himself on having a knowledge of English—though it be only sufficient to enable him to murder it successfully—is the wearing of shoes and stockings. Accordingly there is no reason to distrust the return or to consider the figures of 1881 under-estimated.

Class E, Commerce, transport, and storage.

309. Class **E** contains the occupations on which 324,463 souls, or 4·265 per cent. of the total population, are employed or dependent, and covers our mercantile and trading pursuits. In Group 54, Dealers in money, the most numerically important item is that of money-lenders. Of these there were 847 in Lower Burma in 1881. In 1891, allowing for males under 15 years of age, there were 1,644 money-lenders and pawn-brokers. In this occupation the distribution by the ordinary age limit is not a certain guide to a just discrimination between workers and dependents. There are few professional money-lenders even in Burma under 25 years of age; hence it is possible that the return of 1,644 is in excess of the true number of money-lenders. If we make a proportionate deduction on this account, we find that the number of money-lenders will not probably exceed 997, an increase of 17·7 per cent. As in the last decade the population has increased at the rate of 24·47 per cent., it is possible that the latter calculation, based as it is on excluding all males under 25 years of age, is an under statement of the number of money-lenders. Indeed, it is well known that money-lending is combined with several other occupations in Burma. Paddy-brokers, for instance, are sometimes professional money-lenders, and in nearly every instance brokers, though not always ready to lend money to outsiders, are in the habit of making advances on crops.

General merchants, shopkeepers, and brokers.

310. The returns of merchants, general merchants, brokers, and other business pursuits have been classified and divided on such essentially different lines in the reports of 1881 and 1891 that any comparison of these occupations is apt to be misleading. There were 20,755 persons who were classed as merchants in 1881, while the number of bazaar-sellers was only 10,505 and of brokers of all descriptions there were but 3,086. It is very clear that many of our petty bazaar-sellers had dignified themselves by taking brevet rank and had called themselves merchants. Including the 10,505 bazaar-sellers, the total number of general dealers was but 17,951. In 1891, after making allowance for sex and age, we find that there were in Lower Burma 2,409 merchants, 6,793 brokers, and 13,107 shopkeepers, not counting in those returned as general merchants, shopkeepers, clerks, and pedlars. The term kônthè in Burmese is very misleading. Care was taken during the enumeration of 1891 to enforce the return of these so-called merchants as accurately as possible under the head of the article they dealt in. To suppose that there were 20,000 odd merchants in Lower Burma in 1881 is absurd, and a great number of those returned as merchants should no doubt have been shown as produce-dealers and boat-owners. It is quite clear that unless the same meaning is attached to the terms in use, any comparison is out of question and classification becomes not a logical process, but mere guess work.

Carriers by land and water.

311. In 1881 there were 137 cart-owners and 8,775 cart-drivers in Lower Burma against 12,843 males of over 14 years of age returned under these occupations, an increase of very nearly 44·1 per cent. It is probable that these figures correctly show the num-

bers of those employed on this occupation at the periods given. The increase, which is much greater than the growth of the population, is due to the expansion of trade. In carriers by water the most important items are "ship-owners, companies and agents," of whom there were 48 in Burma as against 14 in 1881 in Lower Burma, and under Item 384, Ship officers, engineers, mariners, and firemen, there were 7,589 males over 14 years of age in Upper and Lower Burma against 2,370 in Lower Burma in 1881 with 325 officers and 194 ship servants, but it is possible that several seamen were included in 1881 under other headings, from which their exact number cannot be ascertained.

312. From remarks made in Chapter I, we would expect that the extension of the railway system in Burma and the growth of the Irrawaddy Flotilla Company would lead to an actual diminution in the number of those employed in the internal water-carriage trade. Thus we find in 1881, 6,482 boat-owners and 34,659 boatmen against 7,454 male boat-owners over 14 years of age and 40,507 boat and bargemen of the same age in 1891. The whole of the Toungoo, Shwegyin, and Pegu rice trade and passenger traffic in 1881 was in the hands of Burmese and Chittagongian boatmen. Launches were not then plying for the passenger traffic of the Syriam creeks. The opening of the Pegu and Sittang Valley Railway naturally diverted the passenger and most of the goods traffic from water-carriage to carriage by land. The failing profits of the boatmen and the enormous extent of land brought under cultivation has no doubt operated on this industry, and hence the comparatively slight increase of 14·9 in the case of boat-owners and 16·8 in the case of boatmen may be taken as a true indication of the position of this industry.

Boat-owners and boatmen.

313. Class **F** includes the professional occupations. The term "profession" is an unfortunate one, as it has an ambiguous meaning. We talk of a profession of faith as well as of a legal or mercantile profession, and the term has another meaning, whereby it denotes those who follow a trade or occupation for hire as opposed to the amateur who follows it for the honour and glory to be gained. There are two orders, XX and XXI; the former embraces the learned and artistic, the latter, professions connected with sports and amusements. Among the former Group 63 is by far the most important. It embraces the religious professions. Among semi-civilized races the religious professions usually far outnumber the other learned professions. In the middle ages in Europe, lawyers, authors and professors were all or nearly all ecclesiastics, and learning was confined to the churchmen. It is not surprising therefore to find that out of the 208,595 persons shown under Order XX, 112,811 should be found under the head of religious services, notwithstanding the fact that the Buddhist religious order is celibate and that the number of dependents under the age of 15 is consequently very small.

Class F, Professions.

314. Item 401 is not confined to Christian priests, ministers, preachers, and missionaries, but includes Hindu and Mahomedan priests. Of these there were 787 in Lower Burma after deducting those under 25 years of age. In 1881 there were but 237 Christian priests, missionaries, and Bible-readers combined. Of Hindu and Musalman priests there were 306, and with one Chinese priest the total return was 544. The difference shown was, so the schedules showed, chiefly due to the great increase in Native Christian ministers. The explanation of the increase is to be found in the comparative tables in paragraph 67 in Chapter III, where it will be seen how largely the number of Christian converts has been increased.

Item 401, Priests, ministers, and missionaries.

315. According to the orders of the Chief Commissioner a slight deviation from or rather expansion of the Imperial return under Item 404 was made with the sanction of the Census Commissioner for India. Item 404 includes religious mendicants, inmates of monasteries, convents, &c. From this category the Buddhist religious orders have been excluded, and they are shown separately under their various headings. Of pôngyis there were in Lower Burma 13,613 and in Upper Burma 11,894. All of these, of course, from the fact that they have taken orders, must be over 14 years of age, and, being celibate, they have no dependents. In

The Burmese religious orders.

1881 there were only 6,498 pôngyis. Of upazins (or probationers) there were in 1891 6,668 in Lower and 14,109 in Upper Burma. In 1881 there were but 626 upazins returned in Lower Burma. Of novices or koyins, of whom rather more than half are under 15 years of age and rather less than half over that age, there were 13,571 in Lower and 31,798 in Upper Burma, while in 1881 there were but 1,386 in Lower Burma. Mr. Copleston noted regarding this obviously wrong return of upazins and novices in 1881 as follows: "The numbers of probationers and "novices are, no doubt, as a rule understated." It is very certain that not only were the lesser clergy understated, but a large number of the pôngyis must have been omitted in 1881, as there is no reason to suppose that they have more than doubled their numbers in the last decade, nor is there any reason to doubt the accuracy of the return of 1891, as special instructions were issued and were carefully carried out by the district officers. Mr. Copleston's explanation that the fault probably lay in the abstraction of the returns will account for the apparent increase. But still some explanation is required for the enormous disproportion in the distribution of upazins and koyins between Upper and Lower Burma. The difference in the latter is due to the fact that there are practically no lay schools in Upper Burma and the monastic schools have the monopoly. Accordingly, we should expect a far greater number of novices in the upper province. There being more novices will account for there being more probationers or upazins, but why there should be fewer pôngyis in Upper Burma is somewhat remarkable considering the large number of probationers. This is due to the fact that a large number of the Lower Burma pôngyis have graduated in Upper Burma, where the standard of Buddhist learning is higher. In the large monasteries of Upper Burma it is not an uncommon thing to find several probationers, while to find more than one in any monastery in Lower Burma is comparatively of rare occurrence. Moreover, the superior sanctity and learning of the Upper Burma monks is to be traced to the fact that, till the annexation, the King of Upper Burma was the head of the Buddhist church in secular matters and the Thathanabaing or "Arch Abbott" lived in Mandalay, the old capital. Hence the greater popularity of the monastic order in Upper Burma is easily accounted for, while the comparatively small number of pôngyis is explained by the emigration of those who have graduated to vacant kyaungs in Lower Burma. It is very probable that, as the cause is now removed, we may expect to find a greater equality in the proportions of the various ranks of the Buddhist hierarchy in 1901.

Besides the regular monastic order, there are in Burma male and female religious mendicants. These are bound by no vows except vows of poverty and celibacy. They pretend to no sanctity and are really only lay brethren and lay sisters. The male mendicants are known as pothudaw and the female as methila. They are more common in Upper Burma, Mandalay possessing by far the largest share. It is difficult to compare these figures with the return of 1881, because they were not shown separately in that enumeration.

Group 65, Literary men.

316. If we exclude private secretaries and clerks and public scribes and copyists from Group 65, Literature, we would find but few literary men in Burma. The number of private secretaries would seem to be disproportionately large, but the return is quite accurate. These men are scribes, one or two of whom are often found attached to some well-known pôngyi or located in the large monasteries. They are employed in transcribing with an iron style or kanyutdan (ကညွတ်တံ) on palm leaves the Burmese sacred writings, of which most monasteries possess a small library. There is good reason to believe that, owing to the extensive and increasing use of the press in the reproduction of Burmese religious books, these private clerks are gradually decreasing in numbers, and at the next census they may have almost entirely disappeared.

Group 66, The legal profession.

317. Of those who are returned under Group 66, the legal profession, 3,108 are either barristers, advocates, or pleaders, or dependent on them for their livelihood. No one has returned himself as a solicitor or law agent, as the solicitors are all of them advocates of the courts, and law agents preferred to call themselves advocates or pleaders.

Of the 1,397 males so returned, 838 were found in Lower and 559 in Upper Burma. Of the 838 in Lower Burma, it has been calculated that 504 were actually engaged in earning their livelihood in this profession, 304 were males under 15 years of age, and they therefore might be considered to be dependents. In 1881 there were in Burma only 10 barristers, 1 attorney, 91 advocates, and 360 pleaders, a total of 462 persons engaged in pleading cases in court. Notwithstanding the fact that the establishment of courts of law in Upper Burma must have attracted away many who formerly practised in Lower Burma, we find that there is an increase of 15·5 per cent. in the number of those who belong to the legal profession. The increase is probably greatest in Rangoon, while in the mofussil the number of pleaders has probably not increased very fast owing to there being now more stringent examinations.

Group 67, The medical profession.

318. There were 49 physicians and surgeons and 21 apothecaries in Lower Burma in 1881 and 102 males over 14 who were returned as practitioners by diploma in Burma in 1891. These do not include Government surgeons, who are returned in Class **A**. Diplomaed chemists were included under this head. Most of those thus returned were found in Rangoon, in the seaport towns, and in Mandalay. Rangoon appears to be particularly well off in medical attendance. Of practitioners without diploma there were 9,724 in Lower Burma over 14 years of age against 7,220 "country doctors" and 488 country drugs and medicine sellers in 1881 or 7,708 in all. The increase of 34·6 is proportionately greater than the increase of the population, and if the returns of the past census are correct, there is evidently no diminution in Burmese credulity or native quackery.

Of midwives there were 290 in Lower Burma in 1881, and after making due allowance for dependents, we find that there were but 317 midwives in Lower Burma in 1891. This small increase of 9·3 per cent. may be due to the trained midwives of the Dufferin Hospital preferring to return themselves as practitioners by diploma.

There were no vaccinators shown separately in 1881; hence there is no means of comparing the returns.

Of astrologers, genealogists, and horoscope casters, there were, after allowing for dependents, 286 in Lower Burma as against 269 in 1881 in the same province. This corroborates the previous inference that Burmese quackery has not yet lost its hold over the people.

Of sculptors there were 58 and of photographers 62 in 1891 against 26 and 11 persons who were returned under these headings in 1881.

Class G, Indefinite and independent.

319. Class **G** embraces the indefinite occupations and those who are independent of any occupation. The first of these orders are the complex and combined occupations. In Burma the instructions issued by the Government of India that only one occupation was to be returned, except when agriculture was combined with another occupation, was strictly carried out. Any attempt to return complex and combined occupations, except thus restricted, would have been in Burma an almost endless and useless task. A Burman is a jack-of-all-trades, and a very large number of them have in their time worked at all sorts of employments. In India, where caste restrictions confine the vast majority of the inhabitants to certain well-defined employments, such a return would present, comparatively speaking, but little difficulty. The strict rule laid down that combined occupations were not to be returned unless agricultural work was one of the items, was strongly impressed on all enumerators, and hence Order XXII, Complex village occupations, is a blank. In Imperial Table XVII-C will be found the occupations combined with agriculture. These persons have already been shown once under Order V. I have, therefore, to make this clearer, shown this Table as if it were an expansion of Order V, just as Item 404, Religious mendicants, has been expanded into 404 *a*, *b*, *c*, *d*. It will be seen that these subsidiary occupations are few and unimportant. The Table is so simple that it requires no comparative statement to explain it.

The indefinite group was intended to include unskilled labourers, men who turn their hands to any kind of manual labour, unspecified labourers, and those who return disreputable and unspecified means of livelihood. Owing to the difference of classification no comparison with the returns of 1881 is of any value, as, owing to the system then adopted, the whole of the non-working population was included under the head of Unspecified. The last order includes those independent of work. There are, in Burma, but 37,541 souls returned as independent of work, of whom 20,900 are beggars and 11,385 inmates of our jails and asylums. Of pensioners there are 2,541, and of those living on their own means or supported by allowances 2,715. These represent the moneyed and leisured class of Burma, and their paucity shows that Burma, as a country, is as yet but little advanced in the race for wealth. In England and Wales, among the moneyed and leisured class, there were 182,282 males between the years of 20—65 who returned themselves of no specified occupation, but, as the Commissioners point out, a large number of them were engaged in managing their own estates. Notwithstanding this voluntary work, they were rightly included in the leisured but should not have been included in the unoccupied class. In Burma we had but 652 males over 15 years of age who could be taken to correspond with this leisured class in England, for pensioners would correspond with those in England of the moneyed class whose age exceeds 65.

CHAPTER XII.

ADMINISTRATION OF THE CENSUS OPERATIONS.

The Agra Conference. The distribution of the area of Burma into Synchronous and Non-synchronous Census tracts and Excluded tracts. The adjustment of Census administration to the lines of the Revenue administration of the province. Changes introduced. Registers prescribed. Translation of Instructions and issue of Schedule Books. House numbering. Revision of indents and reduction in the size of the blocks. Stationery. Areas requiring special arrangements. The Irrawaddy Flotilla. Railways. Ports. Cantonments. Military police and troops on the march. Arrangement made for mill coolie gangs. Boat population. The personnel of the Census staff. The enumeration. The preliminary record and final round. The special plan adopted in Burma to secure the prompt return of the provisional totals. Preparation of the provisional totals. The abstraction, tabulation, and compilation of the figures. The difficulties met with. The Report. Cost of the Census. Printing. The accuracy of the returns.

The Agra Conference.

320. The first step taken in Burma in preparing for the census was the deputation of Mr. F. S. Copleston, C.S., the Deputy Superintendent of the last census of 1881, to attend the Census Conference held at Agra in December 1889. The proceedings at this Conference belong to the Imperial rather than to the Provincial Report. It will be only necessary here to note that at this Conference the date of the census was fixed and several changes in the standard schedule were adopted and the plan and organization of the forthcoming operations discussed. The value of such a Conference can only be estimated by comparing the present with the past census. The experience gained by the several officers was rendered more valuable from the interchange of ideas between those who were present. The sources of error were fully explored and precautions were suggested to avoid them in future. But the value of the Conference would have been much enhanced if the future Superintendents of Census could have been present, not merely to profit by the discussion of past failures, but to learn the work of preparation for the census that lay before them. If, then, a conference of Census Officers be held before breaking ground for the next census, the presence of the Superintendents elect should be considered indispensable. The changes introduced at the Conference in the forms and tables used have already been touched on in preceding chapters, but the alterations introduced subsequently into the organization and administration of the census were initiated by the Census Commissioner when he visited the province in May and October 1890. The work of the Conference was chiefly confined to the discussion of the scope of the census and the best means of utilizing the information gained thereby, but the task of local preparation and organization, varying as it did with the requirements of each province, was necessarily left to be worked out by the Census Commissioner and the Provincial Superintendent.

Appointment of the Provincial Superintendent of Census Operations.

321. Mr. Copleston, the Deputy Superintendent of Census in 1881, was the officer first proposed as Provincial Superintendent, but as his services were not available, Captain (now Major) Temple was appointed in his place. Major Temple, who at the time was on deputation at Simla, was unable to join the appointment on 1st April, which was the date fixed by the Government of India. In the meanwhile Mr. Baines visited Rangoon in May 1890, and after conferring with the Chief Commissioner and Mr. Copleston, arrangements were made to carry on the work pending Major Temple's return. The next step taken was the issue

of the Chief Secretary's letter No. 506-6C.G., dated the 16th May. In this letter, a copy of which will be found at page li. of Appendix **C**, the lines on which the census was to be taken were laid down, and these lines, with some slight modifications, were closely followed. The modifications will be dealt with hereafter. Unfortunately Major Temple fell sick, and when it was found that he would not be able to return to Burma till October, I was deputed to be Provincial Superintendent and took over charge of my duties on the 29th July 1890. Up to this time, beyond the issue of the letter of the 16th May, no further ground had been broken except that, in a few districts, the more energetic Deputy Commissioners had indented for and received Circle Registers **A** and **B** and had proceeded to fill them up.

Distribution of the area of the province.

322. The first thing to be done was to define the areas over which the information required by the census could be collected. In 1881 the whole of Lower Burma was included within the area of operations. In Upper Burma there were, however, in 1891 certain tracts which had not yet been explored, and tributary States whose allegiance was doubtful. In the east the tributary Shan States were not yet ripe for such refinements, and though, no doubt, the schedules could have been filled up, the cost on the one hand would have been prohibitive and the gain but small. The anarchy that had reigned for so many years had succeeded in depopulating some States and in rendering the boundaries of others a matter of doubt. Accordingly the area of the province was divided into two parts—tracts included in, and tracts excluded from, census operations. The excluded tracts are coloured blue on Map II. The tracts included within census operations, that is to say, tracts concerning whose population the information required in the standard schedule could be filled up, varied very greatly. In 1881, over a large tract estimated to extend to about 11,000 square miles, the census schedules could not be synchronously checked in one night. There were two causes that brought this about—the physical features of the country and the illiteracy of the inhabitants. In the recesses of the hills Karen tès or long barrack-like huts, inhabited by several families, are found scattered about. Neither the headman nor his villagers can read or write. In the Chin hills the Chin villages offered the same difficulties. To establish a paid enumerator in each hut or village would entail enormous expense, and the distance separating these scattered hamlets utterly precluded the possibility of one man checking the returns of more than one of them in one night.

Distribution of the Regular Census area in to synchronous and non-synchronous census tracts.

323. In these places the census could not be taken synchronously, and hence the regular census area was distributed into synchronous and non-synchronous census tracts. The selection of these areas was made in every case after consultation with the Deputy Commissioners of the districts in which they were situated. On the map the area over which the census was not taken synchronously was marked yellow. The area thus treated in Lower Burma was reduced from 11,000 square miles in 1881 to about 4,000 square miles in 1891. This was due partly to the fact that the district officers had obtained a firmer grip over their districts and partly to the increased influence of the missionaries and the spread of education amongst the hill tribes. The whole of the Salween district was taken non-synchronously in 1881, but on this occasion the Deputy Commissioner managed to take the census of all the villages synchronously. In Toungoo the American Baptist and Roman Catholic Missionaries cheerfully undertook the task of helping in the census, and each Mission sent out its scholars to act as enumerators in their own villages. No fee of any kind was asked for. In Tharrawaddy, where nearly half the area of the district is forest land, the Deputy Conservator of Forests arranged to undertake the whole of the enumeration by means of his assistants and subordinates. In Amherst the Forest Officer and the Superintendent of Police undertook the Hlaingbwè tract. In Akyab in the Chin Hills special measures had to be adopted by the Deputy Commissioner: special parties were sent out under the Minbya Myoôk. In Kyaukpyu the illiterate Chin villages could only be enumerated by special paid men. In the Arakan Hill Tracts the work was done by the Deputy Commissioner, the Assistant District Super-

intendent of Police, and their subordinates, without extra cost, while they were out on tour. In Shwegyin the non-synchronous census area was reduced and three paid enumerators only were employed. In Tavoy, at the sources of the Tenasserim river, a few villages were taken non-synchronously. In Mergui the Deputy Commissioner and District Superintendent of Police took a warm interest in the work. The Maliwun township was entrusted to Mr. Merrifield, and two special boats and the launch of the Geological Survey Party were employed in the non-synchronous census of the Selôns (or Selungs), and the increase in the large number recorded showed how successful their efforts were. In 1872 no attempt was made to take any census of these sea-gypsies. In 1881 the census was only partially successful. Various expedients were employed in some of these districts to narrow down as far as possible the non-synchronous area. The population of these remote villages is not given to gadding about. When they move, they move like snails, with all their household goods on their backs. The headman was asked to induce the villagers to remain at home on the night of the census, and to each household a bundle of bamboos was given. The big bamboos signified the adults, the smaller the children, and distinguishing marks were sometimes put on each. When the census schedule book was written up by the census clerk, instructions were given to the village headman, who, though he could not read, could count, to tell each householder to prepare a bundle of bamboos, one for each member of his family. These bundles corresponded in number with the entries against each house. On the night of the census, the village headman went round, checked, and collected each bundle of tallies and took them to his house. If a death occurred, the bamboo representing the individual was broken. If one were absent, his bamboo was taken away. If there was any visitor, he was promptly entered by adding a bamboo to the tallies of the house. The enumerator, when he came round soon after the census night, checked the tallies with his book and made the necessary alterations. This plan was adopted with success in the Thayetmyo and Minbu districts, and the Deputy Commissioner of Tavoy himself proposed a somewhat similar method, which he successfully worked.

The agency employed.

324. In India, with the powerful agency we possess in the district revenue administration, any special paid census agency, such as is required in England and America, would be not only a needless expense, but any such staff that could be employed would prove far less efficient than the existing agency. The first problem to be solved, therefore, after defining the area of the operations, was how to organize and adjust the census operations so as to clash as slightly as possible with the ordinary functions of the administrative staff.

The adjustment of the census administration to the lines of the revenue administration.

325. The unit of census administration was the district, and the district was divided into charges, circles, and blocks. The charge was found to coincide with the township, and the chief difficulty of organization lay in the adjustment of the blocks and census circles to the lines of the village and revenue circle, and on the accuracy of this adjustment depended the success of the operations. The existing lines of revenue administration of district, township, and revenue circle were adopted as at the last census. The Deputy Commissioner was the District Superintendent of Census, his Township Officers were the Charge Superintendents, and the census circles in some cases naturally coincided with the revenue circles. Here, however, the variation in the size of the revenue circles made any general rule impossible. The difficulty was increased when the size of the village precluded the possibility of its coinciding with the census block. It became therefore necessary to create to some extent an artificial division of townships into census circles and blocks. The administrative divisions were, however, observed as far as possible, but instead of working down from the township to the block, and then grouping these blocks into census circles, the first thing done was to fix the block. At the last census the value of the village table was much decreased owing to the grouping together of the smaller villages, whereby it became impossible to separate one village from the other. A glance at the Provincial tables of 1881 will show how largely this practice obtained, and I found in my inspection tours that in more districts than one the village had been entirely disregarded and the area had been neatly

parcelled out into tracts of 60 houses, each containing the whole or parts of two or three villages. Accordingly Circular **B**, dated the 29th August 1890, was issued. This circular is important as it placed the arrangement of the census work on a plain logical basis. It laid down briefly that a village, however small, if it be a village and not a mere hamlet of two or three huts, was to be treated as a block, and should be shown apart from its neighbouring village. If a village be too large to be compassed by an enumerator in the three or four hours he is expected to work on the night of the census, then the village should be divided into two or more blocks. The size laid down for a block therefore depends, first, on the size of the village, and, if that be too much for one man to finish in three or four hours at night, then the village is to be broken up into two or more blocks. Of course the amount of work to be done and the time required for its due completion will vary with the size of the village and its compactness and the ability of the enumerator himself. Ordinarily it was found that a man could enumerate about 40 or 50 houses. Experience has shown that these directions were necessary, and the character of the work done was improved by not giving the enumerator too much to do. In the Akyab district the Deputy Commissioner experienced some difficulty in carrying out these orders. He stated that there were villages of one and two and three houses, and wished to know if these villages were to be blocked apart. But as one swallow can hardly be said to make a summer, so one house can hardly be called a village. The Deputy Commissioner was told that of course the houses must be grouped, and that the term "village" was not meant to cover such instances. It was not considered necessary to define what a village was, because, with this one exception, every district officer clearly understood that a village was the administrative unit forming the charge of a ywathugyi, ywalugyi, a kyedangyi, or a kyegaung, according to the local terminology, and corresponded with the Burmese term ywa, whereas the mistake of the Deputy Commissioner of Akyab was that he treated "su" or hamlets as villages. For instance, in the Salween district the Officiating Deputy Commissioner, Mr. Baines, acting on his own initiative, combined the scattered hamlets and tès of the taungyas into census blocks, rightly interpreting that the principle laid down in the circular merely strove to keep apart villages that were villages and recognized as such. The census circle, that is to say, the charge of a supervisor, was estimated to contain about 10 blocks. Here of course, again, the physical conditions of the area enumerated regulated the number of the blocks, for it stood to reason that a supervisor could not so easily supervise many widely scattered blocks. Moreover, it was found that in Lower Burma the revenue circles or "taiks" were, as a rule, far too large to be supervised by one man. In Upper Burma the circles or "daings" were often very small, and in fact sometimes coincident with the village block. If 10 blocks had been arbitrarily fixed as the size of a census circle, while in Lower Burma a revenue circle would comprise and did comprise as many as 10 census circles, in Upper Burma several revenue circles or daings would have been placed under one census circle supervisor. Accordingly no hard-and-fast rule was made, but Deputy Commissioners were advised to adhere as far as possible to the administrative circles, and where, in Lower Burma, the revenue circle was too great to form a single census circle, the taikthugyi was still to be held responsible for his whole circle, but he should be assisted by one or more supervisors; and in Upper Burma, to prevent friction between the ywathugyis and daing thugyis, the size of the circles was left to the option of the district officer. I have dwelt at some length on this point, for I found that while the majority of the more experienced district officers agreed with, and indeed suggested these points to me, a few officers would have imperilled the work of the census by carrying out the instructions of the letter of the 16th May regardless of local requirements.

The Subdivisional and Circle Registers.

326. The next step to be taken was to obtain an accurate list of these blocks. Circle Register **A** was a list of houses and their owners, arranged village by village and revenue circle by revenue circle for each district. These lists formed the basis on which the census blocks were formed, and as it was manifestly impossible for me to check all these circle registers, I asked the Deputy Commissioners and Presidents of Municipalities to give me an abstract of these house-

registers (as they should be called rather than circle registers), showing how they had split up their villages into blocks and the revenue circles into census circles. This register was called the subdivisional register, a name which was given to it by the Government of India. This name, though suitable for India, is unsuitable for Burma. I would propose that the register, which is a most necessary one, be known as the charge or township register. This, however, is a matter of comparatively slight importance.

The register, however, proved itself of the greatest use and was quite indispensable. It served a four-fold purpose—

(1) it enabled the district officers to arrange their districts systematically and prevented any area in their districts being overlooked ;
(2) it enabled the Provincial Superintendent to check the arrangements made and to offer suggestions to the district officers ;
(3) it summarized the work of preparation, and enabled me to relieve district officers of the duty of sending in monthly reports, a duty which was imposed on them in the other provinces of India ;
(4) it acted as a register of schedule books issued from the district office.

But its usefulness was most felt when the enumeration was over. It is not too much to say that it was the basis of the arrangement of the whole of the Provincial tables, and that by its help I was enabled to check every schedule book in the office and to arrange the voluminous records in such a way that I can now assert that not one single book was lost that was received in my office, and that every block in every village and town of the province has been accounted for. The Provincial tables, as they now stand, are nothing but the subdivisional registers with the information collected in the census schedule books compiled for each village and block shown in that register. A modified form of this register was issued for the use of Municipalities. Copies of these registers are given at page lv. of Appendix C. Another great advantage derived from this register is one that is only apparent from a careful study of the Provincial tables. A central abstraction office, such as we have in Burma, without an index such as this register affords, could not detect any omission to include a village or the loss of a supplementary block book.

The translation of the schedule and instructions.

327. The adaptation of the General Instructions issued by the Government of India to local requirements, and their translation into Burmese, was one of the most important of the preliminary operations of the census. Any mistake in the wording is apt to bring about disastrous results. Complaints were rife in 1881 of the orders and counter-orders received, for which the Deputy Superintendent was in no way responsible. Every precaution was taken to prevent this complaint being made on this occasion, and, I believe, with success. The instructions themselves were rigorously scrutinized at my request by some of the ablest officers in the Commission, who kindly read the proofs, and hence they were accepted without any further suggestions by every district officer in the Commission. The translation, too, was very carefully revised, and, with one exception, no objection has been raised against them. One officer, after the census was over, criticized three expressions used in the translation. I have carefully gone over his objections, and I have found that they were based on misconception on the part of the officer who made them. Indeed, it would have been strange if the objections had been sustainable.

A short Handbook of Instructions in English and Burmese, with sample schedules filled in, was circulated with a large number of blank schedules for practice and for the instruction of the enumerators before the issue of the schedule books. Instruction was systematically carried on in every district in Burma. In the course of my tours I visited every district except the Hill Tracts of Northern Arakan and Salween, and had the opportunity of meeting every Deputy Commissioner except one, most of the Subdivisional Officers, and a large number of the Myoôks or Township Officers in the province. The scope and intent of the census operations were discussed with all these officers, and in most of the districts of Lower Burma the thugyis or revenue circle officers were also summoned to headquarters to meet me, and were instructed in the work by Township Officers in my presence. The instruction began in September and was completed by the time the schedule books were issued. That this work was loyally done the schedule books bore testimony. There were few instances of mistakes considering the number of the enumerators, the variety of the entries, and the fact that but 3·35 per cent. of the enumerators were paid for their work. There were 40,183 enumerators, and the task of instructing them was no slight burden on the already well-laden shoulders of the district officers and their subordinates, and I think it but fair to record the fact that the vast majority of the books showed that the enumerators had been instructed, and, what is more, had honestly done their duty. This matter, however, belongs to another section of this chapter which deserves special attention hereafter.

Amendment of Circle Registers A and B.

328. At the same time as the subdivisional registers were issued, it was found necessary to amend the instructions issued in the letter of the 16th May regarding Circle Registers **A** and **B** as misconception had arisen in the minds of the district officers. The registers as at first issued in the letter of the 16th May were undoubtedly tautologous. The registers themselves were cumbersome, and, though they gave a great deal of trouble, were of very little use.

House-numbering.

329. In October the house-numbering was commenced and was generally completed early in November. No difficulty was experienced in carrying this numbering out. The Burmese had no objection to having numbers put up. Some of them with artistic minds, dissatisfied with the simple and cheap expedient of congee-water and lime, carved their numbers on plaques of wood, which they hung up with pardonable pride in front of their houses. As each Burmese family outside our big towns lives in its own house apart from its neighbours, there was no difficulty experienced in ascertaining which houses were to receive numbers. I have already, in Chapter I, dealt with the difficulty experienced in our towns in deciding what was, and what was not, a census house. Just as the house-numbering was being completed, I had the advantage of referring all doubtful points to the Census Commissioner, who came round to Burma on tour in the beginning of November. He himself inspected the numbering in Rangoon, Mandalay, Myingyan, Pakôkku, Minbu, Thayetmyo, and Prome, and was satisfied with the way in which it was done. Only in Pakôkku was there any mistake, and that was due to an excess of zeal on the part of one of the enumerators.

The preliminary and final indents for schedule books and the printing.

330. In paragraph 5 of the letter of the 16th May, No. 506-6C.G., instructions were given for the submission of preliminary indents regarding the probable number of schedules required. The indents should have been sent to the Superintendent of Census, but, as there was no Superintendent then in charge, district officers sent them in to the Superintendent of Government Printing. No time was specified in this letter for the submission of the final indents. These indents began to come in at the end of September and the beginning of October. The subdivisional registers were sent to me at the same time, and were of the utmost service in that they enabled me to check the indents for census books. Owing in Upper Burma to the necessarily short experience district officers had of their charges, and in Lower Burma to the abnormal growth of the population, in many districts I found that, with a few meritorious exceptions, all of the indents for schedule books sent in by the district officers were far too small. Had this not been detected, the rule of the Government of India that each house should be enumerated apart on at least one if not more than one schedule would have been broken through. Although permission to break this rule in case of necessity was granted, though unsolicited by me, I was fortunately able to reply that no necessity for breaking it had arisen in Burma. The Government of India, following the recommendation of the Conference, had ordered that the inhabitants of every house should be enumerated on a separate schedule, and that, if the inhabitants of the house exceeded the number of the eight lines ruled on each schedule, a fresh schedule or schedules should be devoted to that house according to the number of the persons residing in it. Circular

No. 11, dated the 4th November, pointed out that if the average number of inhabitants exceeded 8, however slightly, at least 50 per cent. more schedules were required, since, according to the rules laid down, 9 persons in one house required two schedules just as much as 16 did. Although the revision of these indents by the district officers in some cases delayed the despatch of the schedule books to their destination and thereby caused the preliminary record to be begun after the prescribed date, yet as more than ample time had been allowed for the preliminary record, no real inconvenience or risk was thereby occasioned, and the Government Press in Burma was spared the anxiety occasioned by impassioned appeals for more books such as were sent in almost up to the last moment in more than one of the provinces of India. A short supply of census books would in Burma have meant the ruin of all accuracy in the returns if not total miscarriage of the census itself. Unlike the other provinces of India, many of the districts of this province are difficult of access owing to the physical configuration of the country. Moreover, the revision of the indents was only in part the cause of the late despatch of some of the schedule books. Owing to the original estimate of schedules required being too low, a sufficient number of schedules were not struck off and bound. It is but fair to state that the Government Press was not responsible for this delay, except that the Jail Press worked on the insufficient indents sent in direct by district officers instead of working up to the revised estimate sent them by me on 5th November. The delay thus occasioned was redeemed by cancelling the order that the block lists at the end of each schedule book were to be written up from Register **A** in the district office. This rule was not only unnecessary, but positively dangerous. Owing to the mobility of the Burmese population and the rapidity with which they run up their bamboo and thatch houses, such a register is often absolutely misleading after the lapse of a single month. The Deputy Commissioners of Upper Burma pointed out that their circle registers needed constant revision. Moreover, the mere fact that the block enumerator had not to write out the list himself would, in his own eyes, absolve him from any mistakes in it, and, in nine cases out of ten, would lead to his omitting the new houses that had sprung up. In order that the schedule books should reach the enumerators in time, if the proposed rule had been carried out, they ought to have been in the district offices at least by the end of October. The cancellation of this rule, therefore, compensated for the delay in the issue of the books. Before leaving this matter, which will be more fully considered in the section devoted to Printing, I must here mention that though the books were not issued so soon as was at first considered to be necessary, every schedule book, including the reserve supply, was despatched from the Press a clear six weeks before the night of the census, and the bulk had been despatched before the end of December, the remoter districts being served first. The Press did not issue another book. That in the end the revision of our indents was the means of preventing far more serious delay, may be inferred from the fact that at the Simla Conference it was mentioned that in the other provinces of India the printing and binding of the census schedule books was continued up to within a few days of the census itself. It is clear, then, that since the Press received at the last minute no agonized appeals for more books, this result was due to the district officers remodelling their indents on the lines laid down in the circular of the 4th November. The cancelling of the order that the block list should be copied out in the district offices had another effect. It not only relieved the Deputy Commissioners' establishment of work which they could not perform so well as the enumerator himself, but it made a very appreciable difference in the cost of the census. It saved the necessity, in almost every district, of taking on extra copyists to do this work. The labour of enumerating even one house alone, and entering against the inmates the information required by the 14 columns of the schedule, entails of itself almost as much labour as is caused to an enumerator by making him write up the few particulars required by his block list.

Stationery.

331. An unexpected difficulty arose as regards the means of recording the entries. Pens and ink were prescribed, but the Deputy Commissioners in Upper Burma pointed out that many of their headmen had never handled pen and ink, as all their writing was done with steatite pencils on their black lacquered books which they call

"parabaiks." Pencils were therefore issued, and the unfortunate district officers were obliged to have their headmen taught how to handle a steel-pen. The pencils were used for writing up the entries, which were afterwards carefully "painted in" by the enumerator. And it is remarkable how few entries were under these circumstances rejected as undecipherable. Our stationery was obtained direct from the Stationery Office at Calcutta and was distributed as soon as it was received. The despatch of the census schedule books began in the first week in December. Northern Arakan, Ye-u, Bhamo, and the Upper Chindwin, being the most remote and inaccessible, were first supplied, and by the end of the first week in January the last of the books had been despatched.

Up to the beginning of November I had been working single-handed, and I found that my continual absence on tour, often in places where letters could not overtake me till my return, placed me at a disadvantage. Moreover, I had especial difficulties with which to contend. The province in extent is the largest in India. In Upper Burma, so recently annexed and still more recently pacified, no census operations had ever been attempted, and there were consequently no landmarks for guidance. Many of the district officers were men of comparatively short service and but very few had any experience in census work. Further still, I was handicapped by having been appointed as late as the 29th July, nearly four months after the rest of my fellow Superintendents had begun work. My short experience of the work had already demonstrated to me the necessity of visiting every district. I was now, in October, face to face with the difficulty that I had a great deal of office work to get through which should have been done gradually in April, May, June, and July, and I had yet to travel to the furthest parts of the province, to places beyond the reach of the telegraph wire and with only a weekly post. Under these circumstances I was reluctantly obliged to ask for an assistant. The Census Commissioner endorsed my application, and the Chief Commissioner placed the officer whose services I asked for at my disposal. Mr. Noyce, Extra Assistant Commissioner, at the time Subdivisional Officer of Ngathainggyaung, was placed on special duty in my office. Of Mr. Noyce's services I shall have to speak more fully hereafter.

Areas requiring special arrangements.

332. While these preparations were proceeding in the districts, special arrangements were made for the enumeration of the railways, ports, cantonments, police lines, and forest camps in the province. The Irrawaddy Flotilla was, through the courtesy of the Acting Manager, Mr. Miller, enumerated entirely separately. The plans were prepared and the books and instructions issued through the Manager, and I have much pleasure in placing on record my thanks to him not merely for the willingness with which he took up the work, but for the ability with which he carried the arrangements through. No sort of friction was thereby incurred with the district enumerators, and every steamship or launch schedule book was numbered and assigned to its proper locality. In the samé way special arrangements for the enumeration of the foresters' camps belonging to the Bombay Burma Trading Corporation were made with the Manager, Mr. Glendenning. I have to thank him and Mr. Andrews for the readiness with which they met my proposals, and Messrs. Winser and Bates, their Agents at Pyinmana and Mingin, for the careful way in which they carried out the arrangements that were made.

I do not propose to go into the minutiæ of these arrangements, but I have preserved for my successor the notes I took at the interviews and the instructions issued thereon when these arrangements were considered. In Appendix C will be found the instructions laid down by the Government of India for the enumeration of ports, cantonments, and troops on the march. The military police, a body of Sikhs, many of whom knew no language but their own, could obviously not be enumerated in the ordinary way. Special arrangements were made with General Stedman, the Inspector-General of Police.

Special arrangements for the enumeration of coolies.

333. Last but by no means least, came Rangoon Town. The immigration returns in Chapter II of this report will give some idea of the chief difficulty to be grappled with. During January and February every steamship comes laden with coolies. A preliminary record, taken a fortnight before the census in our

coolie lines, would omit many thousand coolies who were even then on their way hither. This is not the worst of the matter. These coolies swarm in search of work from one mill to another; they go "not single spies, but in battalions." On the occasion of the census of 1881, in one town at least the work of milling had to be stopped while the coolies were counted. This meant not merely vexation, but loss of money, to the firms. The same difficulty, but in a less degree, is felt in Akyab, Moulmein, and Bassein. With the local authorities and the merchants themselves special arrangements were made to ensure the correct and speedy enumeration of these men. This enumeration itself was no light task, as but few Englishmen and fewer Burmans can speak either Tamil or Telugu. Everything, however, was done to render the process of enumeration as little obstructive of the work as possible. Perhaps the best method proposed, and one which was generally adopted, was the plan suggested to me by Mr. Hewitt of Messrs. Steel Brothers. This plan was to treat the maistry and his gang as a small block, and to have him and his gang enumerated separately, and to give him his book and hold him responsible for it and for his men. The book was written out by the clerks of the firm that employed the maistry and was checked by the supervisor a few days before the census was taken. If the maistry, as he often did, left his employer and went to another mill, he took his book with him and produced it and his men on the night of the census. This simple plan obviated the necessity of rushing the work through in the last day or two before the census. It suited the convenience of the merchants, as the books were filled up at the leisure of the clerks, and the work of checking the entries on the night of the census was quickly and accurately done as there were but few corrections to make. In the large towns the preliminary record did not begin till much later than in the rural tracts, but in every case it was finished three clear days before the census.

The enumeration of the population afloat.

334. The boat population had already been partly provided for in the ports and in the arrangements made for the enumeration of the steamships and launches belonging to the Irrawaddy Flotilla. In Circle Register **B** a list had been prepared of all places where boats might be expected; enumerators had already been told off. But provision had to be made for boats on the move. Patrol boats were stationed at certain points and passes were issued to each boat as it was enumerated. It was then permitted to pass on. This occasioned no difficulty when the river channel or creek lay within the limits of one district. But where the channel served as the boundary of two districts, arrangements were made by the Deputy Commissioners for the division of the work of enumeration between their subordinates and for the adjustment of the results. The instructions for the enumeration of ports and cantonments were issued by the Government of India, and were adopted in Burma without modification. They will be found in the appendix to this volume and they need no further comment or explanation here. The instructions for the enumeration of the military police are based on the instructions for enumerating cantonments and troops on the march. A copy of the arrangements made with the Inspector-General of Police will be found in the appendix, and this contains all the modifications that were required.

The *personnel.*

335. There were four grades in the *personnel* of the census staff. First of all there was the Enumerator, who actually wrote the entries of his block in his schedule book; then came the Supervisor, who was in charge of the census circle, which ordinarily consisted of about 10 or 15 blocks. Census circles were grouped into charges, which were under the Charge Superintendent. Nominally there was no grade between the Charge Superintendent and the Provincial Superintendent; as a fact, however, the Charge Superintendents, who in rural tracts were the Township Officers and in Municipalities were chosen out of the executive officers of the Municipal staff, were under the direct orders of the Deputy Commissioners and the Subdivisional Officers in the former and of the Presidents of the Municipal Committees in the latter case. There were 40,183 Enumerators, 4,558 Supervisors, and 365 Charge Superintendents throughout Burma. Of these there were 23,474 of the first, 2,042 of the second, and 199 of the third class in Lower Burma. In 1881 there were 16,974 Enumerators, 2,167 Supervisors, and 151 Charge Superintendents. There was

thus an increase of 38·2 per cent. in the number of enumerators. This increase, which is far in excess of the increase of the population, is due to the lessening of the size of the block and to the introduction of the principle that all villages must be shown apart. On the other hand, we find that there were actually 125 fewer circle supervisors. This is accounted for by the fact that the revenue circle thugyi was made supervisor of his whole circle, and, though he was allowed assistant supervisors when they were necessary, yet he was rightly considered to be in sole executive charge of his circle. In 1881 revenue circles were often split up and the responsibility divided between the thugyi and some outsider. The increase in the number of Charge Superintendents, which is at the rate of 31·7 per cent., while it is greater than that of the total population, is less than that of the enumerators. The reason of this variance is accounted for by the circumstance that Charge Superintendents outside of the Municipalities were the Township Officers, and therefore their numbers depended not on the requirements of the census alone. The proportion between the numbers of these officers in 1881 and 1891 was that in the former year there were 14 supervisors and 112 enumerators and in the latter year 10 supervisors and 117 enumerators to each Charge Superintendent. There was no reason to suppose that any of the charges of the Charge Superintendents was too large and unwieldy, as from the intrinsic evidence of the schedules themselves there was proof that the enumerators had been on the whole well instructed and carefully supervised.

336. The following statement shows the classes from which the census officers were recruited :—

Classes of Census Officers.	Charge Superintendents.	Supervisors.	Enumerators.
Official.			
1. Gazetted Officers of Government	260	7	...
2. Jail Department	2	2	11
3. Education Department	4	2	12
4. Judicial and Revenue clerks	4	481	312
5. Honorary Magistrates	1	7	...
6. Medical Department	1	2	15
7. Municipal Members	12	35	25
8. Municipal clerks and servants	16	64	66
9. Forest Department	5	10	11
10. Public Works Department	5	19	26
11. Military Department	1	1	4
12. Police Officers	5	169	39
13. Thugyis, sawkès, tamôns, shwegunmus, and pawmaings ...	49	2,591	24
14. Railway Department	...	6	122
15. Yazawutgaungs	...	160	73
16. Village headmen, kyedangyis	...	743	28,674
17. Harbour Department	...	1	39
18. Customs Department	...	2	14
19. Bazaar gaungs	...	3	29
20. Excise Department	...	...	...
21. Police constables	...	2	478
22. Telegraph Department	...	1	...
23. Office peons	...	...	6
24. Police Department	...	...	14
Total ...	365	4,308	29,994
Non-official.			
1. Pleaders	...	32	23
2. Teachers and school-boys	...	9	240
3. Merchants, traders, brokers, and brokers' clerks	...	95	336
4. Pensioners	...	5	...
5. Private clerks	...	14	741
6. Burmese doctors	...	41	10
7. Thugyis, village headmen, and kyedangyis' relations ...	...	50	8,798
8. Villagers	...	4	33
9. Petition-writers	...	...	5
10. Contractors	...	...	3
Total ...	...	250	10,189
GRAND TOTAL ...	365	4,558	40,183

Before I leave the matter of the *personnel* of the census staff, I feel it my duty to place on record the careful way in which the work of enumeration was done. Non-officials, to whom the duty imposed brought nothing but trouble and interruption of their work at the busiest time of the year, and officials, of whom but a very few received extra pay for the extra duties imposed on them, with scarcely any exception did their duty cheerfully and well. In two districts only were prosecutions under the Census Act rendered necessary, and there were altogether only four persons prosecuted. In very few cases was the threat of prosecution required. The Census Superintendent, as Mr. Ibbetson, the Punjab Superintendent plaintively remarked, in 1881, is the best abused man in the province. I cannot, however, complain myself of the treatment I received. The work in Rangoon, where a good deal of friction was felt in 1881, was carried through with an alacrity and despatch which could hardly be surpassed. Major Temple, though he had arrived in Rangoon only a few weeks before the census was taken, took up his share as if he himself were alone personally responsible, and Mr. Short, the Secretary, was indefatigable in his efforts to make the census a success. In the Port the Vice-Chairman of the Commissioners, not satisfied with the already sufficiently irksome work, had a preliminary census on his own account. The clerks from the Government offices, to whom the census holidays were but holidays in name, with but one exception did their work cheerfully and well. The way in which Burma, handicapped as it is by the extent of its territory and the poorness of its communications, managed to get in the results of the census, so that it was by no means the last either in the accuracy or promptness of its returns, is the most eloquent proof of the good work done by all alike in the districts outside Rangoon. I shall hereafter deal with the question of the services of the census officers more fully.

The enumeration.

337. The non-synchronous census enumeration was consecutively carried out from its commencement in January till three days after the 26th February. But the synchronous census was in reality two distinct operations—the Preliminary record and the Final record. The preliminary record began on the 8th January and should have been concluded by the 8th February. As a fact, in but few districts was the preliminary record begun on this date, but it was finished in nearly every district by the 10th February, which was sufficiently early. The Provincial Superintendents of the Punjab and Bombay at the Conference were averse to such an early commencement of the record. The area of the block itself, and the number of persons living in it, and the literacy of the enumerator, are in reality the three factors that should be taken into consideration in allotting the time for the preliminary record. The main reason which actuated the Superintendents in granting a month for this preliminary record was that it gave time for inspection to go on while the record was being made. This is, I now think, a wrong principle. Our blocks in Burma are small; they each contain on an average 32 houses and 170 inhabitants. There were two ways in which the preliminary record could be done, either by the enumerator dallying with it day by day, or by "making a meal of it," and finishing his work right off in two or three days at the most. It will be an interesting question for the next census report to settle which of these methods is best suited to the enumerators and which ensures the best work. So far as I have been able to settle this point from my own experience, I am inclined to think that in most of the blocks the actual preliminary record was done within one week of the date the book was issued. I am also inclined to believe that the best policy would be to issue an order that the preliminary record should be finished in rural tracts by a certain date, leaving to the discretion of the district officers the date on which the record should begin. After the date given for the completion of the record, the inspection should be taken in hand at once. In towns, in accordance with the orders of the Census Commissioner, the preliminary record was not begun till much later. In Rangoon the date was left to the discretion of the President of the Municipality and the Deputy Commissioner of Rangoon Town. In some circles in Rangoon the preliminary record was begun as early as the 28th January where the population was known to be stable, but no attempt was made to commence the enumeration of the coolie population till the 11th February.

Census holidays.

338. In 1881 Government offices were closed on the day of the census and on the day immediately preceding and on the day following it. This was done in order that every available Gov-

ernment servant should be able to assist. On this occasion not only was this procedure carried out in towns, but in the districts offices were closed for two days on the 6th and 7th February, so that all Government officials might be enlisted in checking the preliminary record; but as the preliminary record was commenced so much later in the towns, the dates fixed for the closing of Government offices, to enable the establishment to assist in checking the preliminary record, were the 16th, 17th, and 18th February, as these dates were found to be more convenient.

Preparation of the enumerator's abstract.

339. The preparations for taking the census were all complete, and the next step belonged to the compilation of the returns rather than to the actual enumeration itself. An enumerator's duties were two-fold: firstly, he had to fill up the description of the houses required in his block list and to enter the details in the columns of the schedule of every person found in his block. Next he had to add up the totals of the males and females whom he had enumerated and the houses he had found occupied on the night of the 26th February, and enter the total in his enumerator's abstract. The abstract was made as simple as possible. This work is really the first step in the work of compilation. In 1881 the attempt to obtain the filling up of the elaborate enumerator's abstract resulted in failure. In fact the attempt was abandoned. A glance at the complicated abstract form adopted in 1881 will show why the attempt failed. The abstract was not a mere totalling, but an elaborate compilation. The present form was much simpler and there was no difficulty in getting the enumerators to fill it in. Owing to the failure of the attempt to obtain the enumerators' abstracts in 1881, the preliminary totals of the province were not obtained till some months after the census had been taken. This work was done in the central abstraction office. The actual date on which the preliminary totals were obtained is not given, but from the fact that the Hanthawaddy district schedule books were not received till 14th June it may be inferred that the provincial totals were not obtained till after that date. The whole fault lay in the attempt to make the enumerator do a large share of the compilation work. The Census Commissioner pointed out that the simple return required was within the meanest capacity, in fact within the capacity of any man fit to be made an enumerator, and he pointed out the necessity of an early submission of these returns. The time he allowed was six days, so that the returns were due in Simla on 4th March. At first sight such a task seemed to be impossible in Burma. Mistakes would occur in the enumerators' abstracts, in the supervisors' total of the abstracts, and even in the compilation of the supervisors' totals in the Charge Superintendent's office. But it was urged that the tendency of such petty errors, if—and much depended on this "if"—they were made *bonâ fide*, was that they would cancel each other, and the close correspondence of the final with the preliminary totals has proved the truth of this theory. Even then, in our larger Burman districts the attempt to return these totals within six days seemed to be a fore-doomed failure. In some cases an urgent letter sent by the quickest means of transit will take more than seven days to reach headquarters from the outlying villages. In some of the districts telegraph wires do not leave the main lines of communication. The headquarters of four districts are not even connected by wire with Rangoon. Moreover, the totalling of the enumerators' abstracts could not in the non-synchronous tracts and in the boat blocks be finished till 48 hours after the census. The totals of the blocks could not be sent direct to headquarters, but had to be collected by the circle supervisor, who then sent them in to his Charge Superintendent. Verification of the totals was another necessary cause of delay. Hence, at first sight, the collection of these returns within a month seemed to be as much as could be expected.

The special arrangement adopted in Burma to secure an early return of the population.

340. After consultation with the district officers the following plan, which was generally approved by them, was submitted to, and after some consideration received, the sanction of the Chief Commissioner, and was willingly accepted by the Census Commissioner for India; the result justified its adoption. The actual enumeration consists of two distinct operations—firstly, the writing up of the schedule books, which was to be done gradually, and which, as already stated, was to be finished some time before the 26th February; and secondly, the checking of these

entries on the night of the 26th itself. These two operations are called the Preliminary Record and the Final Round. In the remoter villages, where communications are bad, the villagers are of course far less likely to cause much change in the entries in the village schedule books. Next, it must be remembered that what was required in the preliminary totals was a return not village by village, but of district totals, and that these totals were really only valuable as composing the correct total of the province, which was all that was required in these preliminary totals. The preliminary record, then, was practically a correct return of the population. The population of the remoter villages would probably show but slight alteration within the few days that elapsed between the completion of the preliminary record and the 26th February. The population of Burma itself could only be changed in two ways, either, on the one hand, by excess of immigrants over emigrants or of emigrants over immigrants, or, on the other, by variations caused by the excess of births over deaths or deaths over births. What held good of Burma as a whole, held good of each district by itself. Except in Akyab, where they come by the high road from Chittagong, nearly all our immigrants come by sea, as the migration on our frontiers is insignificant owing to the fact that the boundaries are now natural and not artificial boundaries as in 1881. Births and deaths in the 14 or 15 days which might elapse between the final closing of the preliminary record and the census day would not only nearly balance each other, but the variation would, even on the high rate of natural increment that prevailed in Burma, be practically insignificant. The population, it was calculated, in 1881 was increasing at the rate of 26 per cent. by natural increment alone in the decade. This rate is far too high, and it does not probably exceed 22 per cent. for the decade. The rate of increase by natural increment would not exceed ·0054 per diem, and the actual increase during this period, which on the average did not extend to more than 15 days, would amount to 410 souls for the whole of Burma per diem. But it must be remembered that the proposed plan did not contemplate the inclusion of these provisional totals from the preliminary record in the "district summary" total of the population except in the remote and sparsely peopled tracts, where the increment would be infinitesimal and no danger of increase by migration need be apprehended. Arrangements were made, while on tour, with the Deputy Commissioners in anticipation of the sanction subsequently granted. Orders were received and issued in Circular No. 21, dated the 31st January. Although the circular might with advantage have been issued before, as the district officers were already in most instances informed of the intended plan, no inconvenience was actually felt. In those districts of which the area was small and in which communications were good no necessity existed for the adoption of this plan, but in districts like the Upper Chindwin, Bhamo, Amherst, Mergui, Pakôkku, and Minbu, and in fact in the majority of our districts, unless some such arrangement had been entered into, the provisional figures could not possibly have been obtained till at least 15 days later. The following instructions, which are extracted from Circular No. 21 before mentioned, left with Deputy Commissioners the discretion of selecting the census blocks or circles from which the provisional totals could not be obtained in the required time. In these areas the supervisors and enumerators were directed to prepare a provisional abstract, which the supervisors checked when they inspected the census work of their circles, and which they forwarded through the Charge Superintendent to the district office. These were then kept by the Deputy Commissioner. On the conclusion of the enumeration on the night of the 26th February, in all blocks including those in which the provisional abstracts had already been prepared, the abstracts were prepared in the ordinary way, and were forwarded by the circle supervisors to the Charge Superintendents, who sent the circle supervisors' abstracts direct to the Deputy Commissioner. If all of the circle abstracts were received within the six days by the Deputy Commissioner, he was then enabled to compile them and send them on at once. In cases where delay occurred in the submission of the returns of the outlying circles, the Deputy Commissioner could at his discretion use the totals of the preliminary record for these circles. In no case was this discretion abused. Moreover, in the compilation of the returns of the districts, in every case where the final total differed largely from the provisional total, it was invariably found to be due to mistakes of addition in the district office and not to errors in the preliminary record total, where the error was inappreciable. I have thought it necessary to enter into this plan at full length because it was, I believe, adopted in Burma alone, and because, without it, Burma must have been far behind the rest of India in the submission of its returns. The total error in the provisional returns was an omission of 51,150 persons or 0·6 per cent. of the correct population of the area over which the census was taken, most of which was due to the inexplicable omission of 49,272 persons in the Bassein district. And this was evidently due, therefore, not to the few who were omitted in the preliminary record totals, but to the mistakes made in the compilation of the Charge Superintendents' summaries in the district office.

The abstracts on the whole were much better prepared in the newly acquired province. Here the total error is 37,797 souls or 1·2 per cent. in excess. Lower Burma shows a deficiency of 88,947, of which 49,272, as already stated, is due to an absurd mistake in the Bassein district total. But for this mistake, for which the plan adopted for the utilization of the preliminary record totals of the remoter tracts is in no way to blame, the total error in the Burma returns would have been only 1,878 short of the final figures, an error of 0·02 per cent. of the total population of the province. That such an error as that which occurred in Bassein should have been allowed to pass undetected is due to the fact that, just at the critical time while the census schedule books were being written up, a new Deputy Commissioner was put in charge of this district but a few days before the commencement of the preliminary record. As it is, our figures in Burma are proportionately more correct than some of the other provinces of India, and, but for the mistake in Bassein, Burma would have compared favourably not only with Assam, but with Bengal and the Punjab. If we take into consideration the miles the enumerators had to traverse with their abstracts, the distance the circle abstracts had to be carried before they could be compiled into the charge summaries, and, lastly, the long journeys on foot or by boat which had to be undertaken before the charge summary could reach the district office, it must be admitted that no time was lost. On the other hand, when we know that the mass even of our Burmese clerks cannot as compilers compare with the natives of India, it will be admitted that the result reflects credit on the district officers, through whose personal interest and energy the task of submitting these totals so speedily to the Census Office at Simla was, as the Census Commissioner has stated, "very successfully" carried out.

The preparation of the provisional totals.

341. The census was taken on the night of the 26th February, and except in the non-synchronous census areas and in the boat and land travellers' blocks and in ports, the next morning the enumerators assembled together, and in the presence of their circle supervisor wrote up their own abstracts and each checked the return of the other. The circle supervisor checked and wrote up his "circle abstract" and took it to his Charge Superintendent, who, after checking the totals, entered them in his "charge summary," which was sent off direct to the district office. In Rangoon the President assembled his small army of enumerators at the Town Hall, and the work of totalling was taken up at once and the result was in my hands on the 2nd March. The first district whose complete totals I received was Rangoon Town, but Sandoway, Bhamo, Magwe, Toungoo, Shwegyin, and Thayetmyo ran Rangoon very close. Their totals were received on the 4th March. Especial credit is due to the Deputy Commissioner of Sandoway, as not only is his district long and straggling and devoid of good roads, but there is no telegraph office situated there. Moreover, his return was, under the circumstances, wonderfully accurate, the error not exceeding ·5 per cent. In Bhamo, where without doubt the census operations were conducted with the greatest difficulty, especial credit is due for the smartness with which the return was sent in by the Deputy Commissioner. In Minbu the return was the most accurate, the error being but slightly over ·08 per cent. All the districts of Burma had sent in their reports by the 9th April except Shwebo and Sagaing in Upper Burma and Amherst, Northern Arakan and Mergui in Lower Burma. For all of these districts except Sagaing there were good reasons for the delay. The Mergui totals had

to await the arrival of the mail steamer, there being no telegraphic communication. Northern Arakan is a non-synchronous census district, and a large part of Amherst is also included under that head. The enormous distance to be traversed by boat or on foot between Amherst and its outlying circles alone accounted for the fact that the return was only received on the 19th March. The last district to report was Mergui.

342. As in 1881, so on the present occasion, the work of compilation was, with the exception of the preparation of the preliminary totals, entirely performed in one central office. The work was divided into three distinct operations—

The compilation of the figures.

(1) The abstraction of entries.
(2) The tabulation of the contents of the abstraction sheets.
(3) The compilation of the district totals from the tabulation registers.

This last operation may again be divided into two distinct processes—(*a*) the preparation of the Imperial tables, (*b*) the preparation of the Provincial tables. Although these two operations cover the same ground, they differ in two great essentials. The Imperial table is restricted to the district as a unit, but it requires the information regarding that unit to be of the fullest description. The population of the districts is shown in various combinations of age periods, religion, sex, civil condition, education, infirmities, parent-tongue, birth-place, caste or race, and occupation. In the Provincial tables the arrangement is simpler, but the population of each district is shown in great detail by the administrative divisions of each district. Every village, revenue circle, and township is shown apart. Of the labour required in preparing these Provincial tables some idea may be gathered from the fact that they comprise Volumes III and IV of the Report.

343. Returning once more to the three main divisions of the census compilation work, some explanation is necessary of the technical meaning attached to the terms. Abstraction means that the entries in the schedule books are transferred from the books into sheets, in which the information recorded in the schedules is grouped under various heads block by block. There were in all 12 varieties of abstraction sheets. The entries on these sheets were totalled and compared. As the sheets were done independently of each other by separate gangs in different rooms, and as it was impossible in a large office for the abstractor of Sheet I from a schedule book to know who would abstract Sheet II, and who would do the others, these sheets formed of themselves a very fair check on each other; but, besides this, re-abstraction was largely employed, so that the chance of successful fudging in a central office under careful supervision was impossible. Guided by the experience of the last census, every precaution was taken from the very first to show that fudging must be detected. Inter-communication between the rooms being forbidden, the clerks at once recognized that the work they did would be subject to check and scrutiny before the day was over. Every abstraction sheet was collected so soon as the books were given up and were filed together and compared; consequently fudging was at once apparent. The first attempt was detected and the clerk expelled within 24 hours of the commission of the offence, and after this I had no more cases. Careless and grossly careless mistakes there were in plenty, but this, unlike fudging, reveals itself, and is not a dangerous offence such as wilful fudging is.

Abstraction.

The abstraction office consisted of one Manager on Rs. 350, one Inspector on Rs. 150, 2 Sub-Inspectors, 6 Supervisors, 40 Re-abstractors, and the average strength of the clerks was 360.

The preparation of the preliminary totals, the preparation of the district report, and the checking and assorting of the census schedule books preparatory to their despatch to the central office naturally took up some time, and the first district that submitted its books was Tharrawaddy. These books arrived on the 12th March and were quickly followed by those of the other districts. As the consignments arrived, the books were carefully checked with the subdivisional registers before any of them were passed out of the record room.

On the 2nd March the abstraction clerks were engaged. At first but 100 were taken on, and, till the schedule books were available, the clerks were daily instructed in the work of abstracting each variety of sheet. The instruction was commenced by teaching the abstraction clerks how to fill up a census schedule themselves. This not only gave them a connected idea of what their work would be, but it taught them from the very first the mistakes for which they were to be on the look out. They were then made to correct the entries made by other clerks and then shown how to abstract them. This systematic instruction, begun with a few men, was carried out till the whole establishment had been gradually entertained. No clerk was allowed to begin abstraction till he had shown he understood his work. Accordingly, from the very first, the work of abstraction was well done. Time and paper were saved. Abstraction began on 14th March. At first the work was very slowly done. I did not, however, force on the work for the first few days, but by the end of the first week the rate of abstracting, which was at first painfully slow, already showed a general improvement. Hitherto I had no Manager as my assistant, Mr. Noyce, on the 1st of March was appointed to officiate as Secretary to the Financial Commissioner. On the 26th March Mr. Stubbs was appointed Manager of the Abstraction Office and assumed charge of his duties. In March, April, and May the rate of abstraction showed a gradual and steady increase. I was almost as much surprised as pleased at the progress made. The abstraction office reached its maximum number of clerks in May. Burmans composed about 75, Eurasians about 10, natives of India about 8, Karens about 4, and Chinese about 3 per cent. of the *personnel* of the abstraction office. The Chinese and Burmans proved to be the best abstractors. The Burmans, though not good computers, in the mechanical work of hand and eye which quick abstraction requires, showed that they were particularly well fitted for this kind of work. The difficulty was to ensure accuracy. It was perhaps fortunate that from the very first they were trained to work slowly, for as time went on they improved, through acquiring facility, to an extent which surprised me. The work of abstraction took altogether 97 days only, the time allowed being 100. I did not employ the full establishment except for a few weeks in May and June. The work was done in the most economical way. The abstractors were taken on gradually and remained as volunteers till they were qualified. Then, as the districts gradually became exhausted, the slower hands were discharged and others absorbed into the tabulation department, and some were employed in checking and re-abstracting the sheets already finished. In this way, in these 97 working days, the whole of the abstraction sheets were re-checked and compared and errors and discrepancies detected and corrected. Abstraction was estimated to cost Rs. 47,640; as a fact it cost only Rs. 31,028, although the work was so carefully re-checked. We had now a firm basis for the tabulation work. There were 12 sheets abstracted. Specimens of these sheets are preserved in Appendix C of this report. Basing my calculations on the average number of entries, I find that Sheet I, which is perhaps the most important, in which age, sex, civil condition, and religion were abstracted, the average outturn of each man was 2,000 entries per diem and the cost Rs. 5,827. The average strength was 65.

In Sheet II, in which education by religion, three age periods, and sex was abstracted, the work was not so difficult as in No. I, because the age periods were much fewer. The average number of entries amounted to 2,500, the average strength of clerks was 52, and the cost about Rs. 5,060.

Sheet III, sex and occupations by three age periods, gave much more trouble than Sheet II for blocks in towns where occupations are much varied, but in rural tracts this return was less complex and required about the same amount of work as Sheet II. The average number of entries was 2,300, the cost Rs. 4,293, and the average strength of the clerks was 56.

Sheet IV was combined with Sheet X. In this sheet caste or race distributed by religion, sex, education, and knowledge of English was abstracted. This sheet varied greatly in the amount of trouble it gave. The abstraction of towns where natives of India abound, and where, as in Rangoon, we have a polyglot community, occasioned a large amount of labour, but in the rural tracts the entries were generally but few. The average number of men employed was 37 and the cost Rs. 2,530.

Sheet V, parent-tongue, and Sheet VI, birth-place, were comparatively easy. The average outturn was 6,500 entries per diem per man and the average cost Rs. 2,530. The average strength was 15 clerks.

Sheet VII, infirmities by caste, religion, age, and sex, was in reality a difficult return, but as the proportion of those who were shown as infirm is very small, but few entries had to be made. At first I attempted to carry out the orders of the Census Commissioner and allow two men on Sheet I, one of whom was to dictate and write up the entries for Sheet VII when they occurred, and the other to write at his dictation the entries in Sheet I. I very soon found out that dictation would not do, and put on two gangs, one working each man for himself at Sheet I and the other following the plan laid down by the Census Commissioner. I gave both plans as fair a trial as possible by changing the men, and I found out that as work went on, and facility was acquired, one man working alone could turn out very nearly as much as the two men together. Dictation for Burmese clerks was clearly a mistake; and in fact I had abandoned all dictation by the 24th March, except for one couple, who were smart at it, and who were only allowed to keep on at it so long as they showed between them the average outturn of two men. Accordingly I started a separate section for Sheet VII. Picked men were chosen, because the only check on infirmities was by re-abstraction, which is always a costly method. The average strength of the section was 7 and the cost Rs. 1,227. The average number of entries was not a fair index of the work done from day to day, as a man might work all day inspecting the returns of troops without making a single entry.

Sheets VIII and IX refer to Christians only; they were completed in 7 days by 20 men. The abstraction cost Rs. 1,227. The outturn increased from day to day.

Sheet XI was the last regular sheet affecting the whole population; in it caste or race, religion, and civil condition by age periods was obtained. Here, again, the difficulty of abstracting the return varied greatly. In towns the work was slow; in rural tracts fairly fast. The average outturn was 1,100 entries per diem, the average strength 53, and the cost Rs. 4,577.

Sheet XII was not abstracted till I had finished the tabulation and compilation of the age periods. I waited because I was thus able to make a fairer selection of average blocks. The work was done by four tabulation clerks in seven days. It cost Rs. 30.

The tabulation.

344. By the term tabulation is meant the posting up in registers of the totals of the various columns in the abstraction sheets of each village. Specimens of these registers have been preserved for reference in 1901. There were originally 20 sets of registers, each containing ordinarily 10 villages on a page. The work was divided into two portions—posting and page totalling. The revenue circle totals were then posted, and, lastly, the circle totals were added up for the township totals. The sum of the township totals made up the district total. The work was painfully laborious and slow. The registers were, to a certain extent, redundant. In a central office, where the checks are more easily applied and where, by the greater subdivision of labour, greater inter-check between sections can be more easily maintained than in a small district office, I found that Registers II and V were not required except for purposes of check. Accordingly, with the Census Commissioner's sanction, they were not posted up. Again, Registers XIV and XVIII were combined into one register. Not only was there a great saving of time in the tabulation, but time was also saved in the compilation of caste and race, and "literates knowing English by caste and race" from the combined register. Another great saving was effected by using the serial number and letter for villages and blocks instead of writing out the name into the register. So long as the village blocks can be identified by their number, which is more quickly written, there is no necessity to waste time in writing the name. By these means the work of tabulation was greatly curtailed. It was commenced on 20th April with a small establishment, and the strength was increased very gradually. This was an advantage, for it was only by actual experience that these methods of saving time were evolved. Registers I, IV, and VI were first pushed on, and were all com-

pleted by the end of August. Register III was also begun simultaneously, but was not pushed on so fast. Registers VIII to XIII-A were then taken in hand and were completed for all districts by the 10th November. It is exceedingly difficult to gauge the exact amount of work involved in writing up each register, because the work of posting and totalling was in many cases given to separate men. Then, again, the labour of posting up blocks in towns as a rule far exceeded the trouble of posting up rural blocks. For these reasons it is impossible to give the return of the exact amount of labour required. I am only able to give the approximate cost of writing up and totalling each register from the office attendance rolls compared with the dates on which the registers were finished.

Method devised for classifying and tabulating occupations and castes.

345. But these registers were mere child's play compared with the labour of writing up castes and races and occupations. The classification of occupations was begun by me in July and tabulation was started in August. Three districts were fully tabulated by 10th October. I purposely began with the smaller districts in order to feel our way. Here, again, a great deal of time was saved and uniformity gained by not allowing the clerks to have any discretion in the classification. A complete list of occupations in each district was made and the entries in abstraction sheets were numbered accordingly. Hence the posting clerk had nothing but mechanical work to do. Instead of writing down the name of the occupation in the column of the register, he entered the serial number of the occupation in the heading, and in the columns entered the number of those following it. I estimate that about one-third of the trouble in writing up the registers of occupations was saved in this way. Firstly, a list of the occupations found in the abstraction sheets was prepared and the occupations were then classified by me; then their numbers in the list of occupations prepared by the Census Commissioner were affixed to the entries in the abstraction sheets by a select gang of four men, who had the lists pasted up on the wall before them for ready reference; the posting clerk then had no trouble except to write the number down, and for this work ordinary copying clerks were just as good as intelligent men trained to select the right occupation. This division of labour therefore not only saved time, but it saved money. A similar plan was followed in the tabulation of castes. Had this not been done, the tabulation of castes could only have been carried out by natives of India, and even then mistakes would have been multiplied, since we have immigrants from all the provinces of India, and the distribution of blocks containing varieties of castes could not have been given to selected tabulators with success, as so many varieties of race and caste are often found in a single block. The tabulation of occupations by age periods was the severest strain that was felt. The posting and totalling were carried on by a separate gang. This proved to be an exceedingly difficult task. In one block sometimes as many as 40 occupations were found. As these were entered by age periods, several consecutive pages were required for the entries; this entailed a double totalling of the village total at the end of the pages used and a page totalling for the various occupations. The possibilities of error were enormously increased. So many small totals had to be carried forward that the work of tabulating occupations was one long struggle against blunders. None but those who have had practical experience of the work can understand how enormously the mere inclusion of age periods and sex increased not only the volume of the work, but multiplied the liability to error. I have calculated that the tabulation of occupations took 71 days and cost Rs. 1,404.

The tabulation of castes and races.

346. The classification of castes was an exceedingly difficult task in Burma. Caste is unknown among our indigenous population, and the bonds of caste amongst our Indian immigrants are in many cases undoubtedly slackened by their new environment. Besides, we have representatives of all kinds of castes from all three presidencies. The value of such a return depends of course on its accuracy. No attempt was made in 1881 to return caste. The whole question is discussed at length in Chapter X. On the occasion of his tour in Burma during October 1800 the advisability of making this return was discussed with the Census Commissioner. The translation of the schedules had been made purposely to include

the collection of this return should it be decided to attempt it. It was decided that the attempt should be made. If castes were returned, they could be abstracted, and if, on abstraction, the entries appeared to have been carefully made and to be *primâ facie* reasonably correct, they could be tabulated. The experiment appeared to have succeeded beyond our expectation. In the first place a large proportion of the native immigrants are in our native army and military police. Their returns were well made. Next we found that the majority of the other immigrants live in our large towns. Here we had some means of checking the returns made by the enumerated, and the caste names were written down in English. This was important. Only those who have tried to decipher a Burmese enumerator's attempt at the transliteration of a polysyllabic caste name can appreciate the remarkable results that he obtains. In many cases the names were utterly unrecognizable. This will account for the large number of those whose caste is "Not returned." The lists of caste names were checked and revised by my colleagues, and on the return of my lists the tabulation of caste commenced on the 3rd December. While castes and occupations were being tabulated, the compilation of the other returns was pressed on and the Provincial tables were prepared.

Castes were in Burma not so difficult as occupations, because we wisely did not attempt to make the return by age periods. Had the attempt been made, we should still be tabulating them. Caste could not have been tabulated in Burma at all had not the expedient of labelling each caste with a number been adopted. The tabulators, most of whom were perforce Burmans, could write down the numbers just as well as a trained poster who knew all about castes. The tabulation lasted from 3rd December to 20th January. The tabulation of castes and races cost Rs. 1,092. The total cost of tabulation amounted to Rs. 8,580.

Employment of British soldiers in the Census office.

347. In the tabulation office I made the experiment of employing a party of European soldiers belonging to the Norfolk Regiment by the kind permission of the officer in command. The experiment was an interesting one of itself in that it tested the capacity of our soldiers as census tabulators. As abstractors they could not be employed as they were unacquainted with Burmese, the language in which nearly all the schedules were written; but as tabulators I found them honest and steady workers if not very quick. My motive for employing them was, however, one of policy as much as of curiosity. The work of abstraction had begun to wear out the patience of the clerks. Tabulation was almost as dreary, and there were signs that I should have what occurred in Bengal—a strike amongst the Babus. Even the Burmans, docile by themselves, when properly managed, began to catch the infection. I foresaw the trouble, and, in order to prevent it, I felt the only way would be to show the clerks I could be independent of them. I therefore adopted this expedient, and when the dissatisfied ones found that they were not indispensable, the threatened mutiny died out.

Compilation.

348. The meaning of the term compilation has been narrowed down to the preparation of the Imperial tables from our Tabulation registers and the final production of them in the Census Report. The report consists of three parts—the Imperial tables, the Provincial tables, and the Report itself with its comparative statements. In estimating the amount of work to be done, little difficulty was felt so long as the estimate was restricted to abstraction. The estimate could fairly be based on the actual numbers of the population and the various combinations of the returns under the different headings of the schedule required by our Imperial tables. This estimate was based on the same data throughout India. Our abstraction work was well and quickly done and fell far below the estimate of the cost originally submitted. But in tabulation a general estimate for the whole of India could not give such accurate results. Here the unit was not the individual enumerated but the block enumerated. In Burma, for reasons already given at length, our blocks were on the average small. The average block in Burma contained 170 persons. In 1881 the average block in Lower Burma contained 217. In the Punjab in 1881 the average sized block contained 350 souls, and in Bombay 388. These blocks were considered too large, and the original instructions were that in no case were blocks to exceed 300

persons. In Burma, where the number of literates is far greater proportionately than in any province in India, there was no necessity for having large blocks. The Burmese village of the average size contains 336 inhabitants, and, had not the blocks been made to correspond with our villages, the value of our village tables would have been entirely lost. These small blocks, however, made their presence felt in the extra number of entries required in our registers in proportion to the population contained. Our tabulation was all the more elaborate in consequence, and there was not therefore the same saving shown in time or money that we were able to show in abstraction, as the cost of tabulation, instead of being estimated by the number of blocks, was based on the number of the population contained in them. But it was not till I came to compilation and to the preparation of the comparative statements that I fully appreciated that the cost of compilation cannot be based on the total number of the population alone. What is true about tabulation is true about compilation; the unit of compilation is not the block but the district. In Burma we have 36 districts and the Shan States. The preparation of a comparative statement does not depend solely on the population. The calculation up to one more place of decimals is the difference between 7 and 70 millions, but when these figures have to be marshalled into 36 units of compilation, it will easily be understood that the trouble of compiling a report on 36 districts, with an average population of quarter of a million, is far greater than that of 18 districts with half a million each. Compilation was begun in August, when the first compilation slips were prepared and sent in. This work was shared between the tabulation and correspondence office establishments. But as the tabulation registers were completed a regular compilation staff was required to cope with the work.

Imperial tables.

349. The compilation work consists, as I said before, of three parts— Imperial tables, Provincial tables, and the Report. The Imperial Tables I—VI gave but little trouble comparatively speaking. Tables VII—XI are all heavy tables; XII—XV and XII-A to XV-A are not heavy, but Tables XVI, XVII-A, and XVII-B, and Supplementary Table C, from the multiplicity of the totals and cross totals, have proved to be most formidable pieces of work. The compilation of the occupations of the population in urban areas by age periods, although it related to less than 1,000,000 souls, gave proportionately the most trouble of all. Of course the same and even greater difficulty has been experienced in England over this return. The tabulation of this return was heavy, and the compilation of it was proportionately still heavier. The cost of making returns depends, of course, on the complexity of the operations. The compilation of totals unencumbered by age periods and divers headings is comparatively simple work, but where the return is divided into numerous small classes, further subdivided by sex and age, the difficulty of detecting the errors that arise from the numerous postings and re-postings was a very severe strain on the compilation staff. In April 1891 the Census Commissioner foresaw that the sum of Rs. 80,000 he had allowed for abstraction, tabulation, and compilation in Burma would probably be insufficient. As, however, abstraction was done so much more cheaply than was expected, and tabulation—till castes and occupation were started—did not show that it would exceed the budget estimate, I did not ask for a revision of the budget. When the budget was prepared, the question of the compilation of the castes had not been finally settled.

The cost of the report.

350. Lastly we have the cost of the Report. The preparation of the numerous comparative statements was of itself no easy matter. Without these statements the Imperial table would be a sealed book to the general public. It is true that in England the figures are served up without these elaborate statements, but in England the county governs itself; the vestry men and county councillors are not moved from district to district and need not trouble themselves with details about Yorkshire if they live in Somerset. In India and Burma the work of administration is carried on by a few trained men, who are liable to be moved about at short notice, and who are expected to master the details of the administration of their district in a short time. Moreover, if any information is wanted in England, we have there many private persons, not to mention public journals, ready to espouse any cause

and to marshal the facts and figures themselves. In the East we have no men of leisure and but few journals. Moreover, these comparative statements are useful in that the preparation of them is itself a check on the accuracy of the figures compiled. Each statement—and there are, as I know to my cost, a large number of them—covers a certain amount of the census returns, and I trust that they will be of use in placing the returns of the districts of Burma in the right perspective.

I began writing up my report in the intervals of the time I could spare in the compilation of the figures. I had also a vast amount of reading to get through on the subjects dealt with in the report. By the middle of March all the chapters of the report except Chapters X, XI and XII had been drafted and sent in to the press. Chapters X and XI could not be written till the Imperial Tables XVI, XVII A, B, C, and Supplementary Table C, were finally passed. As I found that these tables and reading the proofs did not occupy the whole of my time, and as my services were required for district work, I closed my compilation office in Rangoon on 15th April and went on transfer to Magwe. I have here completed my report in the hours I could spare from district work. Not the least inconvenience felt has been my distance from the press. This has been a source of delay and expense, as it has much prolonged the time taken to return proofs to the press. My transfer, however, has had one benefit, as it has decreased the cost of the census by the curtailment of my census allowance, a piece of economy at which I, as Provincial Superintendent of Census, cannot but rejoice, however much I may deplore it as a private individual.

The following table gives at a glance the number of clerks required and the actual cost of each census abstraction sheet, register, and Imperial table :—

Abstraction.			Tabulation.			Compilation.			Remarks.
Number of abstraction sheets.	Average number of abstractors.	Cost of abstracting each sheet.	Number of tabulation registers.	Average number of tabulators.	Cost of tabulation of each register.	Number of compilation sheets.	Average number of compilers.	Cost of compilation of each sheet.	
		Rs.			Rs.			Rs.	
I	65	5,827	I	2	312	I	1	280	Rs.
II	52	5,060	III	2	312	II	1	280	Record room—
III	56	4,293	IV	5	780	III	1	280	Twenty clerks at Rs. 25 per mensem for three
IV & X	37	2,530	VI	2	312	IV	2	560	months and eleven
V	15	2,530	VII	8	1,248	V	2	560	days ... ... = 1,687
VI	15	2,530	VIII	8	1,248	VI	6	1,680	Re-abstraction—
VII	7	1,227	IX	2	312	VII	6	1,680	Twenty clerks at Rs. 25
VIII	5	1,227	X & X-A	2	312	VIII	6	1,680	per mensem for three
IX	5	1,227	XI & XI-A	2	312	IX	2	560	months and eleven
XI	53	4,577	XII & XII-A	2	312	X	2	560	days ... ... = 1,687
			XIII & XIII-A	2	312	XI	2	560	
			XIV & XVIII	7	1,092	XII	2	560	Total ... 3,374
			XV A & B	9	1,404	XIII	2	560	
			XVI	1	156	XIV	3	840	
			XVII	1	156	XV	3	840	
						XVI	4	1,120	
						XVII A & B	30	8,400	
Total ...	*310	31,028	Total ...	†55	8,580	Total	‡75	21,000	

* Average pay at Rs. 32 per mensem for three months and six days.
† Average pay at Rs. 26 per mensem of each clerk for six months.
‡ Average pay at Rs. 35 per mensem for eight months.

Printing.

351. I have not yet touched on one of the most important parts of the census operations. The printing and the distribution of the schedules, the printing of the abstraction sheets, registers and compilation forms, and last, but not least, of the report and its companion statements and tables. The census of 1891 has given the Government Press of Burma the biggest piece of work it has yet performed. To Mr. Regan, the Super-

intendent of that press, is due no small share of the credit of carrying out the census of Burma. When I compared the trouble and anxiety that must have been felt by my colleagues in India regarding the printing and supply of the schedules, I then knew how much was due to the press for its promptitude in supplying the schedule books. The following statement shows the number and size and description of the schedule books supplied to and used by each district. These returns are taken from the district reports, but in most instances I had to check and revise the statements thus furnished, as I found that they did not tally—

(1) with the statement supplied to me by the press ;
(2) with the subdivisional registers written up in the district office ;
(3) with the record-room registers of my office.

Statement of schedule books used in enumeration.

Class of schedule books.	English.			Burmese.			Remarks.
	Issued.	Used.	Unused or spoiled.	Issued.	Used.	Unused or spoiled.	
Household schedules.							
Book of 16 schedules ...	1,560	1,432	128	25,918	23,440	2,478	
Book of 30 schedules ...	773	624	149	23,941	21,418	2,523	
Book of 60 schedules ...	1,542	1,389	153	19,404	17,270	2,134	
Book of 6 schedules ...	599	535	64	16,954	15,329	1,625	
Total ...	**4,474**	**3,980**	**494**	**86,217**	**77,457**	**8,760**	
Boat schedules.							
Book of 8 schedules ...	575	443	132	8,421	7,699	722	
Book of 16 schedules ...	403	298	105	3,111	2,593	518	
Total ...	**978**	**741**	**237**	**11,532**	**10,292**	**1,240**	
Loose sheets for instruction only	1,137	1,137	...	29,555	29,555	...	
Hand-books	...	...	...	...	...	...	4,269, all used.

From this statement it might at first appear that a large number of schedules were wasted, but, as a large number of these schedules were used in the census offices in the instruction of the clerks, the excess is not so great as it appears. It must be remembered that the growth of the population of Lower Burma was over-rated and that Mr. Copleston, the former Deputy Superintendent, estimated that there would be 5,137,100 souls in Lower Burma in 1891, nearly half a million in excess of our actual return. In Upper Burma we had no previous records to act as a guide. Lastly it must be recollected that the orders of the Government of India necessitated the use of a large number of extra schedules owing to the rule that every house was to be given at least one separate, and if necessary more than one separate schedule. If all of these facts be taken into consideration, and if at the same time the full danger of a short supply of schedules be weighed, then the very slight cost of the extra schedules will be found to be but a slight insurance-fee on the cost of an accurate census. A census wrecked for want of schedules would be a catastrophe for which nothing could compensate.

The actual printing and striking off of the schedules began in October, and the whole of the amount specified in the indents of the Deputy Commissioners had been struck off and bound by the first week in December. These indents had been revised, but unfortunately the Jail Press had neglected to carry out my orders and were working on the old indents. On my return from tour in Upper Burma I found this out, and Mr. Regan, with characteristic energy, soon made up the amount required, and they were all despatched by the first week in January. Meantime the abrogation of the rule of compelling the block lists being written up in the district offices more than compensated for the delay thus occasioned. The actual cost of printing is shown in the statement of account attached. This cost, it must be remembered, includes the very heavy item of carriage. Carriage in Burma is costly owing to the huge distances to be traversed.

After the printing of the schedules was completed, the press began on the abstraction sheets, registers, and compilation forms. The following statement shows the number printed and the number used.

Lastly, we have the printing of the report and tables. This has been a long and wearisome task. Owing to a variety of circumstances and to the character of the work itself, the proofs of these tables and chapters have been kept waiting in type till their contents could be finally compared and checked with the results of other tables. This has resulted in proportionately heavy increase in the cost of printing, and has, I fear, been a tax on the patience of the Superintendent of the press. The impossibility of putting the whole of the figures into proof at once has, on the other hand, been a very considerable drawback to their simultaneous checking, and has thus increased the labour of proof-reading.

352. The following statement gives the cost of the census operations year by year in the form sanctioned by the Government of India:—

	1890-91.			1891-92.			1892-93.			Total.		
	Rs.	A.	P.	Rs.	A.	P.	Rs.	A.	P.	Rs.	A.	P.
A.—ENUMERATION.												
I.—DISTRICT CHARGES.												
1. House numbering	...			...			...			...		
2. Carriage of block-books, &c., to office	179	7	6	110	12	0	...			290	3	6
3. Lights, red ink, &c. ... ... } 4. Petty stationery, &c. ... ... Office expenses, miscellaneous ...	3,224	12	3	...			...			3,224	12	3
5. Travelling allowance to officials, *i.e.*, establishment.	808	8	6	292	9	9	...			1,101	2	3
6. Remuneration of non-officials ...	2,375	5	2	310	0	0	...			2,685	5	2
Total I ...	6,588	1	5	713	5	9	...			7,301	7	2
II.—PRESS CHARGES.												
7. Paper	6,053	7	5	...			...			6,053	7	5
8. Carriage of paper to press ... } 9. Printing ... ... 10. Binding and despatching forms ...	6,407	14	9	...			...			6,407	14	9
Total II ...	12,461	6	2	...			...			12,461	6	2
Total A.—(Enumeration) ...	19,049	7	7	713	5	9	...			19,762	13	4
B.—ABSTRACTION AND COMPILATION.												
III.—DIVISIONAL AND CENTRAL OFFICE CHARGES.												
11. Office rent	569	0	6	4,500	0	0	...			5,069	0	6
12. Furniture	1,169	5	0	1,479	15	3	...			2,649	4	3
13. Office establishment records ... } 14. Office correspondence and accounts ... 15. Office menials	...			5,940	0	0	...			5,940	0	0
16. Working establishment, officials ... }	...			962	1	3	24	0	0	986	1	3
17. Working establishment, non-officials }	...			63,982	2	7	2,627	10	7	66,609	13	2
18. Travelling allowance to officials ...	...			...			120	0	0	120	0	0
19. Carriage of block books from districts	514	6	3	388	10	6	...			903	0	9
20. Contingent charges, postage, stationery, &c.	...			...			...			...		
Total III ...	2,252	11	9	77,252	13	7	2,771	10	7	82,277	3	11
IV.—PRESS CHARGES.												
21. Paper for abstraction and compilation.	1,675	12	6	...			...			1,675	12	6
22. Carriage of do. to press ...	...											
23. Printing ... ... } 24. Despatching charges	267	5	3	5,957	7	9	14,000	0	0	20,224	13	0
Total IV ...	1,943	1	9	5,957	7	9	14,000	0	0	21,900	9	6
Total B.—(Abstraction and Compilation)...	4,195	13	6	83,210	5	4	16,771	10	7	1,04,177	13	5

	1890-91.			1891-92.			1892-93.			Total.		
	Rs.	A.	P.	Rs.	A.	P.	Rs.	A.	P.	Rs.	A.	P.
C.—SUPERINTENDENCE.												
V.—PERSONAL CHARGES.												
25. Deputation allowance of Superintendent.	1,032	4	1	1,536	0	0	363	5	7	2,931	9	8
26. Pay of substitute for Superintendent	...			...			...			...		
27. Travelling allowance to Superintendent.	1,652	3	0	...			...			1,652	3	0
Total V ...	**2,684**	**7**	**1**	**1,536**	**0**	**0**	**363**	**5**	**7**	**4,583**	**12**	**8**
VI.—ESTABLISHMENT & OFFICE CHARGES.												
28. Superintendent's Office establishment.	1,479	0	5	...			990	0	0	2,469	0	5
29. Contingent charges, postage, stationery, &c.	1,745	3	11	1,715	6	8	262	3	0	3,722	13	7
Total VI ...	**3,224**	**4**	**4**	**1,715**	**6**	**8**	**1,252**	**3**	**0**	**6,191**	**14**	**0**
Total C.—(Superintendence) ...	**5,908**	**11**	**5**	**3,251**	**6**	**8**	**1,615**	**8**	**7**	**10,775**	**10**	**8**
GRAND TOTAL A, B, & C ...	**29,154**	**0**	**6**	**87,175**	**1**	**9**	**18,387**	**3**	**2**	**1,34,716**	**5**	**5**
Plus sanctioned amount for Rangoon Municipality.	5,000	0	0	...			...			...		

The total cost of the census operations will therefore amount to Rupees 1,39,716-5-5. This represents a cost of 3·3 pies per head of the population. In 1881 the cost of the census operations was put down at Rs. 76,645-13-11, representing a cost of 3·9 pies per head of the population. But the cost of printing the report in 1881 was, I am informed, very much under-estimated. Hence the cost of the operations amounted to at least 4 pies per head. Unfortunately the actual cost of the printing in 1881 cannot now be ascertained. Taking enumeration and compilation apart, in which latter term abstraction, tabulation, and compilation are now included, we find that in 1881 the cost of enumeration, in which is included a share of the Superintendent's allowance, was 1·4 pies per head of the population, while it is only ·8 pies per head of the population in 1891. Notwithstanding the fact that, as I have already pointed out, the number of districts, revenue circles, and villages has increased in the same proportion as the population itself, and has therefore prevented a similar saving in the cost of compilation, there was a saving of Rs. 35,845-15-6 on the revised estimate of the cost of the enumeration sanctioned by the Government of India. If we deduct the item of printing from the cost of compilation—for in 1881 the actual cost was not entered—we find that even in compilation there is also a saving per head of the population, as the cost of the compilation in 1881 was 2·3 as against 2·1 pies per head of the population in 1891.

353. In the reports of the Deputy Commissioners, extracts from which will be found in Appendix **D**, these officers testify to the general accuracy of the enumeration. The value of the returns depends on three factors—the truthfulness and intelligence of those enumerated, the honesty and care bestowed on the enumeration, and, lastly, the accuracy of the abstraction, tabulation, and compilation of the figures. Of this last factor the Deputy Commissioners could have no knowledge, and their reports of course refer to the enumeration alone. In Burma we find, as a rule, that apart from the fear of increased taxation resulting from the census, the people have no objection to making truthful returns. The only return of the schedule in which errors abounded was the age return. This question has been dealt with at some length in Chapter IV, and I need not recount the points therein mentioned. The inaccuracy there found is common to every census, whether in the East or the West. Our Imperial tables show that greater accuracy was obtained in 1891 than in 1881 in Lower Burma. I am persuaded that the error lies with the enumerated rather than the enumerator, and hence there is greater difficulty in grappling with this error. The efforts of my successor will have to be directed to instructing the

The accuracy of the returns.

enumerated as well as the enumerator. The census schedules themselves testified to the good work of those engaged in collecting the information. There were very few books that showed that the enumerator had not been instructed properly. Mistakes of course there were, but I am glad to be able to testify to the general excellence of the work. As regards the accuracy with which the figures are now produced in my report, this depended in part on the honesty and intelligence of the abstractor and the care taken to instruct him, and the subsequent supervision of his work. Of one thing I may speak with confidence, and that is, that there was not, as in 1881, any appreciable amount of deliberate fudging. This is due to the excellence of the arrangements recommended by Mr. Baines, the Census Commissioner, to the fidelity with which these arrangements were carried out and even supplemented, and, lastly, but by no means leastly, to the unwearying vigilance of the Manager of the office, Mr. Stubbs, and to the staff of Inspectors under him. The advantage of a central office was here felt. It enabled the Superintendent to be in touch with the poorest paid clerk. For a "scratch" office hastily collected and enlisted but for a short time, the feeling of *esprit de corps* that sprung up, and which was fostered as much as circumstances would allow, was, I am glad to testify, most remarkable. The office was engaged, not like ordinary Government offices, in routine work, but in one long endeavour to drive the work through. On two occasions, unasked by me, a squad of clerks sat up all night to finish off district returns.

Absolute accuracy in such a mass of figures is not to be expected, but I trust that the Burma report will be found to be as accurate and trustworthy a representation of the actual condition of the population of Burma as might be expected under the circumstances.

Services of officers.

354. It now remains for me to mention those officers to whom the Government is most indebted for the part they bore in this undertaking. Honour be given to whom honour is due. The long-suffering District officers deserve the greatest share; to them and to the Presidents of the Municipalities is due the actual carrying out of the work. I have already mentioned the excellent work done in Rangoon by Major Temple and Mr. Short. In Mandalay no less credit is due to Mr. Adamson and Count Calderarj. In Akyab Mr. Shaw Brown, the Municipal Secretary, took great pains with the work. In Bhamo Mr. George, hampered with military expeditions and an as yet partially explored district, made a very fair piece of work of what looked like a hopeless task. In all the districts of Burma except one I met with ready and cheerful help from the Deputy Commissioners. With the exception of the Sagaing district, the work in Upper Burma was far better done than in most districts in Lower Burma. In Minbu, Myingyan, Magwe, Yamèthin and Pyinmana, the promptness and accuracy with which the returns were submitted reflected the utmost credit on the District officers. In Lower Burma, in many districts, notably Mergui, Tavoy, Amherst, Akyab, Shwegyin, Sandoway, and Kyaukpyu, the badness of the internal communications and the paucity of European officers severely handicapped the District officers. The work done in Sandoway, Shwegyin, and Toungoo was perhaps the best.

The list of officers who deserve credit for the work they did will be found in the reports of the Presidents of the Municipalities and Deputy Commissioners in Appendix D. I can myself testify in many instances to the fact that these encomiums were well deserved. I have already stated that I laboured under a serious disadvantage in being appointed four months after my colleagues in the other provinces. Consequently I was obliged to be constantly absent on tour. To compensate me for this disadvantage Mr. Noyce's services were put at my disposal. Mr. Noyce had served formerly under me in Pegu, and he fully justified his selection for the work. I regret much that I lost his services immediately after the completion of the enumeration.

The thanks of Government are due to various gentlemen who, as agents or heads of the firms they represent, undertook the labour of enumerating their employés. I have already acknowledged the debt owed to Mr. Miller, the Acting Manager of the Irrawaddy Flotilla Company, who took the entire management of the census of the large fleet of steamers under his command and carried out the work in a way which is deserving of the very highest credit. In the same way Messrs. the Bombay Burma Trading Corporation enumerated their own numerous working camps. The enumeration of the battalions of coolies engaged in the rice-mills was carried out by the merchants and mill-owners of Rangoon, Akyab, Bassein, and Moulmein without a hitch or the least semblance of friction. To Mr. Hewitt, of the firm of Messrs. Steel Brothers, I am indebted for the plan of enumerating coolies that proved so successful at Akyab. In the Port of Rangoon the credit of the arrangement is due to Mr. Darlington, the Vice-Chairman, and his *locum tenens* Mr. Kynoch. Unfortunately the success of the enumeration of Rangoon port was marred by a fatal accident through one of the rowing boats being upset at night in one of the most dangerous parts of the river. In Mandalay Captain Barwick, R.I.M., not only supervised the collection of the returns of the boat population, but was of great assistance in the despatch of the consignments of schedule books.

The Railway returns were collected under the supervision of Mr. Rigg, and special arrangements were made with General Stedman for the enumeration of the military police.

Personally I am myself greatly indebted for advice and assistance in the anxious work of organizing the census operations to the Chief Secretary, Mr. Thirkell White, and Mr. Copleston, the previous Deputy Superintendent. If my circulars have met with the general approval of the District officers of Burma, it is in great measure due to the assistance willingly given me by Mr. Thirkell White. To him and to Mr. Copleston my best acknowledgments are due.

APPENDICES.

A.—The Enumeration in the Tracts excluded from Census Operations.

B.—Index of Castes and Races found in Burma.

C.—Circulars, Instructions, and Specimens.

D.—Extracts from the Reports of local Officers.

APPENDIX A.

The Enumeration of the Tracts excluded from the Census Operations.

A reference to the Census Map No. II will show that large areas included in the province of Burma and the greater part of the Tributary Shan States are coloured blue. The areas thus distinguished, although they were excluded from the regular census operations, were during the dry weather of 1891 subjected to a rough enumeration conducted by the local officers and the native officials. In December 1889 the Government of India proposed to include the Native Feudatory States within the census operations, and the Chief Commissioner of Burma was asked if he thought it advisable to extend these operations to the whole area of Burma and of the Shan States. After consulting the Commissioners of the Northern and Central Divisions and the Superintendents of the Shan States, the Chief Commissioner replied that no regular census could be taken in certain areas within the province and that the Shan States must also necessarily be excepted.

These excluded tracts were—

(1) The State of Wunthò.
(2) The State of Baw in the Kyauksè district.
(3) The State of Momeik in the Ruby Mines district.
(4) The States of Kalè, Taungthut, and Kanti in the Upper Chindwin district.
(5) The Chin Hills in the Upper Chindwin and Pakôkku districts.
(6) The Kachin Hills in the Bhamo district.
(7) The Shan States.

But while a regular census was manifestly impossible both on political grounds as well as on account of the actual impracticability of taking a census, the officers who were consulted stated that a rough enumeration could be made by them during the dry season of 1891. The first proposal was that the enumerations of two years—1890 and 1891—should be taken and compared. The Census Commissioner considered that the results of one season's work would probably be of more value than a computation of the results obtained by two successive enumerations.

The petty State of Baw in the Kyauksè district was subsequently included by the Deputy Commissioner of Kyauksè within the regular synchronous census area. At first it was thought that Baw would have to be excluded, but the arrangements made in concert with the Deputy Commissioner worked so smoothly that no difficulty was experienced in extending the operations so as to include this petty State.

Various forms of village register were proposed. Of these Mr. George's registers were the most complete and Mr. Scott's the most useful for general purposes of administration. But the Census Commissioner was satisfied with the very simple village register proposed by Mr. Daly. A specimen of this village register will be found at the end of this appendix.

The results obtained unsuited for statistical returns.

The returns obtained by these registers do not pretend to absolute accuracy, and although no doubt many of them may be accepted as being fairly accurate, yet as they were not taken simultaneously, and as the returns vary greatly in value, any attempt to include them in our census returns would have destroyed the value of the other figures. Taken as being a rough representation of the actual population of the tracts, the returns of the excluded tracts are worthy of consideration, but for statistical purposes, such as for serving as a basis for deductions as to the dynamical forces at work, they are obviously unsuited. Accordingly, acting under the orders of the Census Commissioner, the returns of the excluded tracts have not been included in the Imperial Tables. I have therefore compiled the returns and prepared a special report, which is added as an appendix to the regular Census Report. For not only are the figures valuable as a record for comparison with future enumerations, but they fill up the blanks left in the regular census operations. Moreover, these returns have been accompanied by interesting monographs prepared by the officers under whose charge the enumerations were conducted.

Excluded Tracts in the Bhamo District.

Of all the districts in Burma, the Bhamo district was on the whole the most difficult. Here, to begin with, the area and boundaries of the district are as yet unknown, so that any systematic parcelling out of the area, a great part of which is still unexplored, was of course impossible. In the next place, the Deputy Commissioner had not, as in the case of the Upper Chindwin district, any responsible Chiefs to whom he could issue instructions. Lastly, the population of the district, even within a few miles of Bhamo itself, is a heterogeneous accumulation of hybrid races. Accordingly the Deputy Commissioner was obliged to abandon all idea of a census over the whole district and to content himself with confining the operations to the Bhamo, Sinkan, Shwegu, Mogaung townships, and a part of the Myitkyina. In order to compass even this restricted area special enumerators were enlisted in Rangoon and despatched to him. Under these circumstances the fact that the returns are, as accurate as they are, reflect credit on his management. As regards the excluded tracts, the returns collected are necessarily somewhat fragmentary. Indeed, their chief value is that they are accompanied by the very interesting monographs on the Kachins and Hpuns with which Mr. George has kindly furnished me. As statistics on which to base calculations or comparisons with the return of future enumerations their value is of course infinitesimal. There were altogether 533 villages enumerated. In these villages there were 8,251 houses, being on an average 15·4 houses in each village. Either the number of houses is understated or the majority of the villages are mere hamlets. The average number of inhabitants per house is 4·6, being below the average in Burma, which is 5·22. The majority of the inhabitants are Kachins, but any systematic classification was impossible. Nor could the return of occupation be filled in. For the rest Mr. George's monographs, which are here inserted, will give the latest and most authentic account of these people :—

Memorandum on the enumeration of the tribes inhabiting the Kachin hills, by E. C. S. George, Esq., c.s., Deputy Commissioner of the Bhamo district.

The only tracts in which a tolerably correct estimate both of the numbers of the houses and the population could be made were Nos. 15 and 16 (*a*) and (*b*), which were traversed by the Eastern Kachin column, the only column which had time to work patiently through the country.

In the case of the returns from the Lower Kaukkwè column—Tract 21 and Tracts 17, 18, and 20 (obtained from native information)—although the returns may be deemed reliable enough, so far as they go, as to numbers of the population, still, admittedly, it is possible there are villages situated in the tract which have not been included in the returns.

Tract 19 is partly in Bhamo and partly in Momeik, and there is at present no definite idea of which villages do or do not belong to one or other of the jurisdictions. Still as the tract was carefully examined by Mr. Saunders, I have included it in our returns as it gives a reliable basis for calculation.

Taking Tract 16 (*a*) and (*b*), we find that the average number of inhabitants to a house is for—

Marips	4·6 (*Vide* Summary).	
Lataungs	3·6	
Szis	4·2	
Marans	4·4	
Maru	5·5	
Kauri Lepai	4·2	
Lakhums	4·3	
Yawyins	2·6	
or generally		4·4

In Tract 19 it is—

Lakhums	4·4 = 4·4

The above areas are those in which we can fairly rely on the returns.

Taking the other Tracts 17, 18, 20, and 21, we find the averages as follows:

In Tract 17—

Hpunkans	4·4 = 4·4

In Tract 18—

Lataungs	4·0
Lakhums	4·4 = 4·2

In Tract 20—

Karas	5·54
Lataungs	5·5
Hpunkans	5·1
Marans	6·5
Lakhums	4·3 = 5·38

In Tract 21—

Kakus	3·6
Karas	6·49
Marans	3·8
Lakhums	5·3
Lataungs	4·45 = 4·9,

which is a coincidence remarkable enough to warrant the conclusion that in the lower portion of the country at any rate the average number of Kachins to a house lies between 4 and 5.

I must here express my deep regret at having been unable to obtain as yet any copy of a report by Lieutenant Eliott of the census of the Kachin hills through which the North-East Exploration column passed. This column's movements were leisurely, and Lieutenant Eliott doubtless has collected information which will be invaluable from a statistical point of view. Failing to obtain information from that quarter, I have submitted returns for the north-east frontier based on local and therefore not fully reliable information. Officers have assured me that the average number of Kachins to a house must be a great deal more than I have made out, and declare further north you get, the more crowded the houses become. Not having Lieutenant Eliott's notes on this point, I am unable to test the truth of this proposition, but from what I have myself seen, I should doubt whether finally much the same average will not be found to prevail in the Jade and Amber Mines tracts as down here nearer Bhamo. The sizes of the houses are always misleading.

The actual tested population of the various tribes is as follows:—

		Houses.	Population.	Average.
Marip	...	25	161	6·4
Kaku	...	81	295	3·6
Lasan	...	75	487	6·4
Kara Lepai	...	228	1,335	5·8
Kauri Lepai	...	621	2,635	4·2
Karwan	...	22	110	5·
Lataung	...	140	670	4·7
Yawyin	...	14	37	2·6
Szi	...	555	2,355	4·2
Hpunkan	...	87	402	4·6
Maran	...	313	1,465	4·6
Maru	...	20	110	5·5
Lakhum	...	1,268	5,577	4·3
Giving a total of	...	3,449	15,639 and average of 4·5 per house.	

The total estimated population (*vide* Summary) over all the tracts is—

Houses.	Population.
4,084	25,253

There is no means at present of estimating even approximately the total population of Kachindom. We are dealing at present with its fringe, where, in successive waves of encroachment, the Kachins have been working south along the high ridges on both sides of the Irrawaddy basin and gradually ousting and driving south the Shan and the Shan-Burman. The wave has now been checked, and subsequent tribes, who are crowded out of the ancestral nidus at the headwaters of the Irrawaddy, will have to come and settle down peaceably, if they care to do so, on the broad plains on each side of the main river which now lie untenanted. At present, like all mountaineers, the Kachins have a horror of the plains and but rarely will come down to settle.

As will be seen from the Summary, the Lakhums are the largest and most widely distributed tribe with which we have to deal. The Lepais, Lataungs, and Marans are not far behind them in strength and distribution. The Szis, Kauris, and Sadans are powerful tribes confined more or less to one or two main centres.

I would beg a reference to Annexure C of Lieutenant Eliott's Report No. 9, dated the 7th May 1891, to the address of the Chief Secretary to the Chief Commissioner. I deal with the origin of the various tribes in the accompanying memorandum, and will confine myself here to taking the main tribes individually as Lieutenant Eliott has done.

1. *Kara.*—A Lepai sub-tribe connected with the Singmas, who are supposed to be an offshoot of the Sadans. They are found in the ridge of hills running due south from the second defile and dividing the Shwegu and Mohlaing townships. They are also met with on the hills to the west of the defile and up the Lower Kaukkwè basin, where their ancestral enmity with the Kwans has hitherto kept the locality in a ferment.

2. *Kauri.*—An offshoot of the Lepai tribe, and tolerably large so far as tribes go. As explained by Lieutenant Eliott, they are confined to the tract embracing the main routes to China from Bhamo lying immediately south of the Tapin and to the east of Bhamo. The peculiar manner in which they are confined to this one tract, instead of being found in scattered portions like other tribes, is probably due to their having a distinct language of their own. They are related closely to the Szis, one of whose main habitats lies just to their south-east, the legend being that the ancestors of the two tribes, namely, Aūrātān and Maingtungla respectively, were brothers, the former being the elder, from whom the Szis are descended. On the death of Aūrātān, Maingtungla took his wife, according to Kachin custom, and had two sons—

> *N'tang*, from whom are descended the *Hpunkan* tribe, who curiously enough speak Kachin, and
>
> *N'tu*, from whom are descended the Numgyun and Wawkhyun tribes, found also in Chinese territory, speaking a dialect of Szis.

3. *Lakhum.*—A Lepai sub-tribe (and possibly, as Lieutenant Eliott states, a branch of the Sadans, though now distinct). They are found in small numbers on the upper reaches of the Nantabet to the east of the Talaw on the Upper Irrawaddy. As Lieutenant Eliott says: "They extend along the Chinese frontier some 20 miles north of the Tapin; "their most northerly village in this section is Munglum. They are likewise found in the

"hills to the east and south-east of Bhamo and along the right bank of the Shweli (*e.g.* "Chauk Taung.—E. C. S. G.), and also in the State of Momeik." Besides they occur in the Kaukkwè basin both in its upper and lower portions. They are, as Lieutenant Eliott rightly says, quite distinct from the 'Nhkum. They have been moving gradually south along the east of the Irrawaddy, and, as this process could not go on without friction with their neighbours, they have been always more or less engaged in hostilities. They began with fighting with the Lepais, who turned them out of a portion of the tract to the north of the Tapin, and they are still in an ill-disguised state of enmity with the Karas, who originally settled in the hills to the east of the Sinkan chaung, and whom they drove across to the latter's present resting-place in Tract No. 20 (*vide* map).

The use of the term "subdivision" by Lieutenant Eliott in this and other instances seems misleading. The names he gives are sometimes not true subdivisions at all, but names of various Sawbwas ruling portions of the same tribe, whose jurisdictions extend over local areas which may in many instances be confined to that of a single village of six or eight huts. According to an easy recognized custom, the name of the Sawbwa is applied to the local area, but the inhabitant of that local area is not always specially distinguished as being a member of a local clan, as Lieutenant Eliott's term would lead one to believe. The inhabitants of each local area look to their own Sawbwa as their sole head, just as a Highland man regarded his Chief, but they form in no sense a clan-family or subdivision, recognized as distinct from a neighbouring clan of the same major tribe or race, like the Campbells, Camerons, &c., of Scottish history.

Of course most, if not all, of the diversity of Kachin tribes rose from the custom described above. When a Sawbwa became very powerful, it became a matter of pride as well as self-interest for his villagers to identify themselves with him, and they thus in some instances adopted the name of his jurisdiction, *e.g.*, a branch of the Lataungs who are ruled by the Sana Sawbwa south of Lake Indawgyi. These might possibly be classed as a distinct subdivision as Sana Lataungs, but in some of the cases noted by Lieutenant Eliott, my enquiries tended to show that the designations had merely local application, and had not yet risen to the dignity of being the nomenclature of true subdivisions. Lieutenant Eliott himself remarks on the "tendency of the Kachins to disintegrate and reform themselves "into minor clans, which after a short time became independent of the parent branch."

4. *Lana.*—As Lieutenant Eliott says, "this is a branch of the Maran tribe. They are "found in the hills to the south of the Lakhum tribe and to the south-east of Bhamo." Unfortunately no census returns for this tribe are available. They cause much trouble by their frequent raids on caravans passing to and from the Shan States.

5. *Lashi* are not a pure Kachin tribe. They are found on our extreme frontier to the south of the Tapin on the borders of China. They have a distinct language of their own, and their customs differ slightly from those of other Kachins. This tribe wâs punished severely this last cold weather for having been engaged in the attack on Lieutenant Burton's camp. They are but a small tribe, probably comprising less than 500 souls.

6. *Lataung*, or *Lataw* as it is sometimes called, is one of the original parent Kachin tribes, and probably the most extensively distributed of all. Lieutenant Eliott describes their habits correctly enough. "Their original home is in the country between the two "rivers, about a week's hard marching north north-east from the confluence." The Lataung tribe is found most wonderfully spread over the country north of the upper defile of the Irrawaddy, namely, in the country from the Malika west to the Kumôn range, along both banks of the N'maika for some way up from the confluence, along the right bank of the Irrawaddy nearly as far south of the Myitkyina, west of this to the Shwedaunggyi hills, far to the south-west of the Indawgyi lake, and finally on the Chinese frontier just below the headwaters of the Molè. They also extend out of the Bhamo district into Momeik.

7. *Lepai.*—One of the original parent tribes from which have sprung the greatest number of distinct Kachin sub-tribes. The following are sub-tribes of the Lepais, many of which have by now become quite as, if not more important than, the parent stem :—

(1) Kara.
(2) Hpunkan.
(3) Szi.
(4) Kauri.
(5) Sadan.
(6) Singma.
(7) Lakhum.

The true Lepais are now found along the east of the Upper Irrawaddy opposite Maingna; in the country above the confluence between N'maika and Malika; in the tract north and north-east of Mogaung between the Nanti and Mogaung chaungs, including the hill tract of Shwedaunggyi, the headquarters of the once powerful Thama Sawbwa; the triangle enclosed by the lower portion of the Mogaung chaung, the Irrawaddy, and a line drawn from Mogaung to Myitkyina, on both sides of the third defile; the Jade and Amber Mines tracts, and the country between Mogaung and Indawgyi; while further south south-east of Bhamo we have them in the Hpunkan tract.

It was with this tribe that the revolutionary movement for the abolition of Sawbwas originated, which has within the last few years spread so extensively, and which will be noted in the accompanying memorandum.

8. *Makaungs.*—An insignificant branch of the Singma Karas. Lieutenant Eliott says: "They live to the south and south-east of Bhamo, also in the hills near the sources "of the Pumwai, which flows into the Nantabet from the north-east. They also have a few "villages in the hills west of Sinbo." A tribe of a similar name, being, however, a sub-tribe of the Marips, is said to exist in the Amber Mines tracts.

9. *Maran.*—Lieutenant Eliott describes their distribution well. "They are found all "along the frontier in scattered villages north of the sources of the Molè. They seem to "live a little to the west of the frontier line. * * * They are also found west of Sinbo and "in the Kaukkwè valley and to the west of the Malika. * * * The Marans are also found in "Momeik, Mohnyin (in Katha), and North Theinni."

It was simply owing to the assistance and protection of this tribe that Lieutenant Eliott was able to explore the tract lying east of the Upper Irrawaddy.

The Marans are also found to the west of the Sinkan chaung between Mohlaing and Shwegu. They have been generally friendly.

10. *Marips* are found mainly in the Jade and Amber Mines tracts, while they have small settlements near Lake Indawgyi. Elsewhere they have a few single villages scattered here and there, the Eastern Kachin column coming upon one to the east of Bhamo. "Their head Sawbwa is Kanmai, who lives at Keungnumpum, some 50 miles to "the west of the Upper Malika and north of the sources of the Mankaung or Mogaung river. "The chief Sawbwa in the Hukong valley is Kalungwa, who lives at Kalung village. In "the Jade Mines the leading Sawbwas are Kansi, Ningcha, and Lôn Kang, who rule the "country round. In authority, however, the latter come a good way below the Kanmai "and Kalung Sawbwas."

So far as we have had experience of them, they appear to be generally friendly, and the Kansi Sawbwa was of much assistance in the establishment of the Jade Mines post.

11. *Maru* are not a pure Kachin tribe and are somewhat looked down on. Where by contact with other tribes they have not got ashamed of the custom, they regard the dog as a delicacy. In appearance and dress they are like other Kachins, and are only distinguishable by their peculiar language. As to their distribution Lieutenant Eliott says: "They are "a very large tribe and are found scattered all along the frontier from Theinni in the far "south-east to the N'maika valley on the north, the latter place and the hills east of the "N'maika being their real home." But they do not render, intermixing freely with other tribes, and odd houses of "Marus" are not unfrequently "found in Kachin villages."

12. *'Nhkum.*—One of the original tribes. I have nothing to add to Lieutenant Eliott's description.

13. *Sadans.*—A Lepai sub-tribe with a branch termed Singma Sadans. They are found all along the frontier *to the north of the Tapin,* as far as the confluence, but are not found to the east and south-east of Bhamo. Lieutenant Eliott remarks they are met with in Theinni. The *Singmas* are mixed up with them, but are apparently confined, from Lieutenant Eliott's information, to the tract lying between Thenlôn on the Upper Molè and a line drawn east of Talaw.

14. *Sassun.*—For this Lieutenant Eliott is my only authority, to whose report I would refer you. Possibly by Sassun he means what have always been described to me as *Sassuns* (sometimes Chasan), a branch of the Lataung tribe said to live all round the Amber Mines.

15. *Szis or Ithis.*—A Lepai sub-tribe. For their origin see under head Karas. They have a distinct language; their main localities are—

(*a*) on the lower portion of the Nanyin valley and on both sides thereof;
(*b*) on the Chinese border in the direction of Maingmaw; also on the east of the Upper Irrawaddy.

Lieutenant Eliott speaks of them as a powerful tribe near the sources of the Molè and the Nantabet. They adopt both Chinese and Shan customs and dress where they abut on these races, and can generally make themselves understood in those languages as well as their own.

16. *Yawyins,* or *Lishaws* as they are called by the Chinese, are scattered along our extreme frontier to the north-east. They, too, have a language of their own. The men wear short drawers, while the women wear long coats. They are also remarkable for wearing large and cumbersome earrings and using bows and arrows.

The above are the principal Kachin tribes with whom we have to deal at present. A few others will be noted in the memorandum.

Besides the Kachins noted in the Summary, there were a few villages of Shans, Shan-Burmans, Shan-Chinese, and Talaings not included in the former census. These aggregate 620 houses, say, 2,500 people, which would make totals for all tracts noted in the map of 4,704 houses and 27,753 people respectively; averages per square mile of surface would be entirely misleading for the reasons already given, namely, that we cannot be sure we have got all the villages down. Taking Tracts 15 and 16 alone, we have an average per square mile of 22·3 and 19·3 respectively.

Summary.

Tribe.	Found in Tract No.	Number of villages.	Number of houses.	Population ascertained.	Average per tract per house.	Assumed average for each tribe per house.	Total estimated population.
1	2	3	4	5	6	7	8
Marip ...	1	4	38	...	...	...	...
	2	33	312	...	...	...	...
	3	18	185	...	...	...	...
	13	1	5	...	...	...	...
	16(*a*)	1	25	161	6·4	...	...
Total ...	...	57	565	161	6·4	5·5	3,107
Kaku ...	21	6	81	295	3·6	...	...
Total ...	...	6	81	295	3·6	...	295
Lasan	1	4	75	487	6·4	...	...
Total ...	...	4	75	487	6·4	...	487
Kara ...	14	3	52	...	...	...	...
	20	20	153	848	5·54	...	...
	21	4	75	487	6·49	...	...
Total ...	...	27	280	1,335	5·8	...	1,335
Kauri Lepai ...	16(*a*) & (*b*)	39	621	2,635	4·2	...	...
Total ...	...	39	621	2,635	4·2	...	2,435
Karwan Lepai ...	15	3	22	110	5	...	...
Total ...	...	3	22	110	5	...	110
Lepai ...	1	1	40	...	40·	4·5	...
	2	5	49	...	9·		...
	3	32	279	...	8·7		...
	5	3	24	...	8·		...
	7	8	52	...	6·5		...
	9	6	282	...	47·		...
	11	1	10	...	10·		...
	12	1	5	...	5·		...
	13	2	11	...	5·5		...
	14	2	12	...	6		...
Total ...	...	61	764	...	...	...	3,488
Singma Lepai	9	9	66	...	...	4·5	...
	7	3	36	...	...		
Total ...	...	12	102	...	...	...	459
Layang ...	2	1	4	...	...	4·5	...
Total ...	...	1	4	...	...	4·5	18
Lataung ...	4	10	132	...	...	4·7	...
	6	2	7	...	...		...
	7	1	12	...	...		...
	10	4	125	...	...		...
	11	4	66	...	...		...
	12	4	19	...	...		...
	14	2	9	...	...		...
	15	2	19	59	3·1		...
	16(*a*)	1	5	18	3·6		...
	18	4	17	68	4·		...
	20	18	79	436	5·5		...
	21	2	20	89	4·45		...
Total ...	...	54	510	670	4·7	4·7	2,397
Kwans ...	13	3	37	...	...	...	...
Total ...	...	3	37	...	...	5·5	203

Summary—continued.

Tribe.	Found in Tract No.	Number of villages.	Number of houses.	Population ascertained.	Average per tract per house.	Assumed average for each tribe per house.	Total estimated population.
1	2	3	4	5	6	7	8
Szis ...	5	8	101	...	...		...
	13	1	5	...	...		...
	15	2	58	256	4·4	4·2	...
	16(*a*) & (*b*)	12	497	2,099	4·2		...
	22	4	29	...	...		...
Total ...	...	27	690	2,355	4·2	...	3,098
Yawyins ...	16(*a*)	1	14	37	2·6	...	...
Total ...	...	1	14	37	2·6	...	37
Hpunkan ...	13	1	22	...	...		...
	17	10	69	309	4·4	4·6	...
	20	2	18	93	5·1		...
Total ...	...	13	109	402	4·6	...	501
Hpauren ...	13	1	4	...	...	...	...
Total ...	...	1	4	...	...	4	16
Tashi ...	13	1	12	...	...	4·5	...
Total ...	...	1	12	...	...	4·5	54
Neinsun ...	13	1	30	...	...	...	...
Total ...	...	1	30	...	...	4·5	135
Nanga ...	13	2	13	...	...	4·5	...
Total ...	...	2	13	...	...	4·5	58
Marans ...	6	2	17	...	...		...
	7	2	10	...	...		...
	8	7	105	...	...		...
	10	2	120	...	...		...
	11	4	105	...	...		...
	13	5	24	...	...	5	...
	14	2	22	...	...		...
	16(*a*)	4	256	1,143	4·4		...
	20	4	38	249	6·5		...
	21	2	19	73	3·8		...
	22	6	70	...	...		...
Total ...	...	40	786	1,465	4·6	5	3,930
Sadan ...	8	5	91	...	...	...	...
	11	14	778	...	...	...	...
	13	2	19	...	...	...	...
Total ...	...	21	888	...	...	4·5	3,696
Singma ...	9	5	174	...	...	...	...
	11	4	40	...	...	...	...
Total ...	...	9	214	...	...	...	963
Maru ...	10	1	20	...	...	...	...
	12	1	3	...	...	...	...
	16(*a*) & (*b*)	2	20	110	5·5	...	...
Total ...	...	4	43	110	5·5	...	110
'Nhkum ...	9	1	8	...	...	...	...
	13	2	11	...	...	...	...
Total ...	...	3	19	...	...	4·5	85

Summary—concluded.

Tribe.	Found in Tract No.	Number of villages.	Number of houses.	Population ascertained.	Average per tract per house.	Assumed average for each tribe per house.	Total estimated population.
1	2	3	4	5	6	7	8
Lakhum	10	8	216	...	...	4·3	...
	15	27	361	1,541	4·2		...
	16(*a*) & (*b*)	8	100	432	4·3		...
	18	38	591	2,604	4·4		...
	19	16	156	695	4·4		...
	20	2	18	79	4·3		...
	21	5	42	226	5·3		...
	22	8	94	...	...		...
Total ...	...	112	1,578	5,577	4·3	...	6,785
Shan ...	1	1	60	...	...	...	...
Shan-Burmans ...	2	1	424	...	...	...	...
Shan-Chinese	8	3	79	...	...	...	...
	9	2	32	...	...	...	...
	11	1	20	...	...	...	...
Talaing ...	18	1	5	38	...	...	...

Memorandum on the Kachins on our Frontier.

All tradition points to the headwaters of the Irrawaddy as the ancestral nidus from which the divers Kachin tribes have emerged. According to widely prevailing belief, their primal ancestor was one Shippawn-Ayawng, a descendant of the nats or spirits who lived on the hill called Majaw-Shingrā-pum (which, so far as I can make out, is equivalent to the "Delectable Mountains" of Bunyan), said to be the hill from which the Irrawaddy rises, the Malika on one face and the N'maikha on the other. Shippawn-Ayawng had still something of divine nature in him, and it was not till the time of his grandson, Wākyetwā, to whom the Kachins more immediately trace their descent, that man became mortal. Shippawn-Ayawng had many sons, of whom I have only been able to learn of the following:—

(1) Sānā-Tengsan, father of Wākyetwā.
(2) N'ting.
(3) Nang.
(4) N'jan Mājā.
(5) Makawng Li-ang.
(6) Karyeng.
(7) Malang.
(8) Pauk Khyeng.

From (1) are descended the *Chingpaws* or true Kachins hailing from the Kaku country (country of the river sources).

From the rest are derived various tribes, which are cognate with the Chingpaws and which by this time have become practically assimilated with them, isolated communities still lingering, however, here and there. They are now said to possess the same language as the true Chingpaws (Singpho of the Assamese frontier), and apparently have much the same customs. I have not been able, however, to personally come across any to institute more minute enquiries.

From (2) the *N'tings*, a colony of which is said to be at Sābya between Mālin on the Uru and the Nantein chaung. A house or two is found occasionally among the Marans.

From (3) the *Nangs*, a few of which are said to exist scattered among the Sadans to the east of the Upper Irrawaddy.

From (4) the *N'jan-Mājā*, said to be found on the road north from Myitkyina to Khampti and also up the Kaukkwè valley at Watu. Their women are said to wear sashes round their waists in place of cane-girdles and to tie their hair in a knot on top of the head without any other head-dress.

From (5) the *Makawng Li-angs*, a few scattered families of which occur among the Sadans. They are also said to have a colony at Saingtaung in the Amber Mines tract.

From (6) the *Karyeng* or *Kharyengs*, said to be met with in the territory of the Lepai Sawbwa of Thama. A large section are at Wudi, north of Moda in Katha district.

From (7) the *Malangs*, said to be found along the Upper Uru.

From (8) the *Pauk Khyeng* or *Bon Khying*, said to reside north of the confluence and to differ from other Kachins owing to a custom of shaving the head so as to leave a top-knot only.

The above is what I have received from native sources, which I have not been able to test. In the ensuing cold weather, when the columns are out, it may become possible to look up the localities indicated and discover what, if any, differences there are between these cognate tribes and the Kachins. The only thing certain about these tribes is that by now they are practically extinct, and only in very rare instances are they found as separate communities.

Passing from the above tribes, which the Kachins admit to be "Chingpaws," we find various other tribes which the Kachins regard as only indirectly connected with themselves (being, of course, descended from the common semi-divine ancestor; else, as a Kachin put it, "Where could they have come from?"), but different, in some cases widely, in manners, habits, and language. These are—

(1) The *Khangs*, said to live on the other side of the Chindwin beyond Bisa. Doubtless we may identify them with the *Chins*.

(2) *Kaphawks*, some of whom accompanied the *Khangs* across the Chindwin, while others remained behind to the east of Khampti (*i e.*, "Kantigyi").

(3) *Kaluns*, a branch of No. (2), but slightly differing from them. (2) and (3) intermarry.

(4) *Kŭmons* and (5) *Kŭmans*, to be found on the east of Khampti, the Kŭmons being nearer to the latter State. Woodthorpe refers to them as "Kunnungs," and describes them as "an extremely gentle, pleasant-looking people, small in stature, rather fair in "complexion, with their hair cut short in a fringe over the forehead. They had melodious "voices and pleasant smiles." He remarks that their language "to a certain extent re-"sembles Singpho, about 5 per cent. of the words being identical."

The Amber Mines pôngyi, who lately came down to Bhamo as an emissary of the Khampti Sawbwa, describes the Kŭmons as going about almost entirely naked, wearing only a breech clout attached to a string, while the women wear a narrow sort of kilt, kept in place by a rattan girdle. They crouch round fires to keep themselves warm at nights, with the result that their skins are scorched and large blisters are usually formed on their backs, chests, and arms.

(6) The *Tarens*, found on the west border of the Chinese State of Sanda. They wear clothes something after the Chinese style. They are also known by the name *Meungsa* or *Maingtha*.

They are a distinct tribe, having a language and customs of their own, and are renowned for the excellence of their das. They are said to be great travellers, and to be mostly itinerant merchants. During the cold weather they desert their villages and scatter over the adjacent countries, returning at the beginning of the rains.

Some of them are found near Khampti, and possibly Woodthorpe confuses them with the Kŭmons in describing the latter as experts in the manufacture of das. If the Amber Mines pôngyi is to be trusted, we could hardly expect the Kŭmons to excel in any manufacture.

Besides the above are three other tribes that hold a sort of midway position between the two sets of tribes, being neither as closely connected as the Malangs, &c., nor so distinct from the true Chingpaws as the Khangs, Kŭmons, &c. They are—

I.—The *Marus*, for a description of whom see my previous letter.

II.—The *Yawyins* or *Lishaws*, for a description of whom see my previous letter.

III.—The *Lashis*, by popular tradition one of the latest of the variations from the great Chingpaw family, being due to hybrid connection between a Chinaman and the daughter of a Maran Sawbwa.

Each of the above tribes has a language of its own, which serves to distinguish it from the other Kachins, and, in the case of the Yawyins, the customs apparently differ considerably.

The only two other branches of the Chingpaw stock that have a distinct language of their own are the Szis and the Kauris. They are each a branch of the Lepai tribes, tracing their descent to two brothers of the Sawbwa or ruling line of the Lepais called (*a*) Aŭrătăn and (*b*) Maingtungla respectively.

Aŭrătăn, according to the legend, lived upon the hills, while Maingtungla lived down on the plains near the river; wherefore naturally, living in the hot atmosphere below, the latter was thin and sallow and sickly, while Aŭrătăn was fat and jolly. Now Maingtungla had a pleasant-looking wife whom Aŭrătăn coveted in addition to his own, and it struck him that as Maingtungla could not have long to live, it would not be a bad plan for the two brothers to enter into an agreement that the survivor should take the other's wife (whence arose the Kachin custom of a brother taking a deceased brother's widow unto himself). This bond was entered into by the unsuspecting Maingtungla, but chance so brought it about that Aŭrătăn was the first to die, and Maingtungla therefore went up to pay his respects to the widow. The result was a child called N'tu, whom at first Maingtungla disowned, and as the widow persisted in saying it was his, he proceeded in Kachin style, with an armed band, to the widow's village with the intention of wiping the village out of existence. As he approached, however, the woman went out to meet him with offerings of Kachin beer, &c., and got him, in an unsuspecting moment, to hold the baby while she went to fetch more drink. She returned with a looking-glass, and Maingtungla seeing, from the reflection therein, how like his own face was to that of the child's, could no longer entertain doubts as to its paternity, and the scene closed with a general reconciliation and drunkenness.

To this N'tu the *Lunggyun* Kachins, who live on the ridge of hills beyond the Namwan chaung on the border-line between China and ourselves, trace their origin. Their language is a dialect of Szi, and they wear much the same dress as the Szis, except that the women are said to wear one single upper garment only, a jacket with long sleeves and no opening down the front or back. This is drawn over the head like a jersey.

From the offspring of the second fruit of the union noted above 'Ntaung, are descended the *Hpunkan Kachins* found on the hills to the south and south-east of Bhamo, who, however, speak ordinary Chingpaw and wear ordinary Kachin dress.

We now come to the origin of the Kachin tribes from Wākyetwā. According to the tradition, Wākyetwā had the following eight sons by his wife Măkawn-kăba Măchan:

	Son's name.		*Title.*	*Race.*
1.	Lăkan	...	Entitled Maripwa Kumgā Măkām	From whom sprung the Marips. A later branch being the Sassāns.
2.	Lănaw	...	Lā-ăn-Nawng-Litaw-wa Nung-lawn.	Latawngs.
3.	Lă Lā	...	Lā-an-lā-Lapaiwa laring ...	Lepai.
4.	Latu	...	Lā-an-tū-an-tū-wā-tū-khum ...	'Nhkum (some say Sassāns).
5.	Latāng	...	Lā-an-tang Mărān-wā-tāng-rān ...	Mărān.
6.	La Yaw	...	Lā-an-yaw-yawng-kun-yawng-tên.	'Nhkum.
7.	La Hka	...	Lā-ăn-ka Litaw-wā-Khāshu Khā-shā.	Latawngs.
8.	'Nkying	...	Lā-an-kying Mărān-wā-kying-nan.	Mărān.

Numbers 6, 7, and 8 are not of the true "Sawbwa Myo" or the Sawbwa stock, while from Nos. 1 to 5 we have the five original parent tribes:

(1) Marips,	(3) Lepai,
(2) Latawngs,	(4) 'Nhkum,

(5) Maran,

and perhaps a sixth, Sassān, which, however, Lieutenant Eliott classes as a later tribe, and, as he got his information from tribes lying nearer to the ancestral home than any I have been able to come across, most probably his information is more correct.

The descendants of the younger brothers, Nos. 6 to 8, mentioned above, are merged in the common folk of their respective tribes, and, although they claim relationship to the ruling line, and apparently can intermarry with it, they are never *admitted* to the post of ruler.

From one or other of the parent tribes all later tribes are offshoots, there being a constant tendency, as Lieutenant Eliott has observed, on the part of the Kachins to disintegrate and "reform themselves into minor clans, which, after a short time, become independent of the parent stock." This disintegration was in past times due, no doubt, chiefly to the natural compulsion to emigrate and seek fresh fields imposed on a growing community by the excess of population on a soil which, worked as they work it, cannot be regarded as very productive. It became the custom, on the death of a Sawbwa, for the youngest son to stay behind, assume the Sawbwaship, and rule in the original homestead; while the elder brothers set out with such following as they could muster and founded fresh settlements which, if they were successful, in time came to be distinct tribes, named after their own founder. Thus from the *Lepais* we have the sub-tribes:

Kără,	Lakhum,	Szi,
Kauri,	Sadôn,	Krawn,

which are recognized as regular tribes, and also a host of minor distinctive appellations struggling to be recognized as the name of true subdivisions, until finally we find Sawbwas ruling over four or five huts, whose inhabitants, for the time being, call themselves by the local appellation of that particular area (which is usually the same as the title of the Sawbwa). These pretensions to be a true sub-tribe or subdivision of a sub-tribe cannot be entertained, otherwise there would be nearly as many tribes as there are villages, and the Kachins themselves, when asked by a stranger who they are, usually give the name of the major and well-recognized tribe or sub-tribe first, and afterwards, if questioned further, give the local distinctive appellation. Materials are still being collected for an authoritative table of tribes, sub-tribes, and subdivisions of sub-tribes, or what may be properly recognized as such; but meanwhile the tribes and sub-tribes given above may be regarded as entitled to the distinction by general consent, and they embrace all the others. Generally and broadly the Kachins divide themselves into two great divisions, the *Kakus*, *i.e.*, Kachins of the river sources, and the Zinpyaw (or Jānpraw) or eastern Kachins, including generally all Kachins to the south of the confluence, and who are found of course in the greatest numbers to the east of the Irrawaddy, distinguished from each other by dress and dialectic differences.

Generally speaking the *Kakus* wear a narrow turban gaungbaung wound round their head, but not concealing completely the top knot of hair, a coat with long sleeves generally dyed with indigo, and without embroidery, and a striped oblong piece of cloth, just about the size of an ordinary bath-towel, which they pass round the waist and secure in front by a twist. They sometimes gird themselves with a narrow cane belt to which are strung a double row of cowries (Shi wan). They also wear two or three thin black cane rings just below the knee, but this is not as a charm, but merely to set the leg off.

The Kaku women are said to wear a white or parti-coloured narrow gaungbaung, which they wear like an ordinary Burman wears his. They wear an under-garment like a jersey with short sleeves (at times they wear but this alone), and over that they wear a coat open down the middle in front, reaching below the waist, with long sleeves, having the cuffs ornamented with cowries, &c. They wear the cowrie girdle noted above, and, as a skirt, an oblong piece of cloth a bit longer than the men's, with a narrower fringe of embroidery at the ends than is customary among the Zinpyaws, which they secure with a twist, so that the opening is towards the left side. They wear no cane rings whatever.

Among the Zinpyaws, on the other hand, the women wear an enormous tall head-dress of folded cloth, reminding one of the tall hat of the Parsis, and also short jackets, barely reaching the waist, and entirely sleeveless. As well as the kinds of jackets noted above, they wear girdles of many folds of thin cane twisted round the waist, as also a few rings below the knees like the men, while their skirts are always worn so as to have the opening to the right. Through the lobes of their ears they thrust long tubes of silver (*Lakan*) with shreds of coloured cloth thrust through, while from the upper portion of the ear descend *litsuns* or lappets of embroidered cloth with small tassels of beads after this shape.*

*

Round their necks, in the case of some tribes like the Kauris, they wear numerous necklaces of small beads called *kăgyi*, while among all the tribes the giri or torque of silver, among such as can afford it, seems universal.

Among the men of the Zinpyaws there is much diversity as to dress, tribes adopting indifferently the dress of Shans or Chinese according as they come in contact with these races. Wide Shan trousers and large round turbans, like those of the Shan-Chinese, are quite common, while there is much diversity in coats—from the long dressing-gown sort of coat of the Yawyin, to the ordinary Burmese coat of white long-cloth found in the hills near Bhamo.

Taken generally, the Kachin is a short man, averaging about 5 feet 4, while the woman averages 3 or 4 inches less. He is by no means as well formed as a Burman, and rarely looks muscular. The number of types met with is bewildering. In a single village one comes across a man who, if he only had short curly hair and rounder eyes, might be taken for a Negro, while next to him is a fair-skinned youth who, if only dressed differently, might, so far as could be guessed from his features, be an inhabitant of Italy. The shades of colour run to everything from almost pure black to a light shade of brunette, though, of course, by far the most prevalent tint is a dirty brown. Anderson, speaking, though of course only of the Kachins near Bhamo, distinguishes two types: "one with a fine "outline of features recalling the womanly features of the Kacharies and Lepchas of Sikkim. "In it the oblique eye is very strongly marked, and the face is a longish, rather compressed, "oval, with pointed chin, aquiline nose, and prominent molars;" while the other, "probably "the true Chinpaw, presents a short round face, with low forehead and very prominent mo-"lars. The ugliness of the slightly oblique eyes, separated by a wide space, the broad nose, "thick protruding lips, and a broad square chin, is only redeemed by a good-humoured ex-"pression. The hair and eyes are usually a dark shade of brown and the complexion is a "dirty buff." The prevailing feature among all the Kachins is the oblique eye and a tendency to high cheek bones, but the nose is not consistent, ranging from aquiline, as noted by Anderson, to a squat blotch on the face. Taken altogether, there can be but little doubt of the Tartar origin of the Kachins. Their traditions point to their ancestral home in a direction south of the desert of Gobi, and their movements have always been south and south-west from the north.

The diversity of the complexion and type, which prevails even in tracts where Shan and Burmese influence could not be felt, seems to me only accountable by the theory of admixture with aboriginal races whom the Kachins supplanted and engulfed in successive waves of migration, and whose fast-disappearing remnants may possibly, when we have fuller knowledge, be identified in the Kŭmons, Malangs, Tarens, &c., mentioned before. To take Dr. Anderson's view that this is due to an admixture of Shan and Burman blood would not explain—

(1) how the diversity is found far up the Irrawaddy;

(2) how the aquiline nose was acquired, neither Shan nor Burman possessing adjuncts of that sort;

nor would it be consistent with the fact that fusion of these races is historically incorrect. From time out of mind the Kachins and Shans have been at constant enmity, and the number of hybrid connections that have ever occurred are so infinitely small in number that they could not have perpetuated a general and widespread type. Unions of Kachins and Chinese are indeed known. Witness the Lashi tribe (see my notes on the

Kachin census), and possibly also the Yawyins or Lishaws (but of these I have no definite information as to origin or connection with Chinese). On the other hand, the Burman is comparatively a new-comer to these parts, the Burmese subjugation of the Shan kingdoms originally existing here being of quite recent date, and although the Burman element has modified to some extent the original pure Shan element prevailing, I can learn of no instances of hybrid connections between Burmese and Kachins.

The theory thrown out is merely a theory, and, in our present state of knowledge, I am unable to suggest who the original tribes were or whence they came. Anderson speaks of the Kacharies and Lepchas of Sikkim as being somewhat alike to the type first noted by him. Not having any books to refer to in this out-of-the-way spot, I am unable to decide whether it would be reasonable to hazard the theory that the mountaineers of Sikkim or part of them originally tenanted the hills now occupied by the Kachins.

The names of the tribes, as above explained, are usually derived from those of the Sawbwas, and do not appear to have, so far as I can learn, any signification. I can find no trace of a totem.

Birth, &c.

Customs.—When a child is about to be born, all friends and neighbours are assembled and two pots of Kachin beer are prepared, one of which is meant for the general company and partaken of by all at birth, while the other is set aside and called after the name of the child, and drunk only after birth. No young man may partake of this latter, otherwise he will always be unlucky in any pursuit; but the aged of either sex; women and children are not debarred. At the instant of birth the *accoucheuse* attending immediately says, "this child is named so-and-so." If she does not do this, some malignant nat or spirit will give the child a name first and so cause it to pine away and die. If the *accouchement* was successful, there is general drinking and a feast, and the happy father gets chaffed. If, however, there is much labour, then it is evident nats are at work, and a Tumsa (whose duties will be described below) is called into requisition. He, stopping at another house in the village, consults the bamboos (Chippawt) for the purpose of discovering whether it is the house-nat who is averse, or whether a jungle-nat has come and driven the guardian nat away. These jungle-nats are termed "Sawn," being the spirits of those who have died in childbed or by violent deaths, and they naturally wish for companions, hence enter the house and try to seize the woman and child. If the bamboo declares that it is the house-nat who is angry, he is propitiated by offerings of spirits or by sacrifice in the ordinary manner. If, however, it appears that a Sawn (*Anglice*, Boojum) has taken possession, then it becomes time for stern measures. Guns are fired off all round the house and along the paths leading into the village, arrows are shot along under the house, das and torches are brandished over the body of the woman, and, finally, old rags, chillies, and other materials likely to produce a sufficiently noisome smell are piled under the raised flooring and set fire to, thereby scaring away any but the most obstinate and wrong-headed spirits.

The birth having satisfactorily taken place, the neighbours make little presents of dried fish, &c., and drink to the health of the parents. Within a day or two afterwards the birth of the child is notified to the house-nats, and it is commended to their protection by the Tumsa, who decides what are the suitable offerings or sacrifice for the occasion.

For three days after birth the mother may not leave the house, but she is not prevented from conversing with any one she chooses. On the morning of the fourth day, very early, the woman goes out with some elderly dame from the village and proceeds to the place whence they usually obtain water. The *chaperon* takes a spear with her. On coming near the spring or well, she casts the spear in that direction and says, "Avaunt all evil spirits!" This is to frighten off any that cherish designs of carrying off the woman or her child. After the casting of the spear, the woman bathes and washes her clothes in safety and thereafter is free to do as she likes.

During pregnancy the woman must take no honey in any shape or form, or eat porcupine flesh, the reason given being that these are likely to cause miscarriage. Otherwise no restriction is put on her food.

There do not appear to be any traces of "the couvade" nor of a suspected subtle connection between the male parent and the offspring, which in other races is shown by restrictions being put on the father's diet, &c. Indeed, relationship is more readily recognized through the female line for reasons stated below.

Naming.

Among the Kachins all personal, or, as they may be termed, Christian names are fixed and used in regular rotation thus:—

The 1st male child born is always called ... 'N Kam.
The 2nd male child born is always called ... 'N Nawng.
The 3rd male child born is always called ... 'N La.
The 4th male child born is always called ... 'N Tu.
The 5th male child born is always called ... 'N Tan.
The 6th male child born is always called ... 'N Yaw.
The 7th male child born is always called ... 'N Hka.
The 8th male child born is always called ... 'N Hkying.

Two other prefixes are common, Mā and Lā for males. Thus the name 'N Kam can also be used as Mā Kam or Lā Kam. It will be noticed that the order follows that of the sons of the legendary Wākyetwā. The names of the females run as follows:—

1st female child born	'N Kaw.
2nd female child born	'N Lu.
3rd female child born	'N Roi.
4th female child born	'N Htu.
5th female child born	'N Kai.
6th female child born	'N Kha.
7th female child born	'N Pri.
8th female child born	'N Yūn.
9th female child born	'N Khying.
10th female child born	'N Nang.
11th female child born	Khying Nang.
12th female child born	Khying Tang.

In the place of prefix 'N, Mā can also be used, thus 'N Kaw or Mā Kaw indifferently; the prefix Lā, however, is peculiar to males.

The above are the ordinary and most commonly used names, but sometimes a few other appellations may be used in exchange. Thus instead of naming the first male infant Mā Kam, he can also be called Kum Rawng or 'N Gam, while for the children of the Sawbwa or ruling line honorific appellations are used thus:—

'N Kam becomes any of these ...	Sau Kam. Sau Ri (among the Lepai). Sau Ing (Lataungs). Sau Sĕng (Lepais, Marans, and Szis). Sau Naw. Jā Lī or Jāle Kam. Kum Saing. Kum Jā Kam.
So 'N Naw becomes ...	Sin Wa Naw. Kumganaw. Sau-awn. An Nawng. Sau Lawn.
'N La becomes ...	Jālā. Lā Ring (Lepai). Sauk 'Nwē La. Jā Yit.
'N Tu becomes ...	Jā Tu. Sau Tu. Sau Hlang.
'N Tan becomes ...	Awrā Awrātan. Sau Tan.
'N Yaw becomes ...	Sau Yaw.

Sau is equivalent to Sawbwa. Jā means gold, and is used similarly to "Shwe" in Burmese. Among the females—

'N Kaw becomes ...	Nang Mun, Ja Taung, Nang Seng,
'N Roi becomes ...	Nang Roi,
'N Htu becomes ...	Nang Hkyeng, Nang Htu,

Nang being an honorific particle. Besides the Christian names, we have in the case of the common folk a large number of family appellations, *e.g.*, we get—

Surnames among the Lakhums ...	(1) M'Bwi. (2) Laban. (3) Paw Sa. (4) Hpaw Tan. (5) 'N Taw. (6) 'N Tap, &c.
Among the Szis ...	(1) Chumlūt. (2) Lăhang. (3) Mălang. (4) Hpau Yu. (5) Hpau Yan. (6) Mi Tun, &c.

These surnames are used before the Christian names; thus the first son of a family of Chumlūt is called Chumlūt Kam, the second son Chumlūt Nawng, and so on.

What, however, is most curious is that, all having the same surname, whether they belong to the same or different tribes, regard themselves as being of one blood and do not intermarry. Thus a Maran Chumlūt cannot take a wife from the Szis Chumlūts. This is interesting as showing that these family distinctions must necessarily be far older than the tribal distinctions, but so far I have been unable to get any account of their origin. Another significant fact is that all Sawbwas, no matter of what tribe, are regarded as of one family and have no surnames, being distinguished from each other by local distinctive appellations. The first question Kachin strangers ask each other is, "Are you a Du Wā, *i.e.*, one of the Sawbwa line, or a commoner." It is customary for those of the Sawbwa family to contract alliances within their own family, but intermarriage with commoners is permitted, the offspring in each case belonging to the father's family. The reason why the people of the same family are found among divers tribes is because, as pointed out in my previous notes on the Kachin census, tribal distinctions are those properly of local area or rather political subordination than of blood. A Szi Chimlūt settling in a Maran Sawbwa's territory and paying dues to the Maran Sawbwa, becomes a Maran, and his children become so too. How or why it is that of the many families in the original Tartar horde composed of the ancestors of the Kachins, one family should have thus risen and arrogated to itself all ruling power, is still an undiscovered passage in Kachin history. The legend of Wākyetwā seems to me to point to a common tendency on the part of a ruling family, which, having raised itself to power by force or fraud, is only too glad to add to the many factors of its prestige the influence of superstition.

In making the remarks just preceding, I am free to confess I do not feel quite certain of my foundation. The Kachins down here do not profess to know, or will not declare if they do know, the origin of the various families, and it might possibly happen that, with further knowledge, the suggestion of one family rising over the rest by its own exertions may appear ridiculous; but, so far as our information goes at present, I think it is reasonably warranted by the facts that—

(1) The *Du Was* are regarded as a separate family from the rest of the commoners.

(2) That families of the same name, regarding themselves as of one blood, exist in different tribes, thus showing that family distinction preceded tribal distinction. The distinction could not have risen after the formation of the tribes, because children always take their father's family name, and therefore no family would ever have been found outside the tribe in which (assuming the latter to have been consolidated and differentiated first) it happened to be at the time of such consolidation.

(3) That widely differing types are found in one and the same tribe, showing a blood relationship among all its members to be unlikely.

Taking from (2) and (3) the distinction of families as primal, and that of tribes secondary, it is a fair inference that it has not happened that in each *separate* tribe the coalition of two or three of its own most powerful families, or that even a single powerful family, has produced a ruling hereditary family. If this were so, the ruling hereditary family of one tribe would not necessarily regard the ruling hereditary family of another tribe as of one blood, which apparently is done at present. The ruling hereditary family must have been in power before the formation of the tribes.

No children are killed at birth; indeed, it is rare to see a large family of children springing from the same couple, owing to the natural difficulty, due to their savage surroundings, of even rearing to maturity those that are born. Every additional hand is so much gain to the family, and there would be no object, from a Kachin point of view, in thus throwing uselessly away a valuable commodity. At the worst, the parent can always sell a useless child as a slave and thus make something out of him.

When the parents belong to different tribes, the children take the name of the father's tribe. This is so even in the case of ningkhis or illegitimate children, the fruit of the licensed intercourse before marriage.

Adoption can usually only take place in the same tribe. There is no restriction as to the age of the adopted child, but the adopted child still retains its own family surname. No particular ceremony is necessary, the adopting parents simply holding a feast (which need not take place at the time of adoption, but can be delayed till the family get in funds), and then, in the presence of elders, declare their intention. The adopted child resides with its adoptive parents, and shares with the other heirs at the former's decease.

Marriage.

A man may not marry a woman of the same surname. It seems to be a general rule that a man should marry a first cousin on the female side, *i.e.*, daughter of a mother's brother. He may not, however, marry his father's sister's child, who is regarded as closely related, blood connection being preferably traced through the female. The rule, however, seems much relaxed among the

"Janpyaw" Kachins, where it is not compulsory; but I have been told that higher north, if there is a marriageable first cousin whom a man out of perversity does not want to marry, he can marry elsewhere only after paying a fine to the injured parents of the damsel. I say injured parents, as it is they who lose in not getting her price from the husband.

The forbidden degrees of consanguinity are:—

(1) Parents and grand-parents.
(2) Children and grandchildren.
(3) Father's sister's child.
(4) Father's brother's child (because of same name).
(5) Mother's sister's child.
(6) Uncle's child.
(7) Aunt's child.

Among the Szis (I am not sure about other tribes) there is an arrangement whereby a family is, so to speak, parent-in-law to another family generally and gives females only to the members of the latter family. The families being thus regarded as connections, it is not competent for the first family to demand females in marriage from the second family, so they have to get theirs from some other one. There appears to be a well recognized series of families to which each family either gives or from which it takes females in marriage.

Thus the following families:—

Mălang,	Mislū,
Hpau Yan,	Taw Shi,
Lăban,	Sinhang,

may take females of the family of Chumlūts, but the Chumlūt family has to go for its consorts to other families, *e.g.*,—

Num Taw.	Hpanyu.
Lŭmaw.	Jang Maw.
Tummaw.	Hpu Kawn.

The only restraining influence compelling adherence to these rules is popular opinion. No particular punishment seems to be inflicted for breach of these sexual rules. Polyandry does not exist, but polygamy is permissible. For a man, however, to take more than two wives is rare; sometimes, however, he cannot help himself. Successive brothers are supposed to take unto themselves deceased elder brother's widows. Occasionally, when the working of this rule would be a hardship from giving one man a plethora of females, it is permissible to make an arrangement for a still younger brother or even a stranger to take the widow. The widow has to be taken care of and fed by her husband's family even if none of them will act the part of the husband by her. If they do not, she returns to her own household, and then this constitutes a "debt," which has to be liquidated in blood or money. The reason given for permitting polygamy is that thereby barrenness is provided against, but, although permissible, it is not always practised, monogamy being said to be fairly prevalent.

As Anderson says: "The ceremony of marriage, besides the religious rites, combines "the idea of purchase from the parents with that of abduction so frequently found to under-"lie the nuptial rites of widely separated races. An essential preliminary is to get the "diviner to predict the general fortune of the intended bride. Some article of her dress or "ornaments is procured and handed to the seer, who, we may suppose, being thereby "brought *en rapport* with her, proceeds to consult omens and predict her destiny." After that there appear to be two forms, one where the abduction of the bride is nominal and the preliminaries and ceremonies adjusted with formality; this is usually done among the Sawbwas and more wealthy or influential households; but the other form, where the abduction is real, is usual among the common people. To take this first.

The Tumsa's verdict being favourable, the husband sends some of his friends to the house of a lugyi or respectable man in the village where his intended resides. This lugyi is termed "Chang Tung." The emissaries inform the "Chang Tung" whom they wish to carry off, and display the presents which the intending husband has sent. There is a more or less recognized scale of presents due according to social standing of the damsel in each case, and the "Chang Tung" goes by it. If he considers the present insufficient, he mentions what is still required. The matter is discussed and the exact presents are finally fixed, agreements being made to make up deficiencies at the first opportunity. By the "Chang Tung's" connivance the girl is decoyed to his house and seized and carried off. This usually occurs at night. Next morning the "Chang Tung" goes over to the parents and informs them of what has happened and displays the presents. As a rule, they, being on the recognized scale, are accepted. Occasionally, however, the parents go in pursuit, and, so long as the religious marriage ceremony has not been performed, and the parties are not man and wife, they can take the girl back. If, however, the religious ceremonies have been gone through, they are too late and must acquiesce.

The religious and other ceremonies performed in case the girl is not recaptured are similar to those used in the more regular or elaborate form of marriage as common among people of high respectability, and may be more fully considered in conjunction therewith.

The proposer sends two messengers bearing Kachin beer and a piece of clothing as presents to make a formal proposal. These go first to the house of a Chang Tung (see above) and by him are introduced to the parents. The amount of dowry is discussed and agreed to, and then the neighbours are summoned and drinks are served round. The girl herself is in no way consulted, being bound by her parents' wishes. This constitutes the betrothal. There is no fixed time necessary to elapse before the marriage ceremony takes place. At that period the groom remains in his house and sends his friends, male and female, in any number, over to the bride's village with the presents agreed on. They go first to the Chang Tung's house and then to the parents' house, where the bride is decked with silver torques (giri) and clothes, with as many silver ornaments as possible (kumpraw palawng). A Tumsa is present and proceeds to divine which two women it would be best to send as bridesmaids. These being selected, each pick up a "nauklwè" (basket carried over the back by a sort of yoke round the neck) in which are clothes, a couple of spears, and a da or two given by the parents and intended to start the couple in house-keeping. Other articles of housewifery, such as cooking-pots, &c., are sent later on; then the bride starts off, attended by her bridesmaids (each carrying one of the nauklwès) and as many other people as the family circumstances permit of, while the parents remain behind. On arrival at the groom's village, the bride is usually conducted to the house of the original messenger or go-between (likyaw); meanwhile the Tumsa has been at work, offering sacrifices to secure a propitious moment, and, when he states all is ready, the bride is brought out and made to sit near the groom's house. Then to quote Anderson: "The Tumsa "arranges bunches of fresh grass pressed down with bamboos at regular intervals so as to "form a carpet between the company (where the bride is) and the bridegroom's house. "The household nats are then invoked and a libation of sheroo and water poured out."

(*Note.*—I have *not* heard of libations ever being poured out. The liquor is presented to the nats in hollow bamboos, which are held before or tied to the shrine, but the liquor is not poured out at all, and usually taken back after an interval and drunk.)

"Fowls, &c. (which means usually pigs), are then killed and their blood is sprinkled on "the grass-path (and also on the bride), over which the bride and her attendants (the two "women with nauklwès only) pass to the house and offer boiled eggs, ginger, and dried fish "to the household deities. This concludes the ceremony, in which the bridegroom takes no "part." He does not even talk to the bride then, she usually going straight into the groom's parents' room till the time of the evening meal, when she is brought out and husband and wife are made to feed each other with a few mouthfuls before the assembled company. "The "marriage feast ends, like all their festivities, in great drunkenness, disorder, and often in a "fight." As a rule, cohabitation does not take place for some days after the marriage, the only reason given being that the parties are ashamed. In some cases, where one or either of the parties is young, cohabitation is delayed indefinitely, it happening often that girls of 10 or 12 are abducted, the intending husband waiting for them to come to a marriageable age before consummation. The bride is not veiled. In cases where the abduction has taken place against the wish of the parents, it is permissible for friends of the intending husband to perform the part of the bridesmaids noted above. A widow, as stated, is usually taken by her husband's brothers. She is not a free agent in choice, and can only marry again outside her husband's household with their consent. Before marriage the young people are allowed to consort as they please. In villages to the north there are always two or three little "bachelors' huts" (dūm 'nta) whereunto any maiden can retire with the man of her choice. If they do not care for each other, they part, and it is no one else's business, each party being free to take up with any one else. If they care for each other sufficiently, they marry. The result is stated to be that unchastity after marriage is practically unknown. In case, however, a child is the result of the temporary union, it is usual to arrange for the *accouchement* to take place in the man's house, and the man has to kill a bullock and pigs to appease the nats of the damsel's house. In addition, he has to pay a fine to the parents of a spear, a gong, a da, and some pieces of clothing, or else marry her; otherwise the parents have a "debt" against him. On payment of the above fine, the man can take or leave the child just as he prefers. Subsequent marriage, however, legitimizes the *ningkyi* or bastard.

Disease.

In case of mild forms of sickness accompanied by not much suffering simple herbal remedies are adopted, but there is no regular profession of medicine, most elders of the village having their own recipes. Where sickness, however, is dangerous or accompanied by pain, then it is ascribed to the effect of a nat or spirit biting the person, who has to be propitiated by offering. The Tumsa is called in, and by his aid the particular nat who is the cause of the illness is discovered and presented with eggs, spirit, fish, or the sacrifice of a buffalo, fowl, or pig, according to the state of the case.

The cause or origin of death is not so clear. The following account has been given me by a Szi from the south-east of Bhamo. Originally, when all men were immortal, a very aged man named A-pauk-kyit-lôk (in the Szi tongue) lived at Majaw Shingra Pum (see above). Nine times had he grown old, lost his teeth, and become grey-headed, and nine times had he become mysteriously rejuvenated, as was the natural state of things in that golden age. He could not die. In this green old age he went out one day to fish and caught a *sĕkhai* (probably a kind of squirrel), which having happened to be asleep on the branch of a tree, had fallen into the water and so got captured. The sĕkhai was put into a big bamboo basket and covered up with clothes while the old man hid himself. The neighbours were taken in by the hoax, and the rumour went round that the old man was dead. Now in the sun there lived the spirit of man termed "sumri," which is the all-pervading life essence, without which man would die. This "sumri" was in the custody of the "Lord of the Sun" (the sun being regarded as a living embodiment). The Lord of the Sun being informed of the occurrence, consulted the "sumri," but he found it in the same state as before—the idea of the "sumri" being that of a nerve centre from which threads of life spread out to each single individual, and, until such thread is snapped or cut, life must and does exist in the individual. The Lord of the Sun discovering the old man's connection with the life-centre still intact, thought that he was being imposed on, so sent several messengers, as if on pretence of dancing at the funeral, but really to enquire. They went to dance, but all they could see was a bundle of clothes enwrapping a form in a wicker basket. It apparently not being permissible to have a free inspection of the alleged corpse, the messengers had recourse to stratagem, and, covering their feet with a composition of honey to make them sticky, they contrived, while dancing round the basket, to touch the clothes with their feet and gradually draw them enough to one side to discover the fraud. They thereon informed the "Lord of the Sun," who in anger cut off A-pauk-kyit-lôk's connection. The latter thereon fell sick. He sent for a Tumsa, and on the messengers going, their path was crossed both by a jungle cat and otter, which were both excellent omens, but in spite of sacrifice and all that could be done, A-pauk-kyit-lôk's folly "opened the door" (as the Kachin put it) for death to enter the world. I doubt, however, so far as my little experience goes, whether the above is a true bit of Kachin mythology. It seems to show traces of Shan and possibly Chinese influence. Elsewhere I have always met with ignorance, not merely of the future nature of the state after death, but of the causes or reason of death. All tales emanating from tribes on the east and south-east frontier of Bhamo must necessarily be looked on with a certain amount of suspicion, and I have had no opportunity of going to the far north to the fountain head of Kachin legendary lore.

Death.

As to the ceremonies that take place at death I cannot do better than quote Anderson, who doubtless had been present at a funeral. "When a Kakhyen (Kachin) dies, the news "is announced by the discharge of matchlocks. This is a signal for all to repair to the house "of death. Some cut bamboos and timber for the coffin, others prepare for the funeral "rites. A circle of bamboos is driven into the ground slanting outwards, so that the "upper circle is much wider than the base. (This is termed kăroi.) To each a small flag "is fastened; grass is placed between this circle and the house, and the Tumsa scatters "grass (nām—long grass) over the bamboos and pours a libation of sheroo (*i.e.*, Chiru—"Kachin spirit)."

Instead of pouring the libation, however, it would appear that liquor is put into a bamboo and offered to the deceased by the bamboo being placed with the spear, bag, and relics of the deceased which are hung up near the kăroi.

"A hog is then slaughtered and the flesh cooked and distributed, the skull being fixed "on one of the bamboos. The coffin (tū-ū) is made of the hollow trunk of a large tree "which the men fell with their das. Just before it falls a fowl is killed by being dashed "against the tottering stem."

The object of this, as explained to me, is to induce the spirit of the departed, by the sacrifice, to make the tree fall fairly so as to be easily split to make the coffin—it being the custom to split the trunk, hollow the inside for the coffin, and use the split pieces as coffin and lid, thereby ensuring that the junction of the two shall be even.

"The body is washed by men or matrons according to sex, and dressed in new clothes. "Some of the pork, boiled rice, and sheroo are placed before it, and a piece of silver is "inserted in the mouth to pay ferry dues over the streams the spirit may have to cross. "It is then coffined and borne to the grave amidst the discharge of firearms. The grave "is about 3 feet deep, and three pieces of wood are laid to support the coffin, which is "covered with branches of trees before the earth is filled in. The old clothes of the de-"ceased are laid on the mound and sheroo is poured on it, the rest being drunk by the "friends around it. In returning, the mourners strew ground-rice along the path, and, when "near the village, they cleanse their legs and arms with fresh leaves. Eating and drinking "wind up the day. Next morning an offering of a hog and sheroo is made to the spirit "of the dead man, and a feast and dance are held till late at night and resumed in the "morning. A formal sacrifice of a buffalo in honour of the household nats then takes "place, and the Tumsa breaks down the bamboo fence, after which the final death dance "successfully drives forth the spirit, which is believed to have been still lingering round its "former dwelling. In the afternoon a trench is dug round the grave and the conical cover "already described is erected, the skulls of the hog and buffalo being affixed to the post."

It must be remembered that the above description applies solely to a funeral among the Kauri Lepais, a tribe, as already pointed out, somewhat distinct, both in curious confinement to one particular locality and in language and customs, to the bulk of true Kachins.

It does not appear to be necessary that the burial and funeral ceremonies should at all be consecutive in point of time. Should a man die at a distance from his village, should it be impossible to collect all friends and relations in time, or, again, should the family finances be too low at the time to provide a sufficiently magnificent "wake," it is quite permissible for the body to be buried at once and without ceremony. An ordinary man can be buried lying in any direction. Although there are recognized burial-grounds, their use is not compulsory, and his relatives can bury a man where they please. In a Kachin burial-ground it is not usual, except in the case of people bearing the same family name, to have the graves as near together as is the case with Burmans and Shans. Among the Szis on the east frontier it is said to be customary to call on a Chinese or Shan-Chinese seer termed "Sen Sen," whose *metier* it is to decide on a favourable spot for the burial, to prevent the survivors being worried by the ghost of the departed. In the case of Sawbwas or influential men, when it has been decided to postpone the funeral ceremonies, it is common for the coffin to be kept sometimes for months supported above ground on posts having a bamboo let into the lower portion connecting it with the earth to permit of the escape of the results of decomposition.

When it is decided to hold the funeral ceremony (mānmăkoi), all friends are invited and a Tumsa is called, who, consulting the spirit of the departed by divination, decides what sacrifice—that of a buffalo, bullock, pig, &c.—he would most prefer. This is killed and eaten, a portion being presented to the spirit of the deceased at his shrine (Mankyang or Mang-jang), the spot usually at the back of the house where the household nats are worshipped, and where, pending the completion of the funeral, the deceased's da, bag, &c., have been hung up. Thereafter, so long as resources hold out, feasting and drinking continue, the monotony being varied by death dances, described by Anderson as follows: "We entered the common hall, round which men, women, and children were dancing, each carrying "a small stick with which each beat time as they circled round with measured steps, "curiously combining a prance and a side shuffle. The instrumentalists were a man and "a girl, who vigorously beat a pair of drums, while ever and anon the dancers burst out "into loud yells and quickened the speed of their evolutions. We at first sat gravely on "the logs brought by a similar girl, but were presently invited by signs to take our places "in the dance; accordingly we stood up and went round, and had hardly taken two turns "when the whole party rushed yelling loudly out of the house, the leader flourishing his "stick wildly as though clearing the way. Much puzzled, we returned into the house, and "found the corpse of a child laid in a corner carefully screened off, and the poor mother "wailing bitterly by its side. The festivity turned out to be the death dance to drive away "the departed spirit from hovering near its late tenement, and our exertions were believed "to have mainly contributed to the happy result. We paid our footing in silver, and departed with a feeling that even the *entente cordiale* we desired with the Kakhyens hardly "demanded an active participation in the death dances."

On the final day, the coffin having already been buried, the "lup" or conical shaped thatch cover seen all over the hills is erected over the grave, and the trench (which is only usually done in the case of Sawbwas and leading men) is finished, the karoi or bamboo circle having been destroyed in the morning. That evening the Tumsa addresses the spirit of the deceased (Man Shippawt Nai), asking it to go away to the place where its ancestors are (I have not been able to get any definite information as to the place to which the unfortunate soul is thus consigned) and never come back. The shrine (Mang-jang) in the house is then destroyed and guns are fired off, a party of friends going out to visit the burial-place, firing and drinking as they go. If the deceased is a man, they make six halts. On arrival at the "lup," they hang up the articles of deceased's dress, and his da, &c., which have been taken off the Mang-jang and fire a fusillade. On returning, they place little heaps of rice-flour here and there on the road, which are inspected next morning and omens drawn from their condition. Should they be found disturbed, it is a sign that some other member of the family or village is shortly about to die. The final death dance having taken place, the company disperse. Six days afterwards in the case of a man, and seven in the case of a woman, the spirit of the deceased is supposed to return for a final look round. It is consequently necessary to propitiate the spirit to go away, and the family set to work to catch some game, generally fish, of which the first captured is presented along with some chiru to the spirit, and he or she is adjured to go and remain with his or her ancestors and not stay and become a nat. Neighbours come in and a general drink ends the proceedings. There is no mourning garb, nor does it appear that any of the relations have to observe any special rules after the death.

Usually, now, burial is resorted to, except in the case of lunatics (mānā), persons dying a violent death (săwā), and women dying in child-birth (ntang), who are burnt. In the latter case, the ashes and bones are simply raked together, covered with a little earth, and a "lup" erected above them. Among the Kauris Anderson says, "Funeral rites are also denied to "those who die of smallpox and to women dying in child-birth. In the latter case, the "mother and her unborn child are supposed to become a fearful compound vampire (swawn). "All the young people fly in terror from the house, and divination is resorted to to dis-"cover what animal the evil spirit will devour and another with which it will transmigrate."

This shows the influence of Buddhist notions introduced through intercourse with Shans, for transmigration appears to be utterly unknown to the Northern Kachins. Anderson continues: "the first (animal) is sacrificed and some of the flesh placed before the "corpse; the second is hung up and a grave dug in the direction to which the animal's head "pointed when dead. Here the corpse is buried with all the clothes and ornaments worn in "life, and a wisp of straw is burned on its face before the leaves and earth are filled in. "All property of the deceased is burnt on the grave and a hut erected over it. The death "dance takes place to drive the spirit from the house in all cases. The former custom "appears to have been to burn the body itself with the house and all the clothes and orna-"ments used by the deceased. This also took place if the mother died during the month "succeeding child-birth, and, according to one native statement, the infant also was thrown "into the fire with the address: 'Take away your child;' but if previously any one claimed "the child, saying 'Give me your child,' it was spared and belonged to the adopting parent, "the real father being unable at any time to reclaim it."

As to this last item the native informant must have been romancing. I have not been able to hear of any such custom, and the Kachins do not recklessly throw away what may afterwards turn out a profitable member of the household.

A tradition exists among the Szis that formerly cremation was the rule. The only explanation I could obtain for its discontinuance is that with altered times came altered customs, and the spread of the custom of chewing betel in recent times was instanced as an example in point.

Government.—As already explained, the ruling family furnishes all the Sawbwas, or Duwas as they are termed. Each Sawbwa has his own recognized hill tract, within which all dwellers look to him as their Chief. The term Sawbwa, however, in most cases conveys a false idea of importance, for though there are Sawbwas, such as the Kansi and Thama Sawbwas, ruling over an extensive tract and having many subordinate Sawbwas under them, the majority of so-called Sawbwas are of no more consequence than the ordinary Burmese village gaung.

The Sawbwaship is hereditary, the youngest son succeeding to the title and the power. The elder sons can stay on in the old homestead if they like, having of course no political power, but in many cases move off with a small personal following to make a fresh settlement. The retention of political importance by the Sawbwa depends entirely on his own personal gifts. If he has a ready tongue and wit, his counsels are attended to, otherwise he is a mere nonentity, and fades into insignificance behind his Pawmaings (also termed Salangs) or councillors. Every Sawbwa appoints two or three of the elders who are renowned in debate or in war his councillors, and they are practically, except in the case of a very strong Sawbwa, all-powerful. They receive no remuneration, but their orders are obeyed with respect, punishment for disobedience being of course ejectment from the community, as the councillors naturally carry the majority of inhabitants with them. This is not the case with the Sawbwa, who often has no means to make his authority regarded. Theoretically the Sawbwa is master of all the land in his territory, but practically individual rights are respected. As Anderson puts it, when speaking of the Kauri tribe, "a suggestion to a villager that the Chief might evict him from his holding, was replied to by "a significant sawing motion of the hand across the throat."

Of course outsiders, before selling or working land, have to get the Sawbwa's permission. All that the Sawbwa gets as a fixed revenue is a yearly due of one or two baskets of rice per house, but he is also entitled to a part, usually a leg, of all game and of all bullocks and buffaloes killed within the limits of his jurisdiction; while such Sawbwas as have their territory along the caravan routes receive also such collections as are made from travellers for free passage. Otherwise the Sawbwa is in the same position as any other villager, and has to work for his living in the same manner, with this one exception, that four times in the year, at jungle-clearing, sowing, weeding, and harvest time, the whole village has to give one day's free labour to the Sawbwa in helping him to cultivate his plot of ground, he feeding them for that day. Curiously enough, he is not usually judge in village disputes, nor does he interfere to keep the peace. The disputants are said usually to refer to the arbitration of the Salangs, sometimes of their own, but more often of a separate village, and, should an award not be accepted, the law of reprisal is resorted to, the Sawbwa, unless he or his relations are personally concerned, having no call to interfere. Inter-tribal or inter-community quarrels are always settled by reprisals, when, of course, the Sawbwa takes the lead in executing vengeance.

By our treatment of the Kachins, and our insistence on the personal responsibility of the Sawbwa for the peace and order of his territories, we are introducing quite a novel view of his authority, with results which will be interesting to watch. As might have been expected from the above sketch, the Sawbwa's power was generally by no means extensive or stable. This will be seen from the recent sudden rise and spread of "Kumlauism." As Major Fenton says, "The term *Kumsa* is applied to all Kachins, irrespective "of their tribe, who are under the rule or influence of a Sawbwa (Du-wa), who receives "presents from his people on certain occasions, the term Kumlau to those that own no "Sawbwa, the headman of each village being called merely Akyi or Salang and receiving "no presents, &c., as a Sawbwa does."

Certainly not more than 30 years ago (the exact year can be fixed by the fact that it was the year in which a very large comet indeed was visible and remained visible for nearly two months) it appears that the daughter of Ning Bauwa, Sawbwa of Sumpawngpum, was demanded in marriage by two men—Khawlè, whom Major Fenton describes as a Maran Akyi (*i.e.*, headman), "hence, perhaps, the *Marangyi* of Alaga's report, whom we could not identify in any other way," and Lapushaung, but she was given in preference to Nawpwè, Sawbwa of Ngumla, a village beyond the confluence, two days' journey north of Wantu. On this account Khawlè and Lapushaung joined and started a revolutionary movement, Khawlè killing the Sawbwa of Ngumla and Lapushaung disposing of the Sawbwa of Sumpawngpum. Thereafter, finding this profitable, they extended the movement, killing or driving away all such Sawbwas as would not yield and efface themselves. Major Fenton remarks that "Simwa Sawbwa, of Sakipum, and numbers of minor Sawbwas saved "their lives by consenting to give up their emoluments, and were made Akyis, apparently "a purely honorary title." This movement is not confined exclusively to the Lepai tribe as stated by Major Fenton, but is found also among the Lataungs and Marans. It is extraordinarily widespread considering its recent origin, as there are villages in the upper defile, just north of Bhamo, that have within the last three or four years driven forth their Sawbwas and established "Akyis." As to how the new system has worked we must quote Lieutenant Eliott, who alone has had a fair chance of observing it. He says the difference between Kumlau and Kumsa "is only mentioned here, as no previous report has noted "how greatly the difficulty of a march through Kachin country is enhanced if the people of "the villages passed through have no Sawbwas, or, short, are Kumlaus and not Kumsas. "With a hereditary Sawbwa, if he is friendly, no trouble need be expected from the villagers; "but in a Kumlau village, which is practically a small republic, however well-meaning the "headman may be, he is quite unable to control the action of any badly disposed villager, "as the latter would strongly resent any restraint on the part of the headman on his liberty "of action." He also remarks that "though the movement may be slowly extending to the "north of the confluence, it is doubtful whether it is really gaining much ground, as certain "Kachin villages near the Chinese frontier are disgusted with the new state of affairs, and "the lawlessness involved thereby, and are negotiating for the return of their Sawbwas. "The Sawbwas, however, do not seem anxious to rejoin, as they are not yet certain of their "position." Occasionally the Sawbwa acts as representative of the whole community in offering sacrifice, *e.g.*, in the yearly celebration of the "nat of the earth," and every member is obliged to assist him and contribute offerings. So, too, at times of general prosperity the Sawbwa, as head of the community, holds high festival for three or four days on end (Manau Kalaw), to which all neighbouring communities are invited. The entire body of nats are then propitiated with offerings, and dancing and drunkenness help to pass the time merrily. The whole community contribute to bear the expense. When a Sawbwa marries, it seems to be customary, but not obligatory, for his subjects to make him offerings.

Law.—As already remarked, the law of reprisal is the only one to which ultimate appeal is made. There does not, so far as our slight intimacy with Kachin customs goes at present, seem to be any body of recognized legal rules. Matters may or may not be referred to the decision of the Sawbwa or some of the Salangs or Pawmaings, but ultimately each man is his own avenger. Compensation for injuries is allowed of course, and there is a tolerably recognized scale of blood-money, *e.g.*, if a Sawbwa is murdered, it requires the cession of half the village lands of the offender, with many slaves and guns, to wipe out the crime; while, in the case of a lesser man, one slave, eight or ten bullocks, and some clothes and gongs will suffice, and so on in proportion. If satisfaction is not thus obtained, it constitutes a "debt," and the Kachin method of reasoning in liquidating these debts is exceedingly whimsical. From actual personal experience I could quote many curious instances, but will only quote one, which shows that whatever administrative grasp we may have over the Kachins, it is still next to impossible to foresee and provide against sudden raids or attacks, from the very fact of the inciting causes being inexplicable to the ordinary understanding and lying dormant for years, only to come into sudden and instantaneous activity without any premonitory symptoms. Last December a caravan of peaceful Chinese traders, returning from Bhamo to their homes, were suddenly attacked *en route* by the Sawbwa of Kasankôn, east of Bhamo, and two Chinamen shot dead. There was no apparent motive for the crime at the time, as the Kachins along that route had been perfectly quiet all the season. Subsequently, on the capture of the Sawbwa, it appeared that in 1868, when Colonel Sladen's mission ascended to Momein, the father of the present Sawbwa of Kasankôn was of assistance to the party, and, in return for his services, Colonel Sladen, on his way back invited him to accompany the expedition to Bhamo, probably with the object of rewarding him on arrival. The father came to Bhamo and died there, apparently from natural causes. This constituted a "debt" against Bhamo, and the memory was carefully treasured up till 1891, when the present Sawbwa suddenly concluded he would wipe it off. Bhamo being the debtor, every one connected therewith, even in the slightest degree, became liable, even a mere merchant visiting it temporarily for trade. Hence a caravan from Bhamo was fair game, with the result above mentioned. The 23 years that had elapsed made no difference as to the ultimate working off of the debt, but even trivial matters are remembered and worked off after long intervals of time. The village of Naungmo was once attacked and burnt, and two villagers shot, because some six years previously a Kachin, who came to the village, lost a cooking-pot there and failed to recover it. This system renders the keeping open of the trade routes a most difficult one. Attacks by Kachins and reprisals by traders have by now furnished a long series of mutual wrongs, which it is inconsistent with Kachin character to forget, and which it would be disgraceful to condone.

It is a point of honour to assist a friend in working off a "debt," and a following can be raised at a moment's notice, and without expense, which will see the avenger through with his business. A poor man is therefore on an equality with a rich one so far as punishing injuries is concerned, and this, I take it, is the main factor conducive to peace and good order. In the case of a murder, a man's relations are his avengers, and divide the compensation, if any, accepted for his death. In other cases a man is his own avenger. In the case of a Sawbwa's death, all his subjects join in exacting an adequate revenge.

Property.—With regard to taungya or hill-cultivation, individual property is not recognized, but the land is regarded as that of the whole community as represented by their Sawbwa, and the system of cultivation does not permit of a constant use of the same plot of ground. In a few cases, however, in the valleys, where ordinary wet-weather paddy is cultivated, the case is different, and individual ownership is admitted with this restriction, that the land cannot be parted with to an alien. It is as a set-off to his theoretical ownership of all the land that the Sawbwa gets one or two baskets of paddy per house annually. Land descends to a household as a whole, and is worked in common for the benefit of all, splitters off from the household losing all right to participate. In the case where the household breaks up voluntarily partition takes place according to no fixed rules, except that the youngest son gets the lion's share as well as the ancestral homestead. If there are no male children, the wife takes all the property.

Religion.—The Kachins worship "nats or spirits," of whom the numbers are endless, for any one may become a nat after his death. The original "nat," according to our Szi informant, was one Chinūn Way Shun, who existed long before the formation of the world and before the other nats came into existence. Subsequently Chinūn Way Shun, now known as the nat of the earth, created the big "nats"—

(1) Chitôn. The "forest nat," a particularly vicious one.
(2) Mū (Mushang in Szi), the nat of the heavens.
(3) Sinlap.
(4) Ponphyoi
(2)–(4): These live in the sky and generally interest themselves in mortal affairs. Sinlap is said to give wisdom to his worshippers.
(5) Mbon, the nat of the wind.
(6) Wăwn or Khyingwăwn, according to Anderson the patron of agriculture.

The last two nats (5) and (6) are worshipped only by the Sawbwa, and only when a festival (Mănau) is being held.

(7) *Jan*, the nat of the sun.
(8) *Shita*, the nat of the moon.
(7)–(8): Both beneficent.

After the formation of these bigger nats, the story runs that Way Shun made a pumpkin and then called in the other nats, who each added a little: Chitôn giving legs, Mū eyes, and so on, and thus the first man-like being, known as Ningkwawnwa or Shingrawa, came into existence. Shingrawa was essentially divine, and from him descended Shippawng Ayawng, above mentioned as the primal ancestor of the Kachin race. At the time of Shingrawa's springing into existence, it is said that the earth was in a parlous condition. The water was undrinkable, the ground unworkable, and every tree and shrub covered with thorns. For some unknown reason the waters began to rise up and cover the land and submerge everything, and after this had happened, Shingrawa created the present earth and plants out of the remains of the old earth. Thereafter the lesser nats began to spring into existence, until now, as Anderson puts it, "every hill, forest, and stream has its "own nat of greater or lesser power; every accident or illness is the work of some malig-" nant or vindictive one of 'these viewless ministers.'"

Additions are also being made to their number by the spirits of the dead. The Kachins seem to have no idea of what happens in a future existence. Beyond consigning the soul to the place "where its fathers and mothers had gone," they care to know naught. There is no scheme among the more northerly Kachins of the good and bad in this life being separated after death. Such legends as there are on this subject come from the Sanpyaw Kachins or Kachins on our eastern border, and are doubtless due to Shan and Chinese influence.

Anderson says of the Kauris that "they believe Tsojah is the abode of good men; and "those who die violent deaths and bad characters generally go to Marai." To questions as to the place and conditions of these, an intelligent Kakhyen answered "How can I tell? "No one knows anything."

A Szi informer gave me a most elaborate and thrilling description of how the wretched soul, after death, had to crawl along a thin bamboo bridge underneath which a set of huge cauldrons were kept continually boiling. If the soul had belonged to a bad man, the cauldrons began to bubble up and boil over and envelop the bridge, thus dragging down the delinquent to perdition (Meungăraitā). The souls of others, not quite so bad, pass on to the end of the bridge, but meeting an almost perpendicular and slippery hill, cannot avoid slipping backwards to the region of the cauldrons, whence they make their escape back to earth and become nats after suffering a parboiling which cannot have improved their tempers. Others get to the top of the mountain, where they meet two roads, one to the right, "straight and narrow," leading to Meungliban, the region of the blessed, and the other, "broad and inviting," leading to Suka, where the soul is subjected to many petty annoyances.

When a man becomes unconscious and then revives, he is said to have got to within sight of the bridge and burning pots, but to have heard the voices of his friends recalling him and to have returned. From the names given for Heaven and Hell, however, I suspect the description will really turn out to be a Shan one in a Kachin dress. I merely insert it as a basis for future investigation. The Northern Kachin, however, has apparently no such notions. It seems a mere chance whether a soul goes to the ancestral resting-place or remains behind and becomes a nat, and apparently the only means of knowing what has happened occurs when, after the death of a member of the family, another member has an accident or falls sick, when, if the Tumsa declares the malignant influence to be due to the soul of deceased, the latter is promptly propitiated and installed among the household gods, who are usually the spirits of ancestors (Kūmkūn Kūmhpai), though Chitôn is occasionally included amongst them. The other nats are worshipped outside with a slightly varying ceremony. As a rule, the nats may be taken as generally malignant, and are not therefore worshipped so long as everything goes on smoothly. Even the beneficent nats apparently do not exert themselves actively to better the condition of their worshippers unless and until their aid is first invoked by offerings. When accident or illness occurs, "to discover "who may be the particular nat, or how he is to be appeased, is the business of the Tumsa "(or regular priest). He prescribes and assists in all sacrifices and calls the nats to receive "their share, which, with economical piety, generally consists of the offal." There are two ways of consulting the nats, either by a possessed medium termed a mi-tway, or by the Tumsa, who is quite distinct. As Anderson observes of the Tumsa, "There is no sacerdo- "tal caste, the succession being kept up by a natural selection and apprenticeship. The "Tumsa practises augury from fowl bones, omens, and the fracture of burned mil-grass, "besides holding communication with a spirit world." The Tumsa is usually resorted to when it is a question of sacrifice or propitiation; the mi-tway when a question of purely human interest (such as the proper time to attack a neighbouring tribe) is being debated.

The Tumsa having by divination discovered which nat is at work, proceeds to deliver a long harangue in esoteric language, which has a sonorous and rhythmical sound, as if he were quoting bits of Homer, but which is not much more intelligible to the ordinary Kachin than to the stranger. There is also a variation in the garb of the Tumsa according to the nature of the nat, thus:

Chitôn is invoked in full dress, with da and bag complete, the Tumsa grasping a hollow bamboo with water therein;

Yūnmū (a nat peculiar to the Szis) is invoked with bare head and in a crouching attitude.

The Earth nat or Kā nat is worshipped in ordinary dress, but with no da.

Meanwhile the devoted animal, buffalo, pig, &c., is brought out, and when the Tumsa has worked himself up to the proper pitch, the word is given and the animal is killed near the bamboo shrine which has been erected somewhere near by, and is divided by the Kyāng Jōng or Khing Jōng, who separates what is known as the "nat's flesh," being parts of the thigh, shoulder, &c. These are boiled and made into little packets with leaves and hung round or deposited on the bamboo shrine. The Tumsa then sets to work again and prays the nat to accept the offering and be appeased. In the case of household nats, as soon as the Tumsa has finished, it is permissible to take back and use the offering for household purposes; with the outside nats Ponphyoi, Wawn, &c., it is different, and the sacrifice may not be taken back. Chitôn and Sinlap, however, being good-natured, it is usual, where the sacrifice has been a pig or a buffalo and tit-bits are going to waste, to run the risk of offending them by taking back these offerings after a decent time has elapsed. Where the offerings have, however, been merely a fowl or dried fish, or spirit, they are left on the shrine. Where there is no sacrifice, but offerings are made, these are tied on to the shrine, it being usual, as a preliminary, to offer thus a hollow bamboo full of spirits. The bamboo shrines referred to are a conspicuous feature near every village, and are fashioned in all sorts of extraordinary shapes, of which some are given below :—

1

2

3

4

5

6

1 and 2 are forms used for the household nats.
3 used for Mū and Ponphyoi.
4 and 6 for Sinlap.
5 for Jān and Shitta.

But there is no fixed form, full scope being permitted to individual imagination. When the three Heaven's nats, *i.e.*, Mosheng, Ponphyoi, and Sinlap, are being worshipped together, Sinlap's shrine is always in the middle, flanked on the right by Mosheng's and on the left by Ponphyoi's.

Certain proportions in the sacrifices seem to be conventional, *e.g.*, the Ka nat and Mu nat get one of each kind of animal sacrificed, while Ponphyoi and Sinlap get two; Mbong, on the other hand, never gets aught but dried fish, eggs, and spirits.

A subdivision of the nats are the swawns or bogies as already described.

The method of consulting the will of the nats by means of a mi-tway cannot be better exemplified than by the narration of an actual instance as described by Anderson. It took place when Colonel Sladen was bargaining for mules to transport his party across the hills, and the Sawbwas, who were to provide them, wished first to consult a mi-tway and propitiate the nâts.

"The mi-tway now entered and seated himself on a small stool in one corner, which had been freshly sprinkled with water; he then blew through a small tube, and throwing it from him, with a deep groan, at once fell into an extraordinary state of tremor, every limb quivered, aud his feet beat a literal devil's tattoo on the bamboo flooring. He groaned as if in pain, tore his hair, passed his hands with maniacal gestures over his head and face, then broke into a short, wild chant, interrupted with sighs and groans, his features appearing distorted with madness or rage, while the tones of his voice changed to an expression of anger and fury. During this extraordinary scene, which realized all one had read of demoniacal possession, the Sawbwa and his pawmaings occasionally addressed him in low tones, as if soothing him or deprecating the anger of the dominant spirit; and at last the Sawbwa informed Sladen that the nats must be appeased with an offering. Fifteen rupees and some cloth were produced—the silver on a bamboo sprinkled with water, and the cloth on a platter of plantain leaves, were humbly laid at the diviner's feet, but with one convulsive jerk of the legs rupees and cloth were instantly kicked away, and the medium, by increased convulsions and groans, intimated the dissatisfaction of the nats with the offering. The Sawbwa in vain supplicated for its acceptance, and then signified to Sladen that more rupees were required and that the nats mentioned sixty as the propitiatory sum. Sladen tendered five more with an assurance that no more could be given. The amended offering was again, but more gently, pushed away, of which no notice was taken. After another quarter of an hour, during which the convulsions and groans gradually grew less violent, a dried leaf rolled into a cone and filled with rice was handed over to the mi-tway. He raised it to his forehead several times and then threw it on the floor. A da which had been carefully washed was next handed over to him and treated in the same way; and after a few gentle sighs he rose from his seat, and laughing, signed to us to look at his legs and arms, which were very tired. The oracle was in our favour, and predictions of all manner of success were interpreted to us as the utterances of the inspired diviner.

"It must not be supposed that this was a solemn farce enacted to conjure rupees out of European pockets; the Kakhyens never undertake any business or journey without consulting the will of the nats, as revealed by a mi-tway under the influence of temporary frenzy, or, as they deem it, possession. The seer in ordinary life is nothing; the medium on whose word hung the possibility of our advance was a cooly, who carried one of our boxes on the march, but he was a duly qualified mi-tway belonging to a Pônsi village. When a youth shows signs of what spiritualists would call a *rapport* or connection with the spirit-world, he has to undergo a sufficiently trying ordeal to test the reality of his powers. A ladder is prepared, the steps of which consist of sword blades with the sharp edges turned upwards, and this is reared against a platform thickly set with sharp spikes. The barefoot novice ascends this perilous path to fame, and seats himself on the spikes without any apparent inconvenience; he then descends by the same ladder, and if, after having been carefully examined, he is pronounced free from any trace of injury, he is thencetorward accepted as a true diviner."

The Jai Wā is a sort of Arch-tumsa occasionally but very rarely met with. He performs ceremonies for only the most powerful Sawbwas, and is supposed to be in more intimate connection with the spirit-world than an ordinary Tumsa.

It should be noted that effigies are not offered up in lieu of a real sacrifice. If the Tumsa declares the sacrifice of a bullock necessary, and the worshipper cannot obtain one at the time, he simply promises the nat to sacrifice one at the first opportunity. Human beings are never sacrificed.

Divination.—The methods of divination usually employed are the following :—

(1) The consultation of the bamboo termed Sāmān or Shimān wōt. The esoteric name of this operation is Ningwōt.

A kind of thin green bamboo is taken and laid across the embers of a fire. The heat causes the wood to split and little hairy fibres stand out all along the edges of the slit thus made. By consulting these, the expert can foretell events.

(2) Consultation of leaf termed Shippa wōt, which is equivalent to the ဝက်လုံးမှန်ထောင်း of the Burmese-Shan. A peculiar kind of leaf is used whose veins do not interlace, but run parallel to each other, something after the fashion of the plantain leaf, and inclined at an acute angle to the midrib. This permits of the leaf being torn into thin shreds, which are taken at haphazard and knotted together. The knots and the number of slips contained in each are then counted, and this, added to other indications, such as form of the knots, &c., known only to the initiated, permits of forecasts being drawn.

(3) Auguries are also drawn from the entrails of cattle and pigs, the brains and sinews of fowls.

(4) The Szis also have a method termed "Shaw sè." Thirty-three short bamboo splints are taken and put haphazard between the clefts of the fingers of one hand. The odd sticks in each group are then taken out and laid on one side. The process is then repeated thrice, and by the result the seer's prognostications are guided.

Omens (*Numdaw Numtan*).—If a snake (lippu), porcupine (tumsi), or wild cat (khan) crosses one's path, it is very fatal, and the journey is about to be unfortunate. Merely seeing them on either side of the path is a matter of indifference. On the other hand, deer (shān ngā), hedge-hog (tu), or rhinoceros (dum pau) crossing the path are good portents. Apparently no omens are drawn from the flight of birds.

Agriculture.—The most common and universal form is taungya or hill-clearing. It is a most wasteful process, large areas being entirely denuded of valuable forest, and the Forest Officers are consequently most anxious to have it stopped immediately within the limits proposed for reservation. The hills to the immediate east of Bhamo, treated in this manner, are now practically bare, which has had an important effect on the climate according to the Kachins. It is said to be generally much warmer than in their father's time, while the rainfall is less. The method employed is to select a virgin site on a hillside and fell the jungle about March, and let it lie on the ground till thoroughly dry. This is set fire to in June and July, and the surface of the earth broken up by hand with a rude hoe, the ashes being thus mixed therewith. The sowing is of the roughest description. As the worker dibbles away with the hoe in his right hand, he throws in a grain or two with his left. The crop is left to take care of itself till it is about a foot high, when weeding takes place. This is repeated once again before the crop gets ripe. In October the crop is usually reaped. The straw is generally regarded as useless. The same area cannot be cropped two years running. Usually it has to lie fallow from 7 to 10 years where the jungle does not grow rapidly, and 4 to 7 years in other cases.

In the hills to the east of Bhamo, where the influence of Shan and Chinese has been felt, wet-weather paddy cultivation has been introduced, the hills being scarped into terraces and water supplied to the topmost terrace (where water is not obtainable on the spot) through bamboo pipes laid from some convenient spring or dammed-up stream. The ground in these cases is worked by means of buffaloes and wooden ploughs. Of course only a paddy crop can be raised in this latter fashion, but in taungyas, paddy, maize, tobacco, indigo, cotton, and sessamum are raised equally well. The poppy plant is extensively cultivated on the eastern hills in little enclosures near the houses, while to the north Kachins come long distances in the cold season to the alluvial lands on the river islands on the Upper Irrawaddy to raise a crop. When the poppy-heads are ripe, they are notched with a da and the exuding juice wiped off on a cloth, which, like everything the Kachin possesses, is generally very dirty. This is dried and rolled up. When required for use, a little bit is torn off and smoked, cloth and all. This opium is, however, very inferior, and by no means as well appreciated as the Chinese opium, which comes across the border in large quantities. This latter is usually imported in the form of a dark viscid liquor, which is prepared for smoking by being soaked up with plantain leaf shredded very fine and toasted brown on the fire. The leaf shreds covered with opium are rolled into little balls and thus smoked. Opium chewing is but little resorted to. The introduction of opium smoking is said to have occurred within the last few generations, and is now almost universal, at least with the Eastern Kachins, young and old alike smoking. It is said that it was unknown before, which either shows that contact with the Chinese, and therefore the advance of the Kachins so far south as this, is of much more recent date than has been suspected, or that the cultivation of the poppy in Yunnan can only recently have been extensively resorted to. What effect this has had generally on the Kachins it is too early to determine. Mr. Shaw remarks on the Kachins at Paraw on the Upper Irrawaddy: "The Paraw Kachins, a fine healthy-looking lot of people, who ought to be exhibited to the opium faddists, "all smoke opium, so they say themselves, men, women, and children alike. The latter are "allowed to begin as early as they please." While Anderson says, "It is worth recording "that the men invariably smoke opium, but not to excess. Rarely, if ever, did we see them "use tobacco for smoking, though they never object to chewing it."

In spite of our restrictive policy, our administrative grasp of the country is yet too weak to enable the importation of opium to be effectively checked.

Each year, before sowing time, the nat of the earth (Ka nât, who is the same as the great original nat Chinūn Way Shun) is worshipped by the Sawbwa on behalf of the whole village, who contribute offerings. The sacrifices take place at the "Numshang" or general prayer-place outside the village on the road, in which a collection of bamboo shrines are usually found. Only the Sawbwa and the Tumsa and Kyang Jōng (or butcher) may be present at the time of the sacrifice, which usually takes place towards the evening, the villagers during the earlier part of the day having worshipped the collective nats at the "Numshang." After the ceremony, for four days no work must be done. After these days of ceremonial holiday (Nā nā ai) the Tumsa, by divination, discovers which particular house of the village should start sowing first in order that the crop may be a good one. The members of this household go out, sow their fields, and two days ceremonial holiday are again indulged in by the whole community.

A general feast and drink is indulged in on that night by the whole village, and eggs, spirits, &c., are offered to the nats to avert all damage from the crops. Two days further ceremonial idleness follow, and thereafter sowing can be commenced indiscriminately.

Altogether there are six recognized holidays a year, when no one is supposed to do any work:—

First.—Two days after the Sawbwa's taungya hut is built. It is customary, owing to the vast distances of the hill-clearings from the village, to erect little huts on the spot each year and remove to the site of the clearing temporarily. On this occasion, too, the Ka nat is worshipped by the Sawbwa, but with more private ceremony than on the latter occasion noted above.

Second.—Two days at the time of first setting fire to jungle-clearings.

Third.—Four days at the time of the great Ka nat worship as noted above.

Fourth.—Two days after the first sowing as described above.

Fifth.—Four days when the crop is ripening at the time of the worship by the whole village of the whole pantheon of nats. Every house presents a distinct offering at the Numshang. This ceremony is termed Chikkhawn Khawn-ai. The ripening crop is commended to the care of the nats in a body and all danger is thereby averted.

Sixth.—Two days after the reaping of the Sawbwa's taungya, which is done for him by the whole village.

In the case of blight, &c., a Tumsa is called in, and by divination proceeds to discover whether some nat is at the bottom of it or not. If the cause is declared to be due to other than nat influence, nothing is done, otherwise the appropriate nat is searched for and appeased.

No reaping whatever may take place till the first-fruits of the crop sown by the first house (see above) have been gathered and offered to the house nats of that particular household. This is usually done before the crop is actually fully ripe, so that the reaping of the other crops may not be delayed.

Among the Szis, after the paddy has been dried and placed in a heap for threshing, all the friends of the household are invited to the threshing-floor and food and drink is brought out. The heap of paddy is divided, and one-half strewed out for threshing, while the other is left heaped up. On this latter heap food and spirits are placed, and one of the elders present, addressing the father and mother of the paddy-plant, asks for plenteous harvests in future, and begs that the seed may bear manifold. Thereafter the whole party eat, drink, and make merry. This is the only time the "father and mother of paddy" are invoked, They are not regarded as nats proper.

Witchcraft.—Some Tumsas have the power to cause sickness and death by bewitching (Marong Măt să ai) the victim. A good price has to be paid, however, and it is usual to consult a *mi-tway* before getting rid of an enemy, to see whether it would not be better (and cheaper of course) to wait for him behind a tree and shoot him out of hand. If, however, it is decided to employ witchcraft, the Tumsa recites charms imprecating the particular ill which it is desired should happen, while the invoker of his power plants a few stalks of long grass by the side of the road leading towards the enemy's abode. Then either a dog or a pig is killed and the body is wrapped in grass and placed by the road and left there, no one eating it. Meanwhile spears are cast and shots fired in the same direction, and the ceremony closes by the Tumsa and each of those present taking up four or five stalks of grass and casting them similarly towards the foe (Kumpă chin Khyen ai).

Besides this there are people who have what is equivalent to the power of the "evil eye." These are said to possess two souls (Numla), the ordinary man having only one. They can therefore afford to keep one in the body to go on with and send the other out to play havoc with their fellowmen. What must be annoying to them, however, is that the victim generally manages to recognize who has been worrying him, and as generally leaves to his family the obligation of wiping out the "debt." In one case that came under my observation short work was made of the evil-dispositioned mortal. *C*, the brother of *A* and *B*, happened to die of fever, and, before dying, declared *D* had bewitched him. Within a fortnight *A* and *B* collected a following, attacked *D*'s house, shot him dead, and capturing the whole of his household and relations, some 13 in all, sold them into slavery. Even on trial *A* and *B* would not admit the possibility of *C* having made a mistake, and were scandalized that the British Government should interfere on behalf of a wizard, who was only to be regarded like Bill Nye's "Injun"—"pisen" to be got rid of wherever found.

Ordeals.—The common one, used in petty cases where one man accuses another of anything, is practised as follows:—Both accuser and accused have to stake something, the magnitude of which depends on the gravity of the crime alleged. The stakes are held by the referee, who wraps some rice in a leaf and boils it. If the rice boils regularly and becomes soft all through, the accused is declared innocent and takes the stakes; if not, the accuser wins.

In however cases of gravity between Sawbwas and leading men, the stakes run to a considerable amount, *e.g.*, several buffaloes, guns, a slave or two, &c. A Tumsa is called in to aid, who proceeds to the jungle with his da, which, after a certain amount of incantation, he casts from him at random. The da, which has become endued with supernatural power, hits a bamboo. This, on being cut down and opened, is found to contain about a cup full of water. This no doubt has been duly arranged for beforehand by the Tumsa. The water is put in a very large pot over a fire, and, when boiling, the accused has to put his hand into it. If he is guilty, the water froths up and bubbles over, taking the skin off the man's hand; if, on the contrary, he is innocent, the boiling subsides and he suffers no hurt. The winner, of course, immediately takes the stakes.

Hunting.—Hunters and fishermen do not appear to prepare themselves for the chase by any special ceremonials, but, on his return, invariably the hunter, by the aid of the "Kyang Jōng" cuts off parts of the body known as "nat's flesh" and puts them in a basket. A friend thereon brings a heap of ashes from a neighbouring fireplace and puts them near the ladder or steps leading into the house. The hunter treads on the heap and thus enters, otherwise he may not. Having entered the house, the basket is placed on the shrine of the house-nats and the Tumsa invites them to eat and be kind, after which the quarry is divided, the Sawbwa getting a haunch and the Tumsa an appropriate share. The ashes are said to be placed there to propitiate the *Tsikhrat* (in Chingpaw dialect) or *Kyam* (in Szi), a sort of "genius" and not a nat. Why he should prefer ashes to any other commodity is not apparent. Besides this, at the moment an animal is captured and slain, a little of the blood is taken and cast towards the jungle to satisfy the Tsikhrat, who is said to possess a sort of radiantly white body, whose aspect so fascinates the quarry that it is unable to stir and so falls an easy victim to the hunter. This belief, however, does not prevail among the Marips and possibly also in some other tribes. The fishermen have apparently no such protecting spirit.

When a hunter dies, it is customary to lay his weapons with him in his coffin as he lies in state before burial. This is done as, after death, his soul has "no road" (whither—as I have before observed—is a matter of conjecture, it being merely alluded to as the place where his ancestors are), because the ghosts of his victims block the way and he has to scare them off. This, curiously enough, does not happen to a man who has killed another. The ghost of the latter is said to have received such a fright during its corporeal existence, that nothing would ever induce it to go near the ghost of the former again. A wounded tiger is never followed up until a Tumsa has been duly consulted, but in the case of other game there is no such restriction.

War.—Of war proper the Kachins have no notion, their hostilities being merely desultory raids from time to time on each other. Sometimes they do not even do this. It is considered sufficient injury to the enemy to attack a peaceable Shan-Burman village under the latter's "protection." This protection is a curious custom which existed in Burmese times. The Burmese rule was not over-vigorous, and nearly all the villages in the Bhamo district were under the "protection" of the Sawbwa of the adjacent hills, who came down occasionally and levied an irregular tribute, ranging from a demand for several buffaloes to a few handfuls of salt. The Shan-Burmans were marvellously afraid of the Kachins and paid without demur. The "protection," however, was an anomalous sort of one, consisting mainly of help in negotiating the release (of course on payment of large sums by the wretched Shan-Burmans) of slaves captured from their village, and an occasionally retaliatory attack on the tribe raiding the village or some village under their protection. It is not surprising that under these circumstances the Shan-Burman found his lot a far from happy one, and was being gradually pushed more and more back to the river's edge and further and further down south. The remains of large Shan villages to the north of our northernmost Shan village at present testify to this. This process has, however, received a sudden check. In the light of the present peaceable state of the Shwegu subdivision, where women are not now afraid to move about unattended, it is curious to learn from Anderson, as late as 1868, how that "at our (*i.e.*, the steamer's) departure in the morning "(from Shwegu, now the headquarters of a subdivision), young women and boys raced "along the river-side, keeping up with us to secure protection from the hillmen on the way "to the villages. We were also informed that the priests' pupils, who collected food from "village to village, were obliged to creep along under the high banks to escape kidnappers. "Subsequent experience has shown that the villagers on the eastern shore as far as Bhamo "are in the habit of sleeping in boats moored in the river; only thus can they be secure "from the nocturnal raids of their dangerous neighbours."

Before a raid by the villagers as a community is taken in hand, the Tumsa is called on to divine which man should or should not take part therein. The nats having been propitiated, the mi-tway is called on to declare which road should be followed and what time is suitable for delivering the attack. Slain enemies have their heads cut off, which are shown to the rest of the band in token that the bearer has really slain a man outright and is entitled to be regarded as a first-class warrior. They are then cast away. The fact of a corpse losing its head apparently has no effect on the future of the soul and makes no difference to the funeral ceremonies, so that mutilation of this kind is not practised out of feelings of spite.

On return after a raid the Sawbwa and his men call in a Tumsa and worship the nats with ordinary rites.

As a rule, the Kachin cannot be said to be courageous. He generally resorts to ambuscade and will not attack unless in what he considers overwhelming force and by surprise. The usual time selected for a night attack is just before the rise of the moon, so that the attack is delivered in a sort of half-light, while the retreat with the booty can be effected in full moonlight with ease. These tactics were adopted with success on the Eastern Kachin column last year.

Slavery is prevalent. The market in former times was supplied by the constant raiding that went on. In fact the stronger would always take the weaker and sell him as a slave. But recently the inhabitants of a village in Thama, regarding a certain household in their community as useless and a nuisance, seized and sold them. So long as the slave behaves well he appears to be treated with uniform kindness. He is an integral portion of the household and works by the side of, and to just the same extent as, his master. Of course refractory slaves are deprived of food or beaten, but never so as to be really injured, for a slave is a valuable article. Now that we have shut off the main source of supply from the Shan-Burmese villages in the plains, and are putting down raids as our hold over the hills extends, he is likely to become more and more scarce and valuable than ever. A slave could always be redeemed by his friends, either by ransoming him, or by the easier method of seizing one of the aggressor's household and effecting an exchange.

A male slave can marry a free woman, though of course only of the lowest and poorest class. The offspring are slaves to the slave's master. A woman slave can be demanded in marriage by any free man. He does not buy her, because that would reflect on his offspring, but he makes offerings to the slave-girl's owner, who is regarded as his father-in-law. For a man to have intercourse with his own female slave is said to occur very rarely, if ever. A personal enemy, when captured, unless sold off at once into distant slavery, is usually put into stocks and not allowed to roam about freely. Early this year I came across one of these wretched victims up the Upper Irrawaddy and ordered his immediate release. He had attempted to murder the owner of the house in pursuance of some old feud, been captured, and at once put into heavy stocks in a dark corner of the house. Over him had been built a sort of cage of bamboos, with two little openings to pass in food by, and he had lain there in one position on his back for about three years in the dark. When released he was quite bleached and could not stand, one of his legs having shrunk. However, his leg began to recover afterwards. He was being kept till his relations could afford to pay for his release. Luckily, these cases are rare, the relations usually ransoming the slave at an early date.

Fire.—The instruments for making fire are now tinder, flint, and steel, though in former times it was usual to notch a bamboo, fill the hollow with tinder, and, using a bamboo splint as a bow, work backwards and forwards along the notch, setting fire to the tinder in a short time. The pop-gun arrangement now found in the Eastern Kachin hills, where tinder is ignited by means of air compressed in a chamber by a piston, is quite a recent innovation, due to Chinese influence.

General.—The Kachins have no form of salutation or obeisance, due, no doubt, to their democratic instincts.

They can count up to 10,000; above that they use general terms "very many," &c. They have different names for cardinals 1 to 10, 20, 100, 200, 1,000, and 10,000. The others are formed in a natural way; thus, 11 is "ten—one" and thirty-three is "three—ten—three." There are no ordinals. They count on their hands, commencing with the little finger in each, also with sticks and pebbles in the case of large numbers. The names of their numbers do not seem derivable from any other roots to show that they were borrowed from the custom of counting on fingers or otherwise.

They possess no knowledge of writing, the legend being that the nats gave all nations writing, but unfortunately that given to the Kachins was written on hide, which, they being hungry and ignorant of the value of what they were destroying, cooked and ate. They can draw rude pictures, as can be seen from the figures on the posts put up outside their villages, descriptive of the offerings they have presented at the Numshang, in order to obtain a good harvest, *vide* sketch below, which I made of a post just outside the Kachin village of Sinlumgate:—

1 represents ears of Indian-corn.
2 ,, the lappet earrings worn by women.
3 ,, the silver torque worn.
4 ,, Kachin rake.
5 ,, trees and jungle.

But they do not seem to have used this picture-writing for the purpose of conveying ideas.

The use of knotted string is common, but the art does not seem to have arrived at the pitch of excellence found among the Mexicans at the time of their conquest by Cortes. The knots are not conventionally distinguished from each other in shape or position on the string, with the result that at best they can only serve as memoranda for the person who made them, and cannot convey ideas to another individuual. Notched sticks are also used.

Time.—The divisions of the day are thus recognized—

(1) Just before early dawn ... Ning htoi maka.
(2) First cock crow ... Wu galang koi yang ... 2 A.M.
(3) Second cock crow ... N'khawng lang koi yang ... 4 A.M.
(4) Dawn ... Ning htoi htoi sa ... 5 A.M.
(5) Sunrise ... Jan pru ... 6 A.M.
(6) Time of morning meal ... Chippawt shat sha tên ... 7 A.M.
(7) ... Jan sin lawng tsan ... 9 to 10 A.M.
(8) Noon (sun vertical) ... Jan pong ding di ... 12 noon.
(8) Midday meal-time ... Shini shat sha tĕn ... 3 P.M.
(9) Fowl roosting-time ... Wu lon tĕn ... 5 to 6 P.M.
(10) Sunset ... Jan shang ... 6 to 6-30 P.M.
(11) Dusk ... Ning rim ... After 6 P.M.
(13) Evening meal ... Shina shat sha tên ... 8 P.M.
(14) Bed-time ... Yup tung tên ... 9 to 10 P.M.
(15) Midnight (full sleep) ... Yup dong ... 12 midnight.

The divisions in the month, which are all lunar, are

Shitta pyaw ... First 10 days of the waxing.
Shitta si ... Last 10 days of the waning.

The intervening space of 10 days has no special name, but the full moon is known as "Shitta lai."

The days of the week are not distinguished by special names. The months are as follows :—

(1) Khrū (roughly January).	(7) Shimari.
(2) Ra.	(8) Kup shi.
(3) Ūt or Wăt.	(9) Kup ton.
(4) Shila.	(10) Kălā.
(5) Chittum.	(11) Măji.
(6) Shingan.	(12) Măkā (roughly December).

They have not got to the stage of inserting an intercalary year or month, with the result that their calendar is somewhat dislocated, and no one, at least down in these parts, seems to have a clear idea of what month it is. No calendars are kept, and there appear to be no recognized beginning or end of the year. The years are not numbered or distinguished from each other. The calendar is therefore made to conform to the natural seasons. When sowing-time comes round, it is considered "this should be such and such a month," and it is regarded so accordingly without further ado.

The seasons are distinguished as follows :—

(1) The rains (beginning)	... Yŭ nām	... July to August.
(2) Rains (middle)	... Yŭ nām kăang	... August to September.
(3) Dry season at hand	... Khengton măkha	... September.
(4) Paddy sprouting	... Mă-ngai-ta	... September to October.
(5) Dry season (beginning-time of harvest).	Kheungton	... October to November.
(6) Cold weather	... Ning-shun-ta	... November to February.
(7) Dry season (middle)	... Kheungton ka ang	... March to April.
(8) Hot weather	... Jan-rawt-te	... April to June.
(9) Paddy-sowing time	... Mam tat ten	... June to July.

The time of this last season is fixed by the rise of a certain constellation over the horizon termed Khru măjan shikkan. I am unable to identify it. It is stated to rise some 30 degrees above the horizon and retire after having remained there a month. After its disappearance it is not good to sow paddy.

The eclipse is said to be due to the efforts of a dog (shitta kwa) to swallow the moon. He appears to be generally frustrated by the firing of guns, beating of gongs, &c.

The rainbow ('Nkoi la tum) is said to come from the mouth of a crab (chikān) which lives in the vast ocean which is supposed to be under the earth. The large marshy hollows occasionally to be met with in valleys are supposed to be connected with this subterranean sea, and the crab comes out of them occasionally for an airing. This chikān is a nat, hence his extraordinary power. If the arc spans the whole heaven, it is a sign that dry weather is in store ; if, however, only portions of the arc appear, rain may still be looked for.

Thunder (Mu ngoi ai) is the voice of the nats of the heavens (Mu or Musheng). *Lightning* (myit hpyap kălam ai) is due to his agency, the literal translation of the phrase being "rolling round and shaking of the eye;" but, whether this is meant to refer to Musheng's eye, to the resultant effect on the eye of the beholder, is not certain. The *earthquake* (shirut ru) is due to the ill-advised antics of the crocodiles (puren) of the subterranean ocean, who insist on going burrowing about in the crevices of the superincumbent earth instead of remaining decorously in their own element.

The nats of the sun and moon are worshipped once yearly by the Sawbwa alone during the cold season. The commoners may not worship them. This ceremony is called "Nat sut ai" and is among the traditions of the Sawbwa stock. No living sacrifice is made, but food and drink are simply offered. The Sawbwa then begs the protection of these nats for the whole village. The only other time they are worshipped is at the "Manau" or general festival described above, which may take place only once in four or five years. As before, the Sawbwa alone may make offerings to them. The kind of shrine appropriate to the ceremony has already figured as No. 5 on page xxv.

(*Note.*—This practice of restricting the privilege of worshipping certain deities to the chief ruler of the State obtains in China. It would be interesting to ascertain if there be any connection between the Taoist rites and the Kachin custom here noted.)

The markings in the moon are said to be due to the foliage of a big India-rubber tree. There must be some legend attached to this which I have been as yet unable to come across.

(*Note.*—My attention has been attracted by Mr. O'Bryen, Assistant Conservator of Forests, to the curious manner in which trees of the Ficus family seem to be generally objects of veneration among many diverse and widely distinct Asiatic races. Thus the banyan by natives of India, the peepul by Burmans, and the India-rubber tree by Kachins, are all respected. Up in the Hukong valley the Maingkwan column found that, as a rule, there were two or three rubber trees near each village which the Kachins venerated and would on no account permit to be tapped. Doubtless, their umbrageous qualities explain why they are a much sought for boon in hot countries, but many other trees, such as the mango and jack, are equally shady, though the fact that the mango and jack appear to be more frequented by red ants, &c., may possibly have some thing to do with the preference shown to a class of trees not so attractive to venomous insects, and therefore more agreeable to man.)

The system of the universe is supposed to consist of three parallel planes whereof the first constitutes the heavens, the second the earth, and the third is known as "Kasangka" or abode of the Kasangs or Lilliputians. These people are formed after the fashion of mortals, but are of such diminutive size that ordinary grass appears to them like trees, while their deer and wild game are of about the bigness of our crickets aud grass-hoppers. When the sun or the moon sets below the plane of our horizon, the region of the Lilliputs gets the benefit of its rays, so that while it is day on earth, it is night in Kasangka, and *vice versâ.*

Alliances between the Sawbwas of diverse tribes are cemented by marriage. In the ceremonial-making of friendship the parties exchange weapons, das, guns, or spears, and call upon the heaven and earth to witness that they are now one in interest, and hope that they may suffer every misfortune, be "bitten" by nats, swallowed by tigers, or killed with their own da, if they prove unfaithful. Thereafter each sacrifices to the household deities of the other.

The Kachins will eat most things, except snakes, wild cats, monkeys, and tigers (though the latter's flesh is sometimes taken). Dogs, as I have before observed, are only eaten by the Marus, who are consequently somewhat looked down on. All birds, except crows and hawks, are fair game for the pot, while no fish are considered unclean, not even eels, which one would think would be regarded in the same light as snakes. Porcupine's flesh and honey are forbidden to pregnant women for fear of miscarriage. Pigs and domestic cattle are rarely if ever killed solely for food, it being usual to offer them in sacrifices and then eat them, but fowls and wild animals are killed simply for the pot. Unless hard set, the Kachin will not, unlike the Burman, eat cattle found dead or that have died a natural death. Blood is not drunk, though the flesh before all the blood is drained off is cooked and eaten. Beyond the notion that eating a tiger's heart subjects a man to uncontrollable fits of sudden fury, there seems to be no superstition in connection with the effect of food.

Cannibalism is unknown among the true Chinpaws, though Captain Fenton, speaking of the Kalangs, Kanôns, or Kamans, says their chief peculiarity seems to be that they eat their elderly relations when they (not the elderly relations) think they have lived long enough, though they do not practise cannibalism wholesale. "My informant said that "when any man or woman became old and decrepit, their relations assembled together, put "the old person upon a high sort of bamboo scaffold, such as the Kachins erect in front of "their villages in connection with their nat-worship, and then poke them off with bamboos, "so that they fall down and die; then they cut them up into small bits and cook and eat "them. Only relations and intimate friends assist at this ceremony."

Lieutenant Master, writing to me from the Jade Mines, says: "There is a tribe called Ling (? Li-angs) who live in the Assam direction, north-west from here, who dispose of their old men and women by making them drunk, killing and eating them by boiling or rather cooking the flesh." This requires confirmation.

The Kachin house is in the form of a long oblong, with a projecting porch at each end, that in front, however, being most spacious. The following ground-plan will serve to explain better than any description in words the usual arrangement:—

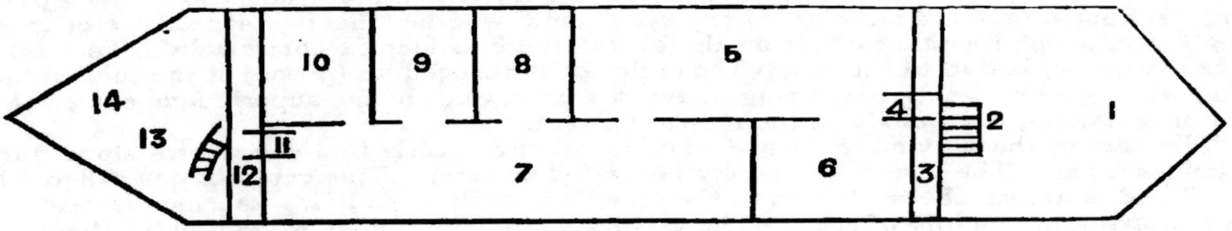

1. Front porch—mpang.
2. Steps—likang.
3. Narrow verandah or landing in front, about 2 feet wide—nau kum.
4. Doorway, usually very narrow—ching-ka.
6. The maiden's apartment—nla. This apartment serves in lieu of the bachelor's hut or dung 'nta, before referred to, in villages where special huts are not built for the purpose.
5. General apartment—can be used as a spare room for guests or for any of the family when the place is crowded.
7. Men's apartment—lupdaw.
8. Room for eldest son and his wife or eldest married couple in the hut.
9. Fireplace—tapnu.
10. Apartment of the parents of the household—ganu-gawa tap.
11. Back door.
12. Back landing.
13. Back stairs.
14. Back porch.

There are no windows, but when the hut is a long one, one or two doors are cut in the sides for easy egress. The back door is not used except by members of the family, otherwise the household nats are offended. The longest house I have met with was about 63 paces in length, say, 150 feet, but these very long houses are by no means so common, at least near Bhamo, as is believed. The houses are raised some 2½ or 3 feet off the ground, the under portion being usually fenced in and forming a happy hunting ground for pigs, fowls, "saltatory hexapods," and other carnivora. A night spent in a Kachin house is an experience not readily forgotten. For absolute dirtiness it is hard to beat a Kachin. Most of them are caked over with real estate and seem to regard it, as Doctor Nansen did in his last Greenland expedition, as an additional and cheaply acquired covering. Luckily for them their climate is tolerably cool and pestilence does not breed. It has been said that the Kachins never wash. This is a libel; they do sometimes. It generally occurs, when there is no help for it, in crossing a stream. There is plenty of opportunity for a boom in soap if some kind-hearted manufacturer would distribute samples free. The houses are constructed of thatch and bamboos, but are far more solidly put together than Burman houses, the posts, particularly in some Sawbwas' houses, having a really fine girth. In front of the porch, on the centre post, are nailed up the heads of buffaloes, &c., that had been sacrificed; the porch itself is used for domestic operations, *e.g.*, paddy-husking and weaving. The paddy is put into a heavy wooden mortar, and two women standing opposite each other pound it in alternate strokes with heavy wooden pestles grasped in the middle.

The weaving is very primitive, there being no frame, the warp being kept stretched by being attached to a bar from which a broad leather strap passes round the back of the operator (a woman), and against which she leans with her legs stretched out straight in front of her. The further end of the warp is attached to a bamboo rod fastened to a peg in the ground. The cloth turned out, though of rough workmanship, is very tough and strong, of a dark blue colour, indigo being the most universal dye. The ends have a narrow strip of variegated pattern, usually in red and yellow. Striped cloths are also met with, but are not as common as others. The Kachin bags—invariable adjunct of Kachin dress—are sometimes very neatly embroidered. As Anderson says: "No hill-man is ever "seen without his da or knife. It is half sheathed in wood and suspended to a rattan hook "covered with embroidered cloth and adorned by a leopard tooth. This is slung over the "right shoulder, so as to bring the hilt in front, ready to the grasp of the right hand."

At the hilt it is an inch and-a-half in breadth, widening to about 2½ inches at the truncated tip. The back is slightly curved.

This is the true Kachin da or linkin. Among the Kachins to the east of Bhamo there is also in use a long straight sword about 2½ feet in length, with a straight wooden half sheath, termed ntu galu. These are said to be manufactured mostly by the Tarens beyond our north-east frontier. Of their instruments of music, dances, &c., I have at present no sufficiently precise knowledge to speak. Gongs of Burmese manufacture are in most request, and of course near Bhamo the Kachins have adopted some of the musical instruments of their neighbours. Speaking generally, the Kachin is lazy and revengeful and treacherous, though how far the last quality is due to the unjust manner in which he in past times has been treated by Shans, Chinese, and Burmans alike, is not clear. So far, going out in columns to punish him for misdeeds, we have not seen him at his best, and perhaps, with fuller knowledge, we shall better appreciate his good qualities.

The above note on the Kachins must necessarily contain inaccuracies. I have been mainly dependent on native information for what has been set down, and have not been able, owing to other duties, to spend the length of time in the hills which would be necessary to test all the statements. There are many points, such as the true doctrine of the soul, which must exist, if only among the esoteric company of the Tumsas,—being shadowed forth by the custom of placing money in the mouth of the dead or in the coffin; the real way in which the Kachin calendar is made to conform to the natural seasons; the characteristics of the different dances; Kachin myth and folklore, which I have been unable to discuss; but the note has been written with the hope of directing the attention of officers accompanying columns to the channels which enquiry might take, and thus leading to a fuller and more accurate knowledge of an interesting and hitherto comparatively unknown race.

The 21st September 1891. E. C. S. GEORGE.

NOTE.—I hear the explorer Alaga described Kachin customs in his report, but it is very difficult to obtain a copy thereof and I have never seen one.

Hpuns.

Mr. George has written a short but suggestive account of another of the broken pre-Chinese tribes as M. de la Couperie styles them. They were first encountered and identified by Captain Hannay, who called them Phwons. Mr. Kincaid, the American Baptist Missionary, also met them and described them under the name of Mwoons. Mr. George and Mr. Kincaid are both inclined to believe that the Hpuns are of Shan extraction. Mr. George, it will be seen, steers clear of the inviting but deceptive derivation of Hpun from the mythical Pong kingdom, and wisely, for, as Dr. Cushing states, so far as he knows the name Hpun is not a Shan name at all. There would have been more excuse for Mr. George had he fallen into this trap than for those who derived Talaing from Telingana, and the fact that he instinctively rejected the fraudulent analogy speaks well for his judgment. I mention this because Mr. George has broken so much new ground that we are bound to accept what he says on trust, as we have not the means of criticising his statements.

Monograph on the Hpuns by E. C. S. GEORGE, Esq., C.S., Deputy Commissioner, Bhamo District.

Another curious race who do not hitherto seem to have been described are the *Hpuns*. These are found only in the third defile, and just above it in the Mankin valley south-east of Sinbo in this district. In features and dress they are now undistinguishable from the ordinary Shan-Burman, while their houses are generally built in the same fashion, with an occasional tendency to the low projecting roof at one end of the house forming a sort of covering over the staircase and the paddy-mill which is affected by the Shan Tayôk.

They state they came from Meungti Meungwan in China about six generations ago. The direction of Meungti Meungwan is described by a semi-circular sweep of the arm towards the east. The distance is unknown. They settled first on the Nanti chaung near Mogaung, but for some unexplained reason, probably early glimmerings of democratic independence, their seven Sawbwas, who had led the exodus, took off the majority of the people to Meungti on the Upper Chindwin, while the radicals came and settled down leaderless in the third defile, where they have remained unmolested ever since, dragging out a precarious existence by means of taungya and timber cutting.

The Forest Department have, however, got their eye on them, and in time the Hpun will be worried into emigration, but who is to take their place is a puzzle. They are invaluable for keeping up communication through the defile in the rains, and, without the help of their villagers, it would be often impossible to tow boats round bad corners, while no other race is likely to take up their village-sites.

They recognize two divisions among themselves—

(1) *Hpun Pyè* or *Meungti Hpuns,* living in the villages of

1. Pulaung.	4. Thamaingyi.	7. Pintaw.
2. Kanti.	5. Nanhè.	8. Hkaungkyè.
3. Htônbo.	6. Hmangin.	9. Hkaungmyè.

Their tones are acute, as opposed to the

(2) *Hpun Samông* or *Meungwan Hpuns,* who speak with a guttural intonation and live in

1. Nansauk.	2. Hnôkkyo (a few).

3. Laungpu.

These latter are said to have emigrated a year or two later from the ancestral home.

Their language is unwritten, and, so far as I know, peculiar. I append a few of their words in case it is possible to trace its resemblance to any other.

Man	=	Yŭsa.	Bullock	=	woālu.
Woman	=	Nŭsa.	Rice	=	tsa.
Water	=	Kheuk.	House	=	aing (Bur. အိမ် evidently).
Land	=	tăm li (Meungti). tăm neuh (Meungwan).	Fire	=	tăm mi (*cf.* မီး).
			Coat	=	hpya.
Foot	=	ăkmuk.	Paso	=	chaukpè.
Hand	=	ă lāw.	Drink	=	kishauk.
Body	=	ă tu.	Eat	=	tsa.

Some words, the last for instance, they have evidently taken from the language of the land of their adoption. Indeed, generally their language is dying out; only the very old men of the villages can speak it properly or understand it. They have words for numerals up to 100,000.

1	=	Taw yôk.	30	=	Sang sik, &c.
5	=	Ha ko.	100	=	Tôk ya (ထဆတ်).
10	=	To sik (ထစ်ဆူ).	1,000	=	Henning.
20	=	Tôk sik.	10,000	=	Meung ngmu.

100,000 = Sawng wun.

Their religion is primitive in the extreme. They worship only one nat, the Natgyi of the hills, once a year, when the whole village present offerings. Otherwise they worship only their immediate deceased ancestors, *i.e.*, mother and father when dead, and not grandfather. This is only done for special reasons, *e.g.*, when sickness occurs. Then food is placed at the *north* end of the house and the *pater familias* prays his parents to partake thereof and help him. Lately, however, Shan practices of having a regular series of nats is creeping in. Divination is practised by the method called "Hpet Tön Hman Taung Kyi" (ဖက်ထုံးမှန်တောင်ကြည်). The leaf of a particular plant called "Shippa Wut" is taken, having parallel veins running at an inclined angle from the midrib to the margin. As these veins do not interlace, it is easy to tear the leaf into long thin shreds, of which a number are taken at random and knotted together, and then another bunch, and so on, whereon by finally consulting the number of the knots and the number of shreds over, it is possible for the initiated to decide whether the fates are propitious or otherwise. This, however, may have been borrowed from the Kachins. It having been, I believe, admitted that the ancient Shan kingdom of "Pông" on the borders of China is more or less a myth, the suggestions that these Hpuns are in any way connected therewith seem hazardous; still it is impossible to doubt, in spite of their distinct language, that the Hpuns had originally something very much in common with the Shans, else in the short space of five or six generations they could hardly have become so modified that it is now difficult to tell the difference.

THE EXCLUDED TRACTS IN THE KATHA DISTRICT.

In the Katha district, as it is now constituted, the greater part of the State of Wuntho is now included. But at the time the census operations were commenced, Wuntho was a semi-independent State; Wuntho therefore was excluded from the operations. The Deputy Commissioner subsequently reported that no regular census could be taken of the Kachin hills, and another tract was also excluded. Finally in February, just immediately before the census was taken and most luckily after the Deputy Commissioner, with commendable punctuality, had prepared his preliminary return as directed in my Circular No. 21, the Wuntho Sawbwa, alarmed at the gradual approach of the railway, broke out suddenly and raided the Kawlin subdivision. He succeeded in burning the court-house of the Subdivisional Officer, and in the confusion that followed, the census schedule books of the Kawlin subdivision that had not been burnt were lost. One result of the rising was the prompt annexation of the Wuntho State and the other was the involuntary inclusion of the Kawlin subdivision in the list of excluded tracts. Still the action of the Deputy Commissioner in carrying out the instructions to obtain a preliminary census lessened the actual loss inflicted.

In Wuntho itself, the area of which is estimated to be 3,000 square miles, there were 502 villages and 6,764 houses, in which there were 33,820 inhabitants of both sexes, that is to say, there were on an average 13·4 houses in each village and 5 persons living in each house. Of the 33,820 inhabitants, 16,921 were males and 16,899 females.

All the information that could be collected regarding the races and religion of the inhabitants has been incorporated in the Census Report. The inhabitants of Wuntho are of mixed descent. As far as can be ascertained, Wuntho was, on account of its poverty and inaccessibility, generally left alone by the Burmans. The origin and history of the Wuntho State is unknown, nor has the Deputy Commissioner of Katha been able to furnish me with any account of it. So far as I have been able to ascertain, this State is a relic of the old Shan kingdom, the existence of which is supposed by Mr. George to be somewhat mythical. But though the name Pông is a name unknown to the Shans, and though tradition has no doubt exaggerated the extent and power and, perhaps, the stability of the Shan kingdom, yet there is abundant evidence to prove that the Tais extended their power across the Irrawaddy and did found a State or series of States in the tract of country now covered by the Katha and Ruby Mines districts and the southern portion of the Bhamo district. Ancient Burmese legends describe how the Tarôk, and Tareks, who after all were Shans, overran and destroyed the Burmese kingdom of Tagaung. The Tais undoubtedly forced their way into Assam and left a colony of Ahoms or Assamese there. Manipur and the Kubo or Kabaw valley is said to have been invaded by them. The Burmans, yielding to the pressure, moved down south and founded the kingdom of Pagan. In course of time the Burmans under Anawratta, re-asserted their power, aided no doubt by the tendency of disintegration which is even yet apparent in the Shans. In his zeal to spread Buddhism, Anawratta extended his conquests as far north as Bhamo. It was probably at this time that this petty State was first separated. Subsequent Shan invasions and internecine wars amongst the Burmans restored the mastery of the Upper Irrawaddy to the Shans, and the fall of the Pagan monarchy which followed the Mongol invasion in the reign of Kublai Khan (Circa) 1284 A.D., was the signal for the establishment of a dynasty of Shan kings at Sagaing. But the power of the Shans was broken, and in A.D. 1554 Bureng Naung again re-asserted the supremacy of the Burmese over the Shans in the valley of the Irrawaddy. The Shans on the western bank escaped the notice of the Burmese only on account of their insignificance and the inaccessibility of their capital, and while the Chiefs of Bhamo, Mogaung, Mohnyin, and Momeit were called in to swear fealty to Alaungpaya when he drove the Talaings out, no mention was made of Wuntho. It is, however, asserted that Sandarit, who was the hereditary Chief or Sawbwa, was recognized as myothugyi by Alaungpaya's son.

No further mention is made of Wuntho till the myothugyi, Maung Shwe Tha, refused to assist the Padein Mintha in his rebellion against Mindôn Min. When the rising was suppressed Maung Shwe Tha was summoned to Mandalay and decorated with the title of Sawbwa. Subsequently, in the reign of Thebaw in 1243 B.E., Maung Shwe Tha was transferred to Mogaung and made Wun of that outlying district. All this, however, tends to prove that Wuntho had no real existence as a separate State. Indeed, until Shwe Tha was recognized as Sawbwa, the myothugyi or Sawbwa was the head rather of a clan than a territorial ruler.

The excluded tracts in the Katha district contained 93 villages and only 613 houses. That the houses are so few is no doubt due partly to the number burnt in the rising and partly to the desire of the local thugyi to conceal the full tale of houses as the thathameda or tax (properly the tithe) is assessed according to the number of houses. There were only 3,814 persons living in this excluded tract, all of whom were Kachins.

Excluded Tracts in the Upper Chindwin District.

There were three States which at the time the census was taken were treated as semi-independent States—Kalè, Taungthut, and Kanti. Besides these three States, in the Upper Chindwin, as in the Katha district, the Wuntho outbreak led to the destruction and total loss of the schedule books of the Uyu township.

Kalè.—The area of this State is returned at 1,078 square miles. There are seven circles, each of which is administered by an amatgyi or agent of the Sawbwa. The Deputy Commissioner's summary showed only 94 villages, whereas 132 were actually enumerated. There were 7,094 male and 6,329 female inhabitants of all ages. In the 132 villages there were 2,862 houses, being 21·6 houses in each village and 4·6 persons to each house. Of the 13,423 inhabitants, 6,730 were Burmese, 4,220 were Shans, 802 natives of India, 295 Chins, 20 Europeans, 13 Manipuris, and 2 Eurasians.

The following statement shows the number of houses and population of each circle :—

Circle.	Area in square miles.	Number of houses.	Population under Sawbwa's administration.	Military in occupation of State.	Total.
Yezagyo	155	373	1,857	135	1,992
Tein-nyin	130	271	1,164	48	1,212
Kalemyo	75	295	838	516	1,354
Indin	115	295	1,555	...	1,555
Sihaung	60	220	997	31	1,028
Kyaukpyôk	138	271	1,222	...	1,222
Kalèwa	405	739	3,500	109	3,609
Total ...	1,078	2,464	11,133	839	11,972

The Kalè Sawbwa, in addition to the seven circles into which the Kalè State was divided, exerted some control over two circles which border on the Chin hills, namely, the Minlèdaung and Tawyan circles. How the connection arose is unknown. In all probability the inhabitants of these two circles voluntarily sought the assistance and protection of the Sawbwa against the Chin raiders from the hills. In the Minlèdaung circle there were 6 villages containing on an average 18·6 houses apiece and 587 inhabitants of both sexes. In the Tawyan circle there were 4 villages containing on an average 37·5 houses each and 850 inhabitants of both sexes. The returns of these two circles are, however, only given approximately, whereas those of the Kalè State are among the most accurately prepared of any returns obtained from the excluded tracts.

Taungthut.—Taungthut is a petty State north of Kindat on the western bank of the Chindwin river. Just at its south-eastern border it extends across the Chindwin, and the villages of Taphanzeik and Waiswè are included in the area of this State. There are 68 villages containing 910 houses and 4,707 persons of both sexes enumerated. The accompanying note by Mr. Moore gives all the information at present available :—

Boundaries.—North, Uyu township; south, Legayaing and Kabaw townships; east, Chindwin river; west, Manipur and Kabaw townships.

Length, about 56 miles; breadth, average 15 miles; area, 840 square miles.

Government.—The head of the government is the Sawbwa, whose power is supreme and uncontrolled. Next to him in rank are the minthas, his three younger brothers, amongst whom the kyamyaing, the eldest of the three, holds the highest rank. Besides these there are two atwin wuns and two amatgyis who form the Sawbwa's privy council and represent him outside of Taungthut.

Civil divisions.—Taungthut is divided into three myos or townships, namely, Sisaw myo, the Northern township; Gamona myo, the western township; and Myoma, the central township.

The place of township officers is taken by the three minthas. They are responsible for revenue collections in their charges, and civil and criminal cases arising in their jurisdiction are dealt with by them with the assistance usually of an amatgyi. Important cases, however, are dealt with by the Sawbwa himself.

The amatgyis receive no pay. They live by cultivation and occasional presents from the Sawbwa.

Revenue—(*a*) *Thathameda.*—A house-tax is levied every year. The assessment per house varies, but is said to average about Rs. 3. The assessment is determined by the Sawbwa himself in consultation with the minthas and amatgyis. The revenue is collected by the thugyis of each village, who pay their collections to the mintha (who pays it to the Sawbwa) who has charge of their villages. No commission is retained by the thugyis or minthas.

(*b*) *Forest and Fisheries.*—No revenue is derived from these sources by the Sawbwa.

(*c*) *Court-fees.*—An *ad valorem* fee of 10 per cent. is levied in civil cases: no fees are levied in criminal cases, but sentences of imprisonment may be compromised by payment of a fine.

Trade.—The principal exports are bamboos, timber, wax, and paddy. Salt is manufactured at three villages—Mawnwè, Mawlun, and Sanan—in the interior. This salt is taken by Chins, who bring in exchange honey, wax, and miscellaneous forest produce. This salt is not consumed by the natives of Taungthut.

Imports.—Salt, earth-oil, sessamum-oil, kerosine, cotton and silk yarn and piece-goods, ngapi, tobacco, blankets.

Opium.—The poppy is not cultivated in Taungthut. Opium-smoking is not encouraged by the Sawbwa, but a large number of the inhabitants smoke it secretly. Opium selling is punished by a fine of Rs. 30 and confiscation of the opium. Opium-smokers are usually whipped if detected.

Cultivation.—Very little cultivation exists beyond paddy. Kaukkyi paddy is grown in the river-side villages. In the interior taungya cultivation prevails. Small patches of tobacco and maize are also grown; but the tobacco grown is not sufficient for the home consumption and it is imported.

Language.—Principally Shan. Burmese is understood in all the larger villages on the river-side; in the interior Chin and Shan only are spoken.

Population.—Principally Shan. There are a few Chins and Manipuris.

Zinglein Kanti.—Kanti, or, as it should be written, Hkamti, is a petty State known by the name of Zinglein to distinguish it from the tract called Kantigyi or Hkamti Lŏng in the Bhamo district. The information afforded me by the local officers regarding this State is of the very barest description. Unfortunately the Deputy Commissioner had been but a short time in the Upper Chindwin district, and the diary of the Burmese officer who made the enumeration contains very little information regarding the people, their origin or customs. The Summary statement at the end of the appendix gives all the information received from this source. The area of the State is not known, but it contains no more inhabitants than may be found in an ordinarily prosperous village. The inhabitants belong to the Hkamti tribe of the Northern division of the Shan race. They speak Shan, but are taught Burmese in the monastic schools; they are but little removed from being mere savages; indeed, the only custom which distinguishes them is one which is distinctly a savage custom,—that the unmarried young men and girls should sleep together, though in the daytime they live and work apart.

THE EXCLUDED TRACTS IN THE RUBY MINES.

Momeit (Mŏng Mit), with its dependency Mohlaing, is included in the area administered by the Deputy Commissioner of the Ruby Mines district. The enumeration of this State was not only performed in a dilatory but in a very perfunctory manner. The returns were submitted very late, long after the returns of every other State had been received, and the delay was not compensated by greater accuracy. Indeed, I am inclined to believe that the returns are of very little value. Moreover, they were received piecemeal, and the first instalment purported to contain the whole of the returns of the Momeik State. Subsequently, after an interval of over one month, a further report was received, submitting the totals of the Myaukkodaung circle. No return of the population of the partially explored

Kachin Hill Tracts in this district was obtained by the Deputy Commissioner. My regret at the failure to obtain these returns is lessened by the fact that I doubt very much, if they had been obtained, whether they would have been worth compiling.

The area of the State of Momeik is unknown. It contains 205 villages, 5,170 houses, and 20,984 inhabitants.

The following statement will show the distribution of the races in this State :—

STATEMENT A.

Race.	Number of villages.	Number of houses.	Population.
Burmese	19	1,610	6,930
Palaung	90	1,353	5.558
Shan	22	710	2,627
Shan-Burmese	7	811	3.370
Shan-Palaung	1	72	251
Kachin	66	614	2,248
Total ...	**205**	**5,170**	**20,984**

Mr. Daniell, the Assistant Commissioner who made the enumeration of the Myaukkodaung circle, is inclined to think that the population is greatly understated. That such is the case throughout the excluded tracts may, I think, be unhesitatingly accepted.

It will be seen that next to the Burmans the most numerous of the races is that of the Palaungs. In the Census Report I have already dealt with this tribe, who are of the Môn Khmer stock. It is stated that till quite recently the Palaungs were even yet more numerous in this State, and indeed had undisputed possession of the Kodaung circle. The Kachins, who are represented by six tribes, have, however, gradually forced their way down southward, driving the Palaungs before them.

Besides the Palaungs there are some half-breed Shan-Palaungs and Shan-Burmans. Of the Shans there are only 2,627 of both sexes, so that Momeik can hardly be included in the list of Shan States. To what tribe these Shans belong the reports of the local officers do not mention.

There are 2,248 Kachins, all of whom are found in the Myaukkodaung circle. The annexed table shows how these Kachins are distributed :—

STATEMENT B.

Tribe of Kachins.	Villages.	Houses.	Population.
Lakum	26	207	810
Pônkan	6	31	92
Saga	1	19	68
Letor	25	289	986
Maru	6	58	253
Lepei	2	10	39
Total ...	**66**	**614**	**2,248**

Regarding these Kachins Mr. Daniell reports that he is informed that the Saga and Pônkan tribes are offshoots of the Lakums. That the Lakums are the fighting tribe, while the Letors and Marus who preceded them have settled down and have become peaceful peasants.

THE SHAN STATES.

The Shan States that lie within the sphere of British influence have already been enumerated at page 2 of the Census Report.

The origin, history, and distribution of the Shan race has already been discussed in Dr. Cushing's note in Chapters VIII and X of the report. All the information that has been obtained by the local officers has been incorporated in reports submitted to the Secretariat, and I have been informed that Mr. Scott (Shwe Yeo) will be commissioned to prepare a Gazetteer of the Shan States. Under these circumstances, any attempt on my part to dilate on the previous history of these States, or to comment on the results obtained by the enumeration, would be mere waste of time. I therefore attach to this appendix the summary of the enumerations carried out in these States and leave to worthier hands the task of dealing with the questions of ethnography and linguistics that may arise from an examination of the returns. I have, however, been favoured by Mr. Hildebrand, the Superintendent of the Southern Shan States, with notes on the Yins, the Zaleins, and the Inthas. These notes I have here reproduced as they contain information hitherto unpublished regarding these tribes :—

Note on the Yang or Yin Tribes of the Monè subdivision, Southern Shan States, by G. C. B. STERLING, Esq., Extra Assistant Commissioner.

THERE are three tribes of Yang or Yin (ယင်) in the Eastern Shan States—the Yang Sek, (ယင်ဆိတ်), Yang Lam, (ယင်လံ) and the Yang Wan Kun (ယင်ဝါင်ကွါင်). The Yang Sek are most numerous in the State of Maingseik (Meung-sit), but are also found in Monè, Maukmè, and (in small numbers) in other States. The Yang Lam extend over all the border States from Maingmang northwards to Kyethi-Bawsan. The Yang Wan Kun are so called by the Shans from the Wan Kun circle of Legya (Laika), which is the stronghold of the tribe. They are not now, however, confined to that circle, but have spread into the adjacent circle of Monè. They are the least numerous of the three tribes.

The Yang Lam have amalgamated with the Shans to a much greater extent than the other two tribes; mixed villages of Shan and Yang Lam are frequent, and the latter are often cultivators of lowland fields. The Yang Sek and the Yang Wan Kun, on the contrary, usually live in villages of their own and are almost always taungya workers. The outward distinction between Yangs and Shans, and between the different tribes of the former, is the dress of the women. The Yang Sek wear a red and white striped blouse; the Yang Lam a closed skirt, belted round the waist, and reaching nearly to the ankles, of dark blue homespun with a jacket of the same colour.

The dress is quite plain, but modest and becoming. The Wan Kun Yang use the same dark material for skirt and bodice, but their garments are more scanty, fit closer to the body, and the bodice is elaborately embroidered and ornamented with beads. Coils of thin bamboo or cane, covered with *thitsi*, are worn round the waist and on the legs below the knee. Similar leg ornaments are often worn by the Yang Sek, but they are made out of brass wire.

Reed pipes (lwi) are played by each tribe, and the music produced, though very monotonous, is not unpleasant. The Yang Sek national dance is a most vigorous performance, and apparently represents courtship. Twenty or thirty men, singing a sort of chant, prance about around some half-a-dozen women, who every now and then turn sharp round and evade the advances made to them by threading their way through the dancers to the other side of the group. The Wan Kun Yang take their amusements stolidly. A line of men, one or two of whom play the pipes, place themselves opposite an equal number of women. Both sing softly, but the dancing consists of the least possible motion of the feet and bodies. The three tribes are Buddhists, but also worship nats, or at all events propitiate them with offerings.

It is difficult to form an opinion as to the origin of the Yang. They look upon themselves and are regarded by the Shans as dwellers in these States from time immemorial, and they certainly must have been here for a very long time. No tradition of an immigration or first settlement appears to have been handed down, but it is to be noted that the Yang Sek and Yang Wan Kun (who have preserved a more distinct nationality) are very timid and not at all disposed to answer questions.

The three tribes are inclined to look upon each other as different races, but their language shows them to be one. The nearer approach of the Yang Lam of the north to the Shans has led to the introduction of many Shan words, but the language is radically the same as that of their brethren further south. The degrees of relationship are apparently designated by separate words, and there is some diversity in the names used. The Yang Sek call themselves Riang (or Riang Rong); the other tribes seem to accept the names given to them by the Shans, or, if they have preserved their tribal names, think it well not to disclose them.

There is no written language. A short vocabulary, which has been drawn up from enquiries made in different States, is appended. The language is quite distinct from Shan, Taungthu, and Karenni. It would be interesting to compare it with the White Karen dialects. If it has no affinities to these, the origin of the tribes must probably be looked for east of the Salween, perhaps in the La and Wa country, or even further east among the "Musos."

The Zaleins are a not very numerous race inhabiting scattered villages in Mobyè State and in the Myelat of Lwèlôn. They have also one village in Sagwe, and I believe one or two in Saga.

They are also known as "Gaungdo" from the fact that the males shave the whole of the head except a small patch over the ear. They are not unlike the Padaungs in appearance, dress, &c., and their dialect is also very similar, both being closely connected with Taungthu. Like the Red Karens they are very shy, but, unlike them, they have the reputation of being of a quiet and peaceable disposition and of having some respect for the rights of property.

Note on the "Nithas or Paunggyan" who reside in the lake district of the Nyaunggwè State, and who are found in the Myelat and a few of the Eastern Shan States.

IN the year 699 B.E. or 1337 A.D. Prince Padrikkhaya, the son of a certain king of India (I cannot ascertain the name of the State), hearing of the wondrous beauty of the daughter named Shwe-ein Si (ရွှေအိမ်စည်း) of the King of Pagan, desired to marry her, and in order to reach her country obtained a piece of charmed quicksilver (it is not related how), which the possessor swallowing, was enabled to travel or be transported to any spot by simply wishing to be at the desired spot. He being much inflamed by the description he had heard of the charms of this princess of Pagan, his first wish was to be at her side, and, owing to the powers of the charm he had obtained, he had no sooner thought the wish than he was traversing the heavens in the direction of Pagan, much in the same manner as a bird would fly. Just outside the town of Pagan he met a Rahanda coming from the town who was also flying, and enquired of him from where he had come. The Rahanda replied that he was returning from the wedding of the Princess Shwe-ein Si of Pagan with the king's adopted son. The news so took Prince Padrikkhaya aback that in his astonishment he opened his mouth and the charmed quicksilver dropped therefrom on to a thingannet tree near the town of Pagan. The prince thus being dispossessed of the charm, fell towards the ground, and was killed by coming into contact with a clump of bamboos, but his spirit is said to have entered the womb of the Princess of Pagan, who had just been wedded, and she gave birth to a male child in the year 700 B.E. or 1338 A.D.

This child was named Manithesee, and on his reaching the age of 15 years, he having heard of the manner in which the Indian prince had lost the charmed quicksilver, set men to work to search for and bring it to him. The search was fruitless and Manithesee determined to have the thingannet tree cut down in the hopes of finding the charm embedded in it; but as the charm was not found, he had the tree cut up and a raft made of it. When this was done, it was discovered that the raft possessed the same miraculous powers as the charm which had fallen on to the tree of which the raft was made, and perceiving this, Manithesee determined on a journey to the Shan States, where he intended to erect some pagodas and religious shrines. He in the first place visited Tavoy, and collecting a number of natives of Tavoy, he hired them as workmen and brought them with him to Mobyè, where he erected a pagoda, and then to Gaya, in which State, at Tagaung, he also erected a pagoda. He continued his journey to Hmawpi, Nampan, Hmaingthaub, Shwe Linbaw, Nankaung, Yatsauk, Maingkaing, Lwemaingôn, Taungbaing, Kaungdaing, Thandaung, Indein, and Taungdo, at all of these places erecting pagodas. From Taungdo he came up to Thalè-u, on the east bank of the lake, and there built a palace, where he lived for a short time.

Before returning to his own country he deposited at Indein five images of Gaudama which he had so far carried in the very front of his charmed raft; hence the name of the images "Paungdaw-u."

These images of Gaudama are objects of great reverence in the lake and are taken round the lake in state to the music of the beating of drums, blowing of trumpets, and beating of cymbals and gongs in the month of Thadingyut every year.

After making over these images at Indein in the year 720 B.E. (1358 A.D.) or about 533 years ago, Manithesee returned to Pagan, leaving the men he had brought as workmen from Tavoy in the lake district, where they remained and were known by the name of "Paunggyan." This name, as they increased and increased in numbers and overspread the lake district, was altered to the one of "Intha" by which they are now known. I have heard that one of the first of these Tavoyans or Paunggyan to take up his residence was one Po Kè, who built his residence at the mouth of the Indein river, and it is now certainly customary, as the "Paungdaw-u" images are being brought out of the river, for the people to pour a chatty of water on the spot where it is believed that Po Kè's house stood.

This is said to be the origin of the race "Intha," and one is always informed by them that they were originally natives of Tavoy.

Language.—Their spoken language is certainly a dialect of Burmese, only spoken with a strong Shan accent, and it is not improbable that they have some Shan blood in their veins, as before their arrival in the lake, the lake was inhabited wholly by Shans, and I have no doubt that they intermixed.

Their written language is Burmese with the substitution of ဆ "Salein" for သ, which they cannot pronounce. For example, in Burmese သင် would be "thin," but the Inthas call it "sang."

Some of their names for things are quite distinct from Burmese and Shan, and I give a few examples which I can recall to mind just now. I am not aware whether these words are used in Tavoy—

Ant	...	"Palang."
Melon	...	"Pakènsi."
Mattress	...	"Pasangkwi."
Water vessel	...	"Yègya."
Basket	...	"Kun."
Trousers	...	"Tanbi."
Shallow	...	"Ti."

Customs.—The marriage, burial, and customs attending child-birth, are similar to those prevalent in Burma, and the only one of which I can hear, which I am certain is not practised in Burma, is the peculiar one of each householder having a "nat" or spirit attached to his or her family. A place is set apart for this spirit, and food is laid on the spot so set apart every day for the use of the spirit. Whatever is done, even if a new coat is bought for the use of the family, the nat or spirit is petitioned, and unless so petitioned the coat cannot be worn. The Taungthus have a very similar custom, but not exactly the same, and I think it possible it may have been learnt from them.

The manner of rowing practised by the Inthas also calls for remark. Although they are able to row or paddle with their hands, they affect the curious practice of rowing with their legs. The rower standing erect on one leg, encircles the oar with the other, and fixing the blade between his toes, seizes the handle of the oar by his hands just at the point where it appears above his shoulder, throws his weight forward, forcing the oar at the same time backwards with his leg, and thus obtains a good way on the boat. It is a curious sight to see a number of men so rowing in a large boat, and the rapidity with which the boat passes through the water is astonishing.

Dress and houses.—The men dress in exactly the same manner as the Shans, namely, the ordinary gaungbaung, coat and trousers, and the women also in the style affected by their Shan sisters, wearing the ordinary coat and tamein, and carrying the "powa" on their heads and not over the shoulder as in Burma ; they also encircle round the legs below the knee threads of black-dyed cotton, about 3 inches deep on the leg, which is exposed when they walk, and about 1 inch or so on the other leg. This is done to make the skin appear fair from the contrast.

The Inthas have a habit of building their dwelling-houses in the water of the lake itself, in some instances being about half-a-mile from the shore. These houses are built as a rule of bamboos, but in some instances have wooden posts and present the appearance of a floating island.

The annexed statement is a summary of the results of the enumerations in the various States that were excluded from the operations of the regular census. It will be noticed that I have for the purposes of ready identification reproduced the Shan names in their ordinary Burmese pronunciation. It is not yet easy to recognize Theinni in its proper Shan dress of Hsen Wi. In page 2 of the Census Report these States will be found with their Shan as well as their Burman names.

Summary statement showing results of the euumerations carried out in the Tracts Excluded from the Regular census operations.

District.	State.	Area in square miles.	Number of villages.	Number of houses.	Population. Male.	Population. Female.	Total population.	Average population per house.	Average population per square mile.	Races. Lushai.	Kachin.	Palaung.	Shan.	Chinese.	Karenni.	Taungthu.	Taungyo.	Danu.	Burmese.	Shan-Chinese.	Danaw.	Intha.
1	2	3	4	5	6	7	8	9	10	11	12	13	14	15	16	17	18	19	20	21	22	23
Bhamo ...	Excluded tract ...	...	533	8,251	...	...	38,403	4·6	...	...	...	28	240	...	...	...	...	...	...	396	...	...
Katha	Kawlin ...	...	...	4,112	...	...	18,448	...	...	...	...	...	...	...	...	...	...	...	...	...	...	...
	Wuntho ...	3,000	502	6,764	16,921	16,899	33,820	5·0	11·27	...	...	...	...	...	...	...	...	...	...	...	...	...
	Excluded tract ...	...	93	613	...	...	3,814	6·2	...	...	3,814	...	...	...	...	...	...	...	...	...	...	...
Ruby Mines ...	Momeik	...	45	2,296	4,773	4,510	9,283	4·0	...	...	...	2,696	2,459	251	3,410	...	...	...	467	...	...	...
		...	18	304	591	627	1,218	4·0	...	...	...	322	112	...	...	...	...	...	784	...	...	...
		...	5	1,290	2,872	2,811	5,683	4·0	...	...	...	...	...	...	...	...	...	...	5,683	..	...	...
Upper Chindwin	Uyu township ...	...	...	3,144	10,855	11,153	22,008	7	...	...	...	...	...	...	..	...	...	...	...	...	...	...
	Kale ...	...	132	2,862	7,094	6,329	13,423	4·6	...	...	...	...	4,220	114	...	...	...	...	6,730	...	...	...
	Taungthut ...	...	68	910	2,275	2,432	4,707	5·1	...	...	...	...	4,506	...	...	...	...	...	...	...	...	...
	Kanti ...	...	18	238	561	557	1,118	4·6	...	...	...	...	964	...	...	...	...	...	...	...	...	...
Myelet States	Nanke ...	...	45	455	...	...	2,610	5·73	...	...	...	...	180	...	...	2,280	...	...	...	...	...	150
	Lwèmaw ...	...	38	400	...	...	2,300	5·75	...	...	...	...	...	...	...	1,500	250	250	...	...	...	300
	Lwèlôn ...	...	243	3,298	...	...	17,682	5·36	...	1,250	...	...	2,000	...	200	10,800	...	432	...	...	...	...
	Bawnin ...	...	15	408	...	...	2,238	5·47	...	...	...	...	160	...	...	1,428	400	...	...	...	...	250
	Lwè-e ...	...	60	590	...	...	3,340	5·66	...	...	...	...	240	...	...	2,700	200	...	...	...	...	200
	Pinhmi ...	...	32	395	...	...	2,145	5·43	...	...	...	...	...	...	...	1,650	75	...	...	...	100	320
	Kyôn ...	...	20	300	...	...	1,620	5·40	...	...	...	...	...	...	...	1,080	300	240	...	...	...	...
	Pwehla ...	...	27	540	...	...	2,700	5·00	...	...	...	...	...	...	...	1,080	900	720	...	...	...	...
	Pindaya ...	...	33	1,030	...	...	4,780	4·64	...	...	...	100	...	...	...	1,080	450	2,400	...	...	750	..
	Bawzaing ...	...	20	300	...	...	1,650	5·50	...	...	...	...	...	...	...	900	375	375	...	...	...	...
	Kyaukuleywa ...	...	22	330	...	...	1,635	4·94	...	...	...	...	...	...	...	630	375	450	180	...	...	...
	Nankôn ...	...	3	40	...	...	208	5·20	...	...	...	...	...	...	...	144	32	32	...	...	...	...
	Thamakan ...	...	131	1,159	...	...	5,745	4·95	...	...	...	60	640	...	...	2,100	1,800	280	...	...	416	...
	Ywangan ...	...	32	428	673	730	1,403	3·26	...	...	...	...	1,403	...	...	...	...	...	...	...	...	..
	Nantôk ...	...	9	182	330	410	740	4·05	...	...	...	...	377	...	...	195	...	...	...	...	...	31

Summary statement showing results of the enumerations carried ont in the Tracts excluded from the Regular Census Operations—continued.

District.	State.	Races—concluded.					Occupation.																									
		Talaing.	Karen.	Yaungsek.	Marip.	Lassan.	Agriculture.	Cooly.	Trade.	Bazaar-seller.	Doctor.	Clerk.	Lead-worker.	Blacksmith.	Cart-driver.	Headman.	Peon.	Dependent.	Merchant.	Pôngyi.	Goldsmith.	Painter.	Official.	Carpenter.	Fisherman.	Military police.	Servant.	Tailor.	Kader.	Sawyer.	Cattle-trader.	Hawker.
1	2	24	25	26	27	28	29	30	31	32	33	34	35	36	37	38	39	40	41	42	43	44	45	46	47	48	49	50	51	52	53	54
Bhamo ...	Excluded tract ...	...	...	...	...	...	...	...	...	...	...	...	...	...	...	...	...	...	...	...	...	...	...	...	...	...	...	...	...	...	...	...
Katha	Kawlin ...	...	...	...	...	...	...	...	...	...	...	...	...	...	...	...	...	...	...	...	...	...	...	...	...	...	...	...	...	...	...	...
	Wuntho ...	...	...	...	...	...	24,615	...	500	1,000	...	...	...	...	...	...	...	2,000	...	...	...	...	1,205	900	3,000	...	...	...	...	...	100	500
	Excluded tract ...	...	...	...	...	...	...	...	...	...	...	...	...	...	...	...	...	...	...	...	...	...	...	...	...	...	...	...	...	...	...	...
Ruby Mines ...	Momeik	...	...	...	...	...	...	...	...	...	...	...	...	...	...	...	...	...	...	...	...	...	...	...	...	...	...	...	...	...	...	...
Upper Chindwin	Uyu Township ...	...	...	...	...	...	...	...	...	...	...	...	...	...	...	...	...	...	...	...	...	...	...	...	...	...	...	...	...	...	...	...
	Kale ...	...	...	...	...	...	5,931	2,066	912	544	9	3	...	44	67	106	85	1,468	76	449	15	5	778	111	214	493	46	1	...	...	...	...
	Taungthut ...	...	...	...	...	...	2,200	1,170	...	10	92	...	...	24	...	...	...	...	...	62	12	...	530	68	25	...	...	...	478	36	...	...
	Kanti ...	...	...	...	...	...	494	77	...	13	...	...	...	...	...	...	...	296	...	31	...	...	78	17	56	...	...	...	...	8	20	28
Myelat States	Nanke ...	...	...	...	...	...	1,263	171	171	286	...	...	...	...	...	...	...	429	...	...	...	...	229	57	...	...	...	...	...	...	...	...
	Lwèmaw ...	...	...	...	...	..	1,000	230	172	287	...	...	...	...	...	...	...	345	...	...	...	...	207	57	...	...	...	...	..	...	...	...
	Lwèlôn ...	...	...	...	...	...	12,376	312	589	611	...	...	...	...	...	...	...	2,144	...	...	...	...	1,195	187	...	...	...	...	...	...	...	...
	Bawnin ...	...	...	...	...	...	1,245	185	109	311	...	...	...	...	...	...	...	295	...	...	...	...	82	11	...	...	...	...	...	...	...	...
	Lwè-e ...	...	...	...	...	...	1,386	283	339	452	...	...	...	...	...	...	...	452	...	...	...	...	328	96	...	...	...	...	...	...	...	...
	Pinhmi ...	...	...	...	...	...	1,126	54	81	239	...	...	...	...	...	...	...	448	...	...	...	...	157	...	...	...	...	...	...	...	...	...
	Kyôn ...	...	...	...	...	...	585	135	167	253	...	...	...	...	...	...	...	378	...	...	...	...	102	...	...	...	...	...	...	...	...	...
	Pwehla ...	...	...	...	...	...	1,400	150	250	350	...	...	...	...	...	...	...	365	...	...	...	...	135	50	...	...	...	...	...	...	...	...
	Pindaya ...	...	...	...	...	...	3,019	185	464	208	...	...	...	...	...	...	...	696	...	...	...	...	139	69	...	...	...	...	...	...	...	...
	Bawzaing ...	...	...	...	...	...	424	...	88	220	...	...	550	...	...	...	...	269	...	...	...	...	99	...	...	...	...	...	...	...	...	...
	Kyaukuleywa ...	...	...	...	...	...	744	98	197	247	...	...	...	...	...	...	...	251	...	...	...	...	98	...	...	...	...	...	...	...	...	...
	Nankôn ...	...	...	...	...	...	101	...	20	31	...	...	...	...	...	...	...	41	...	...	...	...	15	...	...	...	...	...	...	...	...	...
	Thamakan ...	...	...	...	...	...	3,683	198	198	346	...	...	...	...	...	...	...	742	...	...	...	...	529	49	...	...	...	...	...	...	...	...
	Ywangan ...	...	...	...	...	...	737	...	100	...	...	...	...	...	...	...	...	...	...	63	...	8	47	...	...	...	...	...	...	...	...	...
	Nantôk ...	...	137	...	...	...	115	...	82	...	...	...	...	...	...	...	...	...	...	4	...	6	6	...	...	...	...	...	...	...	...	...

Summary statement showing results of the enumerations carried out in the Tracts excluded from the Regular Census Operations—continued.

District.	State.	Area in square miles.	Number of villages.	Number of houses.	POPULATION. Male.	POPULATION. Female.	Total population.	Average population per house.	Average population per square mile.	RACES. Lushai.	Kachin.	Palaung.	Shan.	Chinese.	Panthay.	Taungthu.	Taungyo.	Danu.	Burmese.	Shan-Chinese.	Karen.	Hindustani.	Intha.	Tallaing.	Yin.
1	2	3	4	5	6	7	8	9	10	11	12	13	14	15	16	17	18	19	20	21	22	23	24	25	26
Northern Shan States.	North Theinni ...	...	507	...	...	...	31,103	...	...	...	6,725	4,245	...	385	50	...	...	...	...	...	...	...	...	...	...
	South Theinni ...	...	406	...	...	...	13,262	...	...	...	...	...	...	...	...	...	...	...	...	...	...	...	...	...	...
	Thibaw ...	...	88	...	...	...	3,844	...	...	...	...	...	...	...	...	...	...	...	...	...	...	...	...	...	...
	Taungbaing ...	...	186	2,961	6,985	7,233	14,218	4·80	...	154	2,090	8,661	3,199	114	...	...	...	...	...	...	...	...	...	...	...
Southern Shan States.	Monè (Kyaingtaung)	...	662	6,957	...	...	20,113	2·89	...	...	...	...	16,989	...	...	993	...	...	...	...	...	...	...	...	2,131
	Maingpun ...	...	69	988	1,573	1,517	3,090	3·12	...	...	...	...	2,809	...	...	32	...	...	87	...	...	...	...	...	...
	Maingnaung ...	...	321	3,164	5,833	5,977	11,810	3·76	...	...	...	...	11,164	...	...	...	...	...	42	...	...	...	...	...	604
	Kaingkan ...	...	111	850	1,612	1,654	3,266	3·84	...	...	...	...	3,266	...	...	...	...	...	...	...	...	...	...	...	...
	Kyethi-Bansan ...	...	174	1,984	5,043	5,133	10,176	5·12	...	...	...	...	8,137	...	...	...	...	...	...	...	...	...	...	...	2,039
	Kainglun ...	...	54	1,002	2,140	2,045	4,185	4·17	...	...	...	...	4,037	...	...	...	...	...	...	...	...	...	...	...	148
	Maingshu ...	...	119	1,611	2,962	2,811	5,773	3·58	...	...	...	...	4,637	...	...	...	...	...	...	...	...	...	...	...	1,136
	Maingsin ...	...	32	428	673	730	1,403	3·26	...	...	...	...	1,403	...	...	...	...	...	...	...	...	...	...	...	...
	Yatsauk ...	...	193	2,936	4,233	4,544	8,777	2·98	...	...	...	148	4,110	...	...	1,307	16	3,196	...	...	...	...	...	...	...
	Maingkaing ...	...	218	3,128	5,486	5,694	11,180	3·57	...	...	...	247	10,816	...	...	77	...	...	...	...	...	...	...	...	...
	Lègya ...	...	203	2,848	4,370	4,558	8,928	3·13	...	...	...	...	6,731	...	...	1,613	...	...	71	76	...	...	...	...	40
	Maingseik ...	...	126	1,880	2,689	2,968	5,657	3·00	...	...	...	...	3,962	...	...	450	...	...	38	...	...	...	...	...	437
	Maingpan ...	...	168	2,106	3,317	3,782	7,099	3·37	...	...	...	...	3,783	...	...	3,231	...	...	31	...	...	...	...	...	207
	Thatôn ...	...	122	1,464	3,503	3,823	7,326	5·00	...	...	...	...	1,531	...	...	5,541	...	...	87	...	155	2	...	...	54
	Sagwe ...	...	30	470	833	901	1,734	3·68	...	...	...	...	1,100	...	...	46	...	...	...	...	544	...	17	27	...
	East Nyaungywè ...	...	545	6,559	...	...	33,715	5·14	...	...	...	...	3,352	...	...	10,548	1,585	925	...	...	...	...	17,305	...	...
	Mobyè ...	...	202	3,017	...	...	16,050	3·31	...	...	...	11,250	1,420	...	...	540	...	...	...	...	...	...	400	...	...
	Maukmè ...	...	455	5,000	...	...	15,900	3·18	...	...	...	...	8,100	...	...	6,600	...	...	...	...	...	...	...	...	...
	Hopông ...	...	117	1,458	2,351	2,667	5,018	3·44	...	...	...	...	2,362	...	...	2,629	3	2	22	...	...	...	...	...	...
	Saga ...	...	202	3,685	8,295	8,959	17,254	4·65	...	...	...	...	6,808	...	...	5,010	243	10	85	...	152	...	4,711	...	...
	Naungmun ...	...	65	1,197	2,108	2,552	4,660	3·89	...	...	...	...	4,430	...	8	150	...	...	50	...	...	...	22	...	...
	Nankôk ...	...	88	1,332	2,441	2,721	5,162	3·87	...	...	...	...	3,272	...	...	889	...	...	1	...	...	...	...	...	...
	Banyin ...	...	142	1,895	4,281	5,058	9,339	4·92	...	...	...	...	3,754	...	...	5,220	...	46	...	...	41	...	278	...	...

Summary statement showing results of the enumerations carried out in the Tracts excluded from the Regular Census Operations—concluded.

District.	State.	Races—concld.					Occupation.																							
		Gaungtu.	Yangsek.	Karenni.	Yinbaw.	Unknown.	Agriculture.	Cooly.	Trade.	Tattooer.	Artizan.	Bazaar-seller.	Doctor.	Clerk.	Lime-maker.	Butcher.	Blacksmith.	Fisherman.	Paper-maker.	Carpenter.	Goldsmith.	Shoemaker.	Bamboo-hat maker.	Tailor.	Potter.	Basket-maker.	Oil-maker.	Dancer.	Monk.	Official.
1	2	27	28	29	30	31	32	33	34	35	36	37	38	39	40	41	42	43	44	45	46	47	48	49	50	51	52	53	54	55
Northern Shan States.	North Theinni ...	...	...	...	...	19,698	...	...	...	...	...	...	...	...	...	...	...	...	...	...	...	...	...	...	...	...	...	...	...	...
	South Theinni ...	...	...	...	...	...	...	...	...	...	...	...	...	...	...	...	...	...	...	...	...	...	...	...	...	...	...	...	...	...
	Thibaw ...	...	...	...	...	...	...	...	...	...	...	...	...	...	...	...	...	...	...	...	...	...	...	...	...	...	...	...	...	...
	Taungbaing ...	...	...	...	...	...	4,227	45	399	2	21	22	2	3	4	...	...	...	...	...	...	...	...	...	...	...	...	...	...	...
Southern Shan States.	Monè (Kyaingtaung)	...	...	...	...	...	...	...	...	...	...	...	...	...	...	...	...	...	...	...	...	...	...	...	...	...	...	...	...	...
	Maingpun ...	...	...	...	...	...	741	...	39	...	...	26	12	...	...	...	3	4	...	8	3	...	...	...	...	...	5	6	...	...
	Maingnaung ...	...	...	...	...	...	2,167	...	46	...	...	160	12	...	...	10	3	5	...	8	3	2	5	...	...	...	...	...	...	...
	Kaingkan ...	...	...	...	...	...	603	...	29	...	...	22	4	...	...	12	1	10	11	...	...	...	...	...	...	...	...	...	...	...
	Kyethi-Bansan ...	...	...	...	...	...	1,184	...	341	...	...	...	1	6	...	...	15	...	2	10	5	7	51	5	1	8	...	...	...	...
	Kainglun ...	...	...	...	...	...	738	...	30	1	...	8	5	...	...	...	2	...	1	5	1	...	2	1	...	...	...	...	...	...
	Maingshu ...	...	...	...	...	...	1,305	...	52	...	...	20	...	...	...	7	2	2	...	5	1	...	...	1	...	...	...	...	...	...
	Maingsin ...	...	...	...	...	...	300	...	4	...	...	8	...	...	...	...	...	...	...	...	...	...	...	...	...	...	...	...	...	...
	Yatsauk ...	...	...	...	...	...	2,127	...	243	...	26	...	...	...	...	...	...	...	...	...	...	...	...	...	...	...	...	...	97	52
	Maingkaing ...	...	...	...	...	...	2,507	...	495	...	146	...	...	...	...	...	...	...	...	...	...	...	...	...	...	...	...	...	198	104
	Lègya ...	...	...	...	...	...	2,050	...	518	...	173	...	...	...	...	...	...	...	...	...	...	...	...	...	...	...	...	...	80	24
	Maingseik ...	...	...	...	...	...	1,480	...	183	...	82	...	...	...	...	...	...	...	...	...	...	...	...	...	...	...	...	...	38	12
	Maingpan ...	...	...	...	...	...	1,826	...	183	...	21	...	...	...	...	...	...	...	...	...	...	...	...	...	...	...	...	...	59	14
	Thatôn ...	...	...	...	...	...	1,678	...	272	...	59	...	...	...	...	...	...	...	...	...	...	...	...	...	...	...	...	...	81	18
	Sagwe ...	...	...	...	...	...	375	...	62	...	37	...	...	...	...	...	...	...	...	...	...	...	...	...	...	...	...	...	11	9
	East Nyaungywè ...	...	...	...	...	...	14,854	1,969	4,626	...	...	4,883	...	...	...	...	...	1,028	...	257	...	...	...	...	...	...	...	...	...	2,373
	Mobyè ...	1,400	...	260	780	...	8,062	796	1,327	...	...	1,858	...	...	...	...	...	371	...	265	...	...	...	...	...	...	...	...	...	982
	Maukmè ...	...	450	750	...	...	7,727	1,908	477	...	...	795	63	1,590	...	...	31	31	...	63	19	12	...	...	...	...	...	...	...	...
	Hopòng ...	...	...	...	...	...	979	...	419	...	53	...	...	...	...	...	...	...	...	...	...	...	...	...	...	...	...	...	35	66
	Saga ...	235	...	...	...	...	3,953	...	434	...	148	...	...	...	...	...	...	...	...	...	...	...	...	...	...	...	...	...	82	185
	Naungmun ...	...	...	...	...	...	647	...	535	...	57	...	...	...	...	...	...	...	...	...	...	...	...	...	...	...	...	...	33	39
	Nankôk ...	...	...	...	...	...	1,092	...	283	...	99	...	...	...	...	...	...	...	...	...	...	...	...	...	...	...	...	...	28	51
	Banyin ...	...	...	...	...	...	1,989	...	402	...	16	...	...	...	...	...	...	...	...	...	...	...	...	...	...	...	...	...	52	70

APPENDIX B.

Index of Castes, Tribes, and Races found in Burma—Census, 1891.

Castes, Tribes, and Races.		Class.	Group.
HINDU.			
A.			
Ahir	Hindu	A	2
Aheri	,,	A	4
Agamudayan	,,	A	1
Arain	,,	A	2
Agaria	,,	D	30
B.			
Barai—			
Tamboli	Hindu	A	2
Brahman—			
Trivedi			
Pandè			
Misser			
Sukul			
Pandit			
Lahiri			
Thakur			
Sannyal			
Chaubè	,,	B	5
Gauria			
Halwi			
Banerji			
Ayar			
Chakravarti			
Mukherji			
Chatterji			
Dobè			
Bhat—			
Charna			
Baitali	,,	B	8
Bhujua—			
Barhaniya	,,	A	2
Bhangi—			
Toti			
Lalbagi			
Hela	,,	D	39
Mehtor			
Banya—			
Kansari			
Kundu			
Lohiya			
Soniya			
Bais	,,	C	14
Choti			
Khandelwal			
Jamaniya			
Baidya (Vaidya)	,,	B	10
Bhundauriya	,,	B	5
Balija—			
Naidoo			
Cavarai	,,	D	29
Bhar—			
Raj Bhar	,,	E	45
Barhai—			
Khati	,,	D	20
Bajgi	,,	B	12
Bhotiya—			
Jwar	,,	A	1
Boriya	,,	A	2
Bari	,,	E	45
HINDU—*continued.*			
Bengali	Non-Hindu Buddhist	F	48
	Christian	F	52
C.			
Chatri	Hindu	A	1
Chandal	,,	E	45
Chetti—			
Rowa			
Rana	,,	C	14
Chamar—			
Raedass			
Mochi	,,	D	38
Madiga			
Chero—			
Kharwar	,,	A	4
D.			
Dhobi—			
Chakkalvadu	Hindu		
Dariya	Musalman	D	24
Dogra	,,	A	4
Dom—			
Patwa			
Agaria	,,	E	43
Darzi	Hindu	D	22
Dasari	,,	E	45
Dusadh—			
Kurin			
Palwar	,,	E	45
Maghaiya			
Dhuniya	,,	D	25
Dhangar—			
Oraon	,,	A	2
Dhanuk	,,	A	2
Dholi	,,	B	11
Dosali	,,	E	43
F.			
Fakir—			
Radha			
Bairagi			
Khaki			
Duriya	Hindu	B	6
Gosain			
Vaishnava			
Sadhu			
Fakir	Musalman	B	6
G.			
Gwala—			
Ahir			
Jadavalu	Hindu	D	26
Conan			
Gadariya	,,	D	26
Gujar	,,	A	1
Gandhi—			
Panuri	,,	D	36
Gharuk	,,	A	2
Gujaratti	Hindu / Musalman	C	14
Gurkha	Hindu / Musalman	F	48

Index of Castes, Tribes, and Races found in Burma, Census, 1891—continued.

Castes, Tribes, and Races.		Class.	Group.
Hindu—*continued.*			
H.			
Heri	Hindu	A	4
J.			
Julaha—			
Jugi			
Kori			
Laha	Hindu	D	23
Nath			
Parshutiya			
Julaha	Musalman	D	23
Jat—			
Kudar	Hindu		
Jatki	Sikh	A	1
Nanakas			
Jaiswara	Hindu	A	2
K.			
Kurmi—			
Kunbi			
Murao	Hindu	A	2
Kachi			
Mali			
Koyastha—			
Dey			
Datta			
Pall			
Lalla			
Roy	"	B	9
Das			
Ghosh			
Mitra			
Basu			
Kumhar—			
Pal	"	D	28
Kamhar—			
Lohar	"	D	19
Kalwar	"	D	36
Karar	"	A	2
Kapu	"	A	2
Kahar—			
Gariya			
Bari			
Turha	"	D	35
Mahran			
Komati	"	C	14
Kodulu	"	A	4
Kamsala	"	D	17
Kewat—			
Gurya	"	A	2
Kher	"	A	4
Kanakkan—			
Pillay	"	B	9
Khwa	"	A	2
Kamma	"	A	1
L.			
Lodha—			
Banyan			
Kahar	Hindu	A	2
Lakheya			
Lohar—			
Lohar	Hindu / Sikh do.	D	19
Luniya—			
Agaria	Hindu	D	30
M.			
Maravan—			
Thavar	Hindus	A	1
Meo	"	A	1

Castes, Tribes, and Races.		Class.	Group.
Hindu—*continued.*			
Mallah—			
Marwari	Hindu	D	35
Manjhi			
N.			
Nao—			
Napit			
Ambattan	Hindu	D	18
Paramanic			
Nair	"	A	4
Nat—			
Marpali	"	B	12
Naik	"	A	2
O.			
Oddar	Hindu	E	41
P.			
Paria or Parayan—			
Mala	Hindu	A	2
Palli—			
Padayachee	"	A	2
Pundaram	"	B	5
Pasi	"	D	36
R.			
Rajput—			
Kshatriya			
Singh			
Marwar			
Jaiswara			
Khokar	Hindu	A	1
Chauhan			
Bisen			
Rathor			
Kaushik			
Pundir			
Reddi	"	A	2
Rora	"	C	14
Raj	"	A	2
Reli	"	A	2
S.			
Sathani—			
Satani	Hindu	B	7
Sonar	"	D	17
Sukiar	"	A	2
Savaralu	"	A	2
Sembadavan—			
Besta			
Jalai			
Rajbansi	"	D	35
Rawani			
Shannan—			
Gamalla	"	D	36
Idiga			
Suri	"	D	36
T.			
Teli	Hindu	D	27
Telukulu	"	D	27
Turi	"	E	45
Taga—			
Maheswara	"	A	1
Toti—			
Lalbegi	"	D	39
Tharu	"	A	2
U.			
Udayan	Hindu	D	28

Index of Castes, Tribes, and Races found in Burma, Census, 1891—continued.

Castes, Tribes, and Races.		Class.	Group.
Hindu—*concluded.*			
V.			
Vellala—Mudaliar ...	Hindu ...	A	1
Vaishya ...	,, ...	A	2
Vandayar ...	,, ...	A	2
Vanian ...	,, ...	A	2
Valluvan ...	,, ...	B	5
Y.			
Yalla ...	Hindu ...	A	1
Musalman.			
Shaikh ...	Mahomedan ...	F	48
Pathan—Pathan ...	,, ...	F	48
	Christian ...	F	52
Saiyad ...	Mahomedan ...	F	48
Choliar ...	,, ...	F	48
Mughal ...	,, ...	F	48
Hajjam (Nao) ...	,, ...	D	18
Suratti (Bora) ...	,, ...	F	48
Arab ...	,, ...	F	48
Turk ...	,, ...	F	48
Mappallai ...	,, ...	F	48
Lubbai ...	,, ...	F	48
Burmese.			
Burmese ...	Buddhist ..., Mahomedan ..., Nat-worshipper	F	48
	Christian ...	F	52
Arakanese ...	Buddhist, Nat-worshipper, Mahomedan ...	F	48
	Christian ...	F	52
Chaungtha ...	Buddhist ..., Nat-worshipper	F	48
Selon ...	,, ...	F	48
Talaing ...	Buddhist ..., Nat-worshipper	F	48
	Christian ...	F	52
Tavoy ...	Buddhist ..., Nat-worshipper	F	48
Yabein ...	Buddhist ..., Nat-worshipper	F	48
Zerbadi ...	Buddhist ...	F	49
Chinese.			
Chinese ...	Buddhist ..., Nat-worshipper	F	48
	Christian ...	F	52
Panthay ...	Mahomedan ...	F	48
Chinese-Burmese ...	Buddhist ..., Nat-worshipper	F	49
Chin.			
Chin ...	Buddhist ..., Nat-worshipper	F	48
	Christian ...	F	52
Chin Thet ...	Buddhist ...	F	48
Chin Daignet ...	,, ...	F	48
Chin Kwemi ...	,, ..., Nat-worshipper	F	48
Chin Ann ...	,, ...	F	48
Chin Mro ...	,, ...	F	48
Chin Lushai ...	,, ...	F	48
Chin—Taigma ..., Tainsa ..., Taungyi ..., Mu ...	,, ...	F	48

Castes, Tribes, and Races.		Class.	Group.
Karen.			
Karen Pwo ...	Buddhist ..., Nat-worshipper, Mahomedan ...	F	48
	Christian ...	F	52
Karen Sgau ...	Buddhist ..., Nat-worshipper, Mahomedan ...	F	48
	Christian ...	F	52
Karenni ...	Buddhist ..., Nat-worshipper	F	48
	Christian ...	F	52
Kamu Karen ...	Buddhist ..., Nat-worshipper	F	49
Kachin—Malo ..., Lakun ..., Lamaing ..., Pallaing ..., Yallaing ..., Kaya ..., Mayan ..., Lathaing ..., Moyit ...	Buddhist ..., Nat-worshipper	F	48
	Christian ...	F	52
Kathe ...	Nat-worshipper, Mahomedan ..., Buddhist ...	F	48
	Christian ...	F	52
Chhattri ...	Buddhist ...	A	1
Malay ...	,, ..., Nat-worshipper, Mahomedan ...	F	48
	Christian ...	F	52
Shan ...	Buddhist ..., Nat-worshipper, Mahomedan ...	F	48
	Christian ...	F	52
Maingtha ...	Buddhist ..., Nat-worshipper	F	48
Yun Shan ...	Buddhist ..., Nat-worshipper	F	48
Danu ...	Buddhist ..., Nat-worshipper	F	48
Kamu Shan ...	,, ...	F	48
Lawa Shan ...	Buddhist ..., Nat-worshipper	F	48
Samon Shan ...	Buddhist ..., Nat-worshipper	F	48
Shan-Chinese ...	Buddhist ..., Nat-worshipper	F	49
Shan-Burmese ...	Buddhist ...	F	49
Taungthu ...	,, ..., Nat-worshipper	F	48
	Christian ...	F	52
Palaung ...	Buddhist ..., Nat-worshipper	F	48
Kadu ...	Buddhist ...	F	48
Siamese ...	Buddhist ..., Nat-worshipper	F	48
	Christian ...	F	52
Singhalese ...	Buddhist ...	F	48
	Christian ...	F	52
Yaw ...	Buddhist ..., Nat-worshipper	F	48
Miscellaneous Races.			
Jews ...	Christian ...	F	52
	Judaism ...	F	48
Parsi ...	Fire-worshipper	F	48
	Christian ...	F	52
Madrassi ...	Christian ...	F	52
Eurasian ...	Buddhist ..., Christian ...	F	51
Jamaican ...	,, ...	F	52

Index of Castes, Tribes, and Races found in Burma, Census, 1891—concluded.

Castes, Tribes, and Races.		Class.	Group.
MISCELLANEOUS RACES—*concluded.*			
Goanèse ...	Christian ...	F	52
Japanese ...	" ...	F	52
Egyptian ...	" ...	F	50
African ...	" ...	F	50
EUROPEAN RACES.			
English ...	{ Christian ... { Buddhist ...	} F	50
French ...	Christian ...	F	50
Irish ...	" ...	F	50
Welsh ...	" ...	F	50
Scotch ...	" ...	F	50
German ...	" ...	F	50
Italian ...	" ...	F	50
EUROPEAN RACES—*concluded.*			
Austrian ...	Christian ...	F	50
Portuguese ...	" ...	F	50
Danish ...	" ...	F	50
Dutch ...	" ...	F	50
Russian ...	" ...	F	50
Swiss ...	" ...	F	50
Swede ...	" ...	F	50
Greek ...	" ...	F	50
Norwegian ...	" ...	F	50
Maltese ...	" ...	F	50
Finn ...	" ...	F	50
American ...	" ...	F	50
Australian ...	" ...	F	50
Canadian ...	" ...	F	50
West Indian ...	" ...	F	50

APPENDIX C.

Circulars, Instructions, and Specimen Forms.

From J. E. Bridges, Esq., Officiating Chief Secretary to the Chief Commissioner, Burma, to all Deputy Commissioners, Burma,—No. 506-6C.G., dated the 16th May 1890.

I am directed by the Chief Commissioner to forward to you the following instructions and remarks on the subject of the census to be taken on the 26th February 1891.

2. The method in which the census will be conducted may be briefly explained before the agency to be employed is described and detailed instructions are given.

Lists of houses, monasteries, and other buildings which may probably be inhabited on the night of the census will be prepared for each district, circle by circle, township by township, and subdivision by subdivision, and the buildings enumerated in these lists will be divided into suitable groups called *Blocks*. Books of census schedules will be distributed to District Officers, and after the enumerators and other Census Officers have been instructed in their duties, these (books will be issued to the enumerators with the numbers assigned to the houses) and the names of the heads of the houses entered in a list accompanying the book. Blank schedules for camping-places, new buildings, wayfarers, &c., will be left at the end of the schedule book. The enumerators whose work will be thoroughly tested by the Supervisors of Circles and Superintendents of Charges will, during January, fill in the names and other particulars for all persons belonging to each house and expected to be residing there on the night of the census. This is called the preliminary record. On the night of the census the enumerator will visit every house and add to, or strike out, entries as may be necessary. This is the final enumeration or census. After further testing and totalling, the books will be handed over by the enumerator to his supervisor. The boat population, travellers, persons in camping-places and the like will be enumerated either on the day preceding the census, or during that night, as may be necessary. In towns the preliminary record will be begun somewhat later than in the rural parts of the province.

3. Deputy Commissioners in Lower Burma have in their offices the records of the census of 1881, including the district reports, as well as the Provincial Census Report for 1881. A reference to these records and reports, more especially to Part I of the Report and Appendix B, may be useful in explaining more in detail the system on which a census is conducted in Burma and the difficulties to be encountered.

4. The territorial basis for census purposes will be the revenue circle, *i.e.*, the jurisdiction of the thugyis, which has a defined area, but the unit of enumeration is the enumerator's block which should, so far as is practicable, be a definite part of a circle. An enumerator's block may consist of only village houses, only boats, only fisheries, only camping-places, cutch-boileries, and the like, or of several of these different classes combined. A block should not, as a rule, consist of more than 60 houses or 300 persons, and, where hamlets are small and distant from each other, or houses are scattered, a block will frequently contain many fewer houses than the maximum. From 10 to 15 blocks will form a census circle under the charge of a supervisor, who will generally be the thugyi of the revenue circle. In cases where the revenue circle is large there will be two or more census circles of defined area, each under a supervisor, one being the thugyi, and the others the yazawutgaungs, police officers of the higher grades, or other person to be selected by the Township Officer, and so on. Every part of a revenue circle must be included in a census circle under a supervisor; and every part of a census circle in which any person is likely to be found on the night of the census must be assigned to a census block under the care of an enumerator. Groups of census circles will form *Charges*, generally synonymous with townships, and usually under the care of the Township Officer as *Superintendent*. Each Subdivisional Officer will be responsible for the proper arrangement and carrying out of the instructions in his subdivision. All Government officers serving in the district will be required to assist the Deputy Commissioner in arranging, supervising, and conducting the census.

5. The first step that Deputy Commissioners must now take is to estimate as well they can the number of census schedules that they will require for their districts, remembering that a separate schedule will be required for each house and about 20 per cent. extra for rest-houses, new houses, tès, &c. These rough estimates for house-schedules can be prepared on the basis of the most recent thugyis' rolls, if these rolls show the numbers of houses in their circles. This preliminary estimate should be submitted before the middle of June in the following form :—

Preliminary estimate of Census Schedules required in the district.

Township.	Number of houses.	Number of houses plus 20 per cent. equals number of schedules required.	Remarks.

6. Lists of houses with the name of the head of the house, shown as much as possible in the order in which the houses stand, have then to be prepared village by village for every revenue circle. Monasteries, rest-houses, and camping-grounds near the village, that may perhaps be occupied, should also be shown in their order. These lists will be prepared by the thugyi of the circle in the following form, printed copies of which will be procurable from the Superintendent, Government Printing. He will not fill in column 9.

CIRCLE REGISTER (A).

Name of Township

Name of circle.	Name of village.	Serial No. of house or monastery.	Description of house, &c. (dwelling-house, monastery, &c.)	Name of head of house or monastery, &c.	Zayats.	Camping-grounds, cutch-boileries, &c.	Boat landing-places, fisheries, &c.	Serial No. of the block.	Remarks.
1	2	3	4	5	6	7	8	9	10

The Township Officer will scrutinize the thugyis' lists in consultation with the latter and will determine the blocks to be formed, marking them off in column 9 of the above register. This register then becomes a block statement and will be submitted by the Township Officer to the Subdivisional Officer.

7. If there are likely to be inhabited boats in small numbers near any house block, the number of boats expected to be there should be entered in the column of remarks, and the number of houses to be allotted to a block should be redueed proportionately. A separate series of house numbers should run for each village and there should not be two series of numbers in the same village ; provided that, where a village lies partly in one census circle and partly in another, there should be a separate series of numbers for each part. The Subdivisional Officer, after consulting the Township Officers and, if necessary, making further inquiry, will then submit his house lists, showing blocks and census circles proposed for each township to the Deputy Commissioner and will at the same time nominate the census supervisors and enumerators for each circle and block.

8. A supplementary register in the following form will be prepared of places where inhabited boats are expected to be numerous and where consequently special boat enumerators must be appointed. As a rule, special enumerators should be appointed for boats if they will exceed five in number. In case they do not exceed this number, they can be allotted to a house block as described above. Thirty boats will generally be found sufficient for one enumerator, as the whole schedule will have to be filled up during the day preceding the night of the census.

Circle Register **(B)** *of Boat landing-places District Township.*

Village.	Name of landing-place.	Number of boats expected to be there at the end of February.	If allotted to a house block or not.	Serial No. of boat blocks.	Remarks.

The Township Officer and Subdivisional Officer will submit this list to the Deputy Commissioner with their recommendations and will nominate an enumerator for each block.

9. The Deputy Commissioner will now be in a position to submit a final indent for schedules showing the sizes of books and the numbers of each size required for his district. House schedules will be bound up in book form, the books containing 16, 30, and 60 schedules respectively, each schedule occupying one page. Boat schedule books will be of two sizes containing 8 and 16 schedules respectively and must also be indented for. The house block registers and boat registers should be prepared by the end of July and the final indents for schedules should be submitted before the end of August. Great care should be exercised in the preparation of the lists and submission of the indents, and to ensure the accuracy of the latter. Consideration must be given to the requirements for camping-grounds, fisheries, field huts, cutch and salt boileries, survey parties, and the like, with reference to the season at which the census is to be taken; and, further, the numbers of persons who may be expected to be at each place or travelling along trade routes must be estimated. A list of such places, with the numbers of schedules required, should be subjoined to Register (A) and to the indents for schedules.

Form of Indent for Schedules in the District.

Township.	House schedules.			Boat schedules.		Remarks.
	Number of books of 16 schedules.	Number of books of 30 schedules.	Number of books of 60 schedules.	Number of books of 8 schedules.	Number of books of 16 schedules.	

10. During October and the first half of November Register (A) will be checked and corrected by the thugyis, who will number the houses in accordance with it, as prescribed in paragraph 12 below, and re-submit the list to the Township Officer. During the same period the Census Officers will be appointed by order in writing and their instructions in accordance with rules to be issued separately will be proceeded with.

11. During the latter half of November and the first half of December the names of the heads of houses will be entered in the block lists forming part of the schedule book and the docket on the cover of each book will be filled up. This will be done in the District or Subdivisional Offices. The schedule books must be distributed so as to reach the enumerators through the various grades of Census Officers before the end of December. Specimen schedules and blank schedules for practice and copies of Instructions to Supervisors and Enumerators will be issued in September to District Officers; and the instruction of Census Supervisors and enumerators by the Deputy Commissioner, Subdivisional Officers, Myoôks, and other officers of the district must be systematically carried on, so that when the schedules reach the hands of the enumerators at the end of December the latter may be well acquainted with what they have to do.

12. Numbers will be painted on or affixed to houses by the thugyis according to their lists during October, by means of chalk, lime, charcoal, tickets, or in any other convenient manner, and the enumerator, on beginning his preliminary record, will enter these numbers at the head of the schedules. Zayats may be numbered at the end of the series.

13. Supervisors will be furnished with a summary of the circle register showing the blocks, the names of the enumerators of each block in their circle, the numbers of house and boat schedules made over to them, and so on. This list will be in the subjoined form and, like Register (A), will be printed at the Government Central Press. Deputy Commissioners will see that every schedule issued is used or accounted for and a complete register of issues showing to whom and in what numbers schedules are issued must be kept by each Census Officer for his charge.

SUPERVISOR'S LIST.

District *Township.*

Name of revenue circle.	Name of Supervisor.	Name of block or village.	Name of enumerator.	Total number of inhabited buildings in each block.	Number of boats estimated for.	Series or parts of series of numbers forming the total of column 5.	Number of house schedules issued and in what sized books.	Number of boat schedules issued and in what sized books.	Remarks
1	2	3	4	5	6	7	8	9	10

14. In outlying tracts, such as the Karen Hills, Arakan Hills, the Pegu Yomas, the Mergui islands, and among the wilder tribes it will not always be possible to take a census in the ordinary way, both because the population is sparse and because the inhabitants are illiterate and easily alarmed. Special enumerators will have to be selected, if possible, from among the inhabitants themselves, or deputed by the Deputy Commissioner, where local agency is not available, to enumerate the people during February, as near as possible to the date of the census. In some cases corrections to make the entries correspond with the actual state of things on the night of the census can be effected within the three days succeeding the census.

15. In Municipalities the arrangements for taking the census will be made by the Municipal Committees, who should report at an early date their plans for conducting the operations, and should submit indents for schedules by the end of July.

16. The census of the Port of Rangoon will be undertaken by the Port Officer and the Chief Collector of Customs, who will be addressed on the subject; and in other ports the Port Officer will conduct the arrangements. Special instructions regarding the enumeration of vessels will be sent to these officers.

17. Special instructions will be issued regarding the census in cantonments and on railways.

18. In rural districts enumerators will generally be kyedangyis, or village headmen, and lugyis able and willing to assist. In towns they will be ministerial officers of the lower grades, and such non-officials, lugyis, and others of respectability and intelligence as accept the Deputy Commissioner's invitation to give their assistance. Supervising Census Officers will be selected from the following classes: members of Municipal Committees, Police Officers of superior grades, pensioned Extra Assistant Commissioners, and other pensioners of position and intelligence, thugyis, police gaungs, non-officials of respectability and intelligence willing to give their assistance, and officers of the higher grades in all Government departments.

19. On the 25th, 26th, and 27th February all public offices will be closed in order that there may be more time for the work of supervision, and so as to place the services of officers and clerks as far as may be at the disposal of the officers conducting the census.

20. Permission for pwès and other public entertainments on the night of the census should not be given. Boatmen and others should be persuaded not to move at night, and the inhabitants of villages should be desired not to be abroad after 8 P.M.

21. For census purposes and so far as their duties in this behalf extend, all officials engaged in the enumeration are to consider themselves subordinate to the Superintendent of the Charge in which they are employed.

Circular No. 1 of 1890.

From H. L. EALES, Esq., Superinterdent, Census Operations, Burma, to Commissioners of Divisions,—No. 12-18, dated the 25th August 1890.

WITH reference to paragraph 14 of Chief Secretary's letter dated the 16th May 1890, No. 506-6C.G., I have the honour to request that you will be good enough to furnish me with a list of outlying tracts where the census cannot be taken synchronously owing to the sparsity of the population and the difficult nature of the country. Tracts such as the Northern Shan States and the States of Baw and Wuntho have already been dealt with, *vide* letter No. 1020-3C.G., dated the 28th June 1890, to Superintendent, Northern Shah States, a copy of which was forwarded with Under Secretary's endorsement dated the 28th June 1890. But, besides these States, there are the outlying tracts mentioned in paragraph 14 of the letter of 16th May for which special arrangements must be made. I have therefore the honour to request that, when forwarding the list of outlying tracts, you will favour me with your suggestions as to the special arrangement you propose to make.

Circular No. 2 of 1890.

From H. L. EALES, Esq., Superintendent, Census Operations, Burma, to the Presidents, Rangoon and Bassein Municipalities, &c.,—No. 25-14, dated the 29th August 1890.

WITH reference to Revenue Department No. 506-6C.G., dated the 16th May 1890, from the Chief Secretary to all Deputy Commissioners, I have the honour to request you will be good enough to favour me with the plans you propose to make for taking the Census in the Municipality.

Some Municipalities have already submitted indents for schedules. The plans proposed by the Presidents should deal with—

(1) The division of the Municipal area into Census circles and blocks.

This might be shown on a map, tracings of which should be given to each supervisor.

(2) The *personnel* of the enumerators and supervisors.

(3) The location of the boat-blocks.

(4) The means for the enumeration of boats which might pass through the creeks and rivers included in Municipal limits.

(5) Estimate of cost—

(1) Paid enumerators and supervisors, if it be necessary to employ paid men.

(2) Stationery.

(3) Lights, if necessary.

Circular No. 3 of 1890.

From H. L. EALES, Esq., Superintendent, Census Operations, Burma, to all Deputy Commissioners in Burma,—No. 24-21, dated the 29th August 1890.

WITH reference to paragraph 9 of Revenue Department No. 506-6C.G., dated the 16th May 1890, I have the honour to request that you will furnish me with a copy of the Subdivisional Register in the accompanying form. The information required is necessary in order that I may be furnished with a complete record of the work done in each district and as a means of checking the final indent for block-books. Columns 3 and 7 need not now be filled in. The other columns should be filled in at once and all the Subdivisional Registers should be received in this office by the 20th September.

The Subdivisional Registers will be checked and returned to you in order that the names of supervisors and enumerators may be entered by you, and the registers will then be once more returned to this office on or before the 30th October.

District *Subdivision* *Township.*

Name of revenue circle and serial No. for district.	Census circles by serial letter under revenue circle.	Supervisor's name.	Names of villages, boat-blocks, cutch-boileries, fisheries, and camping-grounds which have been blocked separately by serial No. for each revenue circle.	Number of houses in each village.	Blocks by letter in each village when there are more blocks than one in any village; blocks in towns by serial No. under census circle.	Enumerator's name.	Remarks.
1	2	3	4	5	6	7	8

Circular No. 4 of 1890.

From H. L. EALES, Esq., Superintendent, Census Operations, Burma, to all Commissioners and Deputy Commissioners,—No. 29-22, dated the 4th September 1890.

I HAVE the honour to state that the Chief Commissioner has been pleased to direct that, in order to facilitate the work of the Census office, the Superintendent of Census will be permitted to communicate directly with Deputy Commissioners on all matters of detail. A copy of each letter will be sent by the Superintendent to the Commissioner of the Division. The Deputy Commissioners will be permitted to reply directly to the Superintendent of Census, but they will at the same time send a copy of their letters to the Commissioner of the Division. In future all indents for statements and forms should be addressed to the Superintendent of Census.

Circular No. 5 of 1890.

From H. L. Eales, Esq., Superintendent, Census Operations, Burma, to Presidents of Municipalities,—No. 30-14, dated the 4th September 1890.

The forms of Circle Registers A and B, prescribed in paragraph 6 of the letter of the Officiating Chief Secretary, No. 506-6C.G., dated the 16th May, have been found inapplicable in the case of some of the larger Municipalities. I have therefore the honour to forward a sample of form of a circle register for Municipalities. If, however, the Forms A and B, prescribed in paragragh 6 of the letter of the Officiating Chief Secretary, No. 506-6C.G., dated the 16th May, have already been filled in and the blocking finished, there will be no necessity to indent for the new forms. According to this new form no separate register of boat blocks Circle Register B will be required. I have the honour to request you will be so good as to let me know as early as possible how many copies of Municipal Circle Register you may require.

Circle Register for Municipalities.

Taxation circle.	Census Supervisor's circle by letter under Taxation circle.	Blocks by serial No. under Census circle.	Serial No. of house, monastery, zayat.	Description of "house," dwelling-house, lodging-house, hotel, zayat, &c.	Name of head of house, monastery, &c.	Boat landing-places. (These should be blocked apart from the houses and the blocks divided into circles under separate Supervisors.)	Remarks.
1	2	3	4	5	6	7	8

Circular No. 6 of 1890.

From H. L. Eales, Esq., Superintendent, Census Operations, Burma, to all Commissioners and Deputy Commissioners,—No. 23-21, dated the 29th August 1890.

The outlines of the procedure to be followed in the Census of 1891 have been indicated in letter No. 506-6C.G., dated the 16th May, from the Officiating Chief Secretary to all Deputy Commissioners. Experience has shown that misunderstandings have arisen regarding several of the points raised. The following instructions, which have received the Chief Commissioner's approval, are now issued to clear up points that have been shown to require explanation.

2. In no case shall two or more villages be grouped into one block. As a rule each village will be a block by itself. If, however, any village contains more houses than can be conveniently enumerated within three or four hours by a single enumerator on the night of the 26th February 1891, the village should be divided into two or more blocks. As a rule it will be found that few enumerators can check more than 60 houses within three or four hours at night-time. Accordingly no block should ordinarily contain more than 60 houses; but most blocks will not contain so many as this. From 40 to 50 houses in one block will find ample work for one enumerator.

3. In framing the census circle, it may be laid down that each circle should contain from 10 to 15 blocks according as the blocks are large or small. Where the revenue circle or the charge of a ywathugyi is of a convenient size it is expedient to adopt it as the census circle and to make the thugyi a supervisor. There will be an advantage in making the census circle correspond to the well-known revenue or administration circle. Deputy Commissioners will, however, exercise their discretion in framing the circles so as to facilitate the work of the census.

4. Deputy Commissioners should now proceed to fill up Circle Register A if they have not already done so, and to divide the larger villages into blocks. As some misunderstanding has arisen regarding Circle Register A, I enclose for reference a portion of a sample register for your guidance.

CIRCLE REGISTER A.

Sample Register filled in..................................*Name of Township*..

Name of circle.	Name of village.	Serial No. of house or monastery.	Description of house, &c. (dwelling-house, monastery, &c.)	Name of head of house or monastery, &c.	Zayats.	Camping-grounds, cutch-boileries, &c.	Boat landing-places, fisheries, &c.	Serial No. of the block by letter under village No.	Remarks.
1	2	3	4	5	6	7	8	9	10
Paingkyun...	21 Kamakasè.	1	Dwelling-house ...	Maung Pyu ...	There is only one zayat in this village that is likely to be occupied on the night of the census. The other zayats being ruinous are not likely to be inhabited and have not been numbered.			21	Twenty-one is the serial No. of Kamakasè village in the Paingkyun circle. (If it contained, say, 80 houses and were divided into two blocks, the blocks would be No. 21A and 21B respectively).
		2	Dwelling-house ...	Maung Gyaw ...					
		3	Monastery ...	U Tè Za ...					
		4	Dwelling-house ...	Maung Gale ...					
		5	Zayat	......					
		6	Dwelling-house ...	Maung Talôk ...					
		7	Dwelling-house ...	Maung Se ...					
		8	......	......	......	Kamakasè sakan...	......		A small camping-ground near the village that is sometimes occupied.
		9	......	Maung Gyi ...	......	Maung Gyi's boilery.	......		Small cutch-boilery, in which six men only are employed, situated near village.
		10	......	......	......	......	Kadozeik...		Less than five boats resort here.
	Kamakasè fishery.	...	......	Maung Ké ...	......	......	Fishery ...	22	This fishery is blocked apart as Maung Kè employs over 200 men. It is 4 miles from the nearest village, Kamakasè, whose name it bears. There are only 21 villages in the Paingkyun circle and the fishery and boat blocks are numbered as consecutive blocks at the end of the village list.
	Kama ...	...	......	......	......	......	Landing-place.	23	As more than five boats resort here, this landing-place is blocked separately. Please see Circle Register B.

Sample of Circle Register **B** *of Boat landing-places* *District* *Township.*

Village.	Name of landing-place.	Number of boats expected to be there at end of February.	If allotted to a house block or not.	Serial No. of boat blocks.	Remarks.
Kyauktalôn.	Landing-place.	4	Allotted to house block.	...	Allotted as No. 41, Village No. 24, Block C, Tutalôk circle.
Kamasè ...	Kamasè landing-place.	30	Not allotted ...	4	Blocked as No. 23 in Paingkyun circle.
Kamasè ...	Kadozeik ...	2	Allotted to house block.	...	Allotted as Serial No. 10, Village No. 21, Paingkyun circle.
Myothit ...	Pwezaik ...	22	Not allotted ...	5	Blocked as No. 15 in the Singaing circle.

Circular No. 7 of 1890.

From H. L. Eales, Esq., Superintendent, Census Operations, Burma, to all Deputy Commissioners and Presidents of Municipalities,—No. 45-24, dated the 18th September 1890.

As soon as the Block List, prescribed in paragraph 2 of letter No. 506-6C.G., dated the 16th May 1890, from the Chief Secretary to the Chief Commissioner to all Deputy Commissioners in Burma, is finished, the numbering of the "census houses" in each town and village should be at once taken in hand. Census houses should be numbered serially for each village. In large towns it has been found more convenient to number census houses by serial numbers for each block; but this rule, so far as regards towns and cantonments, need not be followed in cases where it may be advisable to number houses otherwise. This numbering should be completed during the month of October.

A mixture of chunam and rice water "congee" was found at the last census to be the best and cheapest material for painting the numbers on houses.

Circular No. 8 of 1890.

From H. L. Eales, Esq., Superintendent, Census Operations, Burma, to all Deputy Commissioners and Presidents of Municipalities,—No. 57-28, dated the 25th September 1890.

I have the honour to state that special arrangements have been made with the Manager of the Irrawaddy Flotilla Company for the taking of the census on board all steam-ships and launches belonging to the Company.

Deputy Commissioners and Presidents of Municipalities will not be required to submit proposals for the enumeration of any persons who habitually reside on board the Company's steamers. The employés of the Company who live ashore will be enumerated by the District or Municipal authorities. Accordingly, although one of the Company's steamers may be anchored along the shore or landging-stage, the Company will still be responsible for taking the census of those who are on board, but employés who live ashore or on the flats used as landing-stages will be enumerated in the ordinary way.

Circular No. 9 of 1890.

From H. L. Eales, Esq., Superintendent, Census Operations, Burma, to all Deputy Commissioners and Presidents of Municipalities,—No. 108-21, dated the 29th October 1890.

The Subdivisional Registers prescribed in my letter No. 24-21, Census, dated the 29th August, have been checked and returned in order that the names of the supervisors and enumerators may be entered.

The supervisors' lists, prescribed in paragraph 13 of the letter of the Chief Secretary, No. 506-6C.G., dated the 16th May, have been struck off in Burmese and English. Indents for these lists should be submitted with the Subdivisional Register, which should be returned to me corrected as early as possible. These registers will then be again returned to you in order that the issue of the schedule books of various sizes issued to each enumerator may be entered with column of remarks, *e.g.*, $\frac{1}{60}$, $\frac{1}{30}$, $\frac{1}{16}$, will mean that the enumerator against whose name the entry has been made has been supplied with one book of 60, one book of 30, and one book of 16 schedules. The Subdivisional Register will thus act as a record of the books issued and each supervisor's list should tally with it. These registers will be finally submitted with the books of schedules after the completion of the enumeration to this office.

Circular No. 10 of 1890.

From H. L. EALES, Esq., Superintendent, Census Operations, Burma, to all Deputy Commissioners,—No. 109-30, dated the 29th October 1890.

I HAVE the honour to request that you will favour me as early as possible with an estimate of the cost, if any, of census operations in your district. The estimate should contain—

(i) cost of extra copyist establishment;
(ii) cost of numbering houses;
(iii) pay of paid enumerators and supervisors;
(iv) boat-hire for boat enumerators;
(v) cost of lamps on night of census.

The Chief Commissioner has been pleased to approve of the suggestion that a volunteer clerk be entertained in every district, subdivisional, and township office.

These clerks, if they be diligent, will either be offered appointments in the abstracting office in Rangoon or may be appointed to fill up the place of such clerks as the Deputy Commissioner may hereafter be asked to depute to work in the Census Office, Rangoon. Should this assistance be insufficient to cope with the work, Deputy Commissioners should submit through their Commissioners at an early date their proposals for the sanction of the Chief Commissioner.

As regards the cost of numbering houses in most districts the cost has been *nil*.

3. Enumerators should be selected from paid Government officials, such as ywathugyis and village policemen.

In the same way thugyis, taiksayès, yazawutgaungs, and clerks and respectable non-officials should be appointed supervisors.

Paid enumerators may be required in out-of-the-way tracts. Should it be necessary to employ paid men, the Deputy Commissioner should at once submit his proposals through the Commissioner of the Division for sanction.

4. *Boat-hire for enumerators.*—In some districts this may be a necessary charge. In such cases the Deputy Commissioner will submit his proposals through the Commissioner in the ordinary way.

5. *Lighting.*—As the moon will be near the full there is no likelihood of there being any great expenditure of oil. In former census operations house-owners were asked and willingly agreed to have lights burning in their own houses.

The carriage of schedules will incur a small expense. This may, in the first instance, be paid out of contingeucies, but care should be taken to debit the amount spent to the cost of census.

Circular No. 11 of 1890.

From H. L. EALES, Esq., Superintendent, Census Operations, Burma, to all Deputy Commissioners and Presidents of Municipalities,—No. 133-21, dated the 4th November 1890.

FROM a comparison between the sizes of the village blocks shown in the Subdivisional Registers that I have already received from several districts and the indents for the various sized books of schedules it would appear that fuller instructions are needed to explain how these indents should be made up. In calculating the number of pages required to enumerate a block the average population per house must be first considered. The average number of residents in a house throughout Burma at the last census was 5·5 for every occupied house. In towns, however, the average number of residents for every occupied house was much higher. The figures for Akyab were 8·72 and in Rangoon 6·27 residents in every house. It is probable that this average may have slightly increased since last census owing to the large immigration of Natives of India and Chinamen. The schedules contain eight lines on each page. Accordingly, in the town of Akyab, it might be safely assumed that, while in half of the houses in a block the residents would exceed eight, in half there would be eight or less. Accordingly, to enumerate a block of 40 houses in Akyab town, two pages a house, or 40 pages in all, would be required for those 20 houses containing more than eight persons. Hence the whole block of 40 houses would at least require 60 schedules. Lastly, it must be remembered that there may be fresh inhabitants to be enumerated on the night of the 26th February, such as newly-born children and visitors. A few blank schedules must therefore be left at the end of each book in case these new arrivals are found in houses in which there is no room left for the insertion of fresh entries. This contingency, however, should be provided for by careful supervision in checking the entries made at the preliminary record. Supplementary books of six schedules can be obtained and attached to the book or books already issued.

Although it would be impossible to calculate safely the exact number of schedules required for each block, the following table may serve as a guide in the revision of the indents already sent in of the various sizes of books required:—

A village block containing 13 or fewer houses would require a book of 16 schedules.
A village block containing 14 to 25 houses would require a book of 30 schedules.

A village block containing 26 to 40 houses would require a book of 30 schedules and one of 16
A village block containing 41 to 52 houses would require a book of 60 schedules.
A village block containing 53 to 65 houses would require a book of 60 schedules and one of 16.

In towns the number of houses a book of 30 schedules can enumerate will vary with each town. The returns of last census will be found at page (ii) of the Appendix to the report on the Census of British Burma taken on the 17th February 1881, Final Census Form No. I, column 12.

In cases where the number of residents for every occupied house does not exceed seven—

A block of 25 to 35 houses would require one book of 30 schedules and one of 16.
A block of 36 to 45 houses would require one book of 60 schedules.
A block of 46 to 55 houses would require one book of 60 schedules and one of 16.
A block of 56 to 65 houses would require one book of 60 schedules and one of 30.
A block of 66 to 75 houses would require one book of 60 schedules, one of 30, and one of 16.

In towns where the average number per house exceed seven—

A block of 25 houses or less would require one book of 30 schedules and one of 16.
A block of 26 to 35 houses would require one book of 60.
A block of 36 to 45 houses would require one of 60 and one of 16.
A block of 46 to 55 houses would require one of 60 and one of 30.
A block of 56 to 65 houses would require one of 60, one of 30, and one of 16.
A block of 65 to 75 houses would require two of 60.

In Burma there is as a rule very little difficulty in distinguishing what is and what is not a house.. In cases, however, where there are barrack houses in towns and rows of houses adjoining one another, I have while on tour discovered that there has been some diversity of opinion regarding the manner of dealing with such cases. For census purposes a house may be taken to mean either a separate building or a part of a building or tenement completely separated by partitions from the rest of the building, *e.g.*, a house in a terrace in England. If the inhabitants of separate tenements in a barrack house do not mess together, the separate tenements might with safety be numbered as separate census houses. The decision in such matters must, however, be left to the discretion of the District and Municipal Officers. During the present month the numbering should be completed and circle registers checked preparatory to the filling up of the block lists, which will be attached to each book of schedules before the book is issued to the enumerators.

Circular No. 12 of 1890.

From H. L. EALES, Esq., Superintendent, Census Operations, Burma, to all Deputy Commissioners,—No. 134-15, dated the 4th November 1890.

I HAVE the honour to forward copies of the papers cited in the margin and to request that, in accordance with Rule 11 of the rules forwarded with Home Department letter No. 4 Cens.-143, dated the 30th July 1890, you will place yourself in communication with Commanding Officers in your district and afford them such advice and assistance as may be necessary.

Home Department letter No. 4 Cens.-143, dated 30th July 1890, and enclosures.
Letter No. 17-15, dated 26th August 1890, from Superintendent of Census Operations.
Letter No. 849-3C.G., dated 23rd September 1890, to Assistant Adjutant-General.
Letter No. 6478, dated 29th September 1890, from Assistant Adjutant-General.
Letter No. 255-3C.G., dated 6th October 1890, to Superintendent of Census Operations.

I have also the honour to request that you will be so good as to deal with the remaining parts of the Cantonments and Military stations which have not been included in the purely military limits in the same way as villages and towns in your district have already been treated. In the case of large Cantonments the Municipal circle register might be used, and in the case of the smaller Cantonments and Military stations Circle Register A will probably be applicable. The blocking and numbering should be taken in hand at once, and a report on the progress made should be submitted at the end of the present month.

From C. J. LYALL, Esq., C.I.E., Officiating Secretary to the Government of India, Home Department, to the Census Commissioner for India,—No. 4 (Census)-143, dated Simla, the 30th July 1890.

I AM directed to acknowledge the receipt of your letter No. 78-1890, dated the 27th ultimo, forwarding a copy of the proposed rules for the enumeration of cantonments and troops on the march. With regard to cantonments isolated in Feudatory territory, you suggest that the census arrangements should be generally controlled by the chief political authority of the surrounding State, the returns being abstracted and tabulated in some British office and the results communicated to the State concerned. As regards the cost of the operations, you propose that the principle observed in 1881* should be followed, namely, that the cost of compilation and of the enumerators' books should be borne by Government, while that of enumeration should be defrayed from the Cantonment Funds.

* *Vide* Home, Revenue, and Agricultural Department Resolution No. 1—18C. to 34C., dated 18th January 1881.

2. In reply I am to convey the approval of the Governor-General in Council to the proposed rules, which will be circulated for the information and guidance of the local Governments and Military authorities, the co-operation of the latter being invited to the carrying out of the arrangements. Your proposals as to the manner of taking the census in cantonments isolated in Native States and of meeting the general cost of census operations in connection with cantonments and troops on the march are also approved.

Endorsement by J. P. HEWETT, Esq., Under Secretary to the Government of India, Home Department,—No. 4 (Census)—144-153, dated Simla, the 30th July 1890.

COPY of correspondence forwarded to the local Governments and Administrations for information and guidance.

From J. A. BAINES, Esq., Census Commissioner for India, to the Secretary to the Government of India, Home Department,—No. 78-1890, dated Simla, the 27th June 1890.

I HAVE the honour to forward herewith the rules I propose for the enumeration of cantonments and troops on the march. They differ in little from those under which the census was taken in 1881, and the modifications are mostly based on recommendations found in the census reports or extracted from departmental circulars.

2. I would suggest that intimation be given to the Military authorities that the census will be taken under these rules on the night of the 26th of February 1891, and that on matters of detail the local Governments and Administrations will issue supplementary instructions. The co-operation of all military officials concerned should be of course requested, following the precedent * of letter No. 501S.E., dated the 18th October 1880, Military Department, to the Adjutant-General in India.

* See slip A.

3. As regards cantonments isolated in Feudatory territory the arrangements should be generally controlled by the chief political authority of the surrounding State in general accordance with the rules under consideration. The returns should be abstracted and tabulated in some British office and the results communicated to the States within the limits of which the cantonments are located. For instance, the returns of cantonments in Central India and Rajputana will be dealt with at Ajmere, and those of Hyderabad at the Berar Central Office. The Bombay Government will no doubt arrange in like manner regarding Baroda, Deesa, Rajkot, and Bhuj, &c., as will Madras for Quilon.

4. As regards the cost of the operations I would propose to retain the rule of 1881, which was that Government provided the schedules and tabulated the results, the Cantonment Funds bearing the cost of enumeration. On this latter point I would draw attention to Mr. (now Sir Charles) Elliott's letter No. 37, dated the 23rd November 1880, on which was passed Resolution 1-18C., dated the 18th January 1881, which seem worth re-publication for the guidance of those concerned.

Soliciting the early instructions of the Government of India on the above.

CENSUS OF 1891.

ENUMERATION OF CANTONMENTS AND OF TROOPS ON THE MARCH.

A.—Military limits.

1. Within regimental lines, or other purely military limits, the census will be taken by the Military authorities.

2. The determination of these limits should be undertaken as soon as possible after the receipt of these instructions by the Military and Civil authorities in consultation with each other, so that both may know clearly the areas for the enumeration of which they are respectively responsible.

3. To prevent mistakes or double enumeration, it is advisable for the Military authorities to have their limits cleared between sunset on the 26th of February 1891 and sunrise on the 27th idem of all persons who are not residing temporarily or permanently within those limits as officers of any grade, fighting-men, non-combatants attached to the regiments, the servants of the above, regimental followers, or members of the families of any of these.

4. The census to be taken by the Military authorities under the above orders will thus include all persons of whatever age, sex, race, or profession who on the night of the 26th February are temporarily or permanently residing within military limits. Thus it will include all persons who, though ordinarily residing elsewhere, may on that night be stopping temporarily within those limits; and also those who, while actually living at the time and taking their meals within the same, may be absent for a few hours on night duty, &c.

5. Some weeks before the census, a list should be prepared showing every house or other building in the area in question which is inhabited, or is likely to be inhabited, on the 26th February. A convenient form for this list is the following :—

p

Cantonment ________________

House Register of Military Lines, &c.

Serial No. of house.	Description of house (*i.e.*, barracks, guard-room, &c.).	Families.		Remarks.
		Serial No. of each resident family.	Name and occupation of head member of each family.	
1	2	3	4	5

If the lines be divided into blocks, a separate list should be prepared for each block. If any large building has been divided into separate dwellings or tenements, occupied by distinct groups of persons, each of these dwellings should be given a separate number in column 1 of the register. In columns 3 and 4 only those families should be entered who reside *as families* in the buildings. Single individuals living alone and without servants, such as unmarried privates, should not be shown as separate families.

6. The number entered against each house in the above list should be then painted conspicuously upon the building, so that it may be easily noted on the night of the census.

7. The census will be taken, except in the case of European officers who will be provided with separate household schedules, by means of books of schedules bound up with the detailed instructions and other forms required. As soon as the officer responsible for the enumeration has ascertained the approximate number of houses and persons within military limits, he should forward to the Collector or Deputy Commissioner of the district an indent for the requisite number of schedules on the basis of one book for every 300 persons or 60 houses, and one household schedule per officer concerned, a margin of about 10 per cent. being allowed for waste or emergency. He should also specify the language or character in which the former are to be printed. When the cantonment is beyond British territory, this indent should be sent to the Chief Political Officer of the Agency in which it is situated. The books and schedules should be asked for not later than September and should be ready in the cantonment for use as below specified by December.

8. About a week or ten days before the 26th of February, each enumerator should go round his block and enter in the book of schedules full particulars regarding every person, man, woman, or child, whom he finds residing therein. This record should be carefully examined and initialled by the officer responsible for the census and all errors rectified. The houses should be taken in the order in which they are entered in the register, and exact observance of the instructions must be rigidly enforced. Black ink only must be provided for this preliminary record.

9. After gunfire on the night of the 26th February, the enumerator should again go over his block, check and bring up to date the entries previously made as above prescribed, and thus complete the census. The next morning he should go to the households which have been furnished with separate schedules, enumerate the native servants, &c., of each in his block-book and collect the schedules of the house-holder. On this occasion he must be provided with red or magenta ink only, so that the entries of new-born children, of visitors who have arrived since the preliminary record, and the erasure of those who have died or left the lines may be easily distinguished.

10 A register should be kept of the number and description of schedules issued, and each enumerator should account for every one he has received. When the account has been found correct in each case, the officer presiding over the census work should make an index, pack up the books and household schedules, and after filling up the short summary of the abstracts which form part of every enumerator's book, should then forward the whole to the Collector, Deputy Commissioner, or Political Officer, as the case may be. The books and schedules for each regiment or detachment should be packed and registered separately.

11. As it is necessary that the scheme laid down for the census of the whole country should be strictly followed, arrangements will be made by local Governments and Administrations to place a European district official in direct communication with the Military authorities in each cantonment, so that he may give advice to the latter, and otherwise ensure uniformity and punctuality in the arrangements.

B.—Troops on the march.

12. The census of regiments on the march and of detachments of troops on duty within the limits of the province concerned will be taken by the officer in command. This census will include all persons, of whatever sex, age, or profession, who are marching with the troops. It will probably be known beforehand that troops will be on the march on the night of the 26th of February, so that the officer in command should be provided with enumeration books and schedules at the cantonment from which the troops start. There will be no preliminary record taken in this case, unless one has been completed before the troops left their last cantonment.

13. If the regiment or detachment be travelling by rail on the night of the census, the enumeration should be effected at the first place at which the men alight. Such troops will not be enumerated by the Railway authorities.

14. The books and schedules for detachments on the march should be sent to the headquarters of their regiments if it be within the province where they are enumerated. For regiments on the march, the books, &c., should be despatched to the Military authorities of the cantonment at which they were last stationed, and will be then dealt with as prescribed in paragraph 10 above.

C.—Cantonment Bazaars and Civil limits.

15. The census of so much of each cantonment as lies beyond regimental or other purely military limits will be taken by the Cantonment Magistrate acting under the direct orders of the Civil authorities of the district or State. Exceptional cases will probably be found, such as Mhow, in which the whole arrangements will have to be controlled by the Officer Commanding, who will thus be responsible for their efficiency and punctuality.

16. The rules under which the above limits are to be enumerated will be those prescribed for the country at large, and will be found accordingly in the general and provincial circulars. Indents for schedules, based on the circle register of houses and persons, must be submitted as soon as possible after the preparation of the above register. Meanwhile the block-lists can be prepared, the houses numbered as above prescribed, and enumerators nominated and duly appointed.

17. The time allowed for the preliminary record will be slightly longer than in the military limits; but this task should be completely finished by the 15th of February, so as to allow full time for scrutiny and correction.

18. The actual census and the subsequent procedure will be conducted as in the military limits, save that supervision must be closer and more active, owing to the greater variety in the population dealt with.

D.—Legislation.

19. The following provisions of the Census Act are extracted for the information and guidance of those concerned :—

" *Section 5.*—Every military or naval officer in command of any body of men belonging to Her Majesty's military or naval forces, or of any vessel of war * * * * * shall, if so required by the District Magistrate or, in the towns of Calcutta, Madras, and Bombay, by such officer as the local Government may appoint in this behalf, perform such of the duties of a Census officer† in relation to the persons who at the time of the taking of the census are under his command or charge, * * * * * as such Magistrate or officer may, by written order, direct.

" (2) All the provisions of this Act relating to Census officers shall apply, so far as they can be made applicable, to all such persons while performing such duties and any person refusing or neglecting to perform any duty which he is directed under this section to perform shall be deemed to have committed an offence under section 187 of the Indian Penal Code (XLV of 1860)."

From H. L. Eales, Esq., Superintendent, Census Operations, Burma, to the Chief Secretary to the Chief Commissioner, Burma,—No. 17-15, dated the 26th August 1890.

With regard to paragraph 11 of the Instructions for the enumeration of cantonments and troops on the march sanctioned by the letter of the Government of India, Home Department, No. 4 (Census)-143, dated the 30th July 1890, a copy of which was forwarded with your endorsement No. 354-3C.G., dated the 13th August 1890, I have the honour to suggest that the District Magistrate be placed in direct communication with the Military authorities of every cantonment within the jurisdiction of his district.

---

† " *Section 3 (1).*—The local Government may appoint any person by name or by office to take, or aid in, or supervise the taking of, the census within any specified local area.

" (2) Persons so appointed shall be called Census officers.

" (3) The local Government may delegate to such authority as it thinks fit the power of appointing Census officers which is conferred by this section."

" *Section 4 (1).*—A declaration in writing signed by any officer authorized by the local Government in this behalf that any person has been duly appointed a Census officer for any local area shall be conclusive proof of such appointment.

" (2) All Census officers shall be deemed to be public servants within the meaning of the Indian Penal Code (XLV of 1860)."

Endorsement by the Officiating Under Secretary to the Chief Commissioner, Burma,—No. 850-3C.G., dated the 23rd September 1890.

COPY of the following forwarded to the Superintendent of Census Operations, Burma, with reference to his letter No. 17-15, dated the 26th August 1890.

From the Officiating Under Secretary to the Chief Commissioner, Burma, to the Assistant Adjutant-General, Burma District,—No. 849-3C.G., dated the 23rd September 1890.

I AM directed to forward a copy of Home Department letter No. 4 (Census)-143, dated the 30th July 1890, concerning the rules for the enumeration of cantonments and troops on the march in the census which is to be taken on the 26th February next. With reference to Rule 11 of the rules therein sanctioned I am to say that it has been proposed to place the Deputy Commissioner in direct communication with the Officer Commanding each cantonment. I am to enquire whether the General Officer Commanding the Burma District has any objection to this proposal and to ask that a list of the stations in which the enumeration of troops will be undertaken by the Military authorities may be furnished. It will be convenient, the Chief Commissioner thinks, to apply the rules not only to regularly constituted cantonments, but also to all stations where there are troops on the day of the census. The favour of an early reply to this reference is requested.

From the Assistant Adjutant-General, Burma District, to the Chief Secretary to the Chief Commissioner, Burma,—No. 6478, dated the 29th September 1890.

IN reply to your No. 849-3C.G., dated the 23rd September 1890, I am directed to inform you that the General Officer Commanding Burma District has no objection to the proposal contained therein, and that the General Officers Commanding Districts have been instructed to furnish your office direct with lists of the stations in which enumeration will be undertaken by the Military authorities.

From the Officiating Under Secretary to the Chief Commissioner, Burma, to the Superintendent, Census Operations, Burma,—No. 255-3C.G., dated the 6th October 1890.

IN continuation of my endorsement No. 850-3C.G., dated the 23rd September 1890, I am directed to forward a copy of a letter (No. 6478, dated the 29th September 1890), from the Assistant Adjutant-General, Burma District, and to say that the lists of stations at which the Military authorities will be responsible for taking the census within the military lines will be forwarded to you on receipt. In the meantime I am to ask you to circulate to Commissioners and Deputy Commissioners in whose division or district troops are stationed, copies of the papers cited in the margin in order that, in accordance with Rule 11 of the Rules forwarded with Home Department letter No. 4 (Census)-143, dated the 30th July 1890, District Magistrates may place themselves in communication with Commanding Officers and afford them such advice and assistance as may be necessary in this matter.

Home Department letter No. 4 (Census)-143, dated 30th July 1890, and enclosures.
Letter No. 17-15, dated 26th August 1890, from Superintendent of Census Operations.
Letter No. 849-3C.G., dated 23rd September 1890, to Assistant Adjutant-General.
Letter No. 6478, dated 29th September 1890, from Assistant Adjutant-General.
Letter No. 255-3C.G., dated 6th October 1890, to Superintendent of Census Operations.

Circular No. 13 of 1890.

From H. L. EALES, Esq., Superintendent, Census Operations, Burma, to all Deputy Commissioners and Presidents of Municipalities,—No. 293-21, dated the 11th December 1890.

REFERRING to paragraph 11 of the letter No. 506-3C.G., dated the 16th May 1890, from the Chief Secretary, experience has shown that, owing to the mobile nature of the population, the Circle Register A cannot, even when corrected, be taken as a correct block list in many of the villages and towns. The schedule books which are now being forwarded should be written up from these registers; but, in those cases where, as above stated, these registers cannot be accepted as correct, the safer and more expeditious course in most districts will be to fill up the dockets on the cover, enter the books in the column of remarks in the Subdivisional Register and in the supervisor's list, and issue the schedule books at once to the enumerator and direct him to fill up the block list under the supervision of the supervisor of his circle.

2. As on the occasion of the last census, pens, ink, and blotting paper will be supplied from this office. Pencils will be supplied to those districts in Upper Burma where, owing to the illiteracy of the enumerators, difficulty may be experienced in teaching them to use the ordinary pen at first.

Circular No. 14 of 1890.

From H. L. EALES, Esq., Superintendent, Census Operations, Burma, to all Deputy Commissioners, Presidents of Municipalities, and Port Officers, Rangoon, Bassein, Akyab, and Moulmein, and Chairman, Port Commissioners, Rangoon,—No. 300-21, dated the 13th December 1890.

ADVERTING to Circular No. 11 of 1890, issued from this office, I have the honour to request that a revised indent, in the form herewith attached, may be forwarded for such books and schedules as may be required for the census of 1891.

2. The indents submitted by Deputy Commissioners and Presidents of Municipalities should provide for all books and schedules required for enumerating the military police and posts stationed within their respective jurisdictions, and the opportunity should be taken to have the indents carefully checked, so that enumerators may be provided with a sufficient number for the preliminary and final round.

3. As regards household schedules they should be very sparingly used, and their issue should be restricted to the case of persons who are able not only to accurately fill them up, but also to return them to the enumerator concerned on the final day of the census.

4. I would ask that the indent may be forwarded with as little delay as possible, so that the books and schedules may be issued before the end of the current month.

Indent for Schedules required for the...

Serial No.	Name of	House schedules.								Boat schedules.				Household schedules for Europeans and Eurasians in loose sheets.	Number of Charge Superintendents.	Number of Supervisors.	Number of Enumerators.	Remarks.
		Books of 16 schedules.		*Books of 30 schedules.*		*Books of 60 schedules.*		*Supplementary books of 6 schedules.*		*Books of 8 schedules.*		*Books of 16 schedules.*						
		English.	Burmese.	English.	Burmese.	English.	Burmese.	English.	Burmese.	English.	Burmese.	English.	Burmese.	English.*				
1	2	3	4	5	6	7	8	9	10	11	12	13	14	15	16	17	18	19
		No.	No.	No.	No.	No.	No.	No.	No.	No.	No.	No.	No.	No.				

Station
Dated 189 .

....

Circular No. 15 of 1891.

Endorsement by H. L. EALES, Esq., Superintendent, Census Operations, Burma,—No. 476-21, dated the 15th January 1891.

COPY of the following, with copy of letter to which it is a reply, forwarded to all Deputy Commissioners and Presidents of Municipalities for information and guidance.

From H. L. EALES, Esq., Superintendent, Census Operations, Burma, to the Deputy Commissioner, Bassein, —No. 390-24, dated the 6th January 1891.

IN reply to your letter No. 1371-17—1, dated the 14th ultimo, I have the honour to point out that this point might arise under either of three following circumstances:—

(i) the new house might be built in a block in a town where according to my instructions the houses have been numbered consecutively by the block;

(ii) or the house might be built in a village containing only one block;

(iii) or the house might be built in a village where there are more blocks than one, or in a town in which the houses have been numbered serially throughout the town or quarter.

2. In the former two cases experience has shown that the more convenient way would be to give the new house the next number after the last house in the block, while in the last case the proposal to letter the new house under the number of the adjoining one would probably lead to less confusion. Care must be taken to see that in any case the new house gets a separate schedule to itself.

From J. E. BRIDGES, Esq., Deputy Commissioner, Bassein, to the Superintendent, Census Operations, Burma,—No. 1371-17—1 (Revenue Department—Census), dated the 14th December 1890.

THERE is some doubt as to the method of numbering new houses built after the houses in a village have been numbered for census purposes.

2. Should the new houses bear the number of the house adjoining it with a letter allotted, *e. g.*, 85 ထ, or should it bear the number following that of the last house numbered in the village.

3. As the houses are numbered for census purposes only the last method would appear the more appropriate one.

Circular No. 16 of 1891.

From H. L. EALES, Esq., Superintendent, Census Operations, Burma, to Deputy Commissioners and Presidents of Municipal Committees,—No. 477-21, dated the 15th January 1891.

WITH the Chief Commissioner's approval I have the honour to request that the following supplementary instructions may be issued to enumerators as to the manner in which entries are to be made in column 11 of the Enumerator's Schedule.

2. Religious mendicants should be distinguished from members of the Buddhist monastic order. The former, namely, religious mendicants, should be entered as *pothudaw* if of the male sex and as *mèthila* if of the female sex. Buddhist monks or *rahans* should be entered as *pôngyi* or *upazin* according to their status in the order, and acolytes, that is, young persons who have either entered a monastery temporarily and as a matter of custom, or who have not decided whether they will become permanent members of the order or not, should be shown as *thamane* or *koyin*. The enumerator should ascertain in each case whether the person referred to should be classed as a *pôngyi*, *upazin*, or *thamane* or *koyin*. General terms, such as *ahluganpôkgo* or *rahan* should not be used. It is requested that Charge Superintendents and supervisors may be carefully instructed to comply with these directions, which should be clearly explained to them.

Circular No. 17 of 1891.

From H. L. EALES, Esq., Superintendent, Census Operations, Burma, to all Deputy Commissioners,—No. 486-21, dated the 16th January 1891.

I HAVE the honour to enclose for your information and guidance a copy of the instructions for the enumeration of survey camps and of the working camp of the Bombay Burma Trading Corporation, Limited.

Instructions for the enumeration of survey camps and of the working camps of the Bombay Burma Trading Corporation, "Limited."

AFTER consultation with Mr. Glendenning, Manager, and Messrs. Winser and Bates, Agents, Bombay Burma Trading Corporation, Limited, and various officers of the Public Works Department and Survey of India, the following instructions are issued with the Chief Commissioner's approval:—

(1) In order to obviate as far as possible any unnecessary interference with the work of survey and forest camps the Deputy Commissioners of the various

districts in which the camps are situate will appoint the officer in charge of the operations in his District Charge Superintendent.

(2) The Charge Superintendent will select such of his assistants as may be required to be supervisors under him.

(3) He will select his enumerators. Appointment orders will be issued in accordance with the Charge Superintendent's advice by the Deputy Commissioner of the district.

(4) A Handbook of Instructions has already been issued to each Charge Superintendent and supervisor, and the schedule books for the various camps have already been supplied to the Deputy Commissioner, who will issue them to the Charge Superintendent.

(5) The Charge Superintendent will see that these books are duly issued with supervisor's list containing the list of books issued to each enumerator.

(6) The necessary stationery will be supplied by the Deputy Commissioner.

(7) Care should be taken that a sufficient supply of books are issued.

(8) It is most necessary that the instructions be thoroughly understood by the enumerators, and Charge Superintendents should be careful that instructions are explained where necessary.

(9) The preliminary record will commence in January. On its completion the enumerator should, on a slip of paper, write down the total of males and females in his camp or block and the inhabited houses or boats if his camp be located in either houses or boats. The supervisor will collect these totals and submit them to the Charge Superintendent, who will on or before 10th February forward the totals of his charge to the Deputy Commissioner of the district.

(10) During the month of February the enumeration schedule books will be checked by the supervisor, and on the night of the census the enumerator will endorse on the cover of his book the locality of the camp and carry out the instructions which he will find in his schedule-book.

(11) On the morning of the 27th February, or as soon after as possible, each enumerator will in the presence of his supervisor submit the totals of his abstract. The supervisor will check the totals, compare it with the returns sent in after the preliminary record, and will submit them to the Charge Superintendent, who will at once forward the totals of his charge to the Deputy Commissioner.

RANGOON:
The 16th January 1891.

H. L. EALES,
Superintendent, Census Operations.

Circular No. 18 of 1891.

From H. L. EALES, Esq., Superintendent, Census Operations, Burma, to all Deputy Commissioners and Presidents of Municipalities,—No. 487-46, dated the 16th January 1891.

HITHERTO I have not called on you for the submission of monthly reports although in the other provinces of India these reports have been required since the 1st June last. In place of these reports the Subdivisional Registers have been accepted as a brief but clear summary of the progress of census work. As, however, the work of the distribution of schedule books and the enumeration of blocks, the capacity and energy of the Census Officers engaged, and the general progress of the work cannot be gauged by the register, I have the honour to request that you will, on the 1st February, submit a report showing, as far as possible, the actual state of census work in your district on that date. The reports should touch on the following points, but you need not confine your remarks to these points alone. I shall be glad of any other suggestions you may be pleased to make—

(*a*) date of receipt of census schedule books and stationery and issue of the same to the Charge Superintendents and supervisors;

(*b*) date of the commencement of the preliminary record;

(*c*) date of the commencement of the non-synchronous census record; and

(*d*) of the preparation of the register of villages or of tracts excluded from census operations.

Circular No. 19 of 1891.

From H. L. EALES, Esq., Superintendent, Census Operations, Burma, to all Deputy Commissioners and Presidents of Municipalities,—No. 488-21, dated the 16th January 1891.

TRAVELLERS by rail, boat, and road will have to be enumerated at the final record. It will be necessary to issue passes to those enumerated to prevent persons being enumerated more than once or their escaping enumeration altogether. With this view census passes have been attached to the Boat Schedule books, and counterfoil books will be issued to the Railway enumerators through the Manager. I have therefore the honour to request that you will be so good as to inform me how many books of counterfoil passes will be required in your district for the enumeration of travellers by road. There will be two sizes of books, the smaller containing 50 and the larger 100 counterfoils. One counterfoil will be required for each traveller and not as in the case of travellers by river, where one pass is sufficient for the whole boat's crew.

CENSUS PASS.

No...............

District or Municipality...

Circle No.............. Block No............ Boat owner's name.......................

Number of persons enumerated..................................

Dated..........................189 . *Enumerator's Signature.*

RAILWAY AND ROAD PASSENGERS' CENSUS PASS.

No...............

District or Municipality...

Circle No..............Block No...............

Bearer has been enumerated.

Dated...........................189 . *Enumerator's Signature.*

Instructions for the Enumeration of Railway premises and Travellers by Rail.

1. The classes of the population to be enumerated by the Railway authorities are—

A.—Persons residing or working within railway premises;

B.—Persons travelling by rail on the night of the 26th February 1891.

2. Under Class A are included permanent employés of the railway, with their families and servants residing on the railway premises, together with visitors stopping temporarily in their houses; also labourers or others employed on railway work by contractors or Railway Officers, if sleeping within the railway premises. This proviso, however, is not to be applicable to gangs of railway coolies who may have pitched their huts, &c., just beyond railway limits, as these should be enumerated by the agency which collected or is employing them. On the other hand, when convenient, detached houses, &c., of signallers or gatemen may be included in the block of the nearest village or town, and thus be enumerated with the ordinary population of that block. In all such cases the Railway and the District authorities should act in concert with each other, so that there may be neither omission nor re-enumeration of any person. It should be noted that persons who work on railway premises either by day or night, but habitually return to their homes outside railway premises when off work are not to be enumerated in Class A.

3. The first step to be taken is to parcel out the railway premises into circles for supervisors and blocks for enumerators. The tabulation of the returns will be by districts or States, as the case may be, so the mileage included in each of those areas through which the line passes, with the stations, &c., therein, should be registered in a list to be sent to the Superintendent of the Census Operations for the province or agency. It is obvious, therefore, that the partition into the above census areas should be territorial and not departmental, and that in each circle a single officer of the railway should be made responsible for all the census arrangements therein. So, too, not more than one station should be included in one block, as the returns may have to be afterwards distributed between two districts or even two provinces. As a rule, a station will be a convenient circle, though when the premises contain many inhabitants, it may be advisable to divide it into two, each containing not more than ten enumerators' blocks of from 200 to 300 persons or 40 to 60 houses apiece. Where there are a good many houses belonging to the railway, but detached and at a distance from the station, it will be necessary to provide special supervisors and enumerators working, if necessary, in concert with the supervisors of the municipal or village census.

4. A list for each circle should be prepared showing the number and description of buildings, included in each block; and where there are many such buildings, it will be safe to number them with paint or some other material, for the guidance of the enumerator.

5. Supervisors and enumerators should be appointed in writing by the chief railway authorities, and, as far as possible, should be their employés, either European or knowing English well, especially in circles where there is a considerable European or Eurasian colony. At small stations it will be convenient to have the same person to enumerate both residents and travellers, so as to save training two different men.

6. The enumeration will be effected through schedules, of which two kiuds will be issued—(*a*) householder's schedules, to be filled in by the head of each family, and returned to the enumerator on the morning of the 27th February; and (*b*) enumeration books, in which the enumerator fills in the entries for each person at the dictation of the head of the family. The use of the former is restricted to Europeans, Eurasians, and English-speaking employés of the superior grades, and the supervisor of the circle should be distinctly made responsible for seeing that such forms are correctly filled up. Both kinds of form contain room for eight persons per page, or schedule, and in the case of Europeans and Eurasians, the return for native servants and their families on the premises is to be made by the enumerator of the block on a separate schedule. One page is reserved for each house, so that in forwarding indents as below prescribed, allowance to the extent of perhaps 10 per cent. should be made for emergencies. The indents should be sent by the agent or manager to the Superintendent of Census Operations for the province, or in feudatory territory to the Chief Political authority. They should specify—

(*a*) the number of families—European, Eurasian, and native—for whom householder's forms are required;

(*b*) the number of houses, servants' quarters, and police, porter and coolie lines, to be enumerated in the book forms;

(*c*) the number of blocks in each circle, and the number of enumerators to be employed;

(*d*) the number of schedules to be bound up into each book, varying from 12 to 50;

(*e*) the language in which the said books should be supplied.

Each book contains detailed instructions, a sample schedule, an abstract to be filled up by the enumerator after the census, and a list of the houses he has to enumerate, under their serial numbers, as mentioned in paragraph 4 above. The full supply of schedules and books for this class of the population should be indented for in September at the latest, and should be prepared for household distribution and use by enumerators respectively by the middle of January 1891. In writing up the block-list of houses in the book, special note should be made in the last column of the houses where schedules have been left, so that the enumerator may know how many forms, and from whom, he has to collect on the morning after the census.

7. Early in February every enumerator should fill in the schedule for each house in the manner prescribed in the instructions printed in his book. This task should be completed by the 20th, and during its progress the supervisor should test the greater part of the entries by house-to-house visits. This preliminary record may be foregone, as in 1881, in the case of native employés of superior grade in order to diminish the work thrown on the staff engaged as enumerators; but the concession is made on the distinct understanding that it does not interfere with the accuracy of the census, for which the Railway authorities are responsible.

8. The householder's schedules should be left with the head of each family about the 24th of February. On the morning of the 27th idem, they will be collected, examined on the spot by the enumerator, and corrected, where necessary, on his suggestion.

9. On the night of the 26th of February, beginning from about 8 or 9 o'clock, the enumerator will again visit every house in his block, and see that the entries are brought up to date, in accordance with his instructions regarding visitors, births, and deaths not previously recorded. It may be noted that, according to those instructions, employés who are on duty on the night of the 26th February, but are not travelling with any train, should be recorded as present in the houses where they are entered in the book, or where a householder's schedule has been left.

10. On issuing the books and householder's schedules, the supervisor should keep a register of every form thus made over to the enumerator, and on the 27th of February he should recover the same from the latter, and see that each one issued is duly accounted for. He should then certify the list, pack the books and schedules in serial order with it, and despatch the whole without delay to the Collector or Deputy Commissioner of the district if in British territory, or to the resident or the Chief Political Officer of the agency if in a feudatory State, certifying at the same time to the agent or manager of the line that he has done so.

11. On all main points, and in all matters affecting general arrangements connected with the census, the agent or manager should consult with the Superintendent of Census for the province or agency concerned, and in Rajputana, Central India, Quetta, Hyderabad, and Mysore, with the First Assistant to the Agent to the Governor-General and the Resident respectively. All points which cannot be settled by these officials should be referred to the Census Commissioner for India. On minor local details the agent or manager should consult the Collector, Deputy Commissioner, or Political Officer concerned. In order that the arrangements may be carried out successfully, it is important that a list of the railway circles and blocks in each district or State should be sent as soon as they are settled, or before the end of November 1890, to the Provincial Census Superintendent, and also that the instructions above given regarding local and not departmental responsibility should be strictly followed.

CLASS B.—*Travellers by Rail.*

12. A special official should be told off at each station to enumerate all persons alighting from a train at that station during the night of the 26th of February 1891.

13. In the case of 1st and 2nd class passengers and of Europeans and Eurasians travelling intermediate or 3rd class, or on duty with the train, separate schedules should be distributed by the guard in charge of the train on the evening of the 26th February. The rest of the persons in the train will be enumerated in the schedule books described above. Indents for these forms should be sent in with those for the resident population under Class **A**, but under a separate heading. The requirements of each station in this respect should be based on the average number of passengers alighting there on the date specified for the last three years, with special extra provision for the station where the final enumeration under paragraph 15 is to take place.

14. Between 8 P.M. on the 26th February and 6 A.M. on the 27th idem, the station-enumerator should enumerate every traveller,—man, woman, and child,—who alights at the station in question. He should first ask if the person has been enumerated already during the night, and, if he produces an enumeration ticket, or asserts that he has been so counted, the enumerator should accept the answer, and let him go by. If he says he has not, the enumerator should fill up the schedule entries for him in full and give him an enumeration-ticket, a provision of which should also be indented for, telling him to show the same if any enumerator offers to count him again.

15. All passengers found in the train at 6 A.M. on the 27th February, who cannot produce enumeration-tickets, or who otherwise do not appear to have been enumerated during the night, and all employés on duty with the train, shall be counted at the first large station at which the train stops at or about that hour. A place should be chosen where the train is timed to stop for a sufficient period, which may, if necessary, be slightly prolonged.* Enumeration-tickets need not be given on this occasion. The household schedules given the evening before to 1st and 2nd class passengers, &c., who have not alighted during the night should be collected and examined by an employé who should, if possible, be a European or Eurasian. The same official should also fill up the form for those who have omitted to do so for themselves. He should finally see that schedules thus collected are stitched into the enumeration books used for the other passengers.

16. Troops travelling by rail on the night in question will be enumerated by their officers, and the return separately sent in. But the native servants travelling with them, and those travelling with 1st and 2nd class passengers (not being in the same carriage with their employers), should be enumerated with the rest of the persons in the train.

17. The above books and schedules should be separately indexed, and then put up with the returns for Class **A** for transmission to the authorities specified in paragraph 10 above.

18. *Expenses.*—The schedules and books will be supplied by Government. The agency employed will be chiefly people officially attached to the railway. Unavoidable extra expenditure, such as payment for overtime on the night of the 26th, remuneration of outsiders where no officials are available as enumerators, oil, and petty stationery, may be entered in a bill under the above heads and sent through the Provincial Census Superintendent to the Census Commissioner for submission to the Government of India for sanction.

Instructions for the enumeration of the sea-going classes and travellers by sea.

1. *Agency.*—In all places where there is a Port Officer, that officer, aided by the Sea Customs and similar officials, should superintend all arrangements. As regards smaller ports and landing-places the Collector or Deputy Commissioner should arrange with the Customs, Salt, or Marine Departments, &c., for the enumeration of all vessels and persons on board of them at all such landing-places in his district. For the harbours of Bombay, Calcutta, Karachi, and Rangoon special arrangements should be made.

2. *Mode of Enumeration.*—For census purposes vessels may be classed as (**A**) sea-going vessels habitually plying between one coast port and another; by coast port being understood all ports in British India, Burma, and Native States, but not ports in the territory of France and Portugal; and (**B**) vessels habitually plying within the limits of one port, or in the neighbourhood of one village or landing-place, such as fishing, cargo, small passenger boats, &c. The general principle on which the enumeration is to be conducted is that all persons should be counted, as far as possible, at the spot where they happened to be or from which they took their meals, on the night of the 26th February, or else at the place at which they first touched after that night.

---

* Where the local staff is insufficient for the speedy enumeration of passengers at this halt, a few clerks should be sent temporarily from another station. A plan of enumeratian found efficient in 1881 was for two enumerators to enter a carriage as the train drew up, accompanied, if at night, by porters with lamps. Starting from opposite ends of the carriage, each enumerated all the persons on one side of the carriage. They then moved on to the next carriage, which had been locked till their arrival, and repeated the process, the carriage they had left being then unlocked and the passengers allowed to alight.

3. *Enumeration of sea-going vessels plying between coast ports.*—In the first place, it must be noted that vessels sailing under foreign colours are not to be enumerated unless they happen to be laying in a harbour of British India on the night of the 26th February. Vessels whether sailing under British or foreign colours which leave before the 26th and are bound for a port beyond British India or Burma, or which arrive in the latter territory after the 26th, having last touched at such a port, should not be enumerated. In the case of the remaining vessels of this class, it is necessary to provide for the following contingencies :—

(1) vessels laying at anchor in a port on the night of the census ;
(2) vessels having left for a British Indian port shortly before that night ;
(3) vessels arriving from a British Indian port after that night, and
(4) the special case of coasting steamers touching at several ports during that night.

The master of the vessel is in all cases responsible for the due enumeration of all on board on the night of the census. He will be furnished beforehand by a Census Officer at the port where the vessel is laying with the necessary forms and instructions, and will be required to fill in the former with all the details asked for regarding himself, his crew, and the passengers that are on board on the night of the 26th February. The instructions will provide that after entering his own name, he should enter those of the crew, and then, drawing a cross line in column 1 of the form, he should enter below it those of the passengers. Schedules will be distributed to all vessels in port before the 26th February, and either schedules or passes, as hereinafter provided, will be demanded of every vessel arriving from a British Indian port between 8 P.M. on the 26th and the morning of March 15th :—

(1) In the case of vessels laying in port and likely to remain there over the night of 26th, the forms should be distributed at least three days beforehand, with full instructions regarding their completion and return. The master of the vessel should be requested not to allow any of the crew to go on shore between the hours of 8 P.M. and 6 A.M. on the above mentioned date, or, if any are obliged to go on duty, to furnish them with a certificate of enumeration, signed by himself, with directions that it is to be shown to any Census Officer who may wish to enumerate them on shore. On the night of the 26th or morning of the 27th, an enumerator should visit the vessel and collect the returns. examining the entries to see that they are in accordance with the instructions, and mustering the persons on board, if he thinks it necessary to do so. Where the master is illiterate and unable to fill up the schedule, the enumerator should, on the occasion of this visit, fill it up for him.

(2) If a vessel is leaving the harbour between the 12th and the night of the 26th February, and is bound for another coast port in India or British Burma which it is not expected to reach before or during that night, the Census Officer at the port of departure, when distributing the forms, should instruct the master of the vessel to fill them up during the night of the 26th, and deliver them, duly certified, to the Customs or other authority who may ask for them at the port first touched at after 6 A.M. on the morning of the 27th. It is advisable, wherever practicable, to ascertain what port this is likely to be.

(3) If the vessel arrive in harbour from another coast port of India or British Burma between 6 A.M. on the 27th February and the evening of the 14th March, the enumerator of the port must (unless he knows that the vessel has previously touched at a port after the 26th February and that this demand has been made before) require from the master of the vessel a schedule duly filled in, or an enumeration-pass from the port where such schedule was delivered, and if neither of these be forthcoming the enumerator shall at once muster the persons on board and, with the aid of the master and others, fill in the necessary forms, a supply of which should be furnished to him beforehand.

(4) Steamers running at short intervals between coast ports constitute a special case for which arrangements must be made by the proprietors with their agents at the different places where the vessels touch, as nearly as possible after the manner of the enumeration of travellers by railway. It will be advisable to enter the master and standing crew including the servants, on a separate form from that used for passengers. As regards the latter, passengers disembarking at each landing-place at which the vessel touches between 8 P.M. on the 26th and 6 A.M. on the 27th should be enumerated where they land. At the first port in British India or a Native State reached after 6 A.M. on the morning of the 27th, all passengers still on board

should be enumerated, and the schedules relating to them as well as those filled up for the master of the vessel and crew should be made over to the local enumerator, a pass being taken as prescribed below; but all passengers who have embarked after 8 A.M. on the preceding night should be asked if they have been already enumerated on shore at any dwelling or rest-house, and if they say they have, they must not be included in the return for the vessel.

4. Every person, who receives a schedule filled in for any vessel, should give the master an enumeration-pass, containing (1) the name of the port where the schedules are recorded; (2) the name of the vessel; (3) the name of the master; (4) the name of the port from which the vessel started; (5) the signature of the person receiving the schedule. The Charge Superintendent of the larger ports, or in smaller places, the District Officer, should issue these pass-books to persons authorized by name under his signature to grant them, and every master of a vessel receiving a pass should be instructed to keep it carefully on board the vessel until the 25th March.

5. *Enumeration of vessels habitually employed in or near a single port other than those for which special arrangements will be made, as prescribed in paragraph 1.*—With reference to vessels of this class particular care must be taken to enumerate all persons belonging to them at their homes if they happen to be absent for the night only. Crews of fishing vessels and the like should be enumerated at the villages for which no special arrangements have been prescribed above, by the enumerators of the place, as directed by the District Officer. The schedules relating to all vessels belonging to the place should be filled up between the 20th and the 26th February, and an enumeration-pass given to the person in charge of the vessel. Any such vessel entering a port or anchorage after the 26th without this pass should be at once enumerated. Wherever there is a Customs establishment, &c., it will be the duty of the officials belonging to it to do this. Before the night of the 26th the foreshore of the place should be divided into blocks, and an enumerator appointed to each block. His duty will be to go round to every boat on that night and record in his form-book all persons found passing the night in the boat and not taking their meals from other places, and to verify and correct, if necessary, the schedules previously filled in. He should then visit for a similar purpose all vessels at anchor, using a boat provided by the supervisor of the harbour.

6. Provincial Superintendents of Census Operations will supplement the above general rules with any instructions that may seem necessary regarding nomination of agencies, supply of forms, passes, registers, &c. The schedules or enumeration-books, if required of a special form, should be drafted by them, and printed at the press where the rest of the work is being executed. They will also frame special rules for the enumeration of boats plying on rivers, backwaters, and navigable canals.

Circular No. 20 of 1891.

From H. L. EALES, Esq., Superintendent, Census Operations, Burma, to Deputy Commissioners and Presidents of Municipal Committees,—No. 611-45, dated the 31st January 1891.

IT has been brought to notice that sometimes servants sleep in their master's house and not in the usual servants' quarters. The household schedule is for the enumeration of Europeans and Eurasians. There is therefore some danger that servants who live in their masters' houses may escape enumeration. The following notice should therefore be issued to all persons to whom the household schedule is to be supplied.

NOTICE.

THE household schedule has been issued to you for the enumeration of the residents in your own house. You will not be required to enter the servants living on your premises. They will be enumerated by the Block Enumerator. You are requested to be so good as to allow the Block Enumerator to visit your premises for this purpose. Should there be any servants who are not Europeans or Eurasians who live in your own house, you are requested to be so good as to see that they are included by the enumerator along with the rest of your servants. The household schedule is not intended or adapted for showing Native residents.

RANGOON: *The 31st January 1891.*

H. L. EALES,
Superintendent, Census Operations, Burma.

HOUSEHOLD SCHEDULE.

(For Europeans and Eurasians.)

HOUSE No..............

DISTRICT.............................. CHARGE..................................

Subdivision, Cantonment, or Town.............. Village, Ward, or Lines............... Circle..............., Supervisor..............., Block No........., Enumerator...........

Instructions.—The schedule on the next page is to be filled up under the Census Act by the head occupant of the house or tenement, for all Europeans and Eurasians stopping in the house or tenement on the night of the 26th February 1891, counting also as present persons ordinarily residing in the house but absent for a few hours on duty (except with a running train) and still taking their meals from the house. The head occupant aforesaid should deliver or have delivered the schedule, duly filled up and signed, to the enumerator who will call for it on the morning of the 27th February. Every facility and aid is requested for the enumerator, who will probably make two visits to take the census of the native servants and their families residing on the premises. Before filling up the schedule, the instructions on the last page of this form should be carefully read.

SPECIMEN SCHEDULE—(*See Instructions on page* lxxv.)

Serial No. and name.		Religion.	Religious denomination.	Race.	Nationality.	Male or female.	Age.	Married, unmarried, or widowed.	Parent-tongue.	Birth-place.	Occupation or means of subsistence.	Learning, literate or illiterate.	Language known by literate.	Note. Infirmities (see Instructions).
1		2	3	4	5	6	7	8	9	10	11	12	13	14
1	A. F.	Christian ...	Church of England	European	English...	Male ...	38	Married	English...	England ...	Surgeon, Government service.	Literate	English.	
2	B. J.	Christian ...	Roman Catholic ...	Eurasian	Eurasian	Female...	27	Widow...	English...	Calcutta ...	Government Pension	Literate	English.	
3	D. S.	Jew ...	Jew	Jew	Austrian	Male ...	40	Unmarried	Polish ...	Austria ...	Broker	Literate	English.	
4	C. T.	Christian ...	Armenian ...	Armenian	British Indian.	Male ...	Infant	Unmarried	English...	Bombay ...	(Lawyer's clerk) ...	Illiterate	...	Blind.
5	P. N.	Christian ...	Methodist Episcopalian.	European	American	Male ...	48	Widower	English...	United States	Piece-goods Merchant	Literate	English.	
6	A. M.	Christian ...	Presbyterian ...	European	Scotch ...	Male ...	28	Married	English...	Scotland ...	Tea-planter ...	Literate	English.	
7	J. K.	Christian ...	Wesleyan ...	European	English	Male ...	32	Married	English...	Punjab ...	Engineer (Railway)	Literate	English.	
8	H. S.	Christian ...	Lutheran ...	European	Swiss ...	Male ...	35	Unmarried	German...	Switzerland	Watchmaker ...	Literate	German.	
9	M. O.	Christian ...	Roman Catholic ...	European	Irish ...	Female...	14	Unmarried	English...	Malta ...	(Army Officer) ...	Learning	...	
10	I. V.	Christian ...	Greek Church ...	European	Russian	Male ...	52	Married	Russian...	Russia ...	Sailor	Illiterate	...	

HOUSE NO. HEAD OF FAMILY........................... HOUSE NO.

Serial No. and name.	Religion.	Religious sect or denomination.	Race.	Nationality.	Sex.	Age.	Civil condition—married, unmarried, or widowed.	Parent-tongue.	Birth-place.	Occupation or means of subsistence, and for dependents that of the person who supports them.	Learning, literate or illiterate.	Language known by literate.	NOTE.—Infirmities (see instructions).
1	2	3	4	5	6	7	8	9	10	11	12	13	14

Certified to be a correct and complete return of all Europeans and Eurasians in this my house (or tenement) on the night of the 26th February 1891.

(Signed)

INSTRUCTIONS FOR FILLING UP THE SCHEDULE.

GENERAL.—Enter first the head of the family resident in the house on the night of the census, then the rest of the members of the family, and lastly visitors stopping in the house that night. The last column should be filled in only in case of a person afflicted with one of the four infirmities specified in the instructions below, and column 13 only for such as are shown as 'Literate' in column 12, but in every one of the other columns an entry should be made against the name of each person, no blanks being left. General and vague terms for sect and occupation should not be used. The word 'Ditto' should not be used, but each entry made in full.

Column 1.—Enter the names in order, as prescribed above.

Column 2.—(*Religion*).—Enter the main Religion, as shown in the specimen schedule on previous page.

Column 3.—(*Religious denomination*).—Enter the sect or denomination, but do not use general terms such as "Protestant," "Episcopalian," &c. If no sect be returned, enter the word "Unsectarian."

Column 4.—(*Race.*)—Enter *European* (including Australian, Canadian, American, &c.), *Eurasian*, or *Armenian, &c.*

Column 5.—(*Nationality*).—Enter the nationality to which the person considers himself or herself to belong.

Column 6.—(*Sex*).—Enter whether male or female.

Column 7.—(*Age*).—Enter the age *last* birthday, and against children of less than a year old, write "*Infant.*"

Column 8.—(*Civil Condition*).—Show whether each person, infant or grown up, is married, unmarried, or widowed. Persons who have been married, but have no wife or husband living, should be shown as "widowed."

Column 9.—(*Parent-tongue*).—Enter the language ordinarily spoken in the household of the parents.

Column 10.—(*Birth-place*).—If born in India, give the district and province; if born out of India, the country, but do not enter the names of counties, towns, or villages, except in the case of London, or of Calcutta, Bombay, Madras, or Rangoon.

Column 11.—(*Occupation, &c.*)—Enter the occupation of all who do work of any sort, and the source of income of such as live on property, &c. For children of whatever age and for women who do no regular work for wages or profit, enter *in brackets*, the occupation of the head of the family or other person who supports them. If a person has more than one occupation, enter the chief one only, unless one of the other occupations be landholding or cultivation, in which case both should be entered. General terms such as "Government *Service*," or "Railway *Service*," "Commerce," "Clerk," &c., should not be used, but the exact kind of service or dealing must be specified. Persons temporarily out of employ should be returned under their last or ordinary occupation.

Column 12.—(*Education*).—Enter as "Learning" all who are under instruction whether at home or at school or college. Those who are *not under instruction* but are able to both read and write should be shown as "Literate;" and those of whatever age who are not under instruction, and who do not know how to read and write, or who can read but not write, or who can only sign their own name, should be entered as "Illiterate."

Column 13.—(*Language known*).—No entry is to be made in this column except for those shown as "Literate" in column 12, in whose case English should here be specified, or the language, other than Indian vernaculars, which each person can both read and write best.

Column 14.—(*Infirmities*).—If any person be (*a*) of unsound mind; (*b*) deaf-mute from birth, not from accident or disease; (*c*) totally blind; or (*d*) afflicted with the true or corrosive leprosy, an entry accordingly should be made in this column against that person's name.

Circular No. 21 of 1891.

From H. L. Eales, Esq., Superintendent, Census Operations, Burma, to Deputy Commissioners and Presidents of Municipal Committees,—No. 612-44, dated the 31st January 1891.

I have the honour to address you concerning the measures to be taken for securing the early submission of reports of the total population of the province after the taking of the census.

2. The procedure to be adopted to obtain, immediately after the census, an abstract of the results is described, so far as enumerators and supervisors are concerned, in paragraph 14 of the Instructions to Supervisors, and in paragraph 18 of the Instructions to Enumerators. The form of abstract which has to be filled up by enumerators is very simple. All that the enumerator is required to enter in this form is the total number of occupied and unoccupied houses, and the total number of male and female inhabitants, in his block. The supervisor is required to collect these totals and to submit to the Charge Superintendent an abstract of the occupied houses of the male and female inhabitants in his circle. He is not required to enter the total of unoccupied houses. The form in which this abstract is to be prepared is given in the Handbook of Instructions. The supervisor's circle abstract should be sent at once to the Charge Superintendent without the schedule books, which can be sent later. The enumerator's abstracts should not be removed from the schedule books. From the abstracts which he receives from the Supervisors the Charge Superintendent is required to prepare a summary showing the occupied houses and male and female inhabitants of each circle in his charge. This summary should be prepared in the following form:—

Charge Superintendent's Summary.

District.............................Subdivision..........................
Municipality..
Charge or township..

Census circle.	Total number of — Occupied houses.	Persons. — Males.	Persons. — Females.	Total.
1	2	3	4	5
Total ...				

In preparing this summary the Charge Superintendent should be careful to see that no travellers by road or river have been omitted. The summaries should be prepared as quickly as possible and sent by the Charge Superintendents to the Deputy Commissioner without delay.

3. On receipt of the summaries from the Charge Superintendents the Deputy Commissioner should prepare a summary for the district in the following form:

Province Burma District..........................

Name of town, cantonment, &c., and total of rural areas.	Occupied houses.	Persons. — Males.	Persons. — Females.	Persons. — Total	Remarks.
A.—Town A					
Cantonment A					
Town B, &c.					
Total towns ...					
B.—Total rural areas ...					
Grand total districts, &c. ...					

Station..............................
Dated.......................*1891.*

Deputy Commissioner.

The district summaries should be prepared from the charge summaries as received, before the arrival of the schedule books. In the preparation of the district summary the following instructions should be carefully observed. The Deputy Commissioner should see that returns from all cantonments, military police parties, camps of officers on tour, Forest, Survey, and Public Works Department camps, ports, towns, and municipalities are included in the district summary. This should be verified by reference to the Subdivisional Register. The returns from the Railway area and from river steamers in the distrcit should be included in the district summary. For this purpose the Manager and Engineer-in-Chief of the State Railway will be requested to telegraph to the Deputy Commissioner direct, immediately after the census, the number of houses and of male and female inhabitants in the Railway area of each district. In the same way the Manager of the Irrawaddy Flotilla Company will be asked to supply the totals of the steam-boat passenger population. In the case of municipalities the procedure in connection with the preparation of an abstract of the result of the census will be the same as in the case of districts. Where the Deputy Commissioner is not himself the President of the Municipality a summary in the form of the district summary should be sent by the President to the Deputy Commissioner as soon as possible.* In the district summary the totals for towns and cantonments and for rural areas should be separately entered. There will be little difficulty in distinguishing towns and rural areas. Any place where a Municipal or Town Committee has been constituted, and any other place of which the population exceeds 5,000, where there is a market, and where the population is not purely agricultural, should be classed as a town for census purposes. In places where there is a town as well as a cantonment the totals of the town and of the cantonment should be separately entered. In the case of seaport towns the seafaring population should be included.

4. As soon as the district summary has been compiled and the totals have been ascertained each Deputy Commissioner should at once telegraph to the Census Commissioner, Simla, and to me an abstract of the result, as follows:

Houses ... Males ... Females ... Total ...

At the same time he should transmit by post to the Census Commissioner and to this office a copy of the district summary. The despatch of the telegrams and summaries should not be delayed till the schedule books are received in the district office. It is requested that special care may be taken to ensure the early preparation and despatch of the preliminary abstracts of the results of the census in accordance with the above instructions. The Census Commissioner lays great stress on the early submission of these abstracts. He expects to get by telegram from the whole of India an abstract of the result of the census within seven days from the date on which the census is taken.

5. In order that the abstracts from this province may not be later than those from other parts of India it will be necessary to make special arrangements. In some districts the abstracts can be collected in seven days without difficulty. In others, owing to their extensive area and the imperfect nature of the communications, there will be inevitable delay. In order to enable Deputy Commissioners to prepare the district summaries in all cases within the prescribed period of seven days the following plan has been adopted with the Chief Commissioner's approval and sanction. On the completion of the preliminary record, which is now in progress, supervisors should be instructed to add up the totals of occupied houses and of male and female inhabitants. The supervisor should do this when he initials the enumerators' books, as required by Rule 10 of the Instructions to Supervisors, and should enter the results on the supervisor's abstract form, two copies of which will be supplied to him. When he has initialled all the enumerators' books he should send the abstract to the Charge Superintendent. On receipt of these abstracts from the supervisors the Charge Superintendent should at once send them on in original to the Deputy Commissioner, so that they may reach him not later than the 15th February. The Deputy Commissioner will thus be in possession of an abstract of the preliminary record.

6. The preparation of these abstracts of the preliminary record will not affect the preparation of the regular abstracts in the manner prescribed in paragraphs 2—4 of this letter. In the preparation of the district summary the returns sent in after the census has been taken should be used. Deputy Commissioners will issue such directions as may be necessary to ensure the arrival at their offices of all the charge summaries within six days from the date of the census whether all circle abstracts have been received by the Charge Superintendent or not. On receipt of the charge summaries the Deputy Commissioner will ascertain which circles, if any, have not been included and, in compiling the district summary, will supply the totals of those circles from the abstracts of the preliminary record. In most districts it will not be necessary to have recourse to the abstracts of the preliminary record for this purpose as they should on no account be used in respect of places from which the regular abstracts have arrived. It is believed that, as far as the total of the province is concerned, the error resulting from the partial use of the abstracts of the preli-

* In Rangoon special arrangements for the preparation of a summary of the results of the census have been made.

minary record in this manner will be inappreciable. The procedure prescribed in these orders will also be of use in giving enumerators, supervisors, and Charge Superintendents practice in preparing the abstracts which they will have to make when the census has been taken.

Circular No. 22 of 1891.

From H. L. EALES, Esq., Superintendent, Census Operations, Burma, to all Deputy Commissioners and Presidents of Municipalities,—No. 633-24, dated the 2nd February 1891.

I HAVE the honour to forward herewith a copy of a telegram, dated the 29th instant, from the Census Commissioner for India, relative to the rule prescribing a page per house entry in the Census Schedule books which have been issued to you.

2. Although the relaxation of the rule may be necessary in India, it is probable that in Burma the license now allowed will not be required as in Circular No. XI of the 4th November 1890 ample margin was made for the density of the population.

3. If necessary, however, Deputy Commissioners may act on their own discretion, but in all such cases the fact should be communicated at once to this office.

Telegram from the Census Commissioner for India to the Superintendent, Census Operations, Burma,—dated the 29th January 1891.

IF schedules run short, you can cancel rules prescribing page per house either occupied or empty.

Circular No. 23 of 1891.

From H. L. EALES, Esq., Superintendent, Census Operations, Burma, to all Deputy Commissioners,—No. 634-38, dated the 2nd February 1891.

I HAVE the honour to request that you will be so good as to arrange for the enumeration of the jail population in your district in consultation with the Superintendent of the Jail, who will carry out the enumeration under your orders.

2. Every jail should be treated as a separate block. All inhabited buildings should be numbered. For this purpose a jail barrack should be treated as one house. Care should be taken that a sufficient number of schedule books is supplied.

3. In order that there should be as few changes as possible the preliminary record should not ordinarily be commenced earlier than the 20th February. Care should be taken that, when making this record, prisoners who will be released on or before the 26th February are not included.

4. All persons residing on the jail premises, whether Jail officials or prisoners, should be enumerated by the Superintendent of the Jail and not by the ordinary District or Municipal enumerator.

In column 11 of the schedule (occupation) prisoners should be shown as (*a*) convicts, (*b*) under-trial, or (*c*) civil. It is unnecessary to record their employment either before or after their admission into the jail.

Circular No. 24 of 1891.

Endorsement by H. L. EALES, Esq., Superintendent, Census Operations, Burma,—No. 775-14, dated the 19th February 1891.

COPY of the following forwarded to Presidents of Municipalities for information.

Extract from the Proceedings of the Government of India in the Home Department (Census),—No. 1 Cens.-12—23, dated Calcutta, the 26th January 1891.

READ—

Home Department Circular letter No. 5C.-163—172, dated the 27th August 1890.

Read also—

Replies to the Circular of the 27th August 1890.

RESOLUTION.—In the circular letter of the 27th August 1890 the Government of India made suggestions to local Governments as to the principles which should be followed in the rules to be laid down for general adoption regarding the manner in which the cost of Census Operations in Municipalities, other than the presidency towns, should be met and asked for their opinions on the rules proposed to be issued. After considering the replies of local Governments to the circular above cited the Governor-General in Council has decided to prescribe the following rules on the subject for general adoption :—

(*a*) Government will supply to Municipalities, free of all cost, including carriage from the Press, the schedules and enumeration books.

(*b*) Municipalities will provide all the necessary agency and contingent expenditure for the enumeration, supplemented in such manner as the local Government may direct by the loan of Government officials to act as Census Officers.

(*c*) The abstraction and compilation will be carried out by Government agency, the Municipality contributing funds at the rate of three months' salary of one abstracting clerk, on the average scale to be prescribed by the Provincial Superintendent of Census Operations, for every ten thousand of the population dealt with. Fractions of that total will be paid for proportionately on the same scale. Special cases in which the partial exemption of small Municipalities containing less than that number of inhabitants is suggested as desirable will be considered by local Governments.

(*d*) The tabulated registers when done with by the Provincial Superintendent will, in return for the assistance rendered, be made over to the Municipality, provided that the Municipal authority undertakes to preserve them in good order until the next general enumeration.

ORDER.—Ordered that a copy of this Resolution be forwarded to local Governments and Administrations for information and guidance, and that a copy be forwarded to the Census Commissioner for India. / Foreign Department.

(True extract)

C. J. LYALL,

Secretary to the Government of India.

Circular No. 25 of 1891.

From H. L. EALES, Esq., Superintendent, Census Operations, Burma, to all Deputy Commissioners and Presidents of Municipalities,—No. 776-9, dated the 19th February 1891.

I HAVE the honour to request you will be so good as to submit as early as possible a list of the clerks, if any, who have volunteered for work in this office.

2. These clerks will, if recommended by you, be awarded appointments as Abstracting Clerks, commencing at Rs. 20 rising to Rs. 25 per mensem. I hope to introduce a system of payment by piecework, in which case clerks should easily increase their pay. Subject to the Chief Commissioner's sanction clerks who have special claims, or show special aptitude, will be appointed Totallers at Rs. 30 rising to Rs. 40, Tabulators at Rs. 40 to Rs. 50, Supervisors at Rs. 60 to Rs. 70, or Inspectors at Rs. 75.

3. Clerks who are appointed in the districts and who may be employed in bringing down the cases of schedule books on the completion of the census will be paid travelling allowance from the headquarters of the district to this office.

4. The abstraction work will last about four months and the cleverer clerks will find work in my office as Tabulators for about three months more.

Circular No. 26 of 1891.

From H. L. EALES, Esq., Superintendent, Census Operations, Burma, to all Deputy Commissioners and Presidents of Municipalities,—No. 777, dated the 19th February 1891.

As has already been laid down in the Instructions to Supervisors, on the conclusion of the census each supervisor will collect his enumerators' books and, after seeing that the totals of the enumerators' abstract have been duly added up, verified, and entered in the books, he will enter the totals in his own abstract and then compare the number of the books returned to him by the enumerators with the entries in the supervisors' list. On finding that all the books issued have been returned, he will submit his list, with the enumerators' schedule books and any household schedules he may have collected, to his Charge Superintendent, who, after comparing the lists of all the supervisors in his charge with the books returned by them, will submit the books and lists to the Deputy Commissioner through his Subdivisional Officer in the case of rural tracts and to the President in the case of Municipalities. Except in the case of Rangoon Town, where the President, Rangoon Municipality, will forward the books directly to this office, the Presidents will forward the books and supervisors' lists to the Deputy Commissioners of the districts in which the Municipalities are situate. The Deputy Commissioners will finally compare the books with the Subdivisional Register and will see that the books are packed circle by circle and charge by charge, and will then forward the books in charge of a clerk to the Census office. This clerk may be one of the volunteer Census Clerks in those districts where clerks have volunteered for employment in this office. The clerk will be given a passage order on which the number of the cases of books forwarded should be endorsed. The clerk's pay should be advanced by the Deputy Commissioner. The cost of the freight of books despatched by them should be borne by the Municipalities.

2. I have the honour to request that you will be so good as to report on the work of the census in your district. This report should deal with the following points :—

I.—Preparatory work. This should include—

(*a*) the preparation of the Circle Registers A and B and the Subdivisional Register ;

(*b*) the date of the commencement and completion of house-numbering ;

(*c*) the agency employed, showing separately the number of paid and unpaid Charge Superintendents, supervisors, and enumerators, the actual cost compared with the estimated cost of enumeration, and how the enumerators were paid, whether by piecework or by the month.

II.—The Census itself. This should touch on—

(*a*) the preliminary record, which will include the instruction of enumerators and supervisors, dates of commencement and completion of the preliminary record, the testing of this record ;

(*b*) the final census. This portion of your report should include remarks on the quality of the work done by enumerators and supervisors, and Charge Superintendents. I shall be glad if you will be so good as to bring to notice the work done by the unpaid enumerators and supervisors, as well as of those officers who have shown zeal and intelligence in the work, so that I may submit their names to the Chief Commissioner ;

(*c*) the preparation of the enumerators' and supervisors' abstracts and charge summaries, the date of return of the Census Schedule books, and the measures taken for the enumeration of travellers by boat or road ;

(*d*) the progress and date of completion of the non-synchronous census in the outlying tracts, if any, in your jurisdiction ;

(*e*) the progress made up to date in preparing the village registers prescribed for tracts excluded from Census operations ;

(*f*) the prosecutions, if any, that were sanctioned under the provisions of the Census Act and the attitude of the people ;

(*g*) the total actual cost of census operations as compared with the estimates submitted by you ;

(*h*) the number of Census Schedule books and household schedules indented for and used ;

(*i*) the correctness or otherwise of the results obtained.

3. Some Deputy Commissioners and Presidents have already submitted maps of their districts and municipalities. I have the honour to request that, if you have not already done so, you will be so good as to favour me with a map showing in districts revenue circles by their serial number for the whole district and the divisions, if any, of the revenue circles into census circles by letter under the revenue circle. In towns the Municipal maps, being on a larger scale, should show the division of the town into blocks as well as Census circles.

4. In some districts there are tribes regarding whose origin, customs, and traditions little has as yet been published or is known. If District Officers can spare the time to report on any matters of interest connected with these tribes, I shall be very glad to receive them and incorporate them as far as possible in my report. Deputy Commissioners, however, need not delay their district reports in order that these notes should be included by them. The totals required in Circular 21 need not be delayed for the arrival of the Census books in the district office. The Census Schedule books should be collected and despatched to this office not later than the 15th March. The Subdivisional Register should be despatched by post as soon as the books have been finally packed up. The despatch of the books need not be delayed for the district report which has been alluded to in paragraph 4 of this letter. This report should be despatched to this office by the 31st March.

Circular No. 27 of 1891.

From H. L. Eales, Esq., Superintendent, Census Operations, Burma, to all Deputy Commissioners and Presidents of Municipalities,—No. 846-16, dated the 14th March 1891.

With reference to my Circular No. 10 of 1890, being letter No. 109-30, dated the 29th October 1890, and your reply No. , dated , I have the honour to state I have now received the Chief Commissioner's sanction for the expenditure of the sums budgetted by you.

2. It is important that these sums should be paid out of the amount allotted for district charges during the present year. I have therefore the honour to request you will be so good as to pay all charges up to the amount sanctioned before the 31st March. Should any further unforeseen expenditure have been incurred, I have the honour to request that you will be so good as to send in your supplementary budget as early as possible.

Etxracts from the Handbook of Instructions for taking the Census.

It has been considered unnecessary to reproduce the Burmese translations here. A copy of the original handbook has been kept for the use of the Provincial Superintendent of Census in 1901.

INSTRUCTIONS FOR SUPERVISORS.

1. You have been appointed supervisor of the circle containing the blocks named in the list which has been furnished to you.

2. On receiving charge of your circle you will check your list and see that the books entered in it as being distributed to the enumerators are properly distributed. You will at once report the loss of any book to your Charge Superintendent and see that the new book is filled up at once correctly.

3. You will first go round and make yourself thoroughly acquainted with every block in your circle, and you will see that every enumerator knows the boundaries of his block.

4. Carefully read through the instructions to enumerators and see that every enumerator thoroughly understands them. If the enumerators are careless and badly instructed, it will be quite clear that the supervisor has not done his duty.

5. The houses in each block should be entered in the order in which they are entered in the block list. The enumerator should be informed by you that on no account should any page be torn out of the book, however incorrectly it may have been written up. If you find that the page must be written out afresh, let a new page at the end of the book be taken and number it with the number of the cancelled page, write "Cancelled" across the cancelled page, and refer to the number of the page on which the correct entries have been made.

6. You should repeatedly visit every block during the preliminary record, and not only read through entries in the books, but make the enumerators go over the entries with you in the presence of the persons enumerated. You will thus be able to check the entries and not only correct mistakes that may have been made, but show the enumerators how to avoid them in future. Recollect that all columns except 3, 5, 13, and 14 must be filled up, and see that these four columns have not been left blank by mistake.

7. If you find that any house, monastery, zayat, boat, or camping-ground has been omitted, or that there is any mistake in the block list or schedule, you should at once make the necessary correction or addition if you are able to do so. If you have any doubt, you should report the matter to the Charge Superintendent.

8. If it should appear to you that any of the enumerators in your circle will not have enough schedules, you will at once apply for schedule books to the Charge Superintendent.

9. Besides the three sizes of books already issued, namely, books of 16, 30, and 60 schedules, supplementary books of 6 schedules will be issued to you on your requisition. See that these new supplementary books are duly endorsed and entered in your list.

10. See that the enumerators work steadily day by day at the preliminary record. So soon as an enumerator has finished the preliminary record, read through all the entries, and, if you find any mistakes, correct them and initial the books on the day each enumerator finishes his preliminary record.

11. In the rural districts the preliminary record should be finished by the 8th February.

12. As soon as the preliminary record is finished, make the enumerator empty and clean his ink-bottle, and then let him fill it with the red ink which will be supplied to you.

13. On the night of the census, 26th February, you will visit the blocks in your circle and see that the enumerators check the entries. You will particularly enquire and find out whether the zayats, camping-grounds, and landing-places have been duly visited.

14. The enumerator should on the morning of the 27th February come to the place fixed on as your headquarters with his schedule books and add up the number of houses and persons to be enumerated, and note the totals of males, females, and houses occupied and unoccupied which he has enumerated on a slip of paper, which he will hand to you. You will then have the book re-added by another enumerator or person to whom the first totals are unknown, and if the totals agree, you should post up the figures in ink in the abstract at end of the enumerator's schedule book and sign it. You will next enter the totals of each block in your circle in your circle abstract, which is in the following form (form attached).

You will sign the abstract and return it, with the schedule books, as early as possible, to your Charge Superintendent, check your list, and see that every book given out has been returned to you.

SUPERVISOR'S ABSTRACT.

District......................., *Township*......................., *Revenue circle*.......................
Supervisor's Circle.

Blocks in villages by village No. and letter in rural tracts; in towns by number under census circle.	Total number of			
	Occupied houses.	Persons.		
		M.	F.	Total.
1	2	3	4	5

B.—STANDARD ENUMERATOR'S ABSTRACT.

(*Not to be filled up till after the Census on the 26th February 1891.*)

Village.	Block No.	Book No.	Houses.			Persons.		
			Occupied.	Empty.	Total.	Males.	Females.	Total.

(*Signed*)

Re-added by { (*a*) *Enumerator of Block No.* *Enumerator.*
(*b*) *Enumerator of Block No.*

Certified to have been tested and the total found correct.

(*Signed*)

Compiled into Charge Summary on the of 1891. *Supervisor.*

(*Signed*)

Charge Superintendent.

INSTRUCTIONS TO ENUMERATORS.

THE FIRST ROUND.

A.—The Preliminary Record.

1. Beginning from the 8th January 1891, you will visit every house in your block to which a separate number has been affixed, in the order in which they are entered in the list in your book, and enter in the schedules in that book every person residing in those houses in the manner prescribed below. If you find any building which has not been entered in the list, you will enter it and fill up a schedule for it as for the rest.

2. You must use black ink and write very clearly.

3. You must take a fresh page for each house and enter the number of the house from the block list. If there are more than eight persons in a house, you should continue the entries for that house on the next page, repeating at the top of that page the number of the house in question, with the word "continued" after it in brackets. You must never begin the entries for a fresh house in the middle of a page, but should leave the unused lines blank.

4. If the entry for any person in any of the columns of the schedule be the same as that for the person entered on the line above, you must repeat the entry and never write the word "ditto" or make dots.

5. If one of the houses on the list be found unoccupied, you should write the word "empty" after the number of that house on the top of the form and leave the form blank.

6. You are to enter all persons living in, and taking their meals from, the house even though any of them may be at the time of your visit absent for a short time watching crops, fishing, &c., or on a short journey, provided they are to be back at the house before the 26th February. After residents you should enter visitors in the house, if any, but not those who are only stopping there for a short time and will not remain there till the 26th February. In zayats and monasteries you should enter on this occasion only those who permanently reside there.

7. Before beginning to make these entries, you must read carefully the rules for filling up each column which are printed on the next page [See below, C.—Rules for filling up the schedule], and also the specimen schedule on the page opposite those rules. [Not printed.]

8. You should consult your supervisor regarding any points on which you require explanation. You must have completed all the entries in your block by the 8th February 1891.

THE SECOND ROUND.

B.—THE FINAL RECORD.

9. At nightfall on the 26th February 1891 you will take this book, as already filled in, and again visit every house in your block in order.

10. You must summon the chief member of each family residing in the house and read over to him the entries made for his family in the schedule. You will strike out the entries for persons who are not present and fill up the form for any person now in the house who was not there when the first visit was made, such as guests, infants newly born, and others. You are to consider as present all living in, or taking their meals from, the house, even though any of them may be out fishing or watching in the fields, or at a shop, &c., for the night.

11. If there be no room left on the schedule for the fresh entries above mentioned, you will take a fresh page at the end of your book and enter on it the house number with the word "continued" after it, as prescribed in paragraph 3 above.

12. Before you start on your round, you must see that you are yourself enumerated in the house where you are stopping.

13. You must not alter any entry already made against any person, unless you have to strike out the entries altogether, because he or she is no longer present. When you strike out a person, you must draw the line completely through all the entries relating to that person and not merely through column 1.

14. If red ink has been supplied to you, you must use that alone for entries and erasures made at the final record.

15. Whilst going on this round you must visit every house marked "empty" in your book to see whether any person is now living there.

16. After visiting as above all the dwelling-houses, you must go to the zayats, encampments, Shan waings, and landing-places where travellers rest for the night and enter all particulars in the schedules for the wayfarers, the boatmen, or others you may find there, and strike out the entries already made if the persons are not now present.

17. If any householder in your block has been given a separate schedule, you should collect it on the morning of the 27th February and, after seeing that the rules have been complied with in filling up the columns, you should stitch or pin it into your book, next to the last schedule filled up by you.

18. After your book has been inspected by the supervisor, you will prepare the short abstract printed on the back of the specimen schedule in it, and when he has certified it to be correct, he will take charge of your book.

19. According to the Census Act every person is legally bound to furnish you with such information as is necessary for filling up the schedule; but you are forbidden to ask for any information not required for the purpose of the census, as, for instance, the amount of any person's income. Any enumerator detected in extorting money on any pretext connected with the census renders himself liable to punishment under the Census Act or the Penal Code.

C.—RULES FOR FILLING UP THE SCHEDULE.

RULE 1.—Column 1 (*Serial number and name*).—Enter first the chief resident member of the family, whether male or female, then the other members of the family, and their resident servants, if any, and, lastly, visitors or temporary residents. If there be any objection made by natives of India to giving the name of a female, write the word "female" in this column and fill up the rest of the column as usual.

If an infant has not yet been named, enter the word "infant." The serial number must not be added till the Final record.

RULE 2.—Column 2 (*Religion*).—Enter here the religion which each person returns:—

As Buddhist, Hindu, Mussulman, Christian, Nat-worshipper, &c.

RULE 3.—Column 3 (*Sect of religion*).—Enter the sect which each person who has been entered as Christian in column 2 says he belongs to, as Church of England, Baptist, Roman Catholic, &c.

If the sect of Christians cannot be stated, enter "not returned" in this column, but do not leave it blank.

RULE 4.—Column 4 (*Caste, &c.*).—Enter the race of each person, as Burman, Karen, Talaing, &c., European, Eurasian, &c. For Hindus enter the caste, as Brahman, Rajput, Chetty, Paria, &c.

RULE 5.—Column 5 (*Subdivision of Caste, &c.*).—If the caste has been entered in column 4, enter here the subdivison as *Kanaujia* or *Madhava* of *Brahmans, Oswal* of *Banias*; if tribe be entered in column 4, enter here the clan; if race be entered in column 4, enter the tribe or nationality, *e.g.*, for Eurasians enter either Eurasian or Anglo-Burman, Anglo-Indian; for Karens, Sgau or Pwo, &c.

RULE 6.—Column 6 (*Male* or *Female*).—Enter here each person as either *male* or *female*, even though you may have written the word "female" in column 1 already.

RULE 7.—Column 7 (*Age*).—Enter the number of years each person has completed. For infants less than one year old enter the word "infants."

If a person cannot state his or her age exactly, the enumerator should ask the relations *or refer to some well-known event of local importance*, or if the person be present, make a guess at the age from the appearance. He must never insist on seeing any female who is not voluntarily produced before him.

RULE 8.—Column 8 (*Marriage, &c.*).—Enter each person, whether infant, child, or grown up, as either *married, unmarried, or widowed*. This column must not be left blank for any one of whatever age.

Children who have been married should be entered as married even though they may not have begun to actually live with their wives or husbands. Persons who have been married, but have no wife or husband living, should be entered as widowed. The enumerator must accept the statement made by the person, or, in the case of children, by their relatives.

RULE 9.—Column 9 (*Parent-tongue*).—Enter the language which each person returns as ordinarily spoken in the household of that person's parents.

RULE 10.—Column 10 (*Birthplace*).—Enter the district *and State* in which each person was born, and if the person be not born in Burma, add the name of the province to the district of birth.

If the person be born out of India, enter the country, as *China, Kabul, Ceylon*. The names of villages, tehsils, &c., are not to be given.

RULE 11.—Column 11 (*Occupation or means of subsistence*). [*Read this rule very carefully and ask the supervisor about all cases which seem doubtful to you.*]—Enter here the exact occupation or means of livelihood of all males and females who do work or live on private property, such as *house-rent, pension, &c.* In the case of children and women who do no work, enter the occupation of the head of their family, or of the person who supports them, adding the word "dependent," but do not leave this column unfilled for any one, even an infant. If a person have two or more occupations, enter only the chief one, except when a person owns or cultivates land in addition to another occupation, when both should be entered.

No vague terms should be used, such as "service," "Government service," "shopkeeping," "writing," or "labour," &c.; but the *exact service*, the *goods sold*, the *class of writing* or *labour* must be stated. When a person's occupation is connected with agriculture, it should be stated whether the land is cultivated in person or all let to tenants; if he be an agricultural labourer, it should be stated whether he be engaged by the month or year, or is a daily field-labourer. Women who earn money by occupations independent of their husbands, such as *selling firewood, cowdung-cakes, grass* or by *rice-pounding, weaving* or *doing housework* for wages, should be shown under those occupations. If a person makes the articles he sells, he should be entered as "maker and seller" of them. If a person lives on alms, it should be stated whether he is a religious mendicant or an ordinary beggar. When a person is in Government, Railway, or Municipal service, the special service should be entered first, and the word Government, or Municipal, &c., after, as clerk—*Government*; sweeper—*Municipal*; labourer—*Railway*.

If a person be temporarily out of employ, enter the last or ordinary occupation.

RULE 12.—Column 12 (*Instruction*).—Enter in this column against each person, whether grown up, child or infant, either *learning, literate* or *illiterate*. Enter all those as *learning* who are under instruction, either at home or at school or college. Enter as *literate* those who are able to both read and write any language, but are not under instruction as above. Enter as *illiterate* those who are not under instruction and who do not know how to both read and write, and who can read but not write, or can sign their own names, but not read.

RULE 13.—Column 13 (*Language known by literate*).—Enter here the language which those shown as *literate* in column 12 can both read and write, and if a person knows how to read and write English as well as a vernacular, enter "English" also.

This column is to be left blank for those shown in column 12 as *learning* or *illiterate*, and, except when English is known, only one language should be entered, that best known.

RULE 14.—Column 14 (*Infirmities*).—If any person be blind of both eyes, or deaf and dumb from birth, or insane, or suffering from corrosive leprosy, enter the name of the infirmity in this column.

Do not enter those blind of one eye only, or who have become deaf and dumb after birth, or who are suffering from white leprosy only.

BLOCK LIST.

Village *Block No.* *Book No.* *Circle*

Subdivision, *i.e.*, hamlet, quarter, street, &c.	Houses.		Remarks.
	Serial No.	Description. (Dwelling-house, shop, serai, &c.)	
1	2	3	4

RULES FOR THE ENUMERATION OF THE BOAT POPULATION.

1. Circle Register B will show the places in every district where boats are expected to be numerous, and also where boats have been allotted to a house block because they are not numerous.

2. Special enumerators should be appointed for the enumeration of the boat population in all places where boats are expected to be numerous.

3. On the night of the census some boats will probably be moored, while others may be in motion from one district to another.

4. The enumeration of the boats that are moored should offer no difficulty. It would be advisable to mark off the foreshore by bamboo poles and flags, and only permit a certain number to moor between each spot so marked out.

5. As the enumeration will have to be completed in one day and one night, and the average population for all inhabited boats is probably not less than six persons, experience shows that 12 boats or 72 persons will ordinarily find ample work for one enumerator.

6. Ample margin should be left when indenting for boat schedule books to meet a sudden demand caused by the arrival of fresh boats. Care should be taken to provide each Charge Superintendent with spare books, which will be readily accessible on the night of the census.

Care should be taken that boats moored in out-of-the-way places be not omitted.

7. The enumeration of boats in motion will be more difficult. Patrol boats should be stationed at fixed points to be chosen by the District Officers. These patrol boats will start work on the morning of the 26th February and will stop and enumerate all boats whether passing up or down.

8. As soon as a boat has been enumerated, the enumerator will hand the headman of the boat a pass to certify that his boat has been enumerated. The pass will be in the accompanying form :—

CENSUS PASS.

District or Municipality.

Circle No. Block No.

Boat-owner's name—

Number of persons enumerated—

Dated— *(Enumerator's Signature.)*

9. Every boat the headman of which does not possess a pass should be enumerated. If there be found on board any person in excess of the number noted in the pass, he should be enumerated, unless he states he has already been enumerated on shore.

10. The patrol boats should continue to stop all boats for three days after the census and ascertain whether the boatmen have been enumerated or not.

11. Special care and supervision is required lest the enumerators unnecessarily harass or endeavour to obtain fees from boatmen in order to let the latter pass unenumerated.

ABSTRACTION SHEET I.

These Abstraction Sheets are practically the same as those originally prescribed by the Census Commissioner for India.

(Columns 2, 6, 7, and 8 of the Census Schedule).

District..............................

Charge or Township........................ *Circle*.............. *Village*......................... *Signature of* { *Reader*......................... *Abstractor*..................... *Totaller*........................

Block No. or Letter........... *Book No*............ *Date of Abstraction*..............................

Age.	Religion—A. Buddhists.				B. Nat-worshippers.				C. Hindus.				D. Mahomedans.				E. Christians.				F. Sikhs.				G. Others.				Total.
	Married.	Single.	Widowed.	Total.	Married.	Single.	Widowed.	Total.	Married.	Single.	Widowed.	Total.	Married.	Single.	Widowed.	Total.	Married.	Single.	Widowed.	Total.	Married.	Single.	Widowed.	Total.	Married.	Single.	Widowed.	Total.	

[The size of this sheet is $19\frac{1}{2} \times 24$ inches.]

ABSTRACTION SHEET II.

(Columns 2, 6, 7, and 12.)

District....................
Charge or Township..... ....
Circle................................
Village................................
Block No. or Letter..............
Book No..........
Signature of { *Reader**.................. *Abstractor*............... *Totaller*................ }
Date of Abstraction..............(**Optional.*)

Religion.	Males.					Females.				
	Age.	Learning.	Literate.	Illiterate.	Total males.	Age.	Learning.	Literate.	Illiterate.	Total females.

[The size of this sheet is 25 × 10 inches.]

ABSTRACTION SHEET III.

(Columns 6, 7, and 11.)

District...........
Township.........
Circle........
Village..................
Block No. or Letter......
Book No.......
Signature of { *Reader*................. *Re-abstractor*......... *Totaller* .... }
Date of Abstraction.......................

Occupation.	Males.			Total males.	Occupation.	Females.			Total females.
	0—4.	5—14.	15 and over.			0—4.	5—14.	15 and over.	

[The size of this sheet is 13 × 20 inches.]

ABSTRACTION SHEET IV † (COMBINED WITH X).

Columns 2, 4, 5, 12, and 13.)

District..................
Township............... .
Circle.......................
Village.......................
Block No. or Letter...........
Signature of { *Abstractor*.................... *Totaller*........................ }
Book No.............
Date of Abstraction................

Religion.	Caste or race.	Sub-caste, tribe, or nationality.	Parent tongue.	Males.				Females.			
				Learning and illiterate.	*Literate, knowing*			Learning and illiterate.	*Literate, knowing*		
					English.	Other languages.	Total.		English.	Other languages.	Total.

[The size of this sheet is 12 × 10 inches.]

† Where education by caste is not abstracted, the same divisions will serve for language known by the literate (column 13), reserving one column for learning and illiterate combined.

ABSTRACTION SHEET V.

(Columns 6 and 9.)

District..................

Township.....................

Circle.............................

Village............................

Block No. or Letter...........

Signature of {*Abstractor*.................. *Totaller*....................

Book No.........

Date of Abstraction..........................

Language.	Males.	Females.
	[The size of this sheet is 13 × 10 inches.]	

ABSTRACTION SHEET VI.

(Columns 6 and 10.)

District..................

Township.....................

Circle.............................

Village............................

Block No. or Letter...........

Signature of {*Abstractor*.................. *Totaller*....................

Book No.........

Date of Abstraction..........................

Birth, district, &c.	Males.	Females.
	[The size of this sheet is 12 × 10 inches.]	

ABSTRACTION SHEET VII.

(Columns 4, 6, 7, and 14.)

District.................

Charge or Township.......................

Circle.............................

Village............................

Block No. or Letter...........

Signature of {*Abstractor*.................. *Totaller*....................

Book No.........

Date of Abstraction..........................

SECTION I (AGE).										SECTION II (CASTE, &C.).								
Males.					*Females.*					*Males.*					*Females.*			
Age.	Insane.	Deaf-mute.	Blind.	Leper.	Age.	Insane.	Deaf-mute.	Blind.	Leper.	Caste, &c.	Insane.	Deaf-mute.	Blind.	Leper.	Insane.	Deaf-mute.	Blind.	Leper.
					[The size of this sheet is 10 × 12½ inches.]													

ABSTRACTION SHEET VIII—(FOR CHRISTIANS ONLY).

(Columns 2, 3, 4, and 6.)

District..................

Township............. { *Charge*............... *Circle*...............

Signature of { *Abstractor*........................ *Totaller*........................

Village.................. *Block No. or Letter*.................... *Book No*................................

Date of Abstraction...........

Sect.	Males.				Females.			
	European, &c.	Eurasian.	Native.	Total.	European, &c.	Eurasian.	Native.	Total.

[The size of this sheet is 12 × 10 inches.]

ABSTRACTION SHEET IX.

(Columns 2, 4, 6, and 7.)

District..................

Charge or Township..................

Circle..............................

Village..............................

Block No. or Letter...........

Signature of { *Abstractor*........................ *Totaller*........................

Book No.........

Date of Abstraction........................

European, &c., Eurasian, or Armenian, &c.	Males.					Females.				
	0—14.	15—34.	35—49.	50 and over.	Total males.	0—14.	15—34.	35—49.	50 and over.	Total females.

[The size of this sheet is 12 × 10 inches.]

ABSTRACTION SHEET XI—(PROVINCIAL).

(Columns 2, 4, 5, 6, 7, and 8.)

District..................

Charge or Township.................

Village........................

Circle..............................

Village............................

Block No. or Letter............

Signature of { *Abstractor*........................ *Totaller*........................

Book No.........

Date of Abstraction................................

Religion.	Caste, tribe, race, &c., and sub-division of ditto.	Males.					Females.				
		Age periods.	Married.	Unmarried.	Widowers.	Total males.	Age periods.	Married.	Unmarried.	Widows.	Total females

[The size of this sheet is 20 × 12 inches.]

ABSTRACTION SHEET XII—(SPECIAL).

(Columns 6 and 7.)

District..................

Charge or Township..................

Circle..............................

Village..............................

Block No. or Letter...........

Signature of { *Abstractor*........................ / *Totaller*..........................

Book No.........

Date of Abstraction..................................

Age.	Males.	Females.	Age.	Males.	Females.
1					
2	[The size of this sheet is 20 × 8 inches.]				
3					
&c.					

The following forms and registers were prescribed by the Provincial Superintendent of Census for the use of the Abstraction and Tabulation Offices :—

Abstraction No. 1.

INSPECTOR'S PROGRESS REPORT.

Outturn of work done daily in section...........sheet...............Supervisor.

Date.	Number of abstractors.	Number of blocks.	Number of population.	Remarks.

Abstraction No. 2.

INSPECTOR'S CHECKING.

Re-abstraction Register Sheet No............

Date.	District.	No. of circle and village.	Name of abstractor.	Name of re-abstractor.	Population.	Remarks.

Abstraction No. 3.

Room Supervisor's Register of daily outturn of work done in Section on 189 .

Number.	Names of abstractors.	No. of circle and block.	Total block.	Re-abstraction.	Population.

This register is used by the totaller also. Instead of the number of blocks the number of books are entered to check the abstractor from losing any book distributed to him for abstraction.

Abstraction No. 4.

Abstraction-room Book-keeper's Receipt Book.

Date.	Name of district.	No. of circle.	Number of books.	Date of return to Record-room.	Remarks.
					Schedule books received from and returned to the Record-room are entered in this register by the book-keeper of the abstraction-room.

RECORD ROOM REGISTER No. I.

Register of Schedule Books received from each district.

Date of receipt.	District.	Particulars of receipt.				Remarks.
		Number of cases of schedule books.	Number of packets of schedule books.	Subdivisional register.	Loose sheets.	

RECORD ROOM REGISTER No. II.

Outstanding Register of books short received and returned to Deputy Commissioner.

Name of revenue circle and serial No. for district.	Census circle by serial letter under revenue circle.	Supervisor's name.	Names of villages, boat block, cutch boileries, fisheries, and camping-grounds which have been blocked separately. Serial No. for each revenue circle.	Number of houses in each village.	Forwarded from District Officers.	Received from District Officers.	Outstanding.	Remarks.

RECORD ROOM REGISTER No. III.

Register of issue of Schedule Books from the Checking Department to the Record-room.

Circles.		Number of books.	Signature.	Remarks.
Names.	Number.			

RECORD ROOM REGISTER No. IV.

Record-room register of Schedule Books issued to each section.

District.	Circles.		Number of books.	Section for Sheet No. I.		Section for Sheet No. II.		Section for Sheet No. III.		Section for Sheets Nos. IV and X.		Section for Sheet No. V.		Section for Sheet No. VI.		Section for Sheet No. VII.		Section for Sheet No. VIII.		Section for Sheet No. IX.		Section for Sheet No. XI.		Remarks.
	Names.	Number.		Signature.	Date of issue.	Signature.	Date of issue.	Signature.	Date of issue.	Signature.	Date of issue.	Signature.	Date of issue.	Signature.	Date of issue.	Signature.	Date of issue.	Signature.	Date of issue.	Signature.	Date of issue.	Signature.	Date of issue.	

RECORD ROOM REGISTER No. V.

Record-room receipt of Schedule Books from each section.

District.	Circles.		Number of books.	Section for Sheet No. I.		Section for Sheet No. II.		Section for Sheet No. III.		Section for Sheets Nos. IV and X.		Section for Sheet No. V.		Section for Sheet No. VI.		Section for Sheet No. VII.		Section for Sheet No. VIII.		Section for Sheet No. IX.		Section for Sheet No. XI.		Remarks.
	Names.	Number.		Signature.	Date of receipt.	Signature.	Date of receipt.	Signature.	Date of receipt.	Signature.	Date of receipt.	Signature.	Date of receipt.	Signature.	Date of receipt.	Signature.	Date of receipt.	Signature.	Date of receipt.	Signature.	Date of receipt.	Signature.	Date of receipt.	

RECORD ROOM REGISTER No. VI.

Abstraction Sheet received.

Circles.		Number of books.	Sheet No. I, date of receipt.	Sheet No. II, date of receipt.	Sheet No. III, date of receipt.	Sheet Nos. IV and X, date of receipt.	Sheet No. V, date of receipt.	Sheet No. VI, date of receipt.	Sheet No. VII, date of receipt.	Sheet No. VIII, date of receipt.	Sheet No. IX, date of receipt.	Sheet No. XI, date of receipt.	Remarks.
Names.	Number.												

RECORD ROOM REGISTER No. VII.

Subdivisional Register. Issue and Receipt Book.

Name of Subdivisional Register.	Number of books.	Number of sheets.	Signature of receiving party.	Date of	
				Issue.	Returned.

RECORD ROOM REGISTER No. VIII.

Daily Abstraction Register showing number of circles remaining to be abstracted.

Names of sheets.	Akyab.	Northern Arakan.	Kyaukpyu.	Sandoway.	Rangoon Town.	Hanthawaddy.	Pegu.	Tharrawaddy.	Prome.	Thôngwa.	Bassein.	Henzada.	Thayetmyo.	Amherst.	Tavoy.	Mergui.	Toungoo.	Shwegyin.	Salween.	Mandalay.	Bhamo.	Katha.	Ruby Mines.	Shwebo.	Ye-u.	Sagaing.	Lower Chindwin.	Upper Chindwin.	Myingyan.	Pakôkku.	Minbu.	Magwe.	Kyauksè.	Meiktila.	Yamèthin.	Pyinmana.

RECORD ROOM REGISTER No. IX.

*Stock-book of Registers for Tabulation.**

Date.					No. VI.																					VII.																								
	I.	II.	III.	IV.	(a)	(b)	(c)	(d)	(e)	(f)	(g)	(h)	(i)	(j)	(k)	(l)	(m)	(n)	(o)	(p)	(q)	(r)	(s)	(t)	(u)	VII.	(a)	(b)	(c)	(d)	(e)	(f)	VIII.	IX.	X.	X(a).	XI.	XI(a).	XII.	XII(a).	XIII.	XIII(a).	XIV.	XIV(a).	XV	XV(a)	XVI.	XVII.	XVIII.

* The Population Registers themselves are not reproduced here as no alteration was made in them. Tabulation Registers V, XIX, and XX were not used in Burma.

RECORD ROOM REGISTER No. X.

Register of Circles of Abstraction Sheets issued to and received from Checking and Comparing Sections.

Township.	Name of circle.	Circle No.	No. of Sheet.	Date of receipt from record-room.	DISTRICT.		Date of issue to Comparing section.	Date of return by Comparing section.	Date of issue to Final Check section.	Date of return by Final Check section.
					Date of issue to Superficial section.	Date of return by Superficial section.				

RECORD ROOM REGISTER No. XI.

Issue and receipt of Abstraction Sheets to and from the Tabulating Sections.

Township.	Name of circle.	Circle No.	Date of issue for tabulation.	Date of return from tabulation.	Issue.	Returned.	Issue.	Returned.	Issue.	Returned.	Issue.	Returned.	Issue	Returned.

APPENDIX D.

Extracts from the Reports of Deputy Commissioners and Presidents of Municipalities.

IN selecting the extracts that are given in the following pages only the salient points have been considered. The reports naturally cover the same ground in most districts, and in many districts where the census operations were carried out without a hitch the reports are consequently less interesting. I have, moreover, been obliged for want of space to omit much matter, that has already been discussed in the report.

From Major W. F. H. GREY, Deputy Commissioner, Akyab, to the Superintendent of the Census Operations, Burma,—No. 685-16R., dated the 9th April 1891.

* * * * *

The preparatory work commenced late. The first indent for **A** and **B** Forms which was forwarded to the Secretariat through the Commissioner on the 4th June was in some way lost or mislaid. A fresh indent was subsequently submitted, but the registers had to be prepared in manuscript in July. The printed forms were eventually received on the 16th August, when the registers were revised and copied on them.

The instructions for the preparation of Subdivisional Registers were received on the 12th September. They were prepared and submitted by the 29th idem, and were received back in this office on the 7th November.

The numbering of houses was commenced on the 1st October and was not completed till the end of December.

In the district, excluding the Municipality, for which a separate report has been submitted, and the Port of Akyab, the census of which was taken by the Port Officer under special instructions, the following agency was employed :—

	Unpaid.	Paid.	Total.
Charge Superintendents	8	*Nil.*	8
Supervisors	224	*Nil.*	224
Enumerators	1,588	360	1,948
Total ...	...	...	2,180

The estimated cost for which sanction was obtained was Rs. 535, and the actual expenditure Rs. 533. The enumerators were paid by piece-work. Only those received pay who had to work outside their own village. The rate of pay varied from Re. 1 to Rs. 8 (in the Naaf) according to the distance of the scene of work from the enumerator's home.

The highest rate, as shown above, was paid in the Naaf township, which is largely populated by Bengalis knowing no Arakanese. Consequently competent enumerators were scarce and some had to travel far. Before another census is taken it should be considered whether the Naaf schedules should not be prepared in Bengali.

2. Specimen schedules and Handbooks of Instruction were received on the 28th November and were issued to Township Officers on the 1st December. As there were not a sufficient number to allow of issues to each supervisor and enumerator, orders were issued providing for the instruction of the persons concerned at convenient centres. There was not, however, at this date much time left for the process before the actual enumeration began, and in future it would be better to issue the specimen books, &c., either at an earlier date or in greater numbers.

The schedule forms were received on the 3rd January. The Block lists were written up in the office by the sanctioned establishment aided by clerks from different departments, the work being completed in 12 days. They were then distributed and the preliminary enumeration was commenced about the 20th January and was completed about the 15th February.

The final census was carried out on the night of the 26th February by the agency already stated. As noted above there was much difficulty in procuring qualified enumerators in the Naaf, and the same difficulty prevailed elsewhere in a lesser degree owing to the illiterate condition of the people. Judging from the rate of increase shown, I think it may be fairly assumed that so far as figures go the enumeration is very approximately, if not absolutely, accurate. In such matters as the castes of Hindus, sects of Musalmans, and in a lesser degree in the matter of occupation, errors must be expected. Many of the natives of India here do not know accurately themselves the subdivision of creed or caste to which they belong. In Akyab town the question could often be settled by an appeal to a Moulvi or other authority, but in the country districts the enumerator could only enter what he was told. On the whole the work was done willingly, and I think as well as could be expected from the agency employed or from any agency obtainable in the present stage of education except at an excessive cost. The Township Officers of Pauktaw, the Naaf, and Kaladan took trouble over their work. The first two were at one time incapacitated by illness and were assisted by Myoôk Maung Hla Paw Zan and Judicial Clerk Maung Tha Hla placed on special duty for that purpose.

These officers worked well. Mr. Ripley supervised carefully the work of his two subdivisions, and the services of Maung Mra U, the Akunwun, in connection with all the office work required, were most valuable. I regret that I was unable to devote so much personal supervision to the census as I could have wished owing to an accident which incapacitated me from walking for two months from the 18th December.

The enumerators' and supervisors' abstracts and the charge summaries reached this office on dates between the 3rd and the 14th March. The total figures had been previously sent in by special messengers and telegraphed to Simla and Rangoon on the 4th March. The schedule books came in on dates varying from the 3rd to the 18th March. With the exception of those belonging to the Naaf township, they were forwarded to Rangoon on the 16th.

Special measures were taken for the enumeration of travellers on six roads in the district, namely :—

1.	Paungdawbyin	Naaf township.
2.	Letwedet	
3.	Alechaung	
4.	Narigan	Kyelet township.
5.	Mayu	
6.	Myaungbwe :	Myohaung township.

* * * * *

The only part of the district in which a non-synchronous census was taken, comprises the hill tracts in the Minbya township inhabited by Chins. These villages had most of them never paid tribute or been in any way, except nominally, under our administration. All expedition was arranged under Myôok Maung Shwe Hnya for the double purpose of collecting the tribute which they had last year undertaken to pay and of taking the census. The latter was taken in the schedule forms prescribed and was completed on the 4th March, the returns being received in this office on the 13th March.

* * * * *

There were no prosecutions. Two enumerators refused to work, but one of them afterwards thought better of it, and the other advanced reasons for his refusal which were accepted as valid.

The reports of Township Officers do not notice anything remarkable in the attitude of the people except in the case of Myohaung, where the Myoôk says the people believed the enumeration was made as a preliminary to the imposition of a new tax. This is an interesting instance of the longevity possessed by delusions of a certain class. It is perhaps due to the fact that there are a number of Burmans as distinguished from Arakanese in the Myohaung township.

The amount estimated and for which sanction was received as cost of census operations was Rs. 625, namely, Rs. 535 pay of enumerators and Rs. 90 Office establishment.

The actual expenditure on these heads was Rs. 533 and Rs. 45 respectively.

* * * * *

Report by Major W. F. H. Grey, President, Akyab Municipality, on the census for the Town of Akyab.

1. (*a*) The preparation of the Circle Registers **A** and **B** was begun on the 7th August 1890 and was completed about the 15th of September. These registers show the houses and the names of the heads of the houses in the order in which the houses stand, village by village, in every administrative circle.

The town has been divided into eight census charges under Superintendents which include two for the rice mills and godowns, one for the jail, and one for the General Hospital. These charges have been subdivided into 18 census circles under supervisors, and these 18 census circles have been again subdivided into 107 blocks under enumerators. The godown and mill blocks having a very large population, it was necessary to appoint several enumerators to each.

The preparation of Register **B** was commenced at the same time as Register **A**.

Within Municipal limits there was only a portion of two creeks in which to enumerate the boats, namely, Jullia creek above the iron bridge and the Cherogea creek above the Bankshall.

There were 12 boat blocks under one supervisor; 11 of these were in the Cherogea creek and only one in the Jullia creek.

The census of all the boat blocks within the port limits was taken by the Port Department.

(*b*) The numbering of the houses commenced on the 20th October 1890 and was finished by the 17th November after Register **A** had been checked and corrected.

There were 28 villages in the town and separate series of house numbers were run for each village.

Coal-tar was used in the numbering of the houses and answered effectually.

(*c*) The agency employed was as follows :—

Unpaid.

Charge Superintendents	8
Supervisors	19
Enumerators	165

2. (*a*) The supervisors and enumerators of the house blocks were instructed and had the books of schedules given them on the 10th January and those of the godown and mill blocks on the 17th January. The preliminary record of the house blocks was begun on the 12th January and those of the godowns and mills for the permanent hands on the 20th January and completed by the 5th February, and were tested on the 6th, 7th, and 8th February.

In consultation with the Superintendent of Census Operations, who happened to be in Akyab on the 6th and 7th February, it was decided that the best plan of enumerating the coolies at the mills and godowns was by gangs, allotting one book of six schedules to each. A census pass was given to each mangee after the preliminary record of his gang of coolies. The preliminary record of the coolies for the godowns and mills was begun on the 9th February and completed by the 20th February, and the final test of all the preliminary records was done on the night of the 26th February.

It was found that the plan proposed by the Superintendent of Census Operations of having books of six schedules each answered admirably, as on the night of the 26th every thing went off smoothly and without a hitch. Every mangee was called up in turn with his men, who were called out one by one in answer to his name, and new men were entered in red, those being absent were struck out. The whole enumeration of these coolies was finished before midnight.

* * * * *

(*b*) The Charge Superintendent of Myoma circle was Mr. Warde Jones, Extra Assistant Commissioner. The male and female population of his circle was 10,862, of which 7,970 were males and 2,892 were females. Mr. Warde Jones took great pains in the supervision of his circle, which is in the most densely crowded portion of the town.

The following supervisors in his circle have been reported as having done specially good work :—

Maung Hla Aung, Head Judicial clerk, Arakan Commissioner's Office.
Maung Pha Taw U, 3rd clerk, Arakan Commissioner's Office.
Maung Sein U, Judicial Record-keeper.

* * * * *

The Charge Superintendent of Shwe Bya circle was Maung Mra U, Akunwun of the district and Extra Assistant Commissioner. * * This circle is next in importance to Myoma, and Maung Mra U did not spare himself in the supervision of his circle.

The following supervisors in his circle have been reported as having done specially good work :—

Maung Hla Paw U, Akunwun, Municipality.
Maung Hla Paw Zan, District Bailiff.

* * * * *

The Charge Superintendent of the Roagyi circle was Maung Aung Gyawwè, Head Judicial clerk, Deputy Commissioner's Office.

* * * * *

Maung Aung Gyawwè did his work well.

The following supervisors in his circle are reported to have done good work :—

Maung Shwe Min, Municipal thugyi.
Maung Shwe U, Head Judicial clerk, Town Magistrate's Court.

* * * * *

The Charge Superintendent of the Buddawmaw circle was Mr. J. Simon, Head Master, Normal School.

* * * * *

Mr. Simon was very energetic and careful in the discharge of his duties as Superintendent.

The following supervisor under him is reported to have done good work :—
Maung Paw Tun, Myoma thugyi.

* * * * *

The Charge Superintendent of the mills and godowns on the south bank of the Cherogea creek was Mr. C. H. White, Superintendent, Arakan Commissioner's Office.

* * * * *

Mr. C. H. White deserves great praise for the supervision of his circle.

The following supervisors are reported to have given great satisfaction in the discharge of their duties :—

Maung Chan Tun Aung, Advocate.
Mr. P. Cotton, Teacher, High School.
Mr. H. J. D. Wilkinson, Teacher, High School.
Mr. L. Belletty, Teacher, High School.
Mr. A. DeSilva, Clerk, Deputy Commissioner's Office.

* * * * *

The Charge Superintendent of the north bank of the Cherogea creek was Maung Lu Bu, Honorary Magistrate and Head clerk in the office of Messrs. Bulloch Brothers and Company.

* * * * *

Maung Lu Bu was indefatigable in the discharge of his duties and is deserving of special mention.

The following supervisor is reported to have done extra good work :—
Mr. S. Cowell, Head clerk, Deputy Commissioner's Office.

* * * * *

(*c*) All the arrangements connected with the taking of the census in the town were carried out in the Municipal Office under the supervision of the Secretary, Mr. J. Shaw Brown, and the Akunwun Maung Hla Paw U, who is favourably mentioned as a supervisor in the Shwe Bya circle.

* * * * *

(*d*) * * It will be seen that there are three males to one female. This is explained by it being the rice season when the census was taken, at which time it is estimated there must be from 8 to 10 thousand male coolies.

There were no prosecutions under the Census Act, and the people answered the queries of the enumerators without much difficulty and with no seeming reluctance.

(*e*) The Municipal Committee sanctioned a sum of Rs. 250 for cost of census operations.

The amount of estimate which was submitted to the Superintendent of Census Operations, excluding cost of stationery, was Rs. 239-8-0, and the actual expenditure incurred was Rs. 311.

* * * * *

From R. H. Greenstreet, Esq., Deputy Commissioner, Northern Arakan Hill Tracts, to the Superintendent of the Census Operations, Burma,—No. 91, dated Paletwa, the 17th March 1891.

* * * * * *

I.—Preparatory Work.

The census had to be taken in this district in an entirely different manner from that of any other district in Burma.

The inhabitants are mostly wild illiterate hill people, speaking a language of their own and scattered over a large and hilly district ; it was impossible therefore to employ enumerators from inside the district, and to ask for and employ enumerators from outside was equally hopeless, as none know the language of the hill tract. Under these circumstances I was obliged to utilize the staff of Deputy Commissioner's and Police establishments and to carry out the work with their aid. Three writers from the Deputy Commissioner's establishment and two from the Police establishment have been employed in the enumeration of villages and six guard-writers (police) in the enumeration of boat traffic.

By working thus the hillmen, who are naturally suspicious of any strange movement on our side, were not allowed, as they would have been had outsiders been sent to their villages, nor were they brought into contact with other than people knowing their language and whom they had been accustomed to meet on their occasional visits to headquarters.

Preparation of Works.

(*a*) Having thus five persons ready to take the work of enumeration, the district was divided into five portions, keeping as nearly as possible to the thugyi's circles.

(*b*) The plan of numbering the houses was impossible as our officers had to visit sometimes as many as 80 or 90 villages.

(*c*) As there were only five persons available for the whole work, with the Deputy Commissioner as a sort of Charge Superintendent over the whole, the work, was, as may be imagined, a most arduous one.

No Charge Superintendent, supervisors, or enumerators have been paid. All that has been asked for is that the travelling allowance of the court and police officials engaged upon the work should be granted, as it would be if they were travelling with the Deputy Commissioner on town census work.

(*a*) All the enumerators were carefully instructed by the Deputy Commissioner himself in their duties. Rolls of villages in each man's charge were made out and were made over to each enumerator, and they were instructed to visit each and every village on that roll and to take the exact census of that village personally.

(*b*) It was impossible to take such a census in a day or even in a month, as the villages are much scattered and are some of them situated in almost inaccessible places. So that two villages a day and sometimes one may be called good work.

* * * * *

(*h*) * * From the method used and from the reports of the various officers and thugyis' returns, I think we have arrived at a census result as nearly correct as possible.

From F. McBlaine, Esq., Deputy Commissioner, Kyaukpyu, to the Superintendent of the Census Operations, Burma,—No. 320-1—91, dated the 15th April 1891.

* * * * *

The preparation of Circle Registers **A** and **B** was undertaken during the month of July 1890. These were prepared by circle thugyis. It is believed that in some cases they were prepared from the assessment rolls and that the thugyis did not visit every village and house themselves as they were directed to do, the consequence being that the schedules supplied were insufficient in many circles. The Subdivisicnal Register was completed and submitted by the 24th November.

House-numbering was commenced in the latter part of October and finished by the middle of November. The agency employed for the taking of the census was as follows :—

Unpaid.

Charge Superintendents	5
Supervisors	110
Enumerators	982

Paid.

Enumerators	18

The special enumerators were paid by piece-work, each being allotted certain portions of the non-synchronous and wild Chin tracts in the An township.

The estimated cost of special enumerators was put down at Rs. 100.

* * * * *

The supervisors and enumerators were instructed by the Charge Superintendents and had the work well in hand for the taking of the preliminary census, which was commenced about the 8th and finished about the 19th February, all the returns being received at headquarters and the district summary completed by the 24th idem.

The Charge Superintendents in many instances tested the accurary of the records themselves and made corrections where necessary, but this could only be done near their headquarters. On the night fixed for the taking of the final census the enumerators visited each house in many cases accompanied by the supervisors. The enumerators and supervisors all appeared to work well. In a few instances it was found that illiterate men had been appointed as enumerators, but this could not well be avoided as they were headmen of villages and were better able to get the correct information than other persons would. The thugyis or their attendants generally accompanied these men through their villages and made the entries in their schedules.

In the non-synchronous outlying tracts the preliminary record was taken in most cases by the thugyis themselves or their agents or, when available, by fairly intelligent police constables.

For the final record the special enumerators were each accompanied by a staff of three to five writers and went round the villages where the head of each house was called, the entries read over to him, and any names erased or added as required.

Most of the non-synchronous tract which covers a large and sparsely populated area is situated in the An township, where Myoôk Maung Mè was Charge Superintendent. All the special enumerators were under his supervision and his work was extremely well done. He deserves great credit for the way in which he managed to keep his supervisors and enumerators in hand, the whole of the outlying tract being completed at the same time as the synchronous tracts.

The enumerators' abstracts were all filled in the day after the census and the supervisors' abstracts finished by the 2nd or 3rd of March.

All the charge summaries were received and compiled into the district summary by the 6th March. Special arrangements had to be made to ensure the punctual arrival at headquarters of both the preliminary and final records. Special dâks were arranged from each township headquarters to the headquarters of the district, which of course was very expensive. Communications in this district generally are very defective and slow, and it so happened that the P. S. *Hasty*, which runs between Kyaukpyu, Ramri, and Chəduba, was away at Calcutta from the middle of January till the middle of March.

* * * * *

The B. I. S. N. Company's S. S. *Pachumba* was in port during the night of the census and as the Commander had not made any attempt to fill up the census schedules that had been supplied to him at Rangoon, an Inspector of Police with a clerk was sent on board to enumerate the crew and passengers which numbered 400 souls. The population of the steamer was included in the Kyaukpyu Municipal return.

* * * * *

The non-synchronous census in outlying tracts was completed simultaneously with the census of other parts of the district. The special enumerators with their staffs met at certain places in their tracts on the 26th February, and on that and the following day tested the entries in the schedules.

There were no tracts in this district which were excluded from census operations.

There were no prosecutions under the Census Act, nor any complaints against the enumerators.

The attitude of the people was not at all obstructive; they generally gave the required information freely.

The total cost of the census operations was as follows:—

	Rs.	A.	P.
For special enumerators	70	0	0
For contingencies	252	7	3
Total ...	322	7	3

* * * * *

Notwithstanding that the enumerators were in many cases men of little education, there is every reason to believe that the result of the census of the district is accurate as far as the total population is concerned, as every endeavour was made to make it complete; but some of the information regarding the different subdivisions of castes and sects and the occupation of the people may be faulty.

* * * * *

From F. McBlaine, Esq., President of the Kyaukpyu Municipality, to the Superintendent of the Census Operations, Burma,—No. 238, dated the 25th March 1891.

* * * * *

Circle Registers A and B were prepared in August 1890 and the indent for the schedules submitted by the 13th of that month. The Subdivisional Register was completed and submitted on the 2nd October 1890. House-numbering was commenced and finished with the month of October 1890.

There was no paid agency employed within the Municipality.

The Charge Superintendent was the Head Assistant of the Deputy Commissioner's office. There were eight supervisors, five of whom were Municipal Commissioners, one Akunwun, one Inspector of Police, and one Jailer. There were 30 enumerators, 24 of whom were Government clerks, five school teachers, and one police constable.

The preliminary record was commenced on the 12th January 1891. The enumerators were all carefully instructed by the Charge Superintendent and supervisors. Every schedule book was examined personally by the Charge Superintendent and in many instances the entries checked. It was found necessary in some cases to destroy the schedules and issue fresh ones; the preliminary record was finished by the 20th January 1891.

* * * * *

The S. S. *Pachumba* arrived in port on the evening of the 27th February, and as the Commander had not already enumerated the population on board, the Inspector of Police with a clerk was sent on board to do the enumeration after 9 o'clock.

* * * * *

There were no prosecutions under the provisions of the Census Act; the inhabitants were not at all averse to the taking of the census, but on the contrary rendered every assistance to the enumerators. No complaints were made against the men employed.

There was only Rs. 2 expended on account of chunam and rice for numbering the houses; no other cost was incurred on account of census within this Municipality.

* * * * *

I think the census has, on the whole, been well taken, and its accuracy may be relied on as the work was very carefully done.

From B. Houghton, Esq., Deputy Commissioner, Sandoway, to the Superintendent of the Census Operations, Burma,—No. 1356-81—90, dated Camp Gwa, the 12th March 1891.

* * * * *

(*a*) Onr eceipt of letter, Revenue Department No. 506-3C.G., dated the 16th May 1890, from the Officiating Chief Secretary to the Chief Commissioner to all Deputy Commissioners, a preliminary estimate of census schedules required in the district was submitted from this office and the Township Officers were directed to push on the preparation of the circle registers. These registers were completed by the end of August 1890 and a final indent for census house and boat schedules was forwarded direct to the Superintendent of Government Printing, Rangoon, on the 26th August and 1st September 1890. * *

(*b*) On receipt of your letter No. 45-24 of 1890 (Census), dated the 18th September 1890, necessary instructions were issued to Township Officers to start at once numbering the houses, and it may be fairly presumed that this work was completed by 31st October 1890.

* * * * *

(*a*) * * As already explained in my letter No. 1239-81—67, dated the 9th February, the commencement of the preliminary record was somewhat retarded owing to a short supply of schedules being received from Rangoon which necessitated a supplementary indent being despatched. This record, however, may be safely put down as (i) commenced on the 10th January in some parts of the district, (ii) in full progress throughout the district by 28th January, and (iii) completed throughout the district on 15th February 1891.

The testing of the preliminary record was conducted by the Township Officers and by myself to a large extent. The former were specially encouraged to move about in their townships on census duty. In a district like Sandoway, where education is very backward, the brunt of the work fell, as might be expected, on the higher officers and supervisors. In some cases the latter had to write a large portion of the schedules themselves, the enumerators, who outside Sandoway town were as a class very unintelligent, being scarcely able to fill them up correctly in spite of minute instructions. It was in fact in some places very difficult to get persons who could read and write at all, whilst those who could do so committed in filling up the schedules nearly every mistake that it was possible to make. Instructions were issued by me from time to time on those points in the schedules which did not seem to be clearly understood.

* * * * *

All schedule books had been filled up and checked some time before the final census, and the actual enumeration on the night of 26th February came off without any hitch. Few non-officials exhibited much intelligence in the work, though they did this ungrudingly, and of the officials I would bring to notice particularly the work of the three Charge Superintendents Maung Tha Bwin, Maung Chin Hlaw, and Maung Aung Kyaw Zan.

* * * * *

(*c*) * * Notwithstanding the great distances in this district the supervisors' abstracts (with the exception of two in the Northern township) were forwarded to the Charge Superintendent without any unnecessary delay, and by means of a specially arranged police patrol the charge summaries were all received in this office by 3rd March 1891, the district summary being prepared on that date and the result telegraphed to you and the Census Commissioner, Simla, as directed in paragraph 4 of your Circular No. 21, dated the 31st January 1891. The two abstracts mentioned above were received at Taungup and incorporated in the district telegram, so that in no case was it necessary to use the preliminary abstracts which had been prepared in accordance with that letter. The census schedule books have not been returned as yet, but these will be sent after the 15th instant.

Special arrangements were made for the censusing of passengers by the Yebawgyi pass (Taungup-Prome road) and the Yahaing pass leading to the Bassein district.

* * * * *

(*f*) There were no prosecutions sanctioned under the provisions of the Census Act. The people of the district appeared willing to assist in facilitating the work, and no reports of any resistance or unwillingness to afford enumerators particulars were received.

(*g*) As had been anticipated, no expenditure of any kind was incurred in the district on account of census operations.

* * * * *

(*i*) The result of the census in this district may be accepted as fairly correct, though it would be optimistic to suppose that no persons whatever escaped enumeration. For this to be the case it would be necessary to have enumerators and supervisors everywhere as intelligent as those, for example, in Sandoway town; whereas the majority of the enumerators out in the district showed a great want of intelligence, or, in plain English, were very stupid. However, the number of the persons who escaped enumeration must I imagine be very small indeed, and so far as human forethought would allow, no loophole was left for any person to escape. It may be noted here that some of the villages in this district are very much scattered, whilst others (if indeed we may call them such) consist of a single detached house far away in the jungles. I do not believe, however, that any of such "villages" escaped enumeration. No alarmist reports were circulated regarding the census, though Government was currently credited in making it with secret designs to increase taxation. In Taungup, whereas elsewhere investigations connected with the re-settlement of the district are being made, it was rumoured that Government intended to take all the paddy (after deducting sufficient for the actual needs of the people) and store it in a large granary to be built at Taungup. No particularly amusing mistakes were made in filling up the schedules.

* * * * *

From B. HOUGHTON, Esq., President, Municipal Committee, Sandoway, to the Superintendent of the Census Operations, Burma,—No. 32-17, dated the 17th March 1891.

* * * * *

1. (*a*) On receipt of letter, Revenue Department No. 506-3C.G., dated the 16th May 1890, from the Officiating Chief Secretary to the Chief Commissioner, a preliminary estimate of census schedules required for the town of Sandoway was submitted to the Superintendent, Government Printing, Rangoon, and the preparation of the Circle Register taken in hand and completed.

(*b*) The numbering of houses was carried out on receipt of your letter No. 45-24 of 1890 (Census), dated the 18th September 1890.

(*c*) * * There was no expenditure incurred on account of the census, the work being done gratuitously.

2. (*a*) The preliminary record started on and was completed by 6th February 1891, and the schedules were again looked into between the 6th and 7th February 1891 (dates on which the offices were closed).

* * * * *

(*f*) There were no prosecutions sanctioned under the provisions of the Census Act. The people of the town rendered every assist ance towards facilitating the census, and no reports of any resistance or unwillingness to afford enumerators particulars were received.

(*g*) As had been anticipated, no expenditure of any kind was incurred by the Municipality on account of census operations.

* * * * *

(*i*) The result of the census in the town may be accepted as correct, as the intelligence and close supervision displayed by both the enumerators and supervisors render the result of their work to be as correct as could possibly be achieved.

* * * * *

From A. L. HOUGH, Esq., Deputy Commissioner, Rangoon Town District, to the Superintendent of the Census Operations, Burma,—No. 544-69—250, dated the 23rd May 1891.

* * * * *

2. (*a*) The Circle Register **A** and the Subdivisional Register of the Rangoon Cantonment were prepared with the assistance of the Cantonment Magistrate and Cantonment Tax Collector and completed in the latter part of October 1890.

(*b*) The numbering of houses in cantonment was commenced on the 28th December 1890 and completed on the 8th January 1891.

(*c*) The agency employed consisted of four Charge Superintendents, 18 supervisors, and 85 enumerators, who, being Government employés, were paid no remuneration for their services.

3. (*a*) The preliminary record was commenced on the 8th January 1891 and completed on the 15th of the following month. The record was tested by the Charge Superintendents and supervisors, who visited a number of houses at random in each block, and saw the enumerators go over the entries in their books in the presence of the persons enumerated.

(*b*) The final record was commenced at 8 P.M. on the 26th February 1891, and completed at 5 A.M. the next day.

The quality of the work done by enumerators, supervisors, and Charge Superintendents was on the whole good.

* * * * *

(*f*) The attitude of the people was good and there were no prosecutions under the Census Act.

* * * * *

From Major R. C. TEMPLE, President, Rangoon Municipality, to the Superintendent of the Census Operations, Burma,—No. 710-80, dated the 25th June 1891.

* * * * *

2. For census purposes the Municipality was divided into 13 census charges corresponding with the existing taxation circles. The charges were placed under Superintendents as follows :—

North Kemmendine	Mr. R. Grant Brown.
South Kemmendine	Mr. W. B. Addis.
Lamadaw	Maung Po Tsu.
Tarôkdan	Mr. L. Kim Seng.
North-West town	Mr. R. C. Cumming.
North-East town	Mr. A. Malcolm.
South-West town	Mr. H. A. Nelson.
South-East town	Mr. N. Duncan.
Botataung and Yaygyaw	Dr. W. H. Sutherland.
Kungyan	Mr. R. O. Wales.
Theinbyin	Mr. T. J. Metcalfe.
Tamwe	Mr. A. M. Minus.
Dalla	Maung Po Win.

The Municipal Secretary, under the President's orders, exercised a general supervision over the whole of the census work, instructed the Superintendents as to the details, and helped them to instruct the supervisors and enumerators. This plan was adopted in consequence of the experience gained during the census of 1881, when very imperfect results were obtained through want of supervision, as both the President and Secretary had no time to spare, having themselves charge of circles. My thanks are due to the gentlemen unconnected with the Municipality who kindly undertook the duties of Charge Superintendents and carried them out with great zeal, and at the same time at a considerable sacrifice of their time.

3. The Circle Registers A and B prescribed in letter No. 506-3C.G., dated the 16th May 1890, having been found inapplicable to Rangoon, an amended form was prescribed in letter No. 30-14, dated the 5th September 1890. These registers were useful in as far as they showed the numbers of houses in each circle and so indicated the amount of work to be done and the quantity of schedules required, and for these purposes in some form or other such registers are very necessary, but for any other purposes they are useless.

* * * * *

5. The following agency was employed :—

General Superintendent	unpaid	1
Charge Superintendents	paid	1
	unpaid	12
Supervisors	paid	14
	unpaid	34
Enumerators	paid	524
	unpaid	80

The following rates of pay were given :—

	Rs.	
One Charge Superintendent	100	
Supervisors	30	each.
Enumerators	20	each.

They were paid by piece-work.

The following statement shows the actual cost of the census, the estimate having been Rs. 10,000 :—

	Rs.	A.	P.
To remuneration of Charge Superintendent	100	0	0
To remuneration of 14 supervisors at Rs. 30 each	420	0	0
To remuneration of 520 enumerators at Rs. 20 each	10,400	0	0
To remuneration of 4 enumerators at Rs. 15 each	60	0	0
To contingencies	2,027	6	11
Total ...	13,007	6	11

6. * * The house schedules supplied were not issued and were useless. In Rangoon it is better to either enumerate everybody on any premises by the aid of enumerators, or where house schedules are issued, to allow the person filling up the schedule to enter everybody. The house schedules sent only allowed Europeans to be entered, so that wherever there were native servants, a separate enumeration by the public enumerator would have been required, and, as many servants sleep in the houses of their European masters, entry would under any circumstances have been required to the house. As no labour would have been saved and a great deal of confusion and probably incorrectness caused by the use of the house schedules, it was decided not to use them at all.

* * * * *

7. * * On the night of the final enumeration I with the Municipal Secretary saw the enumeration started in the various charges in the town proper, and during the night I inspected every charge and personally satisfied myself that enumeration had been or was being carried out. I visited several collections of kyaungs and zayats, in many burial grounds, and also some of the mills both in Kemmendine and Pazundaung. I found that great care had been taken to make the enumeration correct, and I have no hesitation in saying that it was correct. Only in two cases was I able to discover that any person had been omitted on the night of the census and they were included the following morning. A few cases were brought to my notice where people supposed that they had been omitted, but in every one of such cases I found they had been included. As I said before, my greatest difficulty was to obtain correct returns of the castes, and as so very many of the supervisors and enumerators had little knowledge of Indian caste distinctions, and as a large proportion of the Madrasi population appeared to be equally ignorant on the subject, it is probable that the returns under this head may prove to be wanting in the correctness which will be found under the other heads. I wish to bring to notice the very great trouble and care taken by Mr. Metcalfe, the Assistant Magistrate, Mr. Cumming, the Assistant Superintendent of Police, Mr. Brown, Registrar, Judicial Commissioner's Court, and Mr. Nelson, Head Assistant, Office of the Commissioner of Pegu, who kindly acted as Charge Superintendents. * * As regards Mr. Short, the Secretary, I have no hesitation in saying that the general success of the census is due to his energy, care, and intelligence.

8. The preparation of the abstracts and charge summaries was completed by 8 P.M. on the 28th February in every charge except one, where a delay occurred in consequence of one of the returns not being completed in one mill, which delayed the completion of the returns until the 2nd March. Circular letter No. 3797—209, dated the 20th February, explains the plan I adopted in preparing the abstracts and summaries. Every enumerator appeared at the Town Hall, numbered the entries in his schedules, and filled up his abstracts. The supervisors checked this first and finally the Charge Superintendents checked it, and after the supervisors' abstracts had been filled in, the Charge Superintendents made their charge summaries and delivered the schedules to the Municipal Secretary.

9. No prosecutions were sanctioned under the Census Act, and it was not found necessary to ask for sanction, but in a few cases I had to threaten prosecutions, and the penal sections of the Act were certainly necessary.

* * * * *

12. In paragraph VII I have already stated that I consider that the result of the census gives a correct return of the population.

13. In conclusion I wish to point out that the increase of population shown by the census must really be regarded as having accrued since 1886. There is no doubt that the population actually decreased about the time of the war in Upper Burma and did not commence to recover until the end of 1886. Immigration and emigration were nearly equal until 1886, but since then there has been a large balance in favour of immigrants. There was great trade depression and no increased demand for labour in 1885-86, and it is well known to Municipal Officers that an enormous number of houses and rooms in barracks were empty for nearly two years. I merely mention this fact as one that may be of service to you in making your report and that may not be known to you.

* * * * *

From E. DARLINGTON, Esq., Vice-Chairman, Port Commissioners, Rangoon, to the Superintendent of the Census Operations, Burma,—No. 269-44, dated the 29th May 1891.

* * * * *

2. The Port of Rangoon was divided into 18 stations extending from the boundary pillar at Kemmendine on the north to Elephant Point on the south, including the Pegu river and the Pazundaung creek up to the boundary pillar on each, and also the Bassein creek.

3. Thirteen sets of enumerators were employed in the harbour and the other five as follows :—

(1) From King's Point southward to the Bassein creek. The boat engaged on this station met with an accident at King's Point while returning to town on the morning of the 27th February last, and Mr. A. Jackson lost his life and Messrs G. Brown and F. Lawton their effects. The census schedules, which were also lost at the time have, however, been re-written from memory as far as possible.

(2) From Bassein creek to Elephant Point.

(3) The launch *Cameo* was employed between Bassein creek and the China Buckeer river.

(4) From Syriam Point to opposite Bassein creek.

(5) From a point opposite Bassein creek to the Eastern Grove light-house.

The work done by the enumerators on these five stations was very meagre, the occupants of the boats met with having, in most instances, been previously enumerated by the officials of the district to which the boats belonged.

4. The work of enumeration was performed by 17 boats supervised by three steam-launches. Of this number of boats the Customs Department supplied four, the Harbour-masters' Department five, the buoy vessel *Samson* one, and seven country-boats or dinghies were hired for the occasion. In all 57 officers were employed, of which the Customs Department contributed 17 and the Port Trust 40. A census of the persons on board the European vessels in port was taken by the Harbour-masters' Department, with whom one launch was engaged. There were no paid enumerators, all those engaged being either employés of the Customs or the Port Trust.

5. The enumerators began work about 6 P.M. on the 26th February. Some of them had completed their work by 2 A.M. on the following morning, but those employed in the Pegu river, Pazundaung creek, and beyond the limits of the harbour, were engaged until daylight. The three supervising launches were continually on the move checking the work as it progressed. I was afloat inspecting the work done for between two and three hours.

6. At your suggestion patrols were stationed at Kemmendine, the Pazundaung creek, and between King's Point and Bassein creek on the 28th February, to take a census of any boots which might have escaped enumeration on the night of the 26th

7. The expense incurred by the Trust on the hire of boats, purchase of stationery, &c., amounted to Rs. 52-7-0.

* * * * *

From N. G. CHOLMELEY, Esq., Deputy Commissioner, Hanthawaddy, to the Superintendent of the Census Operations, Burma,—No. 40-94, dated the 8th October 1891.

* * * * *

2. In accordance with the instructions conveyed in paragraph 5 of Revenue Department No. 506-3C.G., dated the 16th May 1890, from the Officiating Chief Secretary, which was received in this office on the 22nd May, a statement of rough estimate for house schedules which would probably be required for the district was prepared on the basis of the latest thugyis' rolls and submitted to your office. The vernacular translation of the circular was also distributed to all the thugyis, Township and Subdivisional Officers with an order that they should keep themselves thoroughly acquainted with the instructions contained therein.

3. In the early part of July the Circle Register **A** was received and distributed to the thugyis with full instructions how to fill it up. The Circle Register **B** was not received from the press till August, when it was at once distributed to the thugyis as in the case of Circle Register **A**.

* * * * *

9. * * The Township Officers all did their work satisfactorily and the services of Maung Shaung the Akunwun who was in special charge of the census operations were of the greatest possible assistance.

10. As suggested in your Circular No. 21, dated the 31st January 1891, two sets of supervisors' abstracts were ordered to be prepared, the first abstract being compiled from the totals of the preliminary record and the second from those of the final census. This enabled me to prepare and send the district abstract to the Census Commissioner, India, and to your office within the appointed time. All the census schedule books were received in this office on the 14th March, and, after they were carefully examined and checked, forwarded to your office on the 24th March.

* * * * *

12. The mass of the people having been previously informed of the object and purpose of the census, their minds were not in any way disturbed and no difficulty was experienced in making the enumeration, the people in every class willingly giving all the information required by the Census officers, and consequently no prosecution under the provisions of the Census Act was necessary in any instance.

13. As already anticipated in my Revenue Department No. 40-34, dated the 26th November 1890, no large expenditure was incurred in this district in connection with the taking of the census. A small sum of Rs. 42-8-0 was shown as charges for carrying the census schedule books.

* * * * *

From S. H. T. DE LA COURNEUVE, Esq., Deputy Commissioner, Pegu, to the Superintendent of the Census Operations, Burma,—No. 18-1061, dated the 16th April 1891.

* * * * *

I.—Preparatory Work.

(*a*) The Circle Registers **A** and **B** were prepared by the taikthugyis under the supervision of Township Officers. The work was completed by the end of July 1890. They were duly checked by the Subdivisional Officers of the Pegu and Kyauktan divisions and then sent in to this office.

The Subdivisional Registers were prepared in September. In the first instance they were revised and submitted in November to your office, and subsequently received back from your office duly approved of by you, and were then returned without delay to the respective Subdivisional Officers.

(*b*) The work of house-numbering was commenced about the beginning of October and completed about the middle of November 1890. The house-numbering was checked by the Subdivisional Officers in a large number of villages and found correct.

* * * * *

II.—The Census itself.

(*a*) The work of instructions of Charge Superintendents and supervisors as well as a large number of enumerators was carried on by both Subdivisional Officers during the months of November and December, and further instructions of enumerators was carried on vigorously by the Charge Superintendents and supervisors during the whole of December 1890.

The census schedules were received in the early part of January 1891, and distributed to both Subdivisional Officers without delay; the Pegu Subdivisional Officer received his books on the 8th and Kyauktan on the 9th January 1891. The entries on the covers of all the schedules were written up in the Subdivisional Offices, and the books were then made into bundles for each census circle, and despatched to the Charge Superintendent for distribution to the respective census officers. When two or more books were given to any enumerator they were sown together before issue; the distribution lasted up to the middle of January 1891.

The work of the preliminary record was commenced as each circle received its schedules. The 14th of January was the earliest date on which the preliminary record was commenced in any part of this district. The preliminary record was, with a few isolated exceptions, finished by the 8th February 1891. During the time the preliminary record was being entered up, the work of the enumerators was constantly supervised by the supervisors, Charge Superintendents, Subdivisional Officers, and my predecessors, and on the completion of the preliminary record, the books were brought in to the headquarters of the respective taikthugyis and checked. Nearly 20 per cent. of the schedules were examined by the Subdivisional Officers during the progress of the preliminary record.

(*b*) The quantity of the work done by the enumerators was on the whole exceedingly good, the hand-writing was in every instance almost clear and legible, and in many cases far above the average expected.

The supervisors with a few exceptions worked well and the Charge Superintendents did their best to give satisfaction. The work was done much better in the Kyauktan subdivision than that done in the Pegu subdivision, and great credit is due to Mr. Sarfas, the Subdivisional Officer, who spared no pains on his part to make the census operation of his subdivision a success. He attributes a great deal of this praise to his Township Officers.

* * * * *

(*f*) There were no prosecutions under the Census Act, and the attitude of the people is favourably reported on by the supervisors and Charge Superintendents; the people seemed perfectly willing and ready to impart all desired information.

* * * * *

(*i*) I have every reason to believe that the results obtained in this district are correct.

* * * * *

From S. H. T. de la Courneuve, Esq., President, Pegu Municipality, to the Superintendent of the Census Operations, Burma,—No. 87-290, dated the 26th March 1891.

* * * * *

I.—Preparatory Work.

(*a*) The preliminary estimate of schedules required was drawn up from the Municipal thugyis' house assessment list. Circle Register **A** was completed by the 15th August 1890; few or no boats being expected, it was not considered necessary to fill in Circle Register **B**.

(*b*) The house-numbering was commenced on or about the 7th July 1890 and completed by the 13th August.

(*c*) The census operations being carried out by the Municipal employés aided by the clerks of the Deputy Commissioner's Court, no expense was incurred on paid enumerators or supervisors. The estimated cost of the census operations was Rs. 29; the actual cost was Rs. 5-8-0, namely:—

	Rs.	A.	P.
Boat-hire	4	0	0
Conveying packages from station and calling notice with a gong	1	8	0
Total ...	5	8	0

II.—Final Census.

(*a*) The preliminary census was commenced on 6th January and completed on 18th February 1891. Supervisors were almost daily instructed at the Municipal Office and their work inspected by the Charge Superintendent.

* * * * *

(*b*) On the 25th February a notice was sent round the town with a gong requesting all persons to make it convenient not to be abroad after 9 o'clock on the following night. On the night of the 26th February at 9 o'clock the enumerators and supervisor of Circle 21A met at the Municipal Office, the enumerators and supervisor of Circle 21B at the Iron bridge, and having been inspected by the Deputy Commissioner and Charge Superintendent, the work was commenced. The enumeration was completed at about 2-30 A.M. on the 27th, each enumerator as he finished his block remained at the last house until visited by the Charge Superintendent or his supervisor and his work examined. * * Mr. Palmer, Secretary and Engineer to this Municipality and Census Charge Superintendent, had the entire arrangement of the census operations here and has been unceasing in his efforts to bring the duties entrusted to him to a satisfactory completion. No hitch was met with in taking the census of the Municipality and I am of opinion the work has been well done.

* * * * *

(*i*) * * The blocking of the town was well done and I have assured myself that no house was omitted or twice entered. Each quarter of the town was dealt with as a distinct village.

* * * * *

From Lieutenant F. D. Maxwell, Deputy Commissioner, Tharrawaddy, to the Superintendent of the Census Operations, Burma,—No. 378-1—8, dated the 16th March 1891.

* * * * *

2. Circle Registers **A** and **B** were submitted by thugyis in August and September, and as submitted originally were found to be very inaccurate, but were corrected and

made as accurate as possible, during the last three months of 1890, by thugyis. Township Officers and Subdivisional Officers went round correcting them. Much attention was paid to this work, as on the accuracy of the Registers A and B depended practically the accuracy of the final census. House-numbering, commenced in October, was finished by the middle of November. While going on and after completion some numbers were corrected, others added, all alterations being shown in Register A.

The district was divided into eight charges, the Deputy Conservator of Forests taking all the reserves on the Yomas; the Assistant Superintendant of Police, North Tharrawaddy, the Taungnyo circle; I took the boat blocks in the Irrawaddy, and each Township Officer was Charge Superintendent in his township exclusive of those parts noted above One hundred and seventy-one supervisors were employed, as also 2,065 enumerators; neither supervisors nor enumerators were paid, so that the actual cost of enumeration was *nil*.

3. Thugyis were first of all instructed as to the filling up of schedules and given blank forms to instruct the various supervisors and enumerators under them. * * I think scarcely a village in the district was not visited by some competent person. Every one worked hard and I find great difficulty in mentioning the names of any individual. Perhaps Myoôks Maung Po of Gyobingauk and Maung Po Ka of Sanywe did more than the others. The preliminary record was completed about the 15th of February. The preparation of the enumerators' and supervisors' abstracts was undertaken sometimes by the latter and sometimes by thugyis. Thugyis, however, tested all, in order that there might be no mistakes. All schedule books with the exception of those from the Taungnyo circle were in my office by the 1st March. Arrangements were made with all thugyis that they were to travel day and night in order to be in time. The Taungnyo thugyi did not send in his books till the 5th March, as he was completely incapacitated by dengue fever. His assistant, however, sent in the supervisors' abstracts by the 1st March. I may mention that the whole of the supervisors' abstracts with one exception were sent in to me by the 1st March and that my totals were delayed through the gross carelessness of one supervisor for four days, namely, until the 5th. There were no prosecutions under the Census Act. The census throughout the district was synchronous.

* * * * *

The most common instances of error I found were under age and occupation. I did not expect the former error and indeed did not notice it till comparatively late; too late, I am afraid, to have it corrected throughout the district.

* * * * *

Under occupation I found the following mistakes very common. The headman of the house would be shown as "landowner," "paddy cultivator," his wife as "landowner," "paddy cultivator (dependent)," notwithstanding that she might assist as women usually do in the transplanting, reaping, and threshing. All the children, of whatever age, whether assisting their parents in the cultivation of their land or not would be shown as "dependent on their parents," there of course being nothing to show who and what their parents are. I am afraid also that many mistakes have been made about natives of India. Many of this class I found on or near the railway who did not know where they were born or their subdivisions of caste or even the name of their language. However, whatever mistakes were made were errors of inadvertence and not carelessness. In conclusion I wish to note on the hard work performed by my Akunwun Sau Pau U in connection with the census. An Akunwun's ordinary daily work is very heavy. The addition of the census has been faced successfully and with diligence.

From D. CAMPBELL, Esq., Deputy Commissioner, Prome, to the Superintendent of the Census Operations, Burma,—No. 27—C.R., dated the 31st March 1891.

* * * * *

I.—Preparatory Work.

(*a*) Circle Registers A and B were compiled in the Revenue office from particulars obtained from Township Officers and thugyis. The blocking of tracts and villages was completed by my predecessor Mr. Bonus. This and the numbering of houses I found finished when I took over charge of the district at the end of November 1890. The Subdivisional Registers were similarly prepared.

(*b*) The numbering of houses was commenced and completed in the several townships on the following dates:—

Name of Township.	*Numbering commenced.*	*Completed.*
Shwele	11th August 1890.	10th September 1890.
Mahathaman ...	14th August 1890.	15th October 1890.
Shwedaung ...	7th August 1890.	15th September 1890.
Padaung	3rd August 1890.	13th October 1890.
Thègôn, Paungdè ...	27th August 1890.	31st October 1890.

(*c*) There were in all nine Charge Superintendents, namely, 3 Subdivisional Officers and 6 Myoôks, 433 supervisors, and 2,585 enumerators; none of these were paid. The supervisors consisted of thugyis, lugyis, &c., and the enumerators, except in the more remote parts, mostly of scholars from the monastic schools.

The total cost of the census has been Rs. 107-9-4, and has been incurred chiefly on freight and cooly-hire for schedules and pay of special messengers for carrying letters. * *

II.—The Census itself.

Preliminary record.—The census schedules were only received from Rangoon on 21st January, and were distributed as soon as possible. The recording of the preliminary census was commenced and finished in the several townships on the following dates:—

Name of Township.	*Commenced.*	*Completed.*
Shwele	25th January 1891.	20th February 1891.
Mahathaman ...	Do.	Do.
Shwedaung ...	27th January 1891.	11th February 1891.
Padaung	31st January 1891.	11th February 1891.
Thègòn, Paungdè ...	27th January 1891.	11th February 1891.

* * * * *

I personally examined many of the schedules in several townships, and saw that supervisors and enumerators understood what they were about.

The Final Census.

(*b*) Everything being complete by the 26th February, nothing was left to be done on that night except the correcting of the schedules as they then stood, and the enumeration of boats and travellers. The drilling of enumerators had been so thorough that this passed off without any hitch.

Where all worked so willingly it is perhaps somewhat invidious to pick out any persons for special commendation, but I would especially mention Maung Shwe Bu, Extra Assistant Commissioner, Subdivisional Officer of Prome subdivision, who went personally through every schedule in his subdivision. He was also the first to send in his Charge Superintendent's summary and supervisors' abstracts on 28th February, the schedule books being also sent in on the same evening. This I consider most creditable, especially as some tracts in the subdivision are very remote and the population very scattered. His two Township Officers, Maung The (Mahathaman) and Maung Kan Tha (Shwele) also deserve credit for their share in procuring this result. The Subdivisional Officer particularly notices the work done by the Karen supervisors in the outlying hilly tracts in Shwele township, and special mention may be made of two of these Pa Lo and Nga Pu.

* * * * *

(*c*) Special boat blocks were fixed and special boat enumerators appointed at points where there were likely to be many boats. Where there were only a few boats they were included in the house blocks. Boats remained stationary as far as possible from the morning of the 26th February, when the enumeration began. Special patrol boats were put on to intercept boats coming up or down the river and enumerate them unless they could show a pass. Travellers in the same way were stopped at certain points and enumerated unless they could show a pass. As a matter of fact people kept very much in their houses.

* * * * *

(*f*) No prosecutions were necessary under the Census Act. The people took the thing very quietly, and gave every possible assistance in furnishing the information required and staying at home as much as possible on the night of the final census.

(*g*) As stated above the total actual cost of census operations was Rs. 107-9-4.

* * * * *

(*i*) From the careful way in which the work of the census was carried out all over the district, I have every reason to believe that the results obtained are as correct as could be.

* * * * *

From D. CAMPBELL, Esq., President, Prome Municipality, to the Superintendent of the Census Operations, Burma,—No. 9-38, dated the 3rd April 1891.

* * * * *

I.—Preparatory Work.

* * * * *

(*b*) House-numbering commenced on 1st August 1890 and was completed on the 8th September 1890.

(*c*) All the Census Officers engaged were unpaid.

There were in all one Charge Superintendent, 18 supervisors, 123 enumerators.

The supervisors were mostly Municipal Commissioners.

The enumerators, clerks, schoolboys, &c.

II.—The Census itself.

The preliminary record commenced on the 18th January 1891 and was completed on the 10th February 1891. It is, however, to be noted that the majority of the enumerators had done their work before the 8th February 1891. After this was done, the schedule books were at the instance of the Charge Superintendent sent in to the Municipal office by most of the supervisors for inspection and returned to them before the final census took place.

The Final Census.

(*b*) On the night of the final census the enumerators experienced no difficulty in doing their work, the majority of the inhabitants actually waited with lighted lamps for the enumerators and shut the doors after being enumerated. All the streets and roads were patrolled by gentlemen who very kindly assisted. * * * Taking all things into consideration, a very accurate census (it is believed) has been taken in the town of Prome. All the supervisors and enumerators did excellent work. I would select for special mention Mr. F. E. James Summers, Secretary and Superintendent of Works, Charge Superintendent; Maung Shan Gyi, Head clerk, Municipal Office, who deserves great credit for an excellent compilation which he made of the various castes of Hindus, which was found of great use; Maung San Pe, 2nd clerk, Municipal office; Maung San Za, 3rd clerk, Municipal office. Among the supervisors U Ne Dun, K.S.M.

* * * * *

(*f*) There were no prosecutions under the Census Act. Only some of the Chetties were served with notices for refusing to give their names, &c. The orders were, however, promptly attended to.

(*g*) The total actual cost of census operations was Rs. 35-10-6 as compared with the estimated amount of Rs. 150.

* * * * *

From MAUNG BA TU, President, Paungdè Municipality, to the Superintendent of the Census Operations Burma,—No. 86, dated the 24th April 1891.

* * * * *

2. The numbering of the houses was commenced on the 1st October 1890 and completed on the 14th of the same month. In consequence of a misunderstanding with regard to numbering of houses occupied by different families, one number at first only being given to each house, the numbering had to be re-done, giving a separate number to each room or part of a house occupied by different families.

* * * * *

4. The preliminary record was commenced on the 16th January 1891. Enumerators were instructed to visit every house in their block to which a separate number was affixed, in the order in which they were entered in their lists, and to show the names of every person residing in each house. If any building was omitted or new ones sprung up, they were all to be entered and filled up in the schedule. This was completed on the 31st January 1891.

* * * * *

5. * * The work done in general by the enumerators, supervisors, and Charge Superintendent was very satisfactory.

I have much pleasure in commending the Secretary of the Municipality and Maung Nya, acting thugyi, the former Charge Superintendent and the latter one of the supervisors, in the zeal displayed by them in conducting the operation of the census from beginning to end.

* * * * *

From G. CARMICHAEL, Esq., Officiating Deputy Commissioner, Ma-ubin, to the Superintendent of the Census Operations, Burma,—No. 402-2—16, dated the 9th April 1891.

* * * * *

I.—Preparatory Work.

* * * * *

(*a*) The preparation of the Registers **A** and **B** and the Subdivisional Registers.—The Registers **A** and **B** were prepared during July and were received at headquarters in August. On the 16th September the Census Superintendent visited Ma-ubin, and at his suggestion certain corrections were made in Registers **A** and **B**. They were returned corrected with the Subdivisional Registers in October. The difficulties met with in preparing the Register **A** were—

(1) After the rains are over the people migrate from the villages to temporary huts near the fisheries in the interior and to the seaside where they gather in sufficient numbers to form considerable villages.

(2) In this district, where an enormous area of waste land has recently been brought under cultivation, each cultivator builds his house on some high ground near his land and over the area newly brought under cultivation. The houses are to a great extent scattered here and there without being grouped together in large villages.

(3) The final census was to be taken just at the close of the reaping season, before the people would in the ordinary course have left their fields.

* * * * *

(*b*) The numbering of houses was done mostly during September and October and was completed about the beginning of November.

* * * * *

Preliminary Record.

* * * * *

2. (*a*) The census schedules were received in the beginning of January and were despatched to the Charge Superintendents on the 6th January. The preliminary record was begun about the 16th January in all the subdivisions except Pantanaw where, owing to the difficulty of communication, the books were not distributed till the 26th January. The preliminary record was completed in the first week of February. In Pantanaw it was not completed about 16th February. * * One difficulty felt by Burman enumerators was in ascertaining the caste, birth-place, and language spoken by the different natives of India. Natives of India were employed to assist the Burmans in this, and where this was not possible, in places where there were a large number of natives of India, the Assistant Commissioner, Pyapôn, and myself called up the men and made the necessary entries. The actual number was correctly taken. While the preliminary record was going on we were ordered to have abstracts of the preliminary record made.

* * * * *

The Final Census.

* * * * *

(*b*) * * Of the Subdivisional Officers the one who worked best and took most interest in the work was Mr. George, Assistant Commissioner, Pyapôn. He took especial pains with his subdivision, with the result that his returns can be relied on as very accurate.

Next I would mention Maung Tha No, Subdivisional Officer, Yandoon, and Maung Hpe, Subdivisional Officer, Ma-ubin.

Maung Tha No showed great energy, and the result of his work is very good. Of the Myoôks, Maung Aung Hla of Dedayè, Maung Tin Gyaw of Danubyu, and Maung Po Thin of Yandoon, deserve mention. Of the thugyis the following deserve special mention :—

Maung Kyauk Lôn of Wakame.	Maung Po Maung of Tomayan.
Maung Shwe Aung of Kyontôn.	Maung Lu Gale of Pathwe.
Maung Myaing of Thazi.	Maung Hlaing of Pantanaw.

Maung Tha Dun of Pyinkatha.

Of the supervisors, I would mention Saya Thit, Ywathugyi of Bogale ; Maung Chan Tha Volunteer clerk in Assistant Commissioner's Office, Pyapôn ; Maung San Min, Yazawut gaung, Kanmekebo ; Maung Kya Yo, Maung Kya Bwin, Maung Nyo, Ywathugyi, Maung Po Myit, Maung Nai Mi.

* * * * *

The census of the travelling boat population of the district was the most difficult to take, but the figures show that the enumeration was very successful on the whole.

The majority of the villages lie on the banks of the rivers and creeks that intersect the district in every direction.

The consequence was that on the census night almost every village was liable to have one or two boats anchored near it for enumeration. Boat schedules were not supplied to every enumerator, but they were supplied with manuscript passes signed by the Thugyi or Myoôk, and were instructed to enter any boats that might come in their ordinary house schedules. The larger boat stations were divided into boat blocks and numbered.

To take the census of the moving boats, enumerators were stationed at the entrance of the main streams of communication with Rangoon, Henzada, Bassein, and Hanthawaddy, and also at several points within the district where the boats were likely to stop for a short time. The enumerator began on the morning of the 26th and continued for three days. An enumerator and an assistant together with boatmen were kept at each station. * * The figures of the boat population show as might be expected a preponderance of males. In the large paddy-boats with 16 to 18 rowers there are rarely any women, but in the smaller boats you very often find a whole family.

* * * * *

Prosecution.—In the Yandoon subdivision two enumerators were prosecuted. The census schedules were delivered to them, but they did not attempt to fill them up, and finally left without giving any warning. The attitude of the people was satisfactory and no difficulty was experienced on this ground. Several people who escaped enumeration on the night of the census, reported themselves for enumeration next morning.

* * * * *

(*i*) *Correctness or otherwise of the result obtained.*—The census on the whole has been accurately taken.

* * * * *

From G. L. Weidemann, Esq., Deputy Commissioner, Bassein, to the Superintendent of the Census Operations, Burma,—No. 302-13—1, dated the 31st March 1891.

* * * * *

I would premise that I took over charge of the district on the 27th December only, and that I am dependent on office records and other sources for the information contained in the report upon census operations prior to that date.

* * * * *

I.—Preparatory Work.

(*a*) Forms of Circle Registers A and B were received and distributed to thugyis; each thugyi prepared the registers, leaving column 9 blank. The registers were then sent to the Township Officer, who scrutinized the list with the thugyi and marked off the blocks in column 9 and submitted the registers to the Subdivisional Officer. The Subdivisional Register was prepared in the Deputy Commissioner's Office from Circle Registers A and B and sent to the Superintendent, Census Operations, Rangoon, who examined and returned it with the remark that the blocks as marked off appeared manageable and that the only error found was that the villages were serially numbered for the whole district instead of for revenue circles.

2. The district was divided into 49 revenue circles, and each revenue circle was again divided into 4 and 5 census circles, each census circle containing on an average 8 to 11 villages. To make the work of enumeration as easy as possible each block was divided so as not to contain more than 40 to 50 houses on the average.

3. (*b*) The dates on which the numbering of houses were commenced and completed stand as follows:—

Township	*Date commenced.*	*Date completed.*
Bassein township	None of the Township Officers report when they commenced numbering.	20th October 1890.
Kangyidaung township		Not reported.
Thabaung township		Not reported.
Yegyi township.		26th October 1890.
Lemyethna township		18th October 1890.
Kyonpyaw township		22nd October 1890.
Myaungmya township		20th October 1890.
Ngaputaw township		14th October 1890.

(*c*) * * There were 9 Charge Superintendents, 161 circle supervisors, 2,172 enumerators. There were no paid supervisors or enumerators in the district. No estimate of cost was submitted.

II.—Preliminary Record.

(*a*) A number of Handbooks of Instructions were issued to Township Officers, who were directed to make their supervisors and enumerators well acquainted with their work. Subdivisional Officers also on tour brought together the supervisors and enumerators and personally explained the duties of taking the census, and in their monthly diaries noted how the work was being carried on. Mr. Bridges while on tour personally explained and examined some of the specimen schedules and corrected errors where they occurred and gave instructions. The schedules were received in this office on the evening of the 30th December 1890, and were issued as fast as the entries on the covers could be completed to the Township Officers in turn with instructions to distribute them to enumerators with the greatest possible despatch. I am unable to state the precise date on which the first and last entries were made, but I saw several books completed on January 18th. Different methods were adopted in different townships. In some cases intelligent enumerators filled in the books off-hand. In the Ngathainggyaung subdivision generally, however, a good deal was done by the supervisors personally. In the centre of the district again, where there is a considerable Karen population, the Charge Superintendents found it advisable to direct the entries to be made upon blank sheets, and fair copies to be made into the schedule books only after they were checked. Many of the columns were for the most part easily understood. Those which created most difficulty were "Occupation," the state of learning of children and the subdivisions in the case of Karens, especially Christian Karens, and natives of India. There were also doubts as to whether a Karen who could read and write Burmese, but not Karen, should be classed as "literate." There were also questions asked as to the mother-tongue in the case, *e.g.*, of the offspring of a Chinese father and Burmese mother. The agency employed naturally varied much in intelligence and there was some waste of schedules. Again, in a few cases the inexcusable error was made of taking a leaf for each house instead of a page, but where discovered this error was corrected without confusion. Whole new villages sprang up in some cases, and indents for fresh books were somewhat hastily and, I fear, recklessly made. No time was, however, left for scrutiny, and it was thought better to incur the risk of wasting books than that the enumeration should be incomplete. * * The Subdivisional Officer reports of the Myoôk of Lemyethna that not only was he in no hurry to distribute the schedules, but so indifferently was the work tested that the Subdivisional Officer had himself to go over a good deal of it again.

The Final Census.

(*b*) The preliminary record was the most important and difficult part of the work done. The final census was comparatively easy, except where there happened to be a large boat population, and in the case of Bassein, where the rice-mill coolies were enumerated off-hand on the 25th and the 26th February. It was deemed advisable to leave these to the last moment, because they were constantly changing from day to day both in numbers and composition, and any preliminary record would have been comparatively useless. * * I placed Mr. Pascal, Myoôk, in special charge of the census in Bassein owing to his familiarity with more than one language, and he is reported to have been of great assistance to the Municipality.

*　　*　　*　　*　　*

(*f*) No prosecutions have been reported. The people have become used to the census and appear to have regarded it with complete indifference. A few questions on the subject showed this.

(*g*) No estimate of cost was submitted. The total expenditure was Rs. 134-14-0 for the district, comprising cost of carriage of schedules and wharfage dues.

*　　*　　*　　*　　*

(*i*) * * It is, I suppose, a truism to say that in this country if the people are to be enumerated in their own permanent houses, the census should be taken during the rains. As far as I can judge, the result of the census as a whole is correct. It was, however, taken upon a much more elaborate scale than the last census, and though I think the enumerators displayed zeal as a body they were necessarily many of them ignorant.

*　　*　　*　　*　　*

From W. J. Addis, Esq., Secretary, Bassein Municipality, to the Deputy Commissioner, Bassein,—No. 17-37G., dated the 11th March 1891.

*　　*　　*　　*　　*

The actual cost of census up to date amounted to Rs. 2,056-7-0, while the estimated cost was Rs. 2,171.

*　　*　　*　　*　　*

From W. J. Addis, Esq., Secretary, Bassein Municipality, to the President, Bassein Municipality,—No. 17-36G., dated the 5th March 1891.

*　　*　　*　　*　　*

I would here beg to call your special attention to the work done by Mr. W. C. Pascal. I cannot say enough in his favour. Knowing the language as he does, he was of the greatest assistance to me in seeing to all the details very necessary in such an undertaking, and I do not know what I should have done had you not placed his services at my disposal, and I shall be glad if this remark be submitted to the Census Superintendent for favourable consideration.

*　　*　　*　　*　　*

Final Report on Census within Municipal limits by Mr. W. C. Pascal, Charge Superintendent, Census Operations, Bassein, dated the 5th March 1891.

1\. (*a*) Circle Register A for houses was commenced on the 18th August and completed by the 5th October 1890. The Municipality was divided into 11 circles, each circle containing an average of 10 blocks.

*　　*　　*　　*　　*

(*b*) House-numbering commenced on the 10th October and terminated on or about 3rd November 1890.

*　　*　　*　　*　　*

2\. (*a*) The preliminary record was commenced on the 31st January 1891 and carried on till the 16th February. As the enumerators were for the most part boys from pôngyi kyaungs, their work had to be carefully checked and the supervisors besides had to be carefully instructed, thus the record could not be completed by the 8th February. The work of enumerators was tested not only by the supervisors but also by the Charge Superintendents, and as the entries in some of the books were found very incorrect and some were in a dirty condition, these had to be replaced by new ones. Some very absurd mistakes were made in the entries, but these were rectified before the final round and the books are now in a fair state.

A preliminary record for coolies employed in the eight mills in the town was begun, but owing to the mobile nature of this population the preliminary record was found impracticable and a feasible plan for the enumeration of this class of people was adopted. The coolies were enumerated on the 25th and 26th ultimo gang by gang, each gang being in charge of a maistry who furnished all the information required to the supervisors, assistant supervisors and enumerators, who were previously instructed as to the manner in which the enumeration should be made.

The work done by the enumerators on the whole was fairly satisfactory and that of the supervisors with one exception was very creditably done. Maung Hmùn, Supervisor of Myoma North Circle C, neglected to convey to the enumerators the instructions given him and the other supervisors for the enumerators caused considerable delay. He took no interest in the work and allowed his enumerators to understand the rules for filling in the schedule books as best they could.

Maung Po Kyaw who had three mills and one godown in his circle, showed great interest in his work, which has been very thoroughly executed.

* * * * *

From J. E. MOULTRIE, Esq., President, Municipal Committee, Ngathainggyaung, to the Superintendent of the Census Operations, Burma (through the Deputy Commissioner, Bassein),—No. 35M., dated the 2nd May 1891.

* * * * *

I.—Preparatory Work.

* * * * *

(*b*) The house-numbering was commenced on the 25th September 1890 and completed on 3rd October 1890.

* * * * *

II.—The Census itself.

(*a*) The preliminary records were commenced on the 12th January 1891 and completed on 9th February 1891.

* * * * *

The Final Census.

* * * * *

(*g*) The total actual cost of census operations amounted to Rs. 22, which was paid from Municipal fund.

* * * * *

(*i*) * * The bulk of the work has fallen on P. C. S. Ramanjulu, who has performed his duties with zeal and intelligence.

* * * * *

From MAUNG OOH, President, Municipal Committee, Myaungmya, to the Superintendent of the Census Operations, Burma,—No. 97, dated the 23rd April 1891.

* * * * *

II.—Census itself.

(*a*) The preliminary record was commenced on the 9th January 1891, as stationery were received only on that day, and completed before the date fixed for its completion.

* * * * *

(*b*) * * Out of the supervisors Maung Kyaw Dun and Maung Po Maung and out of the enumerators Maung Naw took deep interest in the work and performed their duties very satisfactorily.

* * * * *

(*f*) There was no occasion to prosecute any one and the attitude and demeanour of the people were satisfactory, not being in any way aggressive. The work of enumeration was effected without any hitch.

(*g*) No expenditure was incurred for census operations in this Municipality.

* * * * *

From Major J. BUTLER, Deputy Commissioner, Henzada, to the Superintendent of the Census Operations, Burma,—No. 204-187, dated the 12th March 1891.

I.—Preparatory Work.

(*a*) With reference to your Census Circular No. 26, dated the 19th ultimo, I have the honour to report that the time for the preparation of the Census Registers **A** and **B** was given up to the 15th September 1890, but owing to the late supply of the printed register forms from the Government Printing Press, Rangoon, no action was taken up to the 9th August 1890.

* * * * *

(*b*) Immediately after the Circle Registers **A** and **B** were prepared, the numbering of the houses in consecutive order by means of chalk and chunam was begun, and was completed about the middle of October 1890 by the thugyis with the help of their enumerators.

(*c*) No paid men were employed as Superintendents, supervisors, and enumerators.

* * * * *

No difficulty was found in getting non-officials to act as supervisors and enumerators.

II.—The Census itself.

* * * * *

(*b*) The Myoôks of Kyangin, Zalun, and Ôkpo were zealous in pushing on the work of the census in their townships, and Akunwun Maung Shwe Tha deserves especial commendation for superintending all the arrangements, receiving of registers and their distribution, instructing the thugyis, collecting the returns, and pushing on the work from beginning to end.

(*c*) * * Owing to half the town of Myanaung being destroyed by fire on the afternoon of the 26th February 1891 and the schedules of nine enumerators being lost in the fire, it was found impossible to take the final census on the night of the same day as fixed. The preliminary census figures for the town of Myanaung had to be taken in the compilation of the above summary.

* * * * *

(*f*) No single instance of any complaint whatsoever was brought against the men during the whole of the census in the district.

(*g*) The only cost incurred in taking the census was for contingencies amounting to Rs. 36-11-3 for freight and telegrams for which no estimate was made.

(*h*) * * I think the census has on the whole been properly taken and that it may be looked on as fairly accurate.

* * * * *

From Major J. BUTLER, President, Henzada Municipality, to the Superintendent of the Census Operations, Burma,—No. 3-31—24, dated the 31st March 1891.

* * * * *

I.—Preparatory Work.

* * * * *

From the beginning of November 1890 the numbering of houses was taken in hand, and in order to ensure accuracy, Mr. D. Hormusjee, the Head clerk of the Municipal Office, was deputed to accompany the thugyi and check the entries in Register **A** prepared by the latter. In doing so several errors and omissions were discovered and rectified. The numbering and checking was finally completed on the 10th of the following month.

For purpose of census operations the Henzada Municipality was divided into eleven circles, namely :—

A.—Kinywa circle.
B.—Saga circle.
C.—Myoma circle.
D.—Shweku circle.
E.—Uyingyi circle.
F.—Lethama circle.
G.—Yôngyizu circle.
H.—Tangazè circle.
I.—Nyaungbinywa circle.
J.—Yebyan circle.
K.—Pyinmachaung circle.

No paid agency was employed in any case, the whole staff of census operators being selected from Government and Municipal employés consisting of Extra Assistant Commissioners, Myoôks, clerks of the Revenue and Judicial Departments, Police Inspectors, Municipal Commissioners as well as subordinates of the Municipality and Government pensioners of respectable standing.

* * * * *

II.—The Census itself.

From the 15th January 1891 schedule books were supplied to supervisors, who were at the same time instructed in detail as to how to carry out the work. The preliminary record was commenced on the 15th and completed on the 31st January 1891. The entries in the schedule books were made in the first instance by the enumerators *in pencil*, and they were subsequently checked by the house being again visited by the supervisor, who, with the schedule books in hand, compared the entries with the number of inmates. On the test proving correct they were *inked in*.

* * * * *

Final Census.

* * On the whole the quality of the work may be regarded as good and the outturn fairly reliable.

* * * * *

Mr. D. Hormusjee, Head clerk, Municipal Office, has from the commencement to the end of the census operations taken much pains in instructing supervisors and enumerators in their duty, and also in going round checking their work, his former experience in census-taking in 1881 with Lieutenant Eyre, Assistant Commissioner, Henzada, rendering him a fit person as Charge Superintendent.

* * * * *

In no instance was any active opposition or even passive resistance offered by the people, and this may be ascribed to their knowledge of the object of census-taking gained from previous experience, as this was the third time that census operations were carried out in Henzada.

The estimate of probable expenditure of census-taking in this Municipality amounted to Rs. 38, but the actual cost came up to only Rs. 32-8-0.

* * * * *

The result obtained is believed to be correct considering the precautionary measures taken beforehand and the agency employed in carrying out the work.

* * * * *

From Captain A. B. PRITCHARD, President, Myanaung Municipality, to the Superintendent of the Census Operations, Burma,—No. 12, dated the 21st March 1891.

* * * * *

I.—Preparatory Work.

* * * * *

(*b*) House-numbering was begun on the 5th and finished on the 18th October 1890.

(*c*) Charge Superintendent ... ... One, unpaid.
Supervisors ... ... Two, unpaid.
Enumerators ... ... Twenty, unpaid.
Cost of enumeration estimated ... ... *Nil.*
Actual cost ... ... *Nil.*

* * * * *

II.—The Census itself.

(*g*) The total actual cost of census operations was Rs. 11-9-6 for the cost of **A** and **B** Registers.

* * * * *

(*i*) In Myanaung town there were 432 houses destroyed by the late fire of 26th February 1891, the day before taking the census, and six census schedule books in possession of three enumerators were burned up, so I fear that some inaccuracy must have occurred in the enumeration of their blocks.

* * * * *

From Lieutenant G. E. T. GREEN, Officiating Deputy Commissioner, Thayetmyo, to the Superintendent of the Census Operations, Burma,—No. 1274-1—11G., dated the 16th March 1891.

* * * * *

1. (*a*) The preparation of Circle Registers **A** and **B** commenced in July 1890 in the Minhla and Thayetmyo townships of this district and were completed by the end of August. In the Myedè subdivision the preparation of these registers did not commence till about the 20th of August, but were completed, however, in due time.

(*b*) The numbering of houses commenced immediately after the completion of the Circle Registers **A** and **B**, and by the end of October 1890 were completed. Additions and alterations to the numbering of houses were made whenever the inspecting officer found the village he visited incorrectly numbered.

(*c*) No enumerators were paid. There were in all, including the Municipality, 17 Charge Superintendents, 121 supervisors, and 1,373 enumerators.

2. Owing to delay in receipt of schedules, the preliminary record did not commence until about the 25th January. By the 8th February, however, the preliminary record had been completed with the exception of the Kama township.

* * * * *

(*b*) I was agreeably surprised at the manner enumerators did their work. I came across but few cases in which the work had been neglected. The enumerators in Minhla and Sinbaungwe, although probably not so efficient as the enumerators in Myedè and Mindôn, seemed to take more interest in their work.

The supervisors likewise on the evening of the 26th and morning of the 27th must have displayed a good deal of energy by the prompt manner in which the Charge Superintendents came in with abstracts. All these abstracts were on the final record and in no instance had these abstracts to be supplemented by preliminary abstracts.

The Subdivisional Officer, Thayetmyo, reports that the Thayetmyo and Mindôn Myoôks showed great energy in their census work; and the Subdivisional Officer, Myedè, singles out Thugyi Maung Ywet, of the Thambulla circle, as having displayed great zeal and intelligence in the discharge of his duties. He had a large and scattered circle to supervise, and owing to the illness of two of his supervisors he had a treble amount of the work of supervision. My Head Assistant, Mr. Carrapiett, from the careful way in which he has noted receipts and issues and checked errors has been invaluable.

All the Charge Superintendents did their work satisfactorily.

(*c*) * * The quiet condition of the people on the night of the census may be inferred from the fact that not a single cart or traveller was met with either in the interior or in Thayetmyo itself. The district summary was despatched at 5 P.M. on the 4th March 1891.

Had it not been for the travellers by river I could have despatched this summary on the 1st March.

* * * * *

(*d*) The census was taken synchronously, the suggestion made by the Census Superintendent that tally sticks be adopted having been carried out in the Chin Hills with perfect success. The tally stick was as follows: a piece of bamboo 6 inches long was marked with a number corresponding with the number of the house. The side upon which the number was placed was the top side. This stick was handed over to the house-owner with instructions that on the night of the census he was to cut a notch on the right side for every member of his family and a notch on the left side for every stranger who happened to be present. There were no strangers. Had there been, enquiries regarding their age, &c., before submission would have been necessary.

* * * * *

(*f*) * * The bulk of the people were absolutely indifferent, merely looking upon the census as another mark of the eccentricity of the Government.

(*g*) Rupees 30 was estimated for as the total expenditure likely to be incurred on account of census. Up to date Rs. 5-8-0 have been incurred, but much more is expected, as the cost of cooly-hire for carrying the schedules to the District office, the cost of freight and train charges on their being sent to Rangoon, and the expenses of the clerk who will be sent in charge of them has yet to be paid and adjusted.

* * * * *

From Captain T. G. JOHNSON, Deputy Commissioner, Amherst, to the Superintendent of the Census Operations, Burma,—No. 703-16—1, dated the 10th June 1891.

* * * * *

I.—Preparatory Work.

The preparatory work was not done as well as it might have been owing to the fact that there were no Subdivisional Officers in the district to supervise the preliminaries.

* * * * *

(*b*) * * The numbering of houses in the Amherst district commenced in the middle of October 1890 and was completed at the end of January 1891.

* * * * *

II.—The Census.

* * * * *

(*b*) *The Final Census.*

The final census was a greater success than could have been expected from the indifference displayed by the Township Officers in the district and the Secretary and his staff in the Moulmein Municipality towards the preliminary enumeration.

The Charge Superintendents and supervisors in the Moulmein Municipality all worked well; in fact had it not been for their great zeal and activity during the two or three days previous to the final census, the census in the town would have been a failure. In Moulmein town I have especially to bring to notice the following names of persons who worked zealously—

Dr. Slym, Municipal member.
Mr. Forbes, Assistant Superintendent of Police.
Mr. Lamb, Master in the Government school.

Except Dr. Slym and Mr. Benjamin and one Hindu native and one Burmese member, none of the Moulmein Municipal Commissioners took any interest in the census or gave the President the least assistance.

In the district I can only select Myoôk Maung Tu, Myoôk Mr. Moore-Lyons as having done good work. Mr. Moore-Lyons worked indefatigably in January and February checking the preliminary census in nearly every village in no less than three townships.

* * * * *

(*d*) *Non-synchronous Census.*

The census was taken non-synchronously in the following revenue circles of the Amherst district and was completed by the 26th February 1891. This non-synchronous census was virtually taken by the police of the border guards, and the arrangements for taking it were made by Assistant Superintendent of Police Maung Tun Min under whose charge these guards are:—

Paingkyôn and Hlaingbwè.

There appears to have been no great difficulty experienced in taking the non-synchronous census. This census may be considered quite as accurate as the synchronous census.

* * * * *

(*f*) *Prosecutions, &c.*

* * * * *

The general attitude of the people was quiescent and indifferent; many of the Chittagongian boatmen attempted to evade enumeration, and a prevalent idea that Moulmein town would not be enumerated brought in numbers of persons into Moulmein from the district on the night of the census.

(g) Cost of Census.

The total estimated cost of the census in the district (excluding Moulmein town) was Rs. 775; the actual expenditure was Rs. 65-5-6 or Rs. 709-10-6 less than the estimate.

* * * * *

(i) Correctness of results.

The results obtained may be considered satisfactory, far more so than those of the last census; in fact, the results are very fairly accurate. In the worst supervised circles before checking preliminary schedules the error found was not 5 per cent. over or below. In Moulmein town the numbering and blocking was blundered, but owing to the excellent material for supervisors and Charge Superintendents, everything was put right before the census night and the results in Moulmein town may be considered accurate.

* * * * *

4. There are no tribes in this district whose origin and customs need to be reported on as they are already well known; the Taungthus, for example, who inhabit the northern portion of the Thatôn subdivision have peculiar customs and traditions which are well known and have been frequently reported on; they are fast assimilating themselves as regards customs and language and religion with the ordinary Burmese or Talaing population in their vicinity.

From Captain T. G. JOHNSON, President, Moulmein Municipality, to the Superintendent of the Census Operations, Burma,—No. 5-16, dated the 30th June 1891.

* * * * *

Circles Registers were received in the middle of August 1890, and were distributed on the 15th idem to the five Municipal Revenue Thugyis, as they knew the circles. These Circle Registers were completed on the 30th September 1890.

The Census Superintendent visited Moulmein on the 27th November, and finding that the thugyis had entered in the Circle Registers the names of people who had been deceased for the last 8, 10, and even 12 years, ordered the thugyis to recommence with new Circle Registers **A** and **B** and enter none but living and actual owners and occupiers of houses.

These second Circle Registers were completed early in November, and on the 20th idem the Secretary applied for the appointment of 150 census enumerators, being the same number as were employed in 1881.

The Committee, however, being on the eve of vacating office, declined to make any appointment, or to bind the hands of their successors in office by any action of theirs. Matters remained thus until the 7th of January, when Captain T. G. Johnson, Deputy Commissioner, Amherst District, was elected President, and the Secretary having informed the Committee that the census proper should commence the next day, (*i.e.*) the 8th January 1891, the President appointed 10 preliminary enumerators at Rs. 5 per block, whose duties were explained and who filled the block schedules and numbered the houses. This latter was completed about the 20th January 1891.

The President on the 19th idem appointed 10 Charge Superintendents, 21 supervisors, and 162 enumerators.

The Census Superintendent paid a second visit to Moulmein on the 20th February while the President was absent in the district.

The Charge Superintendents appointed for the different revenue circles are as follows:—

1st Division, Revenue Circle Mutpun.

1. E. H. Molloy, Esq., District Superintendent of Police.
2. Vuddy Venketreddy Naidoo, Esq., Municipal Commissioner.

2nd Division, Revenue Circle Maung-ngan.

3. Maung Ngwe Kaing, Assistant Magistrate and *ex-officio* member.
4. T. Coopoosawmy Pillay, Esq., Municipal Commissioner.

3rd Division, Revenue Circle Tavoyzu.

5. Maung Kyaw Gine, Treasury Officer.
6. R. Benjamin, Esq., Municipal Commissioner.

4th Division, Revenue Circle Kaladan.

7. Dr. M. J. Slym, Municipal Commissioner.
8. Ko Hle, Municipal Commissioner.

5th Division, Revenue Circle Daingwunkwin.

9. J. W. Henderson, Esq., Inspector of Police.

General Charge Superintendent, Town.

10. W. W. Forbes, Esq., Assistant District Superintendent of Police.

The Charge Superintendents and 16 supervisors being Government and Municipal servants, received no remuneration whatever. Five supervisors received Rs. 16 each, and 88 enumerators Rs. 5 each per block for the final enumeration.

With reference to instruction of Superintendents, supervisors, and enumerators, the Superintendent of Census himself carefully instructed the thugyis in November 1890 in their duties and the work he expected from them; and on the 6th and 7th of January 1891, as these were holidays specially granted for the purpose, the President had all summoned to the Municipal Office for instruction in the duties devolving on them, and again on the 25th February, on which occasion the President carefully instructed all hands as to the final enumeration on the night of the 26th idem.

The work performed by the Charge Superintendents, supervisors, and enumerators was, I consider, very good, and would specially mention the names of E. H. Molloy, Esq., District Superintendent of Police; W. W. Forbes, Esq., Assistant District Superintendent of Police; Dr. M. J. Slym, Municipal Commissioner; Messrs. J. W. Henderson, Maung Ngwe Kaing, Maung Kyaw Gine, T. Coopoosawmy Pillay, Vuddy Venketreddy Naidoo, as having particularly distinguished themselves by the energy, intelligence, and pains they evinced throughout the census operations.

The supervisors as a rule worked with energy and zeal, and were as follows, namely :—

1st Division, Revenue Circle Mutpun.

1. J. A. Harris.
2. D. A. Ramasawmy.
3. C. W. Lamb.

2nd Division, Revenue Circle Maung-ngan.

4. A. Abreu.
5. T. A. Gregory.
6. C. Baretto.
7. Maung Pan Zôn.
8. W. Martin.

3rd Division, Revenue Circle Tavoyzu.

9. W. Lovett.
10. R. J. Harrison.
11. Maung Shwe Po.
12. M. dePenha.
13. N. Sullivan.

4th Division, Revenue Circle Kaladan.

14. J. W. Crawford.
15. G. H. Jefferson.
16. B. Francis.
17. G. R. Gordon.
18. W. H. Gay.
19. Wm. Pepper.

5th Division, Revenue Circle Daingwunkwin.

20. Maung Thain Maung.
21. Maung Po Maung.
22. R. H. Gill.
23. Wm. Spears.
24. Maung Gyi.
25. Maung Myat Thoo.
26. Maung Shwe Baw.
27. Maung Po Thine.
28. Wm. Donovan.
29. Govindasawmy.
30. H. A. Baker.

* * * * *

The actual cost so far has been Rs. 1,558-11-5 and about seven enumerators still remain to be paid, which will probably amount to Rs. 70, thus making the total cost to the Municipality Rs. 1,630.

* * * * *

The whole number of census schedules received (including a few spoilt) were used in the operations.

* * * * *

From F. C. NISBET, Esq., President, Thatôn Municipality, to the Superintendent of the Census Operations, Burma,—No. 1-356, dated the 19th March 1891.

* * * * *

1. (*b*) The numbering of houses commenced on the 20th October and was completed on the 5th November 1890.

(*c*) Three-fourths of the enumerators were paid servants of the Municipality, clerks from Assistant Commissioner and Myoôk's Courts, and policemen, and the rest were selected persons approved of by the Committee.

No expenses were estimated for and none incurred. The number of unpaid census supervisors and enumerators were respectively 4 and 42.

2. (*a*) The preliminary record was commenced on the 6th February and completed on the 22nd idem. After this the enumerators made over their schedule books for check to their respective supervisors appointed (with one exception) from amongst the Municipal Commissioners.

(*b*) The Thatôn Municipality is only a portion of the Thatôn Myoma Thugyi's circle. It was divided into four census circles which formed two divisions, north and south of the town, under the superintendence of the Vice-President and myself. All the Census Officers gave their gratuitous services in taking the census, and where all endeavoured to do their best, it is difficult to single out any one more deserving of notice than the rest.

* * * * *

(*f*) There were no prosecutions and the general attitude of the people was one of indifference.

* * * * *

(*i*) The mistakes of enumerators in the preliminary record were corrected on the inspection of their schedules by the Vice-President and myself, and the results obtained may I think be fairly considered as correct.

* * * * *

From Major T. M. JENKINS, Deputy Commissioner, Tavoy, to the Superintendent of the Census Operations, Burma,—No. 259, dated the 25th April 1891.

* * * * *

The district of Tavoy has an area of 7,150 square miles, and is divided into 44 revenue circles under four Township Officers. The population consists mainly of Burmans in the plains and Karens in the hills. The arrangements for the taking of the census in the plains was not difficult, but amongst the Karens special arrangements had to be made, as only a few Karens knew how to write Burmese, but the Revd. Mr. Morrow kindly lent me some of his Karen teachers, who proceeded to certain villages and filled in the schedule books, but as they could not themselves attend at all the Karen villages on the night of the 26th February, they, after filling in the schedule books, left with the headman of the village a pencil and a piece of paper on which was written in Karen the numbers of the houses with the names of their owners, and on the night of the census, each house-owner came to the headman of the village and told him the number of men, women, and children there were in the house, which numbers were entered in their respective columns either in figures or by strokes of the pencil to represent the number, and the next day these papers were sent to the teacher and forwarded on to me.

By these means I hoped to make a synchronous census of the district, and with the exception of a few of the outlying Karen villages I have found it to have answered fairly well. On checking over some of these Karen schedules I found that there was a great inclination to make the men, particularly the elderly men, older than they really were, but whether this was, with the hope that they would be exempted paying capitation-tax earlier than they should be, or whether through real ignorance of their age I cannot say. These Karen teachers were the only paid employés in the district.

Amongst the villages in the plains there was not any difficulty shown in the taking of the census as intelligent men were chosen as enumerators and were under the supervision of Township Officers, clerks, and thugyis. At first naturally there were a few mistakes made, which were corrected in time, and, taking it as a whole, I consider that the census is fairly accurate.

* * * * *

Very few men have been shown as fishermen as they objected to this profession being brought against them hereafter, but most of them are shown according to any other trade on which they might be employed ; such as cultivators or dhanni-leaf sowers, &c.

* * * * *

Most of the houses were numbered by the end of December, but on going over the Registers A and in passing through some villages I found that some of the thugyis had numbered all houses in their circle serially, and not village by village. This was speedily rectified, and by the middle of February all houses were properly numbered.

* * * * *

The schedule books were received in this district rather late and it was not until the 25th January that they were all issued, but with the exception of a few villages, the preliminary records were all completed by the 16th February. All Township Officers as well as myself visited several villages and tested these records. I was surprised to find they were so well done, considering that in many places the enumerators were only poor villagers.

* * * * *

I have to thank Myoôks Maung Thaw, Maung Yan Shin, Maung Kyin Yôn, and Maung Myat Kyaw and Mr. Savage of the Telegraph Department at Myittha for the assistance they gave me as Charge Superintendents. All supervisors and enumerators worked hard and did their best, and it would be invidious for me to name any of them.

* * * * *

A non-synchronous census was taken at a few only of the outlying Karen villages at the head-waters of the Kamaungthwè and Banechaung streams, and owing to their schedules not being sent in earlier, this report has been greatly delayed.

* * * * *

The Burmans in the Tavoy district are not pure Burmans; they are supposed to have been descended from certain Arakanese, and their language is to a pure Burman difficult to understand, as it is a dialect of its own, a mixture of Arakanese and Talaing.

* * * * *

Report on the work of the Census by Major T. M. Jenkins, President of the Tavoy Municipality.

* * The town was divided into the Northern and Southern divisions, and each division was divided into blocks, and certain blocks formed census circles, under certain supervisors. For the town there were nine supervisors and 112 blocks, each block being under a different enumerator. In the month of August Circle Registers were prepared and houses numbered, and in October following the Subdivisional Register was completed.

The houses were at first numbered from the thugyis' assessment-rolls, but this proved so complicated that they were all re-numbered consecutively from one end of the division to the other. This numbering was not completed until the 4th January.

* * * * *

The preliminary record was commenced on the 14th January and completed by the 4th February, and this record was tested by the Secretary and myself on the 7th and 8th February 1891.

* * * * *

Maung Lu Han, the Secretary to the Municipality, was the Charge Superintendent for the town. He took great interest in the work, and himself superintended the numbering of the houses, and afterwards greatly assisted the checking of a number of the schedule books. Amongst others, my thanks are due to Mr. Mealin, Maung Po Si, Mr. Gallope, and to Mr. Simeons for the assistance they gave in the taking of the census and in acting as supervisors: also to the following persons, who acted as enumerators, namely, Mr. Culloden, Maung Shwe Hlah, Maung Bah Lay, Maung Shwe Bya, Maung Boo, Ramasawmy, Maung Kya Pe, and Maung Oung Bah.

* * * * *

From H. G. Batten, Esq., Deputy Commissioner, Mergui, to the Superintendent of the Census Operations, Burma,—No. 23-4—1, dated the 23rd March 1891.

* * * * *

I.—Preparatory Work.

* * * * *

(*a*) * * Considerable difficulty occurred in the preparation of these registers as the revenue records and old census returns proved to be of little use. In the greater part of the district villages are only so in name, and are not, as in other parts of Burma, a collection of houses within a small area, but scattered hamlets, the houses of which are sometimes miles apart. The Village Act operations being in hand, I was able to check the census returns with those for the ten-house gaung blocks or charges, and during the preparation I visited every township and most of the circles.

* * * * *

Again the difficulties were increased owing to the different languages spoken in the district. Our officials are nearly all Burmese, and in the Lenya and Maliwun townships and in parts of Tenasserim, Burmese gives way to Siamese, Malay, and Chinese, and in the circles of Pawut in Tenasserim, Pyicha, Tanyet, and Shandut in Palaw Karen is the one language understood.

(*b*) The house-numbering was commenced in Mergui town in December, and in the district in October, but, owing to the ignorance of the thugyis and their assistants, the final and complete numbering was not finished till the end of January. The numbering of the houses in Mergui town had been arranged serially for supervisors' circles, but at the suggestion of the Census Superintendent it was changed, and the number ran serially for enumerators' blocks. Consequently a delay took place, but the work was completed by end of January.

* * * * *

(*c*) * * A paid writer on Rs. 15 a month was also arranged for the Lenya township, where Burmese was unknown; and special enumerators were appointed for the enumeration of the Selong population living amongst the islands of the archipelago. U Shwe I, a leading Chinaman and Municipal Commissioner of Mergui, undertook the difficult task for the Northern Selongs, whilst the Nacoda at Victoria Point undertook the enumeration of the Southern Selongs. Their work was carefully checked by the Myoôk and other officers with result of a really accurate return. I do not think many Selongs escaped enumeration. Shwe I accounted for 216 boats and the Nacoda for 36; the boats checked by my other officers were all found noted amongst these.

The Township Officer, Maliwun, reports that the work done by Maung Gyi was satisfactory.

II.—Preliminary Record.

The Census itself.

(*a*) The schedules, which should, of course, all have been written up by 8th February, were, however, in some parts not ready. There had been errors in the indents and carelessness in the issue, and the consequence was that in many parts of the district the preliminary record was not completed till the actual census came off.

In Mergui town the preliminary work was commenced on 8th January; in the Myoma township on 30th January; in Palaw township on 26th January; in Tenasserim township on 10th February; in Lenya township on 10th February; in Maliwun township on 10th January.

The preliminary record was carefully looked after in Mergui town by Mr. Mackertoom, the Charge Superintendent, who was in constant touch with his enumerators.

The Provincial Superintendent of Census himself on 1st January had called all the supervisors and enumerators together, and with his instructions, followed up by those of Mr. Mackertoom, the work was rapidly and carefully carried out and completed by 8th February.

The Township Officers were constantly on the move and I myself went through all the circles of the Palaw township as it required greater supervision.

* * * * *

Final Census.

(*b*) * * My thanks are chiefly due to A Shwe Kyu and his office assistants for the general supervision, and I may say that without A Shwe Kyu's intelligent direction the census operations would have been an uphill task. Mr. Mackertoom as Charge Superintendent for Mergui town did splendid work, and to him is due the accurate results and careful work done by the enumerators. All the supervisors worked heartily; also the enumerators. I have to thank Mr. Law for the assistance given by his Police Officers.

Maung Gyi, who completed the Maliwun schedules, deserves mention as well as U Shwe I, whose zeal and knowledge of the Selongs has made the enumeration of these people a success. Going out in a small boat through the islands, few boats escaped his eye, and though his expenses were guaranteed, he has refused to accept any remuneration whatever.

* * * * *

(*d*) The only sanctioned non-synchronous census was that of the Selongs; but practically the outlying tracts of Maliwun, Lenya, and Tenasserim were non-synchronous as the enumerators were ignorant and the supervisors had to go round and do the work again.

For any future census, I would recommend that the following tracts be marked off for non-synchronous census:—

(1) Maliwun.
(2) Pawut circle, Tenasserim—all Karens.
(3) Selongs of Archipelago.
(4) Lenya—Siamese.

* * * * *

(*f*) * * On the whole the attitude of the people was satisfactory, and information was readily given.

* * * * *

(*i*) From a scrutiny of the returns and personal inspection of the work during the preparation, I consider that the census of the town has been most accurately done, and that the results of the enumeration in the districts have been decidedly well done, considering the difficulties which had to be contended with.

* * * * *

The Survey parties have added about 1,000 temporary persons to our population, but there has been a steady immigration from Siam and Malaya. This will considerably be added to by the distress in Kopa and Champang, and the bright prospects of the tin industry.

* * * * *

The Palaw township contains a number of persons from Tavoy who may be said to be a different race.

* * * * *

Siamese are spread over Maliwun, Lenya, and parts of Tenasserim. Colonies of Malays exist in Maliwun and along the coasts as high as Lenya, and also are found amongst the islands, and their number is rapidly increasing. Chinese may be found all over the district, but are most numerous in Mergui town and in the tin-mining portions of Tenasserim, Lenya, and Maliwun. All these different races intermarry, and before long the people will be unable to trace their origin in the same way, as the Zarabadis of Mergui are now unable to say to what race they originally belonged and have lost whatever may have been their original tongue.

* * * * *

From A. G. Mackertoom, Esq., Charge Superintendent, Mergui Town, to the Deputy Commissioner, Mergui,—No. 3-C., dated the 28th February 1891.

* * * * *

I beg to report that in compliance with instructions from the Superintendent, Census Operations, Burma, the preliminary round was commenced on the 8th January and completed on the 7th February, the result being submitted on the 14th February.

The final census was commenced at 8 P.M. on the 26th February, all the supervisors and enumerators being present punctually at 7-30 P.M. The enumeration of most of the blocks was completed at a little before midnight, while some of the blocks were finished at 2 A.M. on the 27th.

At 11 A.M. on the 27th all the supervisors and enumerators came together at the Municipal school-house to make up their abstracts, most of which were completed by 6 P.M.

* * * * *

I have much pleasure in specially mentioning Akunwun A Shwe Kyu, Headquarter Myoôk, Maung On Shwe, Maung Shwe Kaing, Maung Tha Oung, Maung Kyin Han, and Maung Tha Han, who were unremitting in their endeavours to obtain an accurate census. Mr. D'Zalazar also deserves great credit for the work done by him on the 26th and following days.

* * * * *

Notwithstanding all this, I am of opinion that the census of Mergui town was a success. The arrangements were excellent, and perfect order was maintained.

From G. M. S. Carter, Esq., Deputy Commissioner, Toungoo, to the Superintendent of the Census Operations, Burma,—No. 1-51, dated the 4th April 1891.

* * * * *

1. (*b*) All the houses in this district were numbered. The numbering commenced early in November and was completed by the end of the month.

(*c*) * * There were six Charge Superintendents, 76 supervisors, and 1,020 enumerators. No remuneration was given in any case.

2. (*a*) The preliminary records commenced from 17th January 1891 and were completed by the end of the month.

These records were carefully tested by circle supervisors under supervision of Charge Superintendents during February. Charge Superintendents, namely, the Township Officers, devoted much of their time to the careful preparation of the preliminary record. In Kyathaundaung and Kanni the Myoôks visited nearly all the villages in their townships and their zeal is worthy of praise.

(*b*) As regards the final census, all the officers employed seem to have done their best. I have no special instances to call to your notice.

(*c*) * * Special measures were taken for the enumeration of travellers by boat or road, but little trouble was experienced in this way, as Burmans seemed to understand that they were required to remain in their homes or some place where they could be easily enumerated and they did so.

* * * * *

(*g*) No cost further than the cost of conveyance and packing charges of census schedules, which amounted to Rs. 8-5-0, was incurred in the census operation in this district.

* * * * *

(*i*) I think it may be said the results obtained were good. Great trouble was taken to make the people thoroughly understand the object of the operations and they appreciated and gave no trouble.

In Toungoo itself I was much struck with the ease and rapidity with which the enumerators were able to complete their work on the night of the 26th February 1891.

* * * * *

From G. M. S. Carter, Esq., President, Toungoo Municipality, to the Superintendent of the Census Operations, Burma,—No. 397, dated the 12th March 1891.

* * * * *

1. The Municipality is divided into two taxation circles called the North and South circles. It was decided by the Committee to form six census circles, three in each taxation circle, and to allot 40 houses to each enumerator.

* * * * *

3. The houses were numbered serially by blocks in the latter part of October. Lime and rice-water was used and answered the purpose.

* * * * *

6. * * All the enumerators, with the exception of the jailer and boat enumerator, were paid at the rate of Re. 1 per 15 houses in their blocks. The total amount paid was Rs. 245-12-10. The estimate was Rs. 210, but this was made before the Circle Register was revised.

* * * * *

13. There were no prosecutions under the Census Act.

* * * * *

16. ** The figures for this year may be taken as correct. There is a large difference in the population of the town in the hot weather and in the rains. At the time of the census large numbers of Karens who attend the Baptist Mission schools were absent on the hills on their annual vacation, and numbers of others were in the district for trading purposes.

* * * * *

From D. WILSON, Esq., Officiating Deputy Commissioner, Shwegyin, to the Superintendent of the Census Operations, Burma,—No. 517-1, dated the 31st March 1891.

* * * * *

I.—Preparatory Work.

(*a*) The preparation of Circle Registers A and B was commenced everywhere in this district about 23rd July 1890, and was completed everywhere by the middle of September 1890. The Subdivisional Registers were completed at the same time.

* * * * *

(*c*) All paid supervisors and enumerators were paid by piece-work, a fixed sum for the whole census, payment being made only after their work had been examined and approved.

* * * * *

Actual cost.

	Rs.
Four paid supervisors at	15 = 60
Two paid supervisors at	10 = 20
Six paid enumerators at	10 = 60
Five paid enumerators at	8 = 40
Paid volunteers at headquarters	10
Total ...	190
Sanctioned estimate	300
Difference not spent	300—190=110

II.—The Census itself.

(*a*) ** When the schedule books came to hand everybody was ready to begin and the preliminary record was commenced in the district on 25th January and completed in most parts of it by the 14th and in all parts of it by the 19th February.

In preparing it the first entries were as a rule made in pencil, then, after the supervisor had examined, corrected, and approved the book, he or the enumerator or both together wrote it out in ink. Thus it happened that comparatively few books were spoiled.

** I observed in examining their work that very few errors of omission were made by the enumerators.

(*b*) ** The following unpaid supervisors have been praised by their respective Charge Superintendents :—

1. Maung Po Chit, Thugyi of Bilin.
2. Maung Po Thwe, Thugyi of Zôkthôk.
3. Maung Nge, Thugyi of Kyaikto.
4. Maung Po Swe, Thugyi of Yehla.
5. Maung Ah Gah, Thugyi of Nyaunglebin.
6. Maung Kin, Head Constable, Nyaunglebin.
7. Mr. Nepean of Thayetkôn.
8. Maung Pan of Pyuntaza.
9. Maung San Dun, Thugyi of Bawni.
10. Maung Kya Win, Thugyi of Kwindala.
11. Maung Po Myit, Thugyi of Mobaw.
12. Maung Tha Khine, Thugyi of Ban.
13. Maung Shwe Byan, Thugyi of Settedaung.
14. Maung Tun, Yazawutgaung.
15. Maung Daik, Yazawutgaung.
16. Maung Thet San, Thugyi of Kyaukkyi.
17. Maung Tha Kyu, Thugyi of Kyaukmaw.
18. Maung Po Myit, Thugyi of Kyaungbya.
19. Maung Tha San, Thugyi of Môn.
20. Maung Po Ka, Thugyi of Thayetpindat.
21. Maung Shwe An, Head Clerk, Myoôk's Court, Kyaukkyi.

The Charge Superintendents Mr. Beale, Mr. Tilly, Maung Shwe Go, Maung Mo, Maung Aung Zan, Maung Pe Gyi were all assiduous, and the Myoôks of Bilin and Kyaikto though nominally only assisting Charge Superintendents, took great pains in instructing the enumerators and supervisors and checking their work. The result of having four gazetted officers to do the census in Kyaikto instead of only two, as in other subdivisions, was seen in the improved quality of the work.

(*c*) ** But the enumerators were men of little education and their abstracts were found on revision to be full of errors. As many of these as possible were corrected before the schedule books were forwarded from the district office to the Superintendent, Census Operations. I enclose herewith a revised district summary based on the corrected figures.

* * * * *

(*d*) ** The results actually obtained by the non-synchronous census of Yinôn taik were probably as correct as could be got in any way. I went through the taik and examined the books, and had reason to be satisfied.

The only other part of the district where a non-synchronous census was found necessary was a small hilly portion of Pyuntaza subdivision comprising Putkya, Mayanky, Aungbya, Pa O, Hlegataung, Kyathaungchaung, and Wingyaung villages, all in Bawni circle. There the villagers were illiterate and scattered thinly over difficult country. The non-synchronous census in this part was made by two paid enumerators, who received Rs. 10 each for their work. It occupied them from 1st February to 25th February.

* * * * *

(*g*) ** The actual cost for enumerators, &c., was Rs. 190, as against the sanctioned estimate of Rs. 300.

During last census certain allowances were paid to salaried clerks at headquarters who assisted. During this census all salaried Government servants available had to assist without extra payment.

* * * * *

(*i*) I tested the schedules at various places and found few errors, and these of a trivial sort.

* * * * *

As to the little known tribes referred to in paragraph 4 of Circular No. 26, I presume the Yabeins alone would come under that designation in this district. But I have come little in contact with them as yet, and have no information regarding them except what has already been made public.

Report by D. Wilson, Esq., President, on the census work in the Shwegyin Municipality.

I.—Preparatory Work.

* * * * *

Register B was not prepared, the boat population in Shwegyin being practically *nil* at this season of the year.

(*b*) *The date of commencement and completion of house-numbering.*—House-numbering was commenced immediately on the completion of Circle Register A, *i.e.*, 2nd October, and was completed by the end of October 1890.

(*c*) *The agency employed, &c.*—There was one Charge Superintendent, 14 supervisors, and 44 enumerators, all unpaid.

* * * * *

II.—The Census itself.

* * * * *

(*a*) *The preliminary record.*—** The preliminary record was begun on 18th January and finished on 3rd February 1891 **

(*b*) The final census was taken on the 26th instant. Great interest was taken in the work in town and it seemed to be correctly and well done. The Circle Thugyi Shwe Don took very great pains with his part of the work, and the supervisors were careful. The following Municipal Commissioners were supervisors: Maung Khaing, Mr. Moss, Maung Kyi Daung, Maung Po, and Maung Kyo.

Other volunteer supervisors were:—

Maung Tha Khway, Honorary Magistrate.
Babu Chowdry, Head Clerk, Deputy Commissioner's Office.
Mr. Gibson, Assistant Teacher.
Maung Thaing, Honorary Magistrate.
Mr. Campagnac, Head Master.
Maung Hmo, Akunwun.
Maung Shwe Don, Thugyi.
Maung Tu, Deputy Inspector of Schools.
Mr. Avietick, Inspector of Police.

There were also 44 enumerators, all unpaid.

(*c*) ** The revised charge summary shows a difference of only three from the charge summary prepared immediately on the completion of the final census.

* * * * *

(*f*) There were no prosecutions under the Census Act. The inhabitants of all races and creeds co-operated willingly with the enumerators.

(*g*) The total actual cost of the census in cash to the Municipality was *nil.*

* * * * *

(*i*) The results obtained may be taken as correct. The number of errors discovered by a pretty close scrutiny was small, and the errors were trivial, *e.g.*, a *Talaing* described occasionally as a Burman, or *vice versâ*, &c.

Report on Census work by A. C. Beale, Esq., President, Kyaikto Municipality.

I.—Preparatory Work.

* * * * *

(*b*) *The date of commencement and completion of house-numbering.*—House-numbering was started immediately on the completion of the above registers, and by the end of the month it was completed.

(*c*) *Agency employed.*—There was one Charge Superintendent, 2 supervisors, and 19 enumerators; none of these were paid. The Myoôk was Superintendent, the Secretary to the Municipality and the Head Clerk of the Assistant Commissioner's Court were the supervisors, and the enumerators consisted of Court and Municipal peons and private individuals who gave their services gratuitously. Up to date the only charges incurred have been those for conveyance of stationery, amounting to Rs. 1-8-0.

II.—The Census itself.

(*a*) *Preliminary record.*—** From the beginning of February till the 25th idem, the President of the Municipality, the Myoôk, and the supervisors went round examining the schedules and testing their correctness by enquiring personally at houses selected at random in each block. Each of the supervisors eventually visited every house in his circle.

(*b*) *The Final Census.*—This was taken on the night of the 26th, when each enumerator visited every house in his block making additions to the preliminary record or scoring out where necessary.

The Charge Superintendent and the supervisors certainly did good work, the Supervisors Maung Ba Din and Maung San Baw being deserving of especial praise for their energy and the pains they took to correct the work of the enumerators, who were most lamentably careless and irregular.

** The schedule books were returned on the 27th February. On the previous night, after the house schedules had been verified, a special look-out was kept for travellers at the boat landing and at the entrances into the town from the main roads east and west. The zayats were also visited more than once, as also vacant dwelling-houses, monasteries, &c.

* * * * *

(*g*) *Actual compared with estimated cost.*—No estimate was ever made; actual cost to date Rs. 1-8-0.

* * * * *

2. *Correctness of results.*—From personal observation I am able to testify that every effort was made to ensure correctness, and so far as my inspection of the schedules entitles me to judge, the results may be accepted as correct.

From W. N. Baines, Esq., Deputy Commissioner, Salween, to the Superintendent of the Census Operations, Burma,—No. 1682-82, dated the 21st March 1891.

* * * * *

(*b*) The numbering of houses was made at the time of making preliminary record and completed before the 8th February 1891.

(*c*) ** No paid agency was employed in this district.

2. (*a*) The census officers entrusted with the schedule books were instructed in their duties by the Charge Superintendent and the office clerks. Preliminary record commenced at Papun on the 1st January 1891 and in the district on the 15th January 1891, and was completed before the 8th February 1891.

* * * * *

(*b*) ** The Charge Superintendent and supervisors got the work done as well as could be expected, but until we get more literate people in these wild places it is impossible to expect much.

* * * * *

(*f*) ** The Karens were perfectly indifferent as to the census and rendered every assistance in their power to the census officers.

* * * * *

(*h*) The number of schedules indented for was 258 house and 34 boat, and the number used 231 house and 11 boat. Out of 12 household schedules only four were used in Papun.

(*i*) The result of census work may be accepted as fairly accurate.

Census Report of Mandalay District by H. Adamson, Esq., Deputy Commissioner.

I.—Preparatory Work.

(*a*) *Preparation of Circle Registers* **A** *and* **B** *and Subdivisional Registers.*—The houses in each village were numbered about the month of August, the numbers being conspicuously attached to each house. From these numbers Circle Registers **A** and **B** and Subdivisional Registers were prepared.

(*b*) *Date of commencement and completion of house-numbering.*—The house-numbering had been completed and thoroughly checked by Myoôks and Subdivisional Officers before the end of October.

* * * * *

II.—The Census.

* * * * *

(*b*) *The Final Census.*—On account of the lateness of preparation of the preliminary record little was left to be done on the night of the census. The enumerators went round and did what they could on that night. The uupaid enumerators and supervisors throughout the district did the work cheerfully and willingly. I would bring to special notice Mr. Carey, Subdivisional Officer of Madaya, and Maung Po Shwe, Myoôk of Kutywa, who took the greatest trouble in instructing supervisors and enumerators.

* * * * *

Boat Census.—Patrol boats were used on various parts of the river and a couple of steam launches at Mandalay. The boat census was conducted in accordance with the rules prescribed.

* * * * *

Attitude of the people.—There was on no occasion any necessity to resort to harsh measures. The people cheerfully numbered their houses and did as they were told. There was not the slightest symptom of apprehension or alarm on the part of the people on account of census operations in any part of the district.

* * * * *

(*i*) *The correctness or otherwise of the results obtained.*—I checked the census in a large number of villages of Madaya subdivision in November and Pyinulwin subdivision in December. I found not a single house without its proper number.

I checked Amarapura subdivision in December and found a considerable number of errors, but these were all corrected and the house-numbering was accurate before the preliminary census began. The preliminary census was carefully checked as I have described above. I am of opinion that the final result is very correct.

From K. G. Burne, Esq., President, Municipal Committee, Mandalay, to the Superintendent of the Census Operations, Burma,—No. 35-32, dated the 22nd April 1891.

* * * * *

REPORT.

1. (*a*) The preparation of the Circle Registers **A** and **B** was commenced on the 10th November 1890 and was ready by the 30th November 1890.

(*b*) The date of commencement of house-numbering was the 10th of October 1890. The numbering was completed in the beginning of November 1890.

(*c*) The census work of the town was carried out by 58 ayat-lugyis (supervisors) and 430 akwetgaungs (enumerators) under the superintendence of the Municipal Secretary. Supervisors and enumerators were not paid.

2. (*a*) The preliminary record, including the instruction to supervisors and enumerators, *began on the 2nd December 1890.* It was completed on the *5th February 1891* and tested on the 6th and 7th of the same month.

(*b*) The Municipal Secretary had the entire charge of the taking of the census of Mandalay, assisted by Maung Po Ka, Municipal clerk and interpreter. Much trouble had been taken to secure accuracy. Most of the ayat-lugyis and akwetgaungs displayed zeal and intelligence.

* * * * *

(*d*) No prosecution under the Census Act has been found necessary. Attitude of people good.

* * * * *

(*i*) The way in which the census operations have been carried out is a guarantee that the results cannot be but satisfactory.

From E. C. S. George, Esq., Deputy Commissioner, Bhamo, to the Superintendent of the Census Operations, Burma,—No. 900-2R., dated the 7th April 1891.

* * * * *

From the early part of December until the middle of February, owing to the withdrawal of the Subdivisional Officers at Shwegu and Mogaung for work on columns, and the fact of Mr. Symington, Extra Assistant Commissioner, Mogaung, being laid up in bed with an accident to his knee during all those months, the work of the census for the whole of this large district fell practically on the Treasury Officer and Deputy Commissioner at Bhamo. Apart from the progress of a regular series of military and police operations in various parts of the district (there have now been five distinct ones already and another is just on the point of starting) entailing a vast amount of extra work and necessarily curtailing freedom of movements on the part of the officials at headquarters, it will be sufficiently obvious that it was impossible to expect a perfect conformity to rule or adoption of an uniform method of procedure in an area extending some 9,800 square miles with hardly any European officials to supervise it. The subordinate element was wretched in the extreme. Out of six Myoôks in the district, only three could read or write. To this was added the additional difficulty of the utter illiteracy of the population as a whole. The Census Superintendent has himself visited Bhamo and I need say no more on this head.

* * * * *

The instructions in each village for the night of the 26th to the headman or enumerator (as he may be called for want of a better title) were simple. If he was absolutely savage and untrained he was shown a number of sticks corresponding to the number of persons in each house. These were wrapped up in a piece of paper bearing the number of the house by the special man and given to each householder. On the night of the 26th the headman went round and counted the inmates, casting away or putting in a stick or two according as the number of people were more or less than that of the bundle (which number corresponded with the number of people therein at the time of the special man's visit and which he wrote down). Next morning the headman brought in these bundles to the special man, who corrected the books accordingly. To remember what strangers were present and what people were absent as evidenced by the altered number of sticks in each case was apparently an easy matter to the untutored mind. In these remote villages it is usual for the headman to know all about every man, woman, and child present and recall it without difficulty, the memory taking the place of pen and paper Homer's works are supposed to have been handed down in much the same way; but this is a digression. The details of age and birth-place given by the headman might in the case of strangers be inaccurate, but the totals and names were not so.

This method was adopted at the suggestion of the Superintendent of Census Operations on the occasion of his visit to Bhamo, and may be regarded as giving fairly accurate results.

If the headman was sufficiently intelligent to be trusted to spell out, with perhaps the aid of one of the small boys of a neighbouring kyaung, the names of the inhabitants, he was given the book ready filled in and a pencil with orders to strike out the names of people not present and subscribe on each schedule pencil marks or such other esoteric characters as would serve afterwards to recall to what served him to mind the names of and particulars about each stranger present.

* * * * *

Now, had there been a sufficient number of special men, I have no doubt that in point of neatness and accuracy in columns 2 to 14 of the schedules, the books of this district would have compared favourably with those of any other, but, as the Superintendent of Census Operations will no doubt discover in time, this was not so, and while maintaining the general accuracy of the totals as obtained, I cannot but express my regret that the schedule books, particularly of Shwegu and Mogaung, which were left mainly through unavoidable necessity to indigenous supervision, were not written with the neatness and regard of explicit instructions that they might have been.

* * * * *

Law is regarded much in the same light as the Sybelline books and approached with feelings of veneration and awe and an inward conviction that it is quite impossible for any non-initiated person to understand its purport. One headman was asked to read over the heading of column 4 and explain it, after I had spent some hours in carefully explaining to a group of enumerators, item by item, what details were to be noted in each column. He read it over 14 times with correct pronunciation, but could only smile woefully at me at the end and say, he really did not know what it meant. I had to give him up. Another man could not make out in what connection the words "female tiger" had been inserted over column 6, but that is another story.

In case, therefore, where the special clerks sent up from Rangoon in February could not be employed and other special men were unobtainable, the books have been considerably dirtied and some were quite spoilt and had to be re-written. The first impulse of a Shan-Burman, when making a slight mistake in writing is to lick his forefinger and use it as an eraser; even when the writing is in pencil, the consequences, owing to the said finger being usually very dirty, are sufficiently disastrous; but when ink is the medium, they are simply appalling.

* * * * *

(*c*) There were only seven paid men, all of whom fulfilled the duties both of enumerator and supervisor. These were distributed as follows:—

One employed alternately at headquarters and at Shwegu. His pay was Rs. 80 a month and he was employed as a sort of Charge Superintendent at Shwegu for a time. He reached Bhamo on 23rd January 1891.

Six were employed at the rate of Rs. 50 a month, paid monthly, of whom one Maung Bah Tè was sent to census the Indawgyi and Nantein tract, and did his work very creditably.

One was sent to Upper Sinkan.

One was sent to help the Sinkan Myoôk. His name was Ah Foung. I had to fine him for deliberate disobedience of orders, and he was mainly useless.

Two were sent to help Mr. Jennings in the final census of the Upper Irrawaddy.

One Maung Lu Galè took the Upper division of Lower Sinkan, and did it creditably.

One Maung Maung was sent to help Captain Gastrell in Upper Sinkan, and though very frightened of Kachins, is reported favourably on.

When it is remembered that these men only reached Bhamo on the last day of January, that all the time previous a persistent and fruitless struggle had been carried on against the prevailing and progress-impeding illiteracy in the remoter portions of the country, that these men were taught their work and sent off to the furthest ends of district in time to enumerate and census synchronously practically the entire district, I think it will be conceded that the need for them was urgent and that the utmost possible results were obtained from their work. Had we been left entirely to our own resources the tracts of Nantein, Indawgyi, Upper Sinkan, and the Upper division of Lower Sinkan would not have been enumerated, while the synchronous censusing of the Upper Irrawaddy from Maingna downwards would have been impracticable.

The total cost of the paid agency was from the last day of January to 19th day of March, the date of their discharge, Rs. 593-3-10.

To this add Rs. 100-14-0 on census contingencies, travelling, &c. Clerks sent to Upper Irrawaddy and Indawgyi could not possibly be expected to pay their own boat-hire (which would be about twice their daily pay), and the need for sending them express to their stations was urgent. It was estimated generally that Rs. 1,000 would be required for census expenditure in this district. A saving of Rs. 305-14-2 has, therefore, been effected.

II.—The Preliminary Record.

* * * * *

(*a*) * * It is true that the District Superintendent of Police went to Upper Sinkan during January, but nothing much could be done there owing to the utter illiteracy of the people till the arrival of a special clerk, and it is entirely due to Captain Gastrell's energy and power of organization during the last weeks of February that it was found possible to census, and not merely to census, but to census synchronously, the Upper Sinkan valley. The commencement of the preliminary record was much delayed owing to the non-arrival of schedule books.

In Mogaung, Koyna, and Sinbo circles, which had been the first to receive regular books, the preliminary record was commenced and completed in January. At Indawgyi and Nantein, and the Sinkan Valley, the preliminary record was commenced and completed in February, while Mr. Jennings started up the Irrawaddy late in January and had finished the preliminary record by about 20th February.

* * * * *

(*b*) My preliminary remarks, and remarks just above on point (*a*), show how the final census was conducted. The enumeration of the military and military police were fairly simple owing to their organization and was carried out departmentally. The enumeration oft he columns out in various parts of the district was effected by taking full particulars before they started out, and by the officer in charge sending down a note on census night of casualties or changes, which of course were but few. The use of launches for river census is noted below. I would specially bring to notice the good work done by Mr. H. W. Godber, Treasury Officer, Bhamo, on whom the burden of conducting the business of the census generally practically devolved, and without whose valuable assistance the census would not have been as successful as it was. Mr. Jennings, Inspector of Police, Mogaung, who was entrusted with the duties of enumerator, supervisor, and Charge Superintendent on the whole of the Upper Irrawaddy, and who accomplished this task practically without skilled assistance at a time when the service was by no means unattended by personal danger. The two special clerks only reached him in time to take part in the final census.

* * * * *

The Census itself.

(*a*) As explained above, the area to be non-synchronously censused, which at first embraced half the district (exclusive of hill tracts excluded from the census) was gradually narrowed down till it was practically *nil.*

The only non-synchronous area finally consisted of some four or five remote villages of Upper Sinkan, which Captain Gastrell could not get enumerated and checked within such time after census night as would render the result trustworthy. This is noteworthy as the tract synchronously censused included wild spots like the Shan-Burman villages up the Molè and Nantabet chaungs, to some of which a white man had not then penetrated, riverine Kachin villages who owned no man as master and ran away to avoid being questioned on Mr. Jenning's approach.

* * * * *

(*f*) No prosecutions were sanctioned : such breaches of the law as occurred being due to natural stupidity rather than perverseness. It was difficult to persuade some old women to leave the numbers outside their houses. They would persist in hiding them away (possibly under the impression they brought good luck).

* * * * *

(*g*) No estimates were submitted, but when the Superintendent, Census Operations, visited Bhamo he mentioned that Rs. 1,000 could be spared for exigencies of this district. Of this sum only Rs. 694-1-10 were spent (see remarks on paragraph 1(*c*).

* * * * *

From G. G. Collins, Esq., Deputy Commissioner, Katha, to the Superintendent of the Census Operations, Burma,—No. 849-10R., dated the 30th March 1891.

* * * * *

The schedule books distributed so far as the Katha and Myadaung subdivisions are concerned have been returned. That for Kawlin, owing to the troubles with Wuntho, have not been collected.

* * * * *

2. (*c*) The abstracts in all cases were not correctly submitted owing to the interruption in the work by Wuntho rebels who recently attacked this district.

* * * * *

It has been impossible to collect any of Kawlin books at present. Kawlin itself was burnt to the ground and many other villages besides, while villagers deserted other villages in large numbers.

(*d*) The non-synchronous returns were received by the 6th of March and varied little with those prepared before the 26th February.

* * * * *

(*f*) No prosecutions were instituted, while the people raised no obstacles to enumerators.

* * * * *

(*i*) I believe the returns for Katha and Myadaung subdivisions are correct.

* * * * *

From Lieutenant H. A. Browning, Deputy Commissioner, Ruby Mines District, to the Superintendent of the Census Operations, Burma (through the Commissioner, Northern Division),—No. 165, dated Mogôk, the 4th April 1891.

* * * * *

Report on Census Operations, Ruby Mines District, 1891.

I.—Preparatory Work.

* * * * *

(*b*) The numbering of houses began in August and was completed in October.

(*c*) The following agency was employed :—

2 Charge Superintendents.
21 Supervisors.
125 Enumerators.

The cost of enumerating was Rs. 25, which sum represents the amount paid for the enumeration of the military police; with this exception no enumerators were paid. The Charge Superintendents and supervisors being all Government officials, were also unpaid.

2. Owing to the difficulty in getting hold of enumerators, many villages not possessing a single inhabitant who could write Burmese, and consequently most of the enumerators having to be imported from the larger villages, the preliminary record commenced somewhat late in most cases. It was completed by the 15th February in all circles.

* * * * *

(*b*) The census took place on the night of the 26th February throughout the district. The day previous to this all the supervisors and enumerators were ready in their circles and blocks. In order to facilitate the work of enumeration orders were issued putting off the bazaar-day at Mogôk two days; thus in a large measure the sudden large increase which always ensues in Mogôk the day before the periodical bazaar-day, which the 26th happened to be, was stopped, thus reducing the work of enumeration at Mogôk and not upsetting the preliminary record of outlying villages.

* * * * *

It was feared at one time that owing to the paucity of enumerators it would not be possible to enumerate all villages synchronously, but by impressing on enumerators who were in charge of two villages, a goodly number, but not so many as was at first feared, *vide* my report No. 804-28R., dated the 21st November 1890, to Commissioner, Northern Division, the necessity of commencing early, namely, on the late afternoon of census night, the villages in no instance being far apart, the whole with one exception were finished before dawn of 27th. The exception represented a small village of ten houses, the census of which was taken on the morning of the 27th.

* * * * *

I would particularly mention in the Mogôk Township Mr. Rees, Executive Engineer, and Mr. Buchanan, Assistant Conservator of Forests, and in the Twinngè Township, Head Constable Maung Aung Bon, as having worked especially hard and taken much pains in the work of supervision.

Mr. Rees was in charge of Mogôk Circle A, where the work was very heavy owing to the number of Maingtha "Camps" about and the necessity of constantly changing arrangements to meet the exigencies of enumerating a shifting population. Mr. Buchanan had charge of the Lishaw circle round Bernardmyo. All the enumerators of his circle had to be imported, and great difficulty was found in enumerating the Lishaw population, who are ignorant and apathetic to a degree.

Besides the Lishaws Mr. Buchanan had to contend with several large camps of muleteers and coolies from the Chinese States. Mr. Buchanan showed great energy and interest in the work.

* * * * *

The Charge Superintendents, Mr. Bear, Extra Assistant Commissioner, and Maung Hmo, Myoôk, Twinngè, both rendered excellent service, and I would particularly bring their zeal and intelligence to your notice. Owing to my being frequently absent from headquarters and sometimes from the district for lengthened periods, the work of directing the census of the district fell in a great measure on Mr. Bear. I always found him most ready and resourceful. He took much trouble with the supervisors and enumerators in his charge, and on the night of the census was engaged till six in the morning going round with the enumerators and seeing that Mogôk town and the neighbouring Maingtha "Camps" were properly enumerated. Maung Hmo at Twinngè did equally good work in his charge. He took much trouble with the preliminary work, such as house-numbering and blocking, and throughout the progress of the census was indefatigable.

* * * * *

I would also mention the good work done by Maung Kyaw Khine, late Township Officer, Mogôk, who had all the preliminary census work of the Mogôk Township in his hands. This he had completed before he was transferred to Moulmein in commencement of November.

This transfer of the Headquarter Township Officer just as he had got a grip of census work was most inconvenient.

* * * * *

(*f*) There were no prosecutions under the Census Act. The attitude of the people throughout the district was most friendly and no trouble whatever was experienced. In even the most remote parts of the district no escorts were required for either supervisors or enumerators.

* * * * *

From Lieutenant F. H. ELIOTT, Deputy Commissioner, Shwebo, to the Superintendent of the Census Operations, Burma,—No. 302-67, dated the 11th April 1891.

* * * * *

II.—The Census itself.

* * * * *

(*d*) The census was taken all over the district at the same time without any great trouble.

(*e*) There were no prosecutions under the Census Act in this district.

The people were at first alarmed, but when they found their fears were groundless and Government had no ulterior motive in taking the census, they calmly submitted to it and in fact helped to expedite the enumeration.

(*g*) The total cost of census was Rs. 178-4-0 as shown in the statement under (*c*) of the preparatory work of this report.

* * * * *

(*c*) I am of opinion that the census taken may be classed as fairly accurate. The whole of the district without exception of any outlying tracts was under immediate control, and there being no very great amount of traffic, or, as in India, any great number of the population on the constant move, the work of enumeration was not very difficult. Great zeal was displayed by enumerators in writing up their books correctly.

* * * * *

From C. A. SOPPITT, Esq., President, Shwebo Municipality, to the Superintendent of the Census Operations, Burma,—No. 16M., dated the 5th March 1891.

* * * * *

I.—Preparatory Work.

* * * * *

(*b*) The numbering of the houses was begun by the Myothugyi in June 1890 and completed in the same month.

* * * * *

(*c*) * * The only expenditure incurred for enumeration was for printed forms, stationery, and lights, which cost Rs. 49 against an estimated cost of Rs. 150.

The reduction was due to the lamps used for the final census on the night of the 26th February 1891 having been hired instead of being purchased.

II.—Preliminary Record.

(*a*) * * The only difficulty experienced by all official and non-official enumerators was caused by the natives of India refusing to give their castes and subdivision of castes. This gave the Charge Superintendent incessant trouble, he having personally to go along with the enumerators and worm out the particulars wanted.

* * * * *

By the 1st February 1891 the books were filled in with pencil. On the 6th February the supervisors with the enumerators had their books examined and errors rectified by house-to-house visit * *. On the 8th February a telegram was despatched to Superintendent, Census, Rangoon, giving the particulars for the preliminary census.

* * * * *

(*b*) *Final Census.*

* * * * *

The Charge Superintendent, Mr. Macnamara, interested himself very much in the matter and has spared no time or trouble to secure a reliable and perfectly correct record. I am much indebted to him and wish to bring his services before the Census Commissioner.

Supervisors Maung Tu and Maung Lin displayed commendable zeal and intelligence in the discharge of the work entrusted to them.

Enumerators Maung Kyaw and Maung Bya, Law Agents; Maung Myin, the son of the Myothugyi of Shwebo; Maung Hla, Treasurer; Maung Tha U, Clerk of the Court of the Headquarter Magistrate; Mr. Denis and Maung Min Gyaw, Clerks of the Public Works Department; Maung Tha Daw, Maung Chwa, and Maung Chaik, traders, showed intelligence and performed the work to my satisfaction.

* * * * *

(*f*) No prosecutions were instituted in this town under the Act.

The majority of the people were first alarmed, being under the impression that it was the object of Government to find out the inmates of each house with a view to increasing the realization under thathameda-tax. A few imagined that it was to discover the total adult population for the purpose of instituting a comparison between the figures which would be realized from capitation-tax and the thathameda, and if the former showed an augmentation, Government intended imposing it and doing away with the latter tax.

* * * * *

(*i*) On the whole I am satisfied with the results of the operations conducted in this town and consider the statistics obtained to be reliable.

* * * * *

---

* * * * *

From R. C. STEVENSON, Esq., Deputy Commissioner, Ye-u, to the Superintendent of the Census Operations, Burma,—No. 294-1N., dated the 27th March 1891.

IN answer to your Census No. 777, dated the 19th February 1891, I have the honour to report that Circular No. 26 was, by the carelessness of my office, left unfiled and that I was unaware of its existence when I wired my No. 87 to you. That on receipt of your No. 266 of the 21st instant I at once called for the Census Circular No. 26. In the meantime the books had already been despatched to your address in charge of Maung Po Mya, Bailiff, who was ordered to go as far as Mandalay.

* * * * *

I.—Preparatory Work.

* * * * *

(*b*) The house-numbering was completed by the end of October and was commenced about the beginning of that month.

(*c*) * * The cost of enumeration up to the present date has been *nil*.

* * * * *

2. (*a*) * * Mr. Warde, Subdivisional Officer, Southern Subdivision, reported that he did not allow a single supervisor to leave until he was able to show that he had mastered the instructions.

* * * * *

Final Census.

(*b*) I consider that the work of bringing the census to a successful issue rested to a very great extent on the energy and zeal of the Charge Superintendents. I consider my two Subdivisional Officers and all my five Myoôks did their work loyally. I specially mention the Ye-u Myoôk, Maung Po Hla, the Mayagan Myoôk, Maung Su, for interest taken in the work. Maung Sein, Akunwun, was also of the greatest assistance in supervising the writing up of block lists and despatch of schedule books. Maung Po Gaung, Head Accountant, who is Supervisor of Municipality, was specially mentioned by the Charge Superintendent of Municipality for good work. This officer has an excellent record of service. I would ask in the interest of the service that his name be not forgotten when a vacancy occurs in 4th grade Myoôkship.

* * * * *

(*f*) There were no prosecutions under the Census Act, and the people submitted to the census inquiries with a good enough grace.

* * * * *

(*i*) I am confident the results obtained are, allowing a very small percentage for errors of accident, correct.

* * * * *

From B. K. S. MCDERMOTT, Esq., Deputy Commissioner, Sagaing, to the Superintendent of the Census Operations, Burma,—No. 1040-1G., dated the 2nd May 1891.

* * * * *

I.—Preparatory Work.

* * * * *

2. (*a*) The preliminary records were begun by the Township Officers explaining to the supervisors, who explained to their subordinates. Every village was afterwards checked by the Township Officers.

(*b*) Just before the final census all clerks in the offices of the Subdivisional Officers were given certain circles to look after. These clerks travelled about, saw enumerators understood their work, and explained to them the difficult points which they could not understand.

* * * * *

(*f*) No prosecutions were sanctioned under the provisions of the Census Act. The attitude of the people towards the census was that they regarded it with suspicion, thinking that the census was taken to enable the Government to assess on them a new tax about to be introduced. The people were quiet and orderly on the night of the final census.

* * * * *

(*i*) The results obtained by the census were on the whole correct. I attach a map of the Sagaing district showing the revenue circles by their serial number, and to explain that the revenue circles are also used as census circles. In conclusion, I have to report that the work of the census being new to almost all the officials in this district, it required a large amount of instruction to make them understand their work.

From B. K. S. McDermott, Esq., President of the Sagaing Municipality, Upper Burma, to the Superintendent of the Census Operations, Burma,—No. 73-9, dated the 1st May 1891.

* * * * *

1. (*b*) House-numbering begun from 20th October 1890 and ended in the middle of November 1890.

* * * * *

2. (*b*) The supervisors went out on the night of 25th February and checked the work done by the enumerators. They again were out on the night of the 26th February, on which occasion the census itself was taken. The enumerators were rather backward in picking up the instructions at first, but after a little patience they clearly understood what was required and gave satisfaction to their supervisors. I have every reason to be thoroughly satisfied with the manner in which the census work within Municipal limits was taken.

* * * * *

(*f*) There were no prosecutions sanctioned under the Census Act. The attitude of the people towards the census was most submissive, although they at first thought there was to be an assessment of a new tax about to be introduced by the British Government; but this idea was soon removed.

* * * * *

(*i*) * * I beg to express my satisfaction with the correctness of the results obtained.

* * * * *

From Major G. S. Eyre, Deputy Commissioner, Lower Chindwin, to the Superintendent of the Census Operations, Burma,—No. 948-47, dated Mônywa, the 26th March 1891.

* * * * *

I.—Preparatory Work.

* * * * *

(*b*) House-numbering commenced in August and completed in September. It was, however, found convenient in large villages to number by blocks instead of by serial numbers for whole village. This was done when checking Register A in October and first half of November.

(*c*) The agency employed was unpaid throughout, and consisted of Government officials chiefly (thugyis and gaungs) and a few private persons. No difficulty was experienced in obtaining volunteers for the post of enumerator in places where the gaungs were incompetent, and as these enumerators worked with the gaungs no jealousy was manifested.

It will be noticed that there are an apparently unnecessary large number of census circles. This is due to the objection small thugyis had to being grouped together under one of their number. I gave way to the objection raised by the thugyis from the first, in anticipation of sanction, which was subsequently accorded.

I attribute the interest taken in census work by the thugyis chiefly to the fact that they were in each case appointed supervisors for their own revenue circles, and were not called upon to submit to what they regarded as supersession.

Where it was necessary to divide a revenue circle into two or more census circles, the thugyi was still in charge of the whole of his circle and looked after and controlled the work of the supervisors appointed to portions of his revenue circle, and the system worked well and without friction of any kind.

* * * * *

II.—The Census itself.

(*a*) *The preliminary records.*—Specimen schedules were received on 26th October and Myoôks at once went round their townships collecting the supervisors and enumerators in neighbourhood of each village they stopped at, instructed them in the filling in of the schedules.

* * * * *

Block lists and schedule books were distributed on 8th January, extra books being issued up to 16th February.

The preliminary record was commenced on issue of schedules and was completed during the first week in February. From this time till 14th February the entries in schedules were checked by Charge Superintendents and supervisors. I myself visited a large portion of the Eastern subdivision and some of the chief villages in the Western subdivision, examined the schedules and pointed out mistakes. The Western Subdivisional Officer was also being engaged in the same work throughout February.

(*b*) *The Final Census.*

* * * * *

The whole of the census work connected with issue of orders and forms, check of Circle A and Subdivisional Registers in the office, has been done by Akunwun U Tha Zan U. He has worked hard and well, and I have very great pleasure in specially recommending him for favourable notice.

The Subdivisional Officer, Western Subdivision, Maung Khep, K.S.M., has also worked hard and done good service in checking the enumerators' and supervisors' work, and has given me great assistance.

I am also greatly indebted to Mr. Durrant, Assistant Superintendent of Police, and to Mr. Inspectors Jenner and Jones, all of whom took great pains in testing the house lists and in bringing to notice omissions therefrom.

Mr. O'Donoghue, District Superintendent of Police, who was in charge of the Civil Station Census Circle, also took great pains in the discharge of his duties.

(*c*) The enumerators' abstracts were made in pencil originally, corrected by them and checked by the supervisors, whose abstracts were in turn checked by the Charge Superintendents, and then submitted to this office.

Ayadaw and Kudaw abstracts were received late owing to the Charge Superintendents detaining those received in time for one or two supervisors' abstracts which had not been received.

The figures given in preliminary record were taken for these two charges, and the resulting difference was not great.

Census schedules were received by 15th March and sent to Census Superintendent by first steamer.

* * * * *

Owing to the river being low, boats did not travel at night, but anchored at villages. There are still 28 schedule books to be accounted for. These are books spoiled or issued as extra. These have been written for and will be duly accounted for. All books used have been received and submitted.

* * * * *

(*f*) No prosecutions were necessary. The people who at first regarded the census as being connected with some new scheme for taxation, were soon re-assured when reminded that such had not been the result of the Lower Burma Census, and I found every one willing to aid work to the best of his ability.

(*g*) The only expenditure on account of the census was for stationery and shipping charges for schedules and for travelling expenses of clerks sent in charge of the schedules. The latter item alone has been paid by this office is not yet adjusted.

* * * * *

(*i*) The census has, I believe, been correctly taken. The enumerators on the whole evinced considerable interest in their work and in many cases prepared the whole of their schedules on blank paper to avoid spoiling their books, and only wrote up the printed forms when satisfied that their entries on manuscript were correct.

The chief errors I noticed were with regard to employment. In one township some 70 per cent. were recorded as "dependent," the occupation of the head of the house having been recorded, and the rest of the household entered as "dependent" on him. As these entries were generally made in pencil they were easily corrected. Another common mistake was the entry of the village at which born instead of the district.

On the whole I consider the census to be as accurate as was possible under the circumstances, and that very few persons have escaped enumeration.

A brief report by H. L. Tilly, Esq., Deputy Commissioner, on the work of the Census in the Upper Chindwin District.

1. In June 1890 I called upon all my Subdivisional Officers to submit indents for Circle Registers A and B. These came to my office by the end of the month, and I submitted indents for my district to the Superintendent, Government Printing, and was supplied with them about the middle of August On receipt the Circle Registers were at once distributed to the different officers and instructions were issued about the mode of filling them up. Unfortunately many of the Myoôks and two of the Subdivisional Officers did not understand the instructions, and a great deal of time was wasted in returning their registers, calling them to headquarters, and getting them to correct their mistakes and issuing further instructions to them.

* * * * *

The house-numbering was being done at the same time as the Circle Registers were being prepared, and was finished everywhere except in Tummu by about the beginning of November.

* * * * *

(*c*) The agency employed throughout the district was unpaid. The enumerating portion of it consisted of ywagaungs and respectable village elders or others able and willing to assist. The supervisors were the thugyis, shwehmus, and police officers of the higher grades. The Subdivisional Officers and some of the Myoôks were made Charge Superintendents. There were only three paid clerks employed during January and February at a cost Rs. 90.

* * * * *

The Subdivisional Officers held census classes and tried their utmost to train the enumerators and supervisors. But very few of the men employed grasped the meaning of what they were taught. Most of them had never used a pen, and many of them had never held or seen such an implement; still with patience and perseverance they were made to do the work which, I believe, is correct, though anything but neat. There was no time to test the preliminary record as it was finished only two days before the final census.

On the night of the 26th February the enumerator met with little difficulty in making his rounds and filling in the necessary information, though in some instances answers were given from within closed doors. In a few cases enumerators to avoid trouble issued orders that no stranger was to come and sleep in their blocks, and no one was to go anywhere during the night, and being the ywagaung could enforce his order. The work done by the enumerators and supervisors has been on the whole satisfactory, and I believe the results are fairly accurate. All the officers in this district worked well.

* * * * *

The only tracts excluded from the synchronous census were the Kalè, Taungdwut, and the Kanti States; the two former were censused by the Extra Assistant Commissioner, Kalè Statè, and the Assistant Commissioner, Paungbyin, respectively, and the Kanti State was done by Lieutenant Loch. No tracts have been excluded from census operations.

* * * * *

There were only two prosecutions under the Census Act in the Paungbyin subdivision for refusing to give information and the accused were fined.

The actual cost of the census has been Rs. 120. Estimates were submitted for Rs. 144.

* * * * *

The schedules and records of the Uyu township were destroyed when the Homalin Court-house was burnt by a band of rebels from Wuntho.

* * * * *

From A. T. A. Shaw, Esq., Deputy Commissioner, Myingyan, to the Superintendent of the Census Operations, Burma,—No. 666-G.4, dated the 2nd May 1891.

* * * * *

(*a*) The preparatory work of the census was started early in this district by Mr. Copleston when Deputy Commissioner, who explained matters to the Thugyis, Myoôks, and Subdivisional Officers during his tours in August, September, and October.

* * * * *

The Subdivisional Registers submitted were returned from the Superintendent's Office with the remark that they appear to have been most carefully prepared.

(*b*) The numbering of the houses in Kyaukpadaung subdivision was commenced on the 20th July and finished on the 30th September; in Pagan the numbers were put in during October. In the Myingyan subdivision the numbering was commenced on the 27th August and completed in the early part of November. At the Central Jail the numbering was finished on the 22nd December, and in the cantonment and civil station on the 23rd January and 8th February respectively.

* * * * *

II.—The Census.

* * * * *

2. (*b*) * * Maung Pyi, Akunwun, was in charge of the work at the district office and rendered valuable assistance to the District Officer.

(*c*) * * The Pagan Subdivisional Officer reports that patrol boats were stationed at Nyaung U, Singu, Salè, and Kyauksè during the final census to ensure the proper enumeration of travellers by boats. These boats patrolled from the 26th to the 28th at Nyaung U (headquarters of the Pagan subdivision), and till the night of the 27th at the other three places. For the enumeration of travellers by road the Pagan Subdivisional Officer reports that scouts were stationed along the six principal roads in the subdivision to see that the travellers were enumerated. In Kyaukpadaung subdivision the village gaung with follow-

ii

ers assisted the enumerators by visiting all roads and camping places distant from the villages, and travellers and cartmen were persuaded to camp inside the village or were enumerated at camps outside.

(*b*) There were no prosecutions under the Act. The attitude of the people was satisfactory. They thought at first that taxation was to be increased, but the Government Officers did their best to explain the object of the census, after which the people readily supplied the information that was required. The Subdivisional Officer, Pagan, reports that the taking of the census was a cause of increase of thathameda in his subdivision, as the thugyis were afraid to hide families whose names appeared in the Census Circle Registers.

(*g*) The total cost of the census was only Rs. 117-9-0 as mentioned above.

* * * * *

(*i*) The results obtained are, I think, fairly correct. The effect of the census will be seen when it is stated that the thathameda increased from Rs. 3,58,037 last year to Rs. 4,28,768 this year, or an increase of 20 per cent.

* * * * *

From A. T. A. Shaw, Esq., Deputy Commissioner and President, Myingyan Municipality, to the Superintendent of the Census Operations, Burma,—No. 7, dated the 29th April 1891.

* * * * *

There are four circles: (1) Pyaungbya, (2) Gwegyi, (3) Myingyan, (4) Thabyebin.

There is a separate numbering of the blocks in each circle, there being 77 blocks altogether.

* * * * *

From M. J. Chisholm, Esq., Charge Superintendent of Census, Myingan Municipality, to the Deputy Commissioner, Myingyan,—No. 1, dated the 8th April 1891.

* * * * *

I.—Preparatory Work.

* * * * *

(*c*) * * With the exception of 54 of the enumerators, the others were all Government servants. The Municipality decided to pay for labour by piece-work. It has not yet been fixed what the rate is to be, but it was proposed that Rs. 3 per head should be the average. The cost was estimated at Rs. 258. The actual cost of the original proposal is carried, but will be Rs. 162 only.

II.—The Census itself.

* * * * *

(*b*) *The Final Census itself.*—The final census took place on the night of the 26th February, when between the hours of 6 P.M. and 2 A.M. each house in the Municipality was visited and noted by enumerators, supervisors, Deputy Commissioner, Messrs. Collins and O'Donnell, and myself. I beg to bring to your notice the names of the following unpaid enumerators and supervisors who I consider took great interest in their work and performed their duties to my satisfaction: Supervisors M. O. Rahaman, Municipal Inspector; Maung San Daw U, Assistant Commissioner's Court Clerk; and Maung Bah Oh, Bailiff, Deputy Commissioner's Office. Enumerators Sergeant Maung Kywe, Maung Sein Gale, Treasurer, Maung Pe, 2nd Judicial Clerk, and Abdool Razee, 3rd Accountant, Myingyan Treasury.

* * * * *

From A. W. Buchanan, Esq., Subdivisional Officer and Vice-President, Pagan Municipality, to the Deputy Commissioner and President, Pagan Municipality, Myingyan,—No. 172-24G., dated the 18th March 1891.

* * * * *

I.—Preparatory Work.

Census work in the Pagan Municipality commenced on the 1st July 1890, the date on which the work was started in the subdivision. The thugyis of East and West Nyaung U, the two villages which form the Municipality, began drawing up their Circle Registers **A** and **B** on this date, completing them within four weeks, the Circle Registers **A** and **B** for the Municipality being sent to Myingyan on the 5th August 1890. Both the lists drawn up by the East and West Nyaung U thugyis were checked by me. Immediately after the submission of Circle Registers **A** and B, census blocks were marked off and enumerators nominated. Both the revenue circles East and West Nyaung U, composing the Municipality, were then numbered in serial order for the district by the Deputy Commissioner, Myingyan, and as soon as this was done, the Municipality was divided into census circles and supervisors nominated, the Pagan Township Officer being appointed Charge Superintendent. The Subdivisional Register, which included all the information required for the Municipality, was submitted to headquarters on the 24th September 1890.

(*b*) House-numbering was commenced on the 1st October and completed on the 1st November 1890.

* * * * *

II.—The Census itself.

(*a*) The census schedule books intended for use in the Municipality did not arrive here till the 28th January 1891. They were distributed without any delay, however, so that the preliminary record was started on the 1st February 1891 and completed on the 10th February 1891, a period of nine days.

* * * * *

(*b*) * * I visited nearly every census block within Municipal limits while the enumeration was going on in company with Mr. D. Philips, Superintendent, Pagan Jail, who had charge of Census Circle 147B. Mr. Philips deserves great credit for the energy and zeal he displayed in his duties as Census Supervisor, the circle allotted to him being a much more difficult one to work than Census Circles 147A and 148 (the remaining two circles within Municipal limits). The work done by his enumerators taken as a whole was much better than that turned out by the enumerators of the other two circles.

(*c*) * * I worked up the river from Singu in the launch *Ant* on the 26th February 1891, accompanied by the boat enumerator belonging to Nyaung U, but found it very difficult work enumerating the travellers in passing boats, a great deal of time being lost every time I boarded a passing boat. I accordingly stationed the enumerator at Nyaung U and made him do all his enumeration at the steamer landing-place, the launch being practically useless for patrol work.

* * * * *

(*g*) The total cost of census operations within Municipal limits was Rs. 4.

* * * * *

(*i*) The results obtained may be looked upon as correct.

* * * * *

From A. S. Fleming, Esq., Deputy Commissioner, Pakôkku, to the Superintendent of the Census Operations, Burma (through Commissioner, Southern Division),—No. 990-1, dated the 29th April 1891.

* * * * *

CENSUS REPORT.

1. (*a*) Circle Registers **A** and **B** were completed by the end of August 1890, and the Subdivisional Register was prepared on receipt of the forms on the 25th September 1890.

The registers were for the most part prepared in accordance with the instructions and were fairly complete. In some cases the blocks were thought to be too large and in few cases houses were found to have been omitted either as being those of officials or exempt from taxation for other reasons. The registers were returned to Subdivisional Officers on the 10th October for check and correction with suggestions for reblocking where it appeared necessary and were re-submitted by the 30th October.

(*b*) The numbering of houses was carried on at the same time as the preparation of Register **A**. They were commenced on the 27th July and completed on the 31st August. In most parts the numbers were written on the outside of the houses with lime, but in some parts each house had its number written on a small board fixed usually outside the house, but sometimes kept inside for safety.

* * * * *

(*c*) * * * The enumerators were in the smaller circles the thugyis themselves and in larger circles gaungs and educated villagers. The total number of Charge Superintendents employed was 11, of supervisors 402, and of enumerators 1,904.

* * * * *

2. (*b*) * * The following officers have given me the greatest satisfaction in their census work:—

Mr. W. B. Tydd, Subdivisional Officer, Pauk.
Maung Lu Tha, Myoôk, Pakangyi.
Maung Maw Lit, Myoôk, Laungshè.
Maung On Gaing, Myoôk, Pakôkku.

Mr. Rama Conar, the head clerk of my office, has also given me invaluable assistance in the office arrangements and work in the town.

(*c*) * * The books issued to the troops that left Gangaw for Thetta on the 29th January accompanied by Mr. Macnabb have been sent to the Political Officer, Haka. The schedules of the Chinbôk Expedition are included in the Yawdwin bundles. The troops and transport between Kan and Rawvan on the Haka road were enumerated from Gangaw.

* * * * *

(*f*) No prosecutions under the Census Act were sanctioned. The people have raised no serious objection to the enumeration. In most parts the idea that the census was a preliminary to increased taxation led to a tendency to omit houses and inmates, but there was as a rule no difficulty in explaining that the census was not connected directly with any taxation scheme and that it was essential that no one should be omitted. In some parts the people took an amused interest in the operation and wondered at so much trouble being taken to record their domestic particulars.

(*g*) The total cost of the census up to date has been Rs. 331-8-0 as compared with Rs. 210 estimated for. The excess is principally due to the cost of telegrams and postage connected with the census which was not estimated for. The cost of freight and carriage was also somewhat under-estimated.

* * * * *

(*i*) The population result of the census will, I believe, be very nearly correct; the details will not, I fear, be of much value, except as regards age and sex.

* * * * *

The preliminary census was, I think, accurate.

* * * * *

From H. S. HARTNOLL, Esq., Deputy Commissioner, Minbu, to the Superintendent of the Census Operations, Burma,—No. 190-1, dated the 20th April 1891.

* * * * *

The house-numbering was commenced earliest in the Salin subdivision, being completed by October 1st; in the Môn valley subdivision it commenced about the third week of September, and was finished by the last week in November; in the Sagu subdivision it was commenced in November and finished in December.

During October and November thugyis checked circle registers. I applied for appointment orders for supervisors and enumerators on October 13th by my No. 1073-11. They were sent me on the 1st January 1891 and I had them distributed as soon as possible.

* * * * *

The paid enumerators were employed in the Yomas. It was estimated that they would cost Rs. 293. They only cost Rs. 213. I obtained sanction for these employed in the Nape township, but in addition to these another man was employed to enumerate the steatite camp in Sidôktaya, which is situated two days' march into the hills. He cost Rs. 6.

The enumerators were paid by the day.

2. With regard to the census itself I did not receive the Handbooks of Instruction till the end of November. They were thereupon distributed by me with clear instructions to Subdivisional Officers. They and the Charge Superintendents, who were the Myoôks, instructed supervisors and enumerators with these books carefully. I checked the work as far as I was able.

The preliminary record was commenced very late. I did not get the schedules till the 15th or 16th of January, and after they had been carefully checked, I distributed them to Subdivisional Officers to fill in the block lists and dockets on the covers and to distribute. We therefore had to make great efforts to get the preliminary records done in time. During the month that followed Subdivisional Officers and Myoôks spent nearly all their time getting the books written up correctly. I was myself on tour in the Môn and Salin subdivisions and did what I could. The preliminary record was begun about January 25th and was finally completed about a week before the night of the census in most parts.

* * * * *

All my Subdivisional Officers, Mr. Hertz, Mr. Graham, and Maung San Pe, did their best. The Myoôk of Legaing, Maung An Taw Ni; Myoôk of Salin, Maung Kan Gyi, and Myoôk of Kyabin, Maung Ba, who were Charge Superintendents, are worthy of notice.

Amongst other men, who have been brought to my notice are Maung Sein, Law Agent, Minbu; Maung Mu, Myothugyi of Padaing; Maung Shan, Head Clerk, Subdivisional Officer's Court, Salin; Maung Mu, Secretary, Salin Municipality; Maung Aung Kyaw Zan, Bailiff, Subdivisional Officer's Court Salin; Maung On Bu, 2nd clerk, Subdivisional Officer's Court, Salin; and the volunteer clerk Maung Chait of that Court. The clerks of the Salin and Kyabin Myoôks' Courts Maung Po Thit, Maung Hman, Maung Tun U, and Maung Lu Thit are also reported to have done well.

Two abstracts were sent in, first those of the results of the preliminary record, secondly, those of the final results. I did not see Circular No. 21 till about February 13th, and so I had little time to get in the results of the preliminary record, but I managed to do so in time. With regard to the record of final results the Subdivisional Officer, Salin, got all his in by March 1st and forwarded the results to me. The Subdivisional Officer, Minbu, sent me his on March 3rd. I also got most of the results of the final record of the Môn subdivision in time. The only figures taken from the results of the preliminary record that were used in making my telegram to send you and to the Census Commissioner were those for the civil police of Sidôktaya and Dabwin and the Sabegyi circle of the Dabwin township. On receiving the results of the final record for these blocks, I found they differed by 64 persons from those of the preliminary record. The figures of two road schedules consisting of 21 persons were also left out of my telegram.

* * * * *

I have no reason to believe that any great error has crept in or that houses have been intentionally omitted.

* * * * *

From H. P. TODD NAYLOR, Esq., Deputy Commissioner, Magwe, to the Superintendent of the Census Operations, Burma,—No. 535-4R., dated the 13th April 1891.

* * * * *

Circle Registers were received in my office on 2nd August 1890, and were sent out to Subdivisional Officers on 4th August 1890. These were received back from Natmauk subdivision on 25th August 1890, but had to be returned as they were not divided into blocks, and supervisors and enumerators were not nominated. They were all received on 18th September and on the 10th October the final indent for schedules was submitted. I calculated that a village containing over 26 houses would want a book of 60 schedules and one containing over 52 would want an additional book of 16 schedules. I also took 5 per cent. for contingencies. Neither of these were sufficient. There were more than 16 per cent. of houses having more than eight inhabitants and new villages were formed and people returned so rapidly that I had to get more books. Circle Register B or the register of boat blocks was not prepared till much later It was impossible to estimate the number of boats which would be at the different stations on the Irrawaddy. All the Circle Registers which had been returned for correction on the 10th October were returned corrected by 9th December. The numbering of the houses was almost completed.

* * * * *

3. The cost of enumeration was *nil*. The Myoôks were Charge Superintendents and the thugyis supervisors. I found it better to make each thugyi supervisor for his own circle, even when there was only one village, and where he was also enumerator, as it would, I found, create jealousy if one thugyi were to interfere with the circle of another.

* * * * *

II.—The Census.

* * * * *

5. The census was finally taken on the night of the 26th February. The enumerators had been thoroughly well prepared. The Myothit Myoôk Maung Po Thaing was a paid supervisor in 1881 and understood the work; he did it thoroughly well, and had made most careful arrangements. Maung Shwe I and Maung Tun Aung also took a great deal of trouble; the former was taken ill just before the census, but had either been to every village or called every enumerator and supervisor and instructed him. The latter went to every village, and saw the numbering of the houses. I visited some of the outlying villages where officials rarely go and found that they were all enumerated and numbered properly. In one circle, Yônbinkwet, beyond the ridge of the Yomas, they were particularly good. The Subdivisional Officers took great pains over the instruction of the men. I especially noticed Mr. Townsend, who personally visited half the villages in Satthwa. The boats were seen to by clerks or head constables. I set my office and that of the Assistant Commissioner to work. There was no preliminary record in the case of boats. It would have been of no use, and for that reason I selected most intelligent clerks as boat enumerators. Boats were stationed at Thittabwe and a boat with Maung Po Than, Head Constable, below Magwe to check passing boats which might have escaped. There was a little difficulty about outlying guards. Lieutenant Brown, Assistant Commandant, who was arranging the work, was called away, but by dint of sending out men I got all the outlying stations enumerated and the Battalion Commandant had the lines counted by his clerks.

The survey people and the cutch camps were provided for at the last moment. I had to give out more schedules and tear up books to enable me to do it. I would especially bring to notice my Head Revenue Assistant Mr. Abraham, on whom the main work fell and whose diligence and care has mainly contributed to the success of the census. He has worked very hard and to him more than to me is due the eminent success which attended the taking of the census. I had to be much out in camp, and he attended to all the census work and often had to act without consulting me. He had harder work than any one in the district.

6. * * The Subdivisional Officer, Natmauk, was unfortunately taken ill and his returns did not arrive till the 4th of March. They were all prepared and telegraphed on that evening to Simla, and the next morning, as it was too late to send any but an urgent telegram to you, thus I got in the abstract on the sixth day. Mr. Townsend, though his

subdivision was the largest and the most distant, had his abstracts in first. Owing to a mistake of the Myothit Myoôk his schedules were not received till the 16th March, but they were all sent off by the 19th. I have noted the means taken for enumerating travellers by boat. Men were stationed on the main roads to enumerate travellers, they were but few, as I had advised people not to move about that night and they generally took my advice.

* * * * *

8. No prosecutions were instituted under the Census Act.

9. The total cost of the census was—

	Rs.	A.	P.
Telegrams	22	8	0
Cooly and cart hire	76	1	0

and advance to volunteer to take the books to Rangoon Rs. 25.

* * * * *

11. I believe the census to have been remarkably correct. The average of men and women is about the same all over. The people understood what was expected of them and did not object to the questions. An idea that it was connected with taxation I did my best to dispell, and did not check the thathameda rolls or census in the same village at the same time. The idea was prevalent that it had something to do with thathameda, and in the village of Bedôkpin the headman made two men, eight women, and three or four children go outside and sleep in the jungle, as he had not entered them in the thathameda rolls. I found in one village that the headman had not put in the extra people when the household exceeded eight, but I had this thoroughly checked. There were a few cases where men failed at the last moment, but I sent out special men to enumerate in all these cases.

* * * * *

From A. R. BONUS, Esq., Deputy Commissioner, Kyauksè, to the Superintendent of the Census Operations, Burma,—No. 450, dated the 31st March 1891.

* * * * *

1. (*b*) It is impossible to give the exact dates as they varied for different villages but the work was completed before the end of November throughout the district.

(*c*) No paid agency was employed. There were 741 enumerators, 63 supervisors, and six Charge Superintendents.

2. (*a*) *and* (*b*) The preliminary record began on 26th January and was completed on 8th February.

* * * * *

The final census was duly taken on 26th February, and I think the results may be taken as accurate. Almost all census officers worked well. The following are especially noted by Subdivisional Officers :—

2. (*a*) *and* (*b*) *Kyauksè.*—Maung Tha Bu, Myoôk of Minzu, Maung Thaw Da, Myothugyi of Yeyaman, *ex*-Wun Hte, *ex*-Myothugyi Maung Ba.

Myittha.—Supervisors Maung An, Po Hlaing, San Gaing, Maung Gyi, Shwè Zin, Maung Ton, Yan Gyi Aung, Maung Gale, Maung Swe, and Paw U.

The Subdivisional Officer, Myittha, also speaks well of his head clerk, Maung David Po Te. I also wish to bring specially to notice the energy and zeal of Mr. R. Wall, Subdivisional Officer of Kyauksè, and Maung Nyo, Akunwun and Charge Superintendent of the Municipality.

(*c*) The abstracts were prepared in the offices of Myoôks and Subdivisional Officers under their personal supervision, and schedule books were returned to the Deputy Commissioner on 4th and 5th March. Arrangements were made at all regular halting-places of boats and travellers for their enumeration, enumerators being supplied with passbooks.

* * * * *

(*f*) There were no prosecutions. The people were quiescent and acquiescent. I do not think they understood the usefulness of the census, which is not surprising, but no sort of opposition was encountered. Many villages displayed some alacrity in assisting the work in such details as the numbering of the houses.

* * * * *

From Lieutenant J. J. CRONIN, Deputy Commissioner, Meiktila, to the Superintendent of the Census Operations, Burma,—No. 685, dated the 17th April 1891.

* * * * *

I.—Preparatory Work.

(*a*) * * The 972 villages of the district forming 144 census circles were divided into 1,368 blocks, the largest block consisting of 60 houses, the smallest of about 10.

* * * * *

(*b*) The numbering of houses commenced on the 20th June in the Meiktila subdivision, but was not begun in the Mahlaing and Wundwin subdivisions till much later, not being finally concluded until the end of the year.

This delay in the final completion of the numbering of the houses was due to the original numbers having had to be altered in most cases as it was found that the thugyis with a total disregard of the rules regarding blocks and serial numbers had numbered the houses according to the position of the villagers; endless worry and unnecessary labour ensued in consequence.

* * * * *

(*c*) * * In the selection of the enumerators great difficulty was experienced in obtaining men sufficiently educated and energetic enough to undertake the work required of them. Of the total of 1,368 enumerators ultimately employed, 1,272 were Government employés, including thugyis, ministerial officers, village headmen, and police.

The remainder were non-officials, lugyis, traders, &c., of intelligence and influence. Of the total number of persons employed in the work of the census, only 96 were paid and those were enumerators. The cost of the census operations was estimated at Rs. 800. The total expenditure incurred, however, under the head of enumeration was only Rs. 379-10-0, showing that the census in this district has been carried out most economically.

* * * * *

II.—The Census.

(*a*) In many cases the record was in the first instance written on parabaiks, which entries were carefully checked and entered in the schedules on the books being received. This was done in order to ensure that the schedules should be correctly filled in at Township headquarters under the personal supervision of the Township Officer; 120 copies of the Handbooks of Instructions were received on the 29th November, and were at once issued with schedule forms in blank for practice to supervisors and enumerators.

* * * * *

The preliminary record was commenced on the 16th January and was completed about the 10th February.

* * * * *

(*b*) * * Of the supervisors and Charge Superintendents who have shown exceptional energy, zeal, and intelligence in the work of the census, I would specially mention Mr. A. J. A. Jardine, District Superintendent of Police, for the careful manner in which the census of the Lônpan daing, a difficult and hilly tract on the border of the Shan States, was carried out under his personal supervision. The Subdivisional Officers of Wundwin, Meiktila, and Mahlaing; Mr. N. S. Field, Assistant Commissioner; Mr. E. S. Skinner, Myoôk; and Maung Po Min, Myoôk, deserve commendation for the care and trouble taken by them in instructing the supervisors and in checking the work throughout their charges.

The Myoôks of Pindalè, Wundwin, and Meiktila, Maung Lat, Maung Po Tha, Maung Tha Aung, were most energetic and hardworking. On the other hand, the Myoôk of Mahlaing, Maung On Thi, and the Myoôk of Thazi, Maung Tha Dun, were very incompetent.

(*c*) * * Although the form of abstract is a simple one, many mistakes were detected; in some cases the occupied and empty houses were shown in one column, in others the totals of persons were omitted. This was due to the natural carelessness of the Burman.

* * * * *

The supervisors' abstracts were prepared strictly in accordance with the orders given in the Handbook of Instructions. These abstracts were as a rule fairly accurately prepared. In some instances, however, owing to want of care in addition, the totals of occupied houses and male and female inhabitants in the circle were incorrectly entered.

* * * * *

For the enumeration of travellers by road 10 books of 100 passes were issued, of which four were issued to the District Superintendent of Police, Mr. Jardine, under whose superintendence all travellers on the main road to the Shan States were enumerated; for this purpose two enumerators were appointed, who were stationed at Kyatsakan, the junction of all roads leading to the Shan States from this district. By these men both the up and down travellers actually moving on the night of the census on the roads to the Shan States were enumerated. All travellers putting up at zayats or sakans on the night of the census were enumerated by the enumerators in whose blocks they happened to be at the time.

Six books of passes were issued to the Subdivisional Officer, Mahlaing, for the enumeration of persons attending the Mahlaing bazaar as the market day fell on 26th February. All the inhabitants of the district were directed to remain indoors after 8 P.M. on the night of the final census.

* * * * *

(*f*) * * In the taking of the census no opposition of any kind was experienced, the attitude of the people being strictly passive. The census was generally associated in the minds of the people with the obtaining of accurate returns for thathameda assessment purposes.

* * * * *

(*i*) * * The only tribe or race in this district regarding whose origin but little appears to be known are the Danus found in this district only in the Lônpan daing adjoining the Shan States of Nankôn and Pwehla. In appearance they somewhat resemble the Shans and dress like them. I believe they have no distinct language, but speak Burmese with a Shan accent. They live by taungya cultivation. Owing to the unhealthiness of the terai at the foot of the hills, the sole inhabitants of the tract are people of this race. I regret that owing to want of leisure I have not yet been able to obtain particulars of their origin or customs.

* * * * *

From N. G. CHOLMELEY, Esq., Deputy Commissioner, Yamèthin, to the Superintendent of the Census Operations, Burma,—No. 239-1R., dated the 25th March 1891.

* * * * *

I.—Preparatory Work.

* * * * *

(*b*) House-numbering was begun in the early part of August and finished by the middle of November.

(*c*) The agency employed with very few exceptions consisted of the thugyis and ywagaungs; there were no paid enumerators.

The numbers were as follows:—

Charge Superintendents	6
Supervisors	162
Enumerators	1,005

II.—The Census itself.

(*a*) The preliminary record was commenced on the 8th January and completed on the 8th February. Its preparation entailed an immense amount of trouble on almost every official in the district. The enumerators were almost all men of very little education, and 80 per cent. of them probably had never held a pen in their hands before. It was therefore necessary, in order to ensure any approach to accuracy, to have first a rough copy made of the record by each enumerator on parabaik, to which they are accustomed.

* * * * *

(*b*) The final census was taken synchronously throughout the district on the night of the 26th. It went off without any trouble or hindrance, created no sort of alarm, and was, I believe, complete in every particular. With regard to the work of the officers employed Mr. Carstairs, the Subdivisional Officer at Yamèthin, and Maung Po Sa at Pyawbwè, worked in such a way as to entirely relieve me of any anxiety as to the result, and the Myoôks, especially those of Pyawbwè and Yindaw, exerted themselves to the utmost, while Mr. Miller as Secretary of the Yamèthin Municipality showed the greatest diligence and energy. I must also mention the names of Maung Pan Tha, 2nd Revenue Clerk in my office, and Maung Po Wing, 2nd clerk in the Subdivisional Office, Yamèthin, who rendered great assistance by their zeal and intelligence. The enumerators and supervisors who must have thought the whole business a great and needless worry, showed much cheerful alacrity, and I was surprised at the way they got to work and did their best.

* * * * *

(*f*) No prosecutions; the people were perfectly indifferent.

(*g*) The cost of census operation was estimated by me at *nil*, but it was found necessary to engage two special messengers or extra peons whose pay amounted to Rs. 20.

* * * * *

(*i*) I believe that the results obtained will be very nearly correct.

From N. G. CHOLMELEY, Esq., President, Yamèthin Municipality, to the Superintendent of the Census Operations, Burma,—No. 22-24, dated the 4th May 1891.

* * * * *

I.—The Preparatory Work.

* * * * *

(*b*) House-numbering was begun in the early part of August and finished by the middle of November.

* * * * *

II.—The Census itself.

(*a*) The preliminary record was commenced on the 8th January and completed on the 8th February. Its preparation entailed an immense amount of trouble. The enumerators were almost all men of very little education and most of them probably had never held a pen in their hands before. It was therefore necessary, in order to ensure any approach to accuracy, to have first a rough copy made of the record by each enumerator on ordinary bazaar paper. These rough copies were carefully checked and corrected by the Charge Superintendent, then entered in the schedule books.

(*b*) The final census was taken synchronously throughout the Municipality on the night of the 26th February 1891. It went off without any trouble or hindrance.

* * * * *

Mr. Miller, Treasury Officer and Myoôk, who is the Honorary Secretary of the Municipality, was in sole charge of the census work in the Municipality, and through his diligence and energy entirely relieved me of any anxiety as to the result.

* * * * *

(*i*) I believe that the result obtained will be very nearly correct. I have reason to believe that there was no desire whatever on the part of those who were engaged on the work to render a false account, and though a small margin must be allowed for human frailty, I have no doubt that the error would form a very small percentage.

From W. N. PORTER, Esq., Deputy Commissioner, Pyinmana, to the Superintendent of the Census Operations, Burma,—No. 225, dated the 31st March 1891.

* * * * *

I.—Preparatory Work.

(*a*) * * The Circle Registers were submitted to the Superintendent, Census, on the 12th September 1890.

* * * * *

(*b*) The numbering of houses was commenced about the end of September and concluded in October 1890.

(*c*) * * It was found necessary to appoint additional enumerators for the straggling foresters and sawyers' camp.

* * * * *

II.—Census.

(*a*) The census schedule books were received on the 3rd January 1891, and were sent out at once to the Subdivisional Officers for distribution to the enumerators through the Superintendents and supervisors, all of whom were instructed in their various duties.

The preliminary record was started at once and finished before the end of January 1891. The testing of the preliminary record was finished by the 20th February 1891.

(*b*) As a rule the census returns were very carefully prepared and considerable interest in the work was shown by the unpaid agency employed.

Extra Assistant Commissioner Maung Kin especially deserves great credit for the time and attention he devoted to the carrying out of the census not only in his own subdivision, but outside it too.

* * * * *

(*d*) 1. In the Ahlaichaung, Bawkata, a special enumerator (Thugyi Maung Lu Gale) was sent out on the 4th February 1891. He had concluded his enumeration and submitted his book schedules by the 24th February 1891.

2. A special enumerator (a head constable of police) was sent to Seikpudaung circle on the 18th February 1891. He concluded his enumeration and submitted his schedule books by the 25th February 1891.

3. A special enumerator (Burmese Inspector of Police) was sent out on the 14th February 1891 to enumerate the four Karen villages situated in the hill east of Kyidaung. He concluded his enumeration on the 20th February 1891, and submitted his books on the 24th February 1891.

* * * * *

(*f*) No prosecutions were instituted under the Census Act.

The attitude of the people towards the census was quite friendly. They had an idea at first that it meant additional taxation, but when re-assured on the point, they showed a good deal of interest in it.

(*g*) The actual contingencies incurred on account of the census operations were as follows:—

	Rs.	A.	P.
Conveying urgent letters and schedule books, &c.	53	8	0
Purchase of pencils	9	6	0
Total ...	62	14	0

* * * * *

	Rs.
(i) Copying establishments	50
(ii) Paid enumerators	

* * * * *

As a rule the schedule books were found to be carefully and intelligently compiled. As was expected, the greater number of mistakes occurred under column 11, head Occupation.

G. B. C. P. O.—No. 4954, B. S., 23-12-92—1,100.